Shell
2
Shell

DAYTONA 24 HOURS

cadillac.com
5
NORTHSTAR
SYSTEM
TOSHIBA
ACDelco
SR
GMAC
PIRELLI
NORTHSTAR
SYSTEM
TOSHIBA
COPIERS • FAX
ROLEX 24
ACDelco
SR
GMAC
McLaren Engines
PIRELLI

DAYTONA 24 HOURS

THE DEFINITIVE HISTORY OF AMERICA'S GREAT ENDURANCE RACE

BY J.J. O'MALLEY

FOREWORD BY HURLEY HAYWOOD

DESIGN BY TOM MORGAN

PHOTOS EDITED BY BUZ MCKIM

RESULTS AND INDEX BY JANOS WIMPFFEN

Library of Congress Control Number: 2003103993.

ISBN: 1 893618 24 2

David Bull Publishing, logo, and colophon are trademarks of David Bull Publishing, Inc.

Book and cover design:
Tom Morgan, Blue Design, Portland, Maine (www.bluedes.com)

Printed in the United States

10 9 8 7 6 5 4 3 2 1

David Bull Publishing
4250 East Camelback Road
Suite K150
Phoenix, AZ 85018

602-852-9500
602-852-9503 (fax)

www.bullpublishing.com

Page 2: Over the years, the Daytona 24 Hours has attracted the world's premier sports cars. Cadillac made its debut at Daytona in 2000, with a pair of LMPs. Butch Leitzinger, Andy Wallace, and Frank Lagorce finished 13th overall and second in SRP in No. 6, one position ahead of No. 5, driven by Max Angelelli, Wayne Taylor, and Eric van de Poele.

Page 3: International stars are another characteristic of the race. In 1964, Frenchman Jo Schlesser, drove a Shelby Cobra.

Pages 4 and 5: Crewmen and officials stand at attention on pit road for the playing of the national anthem prior to the 1963 Daytona Continental. The Corvette of Tony Denman is on the pole, flanked by the No. 41 Corvette of Robert Ryan Brown. Farther back on the grid, there is an open position, and ABC Wide World of Sports commentator Chris Economaki (dark suit) is wondering if defending champion Dan Gurney will make it to the start of the race.

Page 6: The Brumos Porsche, carrying the unfamiliar No. 61, charges through the rain in the closing hours of the 1976 race. Hurley Haywood and Jim Busby teamed to finish third.

Pages 8 and 9: A full moon helps illuminate the action during the 1990 Daytona 24 Hours.

Page 11: The chief starter waves the green flag for the start of the 1973 Daytona 24 Hours from his post atop the wall on the back straight. In the early years of the event, the race started there to allow the field to spread out before entering turn one at the exit of the infield tri-oval.

CHAMPION
CHAMPION
Firestone
MARTINI &
3
41
29

Brumos
Porsche
61

CONTENTS

DAYTONA

Acknowledgments

All of the photographs in this book have been provided by International Speedway Corporation Publications—Archives. Buz McKim, veteran ISC chief archivist, selected the images, with the assistance of his staff, Nancy Kendrick, Randy, and Sandy Sanderson. Bill Oursler and Michael Keyser also helped by providing photos from Bill's collection.

Janos Wimpffen graciously allowed us to use the race results he compiled for his epic two-volume history, *Time and Two Seats: Five Decades of Long Distance Racing.*

Michael Argetsinger, whose father established Watkins Glen, New York, as the hub of American sports car racing, edited the manuscript. This is a continuation of a relationship that began with my two books on the history of racing at Watkins Glen International.

William Lazarus of ISC Publications edited the manuscript and provided grammatical assistance. David Bull and James Penhune of David Bull Publishing provided editorial support, as well.

Jim France, Mark Raffauf, Bob Snodgrass, David Talley, Bob Leitzinger, and Jimmy Kupstas also read the manuscript, and each contributed details and made many helpful recommendations.

More invaluable assistance was provided by the public relations staff of Daytona International Speedway, including Glyn Johnstone, Kathy Catron, Andrew Booth, Mark Lewis, and Donna Freismuth, in addition to former DIS staffers including Fred Seeley, Dave Rodman, Gary Van Voorhis, Larry Balewski, and John Story, and many sanctioning body officials, including Dic van der Feen, Lyn Myfelt, Adam Saal, Dave Arnold, Patrick Murphy and Christie Hyde.

I have worked at the 24 Hours of Daytona since 1984, primarily in the role as a pit reporter, talking with drivers from opening practice through the post-race interviews. Over the past year I talked with many of the key participants in the event, who agreed to be interviewed for this book.

This list includes: Bob Akin, Mario Andretti, Michael Andretti, Carson Baird, Jack Baldwin, Derek Bell, Raul Boesel, Robbie Buhl, Richard Childress, Price Cobb, Jeremy Dale, Wally Dallenbach Jr., Kevin Doran, Jim Downing, Rob Dyson, Vic Elford, Juan Manuel Fangio II, Ron Fellows, Jon Field, Elliott Forbes-Robinson, A. J. Foyt, Bob Garretson, Paul Goldsmith, Jerry Grant, John Graves, Dan Gurney, Janet Guthrie, Hurley Haywood, Dr. David Helmick, Preston Henn, Tom Hessert, Phil Hill, Irv Hoerr, Alex Job, Parker Johnstone, Davy Jones, Max Jones, Mike Joy, Michael Keyser, Jeff Kline, Chris Kneifel, Terry Labonte, Bob Lazier, Jan Lammers, Bob Leitzinger, Butch Leitzinger, Fredy Lienhard, Buz McCall, Rob Morgan, Ray Mummery, David Murry, Paul Newman, Danny Ongais, Jim Pace, Max Papis, Benny Parsons, John Paul Jr., Roger Penske, Andy Pilgrim, Scott Pruett, Jeff Purvis, Bobby Rahal, Brian Redman, Jack Roush, Johnny Rutherford, Lyn St. James, John Schneider, Dorsey Schroeder, Scott Sharp, Guy Smith, Danny Sullivan, Al Unser, Al Unser Jr., Barry Waddell , Tom Walkinshaw, Andy Wallace, James Weaver.

Providing help in spirit through taped interviews were Dale Earnhardt, Al Holbert, and Bob Wollek.

As I researched materials in the ISC Archives, I was grateful to be able to refer to first-hand accounts filed by the Associated Press, *Daytona Beach News-Journal* and its predecessors, *Orlando Sentinel, St. Petersburg Times, Jacksonville Times Union, Miami Herald, On Track, AutoWeek* and *National Speed Sport News.*

Others who graciously provided material include Al Robinson and the Watkins Glen Racing Research Center; Earl Fannin, who allowed me to quote from his unpublished book on Peter Gregg; Mike Semel, who conducted an interview with Dan Gurney; John Gorsline, who provided his hospitality suite for the Phil Hill interview; Don Panoz, who provided his Sebring suite for the interview with Juan Manuel Fangio II; Ken Breslauer, who allowed the use of the Sebring media facilities; and the Road Racing Drivers Club, for their annual pre-event gathering and trackside hospitality.

Reference books used in this project include Janos Wimpffen's *Time and Two Seats*; Leo Levine's history of Ford's racing, *The Dust and the Glory*; Mark Donohue's *The Unfair Advantage*; Smokey Yunick's *Best Damn Garage in Town: The World According to Smokey;* John Bentley's *The Carroll Shelby Story;* Ronnie Spain's *GT40;* J. A. Martin and Ken Well's *Prototypes: The History of the IMSA GTP Series;* and Steve Small's *The Guinness Complete Grand Prix Who's Who.*

I also want to thank Chris Economaki, publisher emeritus of *National Speed Sport News*, for giving a recent graduate of King's College the opportunity to cover auto racing full time. Thanks also to ISC Senior Vice President John Saunders and ISC Publications President Tom Pokorny.

I cannot think about the Daytona 24 Hours without remembering the kindness extended over the years by the late Sandra Leitzinger, who provided encouragement, support and a good scrapple breakfast to get ready for the races. Her presence is sorely missed.

Finally, and most importantly, I want to thank my wife, Suzanne, and daughter, Erin, for their encouragement and allowing me to devote many evenings to this project.

J. J. O'Malley
March, 2003

CHIEF

CAMEL
GOODYEAR
NASCAR
Winston Cup

Foreword

The 24 Hours of Daytona is the most difficult of all sports car races. I've won the event five times, more than any other driver, which is an achievement I'm proud of, and I'm in a position to compare it with other famous international endurance tests, having also won the 24 Hours of Le Mans and 12 Hours of Sebring.

A variety of factors combine to make the race an unequalled challenge. First, people don't realize that there is such a long night at Daytona—there's at least 12 hours of darkness. In the early years, the event would start at 3 or 4 p.m., which meant that you were quickly running in darkness. Then you still had a long way to go after dawn. Now, the race starts at 1 p.m., which usually allows the entire driver rotation to have some time in the car before nightfall. Starting late, you'd get maybe two guys in during the daylight, and the next group would start at nighttime, which is not an easy thing to do.

There are many challenges in the Daytona 24 Hours that competitors in other long-distance races don't have to deal with. By comparison, the actual driving at Le Mans is much easier, physically and mentally. About half the number of cars start that race, around 45, versus 80 at Daytona, so you have fewer cars to worry about.

In addition, there are essentially only two classes at Le Mans, and you don't have the major class distinctions as you have at Daytona. With so many cars competing in different classes at Daytona, there's a vast difference in speeds. When you overtake those cars on the banking, where even the slower cars drift around a lot, it can be tricky getting around them sometimes.

My first victory here, in 1973, was probably the most satisfying. It was a pretty awesome feat. Our Brumos Porsche team, with Peter Gregg and myself driving, was racing our team's sister car, driven by Mark Donohue and George Follmer, and fielded by Roger Penske. We ran wheel to wheel with them, and we were able to beat them. That made Peter very happy, from the standpoint that it was Brumos Racing, the team he owned, against Penske Racing, and it made me very happy that I was competitive driving against Mark Donohue and George Follmer, two of the best guys in road racing at that point.

That Daytona victory put me and my name into the limelight, and really launched my career, establishing me on an international basis. Over the years, all of my victories here have really cemented the event's importance to me. Daytona has a rich history and plenty of drama. I'm proud to say that I have played a small part in it.

HURLEY HAYWOOD

Left: Hurley Haywood (left) was a relative newcomer to major sports car racing when he joined his mentor, Peter Gregg, in winning the 1973 Daytona 24 Hours. Haywood would go on to lead all drivers with five victories in the event. He also won the 24 Hours of Le Mans three times and the 12 Hours of Sebring twice, giving him 10 victories—at least two more than any other driver—in sports car racing's three premier events.

NO SMOKING
LAPS 59
WINSTON 500
CIBIÉ
LIGHTS
rain·x

Prologue

The tradition of automobile racing along the Florida coastline dates back to 1903, when teams began holding speed trials on the sands of Ormond Beach, just a few miles to the north of Daytona Beach. In the decades that followed, Daytona Beach, with its unusually hard-packed sands, attracted international attention with many land-speed record attempts, a quest that climaxed when Sir Malcolm Campbell's *Bluebird* passed 330 mph in 1925.

Eventually, the more stable surface of the Bonneville Salt Flats in Utah made that the most popular location in the world for land-speed record attempts. To keep Daytona Beach active as a major player in lucrative motorsports competitions, city officials embraced stock car and motorcycle racing on a course that used the beach itself and parallel roads. One of the promoters of the beach races was Bill France, who had relocated from Washington, D.C., to Daytona Beach in 1934 as a 23-year-old mechanic. After a rough start, both the beach races and France enjoyed unparalleled success.

France founded NASCAR in 1948, the same year Cameron Argetsinger organized the first post-World War II sports car race in America, in Watkins Glen, New York. Even then, France also had his eye on sports car racing. In 1949, he promoted an event at the Ft. Lauderdale-Davie Airport that included a short race for sports cars. Later, France organized a successful sports car race weekend in 1957 at the New Smyrna Beach airport, just south of Daytona Beach. Well-known bandleader Paul Whiteman was the race director, and the event, won by Carroll Shelby in a Ferrari, attracted many of America's top sports car drivers.

By the 1950s, promoting beach racing had become an increasingly difficult task. Not only did France have to cope with tides and deteriorating condi-

Left: 24-hour races are often won—or lost—in the pits. In 1975, crewmen frantically service Michael Keyser's overheating Porsche 911RSR late in the race. Keyser finished second, co-driving with Bill Sprowls and Andreas Contreras. Above: Many celebrity drivers have raced at Daytona, including Olympic Decathlon gold medalist Bruce Jenner, who made his professional racing debut in the No. 3 Rusty Jones BMW M1 in 1980.

tions on the sand portions of the track, but growing beachside development and the resulting traffic were encroaching on the races. To remain successful, France knew he would have to build a permanent facility, so he began lobbying city officials for a speedway in 1953. It took six years to realize his dream, and proved well worth the effort.

But France wasn't satisfied with making Daytona International Speedway the most important track in NASCAR stock car racing. He also wanted his sparkling new facility to play a major role in international motorsports. To that end, he came up with a brand-new concept, creating an infield road course inside the high-banked, 2.5-mile tri-oval, which would be perfect for major sports car and motorcycle races.

When the speedway opened in 1959, it hosted the first Paul Whiteman Cup, a non-points club race run clockwise on the banked oval and infield, among other sports car events.

By 1962, France was ready to host an international event—the inaugural Daytona Continental, a three-hour race to be run counter-clockwise on the 3.81-mile circuit. To promote the race, France held a media reception at New York City's posh "21" club, hundreds of miles from Daytona, and light-years away from his usual stock car racing milieu. At that time, NASCAR stock car racing was still in its infancy, and was considered by many to be largely a Southeastern United States phenomenon. Although the Daytona 500 was gaining wider attention, the national media was not hesitant to point out the sport's dubious origins in the moonshine liquor business.

Sports car racing, however, was considered the elite division of American motorsports, rivaled only by the Indianapolis 500, and could potentially attract national attention and publicity to the new venue. Sports car racing would help France open doors that would have otherwise been closed to stock car racing.

The inaugural Daytona Continental, run on a course using the monster 31-degree banking, attracted a strong field of international stars, including America's top sports car drivers, plus a few of stock car racing's biggest names.

In 1964, the Daytona Continental was expanded to 2,000 kilometers, and with a race time of 12 hours and forty minutes, it became America's longest endurance test. With the Ford vs. Ferrari battle for international sports car supremacy at its zenith, the race was expanded to the magical 24 hours in 1966. The event has been run at that distance ever since, with the exception of 1972, when the speedway experimented with a six-hour format, and 1974, when the international fuel crisis forced the one-time cancellation of the race.

The 24 Hours of Daytona joined its 24-hour counterpart in Le Mans, France, and the 12-hour test in Sebring, Florida, as the triple crown of international endurance competition. With Daytona as the opening event in the international racing calendar, sunny Florida had become a welcome destination for the winter-weary racing world.

In these pages are stories and photographs of the drivers, the crews, and the machines who have built the legacy of the 24 Hours of Daytona—America's premier sports car race.

Above: Butch Leitzinger chauffeurs his happy team to victory lane at the conclusion of the 1997 race. Leitzinger is a three-time winner of the event, including victories in 1997 and 1999 with Dyson Racing. Left: An aerial view of the action in the International Horseshoe section of the infield during the 1962 Daytona Continental, with the high-banked NASCAR Turn 4 in the background. The race was the first time many of the competitors competed on a high-banked superspeedway.

ARCIERO
RACING INC.
96
18

1962: Continental Began Daytona Tradition

If promoter "Big Bill" France was hoping to attract international attention to Daytona International Speedway for its inaugural Daytona Continental, he couldn't have gathered a stronger roster of cars and drivers.

The impressive list of internationally known stars featured two Americans who were making their mark on the world stage. Phil Hill had become the first American to win the Formula One World Championship in 1961, while his fellow Californian Dan Gurney was one of the fastest-rising stars in Grand Prix racing.

English legend Stirling Moss joined Hill on Luigi Chinetti's North American Racing Team (NART) entry, driving a pair of Ferraris. Scotsman Jimmy Clark was a year away from his first World Championship, and came to Daytona fresh from three winter victories in non-points Formula One races. Fellow Scot Innes Ireland had won the first U.S. Grand Prix at Watkins Glen in 1961 for Team Lotus. Other international stars included Mexican brothers Pedro and Ricardo Rodriguez, Jo Bonnier of Sweden, England's David Hobbs, and Olivier Gendebien of Belgium.

America's best-known sports car stars were also on hand. Briggs Cunningham had Jaguars for Walt Hansgen and Augie Pabst. They were joined by Roger Penske, Jim Hall, Harry Heuer, and Dick Thompson.

Beyond the traditional sports car ranks, the race also attracted Indy Car

Left: A fenced-off area of the infield trioval, between pit road and the front straight, served as a makeshift victory-lane. A crowd surrounds the winning Arciero Racing Lotus Climax 19B to watch the trophy presentations.
Above: Jim Clark poses next to No. 30 Lotus Elite, which he drove to a 29th-place finish. Clark went on to win the 1963 and 1965 Formula One world championships, in addition to winning the 1965 Indianapolis 500.

driver A. J. Foyt, the 1961 Indianapolis 500 winner, plus Rodger Ward and Dick Rathmann. And NASCAR fans came to root for many of their favorites, with Fireball Roberts, Marvin Panch, Joe Weatherly, and Paul Goldsmith competing. The cars were a mixture of imported and domestic machinery, with the Lotuses, Ferraris, Jaguars, Porsches, and Alfa-Romeos competing with a dozen Corvettes, three Pontiac Tempests, and two Chevrolet-powered Chaparrals.

In addition to the stellar lineup of drivers and cars, the speedway itself was another draw. For the first time, sports car fans could watch the entire course from their grandstand seats instead of being limited to viewing the action directly in front of them, as on a traditional circuit.

The monster 31-degree banking quickly captured the attention of the sports car crowd. "I remember going to Daytona for the first time," recalled Gurney. "You'd go through that tunnel and come out inside the speedway, and here is this gigantic dream of Bill France Sr. It was—and still is—an impressive sight. It was the granddaddy of all such tracks. There was an element of the unknown there. We did not know what it would be like. Drafting was something everybody wondered about—it had an ominous atmosphere to it. But race drivers are supposed to be immune to such things, so we all pretended that this was just another race track."

France made sure that Daytona Beach rolled out the red carpet for its visitors. "They had a reception for the drivers, and someone told Big Bill France that I was a top saloon driver in England," Hobbs said. "He was impressed and started introducing me to people as a star British driver. He made me feel important.

"Big Bill made a big deal of this race," Hobbs continued. "We had all sorts of public receptions the week before the race. Big Bill was keen on the international aspect of racing. He wanted to open up the race to the world, and show everyone it was not just a bunch of good old boys racing.

"Obviously, he was successful. They're still running the event 40 years later."

Top left: NASCAR Grand National star Fireball Roberts braves the rain at an airport to inspect the Ferrari he would drive in the Daytona Continental. Top right: Using the start made popular in the 24 Hours of Le Mans, drivers ran to their cars, while race officials scurried to the tri-oval grass. This was the only year the running start was used at Daytona. Opposite page: Winner Dan Gurney enjoys a drink and listens to a crewman while television reporter Chris Economaki queries Stirling Moss, continuing an interview interrupted by the start of the race.

The Continental started with a running start in the fashion made famous at the 24 Hours of Le Mans. Drivers lined up on pit road, and when the signal was given, sprinted to their cars and fired up their engines. The field then raced one lap on the full 2.5-mile tri-oval (to avoid confusion heading into the first turn of the infield portion of the circuit), and then continued the race on the 3.81-mile road circuit.

Foyt boasted that he would lead the first superspeedway lap in his Pontiac Tempest, even betting teammate Rodger Ward. Foyt collected on the bet.

"I'll never forget when Foyt said he was going to lead that first lap, and we all scoffed—that Pontiac thing? But he did," recalled Phil Hill.

Stirling Moss was known for quick getaways on the running starts, but not this time. He was being interviewed by ABC television commentator Chris Economaki when the signal was given for drivers to run to their cars, which delayed his sprint. Indianapolis 500 driver Dick Rathmann was even less fortunate. His Chaparral's engine flooded immediately, and he missed three laps before it finally fired.

After Foyt led the first lap on the superspeedway oval, the field took to the full road circuit for the second lap. Penske used his road-racing expertise to get by Foyt and take the lead in the infield in a Cooper Monaco with a Climax engine. It was only a matter of time, though, before Hill took over the point in the NART Ferrari Dino.

The world champion had a rough day. Hill's car struck a sea gull that lodged in his radiator early in the race, then had to return to the pits to replace his filler cap after his first fuel stop. He then missed

the first turn on the 44th lap. He pitted on the following circuit and was relieved by Ricardo Rodriguez.

Hill's botched fuel stop gave the lead to Gurney in Frank Arciero's Lotus Climax 19B. Meanwhile, Ricardo Rodriguez battled the Chaparral 1 of Hall for second place, taking the position with 15 minutes remaining in the race. Gurney had a seemingly insurmountable lead. But with one minute and 40 seconds remaining before the three hours elapsed, disaster struck.

"As we were coming down to the end of the three hours, with about a two-minute lead, the engine blew between turns three and four of the banking," Gurney recalled. "It actually stuck a rod right through the side of the engine block. I coasted to the finish line, up on the banking in front of the grandstands. I was looking at my watch and decided if I waited a minute, maybe I had enough of a lead so I could go across when they dropped the (checkered) flag."

Gurney knew that to win, he would have to cross the finish line after time expired, and regulations prohibited being pushed across the line. If Gurney crossed the line seconds before the three hours

Above: Preparation continues on pit road on the No. 2 Scarab of Harry Heuer, who did not attempt to qualify. In the background is the No. 0 Chaparral 1 of Dick Rathmann, who enjoyed success in both NASCAR Grand National and Indy car racing. Opposite page top: Roger Penske pits his No. 46 Cooper-Climax. The future successful car owner led the first lap of competition on the road circuit (after A. J. Foyt paced the opening lap on the superspeedway oval), but Penske later retired after losing oil pressure. Opposite right: Phil Hill's No. 1 Ferrari is unloaded from the NART transporter prior to the event.

were up, there was no way he could run another full lap. Waiting on the banked tri-oval, Gurney hoped gravity would propel him to victory.

"So I sat there, four or five feet short of going across the finish line, way up near the wall," said Gurney. "There were shadows up there, and the guys that were coming by were moving along pretty fast. I was pretty happy nobody was quite as high as I was. The flagman was perched just up above me, and I was looking at my watch, and he was looking at his watch, and I was wondering whether in fact we had the kind of lead we thought we had. In the end, he waved the flag, and I turned left and coasted down the banking and that was the win."

Contrary to the popular legend, Gurney did not cross the finish on his starter motor. "No, I just turned left," he said. "I don't know if the starter motor would have turned over because of the connecting rod sticking through the side there, but that's the way history is made. Nobody could believe it just coasted across."

It was the fastest sports car race ever run in the United States—despite having one of the slowest finishes. Gurney completed 82 laps on the 3.81 mile course, averaging 104.101 mph in his red Lotus.

"It was very smart for you to stop as you did just in front of the finish line," American astronaut Alan Shepard told Gurney after the race. Shepard had become America's first man in space the previous May, and joined fellow astronaut Deke Slayton in attending the race.

Rodriguez and Hill finished second in their Ferrari, 46 seconds behind, with Hall taking third. Stirling Moss placed fourth and led all the way to win the GT class. Moss's closest call came when he dented a left-front fender.

"Someone spun in front of Joe Weatherby," Moss recalled, referring to NASCAR driver Weatherly, who lost control of his Lister Corvette on the 20th lap. "Weatherby spun in front of me, and we touched."

Moss's only other complaint was an oil-splattered windshield, which limited his vision late in the race when he was blinded by the setting sun. "I couldn't see a bloody thing out there." Two months later, Moss was involved in an Easter Sunday racing accident at Goodwood, England, which effectively ended his career.

1962

Fireball Roberts offered Moss his stiffest competition for the GT title, but the NASCAR star lost ground during a pit stop when his crew tried to repair a hood latch. He had to pit again on the 51st lap, and had the crew remove the hood. Roberts finished 12th in his hoodless Ferrari 250, second in the GT class.

The race had 10 different classes, so several other competitors were able to go away from the inaugural event as winners. George Constantine placed fifth in a Ferrari 250 TR and won the Sports 3000cc

Above: The checkered flag waves to signal the conclusion of the three-hour race, and Dan Gurney releases the brake on his parked car to roll to victory. Opposite page top: Dan Gurney climbs out from behind the wheel of the winning Lotus-Climax 19B, and is surrounded by members of the Frank Arciero team.
Opposite right: The No. 78 Corvette of Bob Schroeder races past a group of corner workers at a flagging station entering turn one, where the infield section of the circuit branches off from the superspeedway tri-oval.

class, while Bob Holbert was seventh in a Porsche 718 RSK and first in Sports 2000cc.

Robert Donner's Porsche 718RS61 was 11th and first in Sports 1600cc, while Dick Thompson's Corvette won the Grand Touring over five-liter class. Walt Hansgen, driving Briggs Cunningham's E-Type Jaguar, won Grand Touring 4000cc.

Lynn Coleman, a manager at Brumos Porsche dealership in Jacksonville, Florida, joined Pat Corrigan in winning the 1600cc GT class in a Brumos Porsche 356B. This began a long and successful tradition of Brumos competing at Daytona International Speedway.

Taking the 1300cc GT class was Charlie Kolb in an Alfa Romeo Giulietta SZ, which placed 25th overall. Thirty-four of the fifty starters were still running at the finish. An estimated 18,000 fans were on hand, chilled by a stiff northwestern wind.

The Daytona Continental was definitely a promising start. The event's placement near the beginning of the year soon became an annual tradition for winter-weary sports car competitors and enthusiasts, who looked forward to beginning the new season in the Florida sunshine.

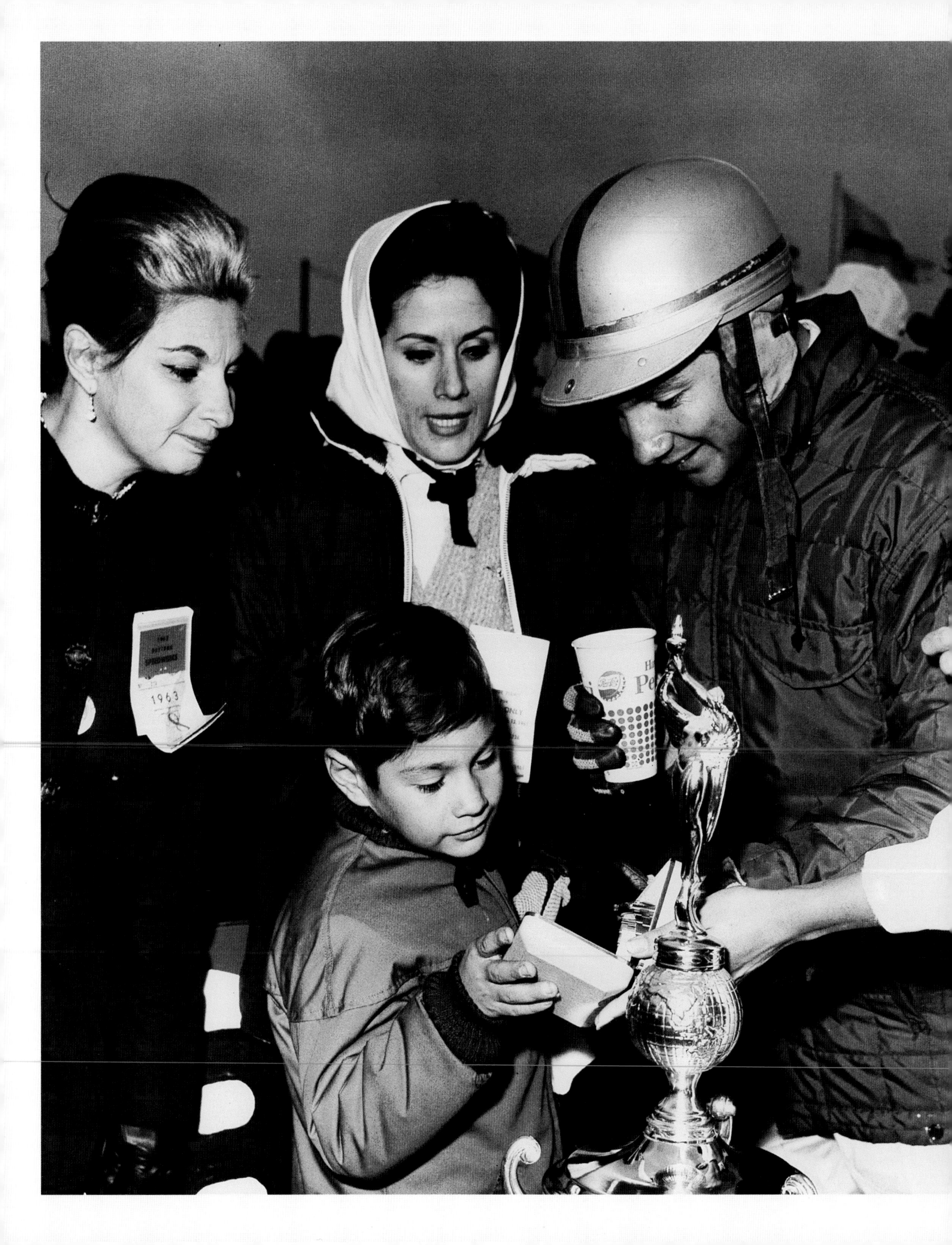
1963

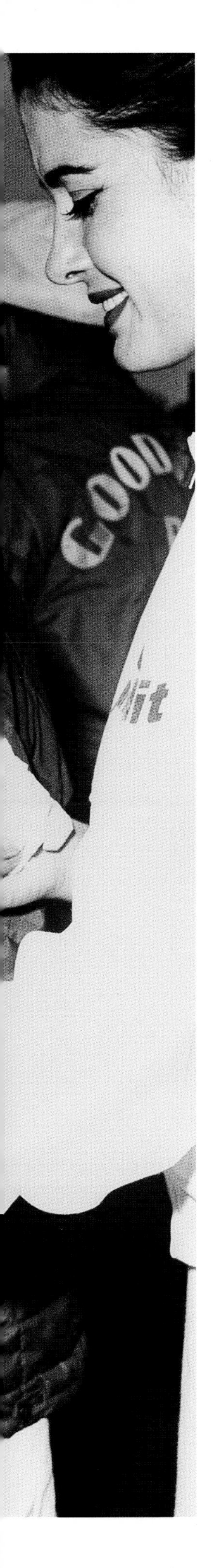

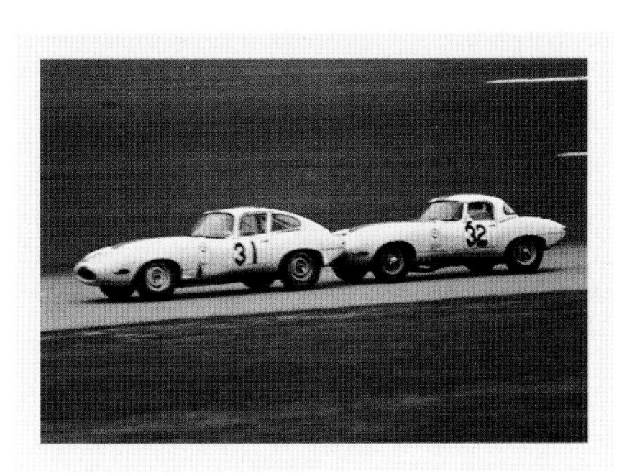

1963: Reluctant Winner

SUNDAY DAWNED DRY BUT WINDY. UNLIKE THE FIRST ANNUAL DAYTONA CONTINENTAL—WHICH ALLOWED GTS AND THE FASTER SPORTS RACING CARS TO ENTER—THE 1963 RACE WAS LIMITED TO GTS. IN CONTRAST TO THE LE MANS-STYLE START USED THE YEAR BEFORE, NO ONE WOULD RUN TO THEIR CARS.

When the 42 cars formed for the start—the grid was based on engine displacement—defending champion Dan Gurney was still in the paddock, waiting for his crew to complete an engine change. His Shelby Cobra had blown out a freeze plug during morning practice, forcing the crew to change engines only two hours before the race. In the meantime, it was rumored that Gurney would switch to the Cobra entered for teammate Dave MacDonald.

Other contenders from the previous year were also having problems. Stirling Moss, still recovering from his Goodwood injuries and now sporting a beard, was at the wheel of the pace car. And although Pedro Rodriguez was driving a new Ferrari GTO, the Mexican racing phenom was reportedly mulling over retirement after the death of his brother, Ricardo, the previous fall in the Mexican Grand Prix.

Both brothers had competed in the inaugural Daytona Continental: While Ricardo finished second behind winner Dan Gurney, Pedro's Lotus 19 dropped out after 28 laps with a broken suspension. Pedro was now part of Luigi

Left: Miss Universe presents the winner's Rolex watch to Pedro Rodriguez, who is joined in victory lane by his mother (far left), wife Angelina, and younger brother Alejandro. Above: Augie Pabst, driving the No. 32 E-type Jaguar, pushes teammate Walter Hansgen on the apron after the latter ran out of fuel while running seventh. The sportsmanlike gesture resulted in Hansgen's disqualification, with Pabst finishing 10th.

Chinetti's North American Racing Team (NART), which once again carried the colors of the Italian manufacturer. Chinetti fielded two bright-red 250 GT cars, the other carrying popular NASCAR Grand National star Fireball Roberts.

In addition, there were three independently entered Ferrari GTOs. Texas oil magnate John Mecom's Rosebud Racing fielded GTO for Roger Penske and Innes Ireland, while David Piper drove his own entry.

Flexing the American muscle were Carroll Shelby's Fords, with Shelby Cobras entered for Gurney, MacDonald, and Skip Hudson. Chevrolet was well represented by a dozen Corvettes, with the driver lineup including A. J. Foyt. Pontiac was also in the field, with a Pontiac Tempest for NASCAR Grand National regular Paul Goldsmith.

When the field took the green flag in a rolling start on the back straightaway, MacDonald was on the track in his Shelby Cobra while Gurney missed the first two laps of the race waiting for his engine change.

A shivering crowd estimated at 9,500, braving bitter cold and wind, watched as Goldsmith jumped to an early lead, but retired his Pontiac after only three laps with a broken fuel pump. A. J. Foyt made

Above: Newspaper publisher and television commentator Chris Economaki works in the makeshift "broadcast central" located in the tri-oval section of the track. Top: Carroll Shelby helped make Ford a force to be reckoned with in international sports car racing. The Texan is pictured with his motorcycle at the sports car race promoted by Bill France at the New Smyrna Beach airport in 1957. Opposite left: Spectators in the circuit infield watch as the No. 59 Triumph TR-3 of George Cornelius is passed by the No. 5 Corvette of NASCAR driver Johnny Allen. Allen went on to finish sixth overall and second in the big-engine class. Opposite right: NASCAR Grand National star Paul Goldsmith, a former motorcycle ace, ran up front in the early going but dropped out after only three laps with a broken fuel pump. He was passed by a pack of Corvette Sting Rays at the completion of lap one.

the first of a series of pit stops on the fourth lap and retired after 41 laps. Ireland's charge ended when he spun on the fifth lap and was hit by a Corvette, putting him out of the race.

Gurney entered the race late, and was never a factor. He soldiered on for 48 laps, fighting throttle trouble in his Shelby Cobra, then calling it quits when his ignition failed. The big-engine Corvettes of Bill Krause and Dick Thompson took their turns out front, while Rodriguez battled his way up through traffic.

Hudson took the lead on lap 10 in his Cobra. He was passed by Rodriguez for the lead on the banking, but battled back to regain the lead in the infield. Rodriguez got by on the next trip to the banking, on the 11th lap. This time, Rodriguez pulled away, averaging 104 mph laps while hitting 160 mph on the straights.

While Rodriguez began to take charge, Penske took over second and watched his pursuers run into trouble. Hudson pressured Penske for the runner-up slot before pitting with a broken fuel line. He later suffered a broken foot when his flywheel came apart and broke through the floorboard of his car. Fireball Roberts worked his way up to fourth before falling back. The NASCAR star felt his engine was running poorly, so he turned the car over to John Cannon, who finished 15th.

Two-thirds of the way into the event, Rodriguez pitted. His NART crew needed only 40 seconds to refuel the Ferrari while Rodriguez watched, standing atop the pit wall. The stop briefly handed the lead to Penske, who pitted four laps later. The Mecom crew changed tires and needed nearly a minute for the service. Penske re-entered the race in second.

David Piper was running third when he spun in oil, missed a shift, and his engine blew. Walt Hansgen and Dick Thompson then battled for third, several laps behind the leading Ferraris.

Suddenly, late in the race, Rodriguez pitted, pointing to the fuel gauge and screaming, "It's empty!"

in three languages. He waited in the cockpit while fuel was quickly added and returned to the race with a one-minute lead over Penske.

Eventually Rodriguez took the checkered flag, 64 seconds ahead of Penske. But the drama wasn't over. The Mecom team filed a protest, stating that the second pit stop was illegal because the driver failed to get out of the car. The protest was studied and upheld. Rodriguez was penalized 50 seconds, which still gave him a 14-second official margin of victory.

"We did not put enough gas in the car during my other stop and came in for more near the end of the race," said Rodriguez afterward. "My pit crew told me to stay in the car because they would only have one man over the wall handling the gas. It was our understanding that the driver could stay in the car if only one man was working over the wall. I did not think I was doing anything wrong."

Penske felt differently.

"Rules are set up for the protection of everybody," he said following the race. "And this rule is perfectly clear: A driver must leave his car at every pit stop regardless. We feel Pedro did not comply with the ruling on either of his stops. The first time he pitted, he stood on top of the wall, and the rule says you must get behind the wall."

Dick Thompson finished third overall in a Corvette—and first in the over five-liter class. Fourth, four laps down, was the Shelby American Cobra driven by Dave MacDonald, winner of the five-liter GT Division III class. Fifth went to the Porsche Speedster of Swedish Grand Prix star Jo Bonnier.

Augie Pabst was awarded the victory in the GT Division III four-liter class. Pabst was running 11th when his Briggs Cunningham teammate, Walt Hansgen, ran out of fuel in the closing laps while running seventh. Pabst pushed his teammate back to the pits, resulting in Hansgen's disqualification for illegal assistance.

Pabst finished behind Hans Hermann, who had an impressive drive in an Abarth-Simca. Hermann was running fifth overall in the 1300cc car before a late fuel stop dropped him to ninth overall, but

Above: Paul Goldsmith is pictured with car owner Ray Nichels and the trophy after winning the Challenge Cup. Goldsmith also won motorcycle and stock car races at Daytona Beach. Opposite right: Competitors at the middle of the pack saw a group of Corvettes and a Pontiac Tempest run up front in the opening laps. Opposite far right: The Shelby American crew works on Dan Gurney's No. 98 Cobra with the No. 97 of Skip Hudson in the background. The defending winner's race got off to a late start following a mechanical problem during pre-event warmups, and his ignition failed after 48 laps.

the German still won his class by six laps.

Bob Holbert, one of America's top sports car drivers and a leading Porsche campaigner, finished seventh overall and second in class, driving a Porsche-Abarth 356B Carrera GTL, two laps and two positions behind class winner Bonnier's Speedster.

The all-GT race featured eight different classes, including other class winners Chuck Cassel in a Porsche-Abarth 356B, eighth overall in GT Division II 1600cc, and Tony Mannino, 17th overall in a Triumph TR-3, in GT Division II 2500cc.

The weekend also included the new Challenge Cup, a 250-mile Saturday race for closed two-seaters on the 2.5-mile oval. A cold, driving rain cut the field to only 14 competitors, led by Goldsmith in a Pontiac, who won easily with speeds averaging 145.16 mph. Foyt finished second in a Sting Ray, two laps back, followed by Bill Krause in a Mickey Thompson Sting Ray, six laps back. NASCAR star Junior Johnson was also part of the four-Corvette Thompson entry, but dropped out while running third, complaining of handling problems.

Also on the schedule was the 200-mile United States Road Racing Driver Championship race, featuring 53 laps of the 3.81-mile circuit. Jim Hall won in a Cooper Monaco over Bob Holbert in a Porsche RS61. Holbert led the first 15 laps before giving way to Hall, who led the rest of the way.

The event was marred by a near-tragedy. NASCAR Grand National veteran Marvin Panch tested a Ford-engined Birdcage Maserati owned by Briggs Cunningham in preparation for the Continental. Panch was turning laps of 103 mph when his car suddenly slowed on the east banking and began flipping, finally coming to a halt on its roof.

Journeyman NASCAR driver Tiny Lund—who was without a ride for the Daytona 500 and hoping to find work on a pit crew—witnessed the accident and rushed to the scene. Lund was removing the stunned driver when the car burst into flames. The injuries from the accident caused Panch to miss both the Continental and the NASCAR season-opening Daytona 500. As repayment to his friend, he personally requested that Lund be allowed to race his Ford in the Daytona 500, and his team owners, the Wood Brothers, agreed. Lund, who at that point had found only limited success in his seven-year career, went out and scored his first NASCAR victory in the 500.

30
FERRARI
30

1964: Continental Lengthened to 2,000 Kilometers

For 1964, the format for the Daytona Continental was changed from three hours to 2,000 kilometers (1,243 miles) for 1964 and 1965, with the eventual goal of racing 24 hours.

Ford was ready for the challenge. Carroll Shelby, who prepared the factory cars, came to Daytona with the first-ever Cobra Coupe, driven by Bob Holbert and Dave MacDonald. Based on the AC-Bristol, the new Peter Brock design was more aerodynamic than its predecessor. After its performance in the Continental, the car would forever be known as the Cobra Daytona. The Shelby American entry also included three teams racing Shelby Cobras: Dan Gurney and Bob Johnson; Jo Schlesser and Jean Guichet; and Tommy Johnson and Zourab Tchkotoua.

The Ferrari entry was in the hands of Luigi Chinetti, whose North American Racing Team fielded a Ferrari 250 GTO 64 for Pedro Rodriguez and Phil Hill. The latter had fallen out with Enzo Ferrari following the 1962 season, but was still on good terms with Chinetti. NART also had a modified GTO for Walt Hansgen and Bob Grossman. There were six privateer Ferraris, including one David Piper shared with Lucien Bianchi, and a Don Fong entry for A. J. Foyt and Charlie Kolb.

The 1964 race started at 10 a.m. under sunny skies, with an attendance estimated at 15,000. Holbert set out at a fast pace, taking an early lead in the Daytona Coupe but stalked by Rodriguez. Holbert averaged 105.605 mph after

Left: A group of observers behind the pit wall watch as service is performed on the eventual-winning Ferrari. Co-driving the No. 30 Ferrari 250 GTO 64 was 1963 Daytona Continental winner Pedro Rodriguez, joined by 1961 Formula One world champion Phil Hill. Above: The Shelby Daytona Cobra Coupe of Bob Holbert and Dave MacDonald (No. 14) leads the Ferrari of Pedro Rodriguez and Phil Hill. Holbert's son Al would carry the number 14 on his Porsches in the seventies and eighties, winning the Daytona 24 Hours twice.

10 laps, with Rodriguez taking the lead at 30 laps. By noon, when driver changes began, Holbert and Rodriguez had lapped the field.

MacDonald took over for Holbert, and extended the lead over Hill to 28 seconds by lap 70. At 3 p.m., Rodriguez cut his left-front tire on the backstretch, taking out most of the fender. A four-and-one-half minute pit stop cost the Ferrari three laps, dropping the team back to fourth behind the Cobras of Holbert/MacDonald and Gurney/Johnson, and the Ferrari of David Piper and Lucien Bianchi. Rodriguez worked his way back to second at the midway point, but was still four laps behind the fleet Holbert/MacDonald Cobra.

After dominating the opening eight hours, the Daytona Cobra pitted on lap 209—around sunset—for routine service. Suddenly, a fire started because of oil leaking from a differential seal. The blaze was quickly extinguished, but the damage was done, and the car was retired. Shelby crewman John Olson, who was under the car when the fire started, was hospitalized with second and third degree burns.

That gave the lead to the Hill/Rodriguez Ferrari, whose only further problems were the frequent pit stops needed to remount their headlights, which had been damaged in the earlier incident. "[Rodriguez] hit something or somebody, and knocked out our most critical headlight, the one that shone on the banking at night," Hill recalled. "That made it particularly difficult when it got dark,

Top: The field is lined up double-file on pit road prior to the start of the 1964 Daytona Continental. Above: A fire on race-leading Shelby Cobra Daytona Coupe was quickly extinguished during a pit stop, but the damage forced the retirement of the car after it dominated the opening eight hours of the race. Above right: Taking the green flag are the No. 36 Ferrari 250 GT of Charlie Dietrich and Dr. M.R.J. Wyllie, No. 50 Porsche-Abarth 356B of Chuck Cassel and Augie Pabst, No. 38 Ferrari 250 GT of Eduardo Dibos and Mario Colabattisti, and No. 54 of Victor Merino. Right: The Pedro Rodriguez/Phil Hill Ferrari (No. 30) chases the No. 20 Cobra of Jeff Stevens and Ralph Noseda, and is followed by the No. 32 Ferrari 250 GTO of William Eve and Larry Perkins.

38
54
36
50
32
30

because the light was pointing straight up in the air."

Rodriguez and Phil Hill completed 327 laps of the 3.81-mile circuit, 1,244.56 miles, averaging 98.199 mph. Because the pair took 12 hours, 40 minutes, and 25 seconds to complete the distance, the event surpassed the 12 Hours of Sebring as America's longest sports car race.

It was the first major endurance victory for Rodriguez, as well as his second consecutive triumph in the Daytona Continental. Hill, a three-time winner at both the 24 Hours of Le Mans and 12 Hours of Sebring, became the first driver to win at all three classic endurance venues.

Second, four laps down, was the Piper/Bianchi car, followed by Hansgen and Grossman to give Ferrari a sweep of the top three positions. The Piper/Bianchi car lost ground when it had to stop to replace a broken alternator mounting, but regained the position when the Hansgen/Grossman car fell back with electrical problems. The Gurney/Johnson Cobra, which was battling ignition problems, finished fourth, 16 laps behind.

Ulf Norinder and John Cannon were running fourth late in the race in Norinder's Ferrari 250 GTO, but a Prancing Horse sweep of the top four was prevented when their car stalled in the pits and had to be restarted using jumper cables. They managed to finish fifth.

Though the race was longer, it included only three classes. Jo Bonnier, Edgar Barth, and Herbert Linge won GT Division II two-liter, finishing sixth overall in a Porsche 356B. Alan Bouverat and Milo Vega won GT Division I 1300cc, sharing a Lotus Elite that placed 16th overall.

A. J. Foyt was frustrated for the third consecutive year at Daytona. In fact, for the second straight year, the feisty Texan didn't even get to drive, as the Ferrari he shared with Charlie Kolb was disqualified after 10 laps for missing technical inspection.

Top left: Dan Gurney smokes the tires in the No. 16 Shelby Cobra. He joined Robert Johnson in finishing fourth. Top right: Action in the banking, as the Daytona Continental races into the night for the first time. The road circuit utilized most of the 2.5-mile tri-oval used for NASCAR competition, including the 31-degree banked turns. Above: The field files off of pit road for a practice session, led by the Howe Sound Ford Special. That car competed in the 250-mile American Challenge race held the day before the 2000-kilometer main event. Right: Phil Hill (left) and Pedro Rodriguez receive the winner's trophy from Miss Universe in a nighttime presentation.

The field also included the debut of Peter Gregg, who shared his Triumph TR-4 with Harold St. John in a 23rd place finish. Gregg would go on to etch his name in the Daytona record books in coming years.

NASCAR Grand National drivers Cale Yarborough and G. C. Spencer shared a Corvette, which retired after 149 laps with gearbox problems. American sports car veterans Charles Dietrich and M. R. J. Wyllie placed ninth overall in a Ferrari 250GT SWB.

The weekend also featured a 250-mile American Challenge Cup, won by Foyt in a Scarab owned by John Mecom. Foyt raced wheel to wheel with Dan Gurney's Lotus 19B, and the pair exchanged the lead 16 times as they pulled away from the other 35 starters. Gurney's car stalled in the pits on lap 38, and retired with gearbox trouble three laps later. Fireball Roberts finished second in a Ford Fairlane prototype, followed by Ed Hugus in a Lotus 23B, and the Porsches of Charles Kurtz, Bob Hagestad, and William Bowman. Next were Walt Hansgen, in a Ford Falcon, and G. C. Spencer in a Corvette. Competition Press called the race the "surprise of the weekend—after all, a stocker beating sports cars in a road race!"

73
72
99
NA·RT

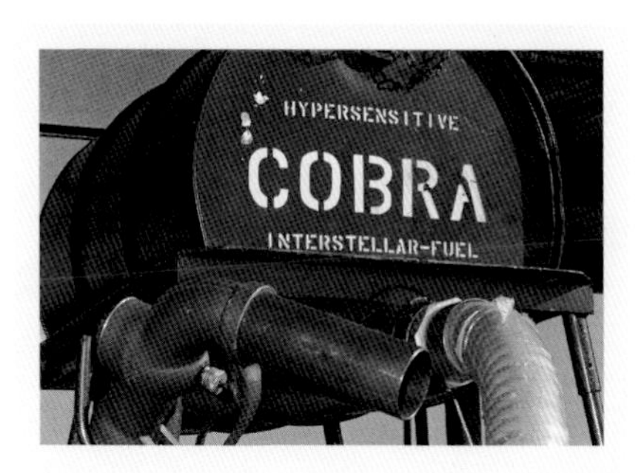

1965: Ford Unveils the GT40

THE FORD VS. FERRARI WAR WAS AT FULL TILT IN 1965, AND THE DETROIT MANUFACTURER SPARED NO EXPENSE IN A BID FOR ITS FIRST MAJOR INTERNATIONAL CHAMPIONSHIP AT THE SEASON-OPENING DAYTONA CONTINENTAL 2000 KILOMETERS. FOR THE FIRST TIME SINCE THE 1962 INAUGURAL CONTINENTAL, THE FASTER PROTOTYPES AND SPORTS CARS JOINED THE GT CARS.

After failing in its bid to buy out Ferrari the previous year, Ford established its own team in England, working with Eric Broadley of Lola. To build the cars, Ford acquired the services of John Wyer, the former racing manager and general manager of Aston Martin. The prototype was based on the popular Mustang I, powered by the 256-cubic-inch Ford Fairlane engine. The prototype, completed on April 1, 1964, was designed in Dearborn, Michigan, by Ford engineer Roy Lunn, who also designed the Mustang I. The vehicle was 40 inches high, hence the name GT40.

Three GT40s competed in the 1964 24 Hours of Le Mans. Though none of them finished, Phil Hill broke the circuit's speed record. Durability problems were also evident in other European races that year.

The winter of 1964 had been spent preparing for the 1965 racing season, with the responsibility for racing the cars given to Carroll Shelby's Shelby American team. The transaxles were modified, the driveshafts replaced, and Cobra 289 cast-iron engines were installed.

Left: The Ferrari started by Bob Grossman attempts to hold off the two Ford GT40s, No. 73 of Ken Miles and Lloyd Ruby and the No. 72 of Bob Bondurant and Richie Ginther. Above: Carroll Shelby had a unique label for the pitside rig that fueled the winning car.

For Daytona, Shelby not only brought a pair of sleek new GT40s, but also four Daytona Coupes. Ken Miles/Lloyd Ruby and Bob Bondurant/Richie Ginther shared the GT40s. Jo Schlesser/Harold Keck, Rick Muther/John Timanus, Ed Leslie/Alan Grant, and Robert Johnson/Tom Payne were entered in Daytona Coupes. NASCAR's Holman-Moody team gave Ford additional depth by fielding a Mustang GT 350 for Skip Scott and Charlie Hayes.

1965

Ferrari, through its North American Racing Team, entered three blue-and-white cars, including a new 275P, with a driver lineup including Walt Hansgen, Pedro Rodriguez, Bob Grossman, and David Piper. NART also entered a pair of 330s, including one for reigning World Champion John Surtees.

Above: The 45-car field follows the Ford Mustang pace car off pit road moments before the start of the race. Right: The No. 13 Shelby Cobra Daytona Coupe of Jo Schlesser, Harold Keck, and Robert Johnson is serviced on pit road during the early evening hours. Far right: The eventual-winning Ford GT40 leads a group of cars, the No 36 Shelby Cobra of Richard Thompson and Graham Shaw, No. 37 Porsche 718 RS 61 of Don Sesslar and Chuck Cassel, and No. 87 Cortina of Buck Baker and Bob Tullius.

The surprise performance of an independent entry had both Ford and Ferrari worried in the early stages of the event. Dan Gurney entered a Lotus 19J dubbed the *Pacesetter*—a highly modified version of his 1962 Daytona winner with a bigger Ford engine—for himself and Jerry Grant. The pair struggled in practice before hitting on the right combination.

"Jerry and I had enormous trouble with the car in practice, mostly aerodynamic problems," Gurney recalled in a 2002 interview. "Suddenly, with just four minutes left in the final practice before the race, we fixed it by putting a little spoiler on the back. Before, it wouldn't even run down the straightaway. The straightaway was the scariest part—I was using up about three lanes just trying to keep it straight, and we could never race it that way. Then, we put this rear spoiler on the back of the bodywork, and, all of a sudden, it was as straight as an arrow. Everything was great."

Bothered by the handling problems, Gurney had only managed to qualify 10th. Once the green flag waved at 10 a.m., however, he quickly got by the Ferraris and then the Fords. The Californian built up a huge lead and showed no signs of slowing down, while the favored competition encountered various problems.

On lap 16, Walt Hansgen ran over debris, cut a tire, and spun down the track in spectacular fashion. A broken driveshaft and suspension damage resulting from the incident sidelined the No.

2 Ferrari, and Hansgen and co-driver David Piper were shifted to the team's third car, started by Bob Grossman.

Surtees kept the lead Ferrari in contention with the Fords during the opening laps. His relief driver, Rodriguez, cut a tire early during his shift on the 64th lap while running second. After changing tires using the on-board spare, the Mexican found that the battery had gone flat, damaged by the shredded tire. By the time Rodriguez hustled back to the pits for a fresh battery, the top Ferrari was out of contention. It was out of the race soon afterward, with suspension problems sustained when the tire went down.

The Ferrari 275P, which was started by Grossman, added Rodriguez to the team, with Hansgen and Piper. The team worked its way up to third until the clutch failed. That left the privateer 250 GTO of Peter Clarke, Bob Hurt, and Charlie Hayes, running well off the pace, to carry the flag for Ferrari.

With the Ferraris out of contention, Ford still faced a very real threat. The Gurney/Grant Lotus had built up a five-lap lead over the GT40 of Miles and Ruby, which was running second. But on lap 215 of 327, during what appeared to be a routine pit stop by Grant, the Lotus was suddenly withdrawn. "Everything was looking real promising," Gurney recalled. "Then, we broke a piston or wrist pin or one of those things, and that was the end of it."

The Gurney/Grant retirement gave the two GT40s a clear run to the checkered flag. Miles and Ruby cruised to win by five laps, giving Ford its first major international victory. They averaged 99.849 mph, needing 12 hours and 27 minutes to cover the 2,000 kilometers.

The Bondurant/Ginther GT40 was in position to win, but a 27-minute stop to cure ignition problems ultimately dropped them to third, behind the Shelby Cobra Daytona Coupe of Jo Schlesser, Harold Keck, and Robert Johnson, who also won the Grand Touring class. The Shelby Cobra Daytona Coupe driven by Muther and Timanus gave Ford a sweep of the top four positions.

Fifth went to the Porsche 904GTS of Charlie Kolb and Roger Heftler, the winners of the Grand Touring two-liter class. Other class winners were the seventh place Ferrari 250 of Bob Hart/Peter Clarke/Charlie Hayes in Grand Touring three-liters; the 11th-place Porsche 356SC 90 of David McClain/Larry Perkins/Leland Dieas in Grand Touring 1.6-liters; the 14th-place Triumph TR-3 of Dana Kelder/Ara Dube in Grand Touring 2.5-liters; and the 20th-place Alfa Romeo Giulietta SC of Charles Mathis/Guido Levetto in Sports-Racing.

Peter Gregg took eighth in a Porsche 904GTS and second in his class, co-driving with George Barber Jr. Two-time NASCAR champion Buck Baker teamed with Bob Tullius in a Lotus Cortina, but failed to finish.

After the race, some people claimed that Gurney had played the role of a "rabbit," and had been funded to do so by Ford to lure the Ferraris into setting a fast early pace. That wasn't the case.

"It was funded by Dan," Gurney recalled of his team. "That part about the rabbit was Carroll Shelby's dream. But I funded it myself, just because I was old fashioned and wanted to do it myself." His co-driver agreed.

"The stories of us dropping out of the race to help out Ford were completely untrue," Grant said. "It was Dan's choice to go with the Lotus 19, and we enjoyed blowing off the Fords until our problem."

Above left: Two-time NASCAR Grand National champion Buck Baker shared this No. 87 Lotus-powered Cortina with Bob Tullius. The car was an early retiree with accident damage. Above right: Carroll Shelby (center) joins winning co-drivers Ken Miles (left) and Lloyd Ruby in front of the winning Ford GT40 as the team celebrates in victory lane. Right: Night action in the pits, as the No. 11 Shelby Cobra Daytona Coupe of Ed Leslie and Allen Grant is in for service.

11
10

25
41
MOBART
X-100

1966: The First 24-Hour Race

THE FORD VS. FERRARI BATTLE WAS AT ITS PEAK IN 1966. THE PUBLIC WAS FOLLOWING THE STRUGGLE WITH GREAT INTEREST, AND BILL FRANCE FELT THE TIMING WAS RIGHT TO EXTEND THE DAYTONA CONTINENTAL TO THE NOW FAMOUS 24-HOUR DISTANCE.

The 24 Hour Daytona Continental not only virtually doubled the 2,000 kilometers raced in 1964 and 1965, it elevated the event to one of the world's top three endurance races, along with the 24 Hours of Le Mans and the 12 Hours of Sebring. Daytona became America's first accredited 24-hour international sports car race, and awarded points towards the FIA World Manufacturer's Championship points and a $52,000 purse.

The 1966 race featured the extreme swings in temperature that would mark the Daytona 24 Hours as one of the world's unique motorsports events. Competitors enjoyed sunny and pleasant conditions at the beginning and end of the event, though the temperature was a chilly 47 degrees at the start. In between, however, they suffered through a bitterly cold night, with freezing temperatures.

No driver was allowed to race for more than four consecutive hours. "What I remember most about that particular year was there was ice on the top lane on the banking," Phil Hill recalled. "It was that cold. Maybe it was frost, but it was enough to make it slippery."

Ford was represented by two factory-backed teams. Shelby American

Left: The No. 25 Ferrari 365P2 of Lucien Bianchi, Gerard Langlois, and Jean Blanton is in the pits for a lengthy evening stop. The team qualified fifth but called it quits after 171 laps with engine problems. Above: Daytona Speedway president Bill France (far left) is joined by (left to right) Miss America Debbie Bryant, Florida Governor Hayden Burns, and astronaut Gordon Cooper during pre-race ceremonies.

fielded three new GT40s, now called Mark IIs and powered by 427-cubic-inch engines. Ken Miles/Lloyd Ruby, Dan Gurney/Jerry Grant, and Chris Amon/Bruce McLaren were the driver pairings for the Shelby-entered cars.

Meanwhile, Ford's main NASCAR team, Holman and Moody, also entered two Mark IIs, for Walt Hansgen/Mark Donohue and Richie Ginther/Ronnie Peterson. The latter car had an experimental

automatic transmission. Hansgen put his ride with the Ford factory team at risk when he insisted that the relatively unknown Donohue be his co-driver. In addition, four of the original GT40s ran in the Sports category, with drivers including Peter Revson.

Ferrari was represented by the North American Racing Team, with an upgraded Ferrari 365—its bodywork modified to P3 specifications—for Pedro Rodriguez and the young American sensation, Mario Andretti. Chinetti also entered Ferrari 250 LMs for Jochen Rindt/Bob Bondurant and George Follmer/Don Wester/Paul Hawkins. In addition, Jacques Swaters' Belgian team fielded a 365P2 for Lucien Bianchi/Gerard Langois von Ophem/Jean Blaton. David Piper, Peter Clarke, and other privateers fielded 250 LMs.

Chevrolet attracted attention with Jim Hall's Chaparral, driven by Phil Hill and Jo Bonnier. The car had a unique automatic transmission and an air spoiler that was controlled inside the cockpit. It had qualified second, but quickly fell out of contention.

1966

While the four previous races started with a full lap of the 2.5-mile tri-oval, the 1966 event began when the field took the green flag on the backstretch. Bonnier led the first lap before yielding to Miles's Mark II, but the Swede pitted after only 16 minutes of racing, spending eight minutes in the pits to repair a loose fan belt. After one hour, two minutes of racing, a steering malfunction cost the team one hour, dropping the Chaparral out of contention.

Above left: Jim Hall (red jacket) makes final pre-race preparations to the No. 65 Chaparral 2D driven by Jo Bonnier and Phil Hill. Bonnier led the first lap, but mechanical problems ranging from a loose fan belt to a steering malfunction quickly dropped the unique car out of contention. Above right: Peter Gregg, driving the No. 14 Brumos Porsche 904 GTS, leads a group of cars on the banking in NASCAR turn 4 of the Superspeedway. Gregg went on to join George Drolsom in a 10th-place finish. Opposite: The Ken Miles/Lloyd Ruby Ford Mk II and the Jo Bonnier/Phil Hill Chaparral lead the field off pit road prior to the start.

Hall explained the Chaparral's steering problems as the result of a stuck pinion. The team also replaced an exhaust pipe during a one-hour-long pit stop, fearing a hole in it might cause a fire. Hill was turning fast laps of 114 mph in the early evening, but the car was running 54th. Bonnier averaged a race record 115.100 on the 197th lap. On his next stint, Hill broke that mark with a lap of 115.8 mph. Their chase ended at 4 a.m. Sunday when the car lost a wheel hub and harmlessly hit a sand bank.

When Miles took the lead on the second lap, it gave Ford an advantage that would hold for the remainder of the event. Miles yielded the lead on his first pit stop to Hansgen, who ran in front for eight laps before the Miles/Ruby Mark II retook the lead, which it held the rest of the way.

Miles and Ruby won by eight laps, followed by Dan Gurney and Jerry Grant, with Hansgen and Donohue in third. The second- and third-place cars also held their positions during most of the event. The best racing was at dawn, when the Ferrari driven by Rodriguez challenged Gurney for third. Gurney kept the position, and broke Hill's race record with a lap of 116.51 mph. Miles and Ruby averaged a blistering 108.02 mph, completing 679 laps in the Mark II.

"It has been a long time since the winning car also led the race for 98.5% of the distance," John Hearst wrote in *Competition Press & AutoWeek*, "and it just may never happen again."

"I think this year the difference was that we [the Carroll Shelby teams] were privileged to pick our target speed for each car," Miles said. The eventual winners picked a 2:04 minute pace, and stuck to it throughout the race. The other teams were more conservative, feeling 2:04 was too fast.

"The first 12 hours was just like last year," said Ruby. "But the last 12 was just a sheer, grinding perseverance." The winning team kept to a schedule of double shifts (approximately three hours), and no sleep for either driver.

Miles said he thought Daytona was twice as tough as Le Mans. "You must make some hectic compromises when you try to set up a car for a road race that also has high-banked turns. They provided entirely different problems," he explained.

Above: The Porsche 906 of Hans Herrmann and Herbert Linge is pushed to the grid. The factory-entered car finished sixth and first in its class. Opposite left: Pedro Rodriguez and Mario Andretti shared the No. 21 Ferrari 365P2, which placed fourth overall behind the top three Fords. Opposite right: An almost-stock Rambler Marlin, driven by Larry and Tommy Hess, looks like it's quite a handful in the infield. The Porsche 904GTS of David Lane and Don Sesslar gets by on the inside. The Marlin managed to outlast the Porsche by six laps, before both cars succumbed to overheating problems.

Taking fourth for Ferrari was the team of Pedro Rodriguez and Mario Andretti. "I really didn't expect it to be such a nice race. I thought only a very few cars would be running at the finish," said Rodriguez after the race. "The Ford engine is almost twice as large as ours and I was surprised that the Fords held up so well. I think they have done a wonderful job."

"It's a long race and it's tiring as hell," added Andretti, who was competing in his first 24-hour race.

"I was grateful to drive with Pedro Rodriguez," recalled Andretti in a 2002 interview. "It was a great opportunity for me, and I learned a lot about long-distance racing. I was actually able to help them a little. I didn't have much experience setting up a car on the road course, but the car was a little light on the banking, and I was able to suggest adding an airfoil to the front which gave a little downforce and made the car handle a little better."

Fifth place went to McLaren and Amon. The other Mark II, with an experimental automatic transmission, was parked by Richie Ginther and Ronnie Bucknum with transmission trouble after 10 hours.

Jochen Rindt and Bob Bondurant finished ninth in a NART Ferrari 250 LM, while the similar NART car for George Follmer, Don Wester, and Paul Hawkins retired with electrical problems. "The course is not the monster it has been made out to be," Chinetti said, pointing out that 34 of the 60 starters were still running at the finish. "I am happy for the Fords, but most of all, I am happy for this country."

A Ford GT40 also won the Sports over three-liter class. Peter Sutcliffe and Bob Grossman placed 14th overall in a Ford Advanced Vehicles–entered Ford GT40, winning the class over the Essex

Wire–entered GT40 of Peter Revson, Masten Gregory, and Ed Lowther. Lowther also saw action in a Shelby Cobra, driving with Oscar Koveleski and Harold Keck.

Once a top American sports car driver, 28-year-old Roger Penske was called "one of the best Porsche drivers in the world" by Baron Huschke von Hanstein, manager of the Porsche racing team. He had retired from racing in early 1965 after purchasing a Chevrolet dealership in Philadelphia.

"I wanted to buy the dealership, and part of the commitment was from the bank. I couldn't get insurance being a race driver, and Chevrolet wouldn't approve me," Penske recalled. "Quitting racing was the right thing, because I could become a business person instead of a race driver at that time.

We had a good career racing. Obviously, I was able to take my experience as a driver and bring that to the team, when to have pressure, and when not to."

While driving did not fit in with Penske's plans, racing played a major role in his business, and his first experience as a car owner was at the first Daytona 24-Hour Continental. He fielded an immaculately prepared Corvette, which finished 12th, and first in the Grand Touring over three-liter class, with drivers Dick Guldstrand, Ben Moore, and George Wintersteen. The team's only problem came when time was lost replacing the headlights and repairing the front bodywork after it tagged the wall.

Competition was held in nine classes. Other winners included Hans Herrmann and Herbert Linge, sixth overall and first in two-liter Prototype in a Porsche 906; Gerhard Mitter and Joe Buzzetta, seventh overall and first in two-liter Sports in a Porsche 904GTS; Jack Ryan, Linley Coleman, and Bill Bencker, 16th and first in Grand Touring two-liter in a Porsche 911; Larry Perkins and Jack Slottag, 19th and first in Sports three-liter in a Ferrari 250 GTO; Dana Kelder, Ara Dudbe, and Red Wilson, 23rd and first in Grand Touring three-liter in a Triumph TR-4; and Ben Scott, Peter Flanagan, and Roger Chastain, 25th and first in Grand Touring 1600cc in an Alfa Romeo Giulia Sprint.

Ryan entered two Porsche 911s in the event, marking the first race for the successor to the 356 in the Continental. The class victory was the first of many for the 911, which would become one of the most successful GT cars in the history of the event.

Peter Gregg finished 10th, joined by George Drolsom in a Porsche 904GTS entered by Gregg's company, Brumos Porsche of Jacksonville, Florida. The pair finished third in the Sports class. Gregg finished just ahead of Sam Posey, the fast qualifier in the Sports class, who teamed with Jim Haynes and Harry Theodoracapulos in a similar Porsche. Gregg would return to Daytona in September to win two SCCA Nationals in a Porsche.

Jacky Ickx of Belgium made his endurance racing debut at the event, but his Ferrari 250 LM retired early. Former world motorcycle champion Mike Hailwood, was scheduled to compete, but the Ferrari 250 LM he was to share with Innes Ireland and pirate radio station owner George Drummond retired after 90 laps with gearbox failure.

Denis Hulme of New Zealand drove a Ferrari 250 LM, which went out after only 53 laps with gearbox trouble. Hulme would go on to win the 1967 Formula One World Championship. Also competing was NASCAR's Bobby Allison, who parked his Corvair after 63 laps with a broken fuel pump.

Two all-woman Autosport Sunbeam Alpine teams attracted considerable publicity. Janet Guthrie, Suzy Dietrich, and Donna Mae Mims drove in a Sunbeam Alpine, which struggled with overheating problems during the final four hours and finished 36th, two positions behind the similar car of Smokey Drolet and Rosemary Smith.

1966

Officially, the race was scored by a 120-person team. For the first time, however, a General Electric 225 computer was used—although the teletype machine ceased functioning during the night due to the freezing conditions.

France announced the two-day attendance at 29,632, breaking all records for the Continental. "It more than tripled what we drew for the Continental in 1965 when it was a 2,000 kilometer race," Bill France told the *Daytona Beach Morning Journal.* "We didn't make a bundle of money on the 24-hour race, but we did start building towards a race that will become one of the great automotive events in the world."

Right: Lloyd Ruby (left) and Ken Miles celebrate their second consecutive triumph in the Daytona Continental, their first at the magical 24-hour distance.

98
98

Firestone
LORENZO BANDINI
Firestone
SHELL
CHRIS
Firestone

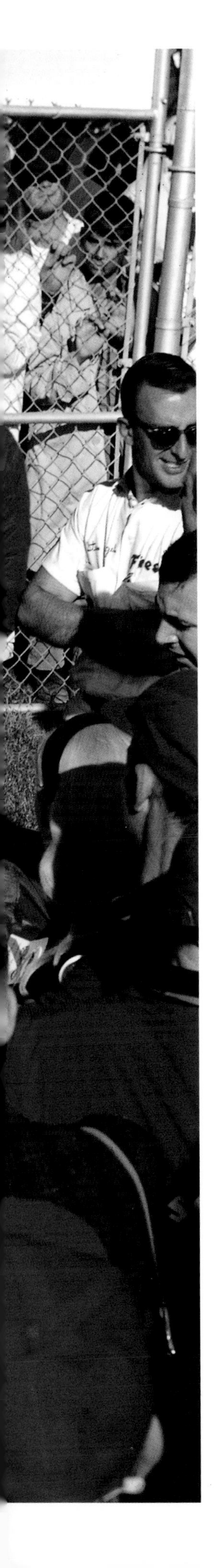

1967: Reversal of Fortune

BEATEN BY UPSTART FORD THE PREVIOUS YEAR IN BOTH 24-HOUR CLASSICS AT DAYTONA AND LE MANS, FERRARI CAME TO DAYTONA LOOKING FOR REVENGE. FERRARI STAGED AN EXTENSIVE, WEEK-LONG DAYTONA TEST OF ITS NEW TWIN OVERHEAD CAM 330P4, WITH A DRIVER LINEUP THAT INCLUDED CHRIS AMON, FROM FORD'S WINNING 1966 LE MANS TEAM.

Unofficially, the team clocked a fast lap of 121 mph (1:53), five mph better than the track record, in the session that was open to the public, although the team was under strict orders from Enzo Ferrari not to break Ford's track record of 1:57.8. Ferrari fired competition manager Eugenio Dragoni for violating the speed orders.

Ford also had a new car, but unlike the Ferrari, it flopped in private testing. The new "J" car (later called the Mark IV) was no faster than the GT 40 Mark II, and was less durable and much slower than the new Ferrari.

Six Mark IIs were built in Ford's Advanced Vehicles plant in England; three of which were turned over to Carroll Shelby and three to Ralph Moody. For

Left: Lorenzo Bandini (left) and Chris Amon are surrounded by Ferrari crewmen in victory lane after winning the 1967 24 Hours Daytona Continental. Above: Fred Opert Racing of Paramus, N.J, entered a Chevron Prototype. Overheating problems sidelined the car very early in the event, with Opert joined by Englishmen Roy Pike and Peter Gethin. Top: The top-three Ferraris approach the finish line in a "photo finish" to the 1967 24 Hours of Daytona. Winning the race is the No. 23 330P4 of Bandini and Amon, followed by the No. 24 of Mike Parkes and Ludovico Scarfiotti, and the No. 26. of Pedro Rodriguez and Jean Guichet.

Daytona, Dan Gurney and A. J. Foyt had their Mk II's suspension privately rebuilt, a move frowned upon by the factory. Then, Gurney posted a record 119.165 mph to win the pole.

In addition to the six Mark IIs, three of the original GT40s competed. One of them was a converted road car loaned by Grady Davis, the vice president of Gulf Oil Corporation, to John Wyer, to be driven at Daytona by Jacky Ickx and Dick Thompson.

An unusual car joined Gurney on the front row. Phil Hill qualified Jim Hall's new Chaparral 2F, which sported a radical high rear wing. Hall also entered and personally qualified eighth a more conventional year-old Chaparral, to be raced by Bob Johnson and Bruce Jennings.

A crowd estimated at 27,000 watched the 58-car field take the green flag on the back straight. By the time the cars cleared the banking and entered the tri-oval, Hill already had opened up a one-second lead in the Chaparral.

By 30 minutes, Hill had a 19-second lead, chased by Ford's rabbit, Mario Andretti. At the 90-

Above: Owner/driver Bill Wonder joined Ray Caldwell in finishing eighth in Ford GT40 chassic number 003, the same car that won the 1965 Daytona Continental. Right: Dan Gurney and A. J. Foyt co-drove the No. 3 Ford GT40 Mk II. Although they won the pole, they joined the remainder of the Ford team in struggling with transmission troubles. Gurney and Foyt rebounded to win the 24 Hours of Le Mans in a GT40 Mk IV.

minute mark, Hill pitted with a 45-second lead over the Ferrari 330P4 of Lorenzo Bandini/Chris Amon, followed by Pedro Rodriguez/Jean Guichet, and Andretti. Hill turned the Chaparral over to Mike Spence.

"We had a similar sort of arrangement as '66, where we had control of the wing being able to trim the car out for a fast run, and then trim it again for road holding, that includes braking, with an extra pedal," Hill said of the unique Chaparral. "We had that feature for both years, but it had been refined for the second year, and it was much more effective."

Three-and-a-half hours into the race, Hill returned to the wheel of the leading Chaparral. On his first lap out, however, Hill slid up the banking and hit the wall tail-first at the transition from the infield road course to the superspeedway. The car retired due to the crash damage.

"We were leading with ease, and Mike Spence came in and never said a word about what was

Above: Dan Gurney (standing) and Jim Hall (kneeling below) talk with Mike Spence, who is at the wheel of Hall's high-winged Chaparral 2F. Right: Team owner John Wyer (left) watches as a crewman extinguishes a small fire on pit road. Wyer's No. 11 GT40 of Dick Thompson and Jackie Ickx finished sixth, the top-placing Ford. Far right: A Ferrari driver listens to shouted instructions from his crew as he assesses damage to his 330P4 while parked near the signaling pits, just before the entrance to the infield horseshoe. Once away from the pits or garage, only drivers were allowed to work on race cars.

happening to the road, over where you exit the infield and go up onto the banking," Hill recalled. "On my first lap, I go over there, and it's all turned to hell. There's gravel, balled up macadam, all the way up to the wall, and I just slid up and tapped the wall, enough to put us out."

Thirty-five years after the race, Hill still bristles when asked if the incident cost his team the race. "I don't think we would have done anything, because we had lost the gearboxes in every other high-speed race in 1967, every single one of them. The only place we finished was Brands Hatch, the last race of the year.

"Anyway, I was blamed, 'We would have won if you hadn't done that sort of thing,' so that was not a pleasant thing.

"We had an easy time of it, that was what was so disappointing about it, because it looked like it would be sort of a walkaway," Hill continued. "But, of course, in a 24-hour race, you can't say anything's a walkaway, because you never know."

The Chaparral's retirement left the door open to Ferrari, which held the top four positions after six hours. The only other cars to lead were the top two Ferrari P4s. The Amon/Bandini car took command during the early morning fog and pulled away throughout the final seven hours.

Meanwhile, the entire Ford team struggled with transmission problems. Each of the Fords required at least one transmission change, with three of the cars needing three changes each. With that much practice during the race, the Ford pit crew was able to get the changes down to 18 minutes.

Ferrari savored its triumph. To show the team had not forgotten its defeat the previous June, the top three Ferraris took the checkered flag in formation, in a staged photo finish.

Mike Parkes and Ludovico Scarfiotti took second in a new 330P4, three laps behind the Amon/Bandini P4, followed by the 330 P3 driven by Pedro Rodriguez and Jean Guichet. The fourth- and fifth-place Porsches also got into the photo, queuing up behind the front trio. Edsel Ford wasn't around for Ferrari's staged finish, having left for Michigan in his private jet before the end of the race.

"We had no problems, nothing that would put us out of the running," said Amon in the post-race interview. "The major task of the pit crews was fueling and changing tires." Amon and Bandini traveled 666 laps, 2,537.46 miles, averaging 105.703 mph.

Asked to compare the Ferrari P4 with the Ford GT40 Mark II, Amon said, "The Mark II is heavy.

The difference is like comparing a truck to a car."

The second-place Ferrari lost 14 minutes in the pits Saturday evening, arising from complications when a brake caliper got stuck during a brake pad change. Hans Herrmann and Jo Siffert took fourth, winning the prototype under two-liter class in a Porsche 910. Fifth went to the Porsche 906LE of Dieter Spoerry and Rico Steinemann.

The top Ford was the original GT40 of Ickx and Thompson, in sixth. The John Wyer–prepared converted road car won the Sports over two-liter class. The only Mark II still running at the finish was the seventh-place Shelby American car of Bruce McLaren and Lucien Bianchi, with Gurney driving the car at the checkered flag.

Other class winners were Grand Touring two-liters, Jack Ryan and Bill Bencker in a Porsche 911, finishing ninth overall; Touring two-liter, George Drolsom and Harold Williamson in a Porsche 911,

Above: Masten Gregory and Peter Gregg co-drove the No. 28 Ferrari Dino, entered by Coco Chinetti, the son of NART owner Luigi Chinetti. Right: Skip Scott assembled a team of many of the world's top female drivers. Left to right are Janet Guthrie, Smokey Drolet, Anita Taylor Matthews, Scott, an unknown Ring Free Motor Oil representative, Donna Mae Mims, and Suzy Dietrich.

10th overall; Touring over two-liter, Paul Richards and Ray Cuomo in a Ford Mustang, 11th overall; and Grand Touring over two-liter, Dana Kelder and Ara Dube in a Triumph TR4, 14th overall.

The pace took its toll, with only 29 of the 59 starters around at the finish. The only major mishap saw the Porsche of Walter Habeggar of Switzerland explode in flames at 9 p.m. He escaped with only minor cuts and bruises. The incident brought out the first full-course caution in the history of the event.

The race again featured two cars driven by all-woman teams, including a Mustang co-driven by Janet Guthrie, Anita Taylor-Matthews, and South Florida short-track racer/stunt driver Smokey Drolet in 20th. Suzy Dietrich and Donna Mae Mims co-drove an ASA to 25th.

"That Mustang had been somebody's street car until the previous week," recalled Guthrie, making her second, and final, appearance in the Daytona 24 Hours. "Anita was one of the fastest woman co-drivers I ever had. She was fast. If we had a slightly faster car under us, it would have been a real good outing."

1968: Porsche Races for Overall Victory

Always a contender but never an overall winner at Daytona, Porsche took advantage of new eligibility rules to flex its muscles in 1968. A mid-1967 ruling by the FIA, the governing body of international endurance racing, limited engine displacement in the prototypes.

Though these changes were made for safety reasons, the ruling sidelined the Chaparrals, seven-liter GT40s, and big-engine Ferraris, but favored cars manufactured by Matra, Renault (both of which, like the FIA, were based in France), and Porsche.

Porsche jumped at the opportunity to run up front, fielding five white, long-tailed Porsche 907s for the race, which was designated the 24 Hours of Daytona for the first time. Jo Siffert and Hans Herrmann shared the lead car, with other Porsches for Jo Schlesser/Joe Buzzetta, Gerhard Mitter/Rolf Stommelen, and Rico Steinemann/Dieter Spoerry. Completing the lineup was Vic Elford, a British driver making his first trip to Daytona.

"I had just won the Monte Carlo Rally a week previous to the Daytona 24 Hours, and I was so excited about winning it, to be honest, I didn't know where Daytona was until I got there," said Elford, a 32-year-old driver who had concentrated on rallying up until that point, and at Daytona would share a 907 with Jochen Neerpasch.

Left: A pair of Porsche 907s lead the nighttime action. No longer satisfied with chasing class victories, Porsche brought a strong contingent to Daytona in hopes of winning the overall title. Above: The Howmet was the first turbine-powered sports car. Pictured in a Daytona testing session, speeds of over 200 mph were anticipated for the highly publicized car. The throttle jammed on lap 34, resulting in a race-ending crash. Pictured with the car at a test session are (left to right) Howmet president John Burke, a Howmet representive, and Bill France Sr.

Grabbing the lion's share of the pre-race attention was another unusual entry, the Howmet turbine. A turbine-powered car had nearly won the 1967 Indianapolis 500. Parnelli Jones, driving Andy Granatelli's STP entry powered by a Pratt & Whitney turbine, led 171 of the first 197 laps at Indianapolis. A $6 transmission bearing failed with only three laps remaining, robbing Jones of a second Indy 500 triumph.

The first turbine-powered sports car, the brainchild of Ray Happenstall and a joint effort between the Howmet Corporation and Continental Aviation, was entered in the 24 Hours. It was originally expected to hit 200 mph. The car had never been tested for longer than an hour at a time and was originally entered to run as an exhibition, before being certified to Group 6 standards by the FIA. It was co-driven by Dick Thompson and Ed Lowther, who qualified an impressive seventh.

Another car attracting attention was a Chevrolet Camaro entered by resourceful Daytona Beach race-car builder Smokey Yunick for Bruce McLaren and Jim Hall. Hall ran fastest of the Trans-Am cars in practice, topping 101 mph. Inspectors disqualified the car, though, citing 27 irregularities.

"It seems like my interpretation of the rules and those of those inspectors were at odds," Yunick related in his memoirs, *Best Damn Garage in Town: The World According to Smokey*. "I believe the rules were being administered by the gentlemen racers of the driving cap and mustache (where you put your cap on backwards, and then your goggles). As bad as France wanted them to run (plus he had two tickets to New Zealand and Australia invested), he couldn't budge the fuzz. There was no way to make the changes they wanted."

Above left: John Wyer's team put a pair of Ford GT40s on the front row, with Jackie Ickx capturing the pole position in a car originally driven on the street. Above right: In addition to attracting international stars, the Daytona 24 Hours traditionally attracts racers of many different levels of competition. Guillermo Ortega Jr. and Fausto Merello of Ecuador joined Miami's John Gunn in taking eighth in a Ferrari 250LM, winning Sports 50 class honors. Opposite: While the Porsches took the top three finishing positions in formations, a group of Alfas queued up behind them for their own "photo finish." Udo Schultzs and Nini Vaccarella placed fifth in the No. 20 Alfa T33, followed by Mario Andretti and Lucien Bianchi in No. 23, and Teodoro Zeccoli and Mario Casoni in No. 22. Also in the photo is the 20th-place No. 24 Alfa GTA of Leo Cella and Giampiero Biscaldi.

20
23
22

1968

Yunick then went down the list of "problems" with his Camaro.

"I believe it was a big aerodynamic problem," he continued. "The bottom [of] my car was clean and shiny as the roof. It also had a strange looking deal that kinda looked like Indy car tunnels on each side. I think maybe brake rotors were accidentally a little too big in diameter and they thought the engine was four inches back and two inches down. You know, a lot of nit picking. They didn't like the air jacks at all. Nor the three-inch wider and lower front bumper, or the full frame using the engine as part of the frame (a stressed member). They were also very critical of the acid dipped body, and Lexan windows, but they never even noticed it was supercharged by clutch fly wheel and bell housing modifications. Probably just as well, seemed like if I got too creative, [the] car would go like hell for a little while then break."

Though Ford was lost in the pre-race publicity, the two-time Daytona winner was not finished. Taking the front row for the race was a pair of John Wyer Ford GT40s. With both the Mark IV and even the Mark II legislated out of racing, Wyer went back to the original GT40 configuration, including the original Ford engine. The car was still fast. Jacky Ickx won the pole with a speed of 119.370 mph in the car he shared with Brian Redman, while teammates Paul Hawkins and David Hobbs qualified second, at 117.230 mph.

"That was my first race in America, and I was teamed with Jacky Ickx, the young Belgian wonder boy," Redman recalled. "Back then, there was no chicane on the backstretch, so you went onto the banking at 200 mph in this GT40, and the transition from the flat on the backstraight to the banking was tremendous—you were thrown up and you couldn't see properly or anything. For lap after lap in practice, I tried to go flat out onto the banking, and I couldn't stop my foot from coming off the throttle a little bit.

"So I said to Jacky at the end of qualifying, 'Jacky, can I ask you a question?' And he said, 'Yes, Breean.' 'Are you flat onto the banking?' He looked at me and said 'Yes! But of course.' And I said, 'I thought you probably were.' To which Ickx added, 'But I think that I fly to zee moon.'"

While there were no factory Ferrari entries, Luigi Chinetti's NART had a 275LM for Masten Gregory and David Piper, which qualified eighth, and a Dino for Pedro Rodriguez and Charlie Kolb, which qualified 10th. The Porsches qualified third, fourth, fifth, sixth, and 12th, led by the Mitter/Stommelen entry.

Hawkins led the first lap, and then gave way to Ickx, who led 67 laps before bowing out with gearbox failure. That gave the lead to Hawkins, who recovered from fuel-feed problems in the early going.

At the four-hour mark, disaster struck. The Ford Mustang of Malcolm Starr and George Winterstein blew its engine at 6:40 p.m. and left debris strewn on the grandstand tri-oval. Mitter cut a tire, turned over, and skidded 250 yards, shedding a wheel. Next, the Ferrari of Masten Gregory hit the loose wheel

Left: Legendary Daytona Beach-based mechanic Smokey Yunick entered a Chevrolet Camaro for Bruce McLaren and Jim Hall, but the car failed technical inspection due to 27 irregularities. Above left: The Corvette of Jerry Grant and David Morgan leads a group of cars in the infield. Above right: The No. 15 Ford Mustang of Bob Grossman and Bob Dini, shown passing the timing and scoring building located at the inside of turn one, was one of the Trans-Am category cars competing in the 24 Hours.

and went end over end three times. Porsche driver Dieter Spoerry attempted to take evasive action to miss his teammate, but lost control and hit the wall twice. Also involved was the Porsche 911 of Marvin Davidson. While no one was injured, three contending cars were eliminated.

Elford, coming up on the accident, was more fortunate. "I saw the dust and debris flying," he said. "I slowed and dipped down under. I was lucky to get through.

"Almost coincidental to that, my co-driver, Jochen Neerpasch, became ill and couldn't continue," Elford continued, "so Rolf [Stommelen], Mitter's co-driver, was drafted into my car as my official co-driver."

Also retiring early was the Howmet Turbine, which was running third in the first hour before it crashed on the 34th lap, when the throttle jammed open. Lowther drove the car back to the garage, but the chassis was too badly bent to continue.

The Hawkins/Hobbs GT40 held the lead until lap 231, when Hawkins pitted for fuel, giving the lead to the Porsche of Buzzetta. Hawkins managed to lead another 16 laps before being passed by the Siffert/Herrmann Porsche, and the Porsches led the rest of the event. The Hawkins/Hobbs Ford was eventually retired after 430 laps with a split fuel bladder.

At 7 a.m., the Siffert/Herrmann Porsche continued to lead, followed by Buzzetta and the Elford

Above: Four Porsche 907s are lined up nose-to-tail on pit road during pre-race practice. Right: Five winning drivers celebrate their 1968 triumph. Left to right are Jochen Neerpasch, Vic Elford, Porsche racing head Huschke von Hanstein, Joe Buzzetta, Bill France, Rolf Stommelen, Jo Siffert, and Hans Herrmann. Elford was happy to extend an invitation to several of his Porsche teammates to share in his car's victory.

car, which was 15 laps behind. With three-and-a-half hours remaining, the lead Porsche lost 22 minutes in the pits to repair a broken throttle linkage. The stop cost the team 14 laps—and the lead. Then Porsche racing director Huschke von Hanstein paid Elford a visit.

"Toward the end of the race, Huschke von Hanstein came over and said, 'Vic, these guys really should have won if it had not been for that little problem. Would you mind letting them each drive a couple of laps so they can be associated with the victory,' and I said, 'Yes, of course.' Jo and Hans each drove about four laps, so technically and officially they were part of the winning team." Overall, the team made five driver changes during the final two hours.

Von Hanstein called the Stuttgart factory with a brief report: "All's gone as planned."

"We had no problems the entire race," Elford added. "Our car was running like clockwork." At the end of 24 hours, a trio of white, long-tailed Porsche 907s rolled to the checkered flag, with Elford leading a five-driver lineup in the winning car. The quintet had completed 673 laps, 2,565.69 miles, averaging 106.697 mph.

Siffert and Herrmann took second, five laps down, followed by Jo Schlesser and Joe Buzzetta, another nine laps in arrears. The three Porsches circulated at 87.5 mph while practicing their formation driving.

Jerry Titus and Ronnie Bucknum took fourth in a Trans-Am, class-winning Shelby Mustang fielded by Carroll Shelby, while the next three positions were filled by Alfa Romeos, including the sixth-place car of Mario Andretti and Lucien Bianchi.

The race featured four classes. John Gunn, Guillermo Ortego, and Fausto Merello won Sports 50 in a Ferrari 250LM under the "Racers of Miami" banner, placing eighth overall—the only finisher in the class. Peter Gregg finished ninth overall and first in Trans-Am under two-liter, joined by Sten Axelsson in a Porsche 911.

The Grand Touring class featured three Corvettes entered by movie star James Garner, who became interested in endurance racing while filming the MGM movie *Grand Prix*. Jerry Grant and Dave Morgan finished 10th overall to win the class.

Peter Revson/Don Yenko and Dick Guldstrand/Ed Leslie/Scooter Patrick/Dave Jordan co-drove the other Corvettes, entered by Garner and the Sunray DX Oil Company. The Corvettes took the checkered flag three-abreast, just behind the winning Porsches and the Titus/Bucknum Mustang. Shelby had also entered a Mustang for George Follmer and Horst Kwech.

Placing 12th was a Roger Penske–entered Camaro for Mark Donohue, Bob Johnson, and Craig Fisher. The car qualified fastest in the class, but had to make two unscheduled stops to change heads in the early morning hours.

Starting last in the 64-car field was a Morgan Plus 4, which was driven for the entire 24 hours by George Waltman. The car was last of 32 still running at the finish, with Waltman—fortified by a two-hour nap Sunday morning—driving solo.

1969: An Eight-Dollar Part Fails, Perseverance Pays

Porsche had rolled to a top-three sweep in the 1968 Daytona 24 Hours, and saw no reason why they couldn't repeat in 1969. To better their chances, the German marque entered five 908 cars, which were more powerful and easier to drive on the high banks than the 907s that had dominated the year before. A solid driver lineup included Jo Siffert, Hans Herrmann, Richard Atwood, Joe Buzzetta, Vic Elford, and Brian Redman.

Leading the opposition were a pair of Ford GT40s entered by John Wyer, which were identical to the cars that raced in 1968 for Jacky Ickx/Jackie Oliver and David Hobbs/Mike Hailwood. There were also five Lola T70s, which were entered by four different teams. James Garner entered two cars, for Lothar Motschenbacher/Ed Leslie and Scooter Patrick/Dave Jordan, while the Swiss-based Sports Cars International entered one for Jo Bonnier and Ulf Norinder. Henri Pescarolo crashed a Matra 630 during night practice prior to the race, which took the car out of contention.

Lost among the list of pre-race favorites was a Chevy-powered, fuel-injected Lola T70 entered by Roger Penske for Mark Donohue and Ronnie Bucknum. The latter driver had fractured a finger in a motorcycle accident

Left: Mechanics take a Sunday morning nap in their team's pit stall. Crew members often do not have the luxury of heading back to a hotel room or motor home, and have to settle for makeshift sleeping quarters during the 24-hour enduro. Above: David Hobbs and Mike Hailwood shared the wheel of John Wyer's Ford GT40, making its final competitive appearance at Daytona.

and withdrawn from the team during practice. To replace him, Penske flew in California veteran Chuck Parsons the day before the race, which allowed him to get only nine laps of practice. Fortunately, Parsons missed the plane he was supposed to take—it ended up being hijacked. "I caught a later flight and prayed all the way it wouldn't go to Cuba," he said later.

The Penske Lola was second-fastest in practice, trailing only the Porsche 908 driven by Redman and Elford. However, Penske felt it would be a race of attrition and ordered his drivers to proceed well below the car's potential.

Penske's orders were forgotten soon after the 3 p.m. green flag. When the top four cars broke away from the 62-car field, Elford grabbed the early lead, trailed by Siffert, Bonnier, and Donohue. The top four exchanged the lead repeatedly throughout the first hour, dodging backmarkers. By the 45-minute mark, only eight cars were still on the lead lap.

The first of the cars to have trouble was Penske's, when Donohue pitted early. "It acts like it's out of gas," he said. The Lola had a fuel-pickup problem that left the car unable to use one-third of its capacity. This meant the team would have to make many more pit stops than planned, considerably reducing their chances for victory.

The next car to pit was Bonnier's Lola, after contact with a backmarker. Shortly after the damage was repaired, Norinder hit the wall after swerving to avoid a slower car, and the Lola was retired.

That gave Porsche the top five positions. Trouble was ahead, however, for the German marque. The first chink in Porsche's armor appeared when Redman, driving in relief for Elford, pitted, overcome by fumes. The team discovered a cracked exhaust pipe. Soon afterwards Kurt Ahrens, who had relieved Rolf Stommelen, and Herrmann, who was in for Siffert, both pitted with the same exhaust problem. Later on, Gerhard Mitter collapsed after he climbed from his car and was taken to the infield care center for oxygen.

The only serious incident of the race came just after dark, when the Richard Robson/Rajah Rodgers Jaguar XKE blew its engine. David Hobbs, driving the second-place Ford GT40, managed to make it through the fog of smoke, but the Alfa Romeo of Mario Calabattisti, the Porsche 911 of Peter Gregg, and the Alex Soler-Roig/Rudy Lins Porsche 907 crashed in the oil and were eliminated.

The Penske Lola experienced more problems shortly afterward, when Donohue pitted with flames pouring from the exhaust. The system was badly cracked and, unlike the Porsche team, Penske had no spares. The crew removed the exhaust system, replaced the gaskets, and welded the fractures, patching a major crack with a sheet of stainless steel held on by Jubilee clips. The stop cost the team

Above: The No. 58 Porsche 907 of Alex Soler-Roig and Rudy Lins is serviced in the pits. An accident eliminated the car after 158 laps. Right: The No. 9 Chevy-Lola T70 of Dave Jordan and Scooter Patrick is in the pits prior to the race. The team finished seventh.

one hour, 19 minutes, and the car returned to action more than 40 laps behind.

While the Porsche team was able to repair its exhaust pipes, a more serious problem eliminated its phalanx during the early morning hours. The leading Attwood/Buzzetta Porsche pitted after midnight with a problem believed to be a broken alternator belt. After the part was replaced, the engine refused to fire. The team found that the intermediate drive shaft between the crankshaft and camshaft had broken, and the car was retired.

Next, Redman's car came to a halt. "The fire extinguisher went off in the cockpit, and that was the original reason Brian went off the road," Elford recalled of the incident. "Eventually, we got it back to the pits, but the car had no oil pressure."

When the team checked the car, the same problem that had eliminated the Attwood car was discovered. One by one, the remaining three Porsches broke down, with the failure of the same small but important part. "Four inches long and only $8 each," explained new Porsche factory team racing manager Gianrico Steinemann. "But we could not replace them, and that killed us."

Porsche's problems helped the Wyer GT40s. At the 3 a.m. midway point, Fords held the top two positions with the Donohue/Parsons Lola seventh, 44 laps in arrears. At 4:30 a.m., Hailwood pitted the leading GT40 with steam pouring from the car, the result of a cracked cylinder head that retired the car. Shortly after dawn, Ickx lost control entering the infield and hit the wall. The car burst into flames as it came to a stop. The Belgian star suffered only minor burns, but the Wyer team was finished.

The Penske Lola, meanwhile, lost an additional 17 minutes when the starter motor failed at 7 a.m. When Parsons rejoined the race, he was 200 miles behind the lone remaining Porsche, driven by Udo Schultz.

At 8:15 a.m., however, Schultz stopped on pit road. After a brief check, Porsche mechanics realized that the car had suffered the same fate as its four teammates, and unemotionally pushed it away, their race finished.

That left the Penske Lola in third place in the scoring, but it was now the leading car still running. It would take the team nearly two hours to make up the distance on the retired Mitter/Schultz Porsche 908 and Ickx/Oliver Ford GT40.

1969

By now, Donohue and Parsons were following the conservative pace Penske had ordered. Their Lola managed to run the remaining hours without any further problems, other than the nuisance of the frequent fuel stops. Despite spending a combined two hours, 10 minutes, and 12 seconds in the pits on 31 stops, the Penske team won by 30 laps. They covered 626 laps, 2,382.63 miles, and averaged 99.268 mph.

Above left: The Chevrolet Camaro pace car leads the 63-car field on the parade lap. Above right: "Captain Nice," Mark Donohue, is glued to Vic Elford's Porsche in early race action in the infield. Although Donohue forgot team orders and raced hard during the first hour, he and Chuck Parsons adapted a more conservative pace after experiencing problems in Roger Penske's Chevrolet-Lola. Their perseverance paid off with the victory. Opposite: Prior to the race, the No. 2 GT40 of David Hobbs and Mike Hailwood is gassed up at the Unocal 76 station behind pit road.

union
76
RACING
Gulf

“Have you ever won a race with so much going wrong?” ABC television commentator Chris Economaki asked the team after the race. According to the *Daytona Beach Morning Journal,* Donohue and Parsons laughed, while Penske roared.

“Our troubles began almost immediately with the fuel problem,” Donohue said. “As a matter of fact, I engineered the system myself so I must take full blame. Normally the tanks hold 37 gallons, but the blockage limited fuel capacity to about 20 gallons, and we were carrying a lot of dead weight.”

“I never gave up when we had that long stop,” Penske told the newspaper. “I knew there were 15 hours to go, and any endurance race takes its toll on the faster cars.” Winning this race would continue to pay dividends throughout Penske’s long career as a car owner.

“Long-distance racing really helped us in 500-mile races,” Penske said in a 2002 interview, shortly after winning his 12th Indianapolis 500, with Helio Castroneves at the wheel. “In fact, running long-

Above: The Porsche team cars enter the speedway under the grandstands. A wingless Porsche 910 is sandwiched by a quartet of long-tailed winged Porsche 908s. Right: When cars broke down on course, it was up to the drivers to make any repairs necessary to get the car back to the pits in the infield. A driver changes the battery of the Ranier Brezinka/Fritz Hockreuter Porsche 906. The Canadian duo finished 20th.

distance races was something that gave us the mode at Indy, that the race will come to you, and that's why we're so successful there. We don't have to lead the first lap. It's nice to lead the first lap, but typically, if you lead the first lap, you don't win that race. You need to be there at the finish, and if you have a car that's reliable and have good pit stops, you can be right up front."

It marked the first time that a Lola had lasted longer than eight hours in competition, and was the first time Chevrolet had won an international endurance race. For Parsons, it was not only his first time in a Lola, but also his first race at Daytona, and his first race at night.

Finishing second, despite heating problems that required frequent stops for water, was the older Chevrolet-powered Lola T70 driven by Ed Leslie and Lothar Motschenbacher, and owned by actor James Garner. "You don't remember any Lolas doing that before," said an exuberant Garner after the race.

Jerry Titus and Jon Ward were third in a Pontiac Firebird, winners of the five-liter Touring class. Ward, a stunt driver, bought the street Firebird after it was recovered by an insurance company following a fire in its interior, and then prepared it for racing.

Fourth went to the Porsche 911T of Tony Adamowicz/Bruce Jennings/Herb Wetanson, the Grand Touring winners, while the Porsche 911 of Bert Everett/Alan Johnson/Lin Coleman placed fifth and first in the two-liter Touring class. Other class winners were Hugh Kleinpeter/Bob Beatty/John Gunn, sixth overall and first in two-liter Sports in a Chevron-BMW, and Claudio Maglioli and Raffaele Pinto, 11th overall and first in Prototype in a Lancia Fulvia HF Zagato.

Astronaut Gordon Cooper was forbidden to race by NASA after being scheduled to co-drive with Charles Buckley in a Mercury Cougar prepared by Bud Moore. The car qualified 25th, second in the over two-liter touring class, but was withdrawn when no replacement driver could be found. Cooper, a backup on the next scheduled Apollo moon mission, got the news only two days before the race.

Later in 1969, the Paul Whiteman Trophy race in July would be won by Dave Heinz. Finishing fifth, and winner of the B Production class, was the Porsche 911S of Jacksonville's Harris Haywood, running in his first race at Daytona. He had met Peter Gregg at Jacksonville University in 1967. Gregg helped him order a Porsche 911, and Gregg's dealership, Brumos Porsche, sponsored the car. While the "Harris" moniker would soon be forgotten, the driver better known as Hurley Haywood would become the winningest professional sports car racer at Daytona.

STP

1970: Battle of the Supercars

THE FIRST RACE OF THE 1970S WAS ALSO THE FIRST MEETING OF TWO NEW GROUP 5 SUPERCARS, THE GULF PORSCHE 917 FIELDED BY JOHN WYER, AND THE FERRARI 512S. WHILE THE FIA WOULD BE PHASING OUT THE FIVE-LITER FORMULA AT THE END OF 1971, PORSCHE AND FERRARI STEPPED UP WITH A PAIR OF EXOTIC CARS THAT DOMINATED THE COMPETITION.

Wyer had won back-to-back victories in the 24 Hours of Le Mans with a GT40. For Daytona, however, he rolled out a pair of light blue and orange Gulf Porsche 917s. His lead drivers were Pedro Rodriguez of Mexico and Leo Kinnunen of Finland, joined by Brian Redman and Jo Siffert in the second car.

Leading the Ferrari entry was the popular Mario Andretti, paired with Italian Arturo Merzario in one of five bright-red 512s. Also competing under the NART banner was Dan Gurney, again paired with Chuck Parsons.

These two teams put on a tremendous battle for second place that kept the large crowd in suspense right up to the checkered flag, despite an early and seemingly insurmountable lead by the flagship 917.

Pedro Rodriguez would score his third triumph at Daytona, but first at the 24 hour distance, driving a fast and disciplined race to join Kinnunen in coasting to a 45-lap margin of victory. After the two Wyer Porsches jockeyed for the point in the early going, Rodriguez took the lead two hours and 35 minutes

Left: Mario Andretti, strapped in to Luigi Chinetti's Ferrari 512S, gives feedback to his team following practice. The versatile Pennsylvanian had already won both the Indianapolis 500 and Daytona 500, and with a win at Sebring in 1967, had made his mark in international sports car racing as well. Above: Coco Chinetti, son of Ferrari importer Luigi Chinetti, and Gregg Young finished seventh overall in the NART Ferrari 250LM.

into the event and led the rest of the way. The winning team averaged 114.866 mph, shattering the record of 107.388 mph set by Lloyd Ruby and Ken Miles in 1966.

It was the battle for second, however, that kept the attention of the crowd. While Rodriguez and Kinnunen ran a relatively problem-free race, the Redman/Siffert entry was not as fortunate.

Redman cut a tire during the third hour, and the flailing tread tore the brake line. Redman fell from the lead to eighth place, although two hours after the stop, he fought back to second. The team lost another 90 minutes to change the clutch in the early morning hours. Redman didn't get to rest while his car was being repaired in the pits.

"They had trouble communicating with the co-driver of the leading car, Leo Kinnunen, who didn't speak much English," Redman related. "They couldn't make him understand that he should slow down a bit because they had a good lead. They put me in the car for a session while my clutch was being replaced. So, I actually drove the first- and second-place cars."

Once the clutch was replaced, Redman rejoined the race in fourth position. Although he quickly moved up to third, the car was 39 laps behind the second-place Andretti/Merzario Ferrari, which was being driven by Jacky Ickx, who had been added to the lineup five hours into the event. Then Ickx lost 45 minutes to weld a broken rear chassis member. The Ferrari returned to the race out of alignment and running slower, but still five laps ahead of Redman.

The Redman Porsche gradually worked its way back and took over second with two hours remaining. Redman then brushed the wall, and lost five minutes in the pits for hasty repairs. That gave the Andretti Ferrari a lap lead in the battle for second.

Siffert took over for Redman, and began slicing into the second-place Ferrari's advantage. It appeared hopeless. The Ferrari maintained a 55-second advantage with 35 minutes remaining, but the

Above left: The eventual sixth-place finishing Corvette of John Mahler and Jerry Thompson gets service on pit road. The team also captured honors in the GT class. Above right: The winning Gulf Porsche overtakes the Camaro of Norberto Mastandrea, Smokey Drolet, and Rajah Rodgers after passing the Mustang of Jim Harrell in the circuit infield. Opposite: Tony Adamowicz (left) and David Piper (center) are joined by Wilbur Pickett on pit road. Adamowicz and Piper teamed to finish fifth overall in a NART Ferrari 312P, while Pickett failed to finish in another Ferrari entry.

Porsche continued to charge. Siffert recorded a 1:48.7 lap—three seconds faster than Andretti's pole time—with 20 minutes remaining to cut the gap to 25 seconds. With only four minutes left, Siffert was on the Ferrari's tail, then swept to the outside and made a 200-mph pass on the east banking above the Ferrari, earning Wyer's Porsches a one-two sweep.

In the end, the battle was exciting but unnecessary. As Redman's team suspected, their car had a lap advantage on the Andretti Ferrari in their fight for second place—three laps, in fact, according to the official scoring. Still, the two teams thrilled the sun-drenched crowd.

A third Porsche 917, driven by Vic Elford and Kurt Ahrens, fell back to ninth place with brake trouble before its retirement in the 11th hour due to a split fuel tank. "What happened was Kurt went past the pits, and he got a puncture on the left rear wheel, so he had to literally do a whole

lap with the body dragging on the ground," Elford explained. "It wore through not only the body, but the fuel tank as well."

The fact that Andretti was still pushing his car was even more remarkable in that the other four Ferrari 512s, which were driven at a more conservative pace, had all broken. This included the NART entry for Dan Gurney and Chuck Parsons. Gurney was running fifth after 18 hours when he lost the transmission. The 512 of Nino Vaccarella and Ignazio Giunti slammed the wall after cutting a tire two hours and 35 minutes into the event. Ickx was playing a waiting game in the car he shared with Peter Schetty, but he also cut a tire and hit the wall. The car was retired with body and suspension damage, and Ickx was added to the lineup on the Andretti/Merzario Ferrari.

A pair of NART Ferrari 312Ps placed in the top five. Sam Posey and Mike Parkes finished fourth in a year-old, three-liter car, winning the Prototype class by 15 laps over the sister car of Tony Adamowicz and David Piper. The fourth-place finisher lost time when Parkes hit a slower car in the infield, and again on three lengthy stops to try and patch a blown oil seal on the alternator drive.

The field included two works Matra 650s, subsidized by the French government. One was for Jack Brabham, who was paired with Francois Cevert in his first visit to Daytona, with Jean-Pierre Beltoise and Henri Pescarolo in the other car. Brabham, a three-time

Top: John Wyer's twin Gulf Porsche 917Ks lead Mario Andretti's Ferrari, Vic Elford's Porsche, and the remainder of the field into turn one early in the race. Above: The 24 Hours of Daytona brings together many types of vehicles with a great disparity in performance. Here, the MGB of John Belperche, Tony Lilly, and Don Pickett is about to be overtaken by the Ferrari 512S of Mario Andretti, Jacky Ickx, and Arturo Merzario. Right: Two-time World Champion Sir Jack Brabham grimly charges on despite damage to his Matra-Simca. Brabham prepped for his final Formula One campaign with a 10th-place finish.

world champion, was embarking on what would be his final Formula One season. Both cars struggled with ignition problems, with the Brabham/Cevert entry finishing 10th. After lengthy stays behind the wall, the two Matras returned to the track in the final minute so they could be credited with "finishing."

Defending Daytona 24 Hours winner Roger Penske entered his new Trans-Am Sunoco Javelin for 1969 winner Mark Donohue and Peter Revson. The car ran out of fuel early, and Donohue had to sprint back to pits for a can of gasoline, losing 11 minutes. Even with the delay, the car was still 23 laps ahead in the Trans-Am class when it lost oil pressure and was sidelined at 11:10 p.m.

Penske also entered his spare Lola Mk 3B Chevrolet from 1969, driven by John Cannon and George Eaton. The red car with white pinstriping was never a factor. Cannon pitted immediately with an overfilled oil tank, and the car was retired without even completing a lap.

DAYTONA
RYDER
PORSCHE
AUDI
UNION 76

Jerry Thompson and John Mahler finished sixth in the Owens-Corning Fiberglas Corvette and first in Grand Touring over two-liters. Bob Mitchell and Charlie Kemp took Touring honors, placing 13th in a Camaro, while the Grand Touring two-liter class went to the 15th-place Porsche 911S of Ralph Meaney, Gary Wright, and Bill Bean.

In under two-liter Touring, Del Russo Taylor and Hank Sheldon's Alfa Romeo GTV finished 22nd and five laps ahead of the Fiat 124 of Amos Johnson and Paul Fleming. Bill Wunder and Ray Cuomo finished eighth in the same Ford GT40 (chassis 103) that won the 1965 Daytona Continental.

Making his Daytona 24 Hours debut was Italian Gianpiero Moretti. While the Ferrari 512 he shared with Corrado Manfredini retired with crash damage, this was the beginning of a quest which would last nearly 30 years, to take the overall victory in the event.

The event continued to grow in popularity. The *Daytona Beach News-Journal* estimated the crowd at 35,000 and contrasted the turnout with the Daytona 500 NASCAR stock-car race, which runs two weeks after the 24 Hours.

"At the Daytona 500—which someday may be rivaled in appeal by this race—the fans are moved by fast cars and brave drivers. They're principally from the Dixie stock-car country," Brad Wilson wrote in the *News-Journal*. "The 24 Hours crowd is perhaps younger and are more familiar with champagne, caviar, jetports, and the cars—like the women—are sleek and exotic. With the exception, of course, of the infield area far, far out near the west banked turn. Here you can find the hippies, with beards, the girls with straight blond hair, Navy pea coats, and bell bottomed jeans."

Houston Lawing, public relations director for the speedway, was quoted in that article as saying, "The ratio of college kids here for this race is 10-1 over the 500."

Left: Ken Squier interviews Pedro Rodriguez while Leo Kinnunen stands to the left in victory lane ceremonies. Above: Brian Redman and Jo Siffert shared John Wyer's No. 1 Porsche 917K, which came back to finish second despite losing time for a nighttime clutch change.

KIRK F. WHITE
PENSKE

1971: The Many Uses of Duct Tape

THE 1971 RACE ATTRACTED ANOTHER RECORD TURNOUT, AND WOULD FEATURE THE CLOSEST FINISH IN THE SIX YEARS SINCE THE SPEEDWAY ADAPTED THE 24-HOUR FORMAT. THE CROWD FAVORITE WAS THE NEW SUNOCO FERRARI 512M ENTERED BY ROGER PENSKE AND KIRK WHITE.

Lead driver Mark Donohue took advantage of the newly paved infield section to shatter Mario Andretti's year-old qualifying record by nine seconds, with a lap of 1:42.42. His average speed, 133.919 mph, bettered Andretti's mark in a factory Ferrari by 11 miles per hour.

Luigi Chinetti's North American Racing Team entered a 512S co-driven by Ronnie Bucknum and Tony Adamowicz. NART was also represented by the unlikely pairing of racing millionaires Sam Posey and Peter Revson, who had been at odds with each other since an incident at Riverside, California, the previous October.

"We still aren't on good terms," admitted Posey before the race, "but we're going to drive together and cooperate with each other and try to go as fast as possible."

The pair shared a Ferrari 512M. A Ferrari 312PB, based on the marque's Formula One car and powered by a three-liter engine, was withdrawn when the only available prototype was destroyed in the 1,000 Kilometers of Buenos Aires, Argentina, in January, killing Ignazio Giunti in the process.

Left: Held together by rolls of duct tape after being badly damaged in a night-time incident, the No. 6 Sunoco Ferrari 512M of Mark Donohue and David Hobbs persevered to a third place finish. Above: Three varieties of American muscle cars in action: the Camaro of Javier Garcis, Luis Garcia, and Richie Small leads the Corvette of John Greenwood, Alan Barber, and Dick Lang, and the Mustang of Warren Matzen and Tom Hayser.

John Wyer returned to Daytona in a bid for his second consecutive 24 Hours victory, with three-time event winner Pedro Rodriguez and Jackie Oliver teamed in a baby-blue-and-orange 4.9-liter Gulf Porsche 917K.

The race started at 2:59 p.m. Saturday under a hot sun, in 78-degree weather. The Penske Ferrari, co-driven by Donohue and David Hobbs, took an early lead, but was forced to the pits five hours into the race with malfunctioning tail lights. Alternator troubles cost the team another twelve-and-a-half minutes in the pits and dropped the Ferrari to third position.

That gave the lead to the Porsche of Rodriguez/Oliver, followed by teammates Jo Siffert and Derek Bell. The lead Porsche quickly lapped the field, while their teammates encountered problems after leading early in the event.

"The car was pretty quick," recalled Bell of his first experience racing at Daytona. "There was no back chicane then, we used to come down the back straight about 225 mph and then just go flat into the banking. It was a pretty nerve-wracking experience, particularly when you watched your teammate doing it, and then realized you were going to have to do it. I was watching Jo from the

infield when we were testing and thought, I can't possibly do that, but of course, I did. But I do have to say I was very relieved when I was sitting in the motor home and he walked in during the middle of the evening. I thought, 'we shouldn't both be here at the same time,' and I realized the engine had gone. That was the only time I ever had a 917 engine blow up, and, of course, I wasn't driving it."

At 11:45 p.m., disaster struck two of the top contenders. The silver second-place Martini and Rossi Porsche 917K of Vic Elford and Gigs van Lenexa hit debris, cut a tire, and spun into the wall on the banking leading onto the speedway's front straight. Donohue, running in third, slowed to avoid the incident but was clipped from behind by a Porsche 911 driven by Charles Perry. The Porsche tumbled

Above left: The field follows the Porsche 914 pace car and pole sitter Mark Donohue in formation down the back straight. Above right: Mark Donohue paces the action in the early going in the Sunoco Ferrari, chased by the John Wyer Porsches. Opposite: Mark Donohue is strapped in and anxious to return to the race as the crew feverishly repairs damage to Roger Penske's Sunoco Ferrari 512M.

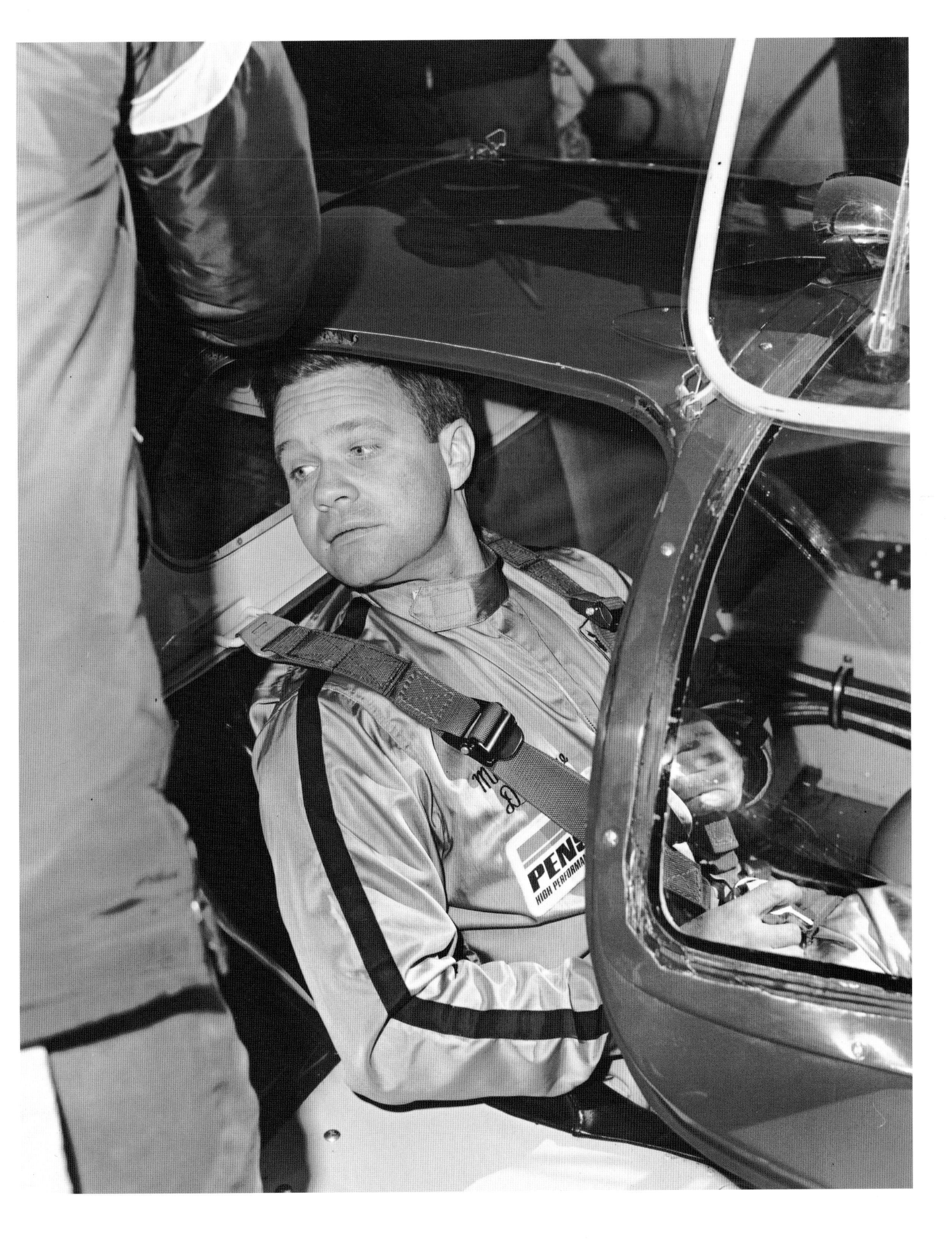
PENS
HIGH PERFORMA

end over end down the banking and into the infield. Neither Perry nor Elford was hurt in the incident.

"As I went up onto the banking flat-out, the right rear tire let go," Elford recalled. "It was right in the middle of the banking, so we were doing about 200 miles an hour. Then, I was instantly spinning. Surprisingly, I didn't actually hit anything. I remembered the rookie meeting when I went there for stock cars [Elford finished 11th in the 1969 Daytona 500 NASCAR race], and Richard Petty told us if you get into trouble on the banking, turn left and put your foot on the brake. So I did, and the car just slowly spun. I went about 400 yards around the banking, spinning. It finally came to rest down on the grass in the infield. There was little left of the car. The entire right-rear corner was gone.

"Porsche 917s weren't made to go 200 mph backwards," Elford continued. "So the first time it went backwards, the whole rear deck came off, and then the doors, one after the other. It finally came to rest. But I'd left so much dirt and dust and filth up there on the banking that Mark [Donohue] in the Penske Ferrari and the [Perry] 911 came along, running together, into a cloud of dust. Neither of them could see. They touched, and Mark hit the wall, and the poor guy in the Porsche came spinning down and literally followed exactly the route I had taken. In fact, I had gotten out of the car wondering which way to run, because I couldn't see. It was so dark I had no idea where to run to until the Porsche started coming down toward me, and he followed the same trajectory and ended up by hitting the right-rear of my car. That launched it into the air, and he rolled a couple times. By then I was out

Above: Pit road is cluttered with tool boxes, a wheel, and loose tools during a lengthy pit stop late in the race. Right: The left-front brakes on the Ronnie Bucknum/Tony Adamowicz Ferrari 512S are serviced on pit road during the night. The NART entry went on to finish second, one lap behind the winning Porsche. Far right: With the rear bodywork high in the air, the gearbox is replaced in the Pedro Rodriguez/Jackie Oliver Porsche 917K. The team lost the lead in the pits, but Rodriguez went back out, made up the difference, and took the smoking car to victory.

of the car, and I immediately went across and started joining in with the rescue workers to see how the guy in the Porsche was. Suddenly there was a cry from my car saying, 'There's no driver!'"

Donohue rolled his battered Ferrari to pit road, with both front and rear wheels broken and the left-side bodywork destroyed. When Ferrari importer Luigi Chinetti, working the pits for his NART team, saw the car rolling down pit road, he dispatched two of his top mechanics to assist Penske with parts and labor. The Penske team lost 53 laps (one hour and 10 minutes) patching up the ruined bodywork with plenty of duct tape. They returned to the race in fifth position.

By 11 a.m. Sunday, the Rodriguez/Oliver Porsche was firmly in control, leading by 55 laps. The car had been smoking for several hours, however, and suddenly slowed at 11:32 a.m., then pitted with a broken part in the gearbox. "We felt like crying," said Oliver after the race. "When our gearbox got sick, so did we."

The Porsche lost more than an hour in the pits as its gearbox was replaced, which handed the lead to the Bucknum Ferrari. Giving chase was the battered Penske Ferrari, which had been gaining over the last 12 hours with inspired driving by Donohue and Hobbs, who were on pace to catch the Bucknum/Adamowicz Ferrari in the final minutes. But the Penske team's chances ground to a halt at 12:42 p.m. when a fuel pump drive belt broke, and the crew needed 13 minutes to replace the not easily accessible part.

Meanwhile, Rodriguez, after a sleepless night, paced pit road as the Wyer team completed its repairs. When the car finally returned with two hours remaining, he began chasing the Ferrari, which was losing ground in the closing hours. A valve spring problem had reduced its maximum RPMs to 7,500—1,000 less than normal—and a fuel pickup problem forced the team to make more frequent pit stops. Rodriguez needed only 33 minutes to make up the two-lap deficit to regain the lead and score his fourth Daytona victory. Smoke trailed the Wyer Porsche over the final laps, due to a broken gasket in the sump oil tank.

"We were making 10 seconds a lap on the lead Ferrari, but I didn't know how many laps we were behind," Rodriguez said in victory lane.

The top two cars, running only a lap and few seconds apart, made for a dramatic finish with the badly smoking Porsche trailed by the Bucknum/Adamowicz Ferrari, which had a valve problem and was belching flames each time it decelerated. The winning team covered 688 laps, 2,621.28 miles,

and averaged 109.203 mph. It was the second consecutive Daytona 24 Hours victory for Rodriguez, who had also won the shorter Daytona Continentals in 1963 and 1964.

The NART Ferrari finished second, one lap behind, while Penske's wounded Ferrari placed third, 14 laps behind. "Putting that Ferrari back together was unbelievable," recalled Penske in a 2002 interview. "In fact, running that Ferrari, and then going on to Le Mans with the same Ferrari, got Porsche's attention. [Porsche head designer] Ferdinand Piech asked me to meet him and his brother [Michael] in Stuttgart, and that's how we got together with Porsche."

The Owens-Corning Fiberglas Corvette team of Tony DeLorenzo, Don Yenko, and John Mahler finished fourth overall and first in the Grand Touring over 2.5-liter class. Fifth, and first in the Prototype class, was the Ferrari 312P of Luigi Chinetti Jr. and Nestor Garcia-Veiga. The team spent a total of one hour, 45 minutes in the pits correcting faulty shift linkage, which cost them fourth place. They refired the car with one minute remaining for a slow final lap.

Taking honors in Grand Touring under two-liters were Jacques Duval, George Nicholas, and Bob Bailey in a Porsche 914/6, placing seventh overall. Taking 11th, and first in Touring, were Vince Gimondo and Charles Dietrich in a Camaro.

Above: Jo Siffert (left) is joined by Miss Universe and Derek Bell, who was making his first appearance in the 24 Hours of Daytona. Bell went on to enjoy success in this event in the mid-1980s, but he admitted he was intimidated by the banking and relieved when the engine failed on their Porsche. Right: The winning team celebrates in victory lane, with Jackie Oliver at the wheel and Pedro Rodriguez on the roof of the John Wyer Porsche 917K, flanked by a pair of crewmen.

1971

Failing to finish was a Mustang entered by Ed Matthews for himself, Swede Savage, and Danny Ongais. Ongais, a successful drag racer from Hawaii, would become a top contender by the end of the decade.

Hurley Haywood, back from duty in Vietnam, renewed his acquaintance with Gregg. Impressed with the younger driver's showing in an autocross, Gregg invited Haywood to join him for the 24 Hours. Gregg set fast time in the GTU class in a Brumos Porsche 914/6, but the duo failed to finish. Gregg would go on to capture the inaugural IMSA GTU championship that year, the first of his six IMSA titles.

After the race, competitors and the remaining spectators looked to the skies in hopes of seeing Apollo 14, which was launched at 4:04 p.m. from Kennedy Space Center, approximately 50 miles southeast of the speedway. But overcast skies prevented them from getting more than a brief glimpse of the spacecraft. The mission commander was Alan Shepard, a frequent visitor to sports car races at Daytona.

"The racing was more competitive this year," said Rodriguez, making his fourth visit to Daytona's victory lane. Unfortunately, it was to be his last. He followed up his Daytona victory with 1,000-kilometer triumphs at Monza, Spa, and the Osterreichring. But in a July Interseries race at the Norisring, Rodriguez crashed after a tire on his Ferrari 512M deflated. The car burst into flames, and Rodriguez succumbed to the injuries. Racing had lost one of its greatest champions.

CARELLO

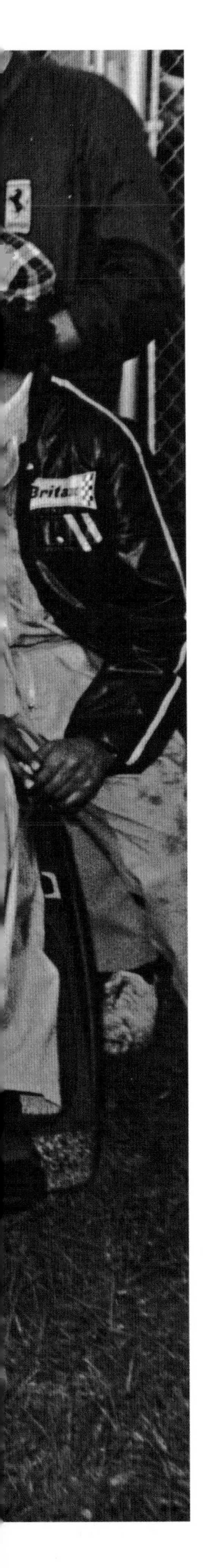

1972: A Return to Six Hours

HANDICAPPING IS NOT PART OF MAJOR ENDURANCE SPORTS CAR RACING, BUT IN 1972 THE FERRARI 312PB OF MARIO ANDRETTI AND JACKY ICKX RACED AT A DISADVANTAGE THROUGHOUT MOST OF THE DAYTONA CONTINENTAL. THE TALENT OF THE DRIVERS, HOWEVER, MADE UP FOR THE PROBLEM.

For 1972, the FIA moved from the five-liter formula to three-liters, making the mighty Porsche 917, Ferrari 512, and Ford GT40 obsolete. The new FIA Group 5 three-liter formula was based on Formula One engines. The other class, Group 4, or Special Grand Touring, was for production-based vehicles. Reliability of the smaller engines was an issue, and the FIA wanted races to last no longer than six hours. Only Le Mans would be allowed to keep its 24-hour race.

Although Sebring fought to maintain its 12-hour format, Daytona went along with the FIA's mandate. Concerned that the loss of the popular big cars would hurt attendance, France agreed, in an experimental move, to shorten the race to six hours. He hoped the shorter distance would bring out larger crowds.

Ferrari and Alfa Romeo each entered a trio of cars for Group 5. In addition to Andretti and Ickx, Ferrari 312PBs were also driven by Tim Schenken/Ronnie Peterson and Clay Regazzoni/Brian Redman. Luigi Chinetti's NART entered a Ferrari 312P for Luigi Chinetti Jr. and George Eaton.

Ferrari's primary opposition came from the Alfa Romeo TT33/3s of Peter Revson/Rolf Stommelen, Vic Elford/Helmut Marko, and Andrea de

Left: Ferrari teammates Mario Andretti (left) and Jacky Ickx, both draped with orange blossom wreaths, flash "V" for victory following their six-hour triumph. Page 93 Above: Tim Schenken, driver of the No. 6 Ferrari 312PB, holds an animated discussion with two crewmen in the pits.

Adamich/Nanni Galli. With their 12-cylinder engine now ruled out, the Alfas were fitted with their old V-8 powerplants, which put them at a distinct disadvantage to the Ferraris, running their Formula One–proven engines. The other top contender was the Ford-Lola T280 of Reine Wisell and Jo Bonnier.

Andretti won the pole with a lap of 131.606 mph, but his car lost a cylinder in the early going of the race. This was the handicap the team would need to overcome. Fortunately for Andretti, the Ferrari still had 11 working cylinders.

"During a pit stop, we found we had a dead spark plug, but the wire to the plug also was dead," said Andretti following the race. "There was nothing we could do about it then, so I didn't think we could win."

Andretti explained that while the Ferrari ran at 11,000 rpm in practice, it was 800 to 900 rpm short during the race, costing the car about 14 mph in top speed. The only thing Andretti and Ickx could do was "drive as hard as we could all day."

Regazzoni set the early pace, pursued by Bonnier. Just before the one-hour mark, the lead Ferrari began to slow due to a gradually deflating tire, enabling the Lola, now driven by Wisell, to close up. Just as Wisell made his bid for the lead on the 27th lap, the Ferrari's tire let go at 185 mph right before the entrance to pit road. The explosion blew away the car's rear bodywork and sent it careening directly into Wisell's path. The impact destroyed the front end of the Lola, just as it had taken the race lead.

"I saw something and ducked," said Wisell, who lost 13 minutes in the pits to repair the damage. The incident dropped their Lola to 15th place. Spectacular driving by Bonnier in the bright yellow car brought his Lola up to eighth place before electrical and fuel-injection problems brought about its retirement during the fourth hour. This marked the final appearance by the Swedish star at Daytona.

Above left: Rain showers dampen the circuit midway through the race. The No. 61 Porsche 911S of Jim Locke and Bob Bailey and the No. 7 Rolf Stommelen and Peter Revson kick up "rooster tails" of spray as they exit NASCAR turn four. Above right: Miss Universe receives the attention of winners Mario Andretti and Jacky Ickx. Opposite top: The pre-race parade lap, taken from the pace car, show pole winner Andretti in the No. 2 Ferrari 312PB and teammate Clay Regazzoni in the No. 4 Ferrari leading the 56-car field. Regazzoni set the early pace, then Andretti and Ickx went on to win the six-hour event. Opposite below: Ickx (No. 2) works to the outside of the Lola T-212 of Sports 2000 class winners Hugh Kleinpeter and Thomas Waugh.

DAYTONA USA
Firestone
Shell 4 Shell
Firestone
Shell 2 Shell

MARIO ANDRETTI
JACKY ICKX
2
Shell
SAVIN
GOODYEAR
MECHANIC
BILL ORR
56
B
Casa Bonita
RESTAURANTS
TOM WAUGH
CHAMPION
union
prestolite

Above: Sam Posey leads NART teammate Ronnie Bucknum in a pair of Ferrari Daytonas in pre-event practice. Neither driver enjoyed success in 1972, with Bucknum failing to start while Posey did not finish. Opposite top: Tim Schenken's No. 2 Ferrari fights off the No. 3 Alfa Romeo T-33 of Vic Elford and Helmut Marko. The Ferrari finished the race second overall, followed by the Alfa. Right: Mario Andretti sits patiently at the wheel of his Ferrari while a half-dozen crewmen work on the car during a pit stop.

Bonnier would lose his life in June after crashing in the 24 Hours of Le Mans.

The other Bonnier-prepared Lola, driven by France's Gerard Larrousse and England's Chris Craft, missed the first seven laps due to ignition problems and retired after a very short run.

Regazzoni was luckier. His Ferrari spun off the banking without hitting anything, and he was able to have the car repaired in the pits, although he lost several laps in the process. The team had another spin and lost more time replacing rear bodywork, and later had a pit fire during a brake change. Miraculously, Regazzoni and Redman persevered to finish fourth.

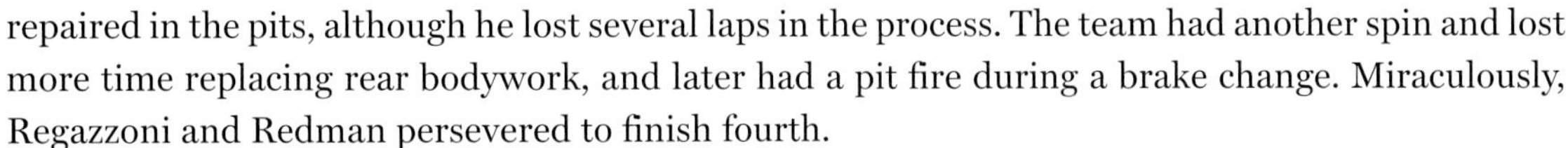

The Regazzoni/Redman incident gave the lead to Andretti's underpowered Ferrari. The Revson/Stommelen Alfa, however, was able to lead twice during pit stops, as the Ferrari crew unsuccessfully attempted to get its car firing on all 12 cylinders. But alternator problems and a steering vibration caused unscheduled pit stops for Revson and Stommelen as well. Finally, the Alfa withdrew

because of engine failure shortly after the halfway point.

After that, Andretti and Ickx led the rest of the way, according to the Daytona International Speedway scoreboard. The Ferrari team scorers showed the pair in second, behind the sister car of Ronnie Peterson and Tim Schenken, which had a slipping clutch throughout the event. Scoring discrepancies were not uncommon in the days before transponders, scoring monitors, and computers, and Ickx wasn't willing to wait until hours after the race for the scoring dispute to be settled.

Despite orders from team manager Dr. Peter Schetty to "cool it," Ickx pressed on and passed Schenken with five laps to go. That gave Andretti and Ickx the lead on everybody's scoreboard.

"We thought we were in second, and when Jacky passed Tim Schenken with five laps to go, that was victory for us," said Andretti. They completed 194 laps, 739.14 miles, and averaged 124.16 mph.

There was a moment of sadness in victory lane when Pedro Rodriguez Sr. presented the winners with a trophy in memory of his son, Pedro Rodriguez Jr., who had won the Continental four times before his death in 1971.

Schenken and Peterson finished second, and were actually two laps down. The Elford/Marko Alfa was third, another two laps behind. Recovering from the early problems to finish fourth was the Regazzoni/Redman Ferrari, 15 laps behind, followed by the remaining Alfa of de Adamich/Galli.

The Tom Waugh/Hugh Kleinpeter Ford-Lola T212 was awarded sixth place and victory in the two-liter Sports class. The Abarth SE of Arturo Merzario and Alex Soler-Roig was fast throughout the race, and was running sixth with 30 minutes remaining when it was disqualified for receiving a push start.

The Lola T212 of Canadians Roger and Maurice McCaig led the two-liter class at the midway point, running sixth overall, but stops to repair an oil leak and starter motor dropped them to ninth overall and second in class. Coming home seventh and first in the 2.5-liter Sports Touring Class was the team

Above left: The Alfa Romeo T-33 of Rolf Stommelen and Peter Revson twists its way through the infield. The car led the event twice before alternator and steering problems dropped the team out of contention, then engine failure put the car out after the midway point. Above right: Tony Dean and Bob Brown co-drove a Porsche 908. The duo started 11th, but failed to finish. Opposite: Clay Regazzoni and Brian Redman swap places behind the wheel of their Ferrari on pit road during pre-event practice.

of Hurley Haywood and Peter Gregg in a Porsche 911S.

"That year, Peter was running the Can-Am, and I was given the task of running for the new IMSA GT championship," said Haywood, who won the GTU title. The pair "never seemed to set a wheel wrong," according to *AutoWeek*.

Other class winners were David Heinz and Bob Johnson in over 2.5-liter Grand Touring (GT), eighth overall in a Corvette, and Bob Mitchell and Bob Christiansen in Touring, 11th overall in a Camaro. The Heinz/Johnson Corvette unveiled a new Goodyear radial tire for the event.

The 10th-place finisher—a Porsche 911S driven by Jim Locke and Bob Bailey—had been stolen two months prior to the race. Locke had had to pay $2,000 in ransom to get the car back. The field also included two-time NASCAR Grand National champion Buck Baker, who completed 43 laps in a Pontiac Firebird he shared with Larry Baker.

Corvettes were involved in three separate incidents. Tom Fraser's Sting Ray lost the brakes in the infield 90 minutes into the event, hurdled a dirt banking, and landed upside-down on a camper. Neither Fraser nor the woman napping inside the camper were injured. Jerry Thompson, driving in the fastest-qualifying FIA GTO entry, cut a tire on the straight and spun twice before hitting the wall. Later, the Vette of Bob Spirgel and Art Mollin caught fire during a pit stop, but the blaze was quickly extinguished.

National Speed Sport News reported a "sun-splashed" crowd of 26,500 was in attendance.

1973: The Flywheel Saga: Warning or Ploy?

After the move to six hours failed to boost attendance in 1972, the FIA approved Bill France's request to return to the 24-hour race format in 1973. A record crowd greeted the return of the twice-around-the-clock enduro.

Not returning, however, were the Ferrari and Alfa Romeo teams, who felt that the endurance format would not favor their cars. A hefty appearance fee could have ensured Ferrari's participation, but Bill France felt the $30,000 request (as opposed to the usual $2,500) was out of line.

Five prototypes led the field. Derek Bell won the pole with a lap of 129.995 mph in John Wyer's Ford Cosworth-powered Mirage M6 he co-drove with Howden Ganley. "The Matra was much quicker than us, but I just got the right lap in during the dry," Bell recalled. "Then, it got wet at the end of the session and that put me ahead of Francois Cevert in a works Matra to win the pole."

Bell managed his fast lap despite a broken seat belt. "I could have gone quite a bit faster than that, but I was holding back a little bit."

The Matra-Simca of Cevert, Jean-Pierre Beltoise, and Henri Pescarolo qualified second, and shared the second row with the Mike Hailwood/John Watson Wyer Mirage and the Reine Wisell/Jean-Louis Lafosse/Hughes de Fierlant Ford Lola T282. The only other three-liter prototype was an aged Porsche 908/3, fielded by Reinhold Joest for himself, Mario Casoni, and Paul Blancpain.

Porsche backed a pair of American efforts to showcase their 911 Carrera

Left: Hurley Haywood and Peter Gregg exchange places during a routine nighttime pit stop for the Brumos Porsche 911 RSR. Above: Sixteen-year-old Richie Panch, son of Marvin Panch and a future NASCAR Winston Cup competitor, made his professional racing debut in the No. 9 Camaro, co-driving with Ray Kessler and Wilbur Pickett. The trio finished seventh overall and first in the Touring class.

RS. The car was technically in the Sports class with the Prototypes. Porsche had already built enough of them (522) to have it homologated and requested that the car be placed in the Group 4 GT class, but the request had not yet been officially accepted by the FIA.

Brumos Porsche entered a new Carrera RS for Peter Gregg and Hurley Haywood. The car, painted in the American red, white, and blue instead of the traditional Brumos' tangerine orange, qualified eighth. A second factory-backed Porsche Carrera RS, fielded by Roger Penske for Mark Donohue and George Follmer, started 13th.

The meticulous Gregg, known in racing circles as "Peter Perfect," had completely disassembled

the car upon receiving it and discovered a loose flywheel. While Gregg warned Penske of the possible flaw, Penske felt it was a pre-race ploy and ignored the advice.

Another contender was the Corvette of Tony DeLorenzo and Mo Carter, which was built by Bud Moore. The car qualified sixth, just ahead of another Corvette fielded by John Greenwood.

The Mirage of Hailwood/Watson took the lead soon after the 3 p.m. start. The pole-winning Bell/Ganley car suffered a loose alternator, then clutch problems in the early going, which led to its retirement. Watson maintained a comfortable lead, with the Matra-Simca of Cevert/Beltoise/Pescarolo keeping pace, but not challenging.

Five hours into the race, the leading Mirage pitted for a lengthy stop to have its clutch replaced. The Joest Porsche had to start at the back of the pack after missing qualifying due to a fire the previous Friday, but worked its way into the top 10 by the 15th lap, and was third by the five-hour mark. The car pitted to have the fuel cell—which was dragging on the track—repaired. The Porsche motored on until 11 p.m., when it lost its transmission.

Meanwhile, the Brumos and Penske Porsches were engaged in a terrific battle for second. That became

Above left: Derek Bell won the pole with a lap of 129.995 mph, running his fast lap despite a broken seat belt in John Wyer's Ford Cosworth-powered Mirage M6. Above right: The sun rises on the first 24-hour race at Daytona in two years, with the No. 57 Porsche 908 of Reinhold Joest leading the No. 77 Porsche 911S of fourth-place finishers George Stone, Bruce Jennings, and Mike Downs. Opposite top: David Heinz, Bob McClure, and Dana English finished third in the No. 5 Corvette, shown battling with another Corvette in the infield. Right: The field takes the green flag from a flagman perched atop the wall on the superspeedway's back straight.

a fight for the lead when the Matra, driven by Cevert at a conservative pace, blew its engine at 12:30 a.m.

"Since we had the prototypes running in that race, we went into it wanting to win over the GT cars," Haywood recalled. "But then all the prototypes started having problems, our car had a lot of speed, and it was prestigious because Roger Penske also had a car with Mark Donohue and George Follmer driving. That was our competition that Peter was most concerned about beating. Yet we were going fast enough that, pretty soon, we found ourselves way up on the leader board."

The Mirage returned to the race after its clutch problems. The Lola struggled after losing its alternator drive, and changed batteries every 30 minutes throughout the evening until the engine began misfiring at 2:30 a.m.

Follmer held the lead when the Penske Porsche encountered engine problems—traced to the loose flywheel Gregg had warned Penske about—shortly after 5 a.m. Two laps after taking over for Donohue, Follmer lost a piston and retired. That left the Brumos Porsche with a 35-lap lead.

At 5:30 a.m. Hailwood crashed the Mirage in the infield after a suspension part broke. The car coasted the rest of the way, slowed only by a cracked windshield when it collected an errant gull. Seemingly assured of the victory, Gregg was approached by representatives of Classic Car Wax on Sunday morning.

"They were the premier car wax at the time," recalled Brumos team manager Bob Snodgrass. "They offered Peter $10,000 if he would pit the car late in the race, and allow their people to wax it. That

was a considerable amount of money at the time, but Peter refused the offer. He was afraid the car wouldn't restart, and didn't want to take any chances."

The Brumos Porsche won by 22 laps over the NART Ferrari Daytona of Francois Migault and Milt Minter, the Grand Touring winners. Another NART car, piloted by factory driver Arturo Merzario and Jean-Pierre Jarier, had led the class much of the race, only to exit with clutch problems. Gregg and Haywood completed 670 laps, 2,552.7 miles, and averaged 106.274 mph.

Third went to the Corvette of David Heinz, Bob McClure, and Dana English, followed by the Porsche 911S of George Stone, Bruce Jennings, and Mike Downs, and the NART Ferrari 365GTB Daytona of Luigi Chinetti Jr., Bob Grossman, and Wilbur Shaw Jr.

Other class winners were the seventh-place Camaro of Ray Kessler, NASCAR's Richie Panch, and Wilbur Pickett in Touring, and the 10th place Porsche 911S of Bob Bergstrom and Jim Cook in two-liter Grand Touring.

Lost in the shuffle was a 911S entered by Al Holbert, the son of veteran Porsche campaigner Bob

1973

Holbert. The car qualified 42nd and dropped out after 213 laps. Like Haywood, Holbert would go on to play a major role in future 24-hour races at Daytona.

The Brumos triumph was the first overall victory for a 911-based Porsche in international competition. The venerable 911 would dominate sports car racing for the next decade. And while it was a watershed moment for Porsche, it also was the turning point in Haywood's career.

"Up until that point, I really had not raced in any international type of events," Haywood explained. "That victory certainly got Porsche's attention, and they started watching what I was doing. It was my first big international win. From there we went to Sebring and won the 12 Hours of Sebring. Winning those two races back to back basically put my name on the map."

Looking back nearly 20 years, Haywood felt this victory was the most satisfying of his five Daytona 24 Hours triumphs.

"It was a pretty awesome feat, because we were racing our sister Porsche, driven by Mark Donohue and George Follmer, and we were able to run wheel to wheel with them and we beat them. That made Peter very happy, from the standpoint that it was Brumos racing against Penske racing. It also made me very happy that I was able to be competitive against Mark Donohue and George Follmer, two of the best guys in road racing at that point."

Haywood would have to wait two years before his next attempt in the 24 Hours, as an OPEC oil embargo late in 1973 led to an international gasoline crisis. The escalating gas prices and long fuel lines led to the speedway's canceling the 1974 event in late 1973.

Ironically, the crisis began to ease in early 1974. The *Daytona Beach Morning Journal* reported on February 19, 1974, that efforts were underway to reschedule the event for July, with the time shortened to 12 hours. However, any change of dates must be approved through the international sanctioning bodies, and the date change was not granted.

Opposite: The outlook is grim for George Follmer and the Penske team in a pre-dawn pit stop. They are about to learn a burnt piston on their Porsche 911 RSR will take them out of the running. Above left: The No. 22 Ferrari 365GTB of Milt Minter and Francois Migault is serviced in the pits. The team finished second overall and won the GT class. Above right: The No. 12 Ford Lola T282 of Reine Wisell and Jean-Louis Lafoose goes to the outside of the No. 88 Porsche 910 of Edwin Abate and William Cuddy. Neither car made it to the halfway point.

SANYO
42
CAMEL
S.E.V. MARCHAL
UNION 76
EQUIPPED WITH
CHAMPION
SPARK PLUGS

1975: Brilliance in the Fog

THE FLEDGLING INTERNATIONAL MOTOR SPORTS ASSOCIATION (IMSA) SANCTIONED THE DAYTONA 24 FOR THE FIRST TIME IN 1975, AND THE RACE OPENED THE SEASON FOR BOTH THE IMSA CAMEL GT SERIES AND THE FIA WORLD CHAMPIONSHIP OF MAKES. THE EVENT HAD A GOOD TURNOUT, EQUIVALENT TO 1973'S RECORD CROWD.

There was plenty of competition, with an untested NART Ferrari Boxer, the BMW factory team of Grand Prix drivers, and John Greenwood's vaunted Super Corvette challenged by a phalanx of Porsches.

Greenwood won the pole with a lap of 119.032 mph in his cream Corvette, powered by a 427-cubic-inch engine. The mustachioed Troy, Michigan, engineer had rebuilt the showroom car with plastic and space-age metals.

"It gives the other guys something to think about," said Greenwood after qualifying. "The pole doesn't mean anything, but when it's easy to do, why not? We didn't want to run any hot laps and really didn't run too fast."

Taking the second and third positions in qualifying were a pair of BMW 3.0 CSLs, with Hans Stuck second quickest in the car he co-drove with Sam Posey, 117.026 mph. They were followed by Swedish Formula One star Ronnie Peterson, third fastest at 117.022 mph, in the car he shared with Brian Redman. The cars were prepared in NASCAR driver Bobby Allison's Hueytown, Alabama, shops. The 24-year-old Stuck, a second-generation Austrian driver

Left: The colorful No. 42 Corvette of John Caruoso and Dick Vreeland is on pit road prior to the start. After qualifying 21st, their engine failed 59 laps into the race. Above: Peter Gregg (left) and Hurley Haywood took their second consecutive victory in the 24 Hours of Daytona, once again at the wheel of the No. 59 Brumos Racing Porsche 911 RSR.

who led BMW to the 1973 European Touring Car manufacturer's championship, had tested the car at the Alabama International Motor Speedway at Talladega, and immediately set a record on the circuit's four-mile road course.

Stuck had been impressed with the banking at Talladega, which is a slightly larger version of Daytona. He asked Bill France if he could get a ride for the Daytona 500. "Perhaps something will come up," France told him. Unfortunately for Stuck, nothing came up, and he never competed in the 500 or any NASCAR event.

"They will be a ton of competition," Greenwood said of the BMWs. "They'll use less fuel than my car and will have to stop less during the race. I'll have to make it up some way."

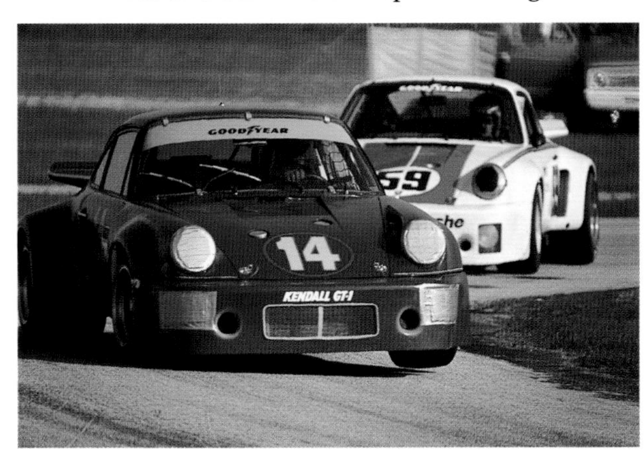

The BMWs were followed by the Camaro of Mo Carter and Gene Felton. Then came the Porsches, led by Al Holbert and Elliott Forbes-Robinson, with Carreras taking five of the next six positions. Qualifying seventh were the 1973 winners, Peter Gregg and Hurley Haywood, returning to co-drive the Brumos Porsche Carrera. Gregg had won both the IMSA and Trans-Am titles in 1973, and repeated as IMSA titlist in 1974.

An unproven NART Ferrari Boxer Berlinetta—one of the wild cards entering the race—proved to be a disappointment. The car arrived late, and Claude Ballot-Lena retired after only one lap with the rear wheels scraping the bodywork.

Greenwood's space-age Corvette led the opening 27 laps after the 3 p.m. start before it began a succession of pit stops for overheating. First, the crew spent 25 minutes changing the radiator. Then they replaced hoses and other parts during ensuing pit stops. All the work was in vain, as the problem was eventually found to be a malfunctioning radiator heat-escape valve, a $3 part that could have been replaced in two minutes. The team's frustration finally ended when co-driver Carl Shafer was squeezed into the wall entering turn one, badly damaging the car. He was uninjured in the only serious accident of the race.

The Peterson/Brian Redman BMW retired one hour into the race after a connecting rod broke. They had been running fourth. The BMW's sister car, driven by Stuck/Posey, took the lead on one of the Corvette's pit stops and held it.

Posey and Stuck went on to dominate the event in their BMW. They led until shortly after 12:45 a.m., when their engine failed, breaking the same part as their teammates had earlier in the race. "Everything was running fine," Stuck told the *Daytona Beach News-Journal,* "and then I heard the noise, and knew exactly what happened."

That gave the lead to the Porsche of Al Holbert and Elliott Forbes-Robinson, and the pair led for nearly six hours before slowing with transmission trouble. The Brumos Porsche encountered

Above: The beginning of a rivalry. Al Holbert, driving the No. 14 Porsche 911 RSR he shared with Elliott Forbes-Robinson, leads the Brumos Porsche of Hurley Haywood. The pair would become America's top drivers in international sports car racing over the next decade. Opposite top: Robert Kirby, John Hotchkiss, and Len Jones pose with their Porsche 914/6 prior to the start. While they qualified fastest in the IMSA 2.5-liter class, they failed to finish, completing just 51 laps. Right: Infield spectators follow the action from behind the guardrail as the 51-car field heads into turn one.

UNION
GOODYEAR
NO SMOKING
TEAM R
51
JOHNSON-BOZZANI
PORSCHE AUDI
GTU
CAMEL
GT CHALLENGE
GT
CHAMPION
UNION

problems early in the event, when Gregg got together with the Porsche of Mexican Guillermo Rojas as they entered the infield portion of the circuit, side by side. Both Porsches continued, with the Brumos car sustaining left-side damage.

"It loused up the rear end a little bit, and it wasn't quite as fast on the straightaways after that," Gregg said. "I guess you'd have to say the fault [for the incident] was divided 50-50. He was to blame for being too aggressive, and I was to blame for pushing too hard that early in the race."

Fog set in during the pre-dawn hours. Some drivers complained about visibility. Haywood,

Above: The Charlie Kemp/Carson Baird Porsche 911 RSR is in for service. The team finished third overall. Right: John Greenwood leads the field from the pole position in his Corvette at the start, followed by the BMWs of Formula One drivers Hans Stuck and Ronnie Peterson. Far right: The No. 73 Corvette of Bill Arnold leads the No. 46 Datson 240Z of Spencer Buzbee in the infield.

however, was not complaining. Driving a brilliant four-hour shift, Haywood gradually cut into the Holbert/EFR Porsche lead, making up 10 to 15 seconds per lap. IMSA was considering red-flagging the race due to the deteriorating conditions, and race official Charlie Rainville asked the Brumos team if Haywood was having visibility problems.

"Put Charlie on the radio," Haywood instructed Brumos crewman Jack Atkinson when told of the situation. Haywood told Rainville to "Time my next lap." Haywood then ran the fastest lap of the race to that point. "How's that, Charlie?" Haywood then radioed, ending all conversation of bringing out the red flag.

Haywood made his pass for the lead at 6:17 a.m. The Holbert/EFR Porsche continued to challenge until the transmission finally gave up in the closing hours. The pair finished eighth, parked on pit road.

"First, we broke a header pipe, then we broke second gear, then we broke third gear, and then it all went away," recalled Forbes-Robinson. "In those years you weren't allowed to change gear boxes, like we are today. We actually had about a one-hour lead on Peter and Hurley at one time. Under today's rules, we could have changed the gearbox and gone on to win the race. We sat on pit road for three-and-a-half hours."

The Gregg/Haywood car was nagged by numerous minor problems, including a faulty oil hose, a loose connection on its two-way radio, and high oil temperatures. A pair of pit miscues led to two of 19 pit stops. During one of the pit stops, the crew forgot to change one of the tires, resulting in an extra stop for Gregg. Later on, he left the pits without the passenger door completely closed and had to return to close it.

In the end, though, it was all Porsche. Bettering the three-car photo finishes of the late sixties, Haywood led a parade of six Porsche Carrera RSRs to the finish line. Only Ted Field's seventh-place Ferrari Daytona, driven by Jon Woodner and Fred Phillips to FIA Group 4 honors, broke up the phalanx, although Porsches swept the next six positions in a dominating performance.

"I just thought it would be neat to have a whole line of Porsches," Haywood explained in victory lane. "When I passed the other guys, I told them to get in line with me. They agreed, and we all passed [the checkered flag] together."

It was the second straight Daytona 24 Hours victory for Haywood and Gregg, backing up their

1973 triumph. The winning Brumos Porsche completed 684 laps, 2,606 miles, and averaged 108.531 mph. "Lordy, am I tired!" Gregg exclaimed in victory lane. "Tomorrow, I've got to go back to selling cars for a living."

"It is incredible," added Haywood, who spent a half hour in the shade getting oxygen before meeting the media. "I thought with all our problems, mostly small ones, we'd never make it. It shows how dedication can perform small miracles.

"I wasn't driving that hard," added Haywood, who was at the wheel for the final four hours. "I guess it was a combination of the heat and all the stuff that hit me. I didn't feel bad until I climbed out of the car in victory lane. Then it just hit me."

While Gregg and Haywood dominated the closing hours of the race, competition was very close behind them, with positions two through six being switched repeatedly.

Michael Keyser, Bill Sprowls, and Andrea Contreras finished second, 15 laps behind. Charlie Kemp and Carson Baird took third, one lap behind second, followed by George Dyer and Jacques Bienvenue in fourth, and Bill Webbe, George Dickinson, and Harry Theodoracopulos in fifth. Sixth went to the Carrera of John Graves, John O'Steen, and Dave Helmick, which spent much of the race stuck in fourth gear. Ninth went to the Porsche that Rojas had tangled with Gregg's car earlier in the race, co-driven by fellow Mexicans Hector Rebaque and Freddie van Beuren.

Rusty Bond, George Rollin, and John Belperche placed 10th overall in a Porsche 911S and won IMSA GTU, while Ray Walle and Tom Reddy placed 14th in a Mazda RX-3 and won in the FIA Touring class. Amos Johnson, Dennis Shaw, and Steve Coleman finished 17th overall in the same near-stock Levi's Team Highball Gremlin that had won Friday evening's Goodrich 100 IMSA RS race.

Fifty-one cars started, with 25 still running at the finish.

The Brumos Porsche had won again, but the performance of the BMW was not lost on Gregg. "You know, I was offered a place on the BMW team and at one point Saturday night I was kicking myself," Gregg admitted during the post-race interview. "They were running away with it and we were having all kinds of troubles—an accident and an oil hose. I thought, 'You dummy! You could have been there in the BMW.'"

Above: Peter Gregg (left) and Hurley Haywood are joined by the Brumos Porsche team in victory lane following their victory. Holding the trophy is team manager Bob Snodgrass, with crew chief Mike Colucci to the right of Haywood. Right: John Greenwood (right) celebrates after winning the pole position while Zora Arkus-Duntov, father of the Corvette, pops the cork on the champagne.

John Greenwood.

CAM2
RICHARD KELLEY Chevrolet
GOODYEAR
ACCEL
2

1976: Water in the Fuel

BMW's performance over the opening 12 hours of the 1975 24 Hours of Daytona had certainly caught Peter Gregg's attention. The long-time Jacksonville, Florida, driver was so impressed that he entered the 1976 edition of the event in a BMW 3.5 CSL, co-driving with Brian Redman.

If Gregg in a BMW sounds odd, it was just one of a number of bizarre and unexpected twists that characterized the 1976 event. NASCAR stock cars were in the field, the race was stopped for a long red flag because of tainted fuel, and race officials made the unprecedented decision to actually turn back the clock.

Redman won the pole in the Brumos BMW, running a lap of 118.61 mph to beat John Greenwood's *Spirit of Sebring* Corvette. Gregg started the pole-winning car and took the early lead, chased by Michael Brockman, who started Greenwood's Corvette. Brockman pitted on lap 39, and after Greenwood got in he had to wait 40 laps while his team worked to repair the transmission. Greenwood rejoined in 28th place, but moved up to 14th after 200 laps.

Defending co-winner Hurley Haywood, who had teamed with Jim Busby in a Porsche, pitted for lengthy service on lap three when a broken intake manifold spilled oil on the exhaust.

By midnight, the race had turned into a BMW parade. The lead Gregg/Redman car was followed by English teammates John Fitzpatrick and Tom Walkinshaw, with 1975 Daytona 500 winner Benny Parsons in third, teamed with David Hobbs.

Left: The CAM2 Chevy Nova of NASCAR regulars Bobby and Donnie Allison pits to change a cut left-front tire. The Allisons were among the stock car regulars to compete in the new Grand International class that competed in the classics at Daytona and Le Mans. Top: Peter Gregg's familiar No. 59 was switched to a BMW 3.5 CSL for the 1976 Daytona 24 Hours. Gregg's move paid off with his third consecutive victory in the classic. (Bill Oursler)

Porsches held the next seven places, including Al Holbert/Claude Ballot-Lena in fifth and John Graves, John O'Steve, and David Helmick in eighth. The Haywood/Busby Carrera had worked its way up to seventh.

During the night, Gregg took ill. "At 11 p.m., I came in and there was Peter, saying 'I don't feel well, can you do another session,'" Redman recalled. By 3 a.m., it became apparent that Gregg could not continue, so Fitzpatrick was moved over from the No. 2 BMW to drive a shift, since his car was being worked on trackside by Tom Walkinshaw after it sustained a broken distributor drive.

At 4 a.m., additional trouble struck the lead BMW. "We had been running relatively conservatively, using 8,500 rpm, and had a very good lead," said Redman. "Part of a valve had broken off. It hadn't broken the piston. It had gone out through the exhaust, and the car was still running. After it went to five cylinders [the engine was an inline-six], we drove it flat-out, using 9,000 rpm, and we were still faster than the fastest RSR Porsche."

The Redman/Gregg/Fitzpatrick BMW continued to run up front and enjoyed a comfortable 17-lap lead with five hours remaining. Suddenly, after a routine pit stop at 9:01 a.m., the engine quit.

"As I pulled out of the pit, the engine misfired and coughed and banged," recalled Redman. "They pushed me back into the pit, and they checked it out. They didn't know what it was at that point. So I set off, but I only got as far as the Horseshoe when it stopped. I ran back to the pits and got tools, and a mechanic came to shout advice."

Following the shouted instructions, Redman disconnected a fuel line, and water began pouring out. He let water spill out until the fuel began running, and then reattached the line, but could not complete a full lap before the car stalled out again.

"I only got as far as the banking out of the infield, when it rolled to a halt again," he explained.

Above left: The No. 59 BMW of Gregg and Brian Redman makes its way through the rain near the conclusion of the race. "You couldn't see through it at all," Redman recalled. Above right and opposite: The No. 71 Ferrari Daytona of Chris Cord, Jim Adams, and Milt Minter is shown in action and during a nighttime pit stop. The Ken Starbird-owned car finished sixth overall. (Bill Oursler)

"This time, I ran across to the spectators, because the battery was going flat, and I asked for a battery and jumper leads, which they got to me through the fence. I bled the system again, and it wouldn't turn over at all, nothing. After forever, 10 or 15 minutes, I asked for new jumper leads, which I got from another spectator, put them on, and it started. We finally got back into the pits."

By that time, other teams were having problems. The second-place Graves/O'Steen/Helmick Porsche stalled on course, while both of the other BMWs had trouble running. "It was water in the fuel," Redman said. "There was no [other] explanation for our problems."

Endurance races traditionally continue, rain or shine. Only extraordinary circumstances bring the racing to a halt. Such was the case in 1976. The weather was not the culprit, nor was there a major

on-track incident. It was this fuel-related problem, which had mysteriously begun to affect the race cars, beginning with the leaders, who had used more fuel up to that point. In this case, race officials even turned back the clock.

Early in the morning, nine of the top cars suffered problems that were traced to water in the racing gasoline. The only teams affected were using overhead fueling rigs, which were supplied by a truck that patrolled pit road, dispensing fuel. Following the event, it was suspected that water in one of the vehicle's tanks had caused the problems. The remaining teams, which shuttled their fuel cans to and from the speedway's Unocal 76 station behind pit road, were fine.

1976

At 10:10 a.m., the red flag waved to bring racing to a halt. For two hours and 40 minutes, the cars were stopped. Ordinarily red flag conditions forbid any work on the race cars, but this time teams were allowed to purge their fuel lines and replace fuel cells. A new fuel truck was dispatched from

Above: The No. 21 Wood Brothers Mercury — a dominant car in Winston Cup competition with David Pearson at the wheel — looks out of place in the Daytona infield. The team finished 16th overall and led the stock cars competing in the Grand International division. Pearson was joined by his son, Larry, and the father-son team of Gary and Jim Bowsher. Right: David Hobbs (left) holds open the door for Benny Parsons as the reigning Daytona 500 champion gets ready to drive their Coca-Cola BMW CSL in testing for the 24 Hours of Daytona. The pair finished 10th overall.

Jacksonville, 90 miles north of Daytona Beach.

While this was taking place, IMSA President John Bishop, after conferring with Charlie Rainville and the other race stewards, ordered that the scoring be reverted to the 18-hour (9 a.m.) standings, using the race time and average speed picked up as recorded just prior to the problem developing. As an example of how this affected the standings, the Redman/Gregg/Fitzpatrick BMW had completed 500 laps at 9 a.m., but only 507 laps at the 10 a.m. red flag.

With the BMW of Redman and Peter Gregg on pit road for a long stop due to the tainted fuel, the Porsche Carrera of Helmick, O'Steen, and Graves had moved into second place at the time of the stoppage. But the team knew they were in trouble.

"We didn't have a spare fuel cell, and the factory teams did," recalled Helmick. His team could only drain their fuel tank, which for safety reasons was lined with foam that was now retaining water.

Also in good position at the time of the stop was the team of Hurley Haywood and Jim Busby, driving the Porsche Carrera that Gregg had taken to the 1975 IMSA Camel GT championship. "I didn't think the decision to stop the race and go back to the 9 o'clock standings was fair," said Haywood after the race.

Bishop defended his position. "The stewards of the meeting felt that resuming the scoring immediately would be unfair to those competitors who had been given the bad fuel," said the IMSA founder. Twenty-nine cars restarted at 12:49 p.m. after a 2:40:37 red flag. Officially, the stoppage was scored as 3:54:05 because the clock had reverted back to the 9 a.m. standings.

When racing resumed, Redman was back in the lead, 16 laps ahead of the Helmick/O'Steen/Graves Carrera, which lost its engine only nine laps later because of the fuel problem. One lap later, the Walkinshaw/Fitzpatrick car also retired due to damage from the bad fuel.

After all the drama that preceded it, the final two hours and 10 minutes were anticlimactic. Redman won by 14 laps over the Al Holbert/Claude Ballot-Lena Porsche. "It rained at the end of the race," Redman recalled. "It was very slippery. We had to change our windshield. You couldn't see through it at all, nothing."

After the checkered flag, Gregg was sufficiently recovered to accept the trophy. "I'm happier than I've ever been after winning a race here," said Gregg, after recording his third Daytona 24 Hours victory. "They made the right decision in stopping the race. A race team should not be expected to anticipate something like this happening." The winning BMW completed 545 laps, 2,092.8 miles, and averaged 104.04 mph over the actual competition time of 20 hours, 11 minutes.

Haywood and Busby finished third, one lap behind Holbert, followed by the Porsche 911 RSRs of Bob Hagstad/Jerry Jolly and Mike Tillson/Dieter Oest/Bruce Jennings. Sixth went to Ken Starbird's Ferrari 365GTB Daytona,

driven by Chris Cord, Jim Adams, and Milt Minter.

Bob Hindson, Dick Davenport, and Frank Carney were seventh overall and winners in the IMSA GTU class in a Porsche 911. Taking FIA Group 4 honors was the 12th place Porsche 911 RSR Carrera of Dieter Schmid/Wilhelm Bartels/Heinz Martin/Egan Evertz.

The field included a new class—Grand International—made up of eight NASCAR Winston Cup cars, with drivers including Bobby and Donnie Allison, David and Larry Pearson, Ed Negre, Joe Ruttman, Buddy Baker, James Hylton, Richard Childress, and Hershel McGriff. The Pearsons, joined by Gary and Jim Bowsher in a Holman-Moody Ford Torino, took class honors, finishing 16th.

"That was really a neat deal," recalled Childress, who at the time was an underfunded independent running the Winston Cup circuit. "James Hylton and myself ran it. It was pretty neat to be out there running against all those cars, with the different formulas. It was a fun deal. I wouldn't take nothing for the experience of it. We had the Winston Cup cars running against cars of every size and speed. We were pretty fast. We weren't going to win it overall, but we were going to win our division, but we lost the clutch and lost too much time replacing it."

The top NASCAR finisher was Parsons, who teamed with David Hobbs in the 10th place *Coke Machine* BMW. Their car was running third before losing 90 minutes to rebuild the transmission.

A joint promotion with Le Mans had doubled the purse to $100,000. In June, two NASCAR teams raced at Le Mans for the first—and only—time. Junie Donlavey fielded a Ford Torino for Dick Brooks, Dick Hutcherson, and Macel Mignot, which lasted 104 laps until the gearbox failed. Herschel McGriff, who competed for more than 50 years before his retirement in 2002, joined his son, Doug, in the other NASCAR stocker, a Harry Hyde Dodge Charger that

Top: The field snakes through the infield during the pre-race warmup, following the pole-sitting Corvette of John Greenwood. Above: The Spirit of Sebring Corvette of John Greenwood and Michael Brockman is serviced in the pits while the Dodge Charger of NASCAR Winston Cup regular Ed Negre and Arturo Merzario goes by. This was the same Dodge that Dale Earnhardt drove in his NASCAR Winston Cup debut in 1975. Right: Peter Gregg, in his immaculate uniform surrounded by two race queens, is joined by a weary Brian Redman in victory lane. Gregg had taken ill during the race, with Redman doing the bulk of the driving. Miss Camel is Patty Huffman, the future Mrs. Kyle Petty.

retired with fuel problems after only two laps.

The Daytona 24 Hours race included the first turbocharged Porsche, a 934 for four-time German champion Sepp Greger, who was paired with Egon Evertz and Jurgen Laessig. The car was the fastest qualifier in Group 4, but retired before the midway point.

Formula Atlantic phenom Gilles Villeneuve entered the race, sharing a Camaro with fellow Canadian Mo Carter. Villeneuve's engine blew in the tri-oval in the only Daytona appearance for the future Formula One star.

Brian Redman memorably summed up his experience that year. "I got a lesson in public relations, because I had never driven with Peter before, but of course, he was the local hero," he recalled. "First of all, I put the car on pole position, but the headline in the Daytona paper the next morning was 'Gregg gains pole' with a photograph and everything.

"Then, the victory lane photographs show me standing at one side. I looked like Peter's grandfather, I'm dirty, my eyes are hanging down, and he's standing there in his immaculate uniform, his arm around the two race queens.

"When I got back to the hotel, I went into the bath and fell asleep, and I didn't wake until three in the morning, so I missed the victory dinner. [Team Manager] Jochen Neerpasch said to me on Monday morning, 'Brian, you missed the victory dinner.' I said, 'I'm very sorry, I fell asleep in the bath.' He said, 'It doesn't matter, Peter Gregg gave a fantastic speech in which he thanked all the German mechanics personally by name.' I said 'Oh great.' Well, that's the story of my life."

18
14
INALTERA
21

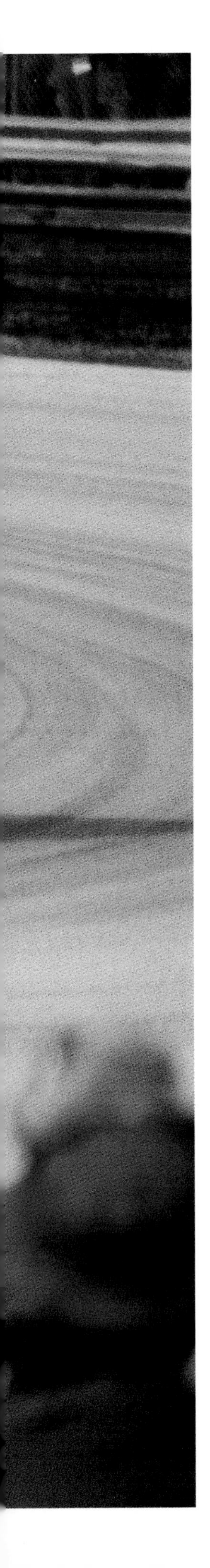

1977: Haywood Skeptical of New Turbos

In 1977, fans got a look at the future when the new Porsche 935 and the Rondeau Inaltera, first of the new breed of GT Prototypes, made their debuts at Daytona. The turbocharged 935, co-driven by Jacky Ickx and Jochen Mass, winners of the 1976 World Manufacturer's Championship, was the first factory-entered Porsche since 1971. But the record crowd also had one last look back at the past, when an older Porsche Carrera 911 RSR made a brilliant showing.

The turbocharged 935 appeared to be the car to beat. In addition to the factory-entered Ickx/Mass car, the factory-assisted Kremer Brothers team entered a 935 for Bob Wollek/Reinhold Joest/Albrecht Krebs, and Martino Finotto had one for himself, and another for Carlo Facetti and Romeo Camathias.

Haywood, however, was skeptical of the reliability of the new cars. "While everyone was switching to the turbos, I was not convinced that the turbocharged car had proven reliability," said Haywood. "When I heard that John Graves and David Helmick were fielding an ex-Peter Gregg Brumos Porsche, and Franz Blam was building the engine, I thought that was the way to go."

Haywood would join them in the Porsche Carrera 911 for Ecurie Escargot. Not offered a ride in one of the factory-fielded Porsche 935s, Gregg accepted

Left: The No. 21 Inaltera-Cosworth of female stars Lella Lombardi and Christine Becker leads the Al Holbert Monza and the No. 18 Camaro of Jack Swanson and Terry Wolters. Above: Paul Newman made his 24 Hours of Daytona debut, finishing fifth overall in Otto Zipper's No. 64 Ramsey Ferrari Daytona. Co-driving were Elliott Forbes-Robinson and Milt Minter.

an offer from rival Camel GT driver Jim Busby to co-drive a turbocharged Porsche 934, which had smaller wings and wheels than the 935. Gregg qualified seventh fastest, but was quickest of the IMSA entries. Ironically, Busby's co-driver in 1976 was Hurley Haywood in a Brumos-sponsored Porsche.

Two Cosworth-powered, French-built Inaltera prototypes, capable of 200 mph, were entered for Jean-Pierre Beltoise/Jean Rondeau and female drivers Lella Lombardi and Christine Beckers. The team was managed by 1968 Daytona 24 winner Vic Elford.

BMW, with the assistance of McLaren, fielded a 320i for David Hobbs, Sam Posey, and Ronnie Peterson. The team was managed by 1968 co-winner, Jochen Neerpasch. The BMW that had won the 1976 24 Hours was also back, co-driven by Rochester, New York, brothers Kenper and Paul Miller, who were joined by John Fitzpatrick.

Mass put the new turbo Martini-sponsored Porsche on the pole with a lap of 127.658 mph, eclipsing John Greenwood's two-year-old mark of 123.368 mph. Bob Wollek, driving in his first Daytona 24 Hours in a Porsche 935 fielded by German Manfred Kremer, also eclipsed the record. Third and fourth

quickest were the Inaltera prototypes of Beltoise and Lombardi. Lombardi became the highest-qualifying woman in any race at Daytona.

Fifty-eight cars took the green flag for the 3 p.m. start, with Ickx leading the opening seven laps. Danny Ongais, driving a winged and turbocharged Porsche 911 owned by Ted Field, challenged for the point on lap eight, and the two cars swapped the lead seven times before both pitted on lap 29. That gave the lead to the Joest Porsche, with Ickx and Ongais both working their way up front until the car retired on lap 36 with a broken piston.

1977

The tremendous horsepower generated by the turbocharged Porsches created tire problems. At 6:43 p.m., Ickx cut a tire, spun in the east banking, and hit the wall. The car suffered from extensive

Above left: Tony Adamowicz, John Cannon, and Dick Barbour failed to finish in the No. 66 Ramsey Ferrari Daytona. Above right: Second-generation Porsche driver Al Holbert switched to a Chevrolet Monza for the 1977 24 Hours. He qualified eighth, but failed to finish. Co-driving were Michael Keyser and Claude Ballot-Lena. Opposite: Al Holbert's team works in vain to repair the engine in the No. 14 Monza. The problem was diagnosed as terminal.

DICKINSON
P+A
14
BOSCH

body damage and he pitted. That gave the lead to the Joest Porsche, which swapped the point several times with the Busby/Gregg Porsche.

At midnight, Porsches held the top five positions. It was an outstanding performance. Even Haywood was impressed. "Midway through the race, I was thinking I made a bad deal," Haywood said. "Then, they all started falling out."

1977

Tenth after the first hour, the Graves/Haywood/Helmick Porsche was up to fifth by the six-hour mark and third by 10 hours. It was still third at the midway point, though six laps down. Haywood drove an eight-hour stint during the night, staying at the wheel because he was gaining so much time.

Above: A pair of turbocharged Porsche 935s lead a pair of Inaltera prototypes on the banking, moments before the start. Jochen Mass started on the pole in the No. 1 Martini Racing entry, flanked by the No. 8 of Bob Wollek, Reinhold Joest, and Albrecht Krebs. Right: Although it didn't win in 1977, the Porsche 935—driven by Jacky Ickx and Jochen Mass—showed it would be the car to beat in the future. Far right: Peter Gregg, driving the No. 61 Brumos Porsche 934, races former teammate Hurley Haywood, at the wheel of the No. 43 Ecurie Escargot Porsche 911 RSR. Rather than race the fast—but unproven—turbocharged 934 or 935, Haywood opted to drive the older but reliable normally aspirated version. Haywood thought he guessed wrong at the midway point, but he came through with his third victory in the 24 Hours.

At 3:45 a.m., the second place Busby/Gregg Porsche pitted with a gear linkage problem that would cost them three hours and 100 laps. They would return to finish 10th. That elevated the Graves' Porsche to second, although the Mass/Ickx Porsche was third and gaining.

The Mass/Ickx Porsche worked its way back to second, four laps down, after 16 hours, when another tire problem put the car into the wall in the same place as the first incident, tearing the right side off the car. This time, the car was retired. The Graves/Haywood/Helmick Porsche moved up to second.

Beckers was running fifth in the Inaltera she shared with Lella Lombardi when a slower car forced her into the wall. Jon Woodner, driving Ted Field's Porsche 911 RSR, ran into Beckers and rolled. Neither driver was hurt.

The Joest Porsche had taken the lead at 2:22 a.m., although it began to experience problems, losing all but fourth gear. The team maintained the lead until Wollek pitted with clutch problems, costing the team 18 minutes. The Graves car took over the lead at 11:57 a.m.

"The 935s were much faster than us, but they all broke," Graves recalled. "We just outlasted them. We got in the top four or five early in the race and just stayed there. We just slowly ground them down."

Their top challenger late in the race was the Jolly Club Porsche 935 of Facetti/Finotto/Romeo. That team encountered brake problems Sunday at noon, which allowed the Graves/Helmick/Haywood Porsche to dominate the final three hours, winning over the Finotto Porsche by three laps.

As the race wound down, Graves did his best to hang on. While the official order of finish was listed as three laps at the time, Ecurie Escargot believed the second-place car was on the lead lap.

"During my last shift, I was driving at a few seconds over our qualifying speed," Graves recalled. "The guys on the radio were yelling, 'He's catching you; he's catching you.' It got pretty hairy, but we managed to hang on. They were eating us up, but the snail outlasted them."

"Forget about what you read," Graves said. "The margin of victory was only 53 seconds." The win earned Haywood his third 24 Hours of Daytona title. It would be the last victory for a normally aspirated car in the Daytona event for many years.

Before his win in 1977, Helmick, a radiologist with 25 years experience, had three top-11 showings at Daytona, and won Sebring in 1975 with Haywood and Peter Gregg. He had left Miami in 1976 to take a staff position at Pocono Hospital in Stroudsburg, Pennsylvania. When Graves proposed running a car in the 1977 Daytona 24 Hours, Helmick took a vacation and finished setting the car up.

"Dave was a genius with the suspensions of those cars," Graves said. "Another reason why we won the race is that we lost only nine minutes total in the pits, in addition to scheduled service."

Helmick came up with the Ecurie Escargot moniker from his days in the service. "It's a team of snails," he explained after the race. "It means we may be slow, but we're still faster than you." It was the final Daytona 24 Hours for both Graves and Helmick.

Third went to the Kremer Porsche 935 of Bob Wollek, Reinhold Joest, and Albrecht Krebs. The team led until just before noon, when they lost 18 minutes to repair a broken front hub. They finished the race with only fourth gear.

Fourth went to the Porsche Carrera of George Dyer and Brad Frisselle, despite a 3 a.m. engine change. "Crew chief Al Lager changed the engine in 32 minutes," Frisselle explained. "We were running

Above: Hurley Haywood, flanked by Dr. Dave Helmick (left) and John Graves, signals No. 3 after winning the 24 Hours of Daytona. It was the last overall victory for a Porsche 911 variant in the event until Kevin Buckler's The Racer's Group won in 2003 in a similar 911-based Porsche. Right: Although the No. 21 Inaltera-Cosworth of female stars Lella Lombardi and Christine Becker failed to finish due to an accident, the car served as an inspiration for IMSA president John Bishop's future IMSA GTP category. (Bill Oursler)

fourth when the engine just went dead. George Dyer had a sprint engine on his truck, with eight or nine hours racing on it, so we put it in and it still finished the race."

The engine change dropped the team to eighth position, and they worked their way back to regain fourth. "We had just too much ground to make up," Frisselle said.

Actor Paul Newman joined Elliott Forbes-Robinson and Milt Minter in the fifth-place Ferrari Daytona.

"The Ferrari Daytona was a tough car to drive at Daytona, because going around the banking, you had to put your arm up on the steering wheel, and then put your elbow into your leg so you could hold the steering wheel, because it got so hard to steer," Forbes-Robinson recalled. "It was very good [running with Newman]. I remember it was a really cold night. It was a group out of California that came out and ran the car, and they had a guy named Otto Zipper running the team.

"We had one toolbox and the tires, there were no spare parts for that car. We just had to make sure it kept on running, and it did. Newman did a good job driving the car, but even then, it was very difficult, because we were involved with other things there. We had Clint Eastwood as one of the entrants for the car, we had Bobby Carradine running a sister car next to us, David [Carradine] was there as an owner in that car, so we had all these stars around there. It was terrible, because you'd go to the garage area and I couldn't even get to my own race car. I had to walk in the back way.

"Fortunately, everybody just took Paul as a race driver after that, which he was. He'd run the SCCA classes, but he hadn't run any of the big cars yet. That was the first time he'd stepped up and run a really fast car that could run down the banking quickly. He was 47 when he started racing. A lot of people think they're over the hill when they're 47, yet he was just beginning."

GTU honors went to the Porsche 911S of Bob Hindson, Frank Carney, and Dick Davenport, placing seventh overall.

While neither of the Inaltera prototypes finished, the cars made a lasting impression on IMSA President John Bishop. "They were purpose-built race car coupes," Bishop recalled. "They didn't win, but they were so pretty. I began to conference with the Le Mans organizers to try to reach a practical formula for this type of car." The idea for the IMSA Grand Touring Prototype (GTP) car had been born.

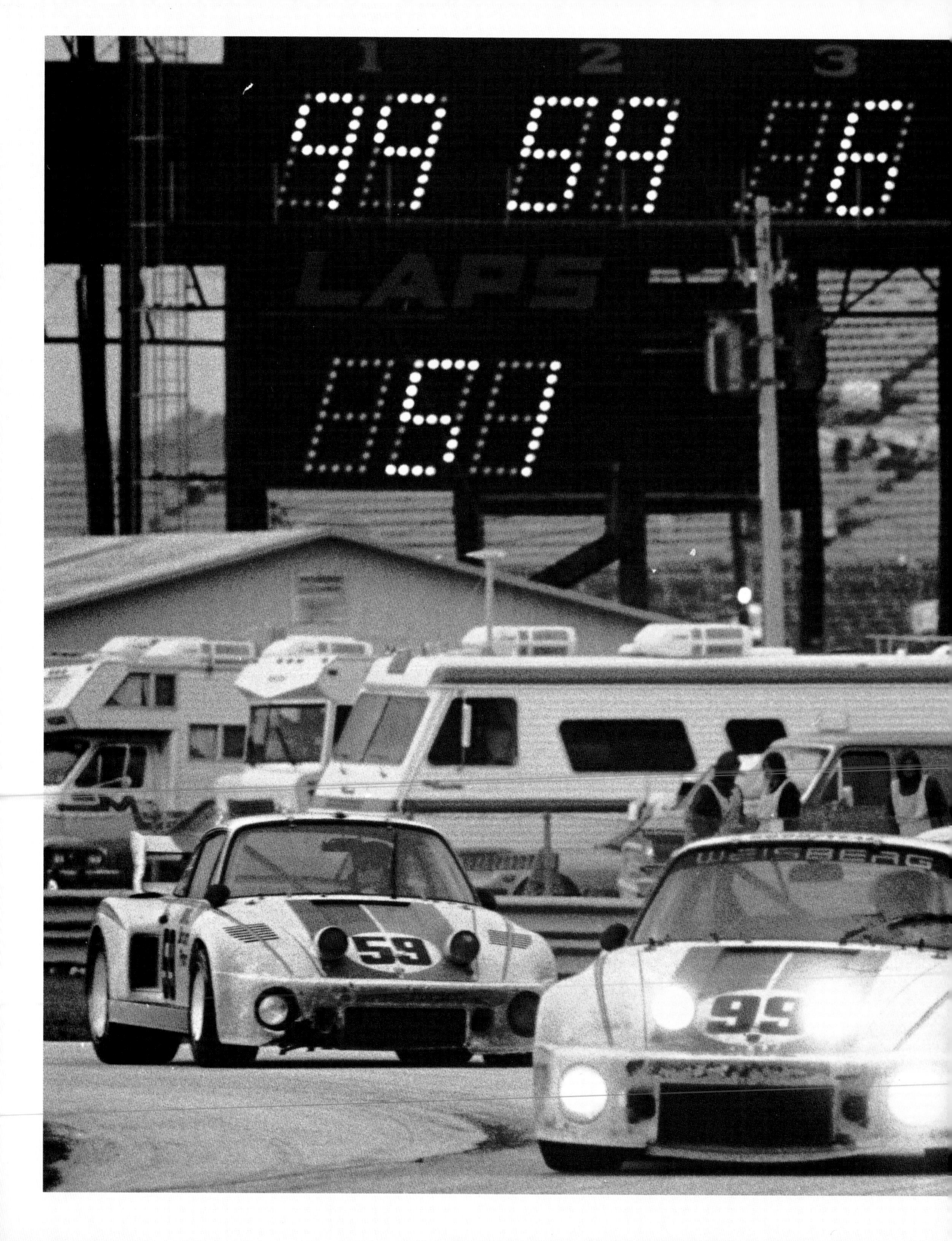
1
2
3
99
59
LAPS
59
99

1978: Porsches on Parade

DESPITE THE FACT THAT THE NEW PORSCHE 935 FAILED TO WIN IN ITS DEBUT DAYTONA 24 HOURS APPEARANCE IN 1977, IT WAS THE CAR OF CHOICE FOR MOST OF THE CONTENDING TEAMS IN THE 1978 CLASSIC. THE RACE FEATURED A DOZEN TURBOCHARGED PORSCHE 935S, INCLUDING A PAIR WITH THE LATEST TWIN-TURBOS: THE KREMER BROTHERS ENTRY FOR BOB WOLLEK AND HENRI PESCAROLO, AND THE BRUMOS PORSCHE ENTRY FOR ROLF STOMMELEN AND ANTOINE HEZEMANS.

Teams had the choice of running under IMSA's new GT regulations, or under special regulations, which included a special refueling rig and a minimum number of laps between pit stops where oil is added, as part of the World Championship of Makes.

The event was also the first race for the World Challenge for Endurance Drivers, administered by Daytona International Speedway. Bill France and IMSA president John Bishop joined with the FIA to develop the concept of the new championship, which would reward the drivers, not the teams. Any international event of six hours (or 1,000 kilometers) could participate by contributing $10,000 towards the year-end point fund. Since the concept rewarded the drivers, competitors could compete around the world in

Left: At dawn, the Brumos Porsches were running one-two, with the No. 99 of Rolf Stommelen and Antoine Hezemans leading the No. 59 of Claude Ballot-Lena and Brad Frissele. Peter Gregg drove in both of his team's cars. The No. 59 had a half-shaft break and puncture the engine block. The team changed engines and returned to finish ninth, 59 laps behind their winning No. 99. Above: Bob Wollek showed indication of future greatness by qualifying second in the Kremer Brothers Porsche, although the car failed to finish.

different cars without the added expense of shipping equipment.

Danny Ongais, who was making his third Daytona 24 Hours appearance, won the pole in wet conditions with a lap of 114.105 mph in a Vasek Polak Porsche 935 leased to Ted Field's Interscope Racing. During testing on the Monday before the event, he unofficially ran a lap of 129.076 mph, quicker than the Jacky Ickx track record of 127.658 mph.

On race day, Ongais, as was his habit, set an early pace for the 68 cars that took the green flag at 4:33 p.m. He was passed twice by the BMW of David Hobbs and the Brumos Porsche of Stommelen, but quickly regained the lead both times and pulled away. "Our strategy will be to stay out front as long as possible, and I'll probably drive the first four hours," Ongais had said just prior to the start.

Ongais's run at the front was short lived, however. He lost the lead on the 14th lap, and then slowed in turn three of the oval on the following lap as the turbocharger failed. The team needed seven laps to replace the turbocharger, and Ongais made one more lap before pitting again. This time, the problem was the engine.

In 1978, engine changes were permitted, so Field replaced the Porsche's powerplant with one purchased for $30,000 from Martino Finotto, who had parked his car after six laps. The Interscope Porsche returned four hours later, only to have a leaking seal get oil on the clutch. The team had to remove the new engine to work on the clutch. The Porsche briefly returned to the track, logging only

1978

Above left: Danny Ongais, a former drag racing star in Hawaii, found a home driving for Ted Field in sports cars, Formula 5000, Indy cars, and even Formula One. He made his second Daytona 24 Hours appearance in 1978, and first driving for Field's Interscope team, winning the pole in the rain with a lap of 114.105 mph. Above right: Lined up prior to the start of the race on pit road are the eventual sixth-place finishing turbo Porsche of Al Holbert, Doc Bundy, and Gary Belcher (No. 09), the fourth place finishing Porsche Carrera of John Paul, Phil Currin, and Bonky Fernandez (No. 33), and the eighth place Ferrari Daytona of Bobby Carradine, John Morton, and Tony Adamowicz. Opposite top: Porsches swept the top seven positions in the 1978 24 Hours of Daytona, taking 14 of the top 15 positions. Escorting the winning No. 99 Rolf Stommelen/Antoine Hezemans Brumos Porsche 935 to the checkered flag are No. 6, Dick Barbour/Johnny Rutherford/Manfred Schurti, second place; No. 59, Peter Gregg/Claude Ballot-Lena/Brad Frissele, ninth place; No. 24, Tom Frank/Bob Bergstrom, 15th place; No. 13, Hal Shaw/Jim Busby/Howard Meister, 10th place; and No. 68, Luis Mendez/Armando Gonzales/Juan Ferrer, 23rd place. Right: Ted Field prepares to take his Interscope Porsche out for a late-night shift. After dominating the opening laps, the team struggled with a succession of major failures.

88 total laps in more than 12 hours of effort.

Bob Wollek had qualified on the outside of the front row in the Kremer Brothers Porsche 935, but his car was parked after 86 circuits with a failed turbocharger.

The main challenge to the Porsches appeared to be the third-qualifying BMW 320i of Hobbs and Ronnie Peterson, which was entered by McLaren North America, but that car lasted only 47 laps.

The Brumos Porsche twin-turbo 935 driven by Stommelen/Hezemans led the eighth circuit, regained the point on lap 14 when the Interscope team had turbo problems, and then motored away to lead the rest of the event. They were followed by the single-turbo Brumos 935 driven by Gregg, Claude Ballot-Lena, and Brad Frisselle. Gregg also drove a shift in the team's lead car, taking over at 1:37 a.m. for one hour, 11 minutes. Stommelen established the race record for 3.84-mile circuit when he averaged 123.600 mph on the 14th lap, the same circuit that he passed Ongais to take the lead.

At dawn, the Brumos teammates were separated by 20 laps, with Diego Febles and Alec Poole running third in an ex-Brumos Porsche RSR. Hopes for a one-two Brumos sweep evaporated when the team's second Porsche had a half-shaft break and puncture the engine block Sunday morning. The team changed engines at 8:37 a.m., then struggled to a ninth-place finish.

With 15 minutes remaining in the race, Stommelen pitted the leading Porsche. Hezemans took over as the Brumos team cleaned up the car and applied fresh decals. When the team washed off the grease and grime, however, they lost a chance at a new race record. Their car also lost time down the stretch, when it formed up for an all-Porsche victory procession by the top five finishers. The winning car still averaged 108.743 mph, just shy of the year-old record of 109.743 mph, completing 680 circuits and 2,611.200 miles, leading 667 laps.

Porsche swept the top seven positions—and 14 of the top 15—

in a dominant performance. Brumos Racing scored its third Daytona triumph, with Stommelen, Hezemans, and Gregg driving their 935 to a 30-lap margin over the Dick Barbour Porsche, with a driver lineup of Barbour, Manfred Schurti, and Indy 500 star Johnny Rutherford. Schurti, the leading sports figure from the tiny principality of Liechtenstein, was a late replacement for Jacky Ickx, who had injured his arm in a skiing accident.

The Barbour team was hurt by two off-track excursions that resulted in a long stop to repair damage, although the team returned to take second from the Febles team.

"Fortunately for Dick Barbour and me, during the event Manfred cut a tire and blew the right rear off of the car and spun," Rutherford said. "He didn't hit anything, but he took everything off the right-rear corner. He limped into the pits, and they bypassed the coolers, put on another suspension, and sent him back out. He drove very hard to catch up and try to gain what he had lost, and about an hour later, he cut the left-rear tire down and tore the left-rear off of the car. Again, he limped back in. It was on his watch both times, thank goodness."

With the Group 5 Porsche 935s scored in the IMSA GTX category, Febles and Poole managed to

win in the new GTO (over 2.5-liter) class. Bonky Fernandez, John Paul Sr., and Phil Currin placed fourth in an RSR, followed by the 935s of Josef Brambring/John Winter/Dieter Schornstein and Doc Bundy/Gary Belcher/Al Holbert. Next was the slope-nosed Porsche RSR of Steve Earle, Bob Akin, and Rick Knoop, which was running in IMSA GTX.

Finally breaking up the Porsche parade was the Ferrari 365GTB Daytona of actor David Carradine, with a driver lineup of his brother Bobby, John Morton, Tony Adamowicz, and Hal Sahlman.

Above left: Bob Akin has a word with co-driver Rick Knoop before a nighttime driving shift. The pair, co-driving with Steve Earle, finished seventh overall in a Porsche Carrera. Above right: New York restaurateur Rene Dreyfus, the event's grand marshal, gives the command to start engines. On the right is IMSA President John Bishop. Opposite top: The McLaren of North America BMW 320i of David Hobbs and Ronnie Peterson qualified third but went out early with mechanical problems. Note the on-board jacks. Right: Rolf Stommelen waits behind the wheel as the Brumos Porsche works on the car during a late-race pit stop. National Speed Sport News' *writer/photographer Bill Oursler is at the left of the car.*

The second Brumos Porsche of Gregg/Ballot-Lena/Frisselle placed ninth. Hurley Haywood co-drove with Doc Bundy in Bob Hagestad's Porsche 935, but failed to finish because of clutch problems.

Winning honors in the GTU (under 2.5-liter) class were Dave White, Gary Mesnick, and J. Dana Roehrig in a Porsche 911. They placed 11th, although the car failed to finish due to engine trouble.

Excited with Paul Newman's fifth-place finish in 1977, the Ramsey Ferrari team had anticipated running a celebrity lineup comprising Newman, Clint Eastwood, Gene Hackman, Dick Smothers, and the Carradines, along with Indy racer Salt Walther. Hackman was expected to run in a Fiat Abart 131 for the three-car team. However, the team's van, which was carrying the Fiat and Newman's Ferrari, was involved in a highway accident that demolished both race cars. That reduced the team's entry to one car for the race.

Although pre-race publicity spoke of Ferrari's most significant assault on Daytona since 1972, Carradine fielded the only front-runner. Among the Ferrari privateers was Preston Henn, who made his first Daytona 24 Hours appearance sharing a 365GTB Daytona with Hal Sahlman and Sandy Satullo. They finished 27th.

The race also featured the first Japanese team for the Daytona 24 Hours. Auto Toyota entered a pair of rotary-engined Mazda RX-3s for Yoshimi Katayama, winner of the 1977 Fuji 1000, and Jojiro Terada, joining Roger Mandeville, with Jim Downing, Walt Bohren, and Stu Fisher in the second car.

In all, the 1978 field featured 29 foreign drivers from 11 countries, with 16 international teams competing.

BOSCH
GOODYEAR
CAMEL
GT CHALLENGE
SIMPSON

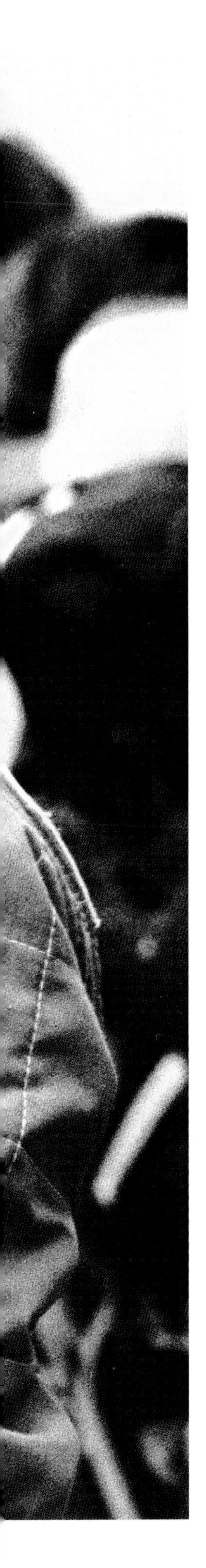

1979: Patience Pays

AFTER LEADING IN THE EARLY STAGES OF THE 1977 AND 1978 EVENTS, DANNY ONGAIS HAD BECOME A RECOGNIZED FACE AT DAYTONA. THOUGH INDISPUTABLY QUICK, "DANNY ON THE GAS" HAD YET TO LEARN THE DISCIPLINE NECESSARY FOR ENDURANCE RACING, AND HE HAD NOT LASTED LONG IN EITHER RACE.

For 1979, car owner Ted Field held back his ace and new recruit, Hurley Haywood, and qualified his Interscope Porsche 935 himself, taking the eighth spot. "I qualified it so Ongais and Haywood wouldn't try to out-race each other and have an argument," Field said afterward. He also drove the early stages of the race, which was now called the 24 Hour Pepsi Challenge.

The Interscope entry, prepared in David Klym's Fabcar shop in Atlanta and powered by a single-turbo 3.1-liter engine, was delivered only one week prior to the race.

Carlo Facetti won the pole in the Jolly Club Porsche 935 he shared with Martino Finotto and Gianpiero Moretti, turning a lap of 130.276 mph. Second was one of Georg Loos's two entries, featuring the all-star lineup of Bob Wollek, Jacky Ickx, and Peter Gregg.

Loos's second car, featuring Manfred Schurti and John Fitzpatrick, started third, joined on the second row by owner/driver/builder Reinhold Joest, who had Rolf Stommelen and Volkert Merl in his lineup.

The international Porsche contingent was challenged by a strong domestic entry of 935s, including the Interscope team joined by Bill and Don

Left: "Do not disturb," requests Hurley Haywood, who scored his fourth Daytona 24 Hours victory in 1979. Above: Paul Newman, racing a turbocharged car for the first time, led the event in Dick Barbour's Porsche. The car retired just before dawn with a blown head gasket.

Whittington, who co-drove with Jurgen Barth; and Dick Barbour, who co-drove with Brian Redman and Paul Newman. Ferrari was expected to offer a formidable challenge to the 935s, but struggled throughout the event.

1979

Race morning began somberly for the Ferrari contingent. Sixty-five-year-old Otto Zipper was found dead at his hotel. The Californian had suffered a heart attack in his sleep. Zipper was team manager of the ancient Ferrari 365GTB Daytona owned by Bill Nicholas and Jim McRoberts, and driven by

Above: Jim Downing (right) waits his turn to drive the No. 77 Mazda RX-7 while a co-driver exits the car. Downing, Roger Mandeville, and Walt Bohren finished sixth overall and second in GTU, marking a successful debut of the RX-7 in competition. Right: The NART Ferrari 512BB of Bob Tullius, J.P. Delaunay, and Pat Bedard leads the No. 67 JMS/Pozzi 512BB of Jean-Claude Ballot-Lena, Michel Leclere, and Jean-Claude Andruet. Suspecting that tire problems caused two accidents, the Ferrari team withdrew to avoid further misfortune. Far right: The No. 06 Corvette of Al Levenson, Gary Baker, and Lanny Hester gets night-time service. When teams encounter problems that will require lengthy work, the cars are moved to the garages in the paddock area for repairs.

Tony Adamowicz and John Morton.

"I asked Otto if he wanted to join us for dinner Friday night, and he didn't want to go," recalled Morton. "He was in pain, and thought he was passing a kidney stone. The following morning, no one saw him at the track, so we called the hotel and had a maid check his room.

"A lot of people on the team didn't want to run," Morton added, "but after we got together we decided to go ahead, because that's what Otto would have wanted us to do."

Luigi Chinetti of the North American Racing Team offered his assistance, and the team decided to run the car in Zipper's honor. Crew chief Bruno Porri ordered a black stripe painted across the hood.

The two "factory" Ferrari teams had problems of their own and were never a serious threat. Three 512BBs, powered by Boxer 12-cylinder engines, were expected to mount a serious challenge, according to pre-event publicity. Two were entered by Charles Pozzi's JMS Racing of France and one by Chinetti's NART. Assisting with the pre-event testing was Jody Scheckter, who would win the 1979 Formula One World Championship for Ferrari. However, both teams struggled during race weekend.

Lead driver Claude Ballot-Lena crashed in Thursday-night practice and badly damaged his car. While all three Boxers were running in the top 10 early in the race, the NART car driven by Frenchman J. P. Delaunay hit the wall on lap 76 in the same location as Ballot-Lena's shunt. It was determined that the high speed on the banking was generating excessive heat in their tires, causing problems for their new Michelins. Rather than risk destroying another car, the remaining two Boxers, running in seventh and eighth positions, were withdrawn at 8 p.m. by Ferrari team manager Jean Marc Smadja.

"I didn't want to risk my drivers' lives," Smadja told *AutoWeek*. "It was not Michelin's fault. They didn't have time to make tires for this track."

With the Ferraris never in serious contention, the race had quickly settled down to a battle among the numerous Porsche 935s. Three different 935s—driven by Facetti, Schurti, and Stommelen—led on the opening lap following the 4:23 p.m. green flag.

By sunset, attrition had played its role. Both of Loos's entries had mechanical problems. The Ickx/Wollek/Gregg car needed to change turbos, while the sister car, driven by Schurti and Fitzpatrick, replaced engines. John Paul, who shared a 935 with Al Holbert, withdrew after electrical problems. Preston Henn crashed in the second Interscope car. The Barbour team also lost its second entry when Rob McFarlin lost the 935 he shared with Bob Akin and Roy Woods to an oil fire.

Stommelen took over the lead, but came to a stop on course. After being penalized for receiving illegal assistance from his crew, the Joest entry continued, only to lose its engine. The lone remaining European Porsche was now the lead Loos's 935, driven back into the lead by Ickx, Wollek, and Gregg. Their challenge ended with engine failure at midnight. That gave the lead to the Porsche 935 Barbour shared with Paul Newman and Brian Redman.

The Barbour and Interscope teams traded the lead several times during the pre-dawn hours. Newman, racing a turbocharged car for the first time, did a pair of solid two-hour shifts before the car was retired just before dawn with a blown head gasket.

The sun rose with the Interscope Porsche enjoying a comfortable lead that kept increasing throughout Sunday morning. Their patience and conservative pace early in the race paid off, as Field and Ongais won by a whopping 49 laps. Haywood earned his fourth victory in the event.

Amazingly, after a near-flawless performance, the turbocharger on the Interscope car failed with 10 minutes remaining. Under IMSA rules, the team would still win, but to gain FIA Group 5 points, the car had to be running at the finish.

Ongais parked the crippled Porsche on the apron and waited for the 24 hours to expire. Then, running very slowly, he rolled across the finish line. The win was reminiscent of Dan Gurney's 1962 Daytona Continental victory. "We still would have won, but it's always better to take the checkered flag," said Haywood.

"Danny radioed he thought the turbocharger packed up," Haywood explained in the post-race news conference.

Above left: Jim Downing prepared a second Mazda RX-7 for Yoshimi Katayama, Yojiro Terada, and Takashi Yorino. They finished fifth overall and first in GTU in the No. 7 entry. Above right: Hurley Haywood (red jacket) and Danny Ongais exchange a quick word during a pit stop for the No. 0 Interscope Porsche. Opposite: A pit stop on the No. 65 Ferrari Daytona of John Morton and Tony Adamowicz. Team owner Otto Zipper died of a heart attack on Friday of race week. The team reluctantly decided to run in the event, with a black stripe painted across the hood of the car.

"I didn't know if it would have made it around for another lap," Ongais admitted in a 2002 interview. "It seemed like the wise thing to do was just sit there with the motor running and wait for the checkered flag." The team completed 684 laps, 2,626.56 miles, and averaged 109.409 mph, all records.

The team's turbocharger problems were not a surprise. Many of the Porsche teams had run into mechanical problems with their normally reliable cars, and all 13 turbocharged 935s had experienced problems. Only four made it to the finish. "They just set too fast a pace for a 24-hour race," Haywood said afterward.

Second went to the Ferrari Daytona of Morton and Adamowicz, winning GTO honors while running in memory of Otto Zipper.

"We had no illusions of doing that well in the race," Morton recalled. "It was a 1973 car, and it had never won a major race before. Tony and I just decided to run the car as hard as we could—our second-place finish was not the result of a steadily paced race. We ran so tired that later in the race, we could only run single shifts between fuel stops. The only break either of us got was when we took the car to the garage for a half hour during the night to work on the rear suspension, because we were burning up the inside of our rear tires. We had no clue we would win our class, let alone finish second overall. We were totally shot at the end of the race."

The Morton/Adamowicz Ferrari was pitted next to the NART team during the race. "Early in the evening, Luigi Chinetti came over and asked me where we were running," Morton recalled. "When I told him we were seventh, he said 'No!' He refused to accept it."

Up-and-coming Indy racing star Rick Mears—who would win his first of four Indianapolis 500s in May—co-drove the third-place Porsche 935 with car owner Bruce Canepa and Monte Shelton. They were followed by the Whittington Brothers/Barth 935. While that car was fast, the team changed turbochargers four times, and finally replaced the engine.

Other present and future Indy 500 stars included Johnny Rutherford and Danny Sullivan. Rutherford, who was one year away from his third victory in the Indianapolis 500, competed in the Daytona 24 Hours for the second straight year. He shared a twin-turbo 935 with Paul Miller and Sebring promoter Charles Mendez, which placed 15th after being damaged in an early morning collision. Sullivan co-drove Anatoly Arutunoff's Lancia Stratos with Jose Marina. They went out shortly after dawn Sunday.

Adding variety were a pair of rotary-engine Mazda RX-7s fielded by Jim Downing, which took fifth and sixth overall and one-two in the GTU class. The Japanese trio of Yoshimi Katayama, Yoiro Terada, and Takashi Yorino drove the fifth-place car, followed by Americans Jim Downing, Roger Mandeville, and Walt Bohren. It was the debut of the Mazda RX-7 in competition, with the factory-backed effort powered by 1146cc Wankel rotary engines. While the overall and GTO classes would remain the domain of Porsche for some time, Mazda RX-7s would become the dominant cars in IMSA's smallest class.

"Our cars were a whole lot better than the cars we had in 1978," said Downing. "We lost two engines in two cars in 1978, and only had one spare. When we came back, we did it right. After some 24-hour testing, the cars were absolutely flawless. This was the first victory ever for the [Wankel] rotary engine in that level of competition. To finish fifth and sixth overall was a thrill for all of us. I had been running for several years in the support races at Daytona and had some success, which was fun, but that was the peak of my experience."

DUNLOP
LM
LIQUI MOLY
wir
halten
Autos
fit
STARCRAFT
STARCRAFT
BOSCH
DUNLOP
Shell
NIGRIN
Autopflege

1980: The Porsche 935 Continues to Dominate

As the 1970s drew to a close, international sports car racing was in a state of flux. The Porsche 935 remained the car of choice for the major teams, although different versions of the car were beginning to be produced by the different race engineering firms. The FIA and organizers of the 24 Hours of Le Mans were frequently at odds, with the American-based International Motor Sports Association often caught in the middle.

IMSA wanted to keep in step with the international scene, but it also wanted to succeed in the United States. The organization was searching for a successful formula that would appeal to American fans and attract new sponsorship, as they had lost Winston's backing.

Recalling the Rondeau, which competed in the Daytona 24 Hours in 1977, IMSA President John Bishop worked on developing a prototype class.

"The French were going towards a fuel-consumption formula for the 24 Hours of Le Mans," Bishop recalled. "That wouldn't sell tickets in the U.S. Instead, we were working towards an engine horsepower-to-weight formula. We thought we had an agreement with the ACO [Le Mans organizers], but it fell through. We wound up going on our own anyway."

As it began to develop the GT Prototype class, IMSA relaxed the GTX

Left: Members of the winning Reinhold Joest crew hitch a ride to victory lane on the No. 2 Joest Porsche. Joining Joest in the winning lineup were Rolf Stommelen and Volkert Merl. Above: Carlo Facetti and Martino Finotto finished 10th and won their class in the No. 4 Jolly Club Lancia Turbo.

("experimental") rules. The change allowed more exotic versions of the Porsche 935, as well as incorporating fledgling prototypes such as the Lancia Beta Monte Carlo and the BMW M1, which entered IMSA competition after the demise of the company's short-lived Procar series in Europe. For 1980, though, the GTP cars would compete in the GTX class.

Three BMW M1s were entered for the 1980 Daytona 24 Hours, including a Procar version for Kenper Miller/David Cowart/Christine Beckers, with sponsorship from the Red Lobster seafood restaurant chain. March Engineering entered a factory car for Michael Korten, Patrick Neve, and Ian Grob in GTX. Rusty Jones sponsored another March fitted with a BMW engine as a GTX entry for Olympic Decathlon gold medalist Bruce Jenner, who made his professional racing debut by joining Rick Knoop and Jim Busby.

Despite the number of new and unproven cars on the scene, there was one given—that the 16 Porsche 935s entered would dominate. Porsche turbos took the top eight slots in qualifying. Don Whittington led the pack with a record lap of 132.782 mph in a twin-turbo Porsche 935 K3 he shared with brothers Bill and Dale. The car was one of several aerodynamic, Kremer-built, Kevlar-bodied versions of the 935 that were holding their own against the Porsche factory originals.

1980

Owner/driver Reinhold Joest fielded his own version of the 935, which was qualified second by Rolf Stommelen, with Volkert Merl completing the trio of drivers. On the second row was the Barbour 935 K3 of Dick Barbour/John Fitzpatrick/Manfred Schurti. They were joined by the Brumos' adaptation of the factory 935, driven by Peter Gregg/Hurley Haywood/Bruce Leven. Defending winner Ted Field again qualified the Interscope entry, clocking in eighth-fastest in the K3 he shared with Danny Ongais and Milt Minter.

Above left: The Joest Porsche 935 of Reinhold Joest, Rolt Stommelen, and Volkert Merl leads the Brumos Porsche of Peter Gregg, Hurley Haywood, and Bruce Levin in the infield in early race action.
Above right: One of the drivers of the Dick Barbour Porsche attempts infield repairs to the No. 6 Porsche. Although the car was badly damaged after tangling with a slower car, the team managed to get it back running to finish the event. Opposite: A pit stop for the No. 5 Herman Miller Coca-Cola Porsche 935, driven by Charles Mendez, Paul Miller, and Brian Redman. An accident eliminated the car from competition.

Although the 1980 race would ultimately be won by a large margin, this was not another battle of attrition. For the first 17 hours, competitors drove with the intensity of a sprint race.

The Whittingtons led the first hour, with Joest taking the lead on the first round of pit stops. For the next five hours, Joest held the lead, with the Barbour, Whittington, and Brumos entries all within striking distance.

Paul Miller crashed the fifth-place Porsche 935 K3 he shared with Brian Redman and Charles Mendez in the early evening. That eliminated his car, and put the Whittington Porsche several laps down when it was penalized for passing during the ensuing caution period.

After midnight, Schurti took the lead in the Barbour 935, and engaged in a furious battle with Stommelen in the Joest entry. The two dueled for more than 100 miles, with the lead changing several times. A loose shock absorber eventually sent the Barbour car to the pits, dropping it to fourth. Schurti battled back to third, but 15 hours into the event he tangled with a backmarker on the banking and was finished.

At sunrise, the Joest car was in the lead, running at a record pace. But it wasn't the fastest car on the track. The Whittington brothers managed to make up a full lap under green flag conditions, and

Bill Whittington passed Joest at 9:25 a.m. to get back on the lead lap with less than seven hours remaining. Moments later, though, Whittington's bright yellow Porsche 935 coasted to a stop in the infield, the victim of a broken distributor shaft. The three brothers pushed the cars back to the pits, but were disqualified for illegal assistance.

"We didn't know that only one person could push the car," said Don Whittington. "We were willing to give up a lap to get it back in the race."

From that point on, the battle was anticlimactic. Unlike the Interscope's Porsche in 1979, Joest did not stumble down the stretch. The team became the first European entry to win at Daytona since 1972. They completed 715 laps, 2,745 miles, and averaged 114.303 mph to shatter the year-old mark by more than five miles per hour.

"This race was much harder than the one in 1978," Stommelen said in his post-race interview, when asked to compare his two Daytona triumphs. "There were so many competitive cars this year. After 17 hours the one-two cars were in the same lap. That makes the race very interesting, and very hard.

"In 1978 we were so much in front of everybody," Stommelen continued. "We went very slowly the last hour in 1978. This time, we didn't slow down. Most of the time, I watched the other cars, but for the last hour I was looking at my watch."

Al Holbert and John Paul Sr. took second, 33 laps back, followed by defending winners Danny Ongais, Ted Field, and Milt Minter in a top-three sweep for Porsche.

"Al Holbert and my father were in Preston Henn's 935," said John Paul Jr., who worked on the pit

Above: Brothers Bill (left) and Dale Whittington talk about how they're going to get their crippled Porsche 935 back to the paddock. The brothers, who led in the early going, were penalized for receiving illegal assistance. Right: Mo Carter, Craig Carter, and Murray Edwards finished fourth overall in the No. 80 tube frame Camaro. "Day 91" on the hood refers to the Iranian hostage crisis; Sunday morning, it was relettered "Day 92." Far right: The Joest Porsche 935 is unloaded in the paddock from the back of a transporter.

crew. "It was a real old car they bought off Interscope. It was so old that the oil line running through the chassis broke. They had to fix it by bypassing that line and running another line through the middle of the car. They basically started an hour behind everyone and finished second—just the two of them. It was an unbelievable race. They did a very impressive job."

Fourth went to the tube-frame Camaro of Canadians Mo Carter, Craig Carter, and Murray Edwards, which underwent two transmission changes. As tribute to the American hostages in Iran, the team had painted the words "91 Days" on the car's hood, and during the night they updated it to "92 Days." Finishing fifth—and first in the GTU category—was the Porsche 914/6 of William Koll/Jim Cook/Greg LaCava. Sixth, and first in GTO, was Tony Garcia/Alberto Vadia/Terry Herman in a Porsche 911 RSR.

The other class winner was the sole surviving Group 5 car, the 10th-place Jolly Club Lancia Beta Monte Carlo of Carlo Facetti and Martino Finotto, which won Group 5 under two-liters.

The three BMW GTP entries were out by the midway point. Jenner worked his way up to eighth place by 7 p.m. when a car spun in front of him. He collected it, causing severe front-end damage. The Rusty Jones M1 continued until 11 p.m., when it retired with a broken driveshaft.

1980 would be the final Daytona 24 Hours appearance for Peter Gregg, who finished 11th in the Brumos Porsche. Later that year, the man nicknamed "Peter Perfect" collided with a French farmer's wagon on the way to a practice session for the 24 Hours of Le Mans. Gregg's head struck the windshield pillar, and although he walked away from the accident, he suffered from double vision for months afterwards.

Gregg skipped five races while the Brumos team built a new Porsche. He entered the Daytona Finale,

but withdrew following the first practice session when he was three seconds off the pace. "We came here to win, not just to run," Gregg told Earl Fannin of the *Jacksonville Times-Union*. "We could attack, but not like I wanted to."

Less than three weeks later, Gregg was found dead on a beach north of St. Augustine, the victim of a self-inflicted gunshot. "I have done all I want to do," he wrote in a brief note.

Not being perfect was too much for Peter Gregg to bear.

ORY LANE
HR. PEPSI
Camel lights
CAMEL GT
union 76
BOSCH Spark Plugs
Bob Garretson
red roof inns
GOODYEAR
Bobby Rahal
BOSCH Spark Plugs
VALVOLINE
MISS CAMEL GT

1981: Trials of a 48-Year-Old Rookie

BOB GARRETSON'S STYLE AUTO PORSCHE 935 WASN'T ON ANYONE'S SHORT LIST OF CONTENDERS FOR THE 1981 DAYTONA 24 HOURS. BUT THAT WAS FINE WITH LEAD DRIVER BRIAN REDMAN, WHO HAD HIS OWN REASONS FOR NOT WANTING HIS CAR TO RUN UP FRONT—AT LEAST FOR THE OPENING 20 HOURS OF THE EVENT.

"Brian qualified the car because he didn't trust me, because he knew—and he was right—that I would try to prove myself," said Bobby Rahal, who joined Redman and Garretson, a 48-year-old rookie, on the driver lineup. "So he was the cool head in the group," Rahal continued. "He just didn't put any importance on qualifying. At the time, there were guys like the Whittington brothers, Danny Ongais, Hurley Haywood, John Paul, who all wanted to prove they were the fastest. Brian didn't want to play that game."

It wasn't that Redman lacked the tools to play. While most of the Porsche competitors opted to go with smaller, slightly detuned 2.8- or 3.0-liter engines, Garretson's factory-built Porsche was powered by a high-boost 3.16-liter sprint-format powerplant. Redman was extremely careful not to put any unnecessary strain on the car, since his primary concern was being able to run fast at the finish.

Rolf Stommelen won the qualifying game, running a lap of 134.078 mph in the Andial-built Porsche 935 he shared with Harald Grohs and Howard Meister. Danny Ongais, the 1979 winner, qualified second in the No. 00 Interscope Porsche 935, but Ted Field—who also disliked the wear and tear of qualifying—withdrew the faster car to concentrate on the No. 0 Porsche

Left: Bob Garretson, Bobby Rahal, Miss Camel GT, and Brian Redman smile in victory lane after their flame-spewing Red Roof Inns Porsche 935 (above) cruised to victory in the 1981 Pepsi Challenge.

935 K3, which he had qualified 10th.

The race started at 3:37 p.m., and the Whittington brothers Porsche 935 grabbed the lead on the first lap and began pulling away. But before the hour was out, the Whittington's $35,000 Porsche turbocharged engine blew. Engine failure would also end the race early for the Porsche of John Paul, who was scheduled to drive with John Paul Jr. and Gordon Smiley.

The twin-turbocharged Jolly Club Ferrari 308 GTB of Carlo Facetti, Martino Finotto, and Emanuele Pirro had qualified a surprising sixth, and quickly moved up to third position in the race. But the car's electronics quit after only four laps, forcing the drivers to switch to the team's turbocharged Lancia. That car went on to finish fifth overall, and first in the Group 5 under two-liter category.

Other front-runners such as Jochen Mass, who was paired with Reinhold Joest and Volkert Merl in a Joest 935, made early exits, along with the Ferrari 365GTB of Pete Halsmer, Jo Crevier, and Al Unser Jr. In fact, neither Mass nor Unser even had the opportunity to race. The 19-year-old Unser

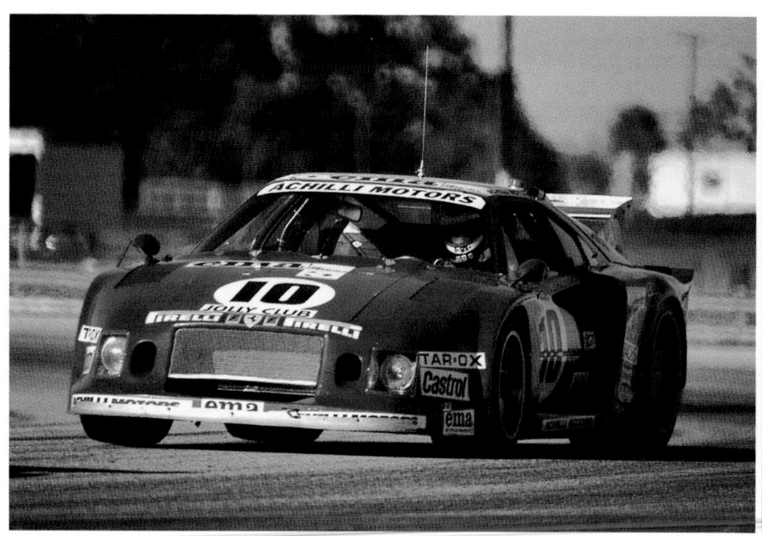

was a sprint car driver looking to make his road racing—and pavement racing—debut. He would go on to win the 1981 Super Vee championship, launching a very successful career.

While the faster teams had trouble, the Garretson Porsche began moving up and led briefly early in the race. But that wasn't where Redman wanted to be. "I said to both Garretson and Bobby, 'It's too soon, it's too soon,'" Redman recalled.

"We were in the lead too soon, which was Brian's scare," Garretson said. "If you get out in front in this race, it's a jinx. But we did, and we kept on going, and we didn't drop out. We stayed ahead,

Above left: The Jolly Club Ferrari 308 GTB qualified a surprising seventh, with Carlo Facetti moving up to third position before the car's electrical system failed in the early laps. Above right: Dirt track racer Al Unser Jr. was scheduled to make his pavement racing debut in this Ferrari 365GTB, but the car retired after only nine laps with Pete Halsmer at the wheel. Opposite top: Gianpiero Moretti poses with a Penthouse *magazine model prior to the race. Moretti was in the early stages of a lengthy quest to win the 24 Hours of Daytona. Right: Bob Akin, Derek Bell, and Craig Siebert finished second overall in Akin's No. 5 Coca-Cola Porsche 935.*

and people kept on dropping out on us."

The team's only real problem came late Saturday evening, when they cracked an exhaust header. "With the turbo, everything was red hot," Redman recalled. "And Jerry Woods changed it. He went under the car on his back, shouting for the wrenches and parts he needed, and he changed the red-hot header in 12 minutes." The Garretson team's only other setback occurred when Rahal had to pit with right-front suspension trouble.

Shortly after midnight, Redman and Rahal crossed paths in the paddock. "I remember I was walking back to our team motorhome," Rahal recalled. "I had just handed over the wheel to Garretson, and Brian was up next. Brian was walking out of the motorhome as I was coming in and he asked me, 'Who's leading?' And I said, 'We are,' and he got mad at me. He said, 'I told you, it's too early, it's too early.' I said, 'Brian, I didn't pass anybody, they're all falling out. Those guys are beating each other into the ground.'"

The Rick Knoop/Tony Adamowicz Ferrari Boxer moved into the top five just before dawn, when Adamowicz tangled with the Porsche 935 of Gianpiero Moretti. The incident eliminated both cars. By sunrise, most of the turbocharged Porsches and Lancias were gone. The Garretson Porsche continued, however, avoiding the turbocharger problems that struck many of the other teams. They led the rest of the way, winning by 13 laps. The winners covered 2,718.72 miles, 708 laps, and averaged 113.153 mph.

"Everybody was wondering what we were adding to our fuel each time we came in for a pit stop, because we had a little additive," Garretson recalled. "So everybody protested, and we got inspected at the end of the race. What we were doing was adding something to make the turbochargers run cooler. It had nothing to do with power or anything like that. So we were exonerated. But we lasted, and most people didn't last."

This was the third time Redman had tasted victory in the 24 Hours, but the first time he had actually celebrated. At his first win in 1970, he had been a late-evening afterthought, running just one shift in the winning car in an effort to slow the pace. In 1976 he had been shoved aside by the media, which was eager to interview winning co-driver Peter Gregg, even though Redman did the majority of the driving in the BMW.

"The last time I gave away the limelight, but not now," Redman said as he savored the victory.

The 1981 race was also a defining moment in the career of young Bobby Rahal. In fact, a pre-race release noted that Rahal had "yet to make a mark in endurance racing."

"Rahal had been running Formula Atlantic and stuff like that, but he was kind of out of places to go," recalled Garretson. "Dick Barbour, who was my partner, heard about him and asked him to drive a few races with us in 1980. The following year, after Dick and I parted ways, I asked Bobby if he would drive with me in my own car."

"That truly was the biggest victory I ever had up until that point in my life," Rahal recalled. "It was great. I look at the pictures

now and chuckle, because we were a lot younger then. It was a great opportunity to drive with Brian—and we drove a lot together—but that was the greatest for me, particularly at that time. I was in career purgatory. I didn't know if I was going to make it or not."

The patience Redman preached paid off for his young teammate, who used the pacing skills he learned at Daytona in a successful career racing Champ Cars, first as a driver and then as an owner/driver.

Bob Akin's Porsche 935K3, which he co-drove with Derek Bell and Craig Siebert, took second place. Bell had hit oil during the night and spun, damaging the suspension.

Third went to the Porsche 911 of GTU winners Jeff Kline, William Koll, and Rob McFarlin. That was highest overall finish ever for a GTU entry in the 24 Hours, and also the highest finish ever for a standard Porsche 911.

"Bill Koll built a real trick Porsche 911, but we had no idea of what to expect in the race," Kline explained in a 2002 interview. "We just kept grinding away. By 6 a.m., we were already third overall. Bill got up around that time, and when he saw the scoreboard, he felt it was a mistake.

"While we were happy to be running third, we knew there were still nine hours remaining in the race," Kline continued. "We knew the chance of our car breaking down was slim, while the chance of a Porsche 935 breaking down was much greater. So we thought we had a good shot at finishing second, or maybe even winning overall. The real key for us was spending only 14 minutes in the pits. We ran an uneventful race, but that's how you finish well in a race like this."

The heralded GTO class failed to live up to its promise, with all but one of the expected contenders

Above: Nighttime view of the field behind the pace car in the tri-oval during a full-course caution period. Opposite top: Young NASCAR star Terry Labonte was teamed with stock car legend David Pearson in Billy Hagan's Stratograph Camaro. Labonte, shown leading the Joest Racing Porsche of Jochen Mass in the infield, wound up dodging fans and a dog during a run back to the pits after running out of gas. Right: John Paul Jr. was scheduled to make his Daytona 24 Hours debut in the No. 18 Porsche 935, but his father retired the car with engine failure early in the race. Far right: A pit stop for the Martini & Rossi Lancia Turbo of Hans Heyer, Riccardo Patrese, and Henri Pescarolo. They team went on to finish 18th.

failing to deliver. The top finisher was the BMW M1 of Hans Stuck/Alf Gebhardt/Walter Brun in sixth, 100 laps behind, which had struggled throughout the race with various mechanical problems. The other M1s and a pair of turbocharged Porsche 924s were not even fortunate enough to make it that far, while the new turbocharged Datsun 280ZX intended for Sam Posey and Fred Stiff arrived late and was never unloaded from the trailer.

Two-time IMSA champion Al Holbert struggled with a new turbocharged Porsche 924, which he co-drove with Indy 500 winner Rick Mears and Doc Bundy in the GTO class. "We need reliability because we haven't got the pace," Holbert said before the race. Reliability became an issue with the new car, though, as problems before the race forced him to replace the entire exhaust system, turbocharger, wastegate, and headers. The car completed 263 laps before retiring with piston ring failure.

NASCAR Winston Cup car owner Billy Hagan entered a Camaro for his young driver Terry Labonte and Winston Cup legend David Pearson, but the engine failed after only 50 laps. Early in the race, Labonte ran out of gas. He stood by his car in the infield, waiting for a ride back to the pits, until he was told by a corner worker that he would have to run back by himself for a can of fuel.

"I did jog a little, but my legs were hurting," Labonte said. "I almost got bit by a dog while running between motor homes. Then one guy tried to fight me because I wouldn't stop and talk to him. Other people wanted me to stop and drink with them. It was great. I had to get three gallons of gas in a can, carry it out, and put it in the car. Then, I threw the can into the lake. I guess it could have been worse. It could have happened in the middle of the night."

The race received a record 97 entries, although no GTP cars were entered. That would change the following year.

Early in the season, the Cooke-Woods Racing Team, owned by Ralph Kent Cooke and Roy Woods, had fielded a new Lola T600. Redman helped engineer and construct the car, which was powered by a Franz Weis–built Chevrolet V-8. Redman drove the Lola to five victories and the IMSA Camel GT championship. By mid-season, Interscope ordered a similar Lola, and young sensation John Paul Jr. won the last two races of the season, backing his three second-place finishes. The IMSA GTP concept had taken off.

18
BILSTEIN
BOSCH
BILSTEIN
SHOCK ABSORBERS

1982: The Team to Beat

IN 1982 ROLF STOMMELEN RETURNED TO DAYTONA SEEKING HIS THIRD VICTORY IN FIVE YEARS. THE GERMAN WAS NOW TEAMED WITH THE FATHER-SON PAIR OF JOHN PAUL SR. AND JR. THE YOUNGER PAUL HAD BEEN SCHEDULED TO RACE IN 1981, BUT HIS FATHER'S PORSCHE 935 EXPIRED AFTER JUST 53 LAPS, SO THIS YEAR WOULD BE HIS FIRST CHANCE TO ACTUALLY DRIVE IN THE EVENT.

Somewhat awed by the competition, Paul Jr. turned to his new teammate. "Before the race I asked Rolf, 'Who's the team to beat here?' He answered, 'We are.'

"He was incredibly cocky, but he was very good," Paul continued. "I had a really good time racing with him. He was an unbelievable driver. He also could hear many subtle little things that the car was doing. I was pretty new to endurance racing then, and I had no idea of what he was talking about, as far as the things he could feel with the car."

Despite Stommelen's confidence, the 21-year-old Paul still found plenty of reasons to be concerned as he looked around the paddock. The face of IMSA competition was changing with the addition of the new Camel GTP class. The new prototypes were classified with the more exotic Porsche 935 derivatives,

Left: The JLP Porsche is in the pits for routine service, with John Paul Jr. standing by the open door. The team experienced no problems—other than running over a bottle—although the elder Paul had a scare in the closing laps when he managed to avoid a slower car blocking his path. Above: The Chevy-powered Lola T600 that took Brian Redman to the 1981 IMSA Camel GT championship was driven in the 1982 24 Hours by Ralph Kent Cooke, Eppie Wietzes, and Jim Adams. The team qualified eighth and failed to finish.

which had been previously classified in GTX.

Leading the GTP entries was a Chevy-powered Lola T600 driven by Ralph Kent Cooke/Eppie Wietzes/Jim Adams—the car Redman had driven to the 1981 IMSA Camel GT championship—plus a Mazda-powered Chevron, a pair of new March 82Gs, and a pair of French Cosworth-powered Rondeau 382s.

A year after his upset victory, which had led him to the World Endurance Driver's Championship, Bob Garretson returned as a car owner, fielding a new Red Roof Inns Chevrolet-powered March 82G. Bobby Rahal put the car on the pole with a lap of 133.063 mph, and was joined in the race by Jim

Trueman and Bruce Canepa. There was also a BMW-powered March for David Cowart/Kenper Miller. Sponsored by Red Lobster, the car was painted with giant claws on the front wheel wells.

Even with the new cars, Porsches were again expected to run up front. Along with the Pauls, the ranks of 935s included Bruce Leven's Bayside Disposal team of Hurley Haywood and Al Holbert; Danny Ongais and Ted Field with Interscope Racing; and John Fitzpatrick's 1981 winner, which he shared with Mauricio de Narvaez and Jeff Wood. It was the first race for Ongais since he had endured a horrible crash in the 1981 Indianapolis 500.

Ferrari's North American Racing Team entered a Ferrari 512BB for reigning Porsche Cup champion Bob Wollek, who was joined by Edgar Doeren and Randy Lanier, a Florida amateur racer. Preston Henn had originally intended the car to be driven by his daughter, Bonnie Henn, and Janet Guthrie. The driver lineup was changed when Guthrie, a veteran of both Indy car and NASCAR Winston Cup racing, contracted the flu.

"We tested it briefly, and the car was a mess," recalled Guthrie. "It didn't know whether to go around the corners forwards or backwards, so I felt sort of lucky to have gotten the flu. But Bob Wollek, a real gentleman, came along and he knew exactly how to tweak it, and he turned it into a competitive

Above left: The No. 18 JLP Porsche 935 on the banking on its drive to victory. Above right: Danny Sullivan, a future Indianapolis 500 winner, was among the drivers of the No. 3 Rondeau 382, a Ford Cosworth-powered prototype. Opposite: Bob Akin waits to get back into his Coca-Cola Porsche 935 during a pit stop. Akin was disappointed after finishing second for the second straight year.

machine. Then I was sorry I had gotten the flu and wished I'd been able to drive it that year."

Bob Tullius' Group 44 entered a Jaguar XJS that was too modified to run in GTO and moved to the GTX class.

The Paul-Stommelen team not only had a proven car, they had history on their side. John Paul Sr. told Larry Balewski of the *Daytona Beach Morning Journal* about a discussion he had had with Stommelen on the eve of the race.

"We were having dinner and I said to Rolf: 'You know, I do good here every other year,'" the elder Paul explained. "'I finished fourth here in 1978, and was second in 1980.' And he said, 'You know John, I win here every other year.'" It would take only two hours for Stommelen to make good on his boast.

The field was greeted by a record crowd estimated by the *Morning Journal* at more than 50,000. While Danny Ongais and Hurley Haywood took turns leading in the early going, pressured by the Fitzpatrick Porsche, the JLP Porsche took the lead at 60 laps—two hours into the event—and led the rest of the way.

The Interscope Porsche of Ongais/Ted Field/Bill Whittington went out at the two-hour mark with a broken connecting rod, while the John Fitzpatrick/David Hobbs/Wayne Baker Porsche 935 K3 exited moments later with cam-drive failure. Both cars retired because IMSA no longer allowed engine changes during races.

"Basically, what turned the race around was when those two went out," said Paul Sr. after the race. "They were our toughest competitors at that point."

Paul Sr. also recalled Brian Redman's concerns about taking the lead too early in the 1981 event. "Like Brian Redman said last year, I thought it was way too early to be in the lead after two hours,"

COWART-MILLER
25
Red Lobster
25
Red Lobster

Paul Sr. told Larry Balewski after the race. "But, it was given to us, and what could we do?"

Despite the Paul-Stommelen team's early dominance, at 10 p.m. the fans were treated to a classic duel between two proven Daytona winners, when Haywood gave Stommelen a stiff challenge for the lead. The Leven Porsche kept the pressure on until 1:30 a.m., when the car developed a fluid leak around the right-rear wheel and was pushed behind the wall to have a transmission mounting welded. Holbert returned 14 laps down, out of contention. The team soldiered on, only to have both turbochargers fail. They spent the final three hours of the race parked on pit road, firing up the car for one slow final lap.

The pole-winning March struggled throughout the race with vibration problems and finally retired with a broken gearbox. But the team was not disappointed in the new prototype.

"Actually, we had a good race," said Rahal. "It was March's first car for this type of racing, and we went a lot further than I thought we would. Franz Weis of Chaparral built us a fantastic engine. I think the exhaust system fell apart in the 20th hour, and then the gearbox finally gave up the ghost. I don't think anybody gave us a chance at all. Yet for most of the race, we were in the top four or five."

The Wollek Ferrari was running third at 2:30 a.m. on Sunday morning when Lanier missed a shift and terminally damaged the car's transmission. Haywood and the Bayside team struggled throughout the second half of the race with broken engine mounts, and later lost both turbochargers. The team spent the final two hours on pit road, waiting for the checkered flag so they could drive one final lap and be classified as finishers, in fifth position.

While attrition took its toll on the others, the JLP Porsche cruised along. Its biggest problem was a cut tire caused by a bottle that the younger Paul had run over during a morning shift.

"It came daytime, and there was nobody left to race," said Paul Sr. in his winner's interview.

Opposite: The Red Lobster BMW March—before it sprouted claws. The car was eventually painted to resemble a lobster. Above left: Yoshimi Katayama, Takashi Yorino, and Yojiro Terado finished fourth overall and first in GTO in a Mazda USA Mazda RX-7. Above right: Bob Tullius' Group 44 Jaguar XJS was deemed too modified to run in the GTO class, so the No. 444 was moved up to the GTX category.

Stommelen's boast to the younger Paul had proven correct: JLP really was the team to beat in 1982, leading a sweep of the top three positions by Porsche 935s.

"We had absolutely no problems at all," Paul Jr. recalled in a 2002 interview. "We never added oil to it, never even opened the hood. We just ran 24 hours with absolutely no problems; it was just unbelievable." The JLP trio won by 11 laps, completing 719 laps—2,760.96 miles—and averaging 114.794 mph. All three were new records.

The winners' closest call came shortly before the checkered flag was waved. Paul Sr. was cruising at high speed, looking to break the race mileage record, when a Mercury Capri moved up the track and into his path as he dove off the tri-oval into the infield.

"That was the only moment I had in the race," said Paul Sr., who managed to avoid the slower car before he had a chance to think about a possibly tragic ending. "I guess I was driving too fast, and the car was running so sweet. It was totally inconceivable that he would come up into the high groove...I guess I could just as easily have been the goat instead of the hero."

Bob Akin, Craig Siebert, and Derek Bell placed second in the Akin Porsche, which lost time after a 9 p.m. incident that knocked the car's brakes out of adjustment. Akin locked up his rear wheels and spun into the barrier entering turn one.

"I thought, 'This is it,' when I saw all kinds of headlights coming at me," Akin said following the race. "Fortunately everybody managed to avoid me on both sides. I hit the guardrail pretty good on the right quarter panel, probably the only place on the car you can hit without much damage."

"Finishing second for the first time in 1981 was very exciting," recalled Akin in 2002, shortly before his death following an accident during practice for a vintage race. "But when I finished second again the following year, I was very disappointed."

Taking third were Garretson, Wood, and de Narvaez. Unlike Akin, the defending winner was far from disappointed. "Just to finish here at Daytona is something to be proud of," said Garretson, whose team had been pulled together at the last minute. He had picked Woods, a Can-Am driver who had neither driven in an endurance race nor competed at night, just a day prior to the event.

Mazda RX-7s captured top honors in both the GTO and GTU divisions. Yoshimi Katayama, Takashi Yorino, and Yojiro Terado placed fourth overall and first in GTO in a Mazda USA entry, while

Top: Bob Leitzinger made his Daytona 24 Hours debut in the No. 4 Gordy Oftedahl Pontiac Firebird, which spins to the inside of the No. 38 Roger Mandeville/Amos Johnson/Jeff Kline Mazda RX-7. Above: "The team to beat" in 1982, John Paul Senior (left) and Junior flank three-time Daytona winner Rolf Stommelen in victory lane. Opposite top: Defending Daytona 24 Hours winner Bobby Rahal accepts the pole position trophy from IMSA President John Bishop (right). His new March prototype had a competitive run before retiring with gearbox problems late in the race. Right: The John Paul/Rolf Stommelen Porsche 935 takes the checkered flag, followed by the third place Porsche of defending winner Bob Garretson.

Kathy Rude became the first woman to win her class in the 24 Hours of Daytona, sharing GTU honors with Lee Mueller and Allan Moffat and placing sixth overall.

The French Rondeau team, which had won the 24 Hours of Le Mans in 1980 and finished second and third in that event in 1981, had high hopes for the Daytona 24 Hour Pepsi Challenge. The team was very optimistic after its first 24-hour test in the U.S. on January 3. They expected their two Cosworth-powered Rondeau 382s, with a driver lineup that included Danny Sullivan, Skeeter McKitterick, and Irv Hoerr, to go farther between stops than the Porsche 935s, as they didn't need to change brake pads as often.

The Rondeaus qualified 14th and 15th, and ran well in the early going, only to suffer from fuel-feed problems later on. Both cars went to backup fuel pumps, and then the alternators failed on both cars, resulting in their retirement.

The race entry was 96 cars, prompting the addition of a 13-lap qualifying race to determine starting positions 51-73. Carson Baird won the race in a Ferrari 512BB Boxer Berlinetta, Paul Miller won in GTO and Anatoly Arutunoff won in GTU.

The 24 Hour Pepsi Challenge was just the beginning of an outstanding season for John Paul Jr. He won nine of the 18 races, an IMSA single-season record, as well as the Camel GT championship. In 1982, he was the man to beat.

BOSCH
BILSTEIN

1983: First-Time Porsche Driver

After Bob Wollek won the pole for the 1983 Pepsi Challenge 24 Hours, A. J. Foyt remarked that he would someday like a try at driving a Porsche. While the four-time Indianapolis 500 winner watched, Wollek had broken his own two-month-old track record with a lap of 135.324 mph. He was driving Preston Henn's Swap Shop Porsche 935, an Andial-built replica of the factory 935-78 that was commonly known as Moby Dick.

Foyt, who had returned to Daytona for his first sports car race in 16 years, was driving an Aston Martin GTP car with NASCAR Winston Cup star Darrell Waltrip. Impressed with Wollek's performance, Foyt made his request of Henn.

"I told him, 'When that piece of crap you're driving breaks,' and he said OK," Henn recalled. Foyt's wish would come true sooner than he realized.

Foyt was a reluctant participant in the 24 Hours, having left his dying father's bedside in order to compete. Waltrip had urged him to join the race as his driving partner, but Foyt remained unpersuaded until his father gave him the encouragement he needed. "He was in the hospital and said, 'Hell, you can't sit here and hold my hand. Go on down,'" Foyt recalled. "The extra push he gave me got me here."

Left: A.J. Foyt, driving the leading Porsche, leads the Avanti of Joe Ruttman and the Chevrolet March of Randy Lanier in the rain late in the race. After Bob Wollek and Claude Ballot-Lena built up a healthy lead during the night (above) in Preston Henn's T-Bird Swap Shop 935, Foyt joined the team Sunday morning and had an impressive run in the unfamiliar car.

Although Wollek won the pole, it was apparent that the influx of faster GTP cars meant the days of the 935 as a front-runner were numbered. To help them stay competitive with the prototypes, the 935s now sported wings and aerodynamic bodywork.

The Interscope team had a Chevrolet-powered Lola T600 for Ted Field, Danny Ongais, and Bill Whittington. Another Lola Chevrolet T600 was entered for Ralph Kent Cooke, Jim Adams, and John Bright.

Marty Hinze, Randy Lanier, and Terry Wolters were entered in a new Chevy-powered March 83G. The Red Lobster team returned in their year-old March 82G, with a Porsche engine installed for David Cowart and Kenper Miller.

Bob Tullius, a Winchester, Virginia, businessman who ran his Group 44 race team with the precision of a military operation, had been on the sports car scene for several years, competing with Triumphs and Jaguars. In 1982 he embarked on a five-year program designed to boost Jaguar's visibility and dealer morale through racing.

Lee Dykstra was commissioned to design the XJR-5, which used the Jaguar V-12 powerplant. The

car finished third in its debut at Road America, its best outing of the season. For Daytona, Tullius was joined by Bill Adam and Pat Bedard in the Group 44 Jaguar XJR-5. Although it would fail to finish, the immaculately prepared, white-and-green car gave Daytona 24 fans a good look at the future of sports car racing.

1983

Aston Martin entered a pair of Nimrods. Foyt and Waltrip were joined by Colombian Guillermo Maldonado, with Lyn St. James, Canadian John Graham, and Drake Olson in the second car. The

Above left: The Group 44 Jaguar XJR-5 of Bob Tullius, Bill Adam, and Pat Bedard gives the field a glimpse of the future of Camel GTP racing. The popular team qualified seventh and led in the early going before experiencing suspension damage. Above right: One of the unique entries in the 1983 Pepsi Challenge was the Avanti, with a driver lineup including NASCAR Winston Cup driver Joe Ruttman. The team lost time for this off-course excursion, but finished 27th. Opposite: Darrell Waltrip, driving the No. 11 Pepsi Aston Martin Nimrod, follows the Pegasus Racing Porsche 935 of Marion Speer, Ken Madren, and Ray Ratcliff on the parade lap.

Mazda of Walt Bohren, Pierre Honegger, and David Palmer was another GTP entry.

In addition to Henn's pole-winning Porsche, six other 935s were entered, and the marque took the top five positions on the grid. A Fabcar-built 935 for John Paul Jr., Rene Rodriguez, and Joe Castellano was second fastest. The younger Paul had followed up his 1982 Daytona 24 Hours victory with eight additional wins that had earned him the Camel GT championship. His team decided to keep its new Lola back in Atlanta, feeling that the endurance format favored the Porsche.

In the second row were the 935s of Frank Rubino/Pepe Romero/Doc Bundy/Dale Whittington and the Kremer-built entry of Bob Akin/John O'Steen. Qualifying fifth was Bruce Leven's Bayside Disposal entry, which he co-drove with Hurley Haywood and Al Holbert.

Wollek led the first four laps, but dropped back to 58th position, 12 laps behind and seemingly out of contention, after two long pit stops to replace both turbochargers. Meanwhile, the Akin and Haywood 935s, along with the Jaguar of Tullius, battled for the lead in the opening hour.

After proving that the XJR-5 could run up front—it was leading at the two-hour mark—the Tullius Jaguar slowed with suspension damage. That gave the lead to Haywood, followed by Paul Jr. The Lanier March took the lead at the fifth hour, followed by the surprising Ferrari 512BB of Carson Baird, Chip Mead, and Tom Pumpelly. The Henn team had quietly worked its way back up to fifth, although they remained eight laps behind.

The Ferrari, which had qualified 21st, led briefly at the six-hour mark, followed closely by Lanier, who quickly regained the point. The Hinze March led hours seven through 15.

The Waltrip/Foyt/Maldonado Aston Martin withdrew after a baffle from the oil sump got into the oil pan and chewed up the timing chain. "We will definitely be back next year," Waltrip said. Henn, meanwhile, remembered Foyt's desire to drive a Porsche.

"When I heard A. J. broke down, my next turn to get in came at 5 o'clock, so I found him and called him and got him down here," Henn recalled. "I'd rather have three race drivers in the car than two race drivers and a businessman when we're so close to winning."

Uncomfortable with the idea of jumping into the unfamiliar car at night, Foyt said he would wait until Henn's scheduled sunrise shift. That information was never relayed to Wollek, who was busy racing.

A terrific battle for the lead had emerged overnight, with the Henn Porsche 935 and the Marty Hinze/Randy Lanier/Terry Wolters Chevrolet March swapping the lead several times throughout the early morning hours. The Baird/Mead/Pumpelly Ferrari hung in until dawn, when it exited with a broken crankshaft.

When Wollek pitted for routine service, he was unhappy to see A. J. Foyt standing at his door, waiting to drive in relief. In fact, Wollek slammed the door shut on Foyt and returned to drive another shift. When he pitted again, Henn was waiting at the door, and "assisted" his driver out of the car. Initially, Wollek was livid.

"I like A. J. now—as I did before—because he's famous and one of the big stars," Wollek said in a 1986 interview. "But I didn't like the situation at that point in 1983, when we had to work very hard with my fellow Ballot-Lena [the other co-driver] to bring the car in the lead after having been delayed twice during the night. When the car was in the lead A. J. just turned up and was going to drive,

Above left: Randy Lanier, Terry Wolters, and Marty Hinze finished second overall in the No. 88 Executone Chevrolet March 83G. One year later, Lanier would capture the Camel GTP championship.
Above right: Dan Gurney returned to Daytona with a pair of GTU Toyota Celicas. Gene Hackman co-drove the No. 99, but it retired early with gearbox failure. Opposite: Darrell Waltrip and A. J. Foyt co-drove the No. 11 Pepsi Aston Martin. When the car retired in the early evening hours, Foyt was asked to drive the eventual-winning Porsche. That was the first time Foyt raced a Porsche.

which I didn't like because I think a team should be a team. You should be a team when you are in the dumps and you're a team when you're in victory lane...It didn't have to do with A. J.; it was just the situation I didn't agree with."

Wollek also had other concerns that he explained in his post-race interview. "I was nervous because he didn't know the car. He didn't know if it had four or five gears, where were the buttons and lights. This car is not easy to drive, but A. J. got away with it," Wollek said. "He learned how to drive a Porsche."

Foyt, who knew nothing about Wollek's comments, went out and turned very competitive laps, even though it had been raining for 30 minutes before his first shift. Foyt and Wollek would share the Henn Porsche for the final eight and a half hours.

Foyt took over with a one-lap lead on the Lanier/Wolters/Hinze March, and returned the car to Wollek with a two-lap lead. Wollek added another lap to the margin, and then handed the car to Foyt for a rain-marred, four-hour, 10-minute shift. Despite the weather, Foyt ran the fastest lap of the race, 126-plus mph. When he turned the car over to Wollek for the final 50 minutes, the lead was seven circuits.

Wollek cruised the rest of the way, winning by eight laps. The Swap Shop team completed 618 laps,

2,373.12 miles, and averaged 98.781 mph, which gave Porsche its seventh consecutive victory in the event. It would also be the final Daytona victory for the 935.

Henn could smile about his "replacement" driver. "A. J. got in and drove it to victory. Driving rain and everything else, he did a great job," Henn recalled. "Wollek was ticked off. He said he's tired of Mr. A. J. Foyt driving for his own publicity. But A. J. did a great job."

"I guess he bad-mouthed me and all, but I knew nothing about that until after the race," Foyt said. "In the post-race interviews, I remember him saying that maybe A. J.'s the champion everybody's talked about."

The victory had special meaning for Foyt, whose last road race was winning the 1967 24 Hours of Le Mans with Dan Gurney. "I didn't care if I ever won another race, because I took the trophy back to the hospital before my father passed on," he recalled.

Finishing second was the Chevy-powered March of Hinze, Randy Lanier and Terry Wolters, which struggled through the rain with ignition problems and several spins. "We were leading and then the rains came in the morning, and we got water in the distributor," said Hinze, a fencing contractor from Fort Lauderdale, Florida. "That cost us four laps, and we were ahead by two laps at the time."

Once again, Mazda RX-7s swept IMSA's production-based classes. Pete Halsmer, Bob Reed, and Rick Knoop won in GTO, finishing third overall and 20 laps behind the winners. Lee Mueller, Hugh McDonough, and Terry Visger took GTU honors, placing 12th overall.

A familiar name in the history of sports car racing returned to Daytona when Dan Gurney fielded a pair of GTU Toyota Celicas under his All American Racers umbrella. Actor Gene Hackman retired after 118 laps with gearbox failure after a noncompetitive run. The other car, driven by Dennis Aase, Al Unser Jr., and Mike Chandler, led the class for several hours before it, too, experienced transmission trouble. Gurney, whose Eagles won the Indianapolis 500 three times, would be a fixture in IMSA competition over the next decade.

Waltrip was so pleased with his experience that the two-time NASCAR Winston Cup champion announced on national television Sunday morning that he would return in 1984. The voluble Waltrip promised to race with Foyt and another driver in a car prepared by legendary NASCAR car owner Junior Johnson, a statement that would be forgotten during the upcoming Winston Cup season.

Foyt was lukewarm when asked about Waltrip's plans following the race. "I'll probably wait another 15 years before I do this again," Foyt said.

Ironically, Waltrip would only return to the Daytona 24 once more, in 1987, while Foyt would have a hand in the competition over the next four years. Joining him in several of those races would be his newfound friend Bob Wollek.

Above: Ralph Cooke, Jim Adams, and John Bright finished sixth in the Chevrolet Lola T600 that Brian Redman had driven to the 1981 Camel GT championship. Right: Bob Wollek, Claude Ballot-Lena, A. J. Foyt, and Preston Henn celebrate in victory lane following the 1983 24 Hour Pepsi Challenge.

VICTORY LANE
24HR PEPSI
DAYTONA
PEPSI
Challenger
Marlboro
BOSCH
'83 PEPSI 24 HR OF
DAYTONA
76

Shell
PORSCHE
DUNLOP

1984: Prototypes Begin to Dominate

FOR THE BRAND-NEW KREEPY KRAULY TEAM, THE FIRST AND BIGGEST PROBLEM IN 1984 WAS FINDING DAYTONA INTERNATIONAL SPEEDWAY, AS MOST OF THEM HAD NEVER BEEN THERE BEFORE. BUT ONCE THEY GOT THERE, EVERYTHING FELL INTO PLACE FOR THE TEAM.

"That was our first race," recalled Ken Howes, crew chief for the Atlanta-based team. "We had Al Holbert's championship car from 1983, and we did some work on it and went to Daytona."

The team was owned by Kreepy Krauly, a South African manufacturer of swimming pool-cleaning equipment. Lead driver Sarel van der Merwe was the only team member who had ever been to Daytona, having run the November, 1983, IMSA finale with Gianpiero Moretti, sponsored by Kreepy Krauly. For the 24 Hours, van der Merwe was joined at the wheel by fellow South Africans Graham Duxbury and Tony Martin.

But being new to Daytona didn't hurt the drivers as much as it might have in previous years, because the course had been changed prior to the 1984 24 Hours. A chicane had been added to the end of the backstraight so that cars would not be carrying top speed into the NASCAR turn three banking. The change also meant that the course length was fractionally lengthened from 3.84 to 3.87 miles.

The race had changed in other ways too. It had a new name—the SunBank 24 at Daytona—courtesy of the Orlando-based banking chain, which used the

Left: Michael Andretti stands by the new Porsche 962 while his father Mario (in car) talks with Porsche engineer Norbert Singer over the intercom. A three-time CART competitor in 1983, Michael and his father finished third in that year's 24 Hours of Le Mans. Above: Sunset found the Group 44 Jaguar XJR-5 of Bob Tullius, Doc Bundy and David Hobbs running up front. A long stop to repair damage from a broken alternator belt took the team out of the lead, although the Jaguar returned to post a solid third-place finish.

race to promote its round-the-clock ATMs. It also boasted a huge entry of 82 cars, with most of the interest focused on cars from IMSA's premier GT Prototypes class.

The Kreepy Krauly entry was one of 18 Camel GT Prototypes, up from just two in the previous year's race. The car attracting the most attention, however, was the first Porsche 962, a plain white car bearing "No. 1." It was co-driven by the father-son team of Mario and Michael Andretti, who had teamed up to finish third in the 1983 24 Hours of Le Mans. Mario's son Jeff was also driving in the GTU class, making this race the first time the 1978 Formula One World Champion had competed with both of his sons.

Porsche had enjoyed success in European Group C competition with its 956 model, which won both Le Mans and the Group C manufacturer's championship in 1983 and 1984. But the car's design, which placed the driver's feet ahead of the front axle, made it ineligible for IMSA competition.

Jurgen Barth, Jo Hoppen, and other Porsche officials visited IMSA headquarters in Bridgeport, Connecticut, to lobby for the 956's acceptance into GTP competition. But President John Bishop and the other IMSA officials stood their ground, blaming the feet-first design for the number of foot and

leg injuries suffered in Formula One, Indy Car, and other sports car series.

"The main difference [between the 956 and 962] was the placement of the driver's feet," Bishop explained. "We require that the footbox be placed behind the front axle. It was a common-sense rule. Porsche didn't want to build a car that way, but we stuck to our guns, and they built it."

1984

Other prototypes included a pair of Group 44 Jaguar XJR-5s, one of which was driven by Brian

Above left: The first Porsche 962 was an immediate attention-getter, winning the pole position for the 24 Hours with Mario Andretti at the wheel. While its debut run was plagued with problems, the 962 would quickly become the car to beat in IMSA Camel GTP competition. Above right: Bob Akin, Bobby Rahal, and John O'Steen shared the Coca-Cola Porsche 935. The team qualified ninth, but retired during the early evening. Akin would be among the Porsche 935 owners who would soon upgrade to the 962. Opposite top: The Kreepy Krawly team raced Al Holbert's 1983 championship Porsche-March, but was not on the list of pre-event favorites. Drivers Sarel van der Merwe (far right) and Graham Duxbury await the start of the race on pit road. Opposite: The 1984 SunBank 24 introduced a chicane at the end of the back straight, designed to slow the cars entering the high-speed banking. Above, the No. 04 Jaguar XJR-5 of Bill Adam, Brian Redman, and Pat Bedard lead the eventual-winning No. 00 Kreepy Krawly Porsche-March and the No. 87 Porsche 924 of Elliott Forbes-Robinson, John Schneider, and Ken Williams at the exit of the new chicane.

Redman; four Marches; two Lola T600s; a trio of Aston Martins; and four Mazda-powered prototypes, including a pair of Lola T616s fielded by Jim Busby using BFGoodrich street radial tires.

Mario Andretti won the pole with a lap of 125.526 mph, immediately demonstrating the potential of the new Porsche. Van der Merwe attracted attention by clocking in second fastest, ahead of the Group 44 Jaguar XJR-5 of Bob Tullius, Doc Bundy, and David Hobbs.

"It was like an old shoe right away," said Mario Andretti of the Porsche 962, which had only 800 kilometers of testing at the hands of Jacky Ickx in France prior to the race. "I just saw it for the first time on Wednesday, and it arrived race-ready. Winning the pole in it is very satisfying."

Bob Wollek qualified fourth in Preston Henn's Thunderbird Swap Shop Porsche 935, but it was apparent that time was running out for the turbocharged version of the venerable Carrera. "I'm a little unhappy about having to go up against the factory Porsche 962 team, but I'll stake my drivers, Foyt and Wollek, against the Andrettis any day of the week," said Henn.

Other Porsche 935s were fielded by Bruce Leven's Bayside Disposal team, including three-time Camel GT champion Al Holbert and Hurley Haywood (who co-drove to victory in the 1983 24 Hours of Le Mans) in the lineup, and Bob Akin, who co-drove with John O'Steen and Bobby Rahal.

A surprise entrant was veteran Innes Ireland, winner of the 1961 U.S. Grand Prix at Watkins Glen, who shared a Porsche 924 Turbo with Tom Winters and Bob Bergstrom.

An hour after the 3:30 p.m. green flag, Mario Andretti held the lead, chased by the Kreepy Krauly March, Group 44 Jaguar, Hinze March, and Henn Porsche 935. Michael Andretti took over for his father and continued to lead before pitting with transmission trouble caused by heat from the turbocharger. The Porsche spent an hour behind the wall for repairs. After a brief return to action, the camshaft failed and the car was retired after 207 laps.

"It was a shame," Michael Andretti recalled. "It drove like we were going to win the race with our eyes closed. Unfortunately, having the first 962 out in a long race, we found out that they didn't have enough heat shielding between the turbo and the gearbox and [the heat] seized the gears together. If this car had been raced before, we would have known about it."

Mario Andretti agreed. "It was a brand new car, and they didn't have everything worked out," he recalled in a 2002 interview. "It was a shame, that's a race we could have won."

After two hours, it was the Chevy March that car owner Marty Hinze shared with Bill Whittington and Randy Lanier in the lead, followed again by the Kreepy Krauly March.

Above: Pole-sitter Mario Andretti is sandwiched at the start by Sarel van der Merwe in the No. 00 Kreepy Krawly Porsche-March and Bob Tullius in the Group 44 Jaguar XJR-5 (far right). Also running up front are A. J. Foyt in Preston Henn's Porsche 935 and the No. 04 Group 44 Jaguar of Brian Redman. Opposite top: Car owner Preston Henn video tapes the action as his Porsche 935 gets plenty of pre-event attention, attracted by his all-star cast of drivers, A. J. Foyt, Bob Wollek, and Derek Bell. Opposite left: Veterans Vic Elford (left) and Richard Atwood teamed to drive a Porsche 928, the only appearance of that model in U.S. competition. They finished 15th overall in the Brumos Porsche-prepared car. Opposite right: The SunBank 24 brought together an impressive mixture of machinery, ranging from the Leon Brothers March (No. 2), Conte Lola (No. 2), Hinze March (No. 16), and other prototypes to a collection of GT cars, including the No. 11 Camaro shared by Winston Cup drivers Joe Ruttman and Tim Richmond, plus the ever-present Porsche 935s.

The Group 44 Jaguar took the lead in the third hour, chased by the Hinze March and the Henn and Bayside Porsche 935s. The Kreepy Krauly team experienced problems with the gear shifter, and fell back to eighth. Then the Hinze March dropped out with transmission problems.

The Tullius team held the lead through six hours, but lost ground when an alternator belt broke, a problem that also occurred with the team's other entry. That gave the lead to the Kreepy Krauly March, which it held until Martin ran out of fuel in the infield and had to jog back to the pits.

"We had only one problem," said Martin. "We had an electrical failure that closed off the auxiliary fuel switch, so we ran out of gas about a third of the way into the race." Van der Merwe carried a five-gallon can of gas "about a mile" to his rescue.

Foyt took the lead in the Henn 935, but fell back with bodywork damage. The Bayside Porsche 935 then took point on lap 197 and began pulling away. At 1:30 a.m., the Leven car rolled behind pit wall to have a crack in the intake system welded.

That returned the Kreepy Krauly March to the lead on lap 254, and the South African trio never looked back. Van der Merwe, Duxbury, and Martin scored a nine-lap victory. The team completed 640 laps, 2,476.8 miles, and averaged 103.119 mph.

"I guess you can say we had beginner's luck," said Howes. "We ran out of gas once, and the gearshift knob came off, but other than that, we had no real problems."

"Except perhaps for Le Mans, Daytona is the greatest name in racing back in South Africa," said Duxbury. "We had hopes, of course. But winning...and winning like we did...well, it won't sink in for a while."

"In South Africa, everybody thinks Florida is warm," added Martin. "It gets into the 40s during the night, and I was cold in the pits. But you Americans think we have lions and tigers walking our streets."

Preston Henn's Porsche 935 soldiered to a second-place finish, driven by A. J. Foyt, Bob Wollek, and Derek Bell, nine laps behind. Al Holbert, Hurley Haywood, and Claude Ballot-Lena took fourth in Bruce Leven's Porsche 935, the last hurrah for the aging model.

The Group 44 Jaguar of Tullius/Hobbs/Bundy placed third, 28 laps behind the winner. While the car ran strong in the early going, it was eventually plagued by electrical problems.

The Red Lobster March was involved in the most serious incident of the race, hitting a Corvette in the chicane and flipping. The car landed on its wheels, and driver Kenper Miller was unhurt. "The car was running beautifully," said co-driver David Cowart. "I had to cut back on my shift points to keep the pace we had set for ourselves. The car really wanted to run."

A pair of IMSA GT categories supported the prototype class. Winston Cup championship–bound Terry Labonte took honors in GTO, co-driving with Billy Hagan and Gene Felton in the Piedmont Airlines Camaro. The trio reached third overall with four hours remaining, but finished sixth overall after struggling with an assortment of minor mechanical problems. Counting support races and class victories, it was Felton's 10th IMSA triumph at Daytona.

In addition to Labonte, three other Winston Cup regulars competed. Sterling Marlin shared a Corvette with Gary Baker, finishing 38th, while Joe Ruttman and Tim Richmond placed 50th in Mike Laws's Corvette.

In the GTU category, Ira Young, Jack Baldwin, and Bob Reed won in the Malibu Grand Prix Mazda RX-7, placing 12th overall. The trio took the lead at the 18-hour mark, after running fourth in the class during the early going. They won the class by three laps over the Porsche 911 of Rusty Bond, Blake Bridgen, and Ben Tilton.

Jack Dunham, Jeff Kline, and Paul Lewis dominated the early going in a Mazda RX-7, but finished 18th overall and third in the class. Malibu Grand Prix head Young had purchased the car from Jim Downing only three weeks prior to the race, with no intention of racing in the SunBank 24. When the car was delivered race-ready, however, Young and his team, led by crew chief Clayton Cunningham, changed their minds.

"I think I've won 30 major races and three championships, and the Daytona trophy sits right in the center of my trophy room at home," said Baldwin in a 2002 interview. "I'm proud of that. It was hard, it was tough, I had to earn that race, I had to race hard to get that one. I didn't have anything in those days, and I kept telling myself, when you've got nothing, you've got nothing to lose: Drive. Everyone else was running a pace, for 24 hours, and I was absolutely jamming it. We fell 12 laps behind, but worked hard and got it back."

Dan Gurney entered a pair of Toyota Celicas in the GTU class. Wally Dallenbach Jr., who would be a rookie in the 1984 Trans-Am competition, shared the wheel with Dennis Aase and Michael Chandler, with the car sidelined after 49 laps. Chris Cord and Jim Adams had better luck in the second car, completing 292 laps.

The 1984 race marked the first—and only—appearance of the Porsche 928 in a professional racing event in the United States. The car was shipped to Daytona by the Porsche factory along with the 962, and the Brumos team fielded it in the race. Veterans Vic Elford and Richard Attwood co-drove with Howard Meister and Bob Hagestad, finishing 15th overall and fourth in GTO.

Above: Graham Duxbury, Tony Martin, and Sarel van der Merwe celebrate their triumph in victory lane. The South African trio won the race by nine laps. Opposite left: Martin (left) and Duxbury relax behind their pit stall. Opposite right: A pensive A. J. Foyt in the Preston Henn pits. The four-time Indianapolis 500 winner was seeking his second consecutive Daytona 24 Hours victory, teamed with Bob Wollek and Derek Bell. The Valvoline Swap Shop Porsche 935 finished second, nine laps behind.

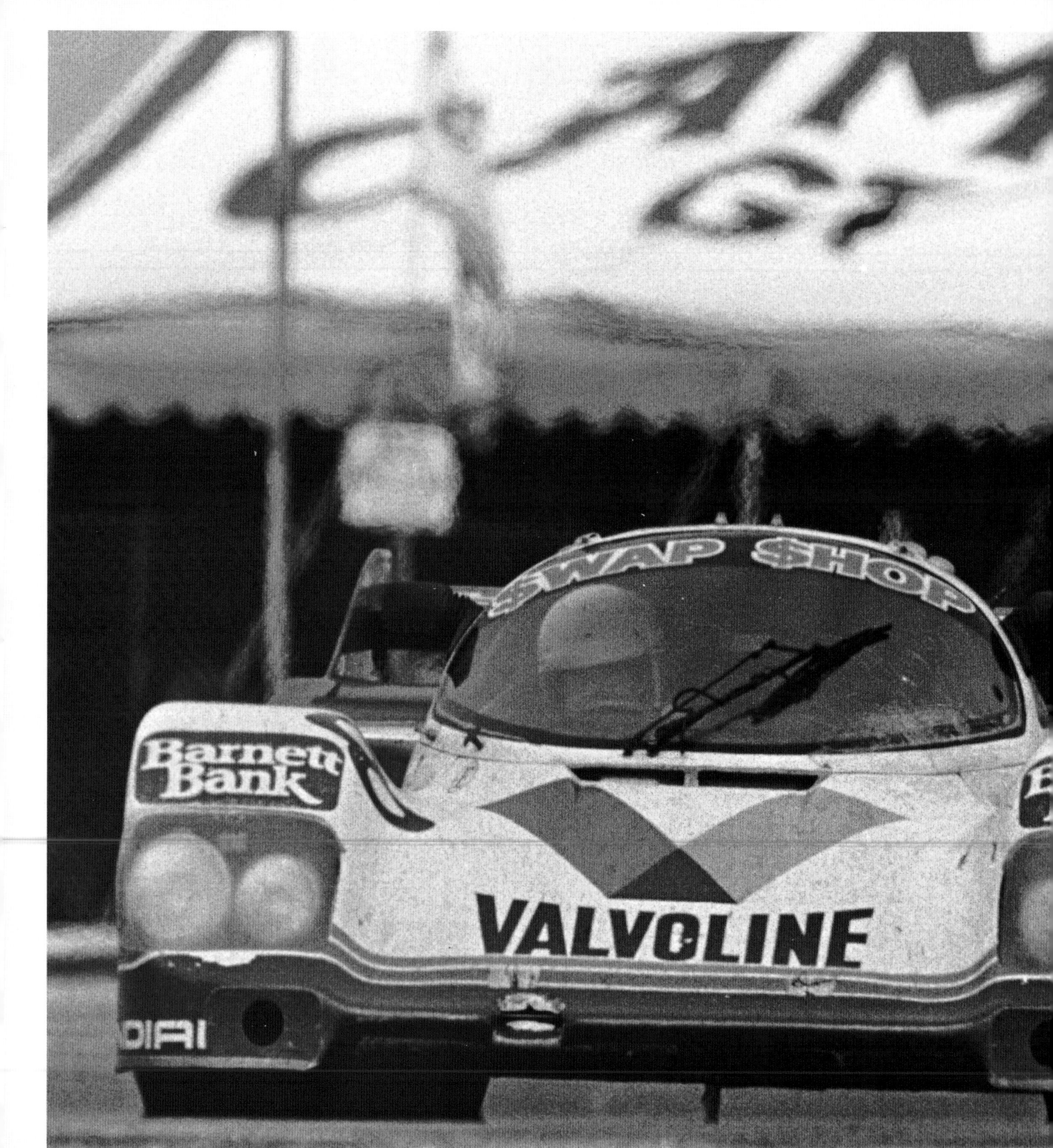
SWAP SHOP
Barnett Bank
VALVOLINE

the car was delivered race-ready, however, Young and his team, led by crew chief Clayton Cunningham, changed their minds.

"I think I've won 30 major races and three championships, and the Daytona trophy sits right in the center of my trophy room at home," said Baldwin in a 2002 interview. "I'm proud of that. It was hard, it was tough, I had to earn that race, I had to race hard to get that one. I didn't have anything in those days, and I kept telling myself, when you've got nothing, you've got nothing to lose: Drive. Everyone else was running a pace, for 24 hours, and I was absolutely jamming it. We fell 12 laps behind, but worked hard and got it back."

Dan Gurney entered a pair of Toyota Celicas in the GTU class. Wally Dallenbach Jr., who would be a rookie in the 1984 Trans-Am competition, shared the wheel with Dennis Aase and Michael Chandler, with the car sidelined after 49 laps. Chris Cord and Jim Adams had better luck in the second car, completing 292 laps.

The 1984 race marked the first—and only—appearance of the Porsche 928 in a professional racing event in the United States. The car was shipped to Daytona by the Porsche factory along with the 962, and the Brumos team fielded it in the race. Veterans Vic Elford and Richard Attwood co-drove with Howard Meister and Bob Hagestad, finishing 15th overall and fourth in GTO.

Above: Graham Duxbury, Tony Martin, and Sarel van der Merwe celebrate their triumph in victory lane. The South African trio won the race by nine laps. Opposite left: Martin (left) and Duxbury relax behind their pit stall. Opposite right: A pensive A. J. Foyt in the Preston Henn pits. The four-time Indianapolis 500 winner was seeking his second consecutive Daytona 24 Hours victory, teamed with Bob Wollek and Derek Bell. The Valvoline Swap Shop Porsche 935 finished second, nine laps behind.

$WAP $HOP
Barnett
Bank
VALVOLINE

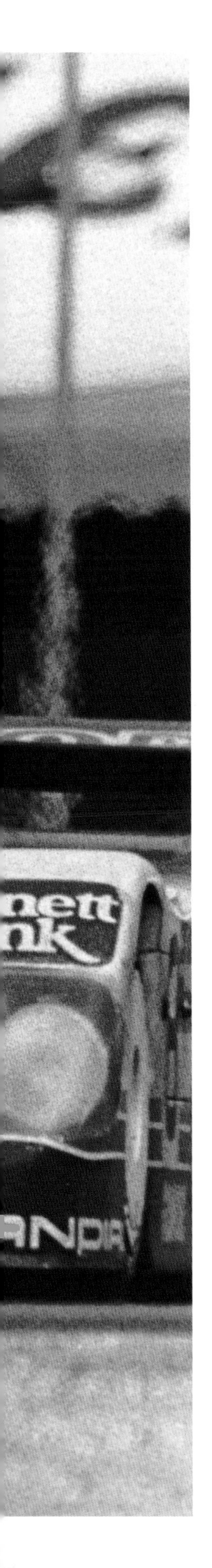

1985: Father vs. Son, Husband vs. Wife

For 1985, the 962 was the car of choice for the leading Porsche teams, with six cars driven by all-star lineups. At that time, there were only eight Porsche 962s in the world.

Preston Henn had upgraded to the Porsche 962, with Valvoline sponsorship and drivers Bob Wollek, A. J. Foyt, and Al Unser. Al Holbert piloted his Lowenbrau Special Porsche 962, joined by Derek Bell and Al Unser Jr., who had won his first CART Champ Car race in 1984.

Bruce Leven co-drove his Bayside Disposal 962 with Henri Pescarolo and Thierry Boutsen. Bob Akin shared his bright-red Coca-Cola 962 with Formula One veteran Hans Stuck, and another endurance-racing legend, Jochen Mass, and veterans Pete Halsmer and John Morton led Jim Busby's two-car BFGoodrich entry.

Seven Porsche 935s were also on hand, but for the first time since 1977, none of them were considered contenders. Akin fielded a Porsche 935 for Jim Mullen, Ray McIntyre, and Kees Nierop. Campaigning Akin's old 935—the car that finished second in 1982—was ex–NFL player Chuck Kendall, whose son Tommy would become an IMSA front-runner.

The sentimental favorite was Group 44. The team finished one-two in the 1984 Grand Prix of Miami and led the 24 Hours of Le Mans. However, Group 44 was still looking for a breakthrough victory at Daytona. Bob Tullius brought a pair of Jaguar XJR-5s, one for himself, Brian Redman, and Hurley Haywood, and a second car for Chip Robinson and Claude Ballot-Lena.

Boosting the Camel GT Prototype entry were eight Marches. The defending

Left: The Preston Henn Valvoline Porsche 962 of Al Unser, A. J. Foyt, Bob Wollek, and Thierry Boutsen scored a 17-lap victory in the 1985 SunBank 24 at Daytona. Above: In victory lane (left to right) are Preston Henn, Al Unser, crew chief Mike Colucci, Bob Wollek, A. J. Foyt, and Thierry Boutsen.

SunBank 24 winners, the Kreepy Krauly team, returned with former Formula One driver Ian Scheckter (brother of 1979 Formula One World Champion Jody) paired with Sarel van der Merwe and Tony Martin in their Porsche-powered entry. Twins Al and Art Leon entered a pair of Marches, with drivers including Randy Lanier, the defending IMSA champion, and Bill Whittington. There were a pair of Buick-powered versions, including one owned by Phil Conte with lead driver John Paul Jr., and another driven by 1983 NASCAR Winston Cup champion Bobby Allison.

Also among the prototypes were a Chevrolet-powered Lola, driven by defending NASCAR Winston Cup champion Terry Labonte, and a Ford Argo for Lyn St. James.

The road-course layout at the speedway had been changed to accommodate an infield road system. The Pedro Rodriguez International Horseshoe was altered, which shortened the course length from 3.84 to 3.56 miles.

John Paul Jr. won the pole in the Conte March with a record lap of 1:41.490, 126.278 mph. He had recently been charged on four counts of conspiracy and racketeering in conjunction with his father's drug-smuggling operation, and released on $125,000 bail. In January, Paul Sr. had been arrested

in Switzerland, where he had fled before his 1983 trial for attempted murder. The majority of the competitors were sympathetic to the younger Paul's plight, knowing he was caught in a family connection. He seemed resigned to his fate and prepared to accept the consequences, but he hoped to continue racing.

"I haven't been proven guilty yet," Paul told Godwin Kelly of the *Daytona Beach Morning Journal*. "When I'm in the race car, I can shove all this behind me and concentrate on racing."

But there was little sympathy for defending IMSA champion Randy Lanier, who co-drove Al Leon's

Above left: Charles Morgan, Bill Alsup, and Jim Miller finished 17th in their battered Buick Royale. Above right: A pit stop for the Rusty Jones Mazda Argo of Don and Kelly Marsh and Ron Pawley, en route to a 10th-place finish and first in the new Camel Lights category. Opposite: The No. 67 BFGoodrich Porsche 962 recovered from this spin to finish third, with Jochen Mass, Rick Knoop, and car owner Jim Busby at the wheel.

No. 1 Porsche March 85G with Bill Whittington. Rumors swirled around the paddock about the source of funding for Lanier's team. Confirmation came when Lanier was later arrested and imprisoned for drug smuggling and possession.

Van der Merwe qualified the Kreepy Krauly Porsche second fastest, making it an all-Porsche-powered front row. March appeared to be holding its own with the Porsche 962, but in reality, its days as a GTP front-runner were numbered.

NASCAR's Allison passed 14 cars on the opening lap after the 3:30 p.m. start, but had to pit only two laps later because he couldn't find the correct switches in the cockpit of his Buick March.

Paul took the lead, while the Kreepy Krauly March struggled with fuel pickup problems. Al Holbert took the lead following pit stops, chased by the Group 44 Jaguar of Brian Redman.

Bob Tullius was driving the Group 44 Jaguar in second place at 10:30 p.m., when it erupted in a ball of fire on the backstretch driving out of the chicane. The fire was quickly extinguished, and Tullius escaped with burns on his right hand. "The tire let go and took the oil line with it, and there was fire all around me," said Tullius. "Until then, the car was running fine and was obviously competitive."

Al Unser was racing for the first time at night, a fact that even surprised his son. The younger Unser's team had built up a 12-lap lead over the Henn Porsche. Both Foyt and Wollek were suffering from the flu, forcing Henn to call on Thierry Boutsen, who was available following the retirement of the Bayside Porsche. Boutsen and Wollek shared the driving during the night, under orders from team manager Mike Colucci to run a fast pace. Also running with the leaders was the Busby Porsche of Jochen Mass, Rick Knoop, and Busby, but it fell back with exhaust problems.

At 7:30 a.m., the Holbert team had its first sign of trouble with clogged fuel filters. At the time, it wasn't considered major. At 10 a.m., Bell reported having no fuel pressure when he went to full power. When he let off the power, fuel pressure would build back up. Bell pitted and the team replaced the fuel filter. Holbert felt he had corrected the problem.

At 12:20 p.m., Unser Jr. pitted after he "barely tapped" a backmarker, the first close call of the race for the leading Lowenbrau Porsche. During the stop, the team blew out the fuel filter and fuel lines. "I don't think it's a problem," Unser said after getting out of the car.

The car continued to struggle on the high-speed banking, however, and the Henn team continued to cut into the lead. While relations between the two teammates may have been strained prior to the event, dating back to their 1983 victory, and though both men were ailing from the flu, Foyt and Wollek rose to the occasion. Foyt handed Wollek his helmet and gloves as the Frenchman prepared to run down the leader in the final two-hour shift of the race. While the men were very different, they shared the same attitude.

"There was no thought of finishing second," Foyt said after the race. "We all agreed to go for broke. We all agreed Bob could run faster and not abuse the car, so we put him in the car for the final two hours. We made a decision to make it or break it. Bob knew what we had to do to win the race."

Though Holbert had his fuel problems fixed, the car continued to lose power, especially on the banking. With the Foyt/Wollek Porsche closing the once wide margin, Holbert's team replaced the voltage box, strapping it in. In a hurry to get back out, Bell fired up the car, left the pits, and quickly got back to speed. However, the box soon came loose and the 962 came to a stop in the chicane.

Bell restarted the car and it seemed to be running fine, so the crew waved him through when he came down pit road. But the car stopped again in the first superspeedway turn. Wollek drove by the

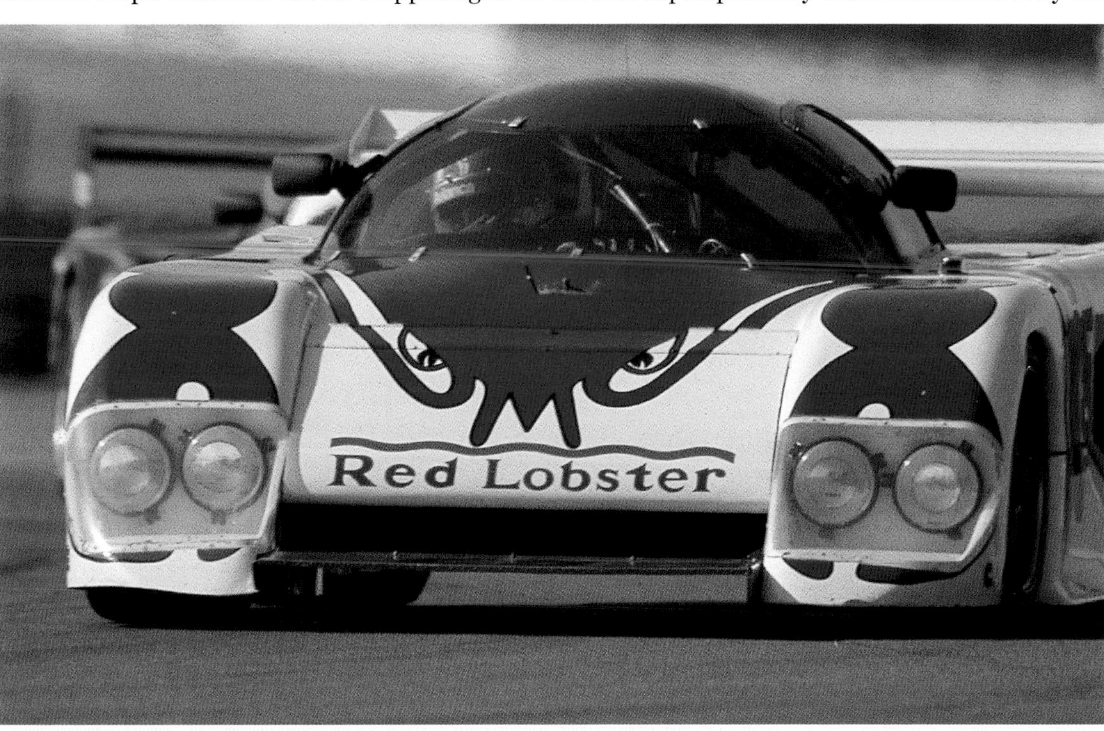

Above: Kenper Miller and David Cowart—joined by Mauricio de Narvaez—returned with the Red Lobster Chevrolet March. An accident sidelined the car after 92 laps. Right: Robin McCall had the opportunity to race against her future husband, Wally Dallenbach Jr., in the Folger's Coffee Camaro she co-drove with Joe Ruttman and Gary Baker. Far right: Bobby Allison, in the No. 3 Buick March, leads a group of cars in the early going. After passing 14 cars on the opening lap, Allison pitted because he was unfamiliar with the switches on the prototype.

crippled car to take the lead. Bell was running laps in the two-minute range before the box was replaced, but afterward his times dropped to the 1:49 range.

"We were going as fast as them after we made the change," Holbert said. "We wouldn't have been caught. We didn't replace it thoroughly, I guess."

"With two hours to go we knew we were picking up 10 seconds per lap on the leaders," Wollek said. "We knew then we were going to win. What we didn't know is they were going to have to stop. Two years ago, we had it all our way. This one was a little different."

The winning Porsche completed 703 laps, 2,505.680 miles, averaging 104.162 mph. Foyt, Wollek, Unser, and Boutsen won by 17 laps, erasing what had been a 13-lap deficit to the second-place Holbert

Porsche in the closing hours. Wollek finished the race severely dehydrated and consumed an enormous amount of Gatorade in victory lane.

Taking third, 29 laps behind the winner, was the BFGoodrich team of Mass/Knoop/Busby. "The only problem was when an exhaust pipe came apart," Mass said. "The car was turning laps as fast as anyone after that."

Was that frustrating?

"No," smiled Mass, "that's 24-hour racing, that's not frustrating at all. Frustrating is what happened to Derek Bell."

Giving Porsche 962s a sweep of the top four was Bob Akin's squad, led by Hans Stuck, co-driving with Akin and Paul Miller. Placing fifth, and carrying Ralph Lauren Polo sponsorship, was Akins's Porsche 935, driven by Mullen/McIntyre/Nierop.

Akin finished the race with a nosepiece borrowed from the Bayside team. "I'm delighted," said Akin after the race. "Even if we didn't have any problems, we couldn't have done any better. This is probably where we would have ended up. The 935 [which finished fifth] went perfectly. It shows the 935 can still do well in some races."

The 1985 race saw a pair of winning streaks begin in the GT ranks. Drag-racing veteran Jack Roush began sports car racing in 1984 in the SCCA Trans-Am Championship, and competed in a limited number of IMSA GTO races, enjoying success in both series. He campaigned Mercury Capris in Trans-Am, but entered a pair of Ford Mustangs in the SunBank 24.

Charlie Selix and Gary Pratt partnered with Roush on the Roush Protofab effort. Wally Dallenbach Jr., John Jones, and Doc Bundy took the class honors, winning by 38 laps. The second team entry was put on the class pole by African-American sensation Willy T. Ribbs. The converted Trans-Am Capri had a brake rotor shatter at 1 a.m., putting Ribbs into the wall at 150 mph. He escaped uninjured. The victory began a nine-year winning streak for Roush.

Roush entered his first Daytona 24 Hours with high expectations—and a solid plan to achieve his lofty goals.

"I was pretty ambitious," Roush admitted in a 2002 interview. "I wanted to sit on the pole, lead every lap, and win the race if I could. I read the rule book, and it said we couldn't change the engine. I wanted to get the pole, so I brought the car down with the engine organized for two sets of cylinder heads, two camshafts, and ran the engine as a qualifying engine to start with. We won the pole. Then we took the engine out of the car, disassembled it on the bench by sitting it on end, changed the camshaft, changed the cylinder heads, put it back in and went out and won the race.

"We kicked their butts, and that was fun. We had a great race car, and we basically smoked them," Dallenbach said in a 2002 interview. "Roush's effort really set the bar on what was to come in the next year. I won a lot of races with Jack here in the 24 Hours. He really knew his stuff when it came to endurance racing. His secret was just preparation."

Selix had called rival GTO car owner Gary Baker's team on Sunday morning to find out when Robin McCall would be racing in Baker's Camaro. He sent out Dallenbach—McCall's fiancé—to race against her. McCall, who met Dallenbach in 1984, had briefly raced in the NASCAR Winston Cup Series.

"I kicked her butt," recalled Dallenbach with a smile. "I remember following her for three laps. She wasn't afraid to wheel it; she had that thing sliding all over the place. However, we had a much better race car. Equipment to equipment, she didn't have a chance."

Amos Johnson's Team Highball Mazda RX-7 began a four-year winning streak in the GTU class. It also was the third class victory for Yojiro Terada, who won GTU in 1979 and GTO in 1981, both in factory RX-7s.

1985

Dan Gurney's All American Racers Toyota team seemed headed for the GTU class victory, only to have the transmission fail, which left the car stranded out on course. Dennis Aase and Chris Cord loaded a spare transmission, jackstands, and tools on an ATV and drove out to change it, which took nearly three hours.

Top: Bob Wollek in the winning Valvoline Porsche 962 and the third-place BFGoodrich 962 take the checkered flag at the conclusion of the 1985 24 Hours of Daytona. Above: In the final glory for the Porsche 935, Bob Akin's now-silver No. 7 finished fifth, driven by Jim Mullen, Kees Nierop, and Ray McIntyre. Within the year, the venerable model would be absent from Camel GT competition. Right: (left to right) Doc Bundy, Wally Dallenbach, and John Jones pose in front of their winning Roush Mustang. Car owner Jack Roush is behind Dallenbach's left shoulder. For the next decade, his team would make winning this class an annual occurance.

Among the GTU competitors was Scott Pruett, who made his Daytona sports car debut in a Mazda RX-7. It was only the fourth sports car race for Pruett, who had competed approximately 20 times at Daytona in go-karts.

The race featured a fourth Camel GT class, Camel Lights. The class, suggested and named by Mazda proponent Jim Downing, showcased smaller and less-powerful versions of the GTP Prototypes. Don Marsh won the first race for the new class in a Mazda-Argo that he'd bought from Downing.

Emerson Fittipaldi, a former Formula One World Champion, was entered in a Buick March, but was scratched on the Thursday prior to the race because the car was not ready.

To run at the front for much of the 24 Hours and not win can be an unexpectedly emotional experience for competitors. "I left the speedway in tears," said Unser Jr., recalling his second-place finish. "I was crushed. We led nearly the whole race and lost. I talked my dad into racing, and he won. I couldn't get out of there fast enough. My car was stopped in traffic, so I pulled to the side of the road and walked back to the hotel, in tears."

14
LÖWENBRÄU
Special

1986: A Reversal of Roles

The 1986 SunBank 24 began as an endurance race, but ended with the intensity of a sprint. It would be a see-saw battle over the closing hours, as the three Porsche teams battled not only each other, but various mechanical problems. The result would be the closest finish to date in the history of the race.

Al Holbert returned with the same drivers he had in 1985, when electrical gremlins cost the Lowenbrau Special Porsche 962 of Holbert, Derek Bell, and Al Unser Jr. the victory. Henn brought A. J. Foyt to drive his Swap Shop Porsche 962, joined by defending Indianapolis 500-winner Danny Sullivan and 1985 Indy 500 Rookie of the Year Arie Luyendyk.

Jim Busby fielded a pair of BFGoodrich Porsche 962s. He co-drove one of them with Jochen Mass and Darrin Brassfield, while Jan Lammers, John Morton, and Derek Warwick piloted the second car.

Bob Tullius had upgraded the Group 44 entry to the Jaguar XJR-7, a totally redesigned car that was only cosmetically similar to the XJR-5. Tullius co-drove with Claude Ballot-Lena and Chip Robinson, with Brian Redman joined by Vern Schuppan and Hurley Haywood in the second XJR-7.

A new entry was a Corvette owned by NASCAR Winston Cup car owner Rick Hendrick and driven by 1984 SunBank 24 winner Sarel van der Merwe,

Left: The No. 14 Lowenbrau Special Porsche 962 of Al Holbert, Derek Bell, and Al Unser Jr. leads the March of John Paul Jr. during evening action. While two lengthy stops seemingly put the team out of contention, they went on to win the race by less than two minutes. Above: Sarel van der Merwe put the No. 52 GM Goodwrench Corvette GTP on the pole, but the car developed an oil leak in pre-race warmups and was withdrawn prior to the start of the event.

Wally Dallenbach Jr., and Doc Bundy. Van der Merwe put the GM Goodwrench Corvette GTP on the pole, but the car fell victim to a vibration during morning warm-ups and was scratched from the race prior to the 3:34 p.m. green flag.

"The car ran normally during warmups, but then we discovered an oil leak," recalled crew chief Ken Howes. "The way those cars were built, we had to remove everything from underneath the car to get a look at the engine. It turned out that the engine block had cracked, and we had no time to change the engine."

Just by making it to the speedway, however, the Corvette had better fortunes than the new BMW GTP, which had lost a car in a test at Road Atlanta on the previous Tuesday. The car was destroyed by fire, but driver John Andretti escaped without injuries.

"This was going to be my first race at Daytona," said Andretti, nephew of Mario Andretti. "It was sad for the entire team. We worked real hard to get to this stage, but with a team like this, it was only a minor setback."

Two Porsche 962s were parked by sunset: the Joest entry of Gianpiero Moretti/Randy Lanier/Paolo Barilla with a broken distributor rotor, and the Brun entry of Thierry Boutsen/Oscar Larrauri/Massimo Sigala with electrical problems.

Hans Stuck crashed Bob Akin's Coca-Cola Porsche 962 early in the race, and the Bayside Disposal Porsche 962 of Bob Wollek/Derek Daly/Bruce Leven tangled at sunset with a slower machine on the banking. The second BFGoodrich Porsche 962 of Jochen Mass/Jan Lammers/John Morton fell out of contention after a 55-minute stop for clutch repairs, then crashed on Sunday morning.

"We had some trouble with the brakes earlier," recalled Lammers. "Then, early on Sunday morning in turn four after the dogleg, I couldn't stop the car, and found out the hard way that the

Above left: John Paul Jr. posted the fastest lap of the race in Phil Conte's Buick Hawk, but the car he shared with Chip Ganassi dropped out of the event early while running in the top three. Above right: The field forms for the start of the 1986 SunBank 24. Up front are a trio of Porsche 962s—the Joest entry of Paolo Barilla (No. 0), the Bayside car of Bob Wollek (No. 86), and the Dyson Porsche of Price Cobb. Opposite: A nighttime stop for the No. 8 Valvoline Porsche 962, co-driven by A. J. Foyt, Danny Sullivan, Arie Luyendyk, and Preston. The team held a 22-lap lead, only to lose due to a sticking throttle.

A. J. Foyt
D. Sullivan
A. Luyendyk
SWAP SHOP
VALVOLINE

Armco barrier *could* stop the car. It was one of my biggest accidents, but that was the race for us."

Both of Bob Tullius' Group 44 Jaguar XJR-7s struggled with various suspension and transmission troubles resulting from drivetrain overload, due to the stiffer chassis. John Paul Jr. posted the fastest lap of the race in Phil Conte's Buick Hawk, 125.011 mph, but the car he shared with Chip Ganassi bowed out while running in the top three. The second Conte Buick, driven by Whitney Ganz, Ken Madren, and Bob Lobenberg, also dropped out early.

Rob Dyson's Porsche 962, which he shared with Price Cobb and Drake Olson for his Daytona 24 Hours debut, held an early lead, but lost time Saturday evening after a brush with another Porsche 962. Early Sunday morning the engine failed, and another 962 was out.

The Holbert team discovered a crack in the left-rear brake line on Saturday evening and lost five laps replacing it, dropping to 15th place. The team then suffered mechanical problems just before dawn, a throttle cable that broke while Unser Jr. was driving. The stop seemingly took the Lowenbrau Porsche out of contention, 22 laps behind the Preston Henn Porsche, which led over the remaining Busby 962.

"I thought we weren't going to win," Unser told *On Track*'s Jonathan Ingram. "But [crew chief] Tom Seabolt calmed me down. He talked to me on the radio and said to take it easy."

Above left: Sunrise found Al Holbert's No. 14 Lowenbrau Special Porsche 962 in third place and seemingly out of contention, 22 laps behind the leader. Above right: Before Daytona International Speedway added lighting in the late 1990s, drivers had to rely solely on their headlights during the nighttime hours. Opposite left: Headlights blaze a trail of light heading to the start/finish line in a time-lapse photograph. Opposite right: After suffering a heartbreaking defeat in 1985, Al Holbert, Derek Bell, and Al Unser Jr. rallied for a come-from-behind triumph in the 1986 SunBank 24.

At the time, Holbert seemed to share Unser's pessimism. "It's a long race, and a lot of things can happen," said a reporter, trying to console the disappointed driver. Holbert just glared.

However, both the Henn and Busby teams later experienced mechanical problems of their own. The Busby team broke a half-shaft, dropping it from a brief turn in front. Hurting the team in the closing hours was a broken seat, which the crew tried to repair by stuffing sweaters and jackets into the cockpit. Compounding the problem were a lost cylinder late in the race, fading brakes, and a loose nosepiece.

"We were just sitting nine laps in the lead and feeling OK, and last night we were down by 15," Brassfield said, after getting out of the Busby car with four hours remaining. "That shows you anything can happen. Right now, I'll just be happy to finish."

Henn's team lost the lead on a succession of three pit stops. The crew replaced a loose banjo fitting underneath the car that was causing an oil leak and had to pit again moments later to replace the turbocharger wastegate.

"I knew they had an oil problem because when I was racing Sullivan earlier this morning, he

was oiling me," Busby said. "So, I raced him harder and harder. Every time he'd shift, I'd see a wisp of oil."

The Henn team decided to take advantage of their huge lead to fix a sticking throttle. "We lost eight laps, and we didn't really get it repaired," Sullivan said in a post-race press conference. "I guess we should have just stayed out there. The throttle-sticking problem was our downfall."

The stop enabled Holbert to catch up and win by one minute and 49 seconds over Foyt. This was the first time that the top two cars finished on the lead lap of the Daytona 24 Hours. Busby's entry took third, only one lap down, and 10 seconds behind the Henn Porsche.

"We had trouble all night long," Bell said. "I didn't think we would ever regain the lead, to be honest."

It was also the fastest running of the Daytona 24 Hours, with the team of Holbert, Derek Bell, and Al Unser Jr. completing 712 laps—2,534.72 miles—and averaging 105.484 mph.

"With Al [Holbert], that was spectacular. We should have won it a few more times, too," recalled Bell in a recent interview. "To drive for Al Holbert was the ultimate, because he was not only the greatest

technical guy I've ever worked with, but he was also a fabulous man and one of the best drivers I've ever driven with. To drive with Al, you knew you were looking in good shape. Al would always do the setup, because that was his passion, his expertise, so Al would set it up and I'd just drive it, and we had good teamwork.

"I don't think we need to walk with our heads down," Foyt said after the race. "I think everyone knew we were here. My biggest problem here was blisters. My hands are like raw meat, and they've hurt for seven hours."

Placing sixth, and fourth in the GTP class, was the Jaguar XJR-7 of Tullius, Robinson, and Ballot-Lena, which had lost an hour for repairs. The second Group 44 Jag, piloted by Redman, Haywood, and Schuppan, failed to finish because of engine problems.

Jack Roush and Amos Johnson both won their respective GT classes for the second straight year. Roush's car, prepared for Lanny Hester, Maurice Hassey, and Lee Mueller, placed fourth overall to

claim the GTO class, finishing one position ahead of heralded teammates Scott Pruett, Olympian Bruce Jenner, and Klaus Ludwig. The latter trio built up a 90-lap lead, only to lose it all late Sunday morning on a long stop to repair an oil leak.

"We dominated for 23 1/2 hours, and it's a 24-hour race," said Jenner. "It was fun. We did our best. Sometimes, you can't help having a mechanical failure."

Roush also fielded a car for NASCAR Winston Cup regulars Bill Elliott, Ken Schrader, Kyle Petty, and Ricky Rudd, but the team dropped out at midnight with mechanical trouble. Also representing

Top: NASCAR Winston Cup stars Ken Schrader, Bill Elliott, Kyle Petty, and Ricky Rudd co-drove Jack Roush's No. 50 Folger's Ford Mustang. While an accident sidelined the car, another Roush car went on to capture GTO honors for the second straight year. Above left: A pit stop on the No. 14 Lowenbrau Special Porsche 962. Two extended stops seemingly dropped the team out of contention. Above right: The A. J. Foyt–led No. 8 Valvoline Porsche 962 passes the No. 76 Corvette of Greg Walker underneath the infield scoreboard and message board. The team led throughout much of the event, only to experience problems in the final hours. Opposite: Derek Bell, Jean Liles (Miss Camel), Al Unser Jr., and Al Holbert celebrate their victory. Kevin Doran is visible standing behind Holbert.

NASCAR was the Skoal Bandit Oldsmobile of Harry Gant, Phil Parsons, and Terry Labonte, which stopped racing after only three laps. Indy 500 veteran Pancho Carter co-drove Buz McCall's Skoal Bandit Camaro with Tom Sheehy and Jim Mueller, but also failed to finish.

Amos Johnson's Team Highball captured the GTU title for the second year running. Joining Johnson were Dennis Shaw and Jack Dunham in the Team Highball Mazda RX-7, which placed eighth overall.

Second in the class, and 10th overall, was Clayton Cunningham's Mazda RX-7, driven by Tom Kendall, Bob Reed, and John Hogdal. The CCR Mazda was the surprise of the race, running as high as fourth overall before the rotary engine failed. Crew chief Dan Binks managed to rebuild the rotary powerplant, only to have the engine let go in the final turn on the final lap, stranding Kendall in sight of the checkered flag. Cunningham was crew chief on Jack Baldwin's 1985 GTU championship team, and bought the car from owner Ira Young following the season.

Ray Mummery, Frank Rubino, and John Schneider took Camel Lights honors in a new Mazda JM Argo 19. Racing under the Outlaw Racing banner, they finished seventh overall.

"It was the loudest car I've ever driven," said Mummery. "I couldn't hear for nearly a week after the race, but I didn't care that much. It's the dream for an amateur driver to win a major race, and that was a very special day."

SHOEI
GOODYEAR
SPEEDWAY
INDUSTRIES

1987: Coming Through in Clutch

AFTER WINNING IN 1986, AL HOLBERT RETURNED TO DAYTONA AS TEAM MANAGER FOR HIS LOWENBRAU SPECIAL 962 TEAM. HE ASSEMBLED DRIVERS DEREK BELL, CHIP ROBINSON, AND AL UNSER JR., AND ADDED HIMSELF AS FOURTH DRIVER AS A PRECAUTION.

"I love to drive, but four drivers is too many," Holbert said on the eve of the race. "I don't want to jump in at seven or eight in the morning after the other guys worked so hard to be there. But after all, I have to wear a driver suit anyway, so we'll wait and see what happens. I'll only drive if something happens." New IMSA rules mandated Nomex fire-retardant uniforms for crewmen.

Once again, A. J. Foyt shaped up as Holbert's top challenger. For the fifth straight year, he played a major role in the drama, joined by co-drivers Al Unser and Danny Sullivan. For 1987, Foyt was also a car owner, fielding a new Porsche 962 that carried No. 1 and sponsorship from Columbia Crest wines and Brumos Porsche. Brumos's Bob Snodgrass was team manager.

Jim Busby, who had placed third behind Holbert and Foyt the previous two years, again entered his BFGoodrich Porsche 962, co-driving with Bob Wollek and Darin Brassfield. Bruce Leven co-drove his Bayside Disposal Porsche 962 with Klaus Ludwig and Jochen Mass. Bob Tullius shared his Group 44 Jaguar XJR-7 with John Morton and Hurley Haywood. Rick Hendrick returned with his GTP Goodwrench Corvette for Sarel van der Merwe and Doc Bundy.

Left: Price Cobb (left), Vern Schuppan, and team manager Pat Smith confer with team owner Rob Dyson, who is set to return his Porsche 962 to the race following a pit stop. The team finished a solid third place. Above: Brothers Tommy (foreground) and Bobby Archer (second from right) relax prior to the start in the tri-oval grass, joined by co-driver Robert Lappalainen and car owner Brooks Fryberger (far right).

The race also featured two Ford V-8-powered prototypes fielded by different teams. Jack Roush tested the GTP waters with the Applicon Mustang for Pete Halsmer and Scott Pruett. Also competing was a Zakspeed Probe for David Hobbs, Whitney Ganz, and Gianpiero Moretti. Roush used a carbureted engine, while Zakspeed opted for fuel injection.

The BMW GTP had won the 1986 fall round at Watkins Glen International, with Davy Jones and John Andretti at the wheel, but the team had folded. Also missing from Daytona were the Nissan and Conte Buick teams.

Mass put Leven's Bayside Disposal Porsche on the pole with a lap of 126.885 mph, and was joined on the front row by the Busby Porsche. Foyt's "dream team" qualified eighth, two positions ahead of the Holbert entry.

Ludwig started the Bayside Porsche and led the opening 10 laps after the 3:34 p.m. green flag. Van der Merwe managed to lead four circuits, but fell back and retired with a broken valve train. The Bayside car regained control and led throughout the next four hours. Then Ludwig encountered trouble.

"I was taking the high line on the banking, passing a couple cars, and one of the idiots came up and hit me in the rear," recalled Ludwig. "I had nowhere to go."

"This cost us the race," Leven added in disgust.

1987

Problems hobbled many of the other front runners as well. The Jaguar XJR-7 of Bob Tullius, John Morton, and Hurley Haywood ran as high as second before exiting with a blown head gasket and related problems. Valve failure also sidelined the Busby BFGoodrich Porsche. The Roush GTP retired with rear suspension problems, while engine failure felled the Zakspeed Probe.

Above left: 1987 marked the last competitive outing for the No. 44 Group 44 Jaguar XJR-7. Bob Tullius, Hurley Haywood, and John Morton ran as high as second before exiting with a blown head gasket. Above right: Bill Elliott waits patiently behind the wheel while the Roush Racing pit crew performs right-front suspension repairs during a stop. Elliott returned to the race and joined Tom Gloy, Scott Pruett, and Lyn St. James in giving Roush his third consecutive GTO victory. Opposite: Walter Brun's Torno Porsche 962 is serviced on pit road. Oscar Larrauri, Gianfranco Brancatelli, and Massimo Sigala teamed to finish second, eight laps behind the winners.

As attrition thinned the ranks, a terrific battle shaped up between the same two teams that had fought it out in 1985 and 1986: Foyt and Holbert. The Foyt Porsche had a slight edge in horsepower, running the 3.0-liter engine compared to Holbert's 2.8-liter, but the Lowenbrau Special was dominant in the infield sections of the circuit.

Sunday morning, Holbert's Porsche was running perfectly. They had lost the driver's side window, however, which caused hot air to blow into the car, and the drivers were exhausted by the heat. Always prepared, Holbert didn't have to look very far for his helmet.

"Al wasn't supposed to drive in that race," recalled Kevin Doran, Holbert's crew chief. "It was just going to be the three guys, Derek, Chip, and Al Jr., but we had some fumes in the cockpit, and all three of them overheated. Al got in the car that morning and did some relief driving, and we won by eight laps."

"The cockpit was really hot. The only air coming in was hot," explained Al Unser Jr. "I started missing corners and not thinking clearly. My dad once told me these cars were fun to drive when everything is working well. But when it's not, Hercules couldn't drive one of these cars."

With Unser struggling, and the Foyt car gaining ground, Holbert decided to take a turn at the wheel. He didn't have a choice, because Robinson and Bell were still recovering from their last driving shifts.

"I was in the motor home Sunday morning and I couldn't even pull my racing underwear on, I

had such terrible cramps from dehydration with two or three hours to go," Bell recalled. "On one side of the motor home, Chip Robinson was being worked on by the medics, and I was at the other end with my wife. Every time I bent down, I got cramps. Little Al was in the car, so we could at least leave Little Al and Chip Robinson, the young guys on the team, to finish the race.

"Then, the next thing they said, Little Al was coming in early; he couldn't take it any more. I said 'Put Chip in,' and they said Chip's had it as well. So how can I do it at 45 when they're 25? So I said, 'You'll have to get Al [Holbert],' who was in the pits as team manager. Al said, 'I'll drive it if Derek

Above: The No. 14 Lowenbrau Special Porsche 962 needed late-race help from team manager Al Holbert to win its second consecutive 24 Hours of Daytona. Right: Dan Gurney moved up to the GTO ranks, with the No. 99 All American Racers Toyota Celica of Ricky Rudd, Juan Manuel Fangio II, and Jerrill Rice falling back in the closing hours with overheating problems.

will do the last stint.' So, that was it. I thought I had another 45 minutes to get myself together.

"Al got in the car and did a magnificent job as always," Bell continued, "but he came in early. The team came up to me after 25 minutes and said he's coming in four minutes. Despite all that cramping, I suddenly realized it came down to me, so I put on my underwear, did up my boots, put the suit on and ran from the motor home to the pit. That shows what the adrenaline did. I ran across, got in the car, and we continued to win the race." The Holbert team completed 753 laps, 2,680.68 miles, and averaged a record 111.499 mph.

The Foyt team ran second until withdrawing in the final hour with engine failure. The engine had a blown head gasket, which caused a main electrical wire to be torched in half. Instead of his third victory in five years, Foyt's fourth-place finish was his lowest showing over that period.

"Until about 20 minutes before the end, it was OK," said Sullivan. "But those things happen. It wasn't a 23-hour, 40-minute race, it was 24 hours, and we didn't make it. A. J. and Big Al were really fun to drive with, and all those 962s were fabulous cars to drive."

"If a guy says he's not tired now he didn't try very hard," said the elder Unser after the race. "I'm disappointed any time I break down. This was just a long race to break down in."

"It's heartbreaking for Dad to lose now after coming this far," said Unser Jr., who recalled leaving the track in tears in 1985 and vowing never to return. "If you break down early, it's no big deal. But, to come this far and lose is the biggest disappointment there is. This race really affects you. It's so far a distance, at the end, your emotions show. You're drained, physically and mentally—no, past drained."

The Walter Brun entry of Oscar Larrauri took advantage of Foyt's problems to take second, eight laps behind, as Porsche 962s swept the top six positions. The Brun team had lost 14 laps in the first hour, falling back to 54th position. But the team ran consistently the rest of the way, making up six of the laps they had lost. John Kalagian, an injured Camel GT veteran, oversaw the German team's U.S. efforts.

Third was the Dyson entry, followed by the Foyt car and the Wynn's Porsche 962 driven by Jim Adams and the father-son duo of John Hotchkiss Sr. and Jr. Placing sixth was Bob Akin's Coca-Cola

Porsche 962, with Englishman James Weaver joining Hans Stuck and Akin.

"We had an absolute blast," recalled Weaver. "The ring and pinion went, and it sounded like we were driving a Mazda, because the noise in the car was unbelievable. It was a fantastic team. Bob Akin was such a gentleman, and Hans Stuck was one of the all-time greats. To come to a big race like this with such a good team was a pretty good start, really."

Akin and Dyson were both New York businessmen, and were good friends. When Akin stopped GTP racing later that season, he asked Dyson if he had a place on his team for Weaver. Fifteen years later, Weaver would still be driving for Dyson Racing.

Two familiar teams won again in the GT ranks, although the GTO champions had to come from behind. NASCAR Winston Cup star Bill Elliott joined Scott Pruett, Tom Gloy, and Lyn St. James on the winning Roush GTO Ford Mustang, which took class honors for the third straight year. However, Ford took a back seat to Chevrolet and upstart Toyota for much of the race.

Chevrolet was represented by the two Protofab Camaros, with drivers Wally Dallenbach and John Jones joined by NASCAR Winston Cup champions Darrell Waltrip and Terry Labonte. The team was leading the race at the midway point, when the car lost a wheel after the wheel nut worked loose, with Labonte in the cockpit.

Dan Gurney moved his All American Racing Toyota Celicas from GTU to GTO competition, with a driver lineup that included NASCAR Winston Cup regular Ricky Rudd, Juan Manuel Fangio II (nephew and namesake of the five-time Formula One World Champion), and Jerrill Rice, plus Chris Cord and Steve Millen.

"I gave Dan a call and said I was interested in running this race car," Rudd said. "It reminded me of driving dirt bikes. This is my first time racing a turbocharged car, and it takes a little getting used to the power under your foot and working with the throttle lag."

The Cord/Millen Toyota led the class until the final 30 minutes, when the team lost time with a broken left-rear suspension upright. Their teammates ran third in the class until falling back in the final two hours with overheating troubles.

"There's so much pounding and miles that are put on these cars that to have a suspension component break is not unusual," said Cord. "But to have it break with only 30 minutes left, that's heartbreaking."

Pruett, who drove the GTO Mustang in addition to the Roush GTP entry, had a scare Sunday morning

Above: Mike Brockman and Steve Durst qualified 17th in their Pontiac Spice, but failed to finish with engine problems. Right: The Lowenbrau Special Porsche 962 team celebrates in victory lane for the second straight year. Left to right are Al Holbert, Derek Bell, Chip Robinson, and Al Unser Jr.

when the leading Foyt Porsche literally blew the nosepiece off his car, folding it into the windshield. The Roush team had a spare nose on hand and quickly returned Pruett to the race.

"We had our bad luck early, and they had their bad luck at the end of the race," said Elliott, who was two weeks away from scoring his second victory in the Daytona 500. "It's the breaks of the game."

Another streak continued in GTU, with Amos Johnson and Dennis Shaw joined by Bob Lazier to give the Team Highball Mazda RX-7 its third straight triumph. It also extended the Mazda RX-7 winning streak that began in 1979.

Clayton Cunningham's team again came up short, despite a change in strategy. "Last year, we broke late in the race and took second," said Tom Kendall, who co-drove with Max Jones. "This year we went more conservative than ever. We were coming off the banking and it went 'ffft!' We didn't lead until just before we went out."

Camel Lights honors went to Jeff Kline, Bob Earl, and Don Bell in a Pontiac Fiero-powered Spice. The car came to a halt on course with electrical failure, but Kline discovered a break in the primary ignition wire and repaired it on the track, allowing the car to continue after losing 20 minutes.

"There's a tool kit in the car, and John Collies of Pontiac told me over the radio what to look for, and I did it," said Kline, who scored his second class victory at Daytona. "I found the coil wire had vibrated off. I had to strip it, fix it, and drive the car back to the pits."

Augie Pabst, who first competed at Daytona in 1959 in a D-type Jaguar, raced in a Camel Lights Mazda Badger and finished 14th overall.

21

1988: New Team on the Block

There was a new team in IMSA Camel GT racing in 1988, TWR Jaguar. For years, Bob Tullius had fielded immaculately turned-out Jaguars for Camel GTP competition. Although they had scored nine victories, the championship and major races, including the Daytona 24 Hours and 24 Hours of Le Mans, eluded the Winchester, Virginia–based team.

For 1988, the English marque turned to its British operation, spearheaded by Tom Walkinshaw, who himself had competed in the 1976 Daytona 24 Hours as part of the BMW factory team.

Walkinshaw had built his own prototype in 1985, the Jaguar XJR-6, which tied for third with Porsche in 1986 Group C competition. He then ran away with the European championship in 1987, winning virtually everything except the 24 Hours of Le Mans. For 1988, TWR prepared a major assault to dominate on both continents. No cost was spared in fielding the best-looking, most competitive cars on the circuit, with perks that included catered meals and professional masseurs.

TWR entered a trio of sleek Jaguar XJR-9s for the 1988 Daytona 24 hours, prepared by Tony Dowe and driven by a formidable lineup that included Formula One veterans John Watson, Eddie Cheever, Jan Lammers, Martin Brundle, Raul Boesel, and Johnny Dumfries; Americans Davy Jones and Danny Sullivan; and sports-car-racing veteran John Nielsen.

Left: Side-by-side action on the high banks in the early evening hours of the 1988 SunBank 24 at Daytona. Above: Racing legend Parnelli Jones made his return to competition, co-driving Clayton Cunningham's No. 76 Mazda RX-7 with his son, P. J. Jones, and John Morton.

The team's pits were surrounded by a mountain of 1,000 Dunlop tires, including special night tires made with a softer compound than those used for daytime driving.

As usual, Porsche was well represented, with eight 962s looking to extend the marque's streak of 11 consecutive victories in the 24 Hours. Al Holbert was seeking to extend his personal streak to three straight triumphs in the Daytona classic. He was back in his capacity as a full-time driver, teamed

with Derek Bell and Chip Robinson in a Porsche 962 with gold Miller High Life livery.

Other top Porsche teams included A. J. Foyt, joined by Al Unser Jr. and Elliott Forbes-Robinson, and Jim Busby with Brian Redman, Bob Wollek, and Mauro Baldi. Bruce Leven withdrew from his driver lineup when Sarel van der Merwe showed up without a ride. That teamed the South African star with Klaus Ludwig and Hans Stuck in the Bayside car. Rob Dyson was joined by James Weaver, Price Cobb, and Vern Schuppan in another Porsche 962.

Group 44 fielded an XJR-7—which was now badged a Goodyear Eagle—driven by Bob Tullius, Hurley Haywood, and Whitney Ganz. It would be a sad farewell for the team that returned Jaguar to the big leagues of international sports car racing. The team qualified 10th, but Ganz would park the car after three and a half hours with a blown head gasket.

Tom Milner originally entered a pair of Ford GTPs, but only raced one, driven by Indy Car driver Arie Luyendyk, Olympian Bruce Jenner, Scott Goodyear, and Tom Gloy.

Mauro Baldi, making his first appearance in the Daytona 24 Hours, qualified Jim Busby's BFGoodrich Porsche 962 on pole with a lap of 129.563 mph. Price Cobb, in the Dyson 962, and Al Holbert pulled away at the start, with the Jaguars driving conservatively. Cobb led the opening 90 minutes and lapped all three Jaguars before losing fifth gear. At that point, Porsches held the top five positions.

Above left: A. J. Foyt's Porsche 962 was painted in Copenhagen's black and orange colors for 1988. Al Unser Jr. and Elliott Forbes-Robinson joined Foyt in an unsuccessful bid for his third Daytona 24 Hours triumph. The team finished sixth. Above right: A late-night altercation took the No. 22 Roush Merkur XR4Ti of Mark Martin, Lyn St. James, Deborah Gregg, and Scott Pruett out of the race after the car dominated the GTO action. Opposite: Al Holbert's Porsche 962 had new sponsorship and new colors for 1988, painted in Miller High Life gold. Above, the No. 14 of Holbert, Derek Bell, and Chip Robinson is in the pits for service.

Many expected TWR to send a rabbit, but the team chose to run a more conservative race. "Why do we need a rabbit?" Jaguar team manager Roger Stillman asked Bill Lovell from *AutoWeek*. "We have three good cars, so why take chances?"

Hans Stuck was leading the race in the Bayside car, but collided with the CCR Mazda RX-7 driven by Johnny Unser in the early evening, sending both cars to the garage for lengthy repairs. The Bayside Porsche later returned to the race, despite being many laps behind.

Holbert, Derek Bell, and Chip Robinson seemed poised to give the Holbert team its third consecutive victory, but turbocharger problems sidelined the leaders at 8:45 a.m. and resulted in a long stop that dropped them from the lead. Engine failure eventually finished the car, although it placed seventh.

The Jaguar of Davy Jones, Danny Sullivan, and Jan Lammers led briefly before retiring with engine problems, shortly after Bell pitted with turbocharger trouble. Then the Jag of Eddie Cheever, John Watson, and Johnny Dumfries led, until an encounter with the leading Busby Porsche driven by Brian Redman. The incident sent both cars to the pits.

Bob Wollek returned the Busby car to the lead, and went on to battle it out down the stretch with the third Jaguar, driven by Martin Brundle, Raul Boesel, and John Nielsen. It made for exciting racing, with the lead changing hands several times.

"This is one of the most incredible sprint races in IMSA history," said Busby during the closing stages of the event. "It's not that often that you see this many lead changes or cars running that close together in a one-and-a-half-hour race, let alone this far into a 24-hour race."

The Busby Porsche and Castrol Jaguar exchanged the lead eight times during the closing hours.

Castrol
Castrol
60
DUNLOP

With the Porsche closing, Walkinshaw decided not to take any chances. He inserted Lammers in place of Boesel in the driver lineup for a two-hour shift. Lammers responded with a brilliant drive. The public-address announcer, however, not knowing of the change, gave the credit to Boesel. Lammer's sidelined teammate was later voted the Norelco Cup by the media for being the outstanding driver in the race.

The fast pace took its toll on the Porsche. With one hour remaining, Baldi was running second, only 15 seconds behind, when he pitted with a cut tire, brake problems, and loose bodywork. The Jaguar went on to win by one lap and 54 seconds over the ailing Porsche, which finished the race minus a door.

The winning Jaguar completed 728 laps, 2,591.68 miles, and averaged 107.943 mph. It was Jaguar's first 24-hour race victory since the 1957 Le Mans event, and ended Porsche's 11-year winning streak in the 24 Hours of Daytona. The race featured 25 lead changes among seven cars.

"It was a very, very demanding and tiring race, and we had to fight the whole race, right up until the end," recalled Boesel in a 2002 interview. "I ran Daytona a few times, but, obviously, that was the one that gratified the most."

"Finishing third is not as good as winning," said Eddie Cheever, then the only American-born driver competing in Formula One. "We started having engine problems eight hours before the finish and stroked the last third of the race."

"Winning's everything," added Redman after the race. "Finishing second is nothing."

The Bayside Porsche of Hans Stuck, Klaus Ludwig, and Sarel van der Merwe battled back from its early incident to take fourth, 34 laps behind, followed by John Kalagian's Porsche 962, driven by Jim Rothbarth and brothers Bernard and Michel Jourdain.

A. J. Foyt's Copenhagen Porsche, which he shared with Al Unser Jr. and Elliott Forbes-Robinson, finished sixth, 53 laps behind, after suffering a crash and the loss of fifth gear. "We started out bad, and then it was one thing after another," said Foyt. "The Jaguars were tough, but they still had to beat us. They kind of backed into it—the Porsches had a lot of problems they normally don't have."

Taking ninth was the Dyson entry, 90 laps off the pace.

In GTO, Roush won for the fourth straight time with Scott Pruett, Paul Miller, Bobby Akin Jr., and Pete Halsmer, coming back from early troubles in a Merkur XR4Ti to triumph in a very competitive finish over Buz McCall's Skoal Camaro.

The Roush car pitted with a broken spark plug and sheared axle-drive pins only three hours into the race, and fell to 54th place, 34 laps behind. That put the team car of Lyn St. James, Deborah Gregg (widow of three-time Daytona 24 Hours winner Peter Gregg), Mark Martin (who would return to NASCAR Winston Cup racing two weeks later in the Daytona 500, driving for Jack Roush's new team), and Pruett into contention. However, their Roush Capri was eliminated when Pruett tangled with

Left: Sunday morning pit work for the eventual winning No. 60 Castrol Jaguar XJR-9 of Raul Boesel, Martin Brundle, John Neilsen, and Jan Lammers. While Lammers is not officially credited with a share in the victory, he drove a critical two-hour shift Sunday morning. Above: Early action in the 1988 SunBank 24 at Daytona, with the pole-winning No. 67 Jim Busby Porsche 962 of Mauro Baldi and the No. 61 Castrol Jaguar XJR-9 running in front.

another car in turn one while running on the lead lap.

Once again, Dan Gurney fielded a pair of very competitive turbocharged Toyota Celicas, and once again, the All American Racers entry was unlucky. The Toyotas, driven by Willy T. Ribbs, Rocky Moran, and Juan Fangio II, and Chris Cord, Dennis Aase, and Steve Millen, both suffered transmission trouble near dawn while running one-two. They returned, only to retire later with engine failures.

Buz McCall's Skoal Bandit Camaro took advantage of his rivals' misfortunes, and seemed headed toward victory. McCall, Paul Dallenbach, and Max Jones built up a 35-lap lead, despite a broken header that sent fumes into the cockpit.

"Rather than take 10 minutes to fix it, we continued on," McCall explained. "It blasted into the firewall and finally burned right through. Every time you would back off, it shot flames right at your leg."

Eventually, McCall, Dallenbach (younger brother of Wally), and Jones were overcome by fumes. Mike Meyer, whose Mazda had been withdrawn, joined the team. Jack Baldwin, who did not have a ride for the event, was watching the team's misfortunes from the Goodyear Tower overlooking the pits and garage.

"We saw them taking Max to the hospital," Baldwin recalled. "I came down and when they saw me walking up, Buz said, 'Jack, do you want to drive, will you drive for us, we're out of drivers.' I got my Levi Garrett [a tobacco product that competes with Skoal] drivers suit, but the president of Skoal was standing right there. They were good-natured about it and they proceeded to put green tape all over my entire driver suit. Then they threw me in the car." The race was nearly over when Baldwin rejoined with a three-lap lead. Heat in the cockpit remained a serious problem.

"The flame from the pipe was coming inside the car and was literally on your leg," Baldwin continued,

Top left: The eventual Camel Lights-winning Chevy Tiga of Tom Hessert, David Loring, and David Simpson snakes to the inside of the No. 15 John Kalagian Porsche 962, driven by Bernard Jourdain, Jim Rothbarth, and Michel Jourdain to a fifth-place finish. Top right: A time-lapse photo of nighttime pit work, braking for turn one and racing in the infield. Opposite: Bob Tullius made his final appearance in the No. 44, now badged a "Goodyear Eagle." Joined by Hurley Haywood and Whitney Ganz, the Group 44 team went out with overheating problems.

"and you'd give it the throttle, and the more gas you'd give it, the hotter your leg would get. I came in the pits, and I told them what the problem was. So they pulled the exhaust pipe off the motor, which now didn't direct it at the firewall." Baldwin returned to the track, but with the engine failing, could not hold off Pruett in the charging Roush entry. Pruett passed Baldwin for the lead with 16 minutes remaining. Baldwin hung on for second, finishing on the same lap as the winners.

"It was not funny," Baldwin said of the car's exhaust problem. "Mike Meyer drove it long enough to actually melt his foot, and he needed to get surgery and skin grafts. All those laps they were leading, if they said, 'let's take a minute and fix the car,' they would have won."

Also unlucky for the third straight year was the CCR Mazda RX-7 team, with Indy Car legend Parnelli Jones making a return to racing, joined by his son, P. J. Jones, and John Morton. Driving a second Mazda was Johnny Unser (nephew of Al and Bobby Unser, and cousin of Al Jr.), Bart Kendall (Tom's brother), G. S. Johnson, and Tom Frank. The Jones' car was sidelined by an accident after 389 laps, with the second car catching fire 57 laps later.

Riley Protofab entered two Corvettes, one for Tommy Riggins, Greg Pickett, and John Jones, and another for Tommy Archer, Chip Mead, and Bill Adam.

An unusual entry in the GTO class was a Buick Somerset entered by Bobby Allison. The car was originally built as a prototype for a specially engineered NASCAR road-course car, but the concept was scrapped when the existing Winston Cup cars were able to put on competitive shows at Watkins Glen International. Allison shared the driving with his son, Clifford, and IMSA Kelly American Challenge driver Dick Danielson. The car dropped out early when a timing gear broke in the engine.

In GTU, Amos Johnson stretched his streak to four in a row, joined by Dennis Shaw and Bob Lazier in the Team Highball Mazda RX-7. The trio finished 15th overall, and won the class by 12 laps over the Porsche 911 driven by the father-son duo of Gary and Bill Auberlen, joined by Cary Eisenlohr and Adrian Gang. The younger Auberlen was just launching a successful career racing sports cars. Their car was serviced by a four-man crew who worked the entire 24 hours in the pits.

Another future star making his first SunBank 24 appearance was Butch Leitzinger, who joined his father, Bob Leitzinger, and brother, Chuck Kurtz, in a family-prepared Nissan 300 ZX. They finished 25th overall, and fifth in GTU. Yet another future star was Dorsey Schroeder, who practiced in the Full-Time Racing Dodge Daytona but did not get to compete because car owner Kal Showket had an early exit.

Camel Lights went to the 12th-place Chevrolet-powered Tiga of Tom Hessert, David Loring, and David Simpson. The trio came back from a broken halfshaft and won by two laps over the Mazda Argo of Jim Downing, Howard Katz, and Hiro Matsushita. Hessert parlayed the victory into the class championship. Third and fourth went to a pair of Spice-powered Fieros, driven by Terry Visger/Paul Lewis/John Woodner and Charles Morgan/Costas Los/Don Bell.

Olympic skiers Phil and Steve Mahre co-drove a BMW Urd, which placed 72nd in the 75-car field. South African Wayne Taylor made his Daytona 24 Hours debut in a Ford ADA, which finished 64th. Lorenzo Lamas of the television show *Falcon Crest* drove a Camel Lights Fabcar, but crashed in the early evening hours and was eliminated. He was co-driving with movie star Perry King.

BRUN
GUFFANTI
sire
3
84
GTP ZX-TURBO
BOSCH
GOODYEAR
DAYTONA BEACH Marriott
CIBA-GEIGY
NISSAN
Castrol
JAGUAR
GTP ZX-TURBO
NISSAN
GTP ZX-TURBO
83
NISSAN
BOSCH
DAYTONA BEACH Marriott
CIBA-GEIGY
NISSAN
83
GOODYEAR

1989: The 20 Hours of Daytona

CHANGE WAS THE ORDER OF THE DAY AT DAYTONA IN 1989. NISSAN AND TOYOTA JOINED PORSCHE AND JAGUAR IN THE PREMIER CAMEL GTP CLASS. LONGTIME IMSA OWNER JOHN BISHOP HAD SOLD THE SANCTIONING BODY OVER THE WINTER TO TAMPA BUSINESSMEN MIKE CONE AND JEFF PARKER. THE NEW OWNERS HAD RELOCATED THE HEADQUARTERS FROM BRIDGEPORT, CONNECTICUT, TO TAMPA, FLORIDA. EVENTUALLY, CONE WOULD BUY PARKER OUT TO RUN THE ORGANIZATION.

Mark Raffauf, who began his career at age 15 as a gofer at IMSA events in 1973, had worked his way up the ladder to become the sanctioning body's chief steward and executive vice president, and had recently been named the new president. Parker and Cone had purchased a healthy organization.

The race fielded a record 21 Camel GTP entries, backed by 17 Camel Lights prototypes. Sixty-eight cars took the 3:30 p.m. green flag under sunny skies. Among the field were a few contenders whose teams were new to endurance racing at the prototype level, but who would quickly make their mark.

Don Devendorf, an engineer with Hughes Engineering, formed Electramotive Engineering in 1975 to design systems for electronic fuel management.

Left: Don Devendorf's Electramotive Nissan team entered the Daytona 24 Hours for the first time, fielding a pair of blue, white, and red Nissan GTP-ZXTs for a driver lineup including Geoff Brabham, Chip Robinson, and future two-time Indianapolis 500 winner Arie Luyendyk. Above: Jim Busby's winning team celebrates in victory lane. Left to right with the Camel Pyramid check are John Andretti, Derek Bell, Jean Liles (Miss Camel), and Bob Wollek.

Campaigning a Datsun 240X, he won the IMSA RS title in 1977 and GTU in 1979, then took a turbocharged Datsun 280XZ to the GTO crown in 1982. His next goal was GTP, but that had proven a long and difficult road.

Devendorf struggled with a Nissan-powered Lola in 1985 and 1986, then Geoff Brabham and Elliott Forbes-Robinson gave the team a breakthrough victory at Miami in 1987, its only win of the season. In 1988, the team skipped Daytona and Sebring, though at Road Atlanta, Brabham came from the back of the pack to win, beginning a strong run that saw Nissan win nine races, and Brabham the GTP title.

Devendorf's team finally entered the Daytona 24 Hours in 1989. Despite its proven speed, the Nissan was an unknown quantity, having never competed in a 24-hour race. Geoff Brabham put the car he shared with Arie Luyendyk, Chip Robinson, and Michael Roe on the pole with a lap of 129.217 mph. The Electramotive team entered two cars, but planned to withdraw one early in the race and concentrate on the better-placed car.

Toyota was another marque looking to succeed in Camel GTP Racing. Dan Gurney, who had successfully fielded Celicas in GTU and GTO competition, was ready for the next step. Toyota provided the All American Racers team with an 88C for Drake Olson, Chris Cord, and Steve Bren. The car was built by Dome in Japan for the European Group C series. Gurney was also building his own Toyota GTP in his California shops, but it was not ready for the race.

Defending champion Tom Walkinshaw Racing had potential winners in his TWR Castrol Jaguar

Above left: The No. 61 Jaguar leads the No. 67 Porsche on the superspeedway turn four banking. The two cars eventually finished in reverse order. Above right: Tom Hessert took his second consecutive Camel Lights victory, joining Charles Morgan and John Morrison in the Cherry Hill Classic Cars Buick Tiga. They won by a whopping 55 laps. Opposite top: Derek Daly's No. 66 Jaguar was eliminated in a first-lap accident, leaving Formula One veterans Patrick Tambay and Martin Donnelly rideless for the event. Opposite bottom: Jack Roush switched to Lincoln-Mercury Cougars for 1989, and recorded his fifth consecutive GTO class victory. The No. 16 finished sixth overall and won the class, with Pete Halsmer and Bob Earl joined by Mark Martin and Paul Stewart late in the race. The No. 11 finished seventh overall, with Martin joining Wally Dallenbach Jr. and Dorsey Schroeder.

DEREK DALY
MARTIN DONNELLY
PATRICK TAMBAY
JAGUAR
Castrol
66
66Castrol
JAGUAR
TWR
BOSCH
DUNLOP

U-HAUL
U-HAUL
U-HAUL
FREEBIRD
STROHS LIGHT
COUGAR
STROHS
LIGHT
16
STROHS LIGHT
COUGAR
STROHS
LIGHT
11

Brian Redman
76
KONI

XJR-9s, driven by Jan Lammers/Davy Jones/Raul Boesel, Patrick Tambay/Derek Daly/Martin Donnelly, and Price Cobb/John Nielsen/Andy Wallace. The Castrol Jaguar team had won in its first IMSA outing at Daytona the year before, but had been frustrated throughout the remainder of the season, winning only the final race at Del Mar, California, with a masterful comeback drive by Martin Brundle.

The fastest of nine Porsche 962s to qualify could manage only fourth overall, driven by Oscar Larrauri with team owner Walter Brun and Hans Stuck. Joest Racing had an entry for Frank Jelinski/Claude Ballot-Lena/Jean-Louis Ricci. Bruce Leven's Bayside Motorsports entered two Porsches, one for Leven, rival owner-driver Rob Dyson, and Indy Car drivers Dominick Dobson and John Paul Jr. Driving the second car were Klaus Ludwig, James Weaver, and Sarel van der Merwe.

Jim Busby fielded a pair of BFGoodrich-backed 962s. One was for Bob Wollek and Derek Bell, and the other was a former Al Holbert chassis prepared by Holbert's former crew chief, Kevin Doran, for Mario and Michael Andretti. John Andretti, nephew of the World Champion, was entered in both cars. Originally, John had hoped to co-drive with his uncle and cousin, but the progress of the race would decide his choice.

"I was going to try and run for the championship, so I was the third driver on both cars," recalled John Andretti. "Whichever car was doing better at the time, then I would get in. Sometimes, you have a car that has problems early, and not have any late, and another guy has problems later, which are bigger. But we got into the race, and Wollek and Bell were having no problems, and Mario and Mike were having some problems, so I got into Wollek and Bell's car. It ended up being the right decision for me."

Ludwig set the early pace, then two of the contenders, the Nissan of Roe and the Jaguar of Daly, collided on the second lap. The Jaguar was out of the race with a bent suspension, and the Nissan was withdrawn after 51 laps.

The Bayside/Havoline Porsche of Ludwig/Weaver/van der Merwe continued to hold off the Brabham Nissan and Davy Jones Jaguar until a broken throttle linkage resulted in a very long stop, dropping the car out of contention. Gurney's Group C Toyota, driven by Olson/Cord/Bren, lasted 180 laps before succumbing to persistent overheating problems.

The Nissan GTP-ZXT of Geoff Brabham was leading the race shortly after midnight, when a blanket of fog brought out the red flag, and racing stopped (though the clock kept running) for almost four hours.

"It was the 20 hours of Daytona, because they had a tremendous amount of fog," said Andretti. "The team called me on the radio and asked me if I thought it was too foggy to drive, and I asked them if we needed it, because we were catching the Nissan. We knew that the more hours there were on the Nissan, the better the chance for us to win with the Porsche. So, we really didn't want

Left: Brian Redman relaxes behind the pits between shifts in Roger Mandeville's 11th-place Mazda RX-7. The fence to his back separates the working pits from the paddock area. Above: Paul Stewart, son of Formula One legend Jackie Stewart, co-drove the winning Roush Lincoln-Mercury Cougar.

them to stop, but they pretty much had to. You couldn't see 10 feet in front of you."

The Nissan of Brabham/Robinson/Luyendyk/Roe held the point until its engine failed with less than five hours remaining. That put the Busby Porsche in the lead, although the Jaguar tried to hang on despite a spin and overheating problems. Cobb had cut the margin to eight seconds before his spin, and the team drafted Lammers from its sidelined sister car to assist in the stretch drive.

Andretti admitted that his team took advantage of the Jaguar's problems. "The Jag was our competition at the end, and they were overheating. They had a front radiator on the car, and they were running right behind. To help their heating problem, I'd—we'd—drop wheels off the track to try to fill their radiator."

The final hour had featured an exciting battle between Wollek and Lammers. Each time the Jaguar would cut into the margin, Wollek would respond. A "gas and go" pit stop in the closing minutes by Wollek cut the margin to one minute and 20 seconds.

Wollek still finished strong, winning by 1:26.665—the closest margin of victory in the history of the event. The Busby team completed 621 laps, 2,210.760 miles, averaging 92.009 mph. It was the 50th victory for the Porsche 962 in Camel GTP competition.

The Brun Porsche of Brun/Stuck/Larrauri finished third, 18 laps behind, followed by the Bayside/Havoline Porsche of Ludwig, Weaver, and van der Merwe, which spent nearly the entire race playing catch-up after their early problems.

Mazda's new four-rotor Mazda 767B finished fifth in the hands of Yoshimi Katayama, Takashi Yorino, and Elliott Forbes-Robinson. "Mazda used that race as a tune-up for Le Mans, rather than try to win it, and I believe we had a shot at doing a lot better," recalled Forbes-Robinson. "They didn't know how the car was going to do, so we ran really easy with the car. As it worked out, they finished that race, and finished all three cars at Le Mans. A top five at Daytona is always a good finish, and there were some very good cars in front of us that we could actually outrun at the end of the race."

Jack Roush's team took GTO honors for the fifth consecutive year, finishing sixth overall with Pete Halsmer and Bob Earl—joined by Mark Martin and Paul Stewart—in a Cougar XJR-7. Roush Cougars

Above: The checkered flag waves for the No. 67 BFGoodrich/Miller High Life Porsche 962 owned by Jim Busby. Right: Bob Leitzinger, joined by his sons Butch Leitzinger and Chuck Kurtz, dominated the GTU competition in their Fastcolor Automotive Art Nissan 240SX. A late-race altercation resulted in a second-place finish in the class. "Fastcolor" refers to the paintings of noted automotive artist Sandra Leitzinger, Bob's wife and mother of Butch and Chuck.

swept the top four positions in the class, all placing in the top 10 overall.

Martin started the car that finished second in the class, but also did some late-race relief. "Earl and Halsmer were the only two guys assigned to the winning car, and it got down to noon on Sunday and they couldn't drive it anymore," Martin explained. "They wanted to put somebody in the car who could run a nice pace and not tear up the car. That is when I came in."

Stewart, son of Formula One World Champion Jackie Stewart, was given the honor of driving the car to the checkered flag.

Dorsey Schroeder, who co-drove with Wally Dallenbach and Martin in the seventh-place Cougar, recalled his first pre-race meeting with Roush. "At the drivers' meeting before the race, Jack Roush told us that he's built the best car that could ever be provided to a driver," Schroeder recalled. "His cars were built perfectly, and then he told what we were not supposed to do was tear up his equipment.

"Then Jack gave us each a $100 bill to put in our driver's suit," Schroeder continued. But Schroeder quickly found out he wasn't getting a pre-race bonus. "He said, 'Bring that $100 with you.' We said 'What do we do with that?' And he goes, 'If you break down on course, the corner workers have sole authority to determine if you're in a safe place or not, or whether you can get towed to a better place. Give them that $100 and get to a damn safe place.'

"During the race, our car broke down. The car just died when Wally Dallenbach was in it, and Mark and I ran out there and it was a long run. I ran up there with five gallons of gas, but the car wasn't out of gas, the battery was dead. By then, many of the guys were pretty drunk by that time in the motor homes, and they were yelling, 'Mark Martin, Dorsey Schroeder.' Mark said, 'Give me your motor home battery,' and he gave a fan the hundred dollars. That got us going, and we got a third place out of it that year."

"I armed the drivers with as many tools as they could manage—the drivers could do virtually anything," Roush said. "I generally gave them a little money in case they needed to buy a tool along the way, or get a little help that money would fix, we availed ourselves of that opportunity, which was common among the teams. I don't know if they ever spent the money, but I never got any of the money back. You know how drivers are."

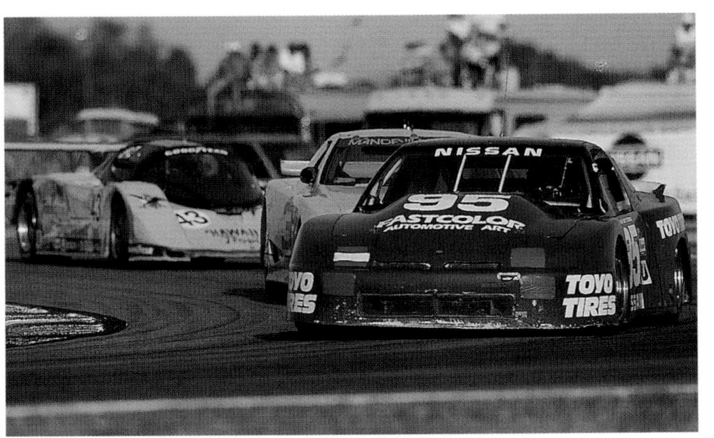

Al Bacon, Bob Reed, and Rod Millen won GTU in a Mazda RX-7 over the Nissan 240SX of Bob Leitzinger, who was joined by his sons Butch Leitzinger and Chuck Kurtz. Amos Johnson made a strong bid for his fifth consecutive GTU class victory, but an engine misfire slowed his Mazda and he had to settle for third in class.

Charles Morgan, Tom Hessert, and John Morrison won in Camel Lights with their Buick Tiga in record fashion, winning by 55 laps. While 17 cars started in the class, only five finished as a close race turned into a runaway. "Just like last year, it was an uneventful race," said Hessert after winning his second consecutive Camel Lights victory in the 24 Hours. "We just kept going and going."

Missing from the lineup for the only time in his career was Hurley Haywood, who was testing for Audi in France.

Bob Holbert took a pre-race lap in the Lowenbrau Special Porsche 962 in tribute to his son, two-time Daytona 24-Hours winner Al Holbert, who had lost his life in an airplane crash in October, two months after retiring from racing.

GTP ZX-TURBO
ROBINSON EARL
BRABHAM DALY
NISSAN
performance
technology, inc.
NISSAN
83
83
NISSA

1990: The High-Water Mark for GTP

As the new decade began, IMSA Camel GTP competition reached its zenith, with Porsche, Jaguar, Nissan, and Toyota teams all on the hunt for overall honors in the 24 Hours. Jaguar, Porsche, and Nissan had all won GTP races in 1989, and Toyota was coming into its own.

Once again, Don Devendorf's factory Nissan team entered two cars at Daytona, with the intention of withdrawing one early in the race. Nissan's disappointment after dropping out with less than five hours remaining in the 1989 race was quickly offset by their domination of the Camel GTP competition throughout the rest of the season. Nissans had won 10 of the 15 races in 1989, and Brabham captured his second straight driver's championship. Nissan had won its first manufacturer's championship.

Jim Busby's team, the defending race winner, switched from a Porsche 962 to an independent Miller High Life/BFGoodrich-backed Nissan, with John Paul Jr., Kevin Cogan, and Mauro Baldi. The car was the ZX-T that Brabham had driven to the 1989 championship. In 1989, Busby had been Porsche's North American development team, but had managed only one other victory, at West Palm Beach, Florida, in addition to the team's Daytona win.

Porsche was well represented, as always. Bruce Leven entered the Bayside Porsche, with major sponsorship from Texaco Havoline, for Bob Wollek, Sarel van der Merwe, and Dominic Dobson. Rob Dyson brought a Porsche 962C, which he planned to co-drive with James Weaver, Scott Pruett, and Vern

Left: The crewmen are a blur of activity during night action in the pits of Geoff Brabham's No. 83 Nissan. Above: Derek Bell joined Gianpiero Moretti and Stanley Dickens in the Momo Porsche 962. Bell flipped the car exiting NASCAR turn four early in the evening, and escaped unhurt in one of the biggest scares of his career.

Schuppan. The father-son team of John Hotchkis and John Hotchkis Jr. joined Jim Adams in the Wynns Porsche 962.

Also among the Porsche contenders were a number of European teams. Owner-driver Rene Herzog, with assistance from Brumos Porsche, fielded a Porsche 962 for Hans Stuck, Harald Grohs, and Hurley Haywood. Dauer had a 962C for Raul Boesel, joined by cousins Al Jr. and Robbie Unser. Joest had a 962C for Oscar Larrauri, Henri Pescarolo, and Frank Jelinski.

Tom Walkinshaw brought a pair of new Castrol Jaguar XJR-12s for Davy Jones/Jan Lammers/Andy Wallace and Price Cobb/John Nielsen/Martin Brundle. The team had switched to a turbocharged car, the XJR-10, midway through the 1989 season, but went back to the normally aspirated V-12 engine for the new XJR-12. The team also switched from Dunlop to Goodyear tires. The Jaguars had momentum on their side, having won the final two races of the 1989 campaign.

"The changes in the car are very subtle, and they've been ongoing," explained TWR team manager Tony Dowe. "This is an endurance car, not as fast as the turbo cars, but it can win a 24-hour race."

Toyota had enjoyed moderate success in 1989, but Dan Gurney's team didn't win any races. They

suffered setbacks when both cars crashed heavily late in the season. For Daytona, All American Racers would enter a Toyota Eagle 89E for Drake Olson, Rocky Moran, and Juan Manuel Fangio II.

"We're proud of what we've achieved," said Gurney. "While 1989 was a good start for our GTP team, we weren't satisfied because we didn't win any races. We came close, but no wins."

Gianpiero Moretti entered a Porsche 962C and a Gebhardt AT8 GTP powered by an Audi engine used in Trans-Am competition. Another new prototype was the Spice SE90C. Jeff Kline, a two-time class winner at Daytona, thought he had a chance at winning overall with the new car.

Above left: A pair of Tom Walkinshaw Racing Castrol Jaguars race through the infield. The two cars finished one-two. Above right: Fire broke out in the Nissan pit only 57 minutes into the race, following a fuel spill during a Derek Daly stop in the No. 84 entry. At that point, it was decided to use the car to scrub in tires for the No. 83 car. Later, when the No. 83 retired with engine failure, the No. 84 returned to the race to get more track time.

Wollek won the pole in the Bruce Leven Texaco Porsche 962 he shared with Sarel van der Merwe and Dominic Dobson, turning a lap of 131.000 mph. He was joined on the front row by the Nissan GTP-ZXT of Brabham. Oscar Larrauri qualified third quickest, but flipped the Brun Porsche 962C and slid on its roof along the front straight. The car was withdrawn from the event.

The Brun car was not the last to experience problems prior to the event. Busby's Nissan lost its timing belt during Saturday morning warmups, and the team barely had a new powerplant installed in time for the 3:30 p.m. start. Also having to change engines was the Essex Racing team, which was seeking its third consecutive Camel Lights victory.

Rob Dyson hit the guardrail after only six laps in the Blaupunkt Porsche and was eliminated from the race. Next to have trouble was the factory Nissan team. Only 57 minutes into the race, a fire erupted in the Nissan pits from a fuel spill when Derek Daly was pitting the No. 84 car. The blaze was quickly extinguished, and the undamaged car was pushed behind the wall to clean up the powder from the fire extinguisher. At that point, Devendorf decided to use the car to scrub in tires for the rest of the race.

The Leven and Joest Porsche teams traded the lead during the first hour, but both had problems. One hour into the race, van der Merwe collided with the Camaro of Mark Montgomery and struggled back to the pits. Nine minutes later, Pescarolo spun in the Joest Porsche and limped back with a broken lower control arm, resulting in a 21-minute pit stop. The car would retire at the five-hour mark with engine failure.

Pescarolo's trouble gave the lead to the No. 60 Jaguar of John Nielsen, which was passed for the point only four laps later by the No. 61 Jaguar of Jan Lammers. "We didn't count on being in the lead quite yet," said Price Cobb. "Maybe by hour 16, but not now. We'll continue to run our own pace and, if anybody wants to go ahead right now that will be all right."

Two hours into the event, the Texaco Porsche again had trouble. Wollek pitted, his car smoking heavily when an oil-line fitting—a $5.29 part—to the turbo failed, resulting in a 15-minute pit stop. The Spice crashed out while running sixth, when a GTU car moved into Jeff Kline's path, resulting in the first caution of the event at 6:15 p.m.

The two Jaguars continued to swap the lead. Lammers broke van der Merwe's five-year-old race lap record by three seconds, with a lap of 1:38.596 at 8 p.m.

During the early evening, Derek Bell had one of the biggest scares in his long career when he flipped the Momo Porsche at 9:24 p.m., coming off turn four of the superspeedway.

"I wish I knew what happened," Bell said after the incident. "I was flat out running the banking when something broke in the rear. It skidded on and on and on. I hit nothing, but I put on the fire extinguisher because I was terrified of a fire. I was still upside down and the engine was on. I switched it off, but I was soaked in fuel, and I started to pass out from the fumes. It was like a dream. I remember having nightmares. I guess I hit my head on the roof. In 20 years, I had never crashed out of a race, but I have now." Bell escaped the incident with only a stiff neck.

"I came around and thought a tractor trailer blew a tire, because there were pieces of debris scattered all over the place," said defending Camel Lights winner Tom Hessert. "Then, I saw it was really the Momo car, upside down."

At 11:25 p.m., the two Jaguars were running only 12 seconds apart, when Davy Jones pitted to replace the rear tail section of the No. 61. He returned to the race in second place, one lap behind the No. 60 Jaguar.

The No. 83 Nissan also ran near the front, and Brabham took the lead at 10:44 p.m. For three hours, it battled near the front against the two Jaguars. Then, at 1:48 a.m., it encountered trouble, running out of fuel in the chicane. Fortunately, Bob Earl was able to coast to the pits. "The fuel light came on, showing we've got one lap of fuel left, but with no further warning, the car immediately ran out of fuel," said Earl.

The problem was more than running out of fuel; the car was pushed behind the wall and retired with engine failure. Meanwhile, the team returned the No. 84 car to the race, which had been used up until that point by Daly to scrub in tires and get more track time.

The factory Nissan's departure left the Jaguars one-two, with the Busby Nissan third. The Nissan began having electrical problems at 4 a.m. that led to its retirement.

At that point, it became a matter of which of the two Jaguars would win. The No. 61 led until 11 a.m., when the team made a long stop to add water to the radiator of the overheating car. The two Jaguars swapped the lead over the next four hours. With an hour remaining, Lammers led teammate Brundle by 47 seconds. Brundle chopped away at the lead and took the point with 45 minutes remaining. The drama came to a halt seven minutes later, when the No. 60 car pitted and lost six minutes—three laps—while coolant was added to the radiator.

The day belonged to Tom Walkinshaw, who scored a one-two sweep, led by Davy Jones, Jan Lammers, and Andy Wallace, who completed 761 laps, 2,709.16 miles, averaging 112.857 mph, four laps over Jaguar XJR-12 teammates Price Cobb, John Nielsen, and Martin Brundle.

""We communicated with each other very well, so that when any one of us got into that car, we wanted the car to believe that it was the same person all the time driving the car," said Jones. "In a 24-hour race, you can get one driver that thinks he might be a bit of a hero or a rock ape, that he's going to set the world on fire, and he's going to make a mistake. That's what costs you a 24-hour race. When we won that race in 1990, honestly, I believe that car could have gone another 24 hours because we took such good care of it."

1990

It was Nielsen's 12th runner-up finish in 23 starts since he won his first Camel GTP start, the 1988 Daytona 24 Hours.

"My most satisfying, and yet most disappointing, race at Daytona was 1990," recalled Price Cobb. "We had a huge lead, but Tom Walkinshaw didn't want our car to win, so he made us sit in the pits,

Above: A competitor's eye view as the field takes the green flag for the start of the SunBank 24 at Daytona. Right: Juan Manuel Fangio II, Rocky Moran, and Drake Olson co-drove Dan Gurney's No. 99 All American Racers Toyota Eagle. The car went out early with overheating problems. Far right: Celebrating Jaguar's triumph with Miss Camel, Monica Hylton, are (left to right) Jan Lammers, Andy Wallace, and Davy Jones.

so our teammates' car passed us to win the race. He told us all kinds of stuff, but apparently, the bottom line was he wanted the guys in the other car to win. It could have been part of a long-range plan, but he didn't share it with us. We went on to win Le Mans that year, but it would have been very satisfying if I could have won the race here, too, as well." Both Jones and Lammers, however, denied that team orders played a role in the outcome of the event.

Wollek settled for third, six laps down, followed by the Rene Herzog Porsche 962 with a driver lineup that included Hans Stuck and Hurley Haywood. "If we didn't have that trouble early in the race and lose all that time, I think we would have been racing with the Jaguars at the end," said Wollek. "It's no shame to be beaten by a factory effort. You have to give credit to [crew chief] Walter Gerber and the Bayside team. They are very good at preparing a Porsche."

Jack Roush took GTO honors for the sixth straight year, with young off-road racing star Robbie Gordon joining Calvin Fish, Lyn St. James, and Robert Lappalainen for fifth overall in a Lincoln-Mercury Cougar XR-7, overcoming a pair of fast Mazda RX-7s built by Fabcar's Dave Klym.

The previous December, Gordon had paid $120 in cab fare for a ride from the Orlando airport to the Sebring race circuit to test for Roush. It proved a worthwhile investment, and launched Gordon on a new career path. "Today was definitely the fastest I have ever driven," Gordon said on the opening day of practice. "Going straight from dirt to pavement on a team like Roush is the chance of a lifetime for a kid like me."

Leading the rotary contingent in GTO were Amos Johnson, John O'Steen, Jim Downing, and Pete Halsmer, placing second in class and seventh overall in the new Mazda, 18 laps behind the class winners.

In GTU, the Team Highball car that had won four of the last five Daytona 24 Hours returned to victory lane in the hands of Peter Uria, Bob Dotson, Jim Pace, and Rusty Scott.

"I've been coming to Daytona for the past five years driving Porsche 911s, and I've always finished second or third, behind Amos Johnson," said Uria, a pacemaker salesman. "I decided that if you can't beat them, lease them. So I talked to Amos, and we came to an agreement in December."

John Grooms, Michael Greenfield, and Frank Jellinek captured Camel Lights honors in a Mazda-Argo JM16. Tom Hessert's bid for three class victories in a row ended when both of Michael Gue's Spice-Buicks faltered during the night with electrical problems.

BAUER RACING
JOEST
PORSCHE
Shell
GMM
BOSCH
Shell
6
TORNO
BOSCH
Shell

1991: The Last Hurrah for Porsche 962

WITH WAR RAGING IN THE PERSIAN GULF, ENTRIES LAGGED FOR THE DAYTONA 24 HOURS IN 1991. IN A MOVE TO BOOST THE NUMBER OF COMPETITORS, IMSA OPENED THE FIELD TO LE MANS–TYPE CARS. HOWEVER, WHILE THE EUROPEAN CARS WERE FASTER THAN THEIR AMERICAN COUNTERPARTS, SEVERE FUEL RESTRICTIONS RESULTED IN ONLY THREE ENTRIES PARTICIPATING IN THE NEW CLASS, A TRIO OF GROUP C NISSANS ENTERED BY THE AMERICAN NISSAN TEAM, WHICH HOPED TO FINALLY WIN THE MAJOR RACE THAT HAD THUS FAR ELUDED THEM.

"I think that by running the C cars here it will help our overall effort," said team leader Don Devendorf before the race. "These cars were built strictly for the purpose of running 24-hour races. The factory wants this race badly, because it carries a lot of prestige. I think we're ready."

The Group C Nissans set the pace in qualifying, with Derek Daly running a quick lap of 116.653 mph during a rain-soaked session, though only IMSA GTP cars were eligible to start from the front row. That put veteran Bob Wollek on the pole for the fourth time in the Daytona 24 Hours with a lap of 115.594 mph in one of two Porsche 962Cs entered by Joest Racing.

Left: Bob Wollek won the pole in the No. 6 Joest Porsche 962C. He's shown leading the Andretti Porsche, and the No. 1 Nissan in early race action. Above: While the No. 48 Comptech Acura Spice dominated the Camel Lights class and finished seventh overall, the car's electrics failed with five minutes remaining, with Parker Johnstone in sight of the start/finish line. Joining him in the class-winning effort were Doug Peterson, Steve Cameron, and Bob Lesnett.

Winning the pole was important for Wollek, who entered the season without a regular ride. "At the end of last season, I spoke to a lot of people, including the Nissan and Jaguar teams, because I wanted to stay in Group C," the 47-year-old Wollek said. "Nobody seemed interested in me as a driver, apparently because they thought I was too old. I wanted to show them they were completely wrong. I wanted desperately to win the pole, and I have been training hard for the last month so I could."

Nissan entered the event as a solid favorite. Geoff Brabham had won his third consecutive Camel GTP championship for Nissan in 1990, and had won 23 of 44 races over that three-year span. Brabham was joined by Chip Robinson in the lead NPTI entry, with Jeremy Dale, Steve Millen, and Bob Earl in the second car. Driving the third car were Arie Luyendyk and Julian Bailey.

A fourth Nissan Group C entry consisted of a Japanese-based Group C car piloted by Masahiro Hasemi, Toshio Suzuki, and Anders Olofsson. However, the Nissan Motorsports International (NISMO) team never made the trip to Daytona because of a corporation-wide restriction on international travel due to the Persian Gulf military action.

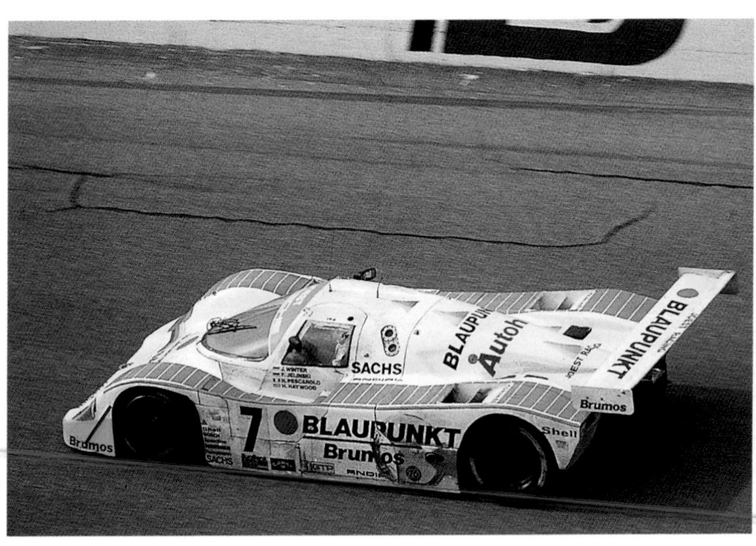

The pole-winning Porsche was fielded by a combination of the Joest and Brumos teams. Paolo Barilla, Bernd Schneider, and Massimo Sigala joined Wollek in the Torno-sponsored 962C. Hurley Haywood, Frank Jelinski, Henri Pescarolo, and John Winter were teamed in the second car, the Blaupunkt Porsche, which qualified seventh.

Only 46 cars were on the starting grid, including a dozen GTP entries. What the field lacked in depth, however, it had in quality, with the Nissans challenged by Toyota, Jaguar, Porsche, and Chevy-Spice teams.

All American Racers had a pair of Toyota Eagles, one for Juan Fangio II, Willy T. Ribbs, and Andy Wallace, and another for Rocky Moran, P. J. Jones, and reigning Toyota Atlantic champion Mark Dismore. The team had had a breakthrough 1990 campaign and won four races.

Above left: Showing the scars of combat, the No. 7 Porsche charges to victory. Above right: Three Roush Racing Ford Mustangs finished in the top 10, giving Roush his seventh consecutive victory in the class. Winner Robby Gordon (right) slides up to nudge Dorsey Schroeder, who later remarked, "Jack would have killed us if we all wrecked!" Opposite: Car owner Dan Gurney (left) chats with driver Andy Wallace. The team struggled with electrical problems that eventually sidelined both AAR Toyota Eagles.

TWR fielded a pair of Jaguar XJR-12s, painted in new Bud Light colors, for Davy Jones/Scott Pruett/Raul Boesel and Derek Warwick /John Nielsen. After Nielsen spun entering the chicane and crashed in Thursday's opening practice, the car was withdrawn. Warwick moved to the team's lone remaining car for the race.

Rob Dyson entered a Porsche 962C for himself, John Paul Jr., James Weaver, and Tiff Needell. Tom Milner brought a pair of Chevy-powered Spices for Brian Bonner, Jeff Kline, Scott Sharp, and defending Daytona 500 winner Derrike Cope; and Michael Brockman, Jeff Davis, Tim McAdam, and Fred Phillips. Paul Newman was originally scheduled to drive the latter car, but withdrew.

Dauer Racing had a pair of Porsche 962Cs for two of America's most famous racing families. Mario Andretti co-drove with sons Michael and Jeff in one car, while brothers Al and Bobby Unser were joined by their respective sons, Al Jr. and Robbie.

"It seemed to be a last-minute effort from the guy that put the package together," recalled Al Unser Jr. "It really wasn't a good deal for us, so the car didn't last very long [only 270 laps].

"That's the only time that ever happened [four Unsers co-driving the same car], and it's the only time it ever *will* happen," he added with finality.

Mario Andretti explained why the situation may have seemed hurried to Unser. "The Persian Gulf situation delayed transport of our car out of Germany, so things have been a bit rushed," Andretti

said before the race. "I've found that once you get these cars balanced, just about any driver will like them. I'm really happy that we are able to do this in a Porsche because of their reliability, which is what you need to be able to do a fast, steady, competitive pace."

1991

Completing the GTP entry was an unusual open-cockpit BFGoodrich Porsche 966 entered by Gunnar Racing for Derek Bell, his son, Justin, and Jay Cochran. The car was parked early in the race, where fans had the opportunity to sign it to show their support for American troops in the Gulf War.

Two of the NPTI Nissans nearly crashed during the first lap on a damp track after the 3:30 p.m. start, with Bailey spinning to avoid hitting Luyendyk. The team withdrew Luyendyk's car to concentrate on the two remaining Nissans, shifting the drivers over to the other cars.

Above: The No. 83 Nissan R90C in the pits for service and a driver change. While the team struggled with handling problems, Geoff Brabham, Bob Earl, Chip Robinson, and Derek Daly held on to finish second.
Right: Falling behind early with electrical problems, Mario, Michael, and Jeff Andretti staged a remarkable comeback, charging from 20 laps down to take the lead in the Dauer Racing Havoline Porsche 962. However, the car broke down shortly after Michael Andretti took over the lead, resulting in a sixth-place finish.

Next, the Andretti Porsche struggled with electrical problems. At the end of two hours, the team was back in 33rd place.

Neither Toyota was a factor, with both cars suffering from electrical problems, traced to the team's radios. The team finally called it quits after 15 hours. "The guys on the crew were like bird dogs," said Willy T. Ribbs, who made on-course repairs to his Toyota. "They pointed, and I did it. I would have been much more frustrated if we had gone 23 hours and had this happen."

Next to suffer disappointment was the Nissan team, which parked its No. 84 car. "It was a great team, Arie Luyendyk, myself, Steve Millen, and Julian Bailey all shared a car, and we qualified well," recalled Dale. "We were leading the race at 11 in the morning. Arie was driving the car through the tri-oval, and it cut a right-rear tire at about 215 mph, and it broke the transmission. We were done. I think we certainly had a real good shot. The car was an unbelievable race car, just incredible."

The pole-winning Porsche went out near the midway point while leading, after the crew found water in a cylinder. "Now, I'm going to drive in the No. 7 car," said Wollek, sarcastically. "They're tired—old. They need a young man to drive."

Sunrise found the Jaguar down by 101 laps, the result of changing two water pumps. Boesel had pitted while leading at 2:04 a.m., but the car went behind the wall for a new water pump and radiator, losing 55 laps in the process. The crew later replaced another water pump, but finally called it quits just before 8 a.m.

"Our engine was way too abused," said Jones. "It was running on steam for the last six hours. If it hadn't been for a recurring water pump problem, I feel we could have won the race."

Taking up the charge for Porsche was the Dyson entry, which challenged the lead Nissan until an oil pump seized. Because he hadn't driven in the race, Dyson did a relief shift in the Wynn's Porsche.

With the No. 84 Nissan out of the race and the No. 83 Nissan struggling with handling problems, the race turned into a battle of Porsches, with the remaining Joest/Brumos Porsche battling to hold off the Andrettis, who had recovered from their earlier problems in the Dauer Porsche. The Andretti Porsche took the lead for four laps just after 9 a.m. and stayed in striking distance for another hour, before mechanical problems took their toll.

"That's a race we would have won," recalled Michael Andretti. "We lost about 20 laps right at the beginning of the race, and we came back. By 9 in the morning, I had taken the lead. Then, the gearbox broke, and we ended up finishing sixth. Or the clutch broke. It was disappointing, because me and Dad drove so hard through the night, and Jeff was my teammate as well. That would have been one of the biggest comebacks ever, and to have it break was a real disappointment."

About 30 minutes before the checkered flag, Jay Cochran took out the Gunnar Porsche from the paddock. The car carried signatures of support from 6,000 race fans, with BFGoodrich donating one dollar for every signature to the USO. Cochran slowed for the final lap and held up an American flag.

With the Andretti car out of contention, the Joest team held on for the victory, surviving three cut tires, a battery failure, and overheating problems during the last two hours. It was the final Daytona triumph for the Porsche 962, the fifth Daytona 24 Hours victory for Haywood, and the fourth for Wollek. Also driving the winning car were Henri Pescarolo, Frank Jelinski, and John Winter. The Joest team completed 719 laps, 2,559.640 miles, averaging 106.633 mph.

"I won at Le Mans four times, so I had to win here," said Pescarolo. "This is a very good team and a great car. I have good teammates. It was perfect."

"This has been the hardest victory here, that's for sure," said Haywood. "We raced hard, and the competition was good. This has probably been the most rewarding one. Racing at night in the rain was pretty exciting, but we had no close calls."

The No. 83 Nissan of Brabham, Robinson, Daly, and Earl finished second, 18 laps behind, with John Hotchkis, James Adams, Chris Cord, and Dyson third in the Wynn's Porsche 962. The Andretti

Above: Celebrating in victory lane are (left to right) Henri Pescarolo, Hurley Haywood, Miss Unocal, Bob Wollek, Frank Jellinski, and John Winter. Right: A solitary car races in the darkness of the infield course. Far right: The Jaguar team carried Bud Light sponsorship in 1991. Davy Jones, Scott Pruett, Raul Boesel, and Derek Warwick drove in the No. 2 Jaguar XJR-12, the team's lone car for the 1991 Daytona event after the No. 3 car crashed in opening practice.

Porsche took fifth, losing its engine with only 13 minutes remaining, while the only other GTP car to finish was the Milner Chevy Spice of Bonner, Kline, Cope, and Sharp, 11th overall.

For 1991, the IMSA GT series had a new sponsor, Exxon Supreme, for the GTO and GTU divisions.

Roush took GTO honors for the seventh straight year, with Mark Martin, Wally Dallenbach, and Robby Gordon driving a Ford Mustang to a 14-lap win over teammates John Fergus, Max Jones, and Dorsey Schroeder. Roush took a podium sweep when the customer car, driven by Jim Stevens, Craig Bennett, Tommy Grunnah, and James Jaeger, placed 10th overall.

"I remember coming across the victory line one-two-three, trying to get lined up in formation," Schroeder recalled. "Then, Robby [Gordon] decided to do an 'Earnhardt donut' on everybody's door, so he slammed me in the side coming across the start/finish line, which shoved me up into Stevens' car. I thought we were all going to have a big wreck, and Jack was going to kill us."

Comptech led start-to-finish in Camel Lights with the debut of its Acura NSX Spice, with Parker Johnstone, Steve Cameron, Doug Peterson, and Bob Lesnett placing seventh overall. While they won

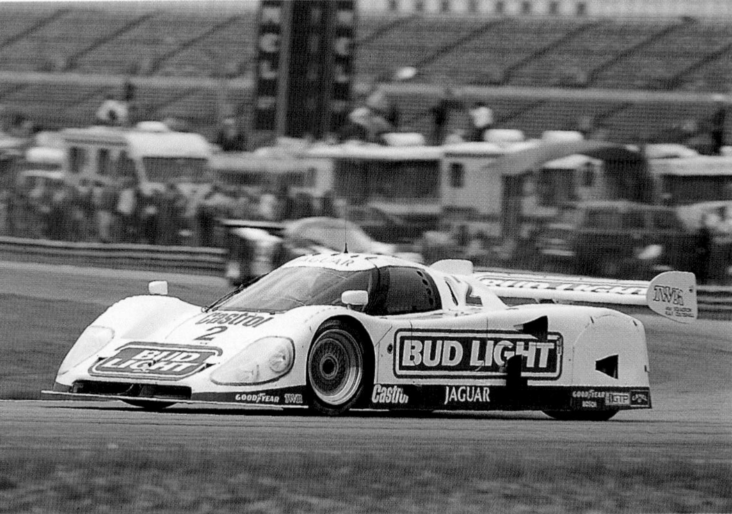

the class by 34 laps, the car failed to take the checkered flag, falling victim to electrical failure in the closing minutes.

"The car was perfect for 23 hours and 55 minutes. Then, the electrics went dead with no warning," said Johnstone. "The only thing I could have wished for was to drive it across the finish line."

Dick Greer won in GTU, joined by Al Bacon, Mike Mees, and Peter Uria, winning the class by 29 laps. It was the second consecutive class victory for Uria and second Daytona 24 Hours GTU title for Bacon, the 1989 co-winner.

Bob Leitzinger entered two Nissan 240SXs for the first time and was the pre-race favorite. However, the second car—started by his son Butch—went out after 13 laps with engine problems. "At least we've got one more car," said Butch after his retirement from the race. "At this time last year, our only car was in the garage with a stuffed-in rear end." Unfortunately for the team, the second car lasted only 192 laps before also succumbing to engine failure.

ENGINE

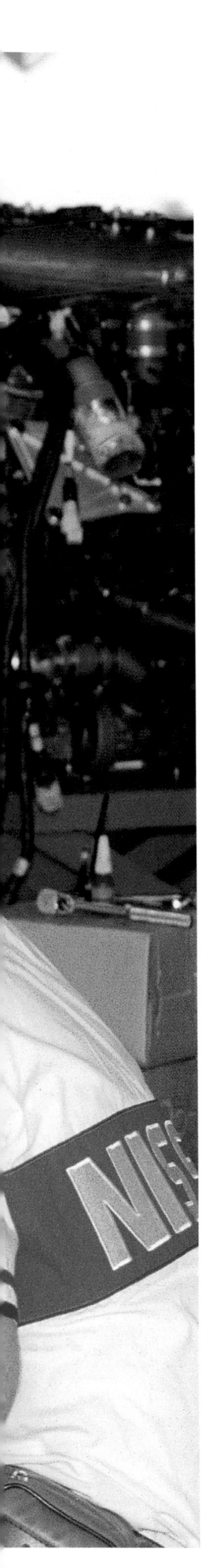

1992: Which Nissan?

THE RACE HAD A NEW NAME FOR 1992—THE ROLEX 24 AT DAYTONA. IN ADDITION TO GIVING OUT ROLEX WATCHES TO THE RACE WINNERS, ROLEX NOW SPONSORED THE 24 HOURS.

Though it had been a year since the Persian Gulf crisis, sports car racing was still in a state of flux. With money tight, the rising costs of racing had driven many of the independent teams out of competition, while the factory-backed teams were beginning to lose funding. The renamed race could only muster a 49-car field—three more than in 1991. Once again, however, what the field lacked in numbers it made up for in quality. Factory teams from Nissan, Jaguar, Toyota, and Mazda were challenged by Porsche and Chevrolet efforts.

Despite the competitive teams that had entered, there was only one question anyone was asking before the race: "Which Nissan will win?" There were five cars to choose from.

Don Devendorf's Nissan Performance Technology Inc. entered a trio of Nissan R90C twin-turbocharged V-8s, Group C cars prepared to IMSA specifications. Leading the driver lineup was Geoff Brabham, who had won his fourth Camel GTP championship in 1991, and had won 29 races in four years. He was joined by Chip Robinson, Arie Luyendyk, and Bob Earl in the lead car, while Derek Daly, Steve Millen, and Gary Brabham were also entered.

In addition to the American team, the Japanese factory wanted to flex its muscle. With its R91CP no longer eligible for the 24 Hours of Le Mans, a pair of Japanese teams fielded entries to showcase the prototype. Nissan Motor

Left: A Nissan engineer runs checks on one of the team's powerplants. Nissan brought along plenty of spares for the event, pulling out all the stops in its quest for the overall victory. Above: Winning drivers Masahiro Hasemi, Kazuyoshi Hoshino, and Toshio Suzuki, joined by reserve driver Anders Olafsson, hold the checkered flag in victory lane.

Sports International (NISMO) entered a Group C car for drivers Masahiro Hasemi, Kazuyoshi Hoshino, Toshio Suzuki, and reserve Anders Olafsson.

The only cars joining the Nissans in Group C were Yves Courage's two-car Group C Porsche Cougar C28S entry, with a driver lineup headed by four-time Daytona 24 Hours winner Bob Wollek. Japanese Sports Prototype Championship rival Nova also entered a car, with a lineup of Mauro Martini, Volker Weidler, and Jeff Krosnoff. Unlike 1991, the Le Mans Prototypes were ineligible to score Camel GT points. Jaguar entered two cars, a new Bud Lite XJR-16 and a proven XJR-12, for Davy Jones, a five-time Camel GTP winner in 1991, and Scott Pruett, Scott Goodyear, and David Brabham. Brabham was joined at Daytona by his brothers, Geoff and Gary, which meant that three sons of three-time Formula One World Champion Jack Brabham would be competing in the Rolex 24.

Toyota's hopes for the event were boosted by three days of virtually trouble-free testing in November, using its new Toyota Eagle Mark III. The newest version of the Dan Gurney–fielded prototype had debuted in the 11th race of 1991 and won two races. The All American Racers' hopes were further raised when the team set fast time in the IMSA January test session.

Mazda, the 1991 24 Hours of Le Mans winner, had put together a Camel GTP team for 1992, with a driver lineup that included 1991 GTO champion Pete Halsmer, but chose to sit out the Daytona opener.

Another contender was a Tom Milner Chevy Spice for Wayne Taylor and Jeff Purner. However, the team struggled early in the race and lost several hours replacing the clutch before finally quitting near the halfway point.

Porsche was represented by three solid GTP teams. Walter Brun fielded the Torno Porsche 962C, with a driver lineup of John Winter, Bernd Schneider, Massimo Sigala, and Oscar Larrauri. Vern Schuppan had the 0123/Artsports Porsche 962C for Hurley Haywood, Roland Ratzenberger, Eje Elgh, and Scott Brayton. Joest, the defending race winner, returned with the Momo Porsche 962C for Gianpiero Moretti, Hans Stuck, Frank Jelinski, and Henri Pescarolo. Stuck, a two-time Le Mans winner, qualified third.

"Daytona is the most difficult race to win," Stuck said after qualifying. "It's at least three times harder to win than Le Mans."

Juan Fangio II put the Toyota Eagle on the pole with a record lap of 133.695 mph, followed by Davy Jones in the Bud Lite Jaguar XJR-16, at 133.131 mph. They were the quickest of eight cars that topped Wollek's two-year-old track record.

Problems struck both the Jaguar and Nissan teams before the race. Jaguar withdrew its new XJR-16 following an internal engine problem during Saturday morning warmup, and would run only one car in the event. Devendorf's team struggled with fuel cell problems in Friday's practice and

Above: The Nissan Motorsports No. 23 R91CP took a nine-lap victory, driven by Masahiro Hasemi, Kazuyoshi Hoshino, and Toshio Suzuki. Opposite top: While denied the victory, both of Dan Gurney's All American Racers Toyota Eagle Mk IIIs finished, with the No. 98 taking fourth and the No. 99 11th. Right: The No. 84 Nissan R90C, shown running ahead of the No. 52 Porsche 962 driven by Hurley Haywood, was running fifth when Gary Brabham tagged the guardrail exiting pit road, putting the car out of the race.

TOYOTA
99
TOYOTA
98

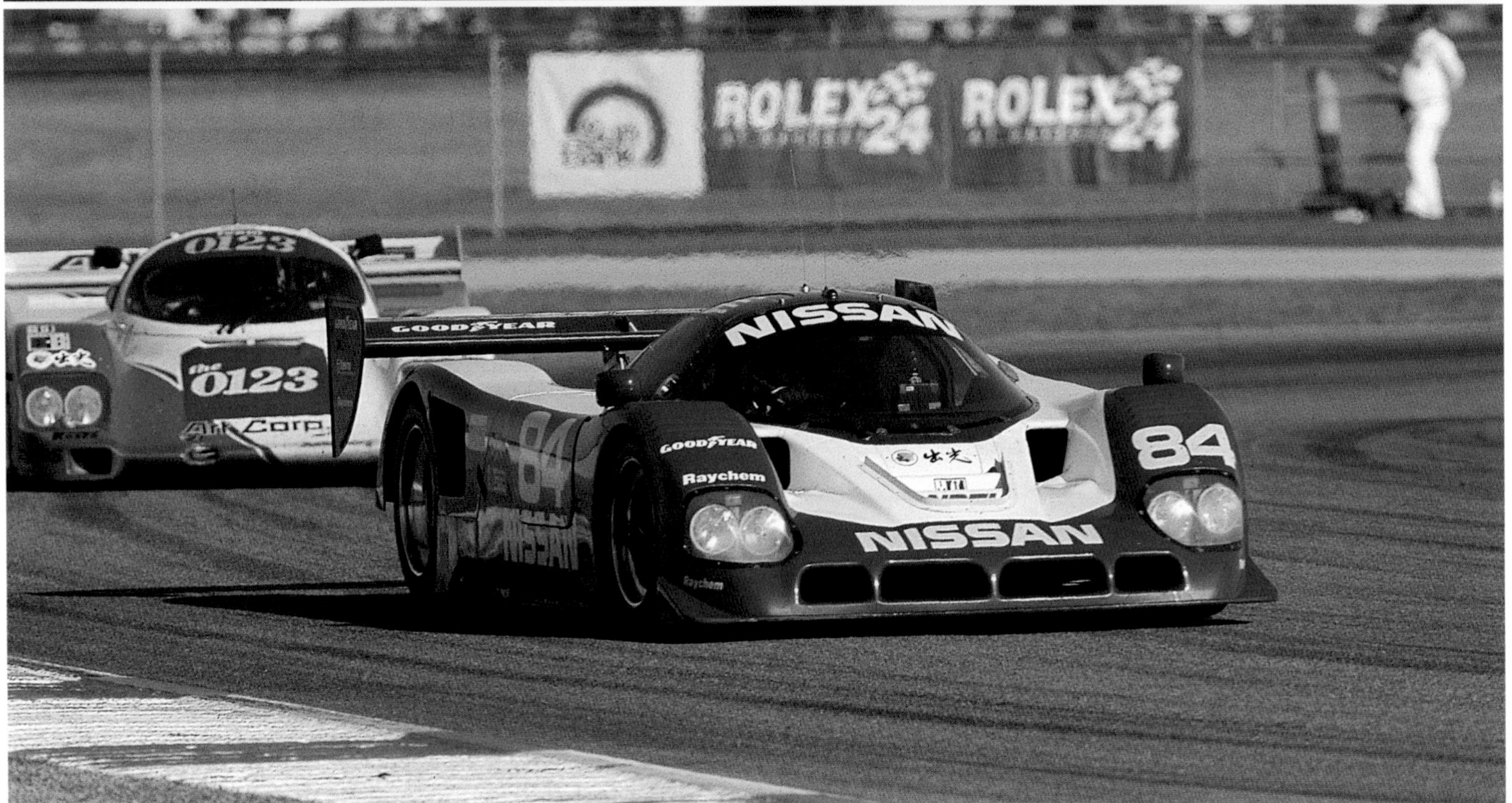
ROLEX 24
ROLEX 24
the 0123
NISSAN
GOODYEAR
84
GOODYEAR
Raychem
NISSAN

Saturday morning's warmup. Rather than start three cars, the team withdrew one Nissan and renumbered its two other entries, voiding their qualifying times.

"We really would have liked to have run three cars," said Kas Kastner, NPTI team manager. "But, we didn't have time to find the problem, so our only option was to shuffle car numbers to have a pair of competitive cars for the race." The team ran numbers 83 and 84 throughout the season, and only used No. 1 for the Daytona event.

Almost from the drop of the green flag at 3 p.m., it was Nissan's race. Pole-sitter Fangio led the first lap, while Stuck led a lap at the hour mark during pit stops, but Nissans led the remainder of the event.

Toyota encountered problems early on. Fangio ran a strong first shift, but relief driver Andy Wallace pitted 15 minutes into his first shift with no power, due to an electrical problem. The car sat on pit road for 21 laps while the alternator was repaired. The team would struggle with damage from a collision that occurred while exiting pit road and various mechanical shortfalls throughout the race.

Shortly after 7:30 p.m., the two younger Brabham brothers encountered problems at the same part of the race course. First, David struck the guardrail exiting pit road, costing the lone Jaguar five laps. Two minutes later, Gary hit the same piece of guardrail, badly damaging the fifth-place No. 84 Nissan.

"That's where Geoff always told me to be very careful," said Gary after the incident. "I went to turn left and went straight into the guardrail. I was on fresh, unscrubbed tires. It's getting cold. It was like ice skating out there."

While the younger Brabhams struggled, big brother Geoff seemed to have matters in hand with the No. 83 Nissan, as he battled the NISMO Nissan for the lead. The two teams exchanged the lead several times during the first nine hours, until the engine in Brabham's car suddenly quit in the infield while leading at 11:22 p.m. "The engine blew up, just like that," Brabham said. "Something must have broken inside the engine, because it just locked up solid. There was no warning."

Not only were Geoff Brabham and teammate Chip Robinson out of the race, neither driver had accumulated enough laps to score Camel GT points. That put the NISMO Nissan in control, but the competition wasn't ready to throw in the towel.

"Look at the pace they're running, it's crazy," Haywood told Godwin Kelly of the *Daytona Beach*

Top: Pole winner Juan Manuel Fangio II leads the field in the early laps, driving the No. 99 Toyota Eagle Mk III. Above: Hans Stuck qualified third in the Joest-entered Momo Porsche 962, but the car he shared with Gianpiero Moretti, Frank Jelinski, and Henri Pescarolo went out at 7 a.m. with electrical problems. Right: Dick Greer repeated in the GTU class, joined by Al Bacon, Mike Mees, and Peter Uria in the Wendy's Mazda RX-7, shown racing the Porsche 911 of ex-NFL quarterback Dan Pastorini, Tim McAdam, Charles Monk, Sam Shalala, and Andre Toennis. Far right: A pit stop for Vern Schuppan's 0123 Art Corp. Porsche 962. Hurley Haywood, Eje Elgh, Roland Ratzenberger, and Scott Brayton drove the car to a third-place finish.

News-Journal. "You don't need to be a brain surgeon to figure out the Nissans are going to have problems."

Porsche took up the challenge, and had cars in the second, third, and fifth positions by the 10-hour mark. However, both the Brun and Joest cars were out by 7 a.m.—one with electrical problems, the other with engine failure—while the Schuppan car continued the chase.

"Our engine suddenly stopped and wouldn't start again," said Frank Jelinski, bidding for his second consecutive Daytona victory, after the Joest Porsche stopped at 7 a.m. "The car was OK, no problems at all. We were not so fast as the Nissan, but we could hold our speed and maybe at the end we could finish first."

At 9 a.m., Schuppan's remaining Porsche 962 hit encountered brake problems, which cost the team

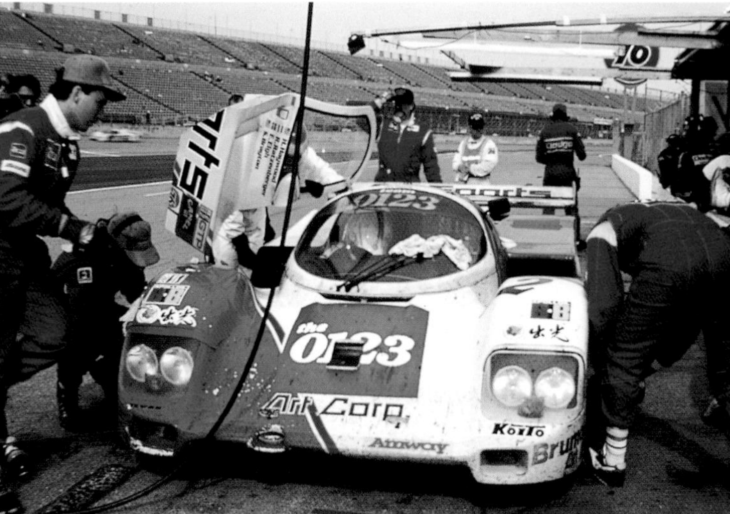

four laps and second place overall.

In the biggest incident of the race, Olympic ski champion Phil Mahre stalled his Mazda MX-6 and was hit by the Buick Spice of Ken Parschauer, which sent the Mazda flying into the path of the Buick Kudzu of Jim Pace. The Buick caught fire, but no one was hurt.

NISMO's only problem the remainder of the race was overheating, caused by sand in the radiator. They quickly diagnosed that problem, and the car ran flawlessly the rest of the way. Hasemi, Hoshino, and Suzuki drove to a nine-lap victory that broke both the speed and distance records for the race. The winning team covered 762 laps, 2,712.720 miles, and averaged 112.897 mph. It was the first 24-hour victory for Nissan, coming on the heels of Japanese rival Mazda's 1991 victory at Le Mans. NISMO had left nothing to chance and brought 150 mechanics to the race.

"I can not express how enjoyable it was to cross the finish line and win this race," said Suzuki. "I was very glad to take the victory. Daytona is very historic, a very prestigious event."

Some late-race drama was provided by Haywood, who squeezed his Porsche into a tight Nissan formation to spoil the checkered-flag photo finish, despite efforts by the Nissan drivers to shove him out of the way.

Finishing second, and first in the IMSA GTP category, was the TWR Jaguar of Davy Jones, Scott Pruett, Scott Goodyear, and David Brabham. "We ran the car very, very hard the whole race," said Pruett. "We didn't have many problems, but the Nissan was just a faster car."

Third went to Schuppan's Team 0123 Porsche 962. The team lost four laps repairing a broken brake caliper at noon on Sunday, which cost them second place overall and the GTP victory.

The Gurney Toyota driven by Jones, Moran, and Dismore managed to place fourth, 23 laps behind. Dismore drove three solid consecutive nighttime shifts, his first road racing since he was injured in the 1991 Indianapolis 500. Their team car of Fangio, Wallace, and Acheson struggled through their early alternator problem, a three-hour front-end rebuild, and other mechanical trouble to place 11th overall and fourth in GTP.

"It's always better to win, but, having our two Toyotas running at the end of the race, it's already a victory," said Fangio. Toyota had proven it was strong enough to finish a 24-hour race. A post-race systems check proved the car could have run faster than the conservative pace chosen for the event. One month later, the team proved itself with a win in the 12 Hours of Sebring after an exciting battle with the American NTPI Nissan team. Toyota would continue its dominance through the remainder of the 1992 season.

The support classes had new names, but familiar winners. GTO was now called Exxon Supreme GTS, but had the same winner, with Roush Racing taking its eighth consecutive title in the class. Dorsey Schroeder, Wally Dallenbach, and Robby Gordon lost a piston with three hours remaining and failed to finish, but were holding a 100-lap lead at the time. The team still managed to place ninth overall and win the class by 24 laps over the Rocketsports Oldsmobile Cutlass of Jeff Kline, George Robinson, Darin Brassfield, and Paul Gentilozzi.

Mark Martin hit the wall early in the race when his feet got tangled up in the pedals of the second Roush Mustang. His team repaired the damage, and the car came back to place third in the class.

Jeremy Dale led GTS early in the event driving Clayton Cunningham's CCR Nissan 300ZX, but broke an oil fitting, which caused a loss of oil pressure, a spin, and a fire that burned the wiring, resulting in a long stop. Dale, joined by Johnny O'Connell and John Morton, recovered to finish fourth in GTS.

Parker Johnstone and Steve Cameron recorded their second consecutive Camel Lights victory, joining Jimmy Vasser and Dan Marvin in the fifth-place Comptech Acura Spice SE91P. They led for all but a few minutes after their first fuel stop. The team took time late in the race to wash the car on pit road and make it look good for the finish.

Doug Peterson's Comptech team had one scare, when the fuel pump failed and the Acura lost power in NASCAR turn three, shortly after noon. Johnstone pushed the car to the entrance

Above: NASCAR Winston Cup driver Mark Martin climbs from Jack Roush's Whistler Ford Mustang to examine the damage from an impact with an infield barrier. Martin crashed after his feet became tangled in the pedals. The team repaired the car, and it came back to finish third in GTS. Joining Martin were Robbie Buhl, Calvin Fish, and Jim Stevens. Right: The infield racing action continues into a brilliant sunset.

of pit road so the team could work on it, and quickly corrected the problem. "I'll never make the bobsled team," he said. "That was one of the most physically demanding things I ever did in my life, pushing a 1,750-pound car. That was a pretty good effort."

Joining the Camel Lights field was Scandia Engineering, which had a Buick Kudzu for Andy Evans, Fermin Velez, and Dominic Dobson. Dobson set a fast time in the car, which finished second in the class, 27 laps behind the Acura.

In GTU, the Mazda RX-7 of Dick Greer repeated its win, with the car owner joined by Al Bacon, Mike Mees, and Peter Uria. It was the 11th consecutive GTU victory and 12th Daytona 24 Hours win for Mazda.

Nissans also ran up front in that class, with Leitzinger Racing fielding a pair of 240SXs. The cars ran one-two after six hours, but both fell back with cracked cylinder heads. Dodge also had a strong entry. John Fergus was running second at the eight-hour mark when he struck an errant wheel, resulting in suspension damage that required lengthy trackside repairs. The team managed to finish sixth, with Bobby Akin, Bob Leibert, and Neil Hannemann co-driving with Fergus.

The Exxon Supreme Series also had a GTO category for 1992 competition, open to cars that once raced in the All American Challenge specification. However, the class did not compete in the Rolex 24.

By itself, the 1992 edition of the Rolex 24 at Daytona had an impressive entry, with a variety of contending GTP cars. As the season progressed, however, numbers would continue to decline.

TOYOTA
99
TIMET

1993: The Last Man Standing

NISSAN, JAGUAR, AND MAZDA ALL WITHDREW FACTORY SUPPORT FROM RUNNING A FULL SEASON IN 1993. THE DAYS OF THE CAMEL GT PROTOTYPE CLASS WERE NUMBERED. IMSA HAD ALREADY ANNOUNCED PLANS FOR THE OPEN-COCKPIT WORLD SPORTS CAR, WHICH WOULD DEBUT IN 1994 AND BECOME THE PREMIER CLASS IN 1995. ADDING TO IMSA'S TROUBLES, LONG-TIME SPONSOR CAMEL WAS ALSO IN ITS FINAL YEAR SUPPORTING THE TOP GTP CLASS.

Dan Gurney's All American Racers Toyota team was now the only factory team planning to run the full 1993 IMSA schedule. Gurney returned to Daytona with a pair of Toyota Eagle Mk IIIs, chased by a handful of privateer Porsches and Nissans. In all, only 10 GT Prototypes were entered, down from 20 in 1992. Overall, however, the field had 60 starters, 11 more than the previous year.

As expected, Gurney's white Toyotas swept the front row. P. J. Jones captured the pole with a record lap of 136.52 mph, breaking teammate Juan Fangio II's year-old record by two seconds. Fangio qualified second, at 135.38 mph. Jones, the son of Indy Car racing legend Parnelli Jones, shared the No. 98 Eagle with Mark Dismore and Rocky Moran, while Andy Wallace and Ken Acheson were teamed with Fangio in the No. 99 entry.

The only other factory team participating in the race was Jaguar, which

Left: A wide-angle view of a pit stop for the No. 99 Toyota Eagle of Juan Manuel Fangio II, Andy Wallace, and Kenneth Acheson. After struggling with electrical issues that began four hours into the race, the car retired with engine failure. Above: Kevin Doran fielded an ex-Geoff Brabham Nissan NPTI-90 for Gianpiero Moretti, John Paul Jr., Derek Bell, and Massimo Sigala. The car led before blowing its engine with one hour, 40 minutes remaining.

entered a trio of TWR Jaguars. The company intended to run one of the cars, No. 32, for only 10 laps as a shakedown for the 24 Hours of Le Mans, with the car set up for the French event.

Gianpiero Moretti entered an ex-Brabham NPTI-90, qualified third by John Paul Jr., Derek Bell, and Massimo Sigala. Kevin Doran, who had enjoyed success at Daytona as crew chief for Al Holbert, made his debut as a car owner in the event.

Skeptics of Toyota's reliability expected Reinhold Joest's entry, a pair of race-proven Porsche 962s, to win with its impressive driver lineup. Chip Robinson was joined by Hurley Haywood, Danny Sullivan, and Henri Pescarolo, with Bob Wollek, John Winter, Frank Jelinski, and Manuel Reuter in the second car. Collectively, the team had earned 19 victories in the 24-hour races at Daytona and Le Mans.

"The best way to win one of these races is in a Porsche," said Haywood, who had already backed up that claim five times at Daytona, three times at Le Mans, and twice in the 12 Hours of Sebring. The fastest Porsche 962 was qualified by Robinson, an ex-Nissan driver.

While spiraling expenses, coupled with a slumping economy, were pricing the GT Prototypes out of existence, the lure of running Daytona continued to attract top teams. "We hadn't planned on running

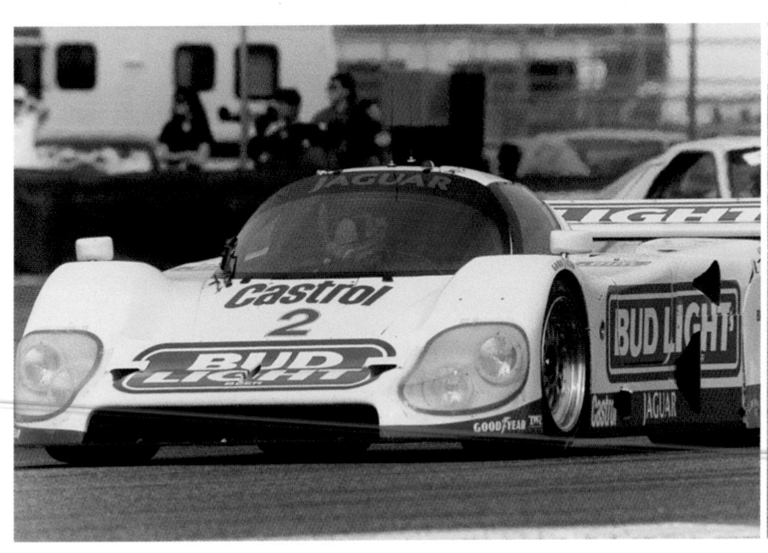

the Rolex 24 that year," recalled Rob Dyson, who sat out the entire 1992 season. "We had even sold our Porsche 962, chassis No. 148. We weren't supposed to deliver that car to the new owner until after the 24-hour race, so we decided at the shop party on Christmas Eve, 'What the heck, why not run it one last time?' I figured we had one last shot at winning the Rolex 24 in the Porsche 962."

To pilot the car, Dyson got together several of his ex-drivers, including Price Cobb and James Weaver. The only driver new to the team was Elliott Forbes-Robinson.

The Toyotas pulled away at the drop of the green flag, with Jones and Fangio trading the lead four

Above left: The TWR Jaguar XJR-12D had a memorable race. Scott Pruett repaired the transmission linkage on course, managing to keep the car in the lead. Then the engine suddenly let go, costing them a chance of victory. Above right: Looking more like a NASCAR modified than a Camel Lights car, Buddy Lazier, Sam Shahala, Michael Sheehan, Chris Ivey, and Anthony Lazzaro managed to finish in a wounded Porsche Fabcar owned by Frank Beard of the rock band ZZ Top. Opposite: Dan Gurney's two All American Racing Toyota Eagles pull away at the start of the 1993 Rolex 24 at Daytona.

times in the opening 30 minutes.

Jaguar was down to two cars in the opening hour, when the No. 3 of John Neilsen and David Brabham retired with an oil leak. At that point, the team returned the No. 32 to the event, after they had already parked it in the early going, as planned. Now, the Le Mans–configured car would really be tested.

Ironically, the proven reliable Porsches were among the first contenders to fall by the wayside. The No. 7 Joest Porsche went out with a blown engine with Henri Pescarolo at the wheel, while the team's other car struggled with overheating problems, finally being parked shortly after midnight.

"I think I was the only guy on the two-car team that didn't have at least one 24-hour win," Sullivan recalled. "With the Porsche 962s, it looked like here's my best chance to win the race. Then, neither car lasted four hours, which was almost unheard of in those days for a Porsche 962. But, *c'est la vie!*"

Another car that withdrew early was Kevin Jeannette's Gunnar Porsche 966, an open-cockpit version of the 962. Driven by Dennis Aase/Bobby Carradine/Jay Cochran/Chip Hanauer/Carlos Moran, it went out after 271 laps with engine problems.

Four hours into the race, the No. 32 Le Mans Jaguar also retired with handling problems. The Momo Nissan struggled to correct an electrical problem and lost time in the pits.

After being the only two cars on the lead lap for four hours, P. J. Jones had a lap on the field when Fangio pitted in the No. 99 Toyota with electrical problems. It was later withdrawn with engine problems. The No. 98 entry would have better luck.

P. J. Jones held the lead until midnight, when the Jaguar of Davy Jones took over, as the Toyota team was having trouble replacing front bodywork. The two cars traded the lead throughout the remainder of the evening in a tight battle. Then, at 5:50 a.m., the second-place Toyota of Mark Dismore tapped the wall in the chicane. Dismore was able to drive back to the pits, and returned to the race seven minutes later after repairs.

The Jaguar was leading at 9:51 a.m., when Pruett pulled off course in the infield with transmission failure. Under the careful supervision of his crew, he then changed one-third of the shift linkage.

Only six minutes after Pruett had pulled off course with transmission trouble, Dismore pitted in the Toyota, which was smoking. The Toyota team spent one hour and 16 minutes on pit road Sunday

Above: Dan Gurney's Toyota Eagles weave their way through traffic in the infield. Boris Said, Peter Cunningham, Lou Gigliotti, and Jim Minneker shared Kim Baker's No. 5 Corvette, while Andy Evans, Charles Morgan, and Lon Bender co-drove the No. 44 Scandia Buick. Right: 1993 marked the final year Bob Leitzinger raced his No. 95 Nissan 240SX with his sons, Butch Leitzinger and Chuck Kurtz. The car was quickest in the GTU and led the class for half the race. Eventually, suspension problems led to a third-place finish. Far right: The No. 1 Nissan 300ZX of John Morton, Steve Millen, and Johnny O'Connell finished fourth overall and second in GTS. The Clayton Cunningham team came within four hours of winning, losing the lead when its turbocharger failed.

morning for a lengthy transmission replacement. "It was an up-and-down emotional roller coaster," said P. J. Jones. "After that long pit stop, we thought, 'No way, we're out of it.'"

By the time the transmission was replaced, the Toyota had fallen 30 laps behind the Jaguar, which was battling with the Momo Nissan NPTI of Gianpiero Moretti, Derek Bell, John Paul Jr., and Massimo Sigala.

While Pruett completed transmission repairs, Davy Jones took over the Jaguar so it could immediately resume racing when Pruett finished his work. The team managed to retain its lead, while the Momo Nissan passed the parked Toyota to claim second. But shortly afterwards, at 11:35 a.m., the Bud Light Jaguar's engine expired in a puff of smoke.

"After we got the shifting problem fixed, the car was perfect," said Davy Jones. "I thought we were ready to win. We had built up such a big lead we were lowering our rpms, running to finish. Then, with no indications at all, the engine let go."

That gave the Momo Nissan a two-lap lead, which was cushioned when the Toyota returned to pit road for new brake pads. But the Nissan was soon in trouble. The engine failed in turn six with one hour and 40 minutes remaining. The last contender had fallen by the wayside.

"After we took the lead, the red light for oil pressure came on in the slow corners," said Moretti. "Then, it just stopped. It did 22 hours and then she said, 'It's enough.' We were 32 laps down at one point and came back, so I was happy with the effort."

The Toyota regained the lead with 96 minutes left, and was unchallenged for the remainder of the race. The team completed 698 laps, 2,484.88 miles, averaging 103.503 mph. Jones became the first pole winner to also win the race since Bob Wollek in 1983.

"We came here with not very high expectations," said Gurney. "But we intended to race and see what would happen. I thought our engine was our weakest link, but our engine people said, 'Run it hard.' We figured we would just go and race, and see what happened. We ran hard so they had to keep up with us. It was the right move."

"This was the jewel we were missing," added Jones. "It's the biggest race I've ever won."

The only other Camel GTP car still running at the finish was Dyson's "borrowed" Porsche 962C, 43 laps behind. But what if the team had wrecked the car, which Dyson had already sold?

"Both of our days would have been ruined," Dyson recalled with a smile.

The Moretti Nissan, which led with two hours remaining before it exited, was classified in sixth. "Gianpiero and I nearly won in our first race," car owner Kevin Doran recalled in a 2001 interview. "In hindsight, he might have retired if he had won that race, so maybe it was a good thing we didn't win then."

Finishing 10th overall was the TWR XJR-12D shared by Scott Pruett, Davy Jones, and Scott Goodyear. Although the team had withdrawn with engine failure, it finished first in Group C1/Category 2.

In the Exxon GTS class, Jack Roush triumphed once again, with Wally Dallenbach, Robby Gordon, Tommy Kendall, and Robbie Buhl. Their Mustang finished second overall, 10 laps down, two laps ahead of teammates Mark Martin, John Fergus, and Jim Stevens, who placed third overall. It was Roush's ninth-straight class victory in the event. "We might not be able to outrun the GTP cars, but we can outlast them," said Dallenbach.

"We thought we had a shot of winning the overall race," said Gordon, who won his fourth class victory for Roush in the event. "We didn't think the Toyota could make it 24 hours, but they proved us wrong and deserved to win."

"This was a big breakthrough for me," said Buhl. "That was the first opportunity that I ever had to run for a big team, where we had tires, transmissions, people taking care of stuff, plenty of food there. It was a first-class operation, and that was the first time I was exposed to that in racing. That was fun." Buhl had tried out for the Roush team three years earlier, after he had captured the Barber Saab Pro Series championship, but had lost out to Robby Gordon.

"We were prepared to run faster than the competition," said Roush. "I think we ran harder than we ever had to for the whole thing, and with less trouble."

Once again, Nissan and Oldsmobile fielded fast two-car efforts, but both ran into trouble. Clayton Cunningham's Nissan 300ZX Twin Turbo came within four hours of winning in GTS, only to have its turbocharger fail late Sunday morning. The crew rebuilt the turbo in 42 minutes, and Steve Millen, Johnny O'Connell, and John Morton managed to finish fourth overall and third in the class, 20 laps behind the winning Roush car.

A second Nissan, co-driven by four-time Camel GTP champion Geoff Brabham, failed at the midway point. Paul Gentilozzi entered two Rocketsports Oldsmobile Cutlasses, but both retired almost simultaneously with camshaft failure six hours into the event.

Jim Downing won in Camel Lights, finishing seventh overall in the Mazda Kudzu DG-1 he shared with John Grooms, Tim Jellinek, and Tim McAdam. The team lost fourth gear but had few other problems in the event.

Above: Future IMSA president Charlie Slater works on trackside repairs after the Alex Job Porsche 911 was badly damaged in an off-course excursion near the infield lake. Slater, Mark Sandridge, and Butch Hamlet managed to get the car running, and the team finished the race. Right: Dan Gurney, Rocky Moran, P. J. Jones, and Mark Dismore celebrate with the first-place trophy, presented by Rolex Watch USA President and CEO Roland Puton. Thirty-one years after winning the inaugural Daytona Continental, Gurney won the final Daytona 24 Hours for the GTP category.

Parker Johnstone was fastest in opening Camel Lights qualifying in the Comptech Acura Spice, and was making a bid for his 15th consecutive class pole, a streak that extended back to 1990. The streak ended the following day, however, when Bob Earl took the pole with a record lap of 122.323 mph in the Motorola Acura Spice. Neither car fared well in the race. Comptech's bid for a third consecutive class victory ended early due to electrical problems, while the engine blew in Earl's Acura Spice.

In GTU, Dick Greer triumphed for the third straight year in a Mazda RX-7, placing ninth overall. At age 61, he became the oldest class winner in the history of the event. Co-driving were Al Bacon, Peter Uria, and Mike Mees. It was Uria's fourth consecutive Daytona triumph, while Bacon, who won in 1989, also scored his fourth Daytona victory. "Every year it seems to get a little easier," said Uria.

Second, 46 laps behind the Mazda, was a Porsche 911 owned and driven by Frank Beard, drummer for the rock band ZZ Top. His lineup included Anthony Lazzaro, Alex Tradd, and Omar Daniel.

A new class called Invitational GT had been added for FIA GT Group A or Group B competitors, or Latin American "GTU Junior" cars. Ten street-legal cars modified for racing participated. Winning the class, and finishing 11th overall, was the Porsche 911 Carrera 2 of Enzo Calderari, Luigiano Pagotto, Sandro Angelastri, and Ronnie Meixner.

With the final appearance of the IMSA Camel GTP Prototypes, the 1993 race marked the end of an era. Fittingly, the man who went out on top was All-American hero Dan Gurney.

Gurney came to Daytona a winner, rolling to a triumph in the 1962 Daytona Continental. In 1993, he also went out a winner. His team followed up its Daytona triumph by winning every IMSA event it entered that year (they sat out the race at Road America), with Fangio steamrolling to the championship, followed by Jones.

EXXON
86
F.A.T.
INTERNATIONAL
GROUPAGES EUROPÉENS
larbre
EL MUNDO
IMSA
BOSCH
76

1994: The World Sports Car Debuts

IMSA had a new owner in 1994. Veteran Porsche campaigner Charles Slater had purchased the beleaguered sanctioning body from Mike Cone in February, 1993. Slater had made his fortune developing disposable medical instruments, and after he sold his company, he undertook the challenge of saving IMSA. His major change was replacing Dan Greenwood as IMSA president with Hal Kelley Jr. Slater kept a hands-off approach during the race weekends, and concentrated on running his Porsche in the GT-2 class.

Eight new open-cockpit World Sports Car prototypes were on hand to start the season for the IMSA series, now known as the Exxon World Sports Car Championship. The new chassis were similar to the flat-bottomed Camel Lights cars, although more powerful engines were permitted.

Teams took different approaches to the new class. Some cut the roofs off GTP or Camel Lights cars. Others used ingenuity. Rob Dyson brought a yellow Ferrari-Spice 348, which he built especially for this race.

Left: The No. 86 Fat Turbo Express Porsche 911S of Bob Wollek, Jesus Parejo, Dominique Dupuy, and Jurgen Barth en route to a second-place finish and first in the Le Mans GT-1 class. Above: In an attempt to come up with the best combination for the new World Sports Car class, Rob Dyson did his research by going through automobile magazines, and then built a Ferrari-powered Spice. James Weaver, Scott Sharp, and John Paul Jr. joined the New York businessman in his debut WSC outing.

"It was built to the letter—and spirit—of the rules," Dyson recalled. "The rules called for a street-derived engine. I picked up a *Road and Track* magazine, the 1993 year-end review of cars. I scanned the tests and engine configurations, and liked the Ferrari 348. It had a V-8 engine with four valves per cylinder. I bought one from a car graveyard, pulled it apart, and shipped the engine to Ted Wentz."

Brix Motorsports switched from Camel Lights to the new class, and ordered a conversion kit from Spice USA, in addition to a brand-new, purpose-built World Sports Car.

Jim Downing, the father of the Camel Lights class, designed a new World Sports Car, designated the Kudzu DG2, in addition to modifying his Camel Lights Kudzus for the new class. For the race, Downing was joined in the cockpit by Wayne Taylor, Charles Morgan, and Hugh Fuller.

Morris Shirazi, of the Auto Toy Store team, fielded a Chevrolet-powered Spice WSC prepared by Mike Colucci for veteran endurance stars Derek Bell, Geoff Brabham, and Andy Wallace.

Andy Evans hadn't waited for Daytona to debut his World Sports Car. He had unveiled his Scandia Motorsports Kudzu DG2 in Miami in 1993 and run it for most of the 1993 season. "The biggest thing is that these are flat-bottomed cars," Evans said. "This is a new experience for drivers who are used to ground effects and 6,000 pounds of downforce, which you had in a Nissan, Toyota, or Jaguar."

While Evans fielded his year-old Kudzu in the Rolex 24 for Don Bell, Steve Fossett, and Andreas Fuchs, he also brought a new Spice WSC that he co-drove with Fermin Velez and Ross Bentley.

With the World Sports Car class as yet unproven, speculation raged that one of the production-based classes could pull out the overall win. But the GT classes would be without their biggest star: Jack Roush had decided to sit out the event to concentrate on his growing NASCAR Winston Cup program. This ended his streak of nine consecutive wins in the GTO/GTS class.

Above left: An off-course excursion for the No. 94 Tommy Morrison Corvette early in the event. John Heinricy, Andy Pilgrim, Stu Hayner, and Boris Said recovered to finish seventh overall and second in the Le Mans GT-1 class. Above right: A pit stop for the No. 63 Mazda Kudzu of Jim Downing, Wayne Taylor, Charles Morgan, and Hugh Fuller. The father of the Camel Lights class, Downing built one of the earliest examples of a World Sports Car. Opposite: Indy car standout Danny Sullivan (left), talks strategy with Brumos Porsche team manager Bob Snodgrass.

Brumos entered a Porsche 911 Turbo for the Le Mans GT-1 category, with a star-studded lineup of endurance greats that included Hurley Haywood and Hans Stuck, joined by World Rally champion Walter Rohrl and Indianapolis 500 winner Danny Sullivan.

FAT Turbo Express had Bob Wollek heading the driver lineup of its 911, while defending Camel GT champion Juan Fangio II, who had no full-time drive for the season, joined the Champion Porsche 911 team of Bill Adam and Brian Redman. Redman was marking the 25th anniversary of his first Porsche factory ride. Tommy Morrison also fielded a pair of Corvettes in the class.

In GTS, Clayton Cunningham's two twin-turbocharged Nissan 300 ZXTs sparkled in the January test session, running first and third fastest. Steve Millen was in the lead car, joined by Johnny O'Connell and John Morton.

Paul Gentilozzi saw the event as an opportunity to win overall. He had entered a partnership with Cunningham to field a second Nissan 300 ZXT, and was joined by Scott Pruett and Butch Leitzinger, who had raced Nissans in GTU for several years, taking a championship. Gentilozzi also brought his team manager, Lee White (formerly with Roush Racing), and three of his crewmen.

"We knew we had a solid chance, but we also knew that some of these other guys, the WSC cars, would have to have problems," Pruett recalled. "We also had to look at some of the Porsches, because they are very tough cars to beat in an endurance race."

In addition to fielding his new World Sports Car, Harry Brix prepared a pair of Oldsmobile Cutlasses bought from Gentilozzi. His driver lineup had Darin Brassfield, Mark Dismore, and John Fergus in the No. 5 car, and Irv Hoerr, Tommy Riggins, and R. K. Smith in the No. 6 entry.

DAYTONA ★ USA
ROLEX
EXXON
NISSAN
AGFA FILM
PIAA
AMERICA
PERRY ELLIS

In qualifying, the World Sports Cars came to the front. Velez put the Scandia Chevy Spice on the pole with a lap of 120.981 mph, joined on the front row by Jeremy Dale in the Brix Olds Spice. WSC entries took five of the top seven positions, but ominously, the CCR Nissans of Millen and Gentilozzi held down the second row. It didn't take them long to move to the front, as the new World Sports Cars quickly began experiencing teething problems.

Soon after the 3 p.m. green flag, Velez sprinted ahead of the 63-car field, the largest for the event since 1989. But the Spice's lead was short lived because of an electrical fire. "There were small flames

inside the engine, so I stopped in front of one of the track marshals, and he put out the fire with a small extinguisher," Velez said. "But the fire reappeared, and I had to go to the pits. It was not a good way to start the race."

While the Scandia Chevrolet Spice returned to the race, with Bentley at the wheel, it headed back to the pits only 30 minutes later. The car would lose two hours while the battery, oil line, and air jack line were replaced. "New car blues," said owner/driver Andy Evans. "You can't do anything about it. Unless everybody else breaks, we're not going to get back in it."

Meanwhile, pit road resembled a parking lot for the open-top prototypes, which struggled in the early going. Six of the eight WSCs suffered some kind of mechanical malady by the two-hour mark, and at 5:30 p.m., five WSC cars were parked on pit road with their engine compartments uncovered. The Dyson Ferrari lost an alternator, the Shirazi Spice encountered numerous problems, and the Brix Olds Spice had a fire while refueling.

With the WSCs struggling, the GTS race was also the battle for the lead, and it was a close fight. Morton, driving one of the CCR Nissans, passed Velez for the lead only 30 minutes into the race, when the Scandia car experienced its fire.

Left: Fermin Velez in the pole-winning Scandia Chevrolet-Spice WSC94 leads at the start of the 1994 Rolex 24 at Daytona. Above left: Brumos Porsche returned with a 911 using the familiar paint scheme that dominated the Daytona 24 Hours in the seventies. The car was driven by the solid lineup of Hans Stuck, Walter Roehrl, Hurley Haywood, and Danny Sullivan. While the car qualified eighth and ran up front, a pair of broken fan belts led to the car's early demise. Above right: Nighttime brake work for the eventual-winning Clayton Cunningham Racing No. 76 Nissan.

The two Nissans, the No. 5 Brix Oldsmobile and the Brumos Porsche, ran in the top four at the end of the fourth hour—all on the lead lap. The Brumos Porsche led overall at the end of two hours and again after five hours. The No. 6 Brix Oldsmobile suffered bodywork damage following an incident in turn two, and the car handled badly for the remainder of the event.

Early in the sixth hour, the fan belt broke in the Brumos car, costing the team 16 minutes for repairs. Moments later, the No. 5 Brix Oldsmobile broke an input shaft. Two hours later, Redman's Champion Porsche tangled with Leigh Miller's GTU Porsche 968 at the fastest part of the course, sending Redman into the wall and out of the race.

A battle at the front between the two CCR Nissans ended at 12:47 a.m., when the Millen Nissan's crankshaft broke. From that point on, the remainder of the field waited in vain for the No. 76 Nissan to have problems.

The pole-winning Scandia Spice finally withdrew at 1:13 a.m. with a fuel pump belt failure. The Dyson team retired its Ferrari-Spice at 7:30 a.m. "A baffle came loose in the sump, and the oil pump came loose," Weaver said. "Scott [Sharp] shut it off. He caught it just in time."

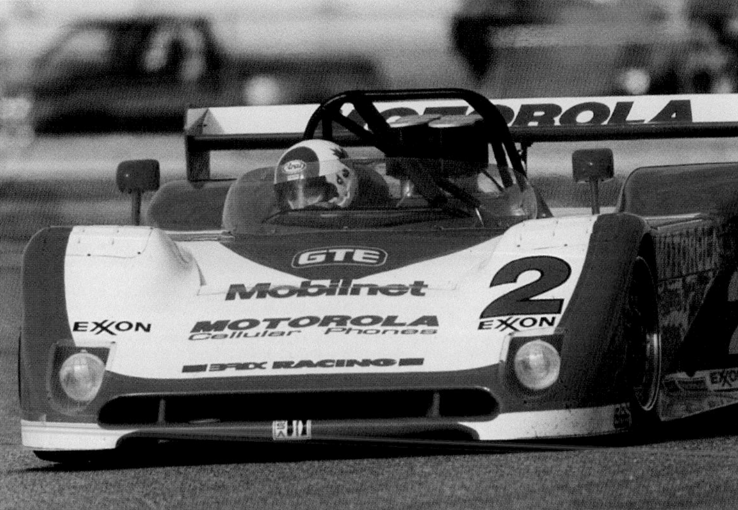

"Blazing trails like this has its drawbacks," said Dyson after the car's retirement. "It also has its opportunities." After seeing the Ferrari 333SP in later 1994 competition, Dyson realized a homemade hybrid would not be competitive in the new class. He commissioned Riley & Scott to construct the first all-new World Sports Car, which would be called the Riley & Scott Mark III.

The Brumos Porsche lost another belt at 7 a.m., but the team was not as lucky this time. The fan belt had broken just as Hans Stuck crossed the start/finish line, and by the time he made it back to the pits, the engine had suffered terminal damage.

Above left: Many of the top WSC cars encountered problems early in the event. Above, the No. 9 Auto Toy Store and No. 16 Dyson teams receive lengthy service on pit road. Above right: The top-finishing car in the new World Sports Car class was the No. 2 Oldsmobile Spice fielded by Harry Brix. Jeremy Dale, Ruggero Melgrati, Bob Shader, and Price Cobb finished the event ninth overall, taking honors in the new class by one lap over Jim Downing's Mazda-Kudzu. Opposite: From left to right Butch Leitzinger, Paul Gentilozzi, Scott Pruett, and Steve Millen pose with the first-place trophy in victory lane.

The Brumos' retirement brought the FAT Turbo Porsche into second, nine laps behind the Nissan. The team added a fourth driver late in the race—Jurgen Barth, Porsche's customer car-racing coordinator. Barth had last driven at Daytona in 1979, when he finished fourth in a Porsche 935.

During a morning shower, the CCR team decided to give Steve Millen a turn in the No. 76 Nissan. "When it started to rain, we got Steve to come out, because he had driven the car for the past five or six years," Leitzinger said. "He was a fantastic driver in the rain in those cars, but also it wouldn't really have been fair to win that race without him getting some exposure, because he did so much bringing that program around."

Nissan went on to win before an estimated crowd of 50,000, covering 707 laps, 2,516.92 miles, and averaging 104.80 mph. The team led all but 111 circuits, including the final 427. Their margin of victory was 24 laps.

A GT car had won for the first time since 1983. It was also the first triumph for a front-engine car since 1976, when Brian Redman, Peter Gregg, and John Fitzpatrick won in a BMW. The win came 10 years after Cunningham won the GTU class in a Mazda RX-7. "If the race looked like we had no problems, it's because they caught things before they became trouble," said Leitzinger. "When we had a small brake problem, they snapped right to it, got just what they needed and corrected it."

Finishing second overall was a familiar car, the Porsche 911, albeit a turbocharged version. Bob Wollek joined Dominique Dupy, Jesus Pareja, Jack LeConte, and Barth in the Fat Turbo Express entry, which finished 24 laps behind. They also took honors in the Le Mans GT-1 class. "It's an achievement, and the worst thing in the world to do, to finish second," Wollek said. "I don't come to race to finish second. I come to win. But we weren't going to win the way the Nissan was running."

Taking third, and first in GTU and Le Mans GT-2, was the Porsche 911 RSR of Dirk Ebeling, Karl Wlazik, Ulrich Richter, and Gunther Doebler. The RSR of Harald Grohs took fourth, followed by the ill-handling Brix Olds Cutlass of Irv Hoerr, Tommy Riggins, and R.K. Smith.

Tommy Morrison's Corvette team struggled in the early going with electrical problems, but ran strong the rest of the race with drivers Andy Pilgrim, John Heinricy, Boris Said, and Stu Hayner. They finished seventh overall and second in the Le Mans GT-1 class.

Jeremy Dale, Price Cobb, Bob Schader, and Ruggero Melgrati won the World Sports Car class in the Brix Oldsmobile-powered Spice, finishing ninth overall. Fuel pickup problems forced the team to make 60 pit stops to complete the distance, and they finished 56 laps behind the overall winners. Second in WSC and 10th overall was Jim Downing's Danka Mazda Kudzu, co-driven by Downing, Wayne Taylor, Charles Morgan, and Hugh Fuller.

Lost in the influx of European GTU Porsches was Dick Greer, who attempted to win his class for the fourth consecutive year in an aged, tube-frame Mazda RX-7. His team rebuilt the engine in a hotel room the night before the race, but the car went out after 258 laps.

Budweiser
70
ROUSH RACING

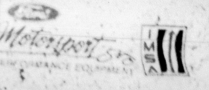
Motorsport
PERFORMANCE EQUIPMENT
IMSA

1995: A 70th-Birthday Present

ACTOR PAUL NEWMAN HAD PLAYED MANY LEADING ROLES THROUGHOUT HIS LONG CAREER IN THE MOVIES. BUT IN 1995, HE WAS CONTENT TO PLAY A SUPPORTING ROLE IN A MAJOR PRODUCTION AT DAYTONA. TO CELEBRATE THE STAR'S 70TH BIRTHDAY, PARAMOUNT PICTURES PRESENTED NEWMAN WITH A RIDE IN THE ROLEX 24. IT WAS A MUSTANG FIELDED BY JACK ROUSH, WHOSE TEAM WOULD BE COMPETING IN THE EVENT AFTER A ONE-YEAR ABSENCE.

Joining Newman in the cockpit were Trans-Am champion Tommy Kendall, NASCAR Winston Cup star Mark Martin, and Michael Brockman, a fellow driver/actor. The car carried the number 70 in honor of Newman's age, along with the name of his upcoming film, *Nobody's Fool.*

The 1995 event included 74 cars, the largest entry in recent years. The Exxon World Sports Cars were the most numerous contingent, with 20 of the open-cockpit cars on hand. Also eligible were the turbocharged Le Mans World Sports Cars. The French endurance event had recognized the American class by making them eligible for its 24-hour classic, and the American sanctioning body reciprocated. European cars would be eligible at the Rolex 24, with minor modifications.

Left: To celebrate Paul Newman's 70th birthday, Paramount Studios had Jack Roush prepare a Ford Mustang for the 1995 Rolex 24. Newman was joined by his friend and fellow racer/actor Michael Brockman, along with Mark Martin and Tommy Kendall. The car carried the name of Newman's upcoming film, Nobody's Fool. *Above: Paul Newman flashes 10 fingers signifying 10 consecutive class victories for Jack Roush, although the streak skipped a year when Roush did not compete in 1994.*

Porsche responded to the challenge by entering a pair of Le Mans WSCs. Mario Andretti joined Bob Wollek, Scott Goodyear, and Scott Pruett in one of Porsche's "X-Machine" prototypes, built by Tom Walkinshaw. Andretti had just completed his "Arrivederci Mario" tour, in which he bade farewell to Champ Car competition. "It was a top-secret project Porsche had," Andretti told Chuck Givler of Pennsylvania's *Easton Express-Times*. "It might have been the most confidential project I have ever been involved with."

Hans Stuck, Thierry Boutsen, Geoff Brabham, and Pruett were scheduled to drive the second Porsche entry.

Porsche's main rival appeared to be the Ferrari 333SP, set to make its Daytona debut. Scandia entered a pair of Ferraris, which between them shared Michele Alboreto, Mauro Baldi, Stephan Johansson, Eric van de Poele, Fermin Velez, Paul Gentilozzi, and Andy Evans. Kevin Doran renewed his partnership with Gianpiero Moretti in the Momo Ferrari 333SP, with Moretti joined by Wayne Taylor, Eliseo Salazar, and Didier Theys.

Brix Motorsports, the defending WSC class winner, brought back Jeremy Dale in the team's WSC car, and also entered a two-car GTS Oldsmobile team for Irv Hoerr, Darrin Brassfield, and Mark Dismore. Television star Craig T. Nelson fielded the Screaming Eagles Racing Lexus Spice, which he shared with Dan Clark, Ross Bentley, and Margie Smith-Haas.

1995

After experimenting with a Ferrari-Spice hybrid in 1994—and seeing the success of the Ferrari 333SP later in the season—Rob Dyson decided to commission a purpose-built World Sports Car. The result: a Ford-powered Riley & Scott Mk III, scheduled to be driven by James Weaver, Butch Leitzinger, Scott Sharp, and Dyson.

There were also a few novel approaches to the class. Scott Flatt of Cortland, New York—who broke

Above left: Jochen Rohr (left) was one of the top Porsche campaigners during the 1990s. In 1995, his driver lineup was led by Hurley Haywood (right), who joined Rohr, David Murry, and Bernd Maylaender in a fourth-place overall finish in a 911. Above right: The two Ferrari 333SPs of Andy Evans take the green flag from the front row for the start of the 1995 Rolex 24. Opposite: James Weaver, driving Rob Dyson's No. 16 Riley & Scott Mk III, races the yellow No. 50 Ferrari 333SP fielded by Antonio Ferrari for Massimo Sigala, Gianfranco Brancatelli, Elton Julian, and Fabrizio Barbazza. While the Ferrari soldiered to an eighth-place finish, the Dyson entry melted a piston and was parked after only 11 laps.

into professional racing with Dyson—cut the roof off a GTO Chevrolet and dubbed it the *Cannibal*.

Just 14 days before the event IMSA, which had said it would adjust its rules following the January test days, announced that the air intakes for the new Porsches would be restricted. Angry with the late notice, Porsche promptly pulled its cars—including the Andretti-led, all-star team—out of the event.

One team, already en route to America when the change was announced, decided to run with the handicap. The factory Kremer team, returning to Daytona for the first time since 1978, fielded a pair of Porsche K8s for Giovanni Lavaggi, Jurgen Lassig, Christophe Bouchut, and Marco Werner, and a customer car for Franz Konrad, Cor Euser, Tiff Needell, and Antonio de Hermann. The K8 was a converted 962 "Spyder." The disadvantage that IMSA's restriction had created became apparent in qualifying, however, when the Porsches placed only 17th and 23rd.

Scandia Ferraris took the front row. Baldi won the pole with a lap of 124.035 mph in the 333SP he shared with Alboreto and Johansson. They were flanked by the team car, co-driven by car owner Evans, defending event winner Gentilozzi, and van de Poele. Third place went to another Ferrari 333SP, the yellow Euromotorsports entry of Massimo Sigala, Fabrizio Barbazza, and Francois Migault.

The 74-car field—the largest since 1988—took the green flag at 3 p.m. before a crowd estimated at 50,000. The Ferraris started quickly and retained the top three positions.

Craig T. Nelson's Screaming Eagles Lexus Spice lost a CV joint during the first hour. Dyson's new Riley & Scott was another early casualty, melting a piston only 11 laps into the event. "For something to go wrong that early is embarrassing," said Weaver.

The Nissan 300 ZX that won the race in 1994 also had early trouble. O'Connell was leading GTS-1 at the one-hour mark when a power steering leak caused a small fire. Repairs would cost the car two hours in the pits.

At 7:33 p.m., the Roush Mustang quietly moved into fifth overall, and first in GTS-1, with Newman at the wheel. Godwin Kelly of the *Daytona Beach News-Journal* asked Paul Newman if the traffic had been courteous during his first nighttime shift.

"Courteous is what you find in office buildings and dentist offices," the actor replied.

At 8:58 p.m., Brancatelli's Ferrari was on pit road for repairs. Meanwhile, both of the Porsche Spyders had worked their way into the top five, and were stalking the Ferraris.

After midnight, trouble struck the three leading Ferraris. The Momo Ferrari began experiencing engine problems around 1 a.m., but was still fast enough to pass Baldi for the lead at 1:53 a.m. But on their next routine pit stop, the Momo team couldn't restart the engine. Moretti sat in the car for half an hour while the team worked to fire it. The car managed to rejoin the race at 3 a.m., and had reached fourth place before the engine blew at 8:04 a.m., sending Theys spinning into the wall. "I thought about retiring after our first problem, but the car was still running quick enough to win," said team owner Kevin Doran.

"The Ferrari engines were running perfectly, but the valves would overheat, because the heat was not allowed to escape," Doran continued, explaining the problem. "We had an accelerated erosion of the valve and the valve seat area. After eight or ten hours of this continued condition, the leakage past the valves eventually got to be so great that we couldn't restart the engines."

"For the first eight hours, it was beautiful," said Moretti, who had announced that 1995 would be his final season. But the lure of running the Rolex 24 would bring him back.

Just before 5 a.m., both Scandia Ferraris endured long pit stops when the cars refused to refire after routine service. The lead Ferrari of Baldi/Alboreto/Johansson pitted at 4:48 a.m. Baldi took over for Alboreto, but the car refused to restart. Ten minutes later, Gentilozzi returned to the race in the other Scandia entry, but encountered mechanical problems on his first lap and pulled off-course. He managed to restart the car, but it failed again in the pits. Simultaneously, both of the Scandia cars were retired with oil-pump problems.

With both Ferraris sidelined, Lavaggi took the lead in the Kremer Spyder at 5:05 a.m. Only 90 minutes later, the Konrad Porsche Spyder crashed in the tri-oval and was also out of the race. The drama was over, and Kremer's yellow Porsche Spyder cruised the rest of the way to a five-lap victory. The team covered 680 laps, 2,456.4 miles, and averaged 102.289 mph.

Bouchut became the first driver to win in both of his first 24-hour races, at Le Mans and Daytona. He had won the French classic in 1993, joined by Geoff Brabham and Eric Helary in a Peugeot.

The Brix team repeated as the WSC class winner, with Dale joined by Jay Cochran and Fredrick Ekblom, finishing second overall. "That Kremer Porsche was a rocket ship in the middle of the night," Dale said. "The turbos just came alive, and we didn't have the speed to match the car. We out-qualified them and won our class, but we really felt that we should have won the race."

Though the overall victory went to the Kremer Brothers Porsche, the headlines went to the third-place overall finishers, Paul Newman and friends in Roush Racing's GTS-1 class-winning Ford Mustang, which finished eight laps behind the overall winners.

"It ain't bad for an elderly gentleman," said Newman in victory lane. "I'm just pleased to have a pulse." He had driven 114 laps, logging four hours and 20 minutes behind the wheel in his first Daytona

Above: The Chevrolet Cannibal of Bruce Trenery, Vic Rice, Grahame Bryant, Buddy Norton, and Jeffrey Pattinson catches fire in the infield. The Scott Flatt team managed to repair the car and return to the race. Right: A pit stop for the eventual-winning No. 10 Kremer Brothers Porsche K8. Giovanni Lavaggi, Juergen Laessig, Christophe Bouchut, and Marco Werner drove to a five-lap victory. Far right: A pit stop for Reeves Calloway's No. 61, whose driver lineup included Indy car driver Johnny Unser.

24 Hours appearance since 1979, when he co-drove a Porsche 935 with Brian Redman and Dick Barbour.

"Winning with Paul Newman was wonderful," said Jack Roush, calling it the highlight of his 10 Daytona victories. "Paul hadn't been in a car for awhile, and he was 70 years old and nervous about whether he would be the reason why we couldn't win, realizing the streak we had. With about four hours to go, Paul got out of the car and said, 'That's it. I've done my part. I'm done.' I said, 'No, Paul, this is your race car, this is your program, this is your name we're under, you got to be in it for the last hour when we finish.'

"So he reached down, and did something that an American hero would do, sucked it up and got back in the car for the last hour. Of course, when he got out of the car and gave everybody high fives, it was a great personal triumph for him as well as keeping the streak alive for the team."

Fourth went to the Porsche 911 Turbo of Hurley Haywood, Jochen Rohr, and David Murry. "We led the race for a long time in the Porsche Turbo over Newman, Brockman, Tommy Kendall, and Mark Martin," Murry recalled. "We saw a crack in the oil cooler earlier, but they didn't think it was a crack. But sure enough, in the middle of the night, it lost pressure on me, and we had to come in with no boost. They changed the intercooler and that put us behind those guys."

Winning in the GTS-2 category, the former GTU class, was the fifth-place Porsche 911 of Lilian Bryner, Enzo Calderari, Renato Mastropietro, and Ulrich Richter. The only Ferrari 333SP to finish was the Sigala/Barbazza/Brancatelli entry, which was running fifth before experiencing a long pit stop at noon because of a stuck throttle. It returned to finish eighth.

Tom Milner's Performance Technology Group fielded a pair of BMW M3s for John Paul Jr., David Donohue, Boris Said, Justin Bell, Pete Halsmer, and Dieter Quester in GTS-2. Both cars went out early with engine trouble.

The *Spirit of Daytona* Mitsubishi, fielded by brothers Todd and Troy Flis, Craig Conway, and Richard Nisbett, started last on the grid but persevered to finish 24th overall and 12th in GTS-2. "We were the only turtle in a race of rabbits," said Conway.

IMSA owner Charles Slater finished 13th overall in the Alex Job Racing Porsche 911, placing sixth in GTS-2. "In one year, to have so many more entries, and to have everyone do as well as they have, I'm completely satisfied," Slater said during the race. "If anyone isn't, they're not thinking long-term, and they're not remembering their history. If you check your old IMSA yearbooks, you can see how long it took the GTP class to become established."

ROLEX
90
43
16
EXXON
BOSCH
MCI
ICE

1996: Quiet Wayne and Mad Max

THE 1996 RACE WOULD ONCE AGAIN PROVE THAT WINNING WASN'T THE ONLY WAY TO SUCCEED AT DAYTONA. WHILE THE SPOTLIGHT FOR THE 1995 RACE SHONE ON THIRD-PLACE OVERALL FINISHER PAUL NEWMAN, THE DRIVER WHO WOULD CAPTURE THE LION'S SHARE OF THE ATTENTION IN 1996 WAS MASSIMILIANO PAPIS, AN ITALIAN WHO WAS LITTLE-KNOWN IN AMERICA.

Papis had briefly raced in Formula One, competing in seven events for the Footwork team. Following the 1995 season, Ferrari hired him to drive in its sports car program. Daytona would be his American debut.

The Italian was joined on Kevin Doran's Momo Ferrari 333SP team by Gianpiero Moretti, Bob Wollek, and Didier Theys, who were looking to end Moretti's winless streak in the 24 Hours. The Momo team intended to run two cars, including one for Bill Auberlen, but last-minute contractual conflicts kept the second car on the transporter, leaving the Californian without a ride. Auberlen wasn't without a car for long, however, joining Roger Mandeville and Henry Camferdam in their Chevrolet Hawk C-8.

By 1996, the World Sports Cars had finally come into their own, with 16 of the open-cockpit prototypes making it into the 76-car grid. Shaping up as the Momo team's top competition was the newly formed Doyle Racing team, which fielded an Olds Aurora-powered Danka/Konica Riley & Scott Mk III

Left: The pole-winning No. 30 Momo Ferrari 333SP of Didier Theys and No. 4 Danka Riley & Scott Mk III Oldsmobile of Wayne Taylor lead the field to the green flag to start the 1996 Rolex 24. Above: Playing fourth overall and first in GTS-2 was the yellow No. 55 Porsche 911 Carrera RSR of Enzo Calderari, Ferdinand de Lesseps, Lilian Bryner, and Ulrich Richter.

for Wayne Taylor, Scott Sharp, and Jim Pace.

Other contenders included the Scandia/Simon Ferrari 333SP of Mauro Baldi/Michele Alboreto/Fermin Velez, and a pair of Dyson Racing R & S Fords for Andy Wallace, Butch Leitzinger, James Weaver, and Rob Dyson. Actor Craig T. Nelson returned to the race in an R & S Ford, joined by Johnny O'Connell, Dan Clark, and Case Montgomery.

The fastest-qualifying speed was turned in by Didier Theys in the Momo Ferrari, with a WSC-record lap of 126.610 mph. He was joined by Doyle Racing's Taylor on the front row.

The event began at 1 p.m., two hours earlier than in previous years. The change allowed two extra hours of daylight, which meant that all four of a team's drivers could take a shift at the wheel before nightfall.

An estimated 40,000 spectators braved chilly, windy, and downright miserable conditions to witness a battle between the Momo and Doyle teams. Taylor took the early lead, with Moretti running the first stint for Momo. The two teams exchanged the lead 17 times from lap 40 through lap 569, their cars never more than five laps apart despite the unpredictable weather conditions.

"I remember after my first stint telling my wife, 'This is going to be pure hell the rest of the race,'" recalled Taylor, a native of South Africa now living in Altamonte Springs, Florida. He was running the Daytona 24 Hours for the 13th time.

The first major casualty was Rob Dyson's Ford R & S Mk III. Andy Wallace started the car in sixth and quickly took the lead. He handed the car over to Dyson, but the car came to a halt in the infield just after the one-hour mark, when it snapped an input shaft. "These things either work forever, or they fail," said Dyson. "This one failed."

But Dyson team manager Pat Smith wasn't ready to throw in the towel. The team had brought—and entered—a second R & S Ford, but had intended to use it only to give the drivers more practice and qualifying time. That car qualified fourth, but was left in the garage on Saturday morning. Now, the team rushed to get the second car on the track. Despite joining the race late with a two-hour, 62-lap handicap, the team went out and finished 20th, completing 555 laps.

Another major retirement in the early going was the Scandia/Simon Ferrari 333SP. Fermin Velez spun in his own oil and crashed exiting the chicane. "The car felt like it was on ice," Velez said. "I spun and hit the outside wall sideways."

The Screaming Eagles Ford R & S qualified fourth, and was running third after five hours, but dropped out when the engine-management system malfunctioned. Other WSC cars to retire early were the Courage, which was damaged in an off-course incident and had no spares available, and

Above: Englishmen Geoff Lees, Kenneth Acheson, and Tiff Needell co-drove the No. 89 Jaguar-powered Lister Storm. The car managed to finish despite a spectacular late-race flip. Opposite top: The badly smoking No. 43 R & S Oldsmobile in the infield. Ross Bentley, Franck Freon, Lee Payne, and Dan Kitch managed to keep the car going, finishing fifth overall. Right: The No. 98 Viper GTS-R of Price Cobb, Tommy Archer, Shawn Hendricks, Mark Dismore, and Vic Sifton at speed in the infield.

98
S1
MICHELIN

O'CONNELL NELSON CLARK MONTGOMERY
2
GOODYEAR
Hella
EXXON
SLICK 50

the Toy Store Spice, which stalled on Justin Bell and failed to refire.

The Doyle Oldsmobile lost four laps on an extended stop to replace the radiator at 8 p.m. The team regained the lost ground, and took the lead at 10:21 p.m., when the Ferrari stopped for new brakes. An hour later, the Momo team replaced the right-side muffler, giving the Doyle R & S a four-lap advantage.

Doyle Racing's Jim Pace realized that he was the new leader when he got a call on the radio during a caution period. "It was dark, we were running around under a full-course caution and the guys came on the radio, 'Safety car's waving cars by, when you get behind the safety car blink your lights,'" Pace recalled. "I knew that meant I was the overall leader, and that was the first time that had happened to me at Daytona. That was a good feeling; I liked it."

Running a strong third at 10 p.m. was the Porsche 911 Turbo of Hurley Haywood, John O'Steen, David Murry, and Scott Goodyear. Not long afterwards, the throttle stuck, which over-revved and destroyed the engine.

At midnight, the Doyle R & S began popping out of second gear, costing the team valuable time in the infield turns. The Doyle team lost its lead at 5 a.m., when Theys passed Sharp on the banking following a full-course caution. At 9 a.m., the Ferrari pitted for 10 minutes to correct a powertrain problem, which allowed the Oldsmobile to build a four-lap margin.

"A bolt on the gearbox cover fell off," Theys explained. "The gearbox cover came loose, and we lost oil. We replaced the bolt and put oil in the gearbox, but it was so cold outside, it took a long time to put in the oil."

Wollek got behind the wheel of the Ferrari, and gained ground until he spun in the chicane following an encounter with the GTS-2 leading Porsche of Ulrich Richter. Theys took over from Wollek, and continued to gain on the Doyle Olds. With two hours remaining, Taylor took over for Sharp in the leading Olds, while Papis replaced Theys in the Ferrari for the stretch drive.

The climax was one of the best finishes in the history of the Daytona 24 Hours. Papis carved six seconds per lap from the leader throughout the final hour, continuing to close on the Doyle Oldsmobile. Television commentator Bob Varsha gave him the nickname "Mad Max" for his efforts.

But Papis ran out of time, finishing 65.518 seconds behind Taylor for the closest Daytona 24 finish to date. The Doyle Olds completed 697 laps, 2,481.32 miles, and averaged 103.324 mph.

It was the first victory for an American-made car since the Ford GT40 Mk II won in 1966. "It was really brilliant, and it was really nice to beat Papis and Ferrari, because they were favorites," Taylor

Left: A pit stop for the Screaming Eagles Racing R & S Mk III Ford of Craig T. Nelson, Johnny O'Connell, Dan Clark, and Case Montgomery. Nelson, a veteran actor and star of the popular television series "Coach," became a serious competitor in the World Sports Car class. Above: The father and son team of Charles and Rob Morgan joined Irv Hoerr, Jon Gooding, and Joe Pezza in winning GTS-1 honors in the No. 5 Brix Racing Oldsmobile Aurora. The team finished seventh overall.

recalled. "It's really strange. They still got more publicity out of finishing second than we did for winning, a very silly thing.

"We were not really [worried about Papis catching him], because we really had the race in hand," Taylor added. "I think if the race had been longer, they might have caught us, but I think we dominated the race from the beginning, and they made a lot of mistakes."

"It was exciting," said Sharp. "You always have certain guys you end up getting in a race-long battle with, and that year it was the Ferrari. You always have more issues at Daytona than you think you're going to. We had some small problems, little tiny ones, nothing too crazy. I think at the end of the race, Papis turned up the rev limiter and tried to catch us. That was similar to what we had done for the last eight hours."

In victory lane, Wayne Taylor received his new Rolex. Papis already had a new nickname, and sports cars—and soon, Champ Cars—had a new star, Mad Max. "Daytona made it possible to turn my career around," Papis recalled. "Without 1996, I would not have the possibility to drive a Champ Car.

"The memories, the emotion, and the feelings that are attached to Daytona are very special. Every time I go there, they are something that no track—maybe only Monza—will be able to provide."

Did Papis realize this event would have such a profound impact on his career? "I didn't know when

Above: Wayne Taylor is at the wheel of the winning No. 4 Danka R & S Oldsmobile. Feeling he had the race in hand, he was puzzled when the second-place team got more publicity for losing than he did for winning. Opposite top: A carnival—complete with Ferris wheel—enhances the nighttime festivities of the Rolex 24. Right: Winners of the 1996 Rolex 24 at Daytona are (left to right) Scott Sharp, Wayne Taylor, and Jim Pace, joined by Rolex President and CEO Roland Puton.

I came here in 1996," he said in a 2002 interview. "I just knew it was a very special event, and I was very proud of being part of it. It turned out to be *the* event for my career, of my life. It was a great thrill, and made a lot of things change in my career."

During his final stint, Papis said he kept his focus. "When you drive, you drive. You think about focus, and you think about doing your job the best. There's nothing else when you sit in the car. If you're a professional driver, you focus about your driving. The emotion comes out later when you're in the winner's circle."

"It's unfortunate that we were not the guys who won," said Moretti, again frustrated in his quest to win at Daytona. "It's never easy to lose, and it's never easy to say, 'That's racing.' When you are 56 years old, you don't have too many more times left to win."

Third overall, but 57 laps behind, was Jim Downing's Mazda Kudzu DHM, which he co-drove with Butch Hamlet, Barry Waddell, and Tim McAdam.

Winning in GTS-2, and finishing fourth overall, was the Porsche 911 driven by Ulrich Richter, Lilian Bryner, Enzo Calderari, and Ferdinand de Lesseps. Cort Wagner, Richard Raimist, Steve Dente, and Mike Doolin finished second in the class, and sixth overall, while the PTG BMW M3 of John Paul Jr., Dieter Quester, David Donohue, and Pete Halsmer were ninth overall and third in GTS-2.

First in GTS-1, and seventh overall, was the Olds Aurora driven by the father-son team of Charles and Rob Morgan, joined by Joe Pezza, Jon Gooding, and late addition Irv Hoerr. Hoerr escaped uninjured during an evening fire that had sidelined the team's other Aurora. When the lead car had suspension bolts break in the closing hours, the experienced Hoerr was nominated to finish the race.

"It was ironic," Hoerr said of his lone Daytona 24 Hours victory. "The car that I started was leading by a good margin, and it burned to the ground. Then, when the other car became lame enough that everyone was afraid to drive it on the banking, they called on me to drive it."

The Lister Storm, an English GTS-1 supercar, was involved in the biggest incident of the race. The driveline failed on the backstraight, sending the car off the track, where it began a series of rolls in the mud. Driver Kenny Acheson escaped uninjured. The car struggled to finish after encountering problems with its V-12 Jaguar engine.

Another unusual entry was the GTS-1 Bugatti EB110, owned and driven by Gilda Pallanco-Pastor. Also co-driving the four-wheel-drive, V-12-powered, four-turbocharger-equipped car were Derek John Hill (20-year-old son of 1963 Daytona winner and Formula One World Champion Phil Hill) and Olivier Grouillard. The car lasted 154 laps before retiring with gearbox failure.

IMSA had had another major personnel change, with long-time employee George Silbermann named the new president the previous May. After the race, Silbermann and the entire organization could boast of a strong headline class—and a new star.

20
ROLEX 24
EXXON
GOODYEAR
EAGLE
EXXON
BOSCH
DYSON
SHOEI
BBS

1997: The Backup Car Comes Through

John Schneider went to the Daytona Beach International Airport on the eve of opening practice for the Rolex 24 to pick up an old friend, Elliott Forbes-Robinson. The pair, who had raced together a decade before, were set to join Rob Dyson and John Paul Jr. in Dyson's second car.

A year ago, the Dyson backup car had been parked in the garage at the start of the race, only to be rolled out two hours into the event when the team's lead car failed. For 1997, Dyson hedged his bets. He slated James Weaver, Andy Wallace, and Butch Leitzinger to drive the lead Ford Riley & Scott Mk III, No. 16. Dyson elected to race the second R & S Ford himself, joining Forbes-Robinson and Schneider behind the wheel of the No. 20 machine. John Paul Jr. would start the race in the No. 20 car, then after eight hours would join the No. 16 team.

"John Schneider and myself talked Rob into running the second car," Forbes-Robinson recalled. "We were just going to go out and have a good time, and let the other guys go for the win in the No. 16 car." Their entry was virtually unnoticed, overshadowed by a strong, 19-car World SportsCar turnout, part of a record 101-car entry.

Five teams were in the front of the World SportsCar field. A second team campaigning Riley & Scott Mk IIIs was the defending event champion Doyle

Left: While smoke billows from the No. 20 Dyson R & S on pit road, the Pat Smith-led crew works to cool down the car. The overheating problems kept the team in suspense right up through the final turn of the race, with Butch Leitzinger managing to pull out the victory. Above: Religious leader Rael, who claimed to be descended from an extra terrestrial being, joined Mark Montgomery, Edd Davin, and Butch Brickell in the No. 19 BMW Argo. In 2003, he would gain national attention following a controversial cloning announcement.

Racing, fielding an Oldsmobile Aurora-powered car for Wayne Taylor, Scott Sharp, and Eric van de Poele. The R & S factory entered a second Olds-powered car for Peruvian Eduardo Dibos, who was joined by Jim Pace and Barry Waddell.

Driving the Scandia Ferrari 333SP were Andy Evans, the new owner of the beleaguered IMSA, joined by Fermin Velez and the father-son team of Charles and Rob Morgan. Kevin Doran's Momo

Ferrari had Gianpiero Moretti making another quest for victory at Daytona. He was joined by veteran Derek Bell, Antonio Hermann, and Didier Theys.

Other top WSC contenders included Darin Brassfield and actor Craig T. Nelson in the Screaming Eagles R & S Ford; Johnny O'Connell in the Support Net Chevy-Hawk; and Danny Sullivan, Ross Bentley, and Jeff Jones in an Essex Racing–prepared R & S Chevy.

Ninety-six cars from the race's huge entry actually practiced before qualifying limited the field to 80 starters. Ferraris dominated, and Velez won the pole with a lap of 127.57 mph in the Acxiom-sponsored Scandia Ferrari 333SP. The car had been set up to take advantage of the high-speed section of the circuit, allowing Velez to hit 203 mph on the banking. Theys made it an all-Ferrari front row in the Momo 333SP.

An estimated 50,000 spectators watched Velez and Taylor battle throughout the first hour, with the veteran Italian holding the upper hand. Weaver began pressuring for the lead after the first hour. But the Doyle R & S Olds began to fade when debris clogged its radiators and caused the engine to overheat.

The Momo Ferrari also ran up front, but an oil leak at the seven-hour mark cost the team three laps—and more. An hour later, some of the oil that had leaked out caught fire, destroying the car's electronics. Kevin Doran replaced the wiring harness in 83 minutes. The team would soldier on to a seventh-place finish, 30 laps down.

Above left: The No. 71 Calloway C7R was co-driven by Boris Said, Ron Fellows, Johnny Unser, and Enrico Bertaggio. It withdrew with electrical problems. Above right: Derek John Hill (left) was joined by his father, Formula One world champion and 1963 Daytona Continental winner, Phil Hill. The second generation driver finished ninth overall, joining Boris Said, Javier Quiros, Bill Auberlen, and Tom Hessert in capturing GTS-3 honors in a Tom Milner–prepared BMW M3. Right: Former motorcycle supercross star and current Indy car driver Jeff Ward was at the wheel of the No. 60 Ford Keiler KII.

At 9 p.m. the No. 16 Dyson machine was leading when the valves on one side of its engine failed. At the time, the No. 20 car was six laps behind.

"It seemed like an early day for everyone—for all of us, anyway," Butch Leitzinger recalled. "James and Andy went back to the hotel. I hadn't done much driving; I only did one or two stints. That didn't seem right, so I went to [team manager Pat Smith] and asked if I could get in the No. 20 car, and he was nice enough to let me do it. For the rest of the night, the five of us—John Paul, Elliott, John Schneider, Rob, and I—just pounded around. I think at that time we were six laps down, but we kept climbing up the leader board.

"Our car was really well balanced. It didn't have much power. They were conservative with that car's engine, but by daylight, we were in the lead."

At 3:45 a.m., Charles Morgan, in the Scandia Ferrari, was passing a Porsche in the infield, when he was hit by another Porsche. While the team spent two laps replacing the Ferrari's damaged rear suspension, the car fell from second, two laps behind, to fourth.

XCEL
ALTA
Natural Spring Water
EXXON
SCANDIA
3
ACXIOM
TEAM SCANDIA
GOODYEAR
PIAA
EXXON
56
KEEWAYDIN GROUP
Hella
BASF
KONRAD
van lent
Hella

At 3:55 a.m., van de Poele was two laps in the lead in the Doyle Racing R & S Aurora when his engine let go with a loud bang. To avoid a similar misfortune, Dibos pitted his R & S Aurora to change the fuel mapping. By 5 a.m., the backup Dyson car was four laps ahead of everyone.

"Around seven in the morning I was in the motor home, waiting for my next shift," Leitzinger recalled. "James and Andy came trundling in after having a nice dinner and sleeping in a normal hotel bed. As they drove into the track, they discovered that our car was on top of the pylon, so they wanted in on it, also. They went running to Pat and begged him to let them into the car. So Pat, being agreeable, let them come aboard."

While Dyson had a pair of fresh aces for the stretch run, his car was getting tired. The team had been treating the engine for overheating since 4 a.m., and the engine had begun to use oil at an alarming rate.

"We would have to come in every hour or so and top off the water," Leitzinger said. "We kept pounding it hard just to have fun while it lasted."

At 9 a.m., Charles Morgan spun in the infield while being pursued by Weaver, and his Ferrari collided with the Riley & Scott. Although both cars continued, the Ferrari got the worst of the incident, and the shunt jolted the Dyson car's electronics.

With two hours remaining, Leitzinger and Velez took over their respective cars for the stretch run. The Dyson team took its time in the pits, adding water and oil, which allowed the Scandia Ferrari to close to within one lap of the lead. Velez carved five seconds per lap and was back on the lead lap with 20 minutes remaining, while the Dyson car was billowing smoke. It was too little, too late, however, and Evans took over when the car pitted for an insurance gas-and-go in the closing minutes.

"With about one hour to go, all of a sudden we dropped a cylinder, which seemed to me like the beginning of the end," Leitzinger recalled. "I figured the engine must be overheating or something. There was nothing else to do but keep running around."

"We were in suspense right up to the checkered flag," Leitzinger continued. "When I came through NASCAR turn four on the checkered-flag lap, I had my hand on the gearshift just because I was certain the engine was going to seize, and I wanted to be able to kick it out of gear really quick and coast to the line, because I could see the smoke billowing out in the mirrors. The engine sounded horrible, and I just didn't think there was any way the car was going to make it to the finish."

Despite the problems, Leitzinger made it to the finish. The Dyson car completed 690 laps, 2,456.4 miles, and averaged 102.292 mph. The team won by one lap and 14.891 seconds over the Scandia Ferrari.

Opposite top: Fermin Velez, Andy Evans, Charles Morgan, and Rob Morgan were competitive all the way in the Acxiom/Scandia Ferrari 333SP, finishing second overall. Opposite bottom: Bob Wollek in the No. 31 Konrad Porsche leads the Tim Allen No. 65 Home Improvement *Ford Saleen and the Martin Snow No. 56 Porsche 911 through the infield in early action. Above: The No. 8 Chevrolet Hawk C8 of Henry Camferdam, Johnny O'Connell, Scott Schubot, and Roger Mandeville leads the Team Peru Riley & Scott Oldsmobile of Eduardo Dibos, Jim Pace, and Barry Waddell, and the Riley & Scott Chevrolet of Danny Sullivan, Jeff Jones, and Ross Bentley.*

"Our team got a lot of teasing from people for taking seven people to win the race," Leitzinger recalled. "But what it came down to, with James and Andy at the end, is when you have talent that good sitting on the sidelines, you want to use it. You don't want to leave your designated hitter on the bench in the World Series."

Schneider received a new Rolex in victory lane. Forbes-Robinson got something bigger—a rejuvenated career. "It was very fortunate for me. Because of that, I was leading the points, either because the other guys in the car didn't get points because they didn't start in that car or get enough time," Forbes-Robinson explained in a 2002 interview. "So leading the championship, I got to come to Sebring. I was able to stay with them the rest of the year, and I haven't left since." He would go on to win the World SportsCar championship.

Paul became the driver with the longest wait between Daytona 24 Hours victories—15 years. "I don't think I appreciated it then what goes in to winning one of these," said Paul, who had joined his father and Rolf Stommelen in winning the 1982 event in a Porsche 935.

Taking third, 18 laps down, was the Dibos Racing R & S Aurora, which lost seven laps after a 10 a.m. incident and cut a tire in the late going.

1997

Ralf Kelleners, Patrice Goueslard, Claudia Huertgen, and Andre Ahrle won GTS-2 in a Porsche 911 GT2, finishing fourth overall. Bob Wollek had been leading the class in the Franz Konrad Porsche, but was knocked out of contention after making contact with another car.

Placing fifth was the GTS-1 winner, the Porsche 911 of Andy Pilgrim, Harold Grohs, Arnd Meier, and Jochen Rohr. They won the class by two laps over the Champion Porsche 911 of Hans Stuck, Thierry Boutsen, and Bill Adam. "Winning that year was huge," recalled Pilgrim. "It was awesome,

Above left: The French Oreca team entered the No. 94 Dodge Viper for Olivier Beretta, Tommy Archer, and Dominique Dupuy. The team finished 15th overall and third in GTS-1. Above right: The No. 30 Momo and No. 3 Acxiom/Scandia Ferrari 333SPs battle side by side in the early going. Opposite: The "Sensational Seven" celebrate in victory lane. Andy Wallace and Butch Leitzinger are up front, while James Weaver, John Schneider, Rob Dyson, Rolex President and CEO Roland Puton, Elliott Forbes-Robinson, and John Paul Jr. are in the back.

because we beat the factory cars, Boutsen and Hans Stuck. That was really cool."

Stuck saw hopes of a class victory go up in a cloud of chemicals shortly after midnight, when a crewman accidentally triggered the on-board fire extinguisher during a routine pit stop. The team lost more than eight laps while the powder was cleaned up.

A pair of European supercar teams also contended in GT1. The British Jaguar-powered Lister Storm, sponsored by the Newcastle United football team, was driven by Geoff Lees, Tiff Needell, and Anthony Reid, and ran as high as fourth overall Saturday evening. The team finished 19th, fourth in class, after falling back with gearbox problems. The French Oreca team fielded a Dodge Viper GTS-R that was quickest in qualifying, with Olivier Beretta at the wheel. Joined by Tommy Archer and Dominique Dupuy, the team led the class at the midway point before losing ground to replace the gearbox. They came back to finish third in class.

Reeves Callaway's Callaway C7R, driven by Johnny Unser, Boris Said, Ron Fellows, and Enrico Bertaggia, was contending for the lead when it went out with an oil fire.

The race included a third GT category, GT3, the successor to the GTU category. Boris Said, Bill Auberlen, Tom Hessert, Xavier Quiros, and Derek Hill won in a Tom Milner BMW M3, two laps ahead of the Porsche 911 of Hurley Haywood, Doc Bundy, David Murry, and Jim Matthews.

The Daytona 24 Hours wouldn't have been complete without a celebrity driver. Filling that role was TV's *Home Improvement* star Tim Allen, who joined Steve Saleen, Price Cobb, and Rob Rizzo in a Saleen Mustang SR.

Two-time AMA Supercross champion and future Indy Racing League star Jeff Ward made his sports car racing debut, joining Owen Trinkler and Roberto Quintanilla in the No. 60 Ford Keiler KII.

One month after the race, IMSA changed its name to Professional Sports Car Racing, or Sports Car. Later that year, Evans sold the organization to a group of investors.

Concerned with the uncertainty of that sanctioning body's future, Daytona International Speedway awarded the sanction for the 1998 race to a newly formed organization—the United States Road Racing Championship, which took its name for the pre-Can-Am sports car championship of the early 1960s.

HOME OF THE PEPSI 400
momo
ROLEX 24
30
DORAN
Enterprises
LiSTA
PROVIMI
GIESSE

1998: Perseverance Pays Off

"WITH ALL THE MONEY I HAVE SPENT AT DAYTONA, I COULD HAVE BOUGHT 1,000 ROLEXES EASILY," SAID GIANPIERO MORETTI ON THE EVE OF THE 1998 EVENT. "BUT I WANTED TO WIN THIS RACE."

The driver from Milan, Italy, first raced in the 24 Hours of Daytona in 1970, running with an underfunded Ferrari team that finished 32nd. In 1979, his second attempt at the Daytona 24, he had made winning his personal goal. Though his team took the pole, the Jolly Club Porsche 935 blew an engine, returned to the race after a lengthy stop, and then spun out. Almost 20 years later, with the advent of the World Sports Car, Moretti had persuaded Ferrari to build him a car that he could race in America—the Ferrari 333SP. This would mark his 15th attempt to win Daytona's endurance classic.

Moretti wanted to win his Rolex, but the 57-year-old driver knew his time was running out. For 1998, he planned to run two shifts, then let teammates Arie Luyendyk, Mauro Baldi, and Didier Theys race for the win.

The race was the first to be sanctioned by the United States Road Racing Championship (USRRC), which was administered by the Sports Car Club of America (SCCA) Pro Racing. Alan Wilson was the new series' operations manager. Borrowing another name from the past, the World SportsCar class was renamed Can-Am.

The race again shaped up as a battle between Ford and Ferrari. Defending champions Dyson Racing returned to carry the flag for Ford with two Riley & Scott Mk IIIs driven by James Weaver, Elliott Forbes-Robinson, and Dorsey Schroeder in the No. 16; and Dyson, Butch Leitzinger, John Paul Jr.,

Left: Mauro Baldi (sitting on the car at left) and Didier Theys (standing in dark glasses) and Arie Luyendyk (right), join the crew for a ride to victory lane in the Momo Ferrari 333SP, with Gianpiero Moretti at the wheel. Above: Ralf Kelleners, Andy Pilgrim, and Thierry Boutsen shared the No. 38 Champion Porsche 911 GT1 Evo, that dropped out late in the race with overheating problems.

and Perry McCarthy in the No. 20.

Henry Camferdam had upgraded to an R & S Ford from a Mazda Hawk, and qualified sixth with his co-drivers Johnny O'Connell and Scott Schubot. Jim Matthews assembled a "dream team" of Hurley Haywood, Derek Bell, and David Murry to co-drive his Riley & Scott Ford, using veteran team manager Mike Colucci.

Ferrari was represented by Scandia and Doyle-Risi, as well as Kevin Doran's Momo team. Denied the sanctioning of the Rolex 24, former IMSA/Sports Car owner Andy Evans wanted to make a strong statement, and assembled the team of Bob Wollek, Max Papis, Yannick Dalmas, and Ron Fellows to run his Scandia Ferrari. The 1996 winner was now known as Doyle/Risi Racing, with Wayne Taylor joined by former Scandia driver Fermin Velez and Eric van de Poele.

The GT1 class featured a pair of new Panoz GTR-1s, powered by Jack Roush Ford powerplants and managed by former Jaguar team director Tony Dowe. Scott Pruett, Raul Boesel, and Andy Wallace were teamed in the No. 5, with Eric Bernard, David Brabham, Doc Bundy, and Jamie Davies in the No. 99.

Dalmas put the Scandia Ferrari on the pole by two seconds with a lap of 129.200 mph. The Momo Ferrari qualified second, followed by the Doyle-Risi Ferrari and the two Dyson Fords of Leitzinger and Weaver.

A record crowd was on hand for the 1 p.m. start. Weaver jumped to second behind Dalmas when the 74-car field took the green flag, and was cruising on the banking during the second hour when a caution waved. Former teammate Andy Wallace was ahead of him in a Panoz, and slowed to prevent him from passing a trio of Porsches under the yellow. Weaver found himself with nowhere to go, and rammed the Panoz, sending both to the pits for repairs. "I painted myself into a corner," Weaver admitted.

Moretti, meanwhile, had a run-in with a Porsche and lost three laps for repairs, allowing the Doyle/Risi Ferrari to take charge. A controversial call cost the Doyle/Risi team the lead, however. A pit marshal waved van de Poele out of the pits during a third-hour caution period while the pit exit was closed, but failed to inform race control of his move. Van de Poele was then penalized two laps for the apparent violation. To be fair, it was a rare mistake by the USRRC officials in their debut race.

Further problems took the 1996 winners out of contention. Van de Poele was hit on the straightaway, breaking a wheel, and later clutch problems required an extended pit stop. The team's race ended at 10 p.m., when van de Poele crashed in the West Horseshoe. He suffered a slight concussion and was released after a precautionary visit to the hospital.

The pole-winning Scandia Ferrari took over, leading through 10 p.m., while the No. 20 Dyson Ford raced into contention. Scandia pitted for 10 minutes with a sticking throttle at 4 a.m., which gave the lead to the remaining Dyson car, with the GT1 Panoz of Bernard, Brabham, and Davies in second,

Above: The No. 20 Dyson Racing R & S races the No. 17 Doyle/Risi Racing Ferrari on the banking. After being in contention for most of the race, mechanical failures eliminated both cars in the closing hours. Right: A large crowd watches as the No. 3 Ferrari 333SP jumps to an early lead in the 1998 Rolex 24.

DAYTO
ROLEX
TOSHIBA

three laps behind. The Scandia Ferrari returned, five laps down, but encountered transmission trouble at 5 a.m. and eventually retired.

"That race was awesome," recalled Ron Fellows, who had won racing a Ferrari 333SP Mosport in 1997 in his only prior WSC race. "Andy Evans called me and asked me to do that race with Max Papis, Yanick Dalmas, and Bob Wollek. We had an awesome team. It was really our race to lose. We were running very strong, before our problem late in the race took us out. Basically, I remember something in the oiling system exploded, and that was the end of our race. That was a big disappointment, but it was a lot of fun."

The Momo Ferrari lost more ground and time when Luyendyk pitted with a cut tire. By dawn, both of the Panoz cars had been retired, while the third-place car was 18 laps behind.

The road to victory seemed clear for the Dyson car. Then, in a development reminiscent of the team's 1997 victory, the car began smoking and slowed by six seconds per lap. Once again, the team hoped to nurse the car home.

"With about three hours to go, I had just gotten out and John Paul had gotten in," recalled Leitzinger.

"I was doing all the mental math for when I'd have to get back in the car again. I went back to the tent and got a big plate of spaghetti. Just being clumsy, I completely dropped the whole plate of spaghetti and sauce all over my driver's suit and shoes. At that same moment, someone said John Paul was slowing.

"Everything all of a sudden went horrible," Leitzinger continued. "I went running to the pits with a badly stained driver's suit, and the car was sitting there and everyone was shaking their heads. It was a horribly despondent feeling, with victory that close. It would have been a real big victory for Perry, John Paul, and myself. It's a horrible thing to happen when you're that close to victory, when

Above left: A trio of Ferraris race to the front as the green flag waves for the start of the race. Above right: The No. 81 Chamberlain Racing Dodge Viper GTS-R of Chris Gleason, Ray Lintott, Ashley Wood, and Matt Turner leaves the pits after being serviced. Opposite: The No. 5 Panoz of Andy Wallace received severe rear-end damage after it was hit from behind by the race-leading Dyson R & S Ford of James Weaver. Wallace, seeing a waving yellow, slowed to avoid passing slower cars, and his former teammate had nowhere to go. Both cars were eventually able to return to the race, but far out of contention.

it all goes up in smoke."

At 9:18 a.m., Paul limped to the pits in the lead Dyson entry, trailing smoke and leaking fluids. "When he got into the pits, he gave me the look that we know only too well, which is, 'This is the end of the road, sunshine,'" said Perry McCarthy. "I was absolutely choked, because I felt we could win."

The team managed to send the car back out, running at slower speeds, to allow Leitzinger to score driver's points en route to his second-place finish (behind Weaver) in the final 1998 USRRC standings. Leitzinger pitted again, while Luyendyk assumed the lead in the Momo Ferrari.

"It's disappointing, of course, to come here and we were running well," said Dyson. "To win this race even once is something, and to put it across the line is tough. We tried, came close, but not close enough." Dyson then walked down pit road to offer his congratulations to Moretti, who was sitting on pit wall.

"I feel the Dyson team has given us a gift," said Moretti. "Last year, Rob won, and I was very happy that he won. Today, he came and said, 'It's your time.' And I said, 'Yes, and I don't care if your car is broken.'"

Moretti then decided that he wanted to finish the race himself. "I thought, 'I want to see a picture of my car—me inside—winning Daytona,'" he said.

With the Dyson car out of the picture, the Momo Ferrari went on to score an eight-lap victory, even taking time to change its rear axle assembly after developing a vibration in the right-rear suspension. Moretti had his car brought back to pit road with 15 minutes remaining, and the popular owner drove the car himself to take the checkered flag. When he returned to pit road, he was carried to victory lane on the shoulders of his crew.

"I love Daytona—but Daytona, she doesn't like me," Moretti said after the race. "I try again, I try again—what the heck—today, I finally did it!"

"That was probably my most satisfying victory, because it was the first Rolex 24 victory for Doran Racing," said Doran. "It was also a great cap on a great career for Gianpiero—it was fun to make that happen for a guy who's been in racing for about 35 years. Winning the Rolex 24 was his drive in motorsports. It was cool to see that come to a successful conclusion after all those years of trying."

"Many times I talked to the man upstairs," Moretti said after the race. "I said, 'If I win, I quit.' This is nature. I'll be 58 in two months, so I win and I quit." With his goal accomplished, Moretti finished the season, which included winning the 12 Hours of Sebring. He then returned to Milan with his Rolex and checkered-flag photo, and quietly retired from the racing scene.

Second in the Can-Am class, and eighth overall, was the Mazda Kudzu of Jim Downing, Howard

Above: With the Ferris wheel in the background, a pack of cars weaves its way through the infield. Opposite top: The No. 36 Colucci/Matthews Racing R & S Ford of Eliseo Salazar, Jim Pace, and Barry Waddell is in for service. An accident put the car out of action after 300 laps. Right: A pit stop for the No. 30 Momo Ferrari 333SP, with Didier Theys set to take over for Arie Luyendyk. Far right: Winners (left to right) Arie Luyendyk, Gianpiero Moretti, Mauro Baldi, and Didier Theys look on as Moretti checks the time on his long-awaited Rolex chronograph.

Katz, Yojira Terada, Frank Freon, and John O'Steen. The team pushed throughout the final two hours to overtake the two Dyson cars, which were out of the running. The Kudzu had started 18th and had a setback when a broken throttle cable left the car briefly stranded on course. The team finished 75 laps behind the winning Ferrari.

Taking second overall, and first in the GT1 class, was the Rohr Motorsports' Porsche 911 GT1 of Danny Sullivan, Allen McNish, Dirk and Joerg Mueller, and Uwe Alzen. "It was fantastic, taking that Porsche to finish second overall against the Prototypes," said Sullivan. "We had a real good shot at winning the race outright, which was fun. It was also neat for me to drive with all those younger guys. I think I was the oldest guy on the team by 24 years or something, I was double everyone's age. They were really good guys. It was fun to be driving the factory Porsche again, and I enjoyed my time there."

Taking third overall, and second in GT1, was the Porsche 911 of Christophe Bouchut, Patrice Gouselard, Carl Rosenblad, and Andre Ahrle. Fourth overall, and winning in GT2, was the Porsche 911 GT2 of Franz Konrad, Peter Kitchak, Toni Seiler, Wido Rossler, and Angelo Zadra. It won the class by one lap, over another 911 GT2 driven by John Morton, John Graham, and Patrick and Duncan Huisman.

BMW repeated as winners in GT3, with Boris Said, Bill Auberlen, Marc Duez, and Peter Cunningham placing sixth overall. Alex Job's Team Seattle Porsche 911 Carrera RSR, driven by Michael Conte, Bruno Lambert, Nick Holt, and Darryl Havens, finished seventh overall and second in GT3. This was the second year for Team Seattle, which raised $200,000 for Seattle Children's Hospital, up from $80,000 in 1997.

Jason Priestley of *Beverly Hills 90210* co-drove a Ford Mustang prepared by Multimatic with fellow Canadian Scott Maxwell. They finished 38th.

In the two weeks following the Rolex 24, the story of Moretti's stirring victory after years of persistence was frequently repeated in the NASCAR garage. The lesson was not lost on Dale Earnhardt, who would finally beat his own 19-year jinx by winning the Daytona 500.

Arai
BOSCH
SHOEI
MULTIVEX
20
R. DYSON
B. LEITZINGER
CANAM
CANAM
CHAMPIONSHIP
DYSON Racing
USRRC
97
98
CHAMPIONS
GOODYEAR
Racing
Hella
PAGID
brake linings
BBS

1999: Once Is Not Enough

GIANPIERO MORETTI WAS TRUE TO HIS WORD: AFTER FINALLY WINNING THE DAYTONA 24 IN 1998, HE RETIRED FROM RACING. BUT WINNING ONCE WASN'T ENOUGH FOR ROB DYSON.

The New York businessman had won the 1997 Rolex 24 after years of trying, and came within three hours of repeating in 1998 before John Paul Jr. pitted, his car trailed by plumes of smoke. Dyson returned to Daytona as determined as ever in 1999, bringing a pair of Ford-powered Riley & Scott Mk IIIs. The No. 16 car would be driven by James Weaver, Stu Hayner, and Dorsey Schroeder, while the No. 20 would carry Butch Leitzinger, Andy Wallace, and Elliott Forbes-Robinson. Dyson was entered as a driver in both cars.

After retiring, Moretti had sold his interest in his team to Kevin Doran. Fredy Lienhard of Switzerland, a maker of ergonomic storage systems, bought Moretti's car. Lienhard would co-drive the team's Doran/Lista Racing Ferrari 333SP with Didier Theys, Mauro Baldi, and Arie Luyendyk.

Doran fielded a second Ferrari 333SP, the Doran/Matthews Racing entry, for Jim Matthews, Jimmy Vasser, Stefan Johansson, and Max Papis. And with 1996 overall winner Wayne Taylor ill, Allan McNish got the call to join Taylor, Max Angelelli, and Didier de Rodriguez in the Doyle-Risi Racing Danka Ferrari 333SP.

The field included two additional Ferrari 333SPs, the Dollahite Racing entry for Bill Dollahite, Paul Dallenbach, Mike Davies, and Doc Bundy, plus the European Auto Sport Racing entry for Lillian Bryner, Enzo Calderari, Angelo Zadra, and Carl Rosenblad.

Left: A fresh and rested Andy Wallace hops in to replace Butch Leitzinger on the No. 20 Dyson Racing R & S Mk III Ford and resume the team's battle with the Risi Ferrari. Above: Team owner Kevin Doran talks to his drivers of the No. 36 Doran/Matthews Racing Ferrari 333SP prior to qualifying. From left to right are Stephan Johannsson, Jimmy Vasser, Doran, and Max Papis.

Other cars to watch included DLW's R & S Ford for Hurley Haywood, Danny Sullivan, and Don and Dale Whittington; German Franz Konrad's Lola Lotus, which he co-drove with Jan Lammers and Vincenzo Sospiri; the InterSport Ford Lola of Jon Field, Ryan Jones, Mike Shank, and Sam Hornish; the Support Net R & S Ford of Henry Camferdam, Eliseo Salazar, Duncan Dayton, and Scott Schubot; and the 74 Hunting Ranch R & S Chevrolet for George Robinson, Jack Baldwin, Irv Hoerr, and Jon Gooding. In all, 21 Can-Am cars were on hand, a record for the open-cockpit class.

Weaver won the pole in the Dyson Ford with a lap of 127.05 mph, two seconds ahead of Theys in the Doran Lista Ferrari 333SP. The 78-car field took the green flag at 1 p.m. Saturday under sunny skies. Weaver set the early pace, chased by McNish in the Doyle-Risi Ferrari, while Lammers worked the Lola Lotus up to third.

Four-time Daytona 24 winner Bob Wollek brought out the first caution when he crashed in the turn four banking after completing seven laps. Lammers was penalized for passing under the caution in the infield. During the second caution, Lammers was again called for passing in the same location, between turn four and the West Horseshoe in the infield—an area of limited visibility. This time, the Lola was held for one minute in the newly-designated USRRC penalty box on pit road. The car overheated during the enforced pause, and the engine expired after 43 laps, ending Lammers' quest for his third Daytona triumph.

The race settled down to a battle among the two Dyson cars and three Ferraris. The Doran Lista Ferrari fell off the pace four hours into the event when Luyendyk broke the gearbox downshifting to miss a slower car entering the back stretch chicane. The car came to a halt on the banking and was towed to the garage, where the team lost 46 laps while the gearbox, starter, and flywheel were replaced. The team would make a second transmission change during the 19th hour.

The No. 20 Dyson Ford also fell back during the fourth hour, losing three laps while the alternator

Above left: A pit stop for the No. 4 Corvette of John Heinricy, Andy Pilgrim, and Scott Sharp. Above right: Tight competition in the infield sees the No. 63 Mazda Kudzu of Jim Downing, Howard Katz, Yojiro Terada, and Chris Ronson leading the 74 Ranch Resort R & S Chevrolet of George Robinson, Jon Gooding, Jack Baldwin, and Irv Hoerr, and the GT3-winning No. 23 Team Seattle Porsche 911 RSR of Anthony Lazzaro, Cort Wagner, Kelly Collins, and Darryl Havens. Opposite: Pole sitter James Weaver leads the field to the green flag for the start.

was changed. At 7 p.m., the pole-winning No. 16 Dyson Ford crashed while leading, when Stu Hayner hit a GT3 car in the chicane. The car lost 90 minutes and would struggle to a 22nd-place finish.

That gave the lead to Jimmy Vasser in the Doran/Matthews Ferrari. The car was still leading at 10 p.m., when Max Papis handed off to Stefan Johansson. As the car was exiting the pits, the left-rear wheel fell off. The car was towed to the paddock, where it lost 14 minutes for repairs.

That put the Risi-Ferrari in the lead, chased by the No. 20 Dyson Ford. The two teams would battle it out the rest of the way. The Ferrari lost its two-lap lead when a brake pad jammed during a 1 a.m. pit stop, giving the Dyson car a one-minute lead. For the second half of the race, the two teams dueled for hour after hour, braving two downpours and numerous cautions.

"For the entire race, we were locked in battle with the Ferrari. Every time we'd leave the pits, the Ferrari would be right there," Butch Leitzinger recalled. "So we had a real battle with the Ferrari trying to get our laps back, and obviously, they were trying to keep us laps down, so they were racing very hard. We finally managed to get back on the lead lap when they had problems of their own, but it was a great race, a very hard-fought race where the car in front was doing a lot of blocking, slicing through traffic, going on both sides of slower cars.

"It was probably the hardest-fought 24-hour race I've ever been in," Leitzinger continued. "Each time you'd finish your stint, you'd go back to the motor home and as soon as you'd open the door, Andy [Wallace] would be standing there, wanting to hear the news. We'd come into the motor

home and say, 'God, that Ferrari's fast.' Every time we'd come in, we'd be so charged up. It was such a good race."

Teams had a new experience driving during the night. Daytona International Speedway had installed lights, and was running its July Pepsi 400 NASCAR Winston Cup race at night. Rolex 24 competitors now found the superspeedway portion of the circuit illuminated, although at only 20 percent of the maximum used to light the tri-oval for stock cars. "The big lights are very good," said Elliott Forbes-Robinson. "In the dogleg, you kind of counted and turned, and now you can see the whole thing."

As the Dyson Ford and Doyle-Risi Ferrari continued to battle, they faced another obstacle—changing weather conditions—that kept the teams guessing. As it turned out, the Dyson team made the best guesses.

"It was one we were destined to win, because in mid-morning, it started to rain," Leitzinger recalled. "Andy got in the car, and he did a fantastic job calling the tire choices. It was very difficult, whenever

Above: Hurley Haywood teamed with brothers Don and Dale Whittington and Danny Sullivan in the No. 3 R & S Ford. Opposite top: While racing continued throughout the night, fans were treated to an infield carnival. Right: Sunday morning, the weather conditions deteriorated. The No. 18 Auberlen Porsche kicks up spray that obscures the No. 72 Lista Ferrari 333SP.

you wanted to go from dries to wets or vice versa, because you needed to know what everyone else was doing.

"At one point, the Ferrari came in to change to dry tires. Andy went by as the Ferrari was coming out of the pits on dry tires and he was still on wets. For the first few laps, Andy watched his mirrors and could see that he was pulling away from the Ferrari. When he could see the Ferrari started to catch up, he knew it was time for him to come in the pits to put on dry tires. He called that perfectly. The Ferrari team just had the bad luck of making the wrong call, and we happened to make the right calls."

Leitzinger took the checkered flag in a driving rainstorm. The team completed 708 laps, 2,504.54 miles, and averaged 104.900 mph. They beat the Ferrari by two laps.

"Last time we won [1997], our car started down in the field, and we didn't even think about winning until late in the race," said Leitzinger. "This weekend was different because we felt like we had a chance. We were in contention the whole race."

Noting the performance of his team's lead car, Dyson said, "One-two would have been really something."

"Ninety-nine was actually the really big one, because Butch and I and Andy Wallace got to win, and we had to race with the Ferrari the whole race," said Forbes-Robinson. "And it was an excellent race. You just couldn't let up. The rain was a little tough at times, but the Riley-Scott and Ford motor ran quite well, and we didn't have problems. The crew actually won it for us, because our pit stops

for brake pads were much faster than those for the Ferraris. So, that put us in the position we wanted to be in."

While they failed to take the overall victory, the Ferraris had a strong showing, taking four of the top eight places.

The Doran/Matthews Ferrari took third, 14 laps down. The car was fast, but a pair of incidents involving lost wheels—the first of which cost the team 14 laps—eliminated them from contention. The Doran/Lista Ferrari, which lost its gearbox four hours into the event, soldiered on to an eighth-place finish.

The Auto Sport Ferrari of Bryner/Calderari/Rosenblad/Zadra came in fourth, while the Support Net Riley & Scott Ford of Camferdam/Salazar/Dayton/ Schubot gave the Can-Am class a sweep of the top five positions.

The first non-Can-Am finisher was the GT3 winner, the sixth-place Porsche 911 RSR prepared by Alex Job Racing with drivers Kelly Collins, Anthony Lazzaro, Darryl Havens, and Cort Wagner. Running under the "Team Seattle" banner, their 1999 effort raised $250,000 for the Seattle Children's Hospital.

"We were in the lower GT3 class, and the turbo Porsches were in GT2," said Alex Job. "We beat all of them, there were only five prototypes ahead of us. We led 22 and a half of the 24 hours. It was a great race. We had the pole and set a new track record."

Winning in GT2 was the Roock Racing Porsche 911 GT2 of Andre Ahrle (who drove 14 stints), Hubert Haupt, and David Warnock, which finished seventh overall and led the class for the final three hours. Second in the class was the Schumacher Racing Porsche 993 of Larry Schumacher/Dirk Miller/John O'Steen/Martin Snow, eight laps behind and 10th overall.

The Corvette of Ron Fellows, Chris Kneifel, and John Paul Jr. finished third in the class. The team led the class for half of the event before being slowed by an oil leak. Teammates John Heinricy, Andy

Above: The scoring pylon in the background affirms that the No. 7 Doyle-Risi Ferrari 333SP of Wayne Taylor, Max Angelelli, Allan McNish, and Didier de Rodriguez is the race leader. Right: Butch Leitzinger holds on to take the checkered flag in a downpour, winning by two laps over the Doyle-Risi Ferrari.

Pilgrim, and Scott Sharp led the class early, but finished well back, the victims of various mechanical problems.

The French Team Oreca Dodge Viper GTS-R of David Donohue, Tommy Archer, and Olivier Beretta went out after 188 laps with suspension problems following an altercation with a backmarker. The race also included a new class for American sedans, GTT, won by the Ford Mustang Cobra of Craig Carter, Kyle McIntyre, Andy Petery, and Gary Stewart. They finished 28th overall, one of seven entries in the new class.

NASCAR Winston Cup star Ernie Irvan was entered in the GT3 class, but his PTG BMW M3 retired with engine trouble shortly after midnight, before he had the opportunity to drive.

USRRC held only two more races, at Lime Rock and Mid-Ohio. With car counts dropping, the series was unable to schedule additional races. Instead, promoters opted to schedule the European FIA GT, Sports Car, or wait for a more attractive series. As a result, the USRRC disbanded. A new independent series, with the strong support of the International Speedway Corporation, was announced at the September meeting of the Madison Avenue Sports Car Driving and Chowder Society in New York City. The Grand American Road Racing Association was born.

musco
16
Hella
2000 INAUGURAL SEASON

2000: Death of a Thousand Cuts

THE 2000 RACE WAS THE FIRST EVENT TO BE SANCTIONED BY THE NEW GRAND AMERICAN ROAD RACING ASSOCIATION, HEADQUARTERED IN DAYTONA BEACH. THE LEAD CLASS, ORIGINALLY KNOWN AS WORLD SPORTS CAR AND RENAMED THE CAN-AM, WAS NOW KNOWN AS SPORTSRACER PROTOTYPE (SRP). THERE WAS ALSO A CLASS FOR SMALLER PROTOTYPES, SRP II. THE GT CLASSES USED THE ORIGINAL IMSA NOMENCLATURE, GTO AND GTU, PLUS AGT FOR TUBE-FRAME, V-8-POWERED AMERICAN RACE CARS.

Three rules would change the traditional strategy for the 24 hours: The Grand-Am required the drivers who qualified their cars to start the race; it placed a four-driver limit on each car; and it forbade switching drivers from car to car. Therefore, a team had to nominate its four-driver lineup before the race, ending the earlier practice of often nominating seven or more drivers on each of a team's three entries. These rules also ended the tradition, started by Porsche back in 1968, that allowed a team to transfer a driver from another car to share in the victory.

Longtime American Motorcyclist Association executive Roger Edmondson had become president of the Grand-Am. IMSA founder John Bishop was named the commissioner, with former American Speed Association stock-car

Left: James Weaver and Dyson Racing planned to compete in a new Reynard, but struggled with the car in testing and opted to bring back their tried and true Riley & Scott Mk III Ford for the event. Above: Grand-Am regulars Ralf Kelleners and Mimo Schiattarella shared the No. 12 Risi Competizione Ferrari 333SP with Alex Caffi and Allan McNish.

standout Dave Watson as the director of competition. Administering the new series were a pair of familiar names, Mark Raffauf, the race director, and Tom Seabolt, the director of operations.

The 2000 race also had a familiar name on the pole. James Weaver set the fastest time in Rob Dyson's Ford-powered Riley & Scott Mark III, winning his second straight pole with a lap of 126.88 mph. Dyson had planned to campaign a new Reynard, but had struggled with the car during January testing, so the team instead hastily prepared its old R & S cars.

Cadillac was also part of the international presence for the event. General Motors' flagship line was practicing to compete at Le Mans, and entered two Cadillac LMPs with a talented lineup that included two of Dyson's former regular drivers, Butch Leitzinger and Andy Wallace.

That international presence also included GTO-class entries from General Motors, with its Corvette, and Dodge, fielding its Viper. While the Corvette was based in the U.S., the goal was racing in the celebrated French enduro; the Dodge Viper effort was run not by a U.S.-based organization, but by the highly-successful French Oreca team, which had steamrolled the competition in the 1999 FIA GT series.

In addition to Dyson, teams expected to challenge for the inaugural Grand-Am championship included the Risi Competizione Ferrari 333SP, with a driver lineup that included regulars Ralf Kelleners and Mimmo Schiattarella, plus guest drivers Allan McNish and Alex Caffi; Kevin Doran's Doran-Lista Ferrari 333SP for Mauro Baldi, Didier Theys, Fredy Lienhard, and Ross Bentley; George Robinson's 74 Ranch Resort R & S for himself, Jack Baldwin, and guest drivers Hurley Haywood and Irv Hoerr; a pair of Banana Joe's–sponsored InterSport entries, which featured a pair of identical twins, team co-owners Jon and Joe Field, plus Don and Dale Whittington; and Philip Creighton's R & S Ford, with a driver lineup that included Scott Schubot.

The 80-car field took the green flag at 1 p.m. on a chilly afternoon, with Weaver sprinting to the lead as Caffi spun in the Risi Ferrari and fell to the back of the field in the opening minutes. Stefan Johannson's Reynard ran over debris in the early going, and lost several hours from the resulting suspension damage. Meanwhile, the Doran-Lista Ferrari of Theys passed Weaver to take the lead.

Since its introduction in 1995, the Ferrari 333SP had established a reputation for speed and reliability. The speed was demonstrated early. The reliability, however, was lacking, and both cars were withdrawn by nightfall. The Risi Competizione entry went out early with transmission troubles, and an airbox fire in the fifth hour claimed the Doran Ferrari.

"The Ferrari had a history of spilling the excess fuel over the top of the inlet trumpets during engine overrun conditions, when you enter the corner and close the throttle for deceleration," Doran explained. "This fuel would collect in the airbox. In our case, it was a little excessive that day. Under normal conditions,

Above: Paul Newman carried No. 75 on the Gunnar Racing/Champion Porsche GT3R to commemorate his age. The car also carried the name of his latest film, Where the Money Is. *The oldest competitor in the race was paired with the youngest, 17-year-old Gunnar Jeannette. Opposite top: The two Cadillac LMPs race in formation. Butch Leitzinger (shown), Andy Wallace, and Frank Lagorce finished 13th overall and second in SRP in No. 6, one position ahead of No. 5, driven by Max Angelelli, Wayne Taylor, and Eric van de Poele. Right: An early evening view of the action from the turn one grandstands.*

cadillac.com
5
TOSHIBA
ACDelco
PIRELLI
GMAC
SR
cadillac.com
6
TOSHIBA
ACDelco
PIRELLI
GMAC
SR

it happens every lap. In our case, with all that excessive fuel in there, it ignited the fuel, the fuel burned, and then in turn burned the injector nozzles off, which were plastic. So at that point you're pumping unrestricted fuel through a three-eighths-inch open hole at 100 psi right into the airbox, feeding it with fuel at a high pressure and a high volume. Once it caught fire, the party was over."

Many of the expected contenders experienced troubles. A series of broken half-shafts plagued the Robinson entry. Meanwhile, both of the InterSport entries were on the sidelines, joined by the Creighton Ford, BMW Norma, Pilbeam Nissan, Multimatic Lola, and Konrad Lola, as the bulk of the 21

Above: The Dyson R & S was leading in the early morning, but struggling to keep up the pace. Opposite left: With the leading SRP car in trouble, the hotly contested GTO race eventually became a battle for the overall victory. The No. 92 Oreca Dodge Viper of Tommy Archer, Marc Duez, Vincent Vosse, and Jean Phillipe Belloc leads the No. 4 GM Goodwrench Corvette of Andy Pilgrim, Kelly Collins, and Franck Freon. The two cars' respective teammates finished one-two in the event. Opposite right: Stephen Watson, Christian Vann, Alison Duncan, and Raffaele Sangluolo finished sixth overall in the No. 45 Dodge Viper GTSR fielded by Champerlain Motorsports.

SportsRacer entries experienced problems in the early going.

The Cadillacs also struggled in their debut race, with a failed wheel hub dropping Leitzinger, Wallace, and Frank Lagorce back to 69th position. The team battled back through the night, however, to take over second place, but then experienced transmission troubles.

"It was the first race for the car. We had very good mileage and led the race for a lap or two, but we ended up having a lot of problems," said Leitzinger. "We kept coming back, and we almost regained the lead."

The team's second car, driven by Wayne Taylor, Max Angelelli and Eric van de Poele, also ran second before its transmission failed.

That left Dyson with a huge, 27-lap lead. The car had led since the eighth hour, and was seemingly on cruise control. Meanwhile, a battle was developing between the Viper and Corvette in the GTO class, many laps behind.

Just past the halfway point, a bent exhaust valve began to slowly rob the Dyson car of power. Weaver, Forbes-Robinson, Papis, and Dyson could only hold on and watch the GTO Oreca Vipers and Corvettes

slowly whittle into the lead, a few seconds per lap. "It hurt, seeing it slipping away, when it's in your grasp," said Dyson. "Seeing that big lead disappearing was the death of a thousand cuts, a real heartbreak."

Seeing Dyson's troubles, Team Cadillac tried to rebound. "Even though the Dyson car was leading, it was slowing, and we kept catching it," Leitzinger recalled. "We were about to be ready to catch it and the gearbox went. We had to change that, and that put us another 45 minutes back. With an hour to go, and I was driving, the engine finally blew. So that was a very long race and disappointing in the end, but it really wasn't unexpected because it was a brand new car."

With two hours remaining, Oreca took the lead. Suddenly, it was a Viper vs. Corvette sprint to the finish. Olivier Beretta, Karl Wendlinger, and Dominique Dupuy took the checkered flag only 30.878 seconds ahead of the Corvette of Ron Fellows, Justin Bell, and Chris Kneifel, the closest finish in Rolex 24 history.

The winning Viper completed 723 laps, covering 2,573.88 miles, and averaged 107.20 mph. "Before

I left the pits in the last half hour of the race, I knew the Corvette could be very fast, and that Ron Fellows was a very fast driver," said Wendlinger, who drove the final shift in the Oreca Viper. "When I passed the Dyson car for the overall lead, the team told me to take care. I concentrated only on my driving, and I didn't worry about reliability or passing anybody for the lead."

"That was my first 24-hour sprint race," said Fellows. "We got behind early, and it was just go as fast as you absolutely could, the whole time. Very difficult physically, because you were going so hard, and then to come up 31 seconds short. I didn't think that it would ever happen again, in the near future, to get a shot at overall again. And you know the next year, there it was."

Above: While the No. 31 Konrad Ford Lola of Jan Lammers, Sascha Maassen, and Franz Konrad prepares to exit, a number of other cars are in for service on pit road. Right: Five SportsRacer Prototypes lead the field at the start of the 2000 Rolex 24 at Daytona. Far right: Elliott Forbes-Robinson (right) is presented with a Road Racing Drivers Club award from RRDC president Brian Redman.

"We came up 30 seconds short," recalled Chris Kneifel. "In reality, we lost that race in the first four hours, with some silly little things that went wrong on us. That really gave us confidence coming back in 2001, that we could take it overall if we did it right. It was almost like we had to screw it up once to get to the top."

Oreca took three of the top five places, with David Donohue, Ni Amorim, and Jean Philippe Belloc third, and Tommy Archer, Marc Duez, Vincent Vosse, and St Belloc fifth.

Dyson's underpowered car hung on for fourth overall and managed to win the class, a boost that helped carry Weaver to the inaugural Grand-Am championship. The British independent Chamberlain team placed a pair of Vipers in sixth and seventh overall. Driving the latter car was Erik Messley, who would continue to campaign a Viper in most of the 2000 Grand-Am events.

Winning GTU and taking eighth overall was the Haberthus Racing's BCBS Porsche 911 GT3 R of Luca Drudi, Gabrio, Fabio Rosa, and Fabio Babini. Fifth in GTU was the Alex Job Racing Porsche GT3 R of Randy Pobst, Bruno Lambert, and Mike Conte. In the 15 consecutive years that Alex Job Racing ran in the Daytona 24 Hours, dating back to 1989, 15 of the team's 17 entries finished the race.

The Grand-Am also included a class for American tube-frame sedans, American GT. The battle in that class also proved to be one of attrition. Comer Racing won AGT with a 27th-place finish, its driver lineup including Andy McNeil and Doug Mills. Listed as second, but not finishing, was the Spirit of Daytona Camaro of Craig Conway, Doug Goad, and brothers Troy and Todd Flis.

Paul Newman, the oldest competitor in the event, was paired with the youngest driver, 17-year-old Gunnar Jeannette, in the Gunnar Racing Champion Porsche GT3 R. The team finished well off the pace.

Petty Enterprises was working on the possibility of having three generations of Pettys—Richard, Kyle, and Adam—in a Team Oreca Viper for the event, but ran out of time to complete the package. Richard was a seven-time champion and 200-race winner in NASCAR Winston Cup competition. Kyle raced in the 1986 Daytona 24 Hours, joining fellow Winston Cup drivers Bill Elliott, Ricky Rudd, and Ken Schrader in 1986. Adam, Kyle's 19-year-old son, was beginning his NASCAR career, but tragically, he would lose his life the following May in a crash at the NASCAR Busch Series practice in Loudon, New Hampshire.

ROLEX
AT DAYTONA

ROLEX 24

GM
MOTORSPORTS

ACTION
SIMPSON

GM

Goodwrench
Service
Plus

Goodwrench
Service
Plus

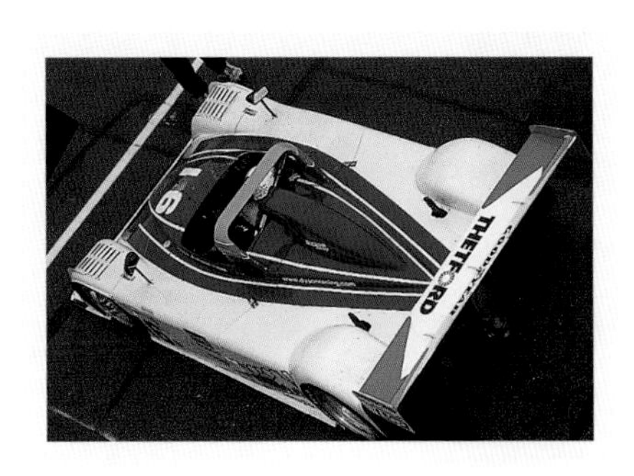

2001: The 24 Hours of Earnhardt

A FIGURE IN A YELLOW CHEVROLET JACKET ENTERED THE GARAGE IN PREPARATION FOR THE 2001 ROLEX 24. THE TALL, MUSTACHIOED MAN WAS SURROUNDED BY A PHALANX OF LAW ENFORCEMENT AND SECURITY PERSONNEL, PROTECTING HIM FROM A THRONG OF WELL-MEANING FANS. "THIS IS TRULY BIG STUFF," KEN WILLIS WROTE IN *THE DAYTONA BEACH NEWS-JOURNAL*. "YOU CAN TELL BY ALL THE GAWKERS STAKED OUT AT GARAGE STALL C-40...THIS IS NIXON-TO-CHINA BIG...WELCOME TO THE 24 HOURS OF EARNHARDT."

Unlike the Winston Cup garage, which is restricted to working personnel, the sports car paddock is open to spectators, who are able to mingle with the participants and see the drivers at close range by purchasing an additional paddock access ticket. Normally, this does not present a problem. Even Paul Newman was usually able to come and go as he pleased, while fans respectfully kept their distance.

Dale Earnhardt's presence, however, attracted a large crowd. Many of the fans visited the paddock, hoping for a glimpse of the seven-time NASCAR Winston Cup champion, or possibly to obtain a photograph or autograph.

Earnhardt was paired with Andy Pilgrim, who had won his class for Corvette in the Petit Le Mans at Road Atlanta in October, 2000, after

Left: Dale Earnhardt is joined by his son, Dale Jr., along with Andy Pilgrim and Kelly Collins to hoist the trophy for finishing second in the GTS category.
Above: For the second straight year, Rob Dyson's Riley & Scott Mk III Ford dominated the Rolex 24, only to have mechanical problems snatch away what appeared to be an easy victory.

executing a fender-banging pass of the Viper of Tommy Archer with two laps remaining. A few days later, Pilgrim was surprised to be handed a Federal Express package with a personal letter from Earnhardt.

"Wow, what a pass," Earnhardt's letter read. "That pass is exactly the reason I want you as my co-driver for the 24 Hours of Daytona. You obviously know how to rub fenders. Now, you got to teach me how to drive that Corvette."

"The first thing he told us was, 'Don't treat me like someone special,'" Pilgrim recalled in a 2002

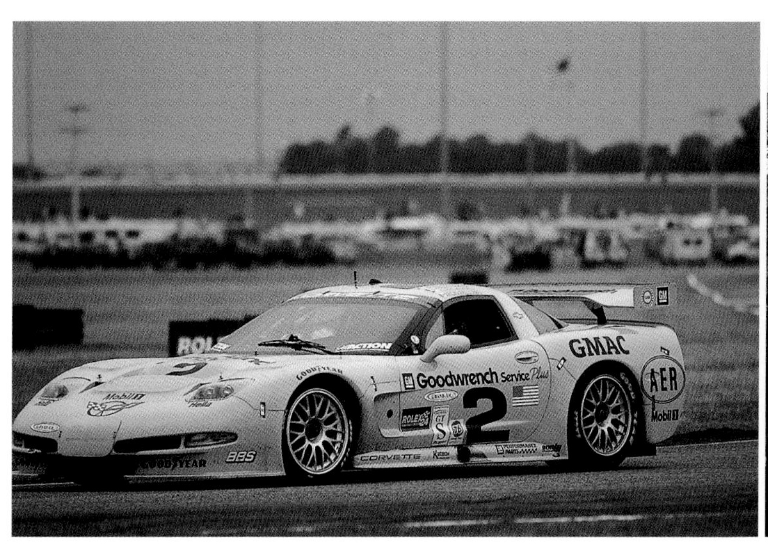

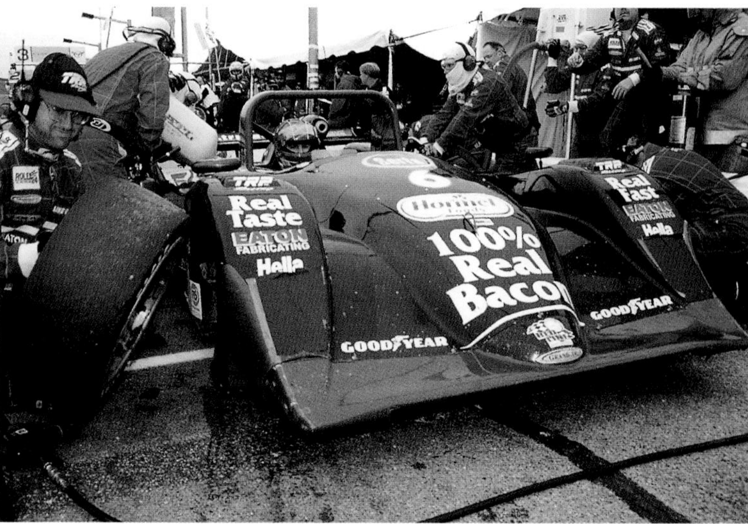

interview. "'I'm part of the team, and you guys need to tell me when I'm screwing up.' That was what he said the first time we met him.

"I sent him a lot of information, and I think he realized how seriously I take racing, this kind of racing, and I think he respected that I had a lot of information he didn't have. From that point on, he was comfortable asking me stuff, which was cool."

Earnhardt would be in one of two yellow, factory-backed Corvettes, co-driving with his son, Dale Earnhardt Jr., who was about to begin his second season racing in the NASCAR Winston Cup Series, as well as Pilgrim, and Kelly Collins. The other Corvette had the veteran lineup of Ron Fellows, Johnny O'Connell, Chris Kneifel, and Franck Freon. The Corvettes were favorites in the GTS category, and some felt they could even win the event overall, as the Oreca Viper team did in 2000.

However, a stronger showing was expected from the SportsRacer Prototype class for the 2001 event. Dyson Racing was back with two cars, with Butch Leitzinger, James Weaver, and Andy Wallace in the No. 16, and Max Papis, Elliott Forbes-Robinson, Nic Jonsson, and Rob Dyson in the No. 20.

There was only one Ferrari 333SP, the Rizi Competizione entry for Ralf Kelleners, Eric van de Poele, David Brabham, and Allen McNish. Kevin Doran's team fielded a new Judd-powered Crawford for

Above left: The overall race-winning No. 2 Corvette of Ron Fellows, Chris Kneifel, Franck Freon, and Johnny O'Connell in action. Above right: The crew goes to work on the No. 6 Miracle Motorsports Riley & Scott Mark III Ford. The car driven by Jeff Bucknum, Gary Tiller, Travis Duder, and Brent Sherman was an early accident victim. Opposite: Jack Baldwin was second-fastest qualifier in the 74 Ranch Resort Riley & Scott Judd, but the car he shared with George Robinson, Irv Hoerr, and Buddy Lazier went out with clutch problems after 563 laps.

Mauro Baldi, Didier Theys, Fredy Lienhard, and Ross Bentley.

The Champion team fielded a Porsche-powered Lola B210K for Bob Wollek, Hurley Haywood, Dorsey Schroeder, and Sascha Maassen. Defending IRL champion Buddy Lazier joined Jack Baldwin, Irv Hoerr, and George Robinson in the 74 Ranch Resort Riley & Scott Mk III Judd. Jon Field was joined by his son, Clint, and brother, Joe, along with Carl Rosenblad on the Banana Joe's InterSport Racing Lola B210K Judd. Car owner Tom Volk joined Indy Racing League driver Jeret Schroeder, Barry Waddell, and Jon Mirro on the TRV R & S Chevrolet.

James Weaver captured the pole in Dyson's Ford for the third consecutive year with a lap of 119.351 mph in the rain. He was joined on the front row by George Robinson, with only the front row set in opening qualifying. During Friday's second round, Kelleners set quick time in the Risi Ferrari 333SP, 126.743 mph, but would start third in the race.

"This is a very easy race to lose," Dyson said after Weaver won the pole. "There are so many things that can happen in 24 hours. You name it, and it can happen."

The 79-car grid took the green flag at 1 p.m., with Jon Field muscling his way into the lead at the end of the first lap, and Weaver, Kelleners, and Baldwin also taking turns out front during the first hour.

The Crawford was on the sidelines early, changing gearboxes. "I didn't have a lot of confidence at the start of the race, and now I've got less," Doran admitted while standing on pit road. Also sidelined early was the Banana Joe's InterSport Lola, with suspension damage, along with Jeret Schroeder's TVR R & S Chevrolet and the Champion Lola, both with engine trouble.

Early in the race, it began to rain. It was the elder Earnhardt's turn to drive. Even though he was used to competing in slick-tired stock cars that only race in dry conditions (although he had once taken a few practice laps at Watkins Glen in the rain using specially grooved Goodyear tires), he felt up to the task. "Keep an eye on my times," he called to his team on the radio. "If I'm going too slow, call me in and put Andy back in."

2001

"No, just keep it up, you're doing fine," Pilgrim radioed back.

"I was telling him where it was slippery and what lines to take," Pilgrim recalled.

Earlier, Earnhardt had said traffic was like, "New York, New York." His son had even tougher going,

Above: Bob Wollek joined Dorsey Schroeder, Hurley Haywood, and Sascha Maassen in the Champion Racing Porsche Lola, in hopes of winning his fifth Daytona 24. The team finished 59th, a victim of engine failure. It was Wollek's final race. The quiet veteran lost his life the following month in a traffic incident en route to practice for the 12 Hours of Sebring, when his bicycle was clipped by a vehicle only a few miles from the track. Right: Genesis Racing fielded the No. 10 BMW M3 for Bill Auberlen, Rick Fairbanks, Chris Gleason, and Chris Miller. The team finished ninth overall and sixth in GT.

spinning twice during his first shift behind the wheel.

"It's a pretty awesome car," the elder Earnhardt said on Sunday morning, following his final turn at the wheel. "I just wish we hadn't had that problem at the start with the transmission, it would have been really good. I felt really good out there in the rain. I was just riding along and doing what the car wanted. I slipped once or twice, but nothing out of the ordinary for a wet race track. It was a fun experience. We're serious about it. I ran second in class. Fellows and them really set the mark with us getting into trouble. I'm happy."

The event settled down to a familiar scenario: Dyson Ford vs. Ferrari. While the other SRPs dropped out, the Dyson R & S Ford Mk III raced on, waging a tactical battle. The Risi Ferrari took the lead at 9 p.m., but lost a wheel on the back straight at 9:45 p.m., resulting in a pit stop that cost the team four laps and allowed the Dyson car to pad its lead.

At 2:25 a.m., the Papis was at the wheel of the third-place No. 20 Dyson Ford when an input shaft snapped, costing the team two hours. At 4:45 a.m., the second-place Risi Ferrari pitted and went behind the wall. The car was eventually retired when the oil temperature rose too high.

That gave the No. 16 Dyson Ford a comfortable lead. For the fifth straight year, the team held the lead at the 21-hour mark with no one in its rearview mirror. The Corvette was second, 27 laps behind. Dyson's race continued to go like clockwork, despite the heavy rain.

"The conditions had been horrible for the entire race, the worst I'd ever seen," recalled Butch Leitzinger. "We had a complete downpour. It was very cold, and we spent so much time behind the pace car that the oil temperature dropped very low, around 120 degrees [normally it's over 200], which is very bad for a racing engine . However, we survived through all that and kept the car on the track."

Suddenly, at 9:33 a.m., things went wrong. "With about three and a half hours to go I was in the car," Leitzinger explained. "As soon as I lifted in the tri-oval to brake for the first turn, there was a big 'pow' out of the engine. It sounded like a war was going on back there. I tried to make it around, but I didn't even make it through the International Horseshoe. The engine seized up. It was just like a hit in the gut. To be winning that convincingly, and we were driving as easily as we possibly could, and still to have that happen. A piston broke. It was horrible to go walking back to the pits and see the guys on the crew. To see the disappointment on their faces and Rob Dyson, to see [our chances] go away that quickly was very difficult."

Meanwhile, Ron Fellows was napping in the team motor coach, barely paying attention to the television. "I saw the Dyson car parked in the infield, but first I thought they were showing a replay of previous Dyson disappointments, because that team was very dominant at Daytona," Fellows recalled. "Then I took a second look, and sure enough, it was this year's graphics on the car. I bolted up, and headed straight for the pits, thinking 'Man, this is an awesome

opportunity here.' I got in the car around 10 a.m. and drove to the end."

By 10:31 a.m. Fellows and the Corvette had made up the distance to the Dyson car, and took the lead. "We were behind by many laps," Fellows said. "As I stepped over the wall to get into the car it started to pour. But we just stayed clean and out of trouble, we were going to make up that deficit, there was still plenty of time to go. We managed to stay out of trouble and win it overall."

Fellows, Kneifel, O'Connell, and Freon completed 656 laps, 2,335 miles, and averaged 97.293 mph, winning by eight laps. Their Corvette teammates, Earnhardt Sr. and Jr., Pilgrim, and Collins, finished fourth overall and second in GTS, 14 laps behind the winners.

"Driving into victory lane was an experience I'll never forget," Fellows said. "It was a tremendous, tremendous high, being there with the Earnhardts and being presented my Rolex by Jackie Stewart, who was a childhood hero of mine. It was probably one of the greatest days I ever had."

Winning the SRP class was the Mazda Kudzu of Jim Downing, Howard Katz, A. J. Smith, and Chris Ronson, finishing 11th overall. The crippled No. 16 Dyson Ford scored second in SRP and 14th overall, with the team's second car continuing after its early problems to take third, 19th overall.

Finishing second, and first in GT, was the White Lightning/Petersen Motorsports Porsche GT3 R of Mike Fitzgerald, Randy Pobst, Christian Menzel, and Lucas Luhr. Third, and second in the class, was the Porsche GT3 RS of Lance Stewart, Wolfgang Kaufmann, and Ciril Chateau.

Michael Johnson's Archangel Motorsports won in SRP II, with Andy Lally, Paul Macey, Peter Seldon, and Martin Henderson finishing 13th overall in a Nissan Lola. A one-two finish in the class had vanished when the team's other car crashed just before dawn while running second, when Tony Dudeck spun and was hit by Doug Goad's Flis Motorsports *Spirit of Daytona Beach* Camaro, which had been running second in AGT.

Above: A pair of Corvettes leads a huge pack of cars to the checkered flag. Right: After scoring overall honors in the 2000 event, Dodge Vipers were not a factor in 2001. The British Chamberlain Motorsports team fielded a pair of Vipers, including the No. 15 for Christian Vann, Chris Bingham, Seigi Ara, and Robert Neam, but neither car finished in the top 30. Far right: Ron Fellows pumps his fist in victory lane after scoring the overall triumph.

The American GT victory went to the Hamilton Safe Motorsports Camaro, which car owner Kenny Bupp co-drove with Simon Gregg, Doug Mills, and Dick Greer, a class winner for the fourth time at Daytona. They finished 28th overall. Amazingly, the Flis Camaro—running without much of its bodywork after the dawn collision—managed to take second in the class for Goad, Craig Conway, Rick Maugeri, and Erik Messley.

Hans Stuck, Terry Borcheller, Boris Said, and Toney Jennings led much of the race in the GT class and were as high as third overall in Tom Milner's JET Motorsports BMW M3, powered by a V-8 engine, which had the air filter plugged in the rain, leading to a burned piston.

NASCAR Winston Cup driver Kyle Petty finished seventh overall, and fourth in GT, joined by Peter Baron, Leo Hindery, and Gian Luigi Buitoni in an Orbit Racing Porsche GT3 R. Petty snared the seventh position on the final lap of the race, when he passed a group of nearly 20 slow-moving cars queued up for the finishing photo on the banking entering turn four, getting by Darrin Law in the G&W Motorsports Porsche in the process. "Since I'm new to this, I didn't know if I was breaking some kind of sports car rule by passing everyone, but I wanted that position for the boys on the team," Petty said.

Mike Colucci, a respected crew chief and team owner in the 24 Hours of Daytona since 1975, and five-time winner of the event, drove in the race for the first time in the other Orbit Porsche, which retired early with engine problems.

Former Camel GTP driver Bob Akin fielded a Riley & Scott Ford, driven by Michael Lauer, Brian DeVries, Mark Simo, and Norman Simon, which was the victim of a lap-one incident and eventually retired after 93 laps.

Joining the winning Corvette team in victory lane was Earnhardt, a 34-time Daytona winner in Winston Cup, Busch Series, and IROC competition. It would also be his last visit there. Exactly two weeks later, the celebrated seven-time NASCAR champion would lose his life in a crash while running third, entering the final turn on the last lap of the Daytona 500.

Just one month later, sports car racing would also lose one of its greatest stars, when Bob Wollek was struck and killed by a car while bicycling to a practice session for the 12 Hours of Sebring.

LISTA
27

2002: The SRPs Are Finally Redeemed

AFTER FAILING TO WIN OVERALL IN THE DAYTONA 24 HOURS FOR TWO CONSECUTIVE YEARS, SPORTSRACING PROTOTYPE COMPETITORS WERE LOOKING TO REDEEM THEMSELVES IN 2002. WITH THE NEW DAYTONA PROTOTYPE ANNOUNCED AS THE LEAD CLASS FOR THE GRAND AMERICAN ROLEX SPORTS CAR SERIES BEGINNING IN 2003, THIS WAS EXPECTED TO BE THE FINAL OPPORTUNITY FOR THE OPEN-COCKPIT CARS. THERE WERE THREE BRAND-NEW SRP MODELS READY FOR THE RACE, TWO OF THEM FIELDED BY FACTORY TEAMS.

The Crawford, which had been rejected by Doran Racing after three races in 2001, was back. Fielded by Max Crawford and powered by a 12-cylinder Judd engine, the team was anchored by two-time Rolex 24 winner Jan Lammers, NASCAR Winston Cup star Tony Stewart (who was making his sports car racing debut), and Johnny Mowlem.

The Riley & Scott Mk III had been winning races since 1995. But its successor, the Mk IIIC, had been turned down by Dyson Racing after a 2001 test. Jim Matthews now fielded the factory-backed team, co-driving with Robby Gordon, Scott Sharp, and Guy Smith. The car was powered by a Ford-based Elan engine from the Don Panoz shops. An additional R & S Mk IIIC was

Left: Didier Theys is at the wheel of the Doran Lista Racing Judd Dallara he co-drove to an overall victory with Fredy Lienhard, Max Papis, and Mauro Baldi. Above: Tony Stewart slips into the cockpit of the new Crawford SRP. A man who had already won championships in IRL IndyCar Series, USAC Silver Crown, Midget, and Sprint cars, Stewart would go on to win the 2002 NASCAR Winston Cup championship.

entered by George Robinson's 74 Ranch Resort team, with the owner joined by Jack Baldwin, Wally Dallenbach Jr., and Mark Simo.

Doran Lista Racing had debuted a Judd-powered Dallara in the finale, a three-hour race at Daytona International Speedway in November. Doran's team had been running third when its gearbox exploded with 15 minutes remaining. The car was fast, but a Judd engine had never finished a 24-hour race, and the endurance of the new car was definitely in doubt. Doran had again assembled Didier Theys, Max Papis, Mauro Baldi, and Fredy Leinhard as his drivers.

Despite the new cars, many looked for one of the veteran SRP cars to win overall. Risi Competizione returned to Daytona with what was billed as the final showing for the venerable Ferrari 333SP. With driver Eric van de Poele, the team entered as a leading contender.

Dyson Racing entered a pair of well-tested R & S Mk IIIs, and was determined to overcome the failures that had cost the team victory the past two years. James Weaver and Butch Leitzinger were joined by Oliver Gavin in the No. 16 car. Rob Dyson was accompanied by his 23-year-old son, Chris, along with Elliott Forbes-Robinson and Dorsey Schroeder in the No. 20.

Other cars to watch included a pair of Lola B210Ks. Champion entered a Porsche-powered Lola for Hurley Haywood, Andy Wallace, Sascha Maassen, and Lucas Luhr, while Banana Joe's InterSport had a Judd-powered Lola for Jon Field, Duncan Dayton, Michael Durand, and Rick Sutherland. Ascari also fielded a pair of Judd-powered cars. Werner Lupberger, Timothy Bell Jr., and Harri Toiven drove the No. 49 entry, with Ben Collins, Klaas Zwart, and Christian Vann in the No. 23.

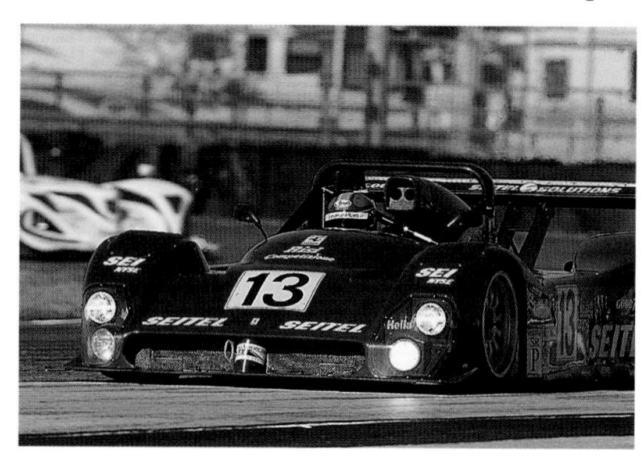

With that SRP entry, the GT classes, including Paul Gentilozzi's Rocketsports Jaguar and Irv Hoerr's Sky Blue Ford Mustang, were relegated to the background. Paul Newman drove a Panoz in pre-event testing, but the team felt that the car was not competitive and did not enter the event.

Doran's off-season work on top-end speed paid off when Theys won the pole for the Rolex 24 with a lap of 125.576 mph. Second fastest was the surprising Ascari, driven by Lupberger. As teams prepared for the 1 p.m. start on pit road, Doran huddled with his drivers. His mood was far from sanguine. "Expect to have problems," Doran told his team. "The challenge is to work through the problems. Keep your chins up."

Jon Field was a little more optimistic, although his car had only qualified 10th. "We were bad in qualifying. We were going for a low downforce setup, and it hurt us. It made us about nine mph faster down the straightaway, but hurt us four seconds on our overall time. So we went back to our high-downforce setup for the race, and it was quick again."

NASCAR Winston Cup champion Jeff Gordon was in the crowd, estimated at 50,000 for the 1 p.m. start, enjoying overcast skies and cooler temperatures while watching the lead SRPs battle with the intensity of a sprint race.

Above: The race marked the last hurrah for the Ferrari 333SP, but the Risi Competizione entry driven by Eric van de Poele, David Brabham, Stefan Johansson, and Ralf Kelleners was not a factor in the race. Right: The No. 8 Rand Racing Nissan Lola, raced for only the second time, captured SRP II honors with a third-place overall finish. Driving were Bill Rand, Anthony Lazzaro, Terry Borcheller, and Ralf Kelleners.

The Champion Lola was first to fall off the pace, pitting on the warm-up lap to change a spark plug. The team spent most of the opening hour in the pits, losing 14 laps and falling to 67th place. Doran Lista's Dallara led at the end of the first hour, challenged by the surprising Ascari of Werner Lupberger.

The Dyson team had a surprisingly early exit in 2002. Their lead car was in the pits 49 minutes into the event because of a power-steering fluid leak. "It was right over our feet and dropping power-steering fluid right on to the brake pedal," Leitzinger recalled. "So every time you'd go for the brakes, your foot would go flying off of it, which is very disconcerting." They lost four laps and fell back to 44th position. The team's problems were just beginning.

Dyson's second car—driven by the team owner himself—took the lead in the second hour, but was soon passed by Brabham in the Risi Ferrari. The race in front was shaping up as a battle among the Risi, Matthews, InterSport, and Doran teams. After five hours, all remained on the lead lap, even

as Dyson's troubles multiplied.

With the No. 16 car already behind the wall for transmission repairs, the No. 20 Dyson Ford pitted without fifth gear. Rather than go back to the garage, the team cannibalized parts from the other car's new transmission to get the No. 20 back in action after a 45-minute stop. The No. 20 continued until 3 a.m., when it retired with terminal engine problems, running well off the pace. "From the beginning, it just seemed we weren't going to have it," Leitzinger recalled.

The Risi car lost ground when the team had to change the gearbox, giving the lead to the Doran Lista Dallara. The Ferrari dropped 30 laps off the pace and was out of contention.

Nine hours into the event, the Matthews R & S Mk IIIC lost 14 laps to replace the alternator. Next to experience problems were the No. 49 Ascari, which ran near the lead for the opening 10 hours before retiring with engine failure, and the Crawford, which lost ground to repair bodywork after Lammers was pinched into the wall entering turn one on a restart. The car was retired soon afterwards.

At the 10-hour mark, the Banana Joe's InterSport Lola took the lead when the pole-winning Doran Lista Dallara lost two laps to change the battery on pit road. Then, at the midway point, the Doran

Above: A red sky at dawn in the 40th running of the Daytona sports car classic. Right: After winning the race overall in 1997 and 1999, and falling just short the past two years, Dyson Racing entered the event as the favorite. However, neither of the team's cars—including the No. 20 driven by Elliott Forbes-Robinson, Dorsey Schroeder, and the father-son team of Rob and Chris Dyson—were a factor in the event. Both cars experienced problems in the early going. Far right: Paul Newman (right) tested the Panoz in January. However, the actor did not feel the car was competitive enough for the Rolex 24, and the car was not entered.

car endured an extended stop for electrical repairs, and lost an additional seven laps. Also struggling with electrical problems throughout the night was the Matthews R & S Mk IIIC.

"Everything was running real well, probably until around midnight," Guy Smith recalled. "First of all, the alternator went down. Changing the alternator cost us about 10 laps. Then we had a problem with the electronics and the lights, which cost us another 10 laps. Then, we had a problem with a cracked header. After we changed that, all our problems were over with, but we lost so much time in the middle of the race. It cost us at the end."

At sunrise, the InterSport team led the Doran Lista Dallara by seven laps, with the Matthews R & S 19 laps behind. Working its way back from opening-hour struggles was the Champion Lola, which had moved up to fifth overall, 29 laps back. At 8:07 a.m., the car came to a stop exiting the infield, and the team lost more time, dooming its chances of taking the overall victory.

While leading throughout the early morning hours, the InterSport Banana Joe's team had troubles of its own. Their Lola lost its clutch after midnight, but managed to retain the lead. At 8:35 a.m., the pace took its toll, and the car came to a stop in the infield. The team lost several laps after

driveshaft repairs and continued, but was now chasing the lead Dallara. The chase didn't last very long, however. At 9:19 a.m., the Lola stopped in the infield with a failed input shaft.

"At Daytona, you always got to plan for trouble," Jon Field said. "We just had a lot of luck going our way for a good part of that race. Then, we lost the clutch around 1 a.m. At that point, I was not as optimistic as I had been, because that's a tough deal, to drive without a clutch in those cars. So we drove until around 8:30 a.m., then we lost a half-shaft, but that was definitely because of driving without the clutch. Then the gearbox went right after that, and it was over. It was tough for the team. There were a lot of people rooting for us, which was kind of neat."

After the InterSport Lola went behind the wall, the Doran Lista Dallara regained the lead at 8:46 a.m. At that point, the Matthews R & S was charging, trying to make up the eight-lap deficit, and waiting for the Dallara to stumble. Given the ebb and flow of the event, it appeared likely that Doran would encounter some type of problem during the final four hours.

"It looked that way," said Scott Sharp. "They were having some oil temperature problems.

Unfortunately, we had different problems earlier. Bill Riley said, 'Just hammer it, go for it. If it breaks it breaks, but we've got to start trying to catch up.' That was the smart thing to do, and it was fun. It was a lot better than sitting around and waiting for the Doran car to drop—it never happened anyway—but we were able make up 16 laps back, a slight bobble on their part probably would have been enough for us to go and win the race."

Waiting on pit road for the final hour to wind down, the haggard Doran Lista team was joined by a rested Rob Dyson, smiling underneath his trademark Goodyear hat. "I can't believe how happy I am," Dyson said. "I feel like I won it with Fredy."

With 20 minutes remaining, Lienhard was given the honor of driving to the checkered flag. "I talked to Mauro Baldi in the closing minutes of the race, and I said, 'If it's OK with you, I would like to do the final laps,'" Lienhard recalled. "Then he said 'Yes, for you, I'll do it, I wouldn't be agreeable for anybody else.' I could feel there was goodwill from everyone. That was very nice. It was a one-time opportunity. You probably won't see that again in your life."

Lienard, owner of Lista, a Swiss-based manufacturer of ergonomic work-space materials, had been

racing since 1968. Like Gianpiero Moretti before him, it was his personal dream to win at Daytona. Like Moretti in 1998, he finally achieved his goal. The team averaged 106.142 mph, completing 716 laps, 2,548.96 miles. The final margin of victory was six laps.

2002

"To me, winning the Rolex 24 at Daytona was the biggest thing," said Lienhard. "It was like a crown on my racing career after all the years, and it was also very nice because I got a lot of response in Switzerland. In Europe, this race is really well known and has a very high reputation. It was also good for my company and my employees, I got really big parties and a nice welcome when I came back. It was not only a big success for my racing, but also it was great for my business." Ironically,

Above left: A pair of eventual class winners battle it out, with the No. 3 GTS Rocketsports Racing Jaguar of Paul Gentilozzi, Scott Pruett, Brian Simo, and Michael Lauer racing the No. 66 GT The Racer's Group Porsche GT3 R of Kevin Buckler, Michael Schrom, Timo Bernhard, and Jorg Bergmeister. Above right: The winning Doran Lista Racing Dallara is surrounded by well-wishers and the team on pit road following the race. Opposite: (left to right) Mauro Baldi, Max Papis, Fredy Lienhard, and Didier Theys celebrate in victory lane.

Lista's business grew so much in the months following the Rolex 24 that Lienhard had to curtail his racing. His son, Fredy Jr., took his place with the team.

The fast Matthews R & S Mk IIIC settled for second. "We saw on the TV when Didier went out there was fire at the back of the car. It had some kind of leak of something, and we thought the engine was going to blow," Guy Smith said. "But the Dallara kept running and running."

"If I said we didn't wish bad luck on them, I would be lying," Robby Gordon said. "I think all of us thought we could win until we got to 13 minutes to go."

Bill Rand's team was the third-place overall finisher, and was the biggest surprise of the event. Rand had entered his Nissan Lola in the 2001 Daytona Grand-Am Finale and won the SRP II class with Anthony Lazzaro and Terry Borcheller driving. It was the Texan's debut as a professional car owner. Rand returned to Daytona for the 24-hour race, with his car prepared by Risi Competizione. This was Rand's first professional race as a driver, and he was joined by Ralf Kelleners, Lazzaro, and Borcheller in a dominant showing. They led their class virtually the entire distance.

Taking third in SRP and fourth overall, after playing catch-up for 23 hours, was the Champion Porsche Lola of Wallace/Haywood/Maassen/Luhr, the only SRP entrant other than the Matthews R & S that was running at the finish.

Paul Gentilozzi, overall winner of the 1994 race, scored the victory in the GTS division, joined once again by Scott Pruett, with Brian Simo and Michael Lauer. The Rocketsports team fielded the same Jaguar that carried Gentilozzi to his third Trans-Am championship in 2001.

Winning in GT was Kevin Buckler's The Racer's Group Porsche GT3 R, finishing seventh overall. Co-driving with Buckler were Michael Schrom, Timo Bernhard, and Jorg Bergmeister. Buckler backed up his Daytona triumph with a GT class victory in the 24 Hours of Le Mans.

The No. 09 Flis Motorsports Corvette finished 22nd overall and won in American GT, driven by Craig Conway, Doug Goad, Michael Ciasulli, and Andy Pilgrim. The victory came the same year that they had shed the *Spirit of Daytona Beach* moniker.

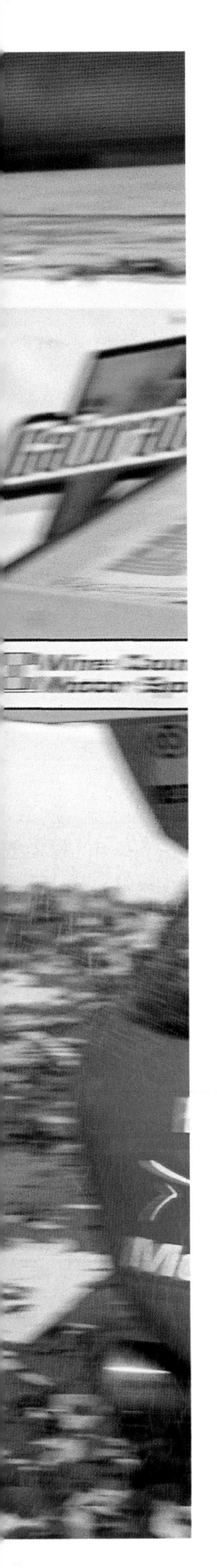

2003: Baptism Under Fire

After taking a late flight from California to Orlando, Kevin Buckler stopped his rental car in front of Daytona International Speedway at 3 a.m. on the eve of opening practice for the 2003 Rolex 24. "After all these years of trying to win here and getting my butt kicked, we finally got you last year," Buckler said to the back of the empty grandstands. "This year, we're going to try to get you again."

Buckler won the GT class in 2002, driving The Racer's Group Porsche GT3 R. His victory led to a career year, winning his class in the 24 Hours of Le Mans and then being named the winner of the international Porsche Cup.

For 2003, Buckler would experience the full gamut of emotions that the 24 Hours of Daytona has to offer—both the thrills of victory and the agony of defeat.

Buckler wasn't alone in approaching the race with optimism. Grand American's new rules package drastically reduced the speed differential between the fastest and slowest classes. Some thought the evolution of the Porsche 911, the GT3 RS, with its legendary reliability, could come from the "slowest" class, GT, and win overall honors.

Others looked at the revamped GTS category, which now combined the sports car "supercars" with tube-frame American V8s, to outrun Grand American's new lead class.

Left: Kevin Buckler (foreground) and Michael Schrom spray the champagne in victory lane. After winning GT class honors in 2002, The Racer's Group captured the overall title. Above: Dr. Steve Earle fights a fire on the No. 22 JMB Racing Ferrari 360 GT two hours into the race. The car was withdrawn after the fire.

Simon Gregg, son of the four-time Daytona 24 Hours winner and now a top Trans-Am competitor, had his Trans-Am owner, Jim Derhaag, build a Corvette to GTS specifications for this race. For his co-drivers, Gregg selected Derek and Justin Bell, which was the first time father and son had shared a race car. The younger Bell, who ran a driving school near West Palm Beach, Florida, promptly set the fastest time in the Corvette with a lap of 117.155 mph.

"This year, it's such an open field," said the elder Bell, a three-time overall winner of the event. "I don't think it's been this wide open in 20 years. My car certainly can win it, but so can many others."

Among the other tube-frame entries was the Acxiom Corvette driven by the father-son team of Charles and Rob Morgan, joined by Jim Pace and Lance Norick.

Also new to the GTS class was the Mosler MT900R. Perspective Racing won the race at Homestead-Miami Speedway and several poles running the full Grand American schedule in 2002, and added Andy Wallace to join regular drivers Joao Barbossa, Michel Neugarten, and Jerome Policand. The British Martin Short team, second overall in a new 2002 24-hour race at Bathurst, Australia, also brought a pair of Moslers for the race. A highly publicized fourth Mosler, with a driver lineup led by 1990 Daytona 24 Hours winner Davy Jones, failed to show up for the race.

2003

Ferrari had its biggest Daytona 24 entry in years, with five 360 GTs entered in the GT class, and a driver lineup led by 2002 Rolex 24 winners Max Papis and Mauro Baldi, plus Cort Wagner, Ralf Kelleners, Anthony Lazzaro, and Ryan Hampton.

The open-cockpit SRP II class was grandfathered in for 2003, although severely restricted. Five cars were on hand, including a pair of Essex entries prepared by Tony Dowe, who had been behind TWR Jaguar's winning effort.

Above left: Three long pit stops cost the new Multimatic Ford Focus an overall victory. Unlike former years, when the faster GTP or SRP classes had a distinct advantage over the slower classes, the Daytona Prototype had to slowly work its way back through the field. Above right: Ferrari of Washington's 360 GT (No. 33) leads the No. 21 Archangel Nissan Lola and the No. 40 Derhaag Corvette in the infield. New rules had all four Rolex Series classes running within a few seconds of each other. Opposite: To showcase the new class, Grand American placed the six Daytona Prototypes at the front of the grid, with Scott Maxwell in the No. 88 Multimatic Ford Focus taking the lead at the start.

While there was talk of a support class scoring an overall victory, most of the pre-race attention was centered on the new stars of the Rolex Sports Car Series. The new Daytona Prototypes class had been announced on the eve of the 2002 Rolex 24. Unlike other leading sports car classes, such as the IMSA Camel GTP and World Sports Car/Sports Racing Prototypes, there was no gestation period for the new cars, and the Daytona Prototypes would be the lead class in their first race.

Six of the new cars were on hand. Brumos Motorsports, which had provided an artist's conception of the new car at its 2002 unveiling, brought a pair of the new cars. One of the Porsche-powered FABCARs was painted in the historic red, white, and blue paint scheme made famous by Peter Gregg and Hurley Haywood, with Haywood himself leading the driver lineup in his quest for his sixth Daytona 24 Hours victory. Joining him in the No. 59 were J. C. France, son of International Speedway Corporation President Jim France, plus Indy Racing stars Scott Sharp and Scott Goodyear. The second Brumos car also had a formidable lineup, with David Donohue and Mike Borkowski paired with Chris Bye and Randy Pobst. Brumos had several months of testing behind them, including a nearly flawless 27-hour test in January.

A third FABCAR featured Toyota power, with owner/driver Darius Grala, a native of Poland who won the 2002 Ferrari Challenge championship, joined by three relative unknowns, Guy Cosmo, Joshua Rehm, and Oswaldo Negri.

The Multimatic Ford Focus was powered by a four-valve V-8 Ford Taurus engine built by NASCAR Winston Cup legend Robert Yates, with Canadian stars Scott Maxwell and David Empringham joined by David Brabham.

G&W presented a BMW-powered Picchio, driven by Darren Law, Boris Said, Dieter Quester, and Luca Riccitelli.

Although defending Rolex 24 winner Doran Racing was absent from competition, Kevin Doran built a Daytona Prototype for Bell Motorsports, with Forrest Barber and Terry Borcheller, joined by defending 24 Hours winner Didier Theys and Christian Fittipaldi, a veteran of Formula One and CART competition, who was making a transition to stock car racing. Doran struggled to prepare the

new car in time for the race, and had no testing prior to unloading the car at Daytona.

The new class was considerably slower than the SRP cars, and Grand American took steps to slow the GTS class, which were as fast as—or faster than—the new Daytona Prototypes. To showcase the new class, Grand American reserved the first six positions for the new Daytona Prototypes. Scott Maxwell led the new class with a lap of 115.969 mph in the Multimatic Ford, the third fastest overall speed. The Ford was followed by David Donohue in the No. 58 Porsche FABCAR. Only four Daytona Prototypes qualified, with both Piccho and Doran struggling to get their cars ready for their third-row starting positions.

The new rules, coupled with an economic downturn and anticipated war with Iraq, led to only 45 entries, of which 44 actually started. Four hours before the green flag, word trickled in that the

Above: The crew of the Racer's Group No. 66 Porsche GT3 RS executes another flawless pit stop. While the other two entries were hauled off on wreckers, the team's lead vehicle had a trouble-free race to score the overall victory. Right: The Orbit Porsche of Kyle Petty, Leo Hindery, Peter Baron, and Marc Lieb (No. 43) leads the No. 10 MAC Racing Porsche GT3 RS in tight infield action. The Orbit team finished sixth overall and fourth in GT. Petty, a NASCAR Winston Cup veteran, said the new Grand American rules that eliminated the faster overtaking cars made the racing more enjoyable.

space shuttle Columbia had been lost over Texas on its approach for a landing at Cape Canaveral. Flags were at half-mast for the start in brilliant sunshine.

Once the green flag waved, the Daytona Prototypes showed promise of a bright future, tempered by many teething problems. Maxwell's Multimatic Ford quickly pulled ahead, followed by Donohue and Haywood in the two Porsches.

Meanwhile, two of the Daytona Prototypes began experiencing problems in the opening 15 minutes. The untested Doran lost most of opening practice with a blown engine, and struggled with new car gremlins before retiring for good after 67 laps.

The Picchio struggled with overheating problems throughout the race. Despite several lengthy trips behind the wall for repairs, the team managed to finish the race, albeit in 24th overall position.

The Multimatic Ford was running second overall when a broken throttle cable only one hour and 39 minutes into the race resulted in a lengthy pit stop, dropping the team far back in the running. Unlike the former rules, in which the lead class had a significant speed advantage and could quickly work its way past the slower classes, the Ford had to slowly claw its way back up the standings.

While several of the Daytona Prototypes struggled, the GTS front runners had problems of their own. The Konrad Saleen was the fastest car on course—when it was running. However, the team spent much of the race repairing the car on pit road. The Morgan Corvette had several tire failures, dropping them 30 laps behind the leaders, while both the pole-winning Corvette of Gregg and the Bells and the Tommy Riggins–led Heritage Mustang went out with engine failure.

The No. 58 Brumos Porsche enjoyed a solid lead, stalked by their teammates plus the Grala Toyota FABCAR, the GT class Porsches of Buckler and Rennsport, and the Perspective Mosler. Suddenly, at 7 p.m., the complexion of the race changed when the engine suddenly quit in the leading Porsche, sending a disconsolate Donohue coasting to the pits. "After the second yellow flag, the motor definitely had a problem in a certain rpm band," Donohue said. "Then, it just finally let go. That was the last part on the car we expected to break."

That elevated the Buckler's No. 66 Porsche in the overall lead, two laps over the remaining Brumos Porsche. Simultaneously, The Racer's Group lost one of its three cars on a restart following a caution period when the Archangel Motorsports Nissan Lola spun between two lines of cars entering turn one, facing race traffic. The No. 67 Porsche sped into the open lane, collected the Lola head on, then went airborne. The incident put the Porsche out of the race, while the Lola went behind the wall for lengthy repairs.

The remaining Brumos and Buckler Porsches traded the lead throughout the remainder of the evening, until a cut tire by the FABCAR returned Buckler's Porsche into the lead shortly after midnight. It never gave it up.

Two of the remaining Daytona Prototypes encountered problems in the early morning hours. Haywood took a trip through the grass to avoid a GT car that spun and blocked the course. "The alternative was a lot worse," said Haywood, although the incident tore a hole in the bottom of the car, sending up dirt and debris. The larger problem was the radiators were clogged and damaged. The team nursed the car through several long stops and continued, although out of contention.

The Grala-led Cegwa Toyota reached fourth overall and second in class at 4 a.m. when an electrical fire damaged the bodywork with Negri at the wheel, and put the car out of the race.

Buckler's Porsche continued to lead, although a different car was doing the chasing. The Multimatic Ford managed to finally gain back all of its lost laps, and closed to within 30 seconds of the overall lead when another lengthy pit stop to replace the throttle cable cost the team valuable time. Another stop to change the headers ended any further hopes of a comeback.

At 8 a.m., another disaster struck The Racer's Group. Jim Michaelian was racing through the infield when he was tagged from behind, sending his Porsche sideways through a barrier and flipping. The car was destroyed but Michaelian emerged unhurt. Ironically, the promoter of the Long Beach Grand Prix was bumped by a golf cart behind pit road as he was describing his accident on the track's public address system.

Buckler's closest pursuers, the Rennsport Porsche, dropped out of the hunt for overall honors at 8 a.m., when the team lost several laps to change radiators. Problems also befell the Ferrari teams, including a lost wheel, a fire, and a broken gearbox. In GTS, Multimatic's big advantage evaporated when the transmission quit, handing the lead to the Morgan Corvette.

At the end, Buckler won handily, covering 695 laps, 2,474 miles, with Schrom taking over for the final shift to the checkered flag. Taking second was the Risi Ferrari 360 GT of Anthony Lazzaro, Ralf Kelleners and Johnny Mowlem, nine laps behind. The Rennworks Porsche GT3 RS of Johannes Van Overbeck, Richard Steranka, Dave Standridge, and David Murry took third.

The Multimatic Ford finished fourth overall to win the Daytona Prototypes class, one position ahead of the Brumos Porsche.

"It takes some time to develop these cars," Haywood said. "We thought we had a handle on it from all the prior testing that we had done, but racing and testing are two completely different animals. We are going to learn from the things we learned down here, and next year come back and hopefully not get into the problems we had. Overall, the car's running, it's running strong, and we just had a bunch of fluky things that all started with my off-road excursion."

The battle in GTS was dramatic. The Morgan Corvette seemed headed to victory, leading by 45 minutes entering the final two hours. With less than one hour left, the team led the resurgent Perspective Mosler by 12 laps, but pitted to repair the rear-end gear. Rob Morgan came off the jacks with a three-lap lead, but the shifter snapped off in his hand while he was exiting his pit stall. He tried in vain to drive around the circuit in fourth gear, with the Mosler taking the lead in the final half-hour and going on to win. "If the shifter had broken before I left the pits, we still had plenty of time to fix it," Morgan said.

Above: Brumos owner Bob Snodgrass had the new Porsche-powered Fabcar Daytona Prototype painted in the colors that won the race overall 30 years earlier. Hurley Haywood, who co-drove to that historic victory, joined J. C. France, Scott Sharp, and Scott Goodyear in the first race for the new class. Opposite left: The No. 46 Morgan Dollar Motorsports Corvette of Charles and Rob Morgan, Lance Norick, and Jim Pace seemed headed to the GTS class victory when mechanical problems struck in the final hour. Here, they lead the G&W Picchio and the two Martin Short Moslers. Opposite right: The Red Bull BMW-powered Picchio sits on the grid. While the Cole Scrogham and Price Cobb-led team struggled with overheating problems throughout the event, Darren Law, Boris Said, Dieter Quester, and Luca Riccitelli were still running at the finish.

Dowe's Team Seattle raced to a one-two victory in SRP II, finishing seventh and eighth overall. The Archangel entry, badly damaged in the evening accident, was repaired when Michael Johnson scavenged parts from a car he'd hoped to sell and rebuilt the right-front corner. After several hours behind the wall, the car ran faster laps than earlier in the race, and finished 18th overall and third in class.

For Buckler, the victory exceeded anyone's expectations—except the team's. "We didn't expect to win, but I don't want to say we really didn't expect it," Buckler tried to explain. "We came down here focused, cohesive, and prepared. And then we drove our butts off. Our drivers got together before the race, and we decided to run as hard as we could for the entire race. We knew our car and our team was probably as good as it gets, in terms of reliability and preparation, so if we pushed everybody else, maybe we would push them into mistakes. That was our unwritten strategy, so on one hand, I'm surprised to win the race overall, but at the same time, I'm not surprised with our car's performance."

Although the Daytona Prototypes failed to score overall in their first outing, many felt it would be only a matter of time for the new cars to shine. "I just think they're going to get better and better," Boris Said commented following the race. "The more we develop the cars, the more reliable they're

going to become, and they'll be faster. I think the race was exactly what Grand-Am wanted. There were a lot of different cars in the top 10, dicing for it. Everybody had a shot at it. The idea was to get the competition back into it. They all think they could win, and that was proven here today."

Also surviving the baptism of fire was J. C. France, who had a strong showing in the Brumos Porsche. "He really had a lot of responsibility on his shoulders, driving this car without any experience road racing in the prototypes, and he adapted like a duck to water," Haywood said. "He's quite good now, but he's just inexperienced with all the conditions you have to adapt to in order to win these races. He gets an A-plus from me."

One month later, France and Haywood teamed to win overall honors at Homestead-Miami Speedway, putting the Daytona Prototype on top for the first time. Already, the team was looking forward to returning to Daytona for the 2004 Rolex 24, along with everyone else in endurance sports car racing, anticipating America's greatest endurance event.

DAYTONA

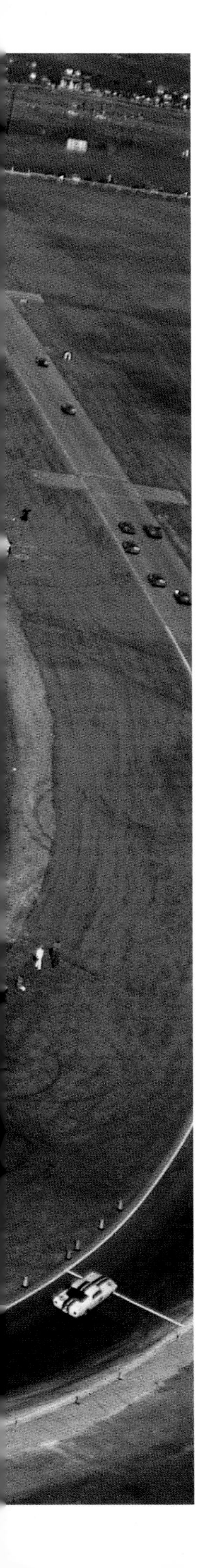

Epilogue

In 1962, the first Daytona Continental began a tradition when it drew many of the world's greatest sports car drivers and teams to the speedway, and with them the international stature Bill France desired for his track.

Over the years, France, followed by his sons Bill and Jim, continued to build on that legacy. The race has played host to many contests, from the dramatic battle for supremacy between Ford and Ferrari, to upset victories where less powerful, production-based cars have triumphed over exotic, purpose-built prototypes.

France had more than stock car racing in mind when he designed and built Daytona International Speedway. The competition and commercial success of the Daytona 24 Hours has made a subtle but fundamental contribution to racing as a whole. France's concept for an infield road course tucked inside a high-banked oval, allowing spectators to view the entire circuit from their grandstand seats, was unique in 1959. Today, this design has become the standard for virtually every speedway.

The competition has changed over the decades. The GT40s, Chaparrals, and Ferraris of the sixties gave way to the Porsches of the seventies, the Camel GT Prototypes of the eighties, and the World Sports Cars of the nineties, which were in turn replaced by the Daytona Prototypes in 2003.

The cars have come and gone, but the test of stamina and endurance faced by the world's top drivers and teams remains much the same. That test keeps legions of sports-car racing aficionados coming back to Daytona every year, as the legacy of America's most challenging sports car race continues to evolve.

Left: An aerial view of the action entering the infield portion of the circuit during the 1966 event, the first race at the 24-hour distance. Above: Dan Gurney was the pacesetter in the No. 44 Lotus-Ford 19J in the 1965 event. The car Gurney shared with Jerry Grant built up a five-lap lead over the factory Fords before being sidelined with an engine problem.

A Note to the Reader about the Results Charts

The cars are arranged in the main body according to the number of laps completed. The "finish" column lists this order, whether or not the car finished. "DQ" (disqualified) means that the car finished, but was later removed from the results.
Drivers are listed in the order that they took the wheel. An asterisk indicates that the driver was scheduled to race, but the car retired before he was able to do so. In some cases, a driver with an asterisk drove the car during practice, but was not planning to do so during the race.
Whenever possible, the principal of the team is noted in the entrant column.
All class winners are highlighted in bold. The names of the class are noted in the column marked "class." The column to the left of the class information shows the starting position for each car.

Daytona Continental

February 11, 1962

3 hour event on the 3.810 mile circuit.
Distance covered: 82 laps for 311.110 miles.
Winning time: 3 hours, 0 minutes, 4.0 seconds for a speed of 103.665 mph.
Fastest lap: #1 Ferrari Dino 246SP (Ricardo Rodriguez) 2:06.0, 108.857 mph.

FINISH	CAR NO.	DRIVERS	CAR	ENTRANT	LAPS	CLASS
1	**96**	**Dan Gurney (USA)**	**Lotus-Climax 19B**	**Frank Arciero**	**82**	**S 2500**
2	1	Phil Hill (USA)/Ricardo Rodriguez (MEX)	Ferrari Dino 246SP	Luigi Chinetti, Sr.	82	S 2500
3	**66**	**Jim Hall (USA)**	**Chaparral 1 (Troutman and Barnes)**	**Jim Hall**	**82**	**S+5000**
4	**18**	**Stirling Moss (GB)**	**Ferrari 250 GT SWB EXP**	**Luigi Chinetti, Sr.**	**80**	**GT 3000**
5	**49**	**George Constantine (USA)**	**Ferrari 250 TR 59/60**	**John T. Bunch**	**79**	**S 3000**
6	0	Dick Rathmann (USA)/Harry Heuer (USA)	Chaparral 1	Peter Hand Brewery	79	S+5000
7	**14**	**Bob Holbert (USA)**	**Porsche 718 RSK**	**Bob Holbert**	**79**	**S 2000**
8	9	John Fulp (USA)/Skip Hudson (USA)	Ferrari Dino 196SP	Luigi Chinetti, Sr.	78	S 2500
9	16	Chuck Cassel (USA)	Porsche 718 RS61	Brumos Porsche	78	S 2000
10	99	Herb Swan (USA)	Porsche 718 RS61	Herb Swan	78	S 2000
11	**23**	**Robert Donner (USA)**	**Porsche 718 RS61**	**Robert Donner**	**77**	**S 1600**
12	22	Fireball Roberts (USA)	Ferrari 250 GT SWB	Luigi Chinetti, Sr.	77	GT 3000
13	**11**	**Richard Thompson (USA)**	**Chevrolet Corvette**	**Grady Davis**	**76**	**GT+5000**
14	6	Peter DaCosta (USA)	Porsche 718 RS61	Peter DaCosta	76	S 1600
15	50	Ricardo Rodriguez (MEX)/Peter Ryan (CDN)	Ferrari 250 Testa Rossa 61	Luigi Chinetti, Sr.	76	S 3000
16	28	Olivier Gendebien (B)	Ferrari 250 GT SWB	Giovanni Volpi di Misurata	75	GT 3000
17	**62**	**Walt Hansgen (USA)**	**Jaguar E-type**	**Briggs Cunningham**	**75**	**GT 4000**
18	77	Doug Thiem (USA)	Ferrari 250 GT SWB	Luigi Chinetti, Sr.	75	GT 3000
19	10	Don Yenko (USA)	Chevrolet Corvette	Grady Davis	75	GT+5000
20	20	Marvin Panch (USA)	Chevrolet Corvette	Red Vogt	75	GT+5000
21	25	Dave Morgan (USA)	Chevrolet Corvette	Delmo Johnson	73	GT+5000
22	80	Guido Lollobrigida (I)	Maserati 200SI	Sorocaima	72	S 3000
23	75	Jack Knab (USA)	Chevrolet Corvette	John Walker	71	GT+5000
24	15	Jo Bonnier (S)	Porsche-Abarth 356B Carrera GTL	Porsche	70 DNF	GT 1600
25	**83**	**Charlie Kolb (USA)**	**Alfa Romeo Giulietta SZ**	**Alfa Romeo**	**70**	**GT 1300**
26	**44**	**Pat Corrigan (USA)**	**Porsche 356B 1600**	**Brumos Porsche**	**70**	**GT 1600**
27	82	Paul Richards (USA)	Alfa Romeo Giulietta SZ	Alfa Romeo	70	GT 1300
28	21	Rodger Ward (USA)	Pontiac Tempest	Frank Nichels	67	GT 4000
29	46	Roger Penske (USA)	Cooper-Climax T61 Monaco	Roger Penske	66 DNF	S 2500
30	91	Ross Durant, Jr. (USA)	Alfa Romeo Giulietta SZ	Ross Durant, Jr	65	GT 1300
31	30	Jim Clark (GB)	Lotus Elite	Peter Berry	60	GT 1300
32	7	Innes Ireland (GB)	Ferrari 250 GT SWB	UDT-Laystall	59 DNF	GT 3000
33	48	William Storey (USA)	Lotus Elite	William M. Storey	58	GT 1300
34	8	Joe Weatherly (USA)	Lister-Chevrolet Corvette	Bill Frick	57	S+5000
35	24	Art Huttinger (USA)	Lister-Chevrolet Corvette	Art Huttinger	54 DNF	S+5000
36	27	Milo Vega (USA)	Lotus Elite	Milo Vega	51	GT 1300
37	63	Robert Keyes (USA)	A.C.-Bristol Ace	Robert Keyes	51	GT 2000
38	17	Robert Johnson (USA)	Chevrolet Corvette	Ronnie Kaplan	42 DNF	GT+5000
39	29	Jef Stevens (USA)/	Chevrolet Corvette	Fred Kappler	37 DNF	GT+5000
40	35	Skip Hudson (USA)	Chevrolet Corvette	R. D. Doane	34 DNF	GT+5000
41	78	Bob Schroeder (USA)	Chevrolet Corvette	John Mecom	31 DNF	GT+5000
42	51	Anson Johnson (USA)	Lister-Chevrolet Corvette	David Lane	30	Sports 5000
43	12	Pedro Rodriguez (MEX)	Lotus-Climax 19	Rosebud Racing	28 DNF	S 2500

FINISH	CAR NO.	DRIVERS	CAR	ENTRANT	LAPS	CLASS
44	47	David Lane (USA)	Porsche 356B 1600	Brumos Porsche	20 DNF	GT 1600
45	32	David Hobbs (GB)	Jaguar E-type	Peter Berry	15 DNF	GT 4000
46	42	Harry Heuer (USA)	Pontiac Tempest	Frank Nichels	14 DNF	GT 4000
47	71	Bill Bencker (USA)	Porsche 356B 1600	Bill Bencker	12 DNF	GT 1600
48	5	Alan Connell, Jr. (USA)	Maserati-Ferrari Tipo 61	Alan Connell, Jr.	7 DNF	S 3000
49	19	Paul Goldsmith (USA)	Tempest	Frank Nichels	2 DNF	GT+5000
50	53	A. J. Foyt (USA)	Pontiac Tempest	Frank Nichels	2 DNF	GT+5000

Daytona Continental

February 17, 1963

3 hour event on the 3.810 mile circuit.

Distance covered: 81 laps for 307.300 miles.

Winning time: 3 hours, 0 minutes, 38.0 seconds for a speed of 102.074 mph

Margin of victory: 1:12.0.

FINISH	CAR NO.	DRIVERS	CAR	ENTRANT	LAPS	CLASS
1	**18**	**Pedro Rodriguez (MEX)**	**Ferrari 250 GTO**	**Luigi Chinetti, Sr.**	**81**	**GT Div III 3000**
2	29	Roger Penske (USA)	Ferrari 250 GTO	John Mecom	81	GT Div III 3000
3	11	Richard Thompson (USA)	Chevrolet Corvette	Grady Davis	78	GT Div III 5000
4	**99**	**Dave MacDonald (USA)**	**Shelby Cobra**	**Shelby American**	**77**	**GT Div III 5000**
5	**15**	**Jo Bonnier (S)**	**Porsche-Abarth 356B Carrera GTL**	**Porsche**	**77**	**GT Div II 2000**
6	5	Johnny Allen (USA)	Chevrolet Corvette	Dixie Motor	76	GT Div III +5000
DQ	31	Walt Hansgen (USA)	Jaguar E-type	Briggs Cunningham	75	GT Div III 4000
7	14	Bob Holbert (USA)	Porsche-Abarth 356B Carrera GTL	Porsche	75	GT Div II 2000
8	**16**	**Chuck Cassel (USA)**	**Porsche-Abarth 356B Carrera GTL**	**Chuck Cassel**	**75**	**GT Div II 1600**
9	**70**	**Hans Herrmann (D)**	**Abarth-Simca 1300 Bialbero**	**Abarth**	**74**	**GT Div II 1300**
10	**32**	**Augie Pabst (USA)**	**Jaguar E-type**	**Briggs Cunningham**	**73**	**GT Div III 4000**
11	77	Bruce Jennings (USA)	Porsche 356B	Bruce Jennings	72	GT Div II 1600
12	44	Bill Bencker (USA)	Porsche 356B Carrera 2	Brumos Porsche	71	GT Div II 2000
13	91	Ross Durant, Jr. (USA)	Alfa Romeo Giulietta SZ	Durant/Swanson	68	GT Div II 1300
14	82	Charlie Kolb (USA)	Porsche 356B Carrera	John Norwood	66	GT Div II 1600
15	22	Fireball Roberts (USA)/John Cannon (CDN)	Ferrari 250 GTO	Luigi Chinetti, Sr.	65	GT Div III 3000
16	48	Bill Storey (USA)/Ray Heppenstall (USA)	Lotus Elite	Bill Story	64	GT Div II. 1300
17	**52**	**Tony Mannino (USA)**	**Triumph TR3**	**Cannon Auto**	**62**	**GT Div III 2500**
18	43	Dana Kelder (USA)	Triumph TR3	Cannon Auto	62	GT Div III 2500
19	33	John E. Hill (USA)	MG A Twin-Cam	John E. Hill	62	GT Div II 1600
20	59	George Cornelius (USA)	Triumph TR3	Cannon Auto	59	GT Div III 25003
21	26	David Piper (GB)	Ferrari 250 GTO	David Piper	58 DNF	GT Div III 3000NRF
22	19	Tony Denman (USA)	Chevrolet Corvette	Tony Denman	57	GT Div III +5000
23	97	Skip Hudson (USA)	Shelby Cobra	Shelby American	54 DNF	GT Div III 5000
24	46	Mike Kurkjian (USA)	Porsche 356B Carrera	Chuck Cassel	52	GT Div II 1600
25	83	Paul Richards (USA)	Alfa Romeo Giulietta SZ	John Norwood	50	GT Div II 1300
26	71	Mauro Bianchi (B)	Abarth-Simca 1300 Bialbero	Abarth	49 DNF	GT Div II 1300
27	98	Dan Gurney (USA)	Shelby Cobra	Shelby American	48 DNF	GT Div III 5000
28	63	Jere Mosiman (USA)	TVR Grantura	Russell Beazell	46 DNF	GT Div II 2000
29	10	Don Yenko (USA)	Chevrolet Corvette	Grady Davis	44	GT Div III +5000
30	4	Billy Krause (USA)	Chevrolet Corvette	Mickey Thompson	41 DNF	GT Div III +5000
31	17	Robert Johnson (USA)	Chevrolet Corvette	Nickey Chevrolet	41	GT Div III +5000
32	62	Charles Mathis (USA)	Alfa Romeo Giulietta SV	Jesse Emerson	38	GT Div II. 1300
33	1	Ed Cantrell (USA)	Chevrolet Corvette	Ed Cantrell	32 DNF	GT Div III +5000
34	6	Jef Stevens (USA)	Chevrolet Corvette	Dixie Motor	28 DNF	GT Div III +5000
35	7	Jerry Grant (USA)	Chevrolet Corvette	Alan Green	26 DNF	GT Div III +5000
36	3	Doug Hooper (USA)	Chevrolet Corvette	Mickey Thompson	14 DNF	GT Div III +5000
37	9	Ralph Salyer (USA)	Chevrolet Corvette	Ralph Salyer	6 DNF	GT Div III +5000
38	25	Innes Ireland (GB)	Ferrari 250 GTO	Rosebud Racing	4 DNF	GT Div III 3000
39	50	Paul Goldsmith (USA)	Pontiac Tempest	Ray Nichels	3 DNF	GT Div III +5000
40	41	Robert Ryan Brown (USA)	Chevrolet Corvette	Robert Ryan Brown	2 DNF	GT Div III +5000
41	42	Tom Kneebone (USA)	A.C.-Bristol Ace	Tom Kneebone	1 DNF	GT Div II 2000

Daytona Continental

February 16, 1964

12 hour event on the 3.810 mile circuit.

Distance covered: 327 laps for 1244.560 miles.

Winning time: 12 hours, 40 minutes, 25.8 seconds for a speed of 98.199 mph.

Margin of victory: 4 laps.

Fastest lap: #14 Shelby Cobra Daytona Coupe (Dave McDonald) 2:08.2, 106.989 mph.

Fastest qualifier: #14 Shelby Cobra Daytona Coupe (Bob Holbert) 2:08.8, 106.491 mph.

FINISH	CAR NO.	DRIVERS	CAR	ENTRANT	LAPS	START	CLASS
1	**30**	**Pedro Rodriguez (MEX)/Phil Hill (USA)**	**Ferrari 250 GTO 64**	**Luigi Chinetti, Sr.**	**327**	**3**	**GT Div III +2000**
2	35	David Piper (GB)/Lucien Bianchi (B)	Ferrari 250 GTO	David Piper	323	4	GT Div III +2000
3	31	Walt Hansgen (USA)/Bob Grossman (USA)/* John Fulp (USA)	Ferrari 250 GTO LMB	Luigi Chinetti, Sr.	319	10	GT Div III +2000
4	16	Robert Johnson (USA)/Dan Gurney (USA)/Bob Bondurant (USA)	Shelby Cobra	Shelby American	311	7	GT Div III +2000
5	33	Ulf Norinder (S)/John Cannon (CDN)/Picko Troberg (S)	Ferrari 250 GTO	Ulf Norinder	311	14	GT Div III +2000
6	**52**	**Edgar Barth (D)/Herbert Linge (D)/Jo Bonnier (S)**	**Porsche 356B 2000GS GT**	**Porsche**	**311**	**17**	**GT Div II 2000**
7	10	Charlie Rainville (USA)/Edward J. Butler (USA)	Shelby Cobra	Edward J. Butler	310	39	GT Div III +2000
8	51	Jo Bonnier (S)/Don Wester (USA)/Edgar Barth (D)	Porsche 356B 2000GS GT	Porsche	303	15	GT Div II 2000
9	36	Charles Dietrich (USA)/M. R. J. Wyllie (USA)/John W. Baxter (USA)	Ferrari 250 GT SWB	Robert E. Amey	302	18	GT Div III +2000
10	18	Tommy Hitchcock (USA)/Zourab Tchkotoua (USA)/Jo Schlesser (F)	Shelby Cobra	Shelby American	295	2	GT Div III +2000
11	32	William Eve (USA)/Larry B. Perkins (USA)	Ferrari 250 GTO	Larry B. Perkins	293	16	GT Div III +2000
12	38	Eduardo Dibos-Chappuis (PE)/Mario Colabattisti (PE)	Ferrari 250 GT SWB	Eduardo Dibos	280	40	GT Div III +2000
13	71	Don Streeter (USA)/Mike Kurkjian (USA)	Porsche-Abarth 356B Carrera GTL	Mike Kurkjian	277	21	GT Div II 2000
14	72	Jack Ryan (USA)/Bill Bencker (USA)	Porsche 356SC	Jack Ryan	272	23	GT Div II 2000
15	43	Dana Kelder (USA)/Ara Dube (USA)	Triumph TR3	Cannon Auto	253	27	GT Div III +2000
16	**98**	**Alan Bouverat (USA)/Milo Vega (USA)**	**Lotus Elite**	**Milo Vega**	**245**	**31**	**GT Div I 1300**
17	27	Brian Hetreed (GB)/Chris Kerrison (GB)	Aston Martin DP214	John Dawnay	243 DNF	9	GT Div III +2000
18	61	Bill Buchman (USA)/Jerry H. Morgan (USA)/Don Bolton (USA)	Sunbeam Alpine	Jerry Morgan	243	32	GT Div II 2000
19	74	Kenneth Stevenson (USA)/Walter Howell (USA)	Porsche 356 Carrera	Kenneth Stevenson	243	46	GT Div II 2000
20	57	Ike A. Maxwell, Jr. (USA)/George Barnard (USA)	Volvo 1800S	Ike A. Maxwell, Jr.	240	26	GT Div II 2000
21	3	Conrad M. Krause (USA)/Jack Moore (USA)	Chevrolet Corvette	Sports Car Service	236	35	GT Div III +2000
22	9	Skip Hudson (USA)/Jerry Grant (USA)	Chevrolet Corvette	Nickey Chevrolet	234	36	GT Div III +2000
23	44	Peter Gregg (USA)/Harold St. John (USA)/* Ronald Hutchinson (USA)	Triumph TR4	Peter Gregg	234	29	GT Div III +2000
24	56	Roger West (USA)/Tommy Charles (USA)	MGB	Tommy Charles	234	50	GT Div II 2000
25	90	George Parsons (USA)/John W. Harden (USA)	Austin-Healey Sprite	George Parsons	230	34	GT Div I 1300
26	14	Bob Holbert (USA)/Dave McDonald (USA)/Jean Guichet (F)	Shelby Cobra Daytona Coupe	Shelby American	202 DNF	1	GT Div III +2000
27	20	Jef Stevens (USA)/Ralph Noseda (USA)/* Ed Wilson (USA)	Shelby Cobra	Ralph Noseda	202 DNF	28	GT Div III +2000
28	7	Tom Rizzo (USA)/Fred Darling (USA)	Chevrolet Corvette	Kenneth G. Hablow	169 DNF	13	GT Div III +2000
29	4	G. C. Spencer (USA)/Cale Yarborough (USA)/Billy Wade (USA)	Chevrolet Corvette	John D. Lewis	149 DNF	12	GT Div III +2000
30	86	Charles Mathis (USA)/Robert Richardson (USA)	Alfa Romeo Giulietta SV	Charles Mathis	147 DNF	25	GT Div I 1300
31	50	Chuck Cassel (USA)/Augie Pabst (USA)/Ed Hugus (USA)	Porsche-Abarth 356B Carrera GTL	Chuck Cassel	127 DNF	49	GT Div II 2000
32	80	Walt Hane (USA)/John E. Hill (USA)	MGA	John P. Hill	123 DNF	24	GT Div II 2000
33	24	Graham Shaw (USA)/Charlie Hayes (USA)/Ed Rahal (USA)	Shelby Cobra	Graham Shaw	116 DNF	38	GT Div III +2000
34	15	Jo Schlesser (F)/Jean Guichet (F)/Bob Holbert (USA)	Shelby Cobra	Shelby American	109 DNF	8	GT Div III +2000
35	64	Richard Robson (USA)/John Jacobson (USA)	MG A	Richard Robson.	101 DNF	33	GT Div II 2000
36	73	Newt Black (USA)/N. C. Zitza (USA)/* John Belperche (USA)	Porsche 356 S90	Newt Black	100 DNF	45	GT Div II 2000
37	11	John A. Everly (USA)/Johnny Allen (USA)	Shelby-Ford Cobra	John A. Everly	70 DNF	11	GT Div III +2000
38	62	E. Linley Coleman (USA)/Lee Cutler (USA)/* Duncan Furlong (USA)	Porsche 356 Carrera	E. Linley Coleman	46 DNF	43	GT Div II 2000
39	58	Art Riley (USA)/* Nick Cone (USA)/* John W. Forte (USA)	Volvo P1800	Art Riley	35 DNF	22	GT Div II 2000
40	26	Roy Salvadori (GB)/* Mike Salmon (GB)	Aston Martin DP214	John Dawnay	34 DNF	6	GT Div III +2000
41	54	Victor Merino (PR)/* Jorge Torruellas (PR)/* Candido Higluera (PR)	Porsche-Abarth 356B Carrera GTL	Victor Merino	23 DNF	19	GT Div II 2000
42	39	Charlie Kolb (USA)/* A. J. Foyt (USA)	Ferrari 250 GTO	Don Fong	10 DQ	5	GT Div III +2000
43	47	Al Rogers (USA)/* Richard Holquist (USA)	Morgan Plus 4 SS	Nuclear Electronics	2 DNF	48	GT Div III +2000

Daytona Continental

February 28, 1965

12 hour event on the 3.810 mile circuit.

Distance covered: 327 laps for 1243.370 miles.

Winning time: 12 hours, 27 minutes, 9.0 seconds for a speed of 99.849 mph.

Margin of victory = 5 laps.

Fastest lap: #88 Ferrari 330 P2 (Walt Hansgen) 2:01.8, 112.611 mph/181.229 kph

Fastest qualifier: #77 Ferrari 330 P2 (John Surtees), 2:00.6, 113.731 mph.

FINISH	CAR NO.	DRIVERS	CAR	ENTRANT	LAPS	START	CLASS
1	**73**	**Ken Miles (USA)/Lloyd Ruby (USA)**	**Ford GT40**	**Shelby American**	**327**	**3**	**GTP**
2	**13**	**Jo Schlesser (F)/Harold Keck (USA)/Robert Johnson (USA)**	**Shelby Cobra Daytona Coupe**	**Shelby American**	**322**	**7**	**GT+3000**
3	72	Bob Bondurant (USA)/Richie Ginther (USA)	Ford GT40	Shelby American	318	2	GTP
4	14	Rick Muther (USA)/John Timanus (USA)/* Tom Payne (USA)	Shelby Cobra Daytona Coupe	Shelby American	317	8	GT+3000
5	**16**	**Charlie Kolb (USA)/Roger Heftler (USA)**	**Porsche 904GTS**	**Charlie Kolb**	**313**	**16**	**GT2000**
6	11	Ed Leslie (USA)/Allen Grant (USA)	Shelby Cobra Daytona Coupe	Shelby American	312	5	GT+3000
7	**23**	**Bob Hurt (USA)/Peter Clarke (GB)/Charlie Hayes (USA)**	**Ferrari 250 GTO**	**Peter Clarke**	**308**	**13**	**GT3000**
8	10	Peter Gregg (USA)/George Barber, Jr. (USA)	Porsche 904GTS	Peter Gregg	306	19	GT2000
9	6	Jack Ryan (USA)/Bill Bencker (USA)/Ted Tidwell (USA)	Porsche 904GTS	Jack Ryan	282	18	GT2000
10	36	Richard Thompson (USA)/Graham Shaw (USA)	Shelby Cobra	Graham Shaw	275	15	GT+3000
11	**7**	**David H. McClain (USA)/Larry B. Perkins (USA)/Leland Dieas (USA)**	**Porsche 356SC 90**	**David H. McClain**	**270**	**33**	**GT1600**
12	5	Don Bolton (USA)/Arthur M. Latta (USA)	Sunbeam Tiger	Imported Car	251	25	GT+3000
13	15	Lance Pruyn (USA)/Newton Davis (USA)/Peter Pulver (USA)	Lotus Elan	Pete Pulver	250	24	GT1600
14	**34**	**Dana Kelder (USA)/Ara Dube (USA)**	**Triumph TR3**	**Cannon Auto**	**250**	**40**	**GT2500**
15	25	Roger West (USA)/Tommy Charles (USA)	MGB	Roger West	247	36	GT2000
16	26	David Lane (USA)/Robert Stoddard (USA)	Porsche 904GTS	David Lane	245	29	GT2000
17	33	Fred Ashplant (USA)/Harry Carter (USA)	Lotus Elan	Fred Ashplant	245	28	GT1600
18	2	Jesse Emerson (USA)/John Hood (USA)	Alfa Romeo Giulia	Jesse Emerson	245	37	GT1600
19	24	Ike A. Maxwell, Jr. (USA)/William J. Martin (USA)	Porsche 356B	Ike A. Maxwell, Jr.	243	38	GT1600
20	**48**	**Charles Mathis (USA)/Guido C. Levetto (USA)**	**Alfa Romeo Giulietta SV**	**Cannon Auto**	**237**	**41**	**S-R**
21	35	George Frey (USA)/John Norwood (USA)/Hans Ziereis (USA)	Porsche 356 Carrera	John Norwood	220	26	GT1600
22	44	Dan Gurney (USA)/Jerry Grant (USA)	Lotus-Ford 19J	Dan Gurney	engine	10	S-R
23	30	Scott Harvey (USA)/Peter Hutchinson (USA)	Plymouth Belvedere	Plymouth	DNF	11	GT+3000
24	12	Robert Johnson (USA)/Tom Payne (USA)	Shelby Cobra Daytona Coupe	Shelby American	DNF	6	GT+3000
25	99	Bob Grossman (USA)/Walt Hansgen (USA)/David Piper (GB)/ Pedro Rodriguez (MEX)	Ferrari 275P	Luigi Chinetti, Sr.	DNF	9	GTP
26	21	Dick Irish (USA)/Bill Pryor (USA)	Lancia Flaminia Zagato	Anatoly Arutunoff	DNF	43	GT2500
27	19	Pete Harrison (USA)/E. Linley Coleman (USA)	Shelby Cobra	Arthur Harrison	DNF	12	GT+3000
28	77	John Surtees (GB)/Pedro Rodriguez (MEX)	Ferrari 330P2	Luigi Chinetti, Sr.	DNF	1	GTP
29	46	Paul Richards (USA)/Ed Wilson (USA)	Alpine-Renault M63	John Norwood	DNF	27	GTP
30	3	Sheldon Dobkin (USA)/Jack Slottag (USA)	MGA	Larry B. Perkins	DNF	42	GT1600
31	87	Buck Baker (USA)/Bob Tullius (USA)	Lotus-Ford Cortina	Harley Cunningham	DNF	30	GTP
32	27	Art Riley (USA)	Volvo P1800	Art Riley	DNF	31	GT2000
33	1	Simeon Shortman (USA)/Rajah Rodgers (USA)	Austin-Healey 3000	Simeon Shortman	DNF	35	GT3000
34	71	Skip Scott (USA)/Charlie Hayes (USA)	Shelby GT350	Holman and Moody	DNF	20	GTP
35	4	John D. Lewis (USA)/Art Huttinger (USA)/* Larry Huttinger (USA)	Chevrolet Corvette	John D. Lewis	DNF	22	GT+3000
36	37	Don Sesslar (USA)/Chuck Cassel (USA)	Porsche 718 RS61	Carl W. Lindell	DNF	14	S-R
37	42	Hamilton Vose (USA)/Roger McCluskey (USA)	Maserati-Ford Tipo 64	Hamilton Vose	DNF	17	S-R
38	88	Walt Hansgen (USA)	Ferrari 330P	Luigi Chinetti, Sr	DNF	4	GTP
39	28	John Bushell (USA)/Don Yenko (USA)	Chevrolet Corvette	Kenneth G. Hablow	DNF	21	GT+3000
40	22	John E. Hill (USA)	MGA Twin-Cam	John E. Hill	DNF	39	GT1600
41	17	Gene Parsons (USA)	Lotus Elan	George Parsons	DNF	23	GT1600
42	47	Dave Hull (USA)	Jaguar E-type	Winter Haven Jaguar	DNF	45	S-R
43	20	Michael Reina (USA)	Triumph TR3	Michael Reina	DNF	44	GT2500
DNS	41	Rolf Soltan (USA)/Everett A. Lewis (USA)	Porsche 356 Carrera	Rolf Soltan	DNS	32	S-R
DNS	8	Richard Robson (USA)/Art Baggely (USA)	Jaguar E-type	Richard Robson	DNS	34	GT+3000

1st lap run on the 2.5 mile/4.023 km. tri-oval;
top 10 grid positions reserved for 1st day qualifiers.

24 Hour Daytona Continental

February 5-6, 1966

24 hour event on the 3.810 mile circuit.

Distance covered: 678 laps for 2583.180 miles.

Winning time: 24 hours, 1 minute, 2.0 seconds for a speed of 107.555 mph.

Margin of victory: 8 laps.

Fastest lap set: #97 Ford Mk II (Dan Gurney) 1:57.7, 116.534 mph.

fastest qualifier: #96 Ford Mk II (Ken Miles) 1:57.8, 116.435 mph.

FINISH	CAR NO.	DRIVERS	CAR	ENTRANT	LAPS	START	CLASS
1	**98**	**Ken Miles (USA)/Lloyd Ruby (USA)**	**Ford Mk II**	**Shelby American**	**678**	**1**	**P+2000**
2	97	Dan Gurney (USA)/Jerry Grant (USA)	Ford Mk II	Shelby American	670	11	P+2000
3	95	Walt Hansgen (USA)/Mark Donohue (USA)	Ford Mk II	Holman and Moody	669	3	P+2000
4	21	Pedro Rodriguez (MEX)/Mario Andretti (USA)	Ferrari 365P2/3	Luigi Chinetti, Sr.	664	4	P+2000
5	96	Chris Amon (NZ)/Bruce McLaren (NZ)	Ford Mk II	Shelby American	651	7	P+2000
6	**15**	**Hans Herrmann (D)/Herbert Linge (D)**	**Porsche 906**	**Porsche**	**623**	**18**	**P2000**
7	**16**	**Gerhard Mitter (D)/Joe Buzzetta (USA)**	**Porsche 904GTS**	**Porsche**	**612**	**24**	**S2000**
8	17	Guenther Klass (D)/Udo Schuetz (D)	Porsche 904GTS	Porsche	610	26	S2000
9	22	Jochen Rindt (A)/Bob Bondurant (USA)	Ferrari 250LM	Luigi Chinetti, Sr.	591	14	P+2000
10	14	Peter Gregg (USA)/George Drolsom (USA)	Porsche 904GTS	Brumos Porsche	589	28	2000
11	20	Sam Posey (USA)/Jim Haynes (USA)/Harry Theodoracopulos (USA)	Porsche 904GTS	Sam Posey	577	22	S2000
12	**6**	**Dick Guldstrand (USA)/Ben Moore (USA)/George Wintersteen (USA)**	**Chevrolet Corvette**	**Roger Penske**	**575**	**21**	**GT+3000**
13	23	Mark Konig (GB)/Peter Clarke (GB)/Bob Hurt (USA)	Ferrari 250LM	Peter Clarke	574	32	P+2000
14	**86**	**Peter Sutcliffe (GB)/Bob Grossman (USA)**	**Ford GT40**	**Ford Advanced Vehicles**	**571 DNF**	**19**	**S+3000**
15	27	David Piper (GB)/Richard Attwood (GB)	Ferrari 250LM	David Piper	556	12	P+2000
16	**18**	**Jack Ryan (USA)/E. Linley Coleman (USA)/Bill Bencker (USA)**	**Porsche 911**	**Jack Ryan**	**548**	**39**	**GT2000**
17	92	Peter Revson (USA)/Masten Gregory (USA)/Ed Lowther (USA)	Ford GT40	Essex Wire	531	15	S+3000
18	90	Don Kearney (USA)/Michael Reina (USA)	Ford Mustang	Michael Reina	527	34	GT+3000
19	**30**	**Larry B. Perkins (USA)/Jack Slottag (USA)**	**Ferrari 250 GTO**	**Jack Slottag**	**526**	**33**	**S3000**
20	67	George Cornelius (USA)/Dick Boo (USA)/Robert Ryan Brown (USA)	Chevrolet Corvette	Cannon Auto	501	38	GT+3000
21	91	Richard Thompson (USA)/Skip Scott (USA)/Peter Revson (USA)	Ford GT40	Essex Wire	500 DNF	10	S+3000
22	56	Ike A. Maxwell, Jr. (USA)/William J. Martin (USA)	Volvo P1800	William J. Martin	496	54	S2000
23	79	Paul Richards (USA)/Ray Cuomo (USA)	Austin-Healey Sprite	Autosport	491	36	2000
24	41	Hugh Kleinpeter (USA)/Harry Fry (USA)/George Parsons (USA)	Triumph LM	E. P. Drescher	490	45	P2000
25	**43**	**Dana Kelder (USA)/Ara Dube (USA)/Red Wilson (USA)**	**Triumph TR4A**	**Cannon Auto**	**487**	**50**	**GT3000**
26	45	Herb Byrne (USA)/Milo Vega (USA)	Triumph TR4A	John Kingham	482	43	GT3000
27	**84**	**Ben Scott (USA)/Peter Flanagan (USA)/Roger Chastain (USA)**	**Alfa Romeo Giulia**	**Sprint Pompano Sports Cars**	**474**	**55**	**GT1600**
28	54	Raymond Stoutenburg (USA)/Gene Jones (USA)/Larry Isley (USA)	Plymouth Barracuda	Raymond Stoutenburg	466	41	GT+3000
29	75	Art Riley (USA)/Ross MacGrotty (USA)	Yenko Stinger	Russ MacGrotty	448	37	P+2000
30	40	George Waltman (USA)/Nick Cone (USA)/Arthur W. Swanson (USA)	Triumph TR4	Genser Forman	432	56	GT3000
31	32	George Follmer (USA)/Don Wester (USA)/Paul Hawkins (AUS)	Ferrari 250LM	Luigi Chinetti, Sr	428 DNF	8	P+2000
32	44	Ernie Croucher (USA)/Walter Glenn (USA)/William Eve (USA)	MGB	Kenneth G. Chambliss	426 DNF	49	GT2000
33	29	Paul Hawkins (AUS)/Jackie Epstein (GB)	Ferrari 250LM	Jackie Epstein	425 DNF	17	S+3000
34	94	Ralph Noseda (USA)/Grant Clark (CDN)/Bob Thorpe (USA) Harry Heuer (USA)	Shelby Cobra	Ralph Noseda	419 DNF	35	S+3000
35	7	John Bolander (USA)/Bob Winkelmann (USA)/John Olson (USA)	Ford Cortina	John Olson	416	46	P2000
36	78	Rosemary Smith (IRL)/Smokey Drolet (USA)	Sunbeam Alpine	Autosport	416	58	S2000
37	73	William McKemie (USA)/Terry Petmecky (USA)/Fred Opert (USA)	Elva Courier Mk IV	Fred Opert	391	51	S2000
38	80	Donna Mae Mims (USA)/Janet Guthrie (USA)/Suzy Dietrich (USA)	Sunbeam Alpine	Autosport	389	57	S1600
39	55	Al Weaver (USA)/John Fraim (USA)/Chet Freeman (USA)	Lotus Elan	J Randall	383 DNF	47	GT1600
40	93	Harold Keck (USA)/Oscar Koveleski (USA)/Ed Lowther (USA)	Shelby Cobra	Archway Ford	371 DNF	23	S+3000
41	87	Richie Ginther (USA)/Ronnie Bucknum (USA)	Ford Mk II	Holman and Moody	329 DNF	6	P+2000
42	89	Dan Gerber (USA)/Robert Johnson (USA)/Peter Learch (CDN)	Shelby Cobra	Dan Gerber	328 DNF	25	S+3000
43	65	Jo Bonnier (S)/Phil Hill (USA)	Chaparral 2D	Jim Hall	318 DNF	2	P+2000
44	36	Wilbur Pickett (USA)/Bill Bean (USA)	Alfa Romeo Giulia Zagato	Cannon Auto	278 DNF	44	S1600
45	42	Ken Hughes (USA)/Fred Salo (USA)/John Addison (USA)	Triumph TR4	John Addison	244 DNF	52	GT3000
46	59	Don Yenko (USA)/John W. Forte (USA)/Art Riley (USA)	Volvo P1800	Art Riley	216 DNF	40	S2000
47	31	Fulp (USA)/Bill Rutan (USA)/Bruce Jennings (USA)	Ferrari 330P	John Fulp	193 DNF	13	P+2000
48	88	William Wonder (USA)/Herb Wetanson (USA)	Ford GT40	William Wonder	178 DNF	27	S+3000
49	25	Lucien Bianchi (B)/Gerard Langlois von Ophem (B)/Jean Blaton (B)	Ferrari 365P2	Jacques Swaters	171 DNF	5	P+2000
50	99	Roger West (USA)/Richard Macon (USA)	Ford Mustang	Joe Treadwell	168 DNF	29	GT+3000
51	24	Innes Ireland (GB)	Ferrari 250LM	George Drummond	90 DNF	16	P+2000
52	19	Duncan Forlong (USA)/Leland Dieas (USA)/* David H. McClain (USA)	Porsche 356B S90	David H. McClain	80 DNF	42	T1600

FINISH	CAR NO.	DRIVERS	CAR	ENTRANT	LAPS	START	CLASS
53	26	Leon Dernier (B)/Jacky Ickx (B)/* Jean Blaton (B)	Ferrari 250LM	Jacques Swaters	80 DNF	20	P+2000
54	74	Larry Hess (USA)/Tommy Hess (USA)	Rambler Marlin	Larry Hess	80 DNF	59	P+2000
55	47	David Lane (USA)/Don Sesslar (USA)	Porsche 904GTS	David Lane	74 DNF	30	S2000
56	77	John Bentley (USA)/John E. Hill (USA)	Sunbeam Tiger	Space Science	71 DNF	48	GT+3000
57	5	Spurgeon May (USA)/Bobby Allison (USA)	Chevrolet Corvair	Robert Harper	63 DNF	53	GT3000
58	28	Denis Hulme (NZ)	Ferrari 250LM	Bernard White	53 DNF	9	P+2000
59	12	Dave Hull (USA)	Jaguar E-type	Jaguar of Florida	41 DNF	31	GT+3000

24 Hour Daytona Continental

February 4-5, 1967

24 hour duration event on the 3.810 mile circuit.

Distance covered: 666 laps for 2537.460 miles.

Winning time: 24 hours, 0 minutes, 32.0 seconds for a speed of 105.688 mph.

Margin of victory: 3 laps.

Fastest lap: #15 Chaparral 2F (Phil Hill), 1:55.69, 118.558 mph.

Fastest qualifier: #3 Ford Mk II (Dan Gurney), 1:55.1, 119.166 mph.

FINISH	CAR NO.	DRIVERS	CAR	ENTRANT	LAPS	START	CLASS
1	**23**	**Lorenzo Bandini (I)/Chris Amon (NZ)**	**Ferrari 330P4**	**Ferrari**	**666**	**4**	**P+2000**
2	24	Mike Parkes (GB)/Ludovico Scarfiotti (I)	Ferrari 330P4	Ferrari	663	6	P+2000
3	26	Pedro Rodriguez (MEX)/Jean Guichet (F)	Ferrari 330P3/412P	Luigi Chinetti, Sr.	637	3	P+2000
4	**52**	**Hans Herrmann (D)/Jo Siffert (CH)**	**Porsche 910**	**Porsche**	**618**	**17**	**P2000**
5	55	Dieter Spoerry (CH)/Rico Steinemann (CH)	Porsche 906LE	Dieter Spoerry	608	20	P2000
6	**11**	**Richard Thompson (USA)/Jacky Ickx (B)**	**Ford GT40**	**John Wyer**	**601**	**13**	**S+2000**
7	1	Bruce McLaren (NZ)/Lucien Bianchi (B)	Ford Mk II	Ford/Shelby American	593	7	P+2000
8	20	William Wonder (USA)/Raymond Caldwell (USA)	Ford GT40	William Wonder	573	24	S+2000
9	**54**	**Jack Ryan (USA)/Bill Bencker (USA)**	**Porsche 911S**	**Jack Ryan**	**555**	**35**	**GT2000**
10	**61**	**George Drolsom (USA)/Harold Williamson (USA)**	**Porsche 911**	**George Drolsom**	**542**	**42**	**T2000**
11	**72**	**Paul Richards (USA)/Ray Cuomo (USA)/John Norwood (USA)**	**Ford Mustang**	**Jim Baker**	**526**	**39**	**T+2000**
12	19	Ray Heppenstall (USA)/Bill Seeley (USA)	Ford Falcon	Howmet	518	38	T+2000
13	73	J. Peter Marinelli (USA)/John Tremblay (USA)/William G. Dunn (USA)	Volvo P1800	J. Peter Marinelli	500	45	GT2000
14	**43**	**Dana Kelder (USA)/Ara Dube (USA)**	**Triumph TR4A**	**Cannon Auto**	**499**	**57**	**GT+200**
15	21	Brock Yates (USA)/Charles Krueger (USA)	Dodge Dart	Brock Yates	498	36	T+2000
16	66	Thomas D. Yeager (USA)/Walt Hane (USA)/Peter Feistman (USA)	Ford Mustang	Thomas D. Yeager	498	28	T+2000
17	86	William Eve (USA)/Ernie Croucher (USA)/Pete Glenn (USA)	MGB	Kenneth G. Chambliss	493	44	GT2000
18	42	Steven Somner (USA)/Guido C. Levetto (USA)	Triumph TR4A	Cannon Auto	491	54	GT+2000
19	75	Ike A. Maxwell, Jr. (USA)/William J. Martin (USA)	Volvo 122S	Ike A. Maxwell, Jr.	485	55	T2000
20	71	Anita Taylor-Matthews (GB)/Smokey Drolet (USA)/Janet Guthrie (USA)	Ford Mustang	Jim Baker	484	50	T+2000
21	32	Peter Clarke (GB)/Edward Nelson (GB)	Ferrari 250LM	Peter Clarke	484	26	S+2000
22	89	Ross L. Bremmer (USA)/Don Kearney (USA)/Billy Turner (USA)	Lotus-Ford Cortina	Ross L. Bremmer	477	56	T2000
23	77	John Bentley (USA)/Brian Beddow (USA)	Alfa Romeo GTA	Precision Auto	465	59	T2000
24	3	A. J. Foyt (USA)/Dan Gurney (USA)	Ford Mk II	Ford/Shelby American	464 DNF	1	P+2000
25	96	Donna Mae Mims (USA)/Suzy Dietrich (USA)	ASA 411 [21004]	Jim Baker	459	53	P2000
26	36	George Wintersteen (USA)/Joe Welch (USA)/Bob Brown (USA)	Chevrolet Camaro	Roger Penske	456 DNF	22	T+2000
27	84	Dick Ganger (USA)/Al Weaver (USA)/Ken Goodman (USA)	MGB GT	Richard N. Ganger	406	58	P2000
28	33	Willy Mairesse (B)/Jean Blaton (B)	Ferrari 330P3/412P	Jacques Swaters	401 DNF	11	P+2000
29	74	Arthur Mollin (USA)/Art Riley (USA)	Volvo 122S	Arthur Mollin	400	51	T2000
30	90	Del Russo Taylor (USA)/Bob Pratt (USA)/Charles Lyon (USA)	Alfa Romeo GTA Junior	Del Russo Taylor	360	41	T2000
31	18	Roger West (USA)/Bobby Allison (USA)	Shelby GT350	Roger West	343 DNF	27	GT+2000
32	34	Charlie Kolb (USA)/John Fulp (USA)	Ferrari Dino 206S	Modern Classic	341 DNF	15	P2000
33	28	Jo Schlesser (F)/Masten Gregory (USA)/Peter Gregg (USA)	Ferrari Dino 206S	Luigi Chinetti, Sr.	338 DNF	60	P2000
34	14	Robert Johnson (USA)/Bruce Jennings (USA)/* Phil Hill (USA)	Chaparral 2D	Jim Hall	334 DNF	8	P+2000
35	46	Richard Robson (USA)/Rajah Rodgers (USA)/Bill Buchman (USA)	Jaguar E-type	Richard Robson	320	40	GT+2000
36	67	Freddie Van Beuren, Jr. (MEX)/Paul Jett (USA)/Don Pike (USA)	Shelby GT350	Dos Caballos	313 DNF	25	GT+2000

FINISH	CAR NO.	DRIVERS	CAR	ENTRANT	LAPS	START	CLASS
37	76	John McComb (USA)/Dave Dooley (USA)	Ford Mustang	John McComb	312 DNF	30	T+2000
38	31	David Piper (GB)/Richard Attwood (GB)	Ferrari 365P2/3	David Piper	311 DNF	14	P+2000
39	6	Lloyd Ruby (USA)/Denis Hulme (NZ)	Ford Mk II	Ford/Holman and Moody	299 DNF	9	P+2000
40	5	Mario Andretti (USA)/Richie Ginther (USA)	Ford Mk II	Ford/Holman and Moody	298 DNF	5	P+2000
41	2	Ronnie Bucknum (USA)/Frank Gardner (AUS)	Ford Mk II	Ford/Shelby American	274 DNF	10	P+2000
42	48	Tim E. Burr (USA)/Buell Owen (USA)/Clint Cavin (USA)	Triumph TR4	Tim E. Burr	264	49	GT+2000
43	40	Craig Fisher (CDN)/George Eaton (CDN)	Chevrolet Camaro	Craig Fisher	258 DNF	31	T+2000
44	4	Mark Donohue (USA)/Peter Revson (USA)	Ford Mk II	Ford/Holman and Moody	236 DNF	12	P+2000
45	51	Gerhard Mitter (D)/Jochen Rindt (A)	Porsche 906	Porsche	194 DNF	16	P2000
46	16	Joie Chitwood (USA)/Jack McClure (USA)	Chevrolet Camaro	Chitwood Racing	186	37	T+2000
47	45	C. C. Canada (USA)/Joe Hines, Jr. (USA)/T. J. Kelly (USA)	Triumph TR4	Joe Hines, Jr.	186 DNF	48	GT+2000
48	53	Udo Schuetz (D)/Rolf Stommelen (D)/Gijs van Lennep (NL)	Porsche 906	Porsche	170 DNF	21	P2000
49	56	Charles Voegele (CH)/Walter Habegger (CH)/* Herbert Mueller (CH)	Porsche 906	Charles Voegele	146 DNF	18	S2000
50	29	Carlos Salas Guterrez (MEX)/Hector Rebaque, Sr. (MEX)	Ferrari 275GTB/C	Pedro Rodriguez	136 DNF	29	GT+2000
51	47	Peter Gethin (GB)/Fred Opert (USA)/Roy Pike (USA)	Chevron-BMW B4	Fred Opert	106 DNF	43	P2000
52	9	Umberto Maglioli (I)/Mario Casoni (I)	Ford GT40	Brescia Corse	93 DNF	19	S+2000
53	15	Phil Hill (USA)/Mike Spence (GB)/* Jim Hall (USA)	Chaparral 2F	Jim Hall	93 DNF	2	P+2000
54	8	Tony Denman (USA)/Robert Ryan Brown (USA)	Chevrolet Corvette Grand Sport	Jim White	72 DNF	61	P+2000
55	82	Harry Theodoracopulos (USA)/Sam Posey (USA)/* Jim Haynes (USA)	Alfa Romeo GTA Junior	Harry Theodoracopulos	69 DNF	33	T2000
56	7	Herb Byrne (USA)/Dick Thetford (USA)/* Russell Beazell (USA)	Shelby Cobra	Herb Byrne	56 DNF	32	S+2000
57	44	Raymond Stoutenburg (USA)/* James Taylor (USA)/* Roger McCluskey (USA)	Triumph TR4A	Raymond Stoutenburg	22 DNF	52	GT+2000
58	87	Chet Freeman (USA)/* Al Weaver (USA)/* John Marshall (USA)	Lotus-Ford Cortina	Chet Freeman	18 DNF	62	T2000
59	63	Bob Grossman (USA)/* Martin Krinner (USA)	Shelby GT350	Dockery Ford	0 DNF	34	GT+2000
DNS	58	Tony Dean (GB)/Trevor Taylor (GB)	Porsche 906	Rod Sawyer	0	23	S2000
DNS	22	Frank Karmatz (USA)/Raymond Caldwell (USA)	Plymouth Barracuda	JoKar Racing	0	50	T+2000
DNS	85	Ken Goodman (USA)/Jim Baker (USA)	Alfa Romeo GTA	Jim Baker	0	51	T2000

Race started on backstretch, total distance includes .64 lap (2.43 miles/3.911 kms.) of paced formation;
1 full course caution period.

24 Hours of Daytona

FEBRUARY 3-4, 1968

24 hour event on the 3.810 mile circuit.
Distance covered: 673 laps for 2564.130 miles.
Winning time: 24 hours, 2 minutes, 4.0 seconds for a speed of 106.686 mph.
Margin of victory: 14 laps.
Fastest lap: #8 Ford GT40 (Jacky Ickx), 1:56.86, 117.371 mph.
Fastest qualifier: #8 Ford GT40 (Jacky Ickx), 1:54.91, 119.363 mph.

FINISH	CAR NO.	DRIVERS	CAR	ENTRANT	LAPS	START	CLASS
1	**54**	**Vic Elford (GB)/Jochen Neerpasch (D)/Jo Siffert (CH) Rolf Stommelen (D)/Hans Herrmann (D)**	**Porsche 907**	**Porsche**	**673**	**5**	**P**
2	52	Jo Siffert (CH)/Hans Herrmann (D)/* Gerhard Mitter (D)	Porsche 907	Porsche	659	4	P
3	51	Jo Schlesser (F)/Joe Buzzetta (USA)	Porsche 907	Porsche	659	6	P
4	**1**	**Jerry Titus (USA)/Ronnie Bucknum (USA)**	**Ford Mustang**	**Carroll Shelby**	**629**	**22**	**TA+2000**
5	20	Udo Schuetz (D)/Nino Vaccarella (I)	Alfa Romeo 33/2	Autodelta	617	9	P
6	23	Mario Andretti (USA)/Lucien Bianchi (B)/Leo Cella (I)	Alfa Romeo 33/2	Autodelta	609	11	P
7	22	Mario Casoni (I)/Giampiero Biscaldi (I)/Teodoro Zeccoli (I)	Alfa Romeo 33/2	Autodelta	594	13	P
8	**34**	**John Gunn (USA)/Guillermo Ortega (EC)/Fausto Merello (EC)**	**Ferrari 250LM**	**Raceco of Miami**	**592**	**14**	**S**
9	**59**	**Peter Gregg (USA)/Sten Axelsson (S)**	**Porsche 911T**	**Brumos Porsche**	**589**	**35**	**TA2000**
10	**31**	**Jerry Grant (USA)/Dave Morgan (USA)**	**Chevrolet Corvette**	**Sunray DX Oil**	**586**	**17**	**GT**
11	77	Robert Stoddard (USA)/George Drolsom (USA)/Marty Gifford (USA) Lewis Williams, Jr. (USA)	Porsche 911	Lewis Williams, Jr.	575	41	TA2000
12	6	Mark Donohue (USA)/Robert Johnson (USA)/Craig Fisher (CDN)	Chevrolet Camaro	Roger Penske	565	20	TA+2000
13	56	Jim Netterstrom (USA)/John Kelly (USA)/John Sabel (USA)	Porsche 911	John Kelly	565	40	TA2000
14	3	Jim McDaniel (USA)/Glen Sullivan (USA)	Porsche 911R	HRH	562	27	P
15	36	Wilbur Pickett (USA)/Bill Bean (USA)/Bill Bencker (USA)	Porsche 911	Wilbur Pickett	545	49	TA2000

FINISH	CAR NO.	DRIVERS	CAR	ENTRANT	LAPS	START	CLASS
16	68	Bill Boye (USA)/Billy Yuma (USA)	Chevrolet Camaro	Bill Boye	540	33	TA+2000
17	71	Joie Chitwood (USA)/Buzz Barton (USA)/Richard Hoffman (USA)	Chevrolet Camaro	Chitwood Racing	536	29	TA+2000
18	61	Jean-Pierre Hanrioud (F)/Sylvain Garant (F)	Porsche 911S	Jean-Pierre Hanrioud	534	42	GT
19	64	Del Russo Taylor (USA)/Bob Pratt (USA)/Bruce Myers (USA)	Alfa Romeo GTA	Bruce Myers	533	44	TA2000
20	24	Leo Cella (I)/Teodoro Zeccoli (I)/Giampiero Biscaldi (I)	Alfa Romeo GTA	Autodelta	529	47	TA2000
21	78	Sam Posey (USA)/Jim Kauffman (USA)	Ford Mustang	(no entrant listed)	523	48	TA+2000
22	28	Edward Ross (USA)/H. Craige Pelouze (USA)	Chevrolet Corvette	Corvette Racing Associates	515	39	GT
23	15	Bob Grossman (USA)/Bob Dini (USA)	Ford Mustang	Randy's Auto Body	514	32	TA+2000
24	67	Hugh Kleinpeter (USA)/Ray Mummery (USA)/Bruce Hollander (USA)	Shelby GT350	Bruce Hollander	510 DNF	54	GT
25	18	Edward Nelson (GB)/Mike Hailwood (GB)	Ford GT40	Edward Nelson	507 DNF	21	S
26	10	Tony Lanfranchi (GB)/Mark Konig (GB)	Nomad-Ford Mk1	Nomad	506	31	P
27	29	Peter Revson (USA)/Don Yenko (USA)	Chevrolet Corvette	Sunray DX Oil	496	19	GT
28	73	Fred Opert (USA)/Joe Grimaldi (USA)	Porsche 911	Fred Opert	471	45	TA2000
29	30	Jerry Thompson (USA)/Tony DeLorenzo (USA)	Chevrolet Corvette	Sunray DX Oil	470	24	GT
30	9	Paul Hawkins (AUS)/David Hobbs (GB)	Ford GT40	John Wyer	430 DNF	2	S
31	32	Jack Ryan (USA)/Pete Harrison (USA)	Porsche 911	Jack Ryan	393	37	TA2000
32	44	Dick Guldstrand (USA)/Ed Leslie (USA)/Scooter Patrick (USA) Dave Jordan (USA)	Chevrolet Corvette	James Garner	373	15	GT
33	35	George Waltman (USA)	Morgan Plus 4	Aztec Racing	338	64	GT
34	12	Paul Vestey (GB)/Roy Pike (USA)/Paul Ridgway (GB)	Ferrari 250LM	Paul Vestey.	264	18	S
35	45	Scooter Patrick (USA)/Dave Jordan (USA)/Herb Caplan (USA)	Chevrolet Corvette	James Garner	262 DNF	16	GT
36	25	Enrico Pinto (I)/Spartaco Dini (I)	Alfa Romeo GTA	Autodelta	235 DNF	51	TA2000
37	41	James Rushin (USA)/Thomas D. Harris (USA)/Chris Waldron (USA)	MGB	Thomas D. Harris	226 DNF	62	GT
38	49	Ike A. Maxwell, Jr. (USA)/William J. Martin (USA)	Volvo 122S	Ike A. Maxwell, Jr.	188 DNF	59	TA2000
39	27	Carlo Facetti (I)/Giancarlo Baghetti (I)/Ove Andersson (S)	Lancia Fulvia HF	Algar Enterprises	180 DNF	58	P
40	48	Doyle Poole (USA)/Phil Stott (GB)/Bruce Morehead (USA)	Triumph TR4A	Doyle Poole	179 DQ	61	GT
41	2	Allan Moffat (AUS)/Horst Kwech (USA) (USA)	Ford Mustang	Carroll Shelby	176 DNF	23	TA+2000
42	43	Carl Schwenker (USA)/Ara Dube (USA)/Dana Kelder (USA)	Triumph TR4A	Cannon Auto	166 DNF	57	GT
43	57	Richard Cline (USA)/Michael Pickering (USA)	Triumph GT6	Richard P. Cline	120 DNF	60	GT
44	7	Billy Hagan (USA)/John McVeigh (USA)/Frans Gillebard (USA)	Mercury Cougar	Billy Hagan	119 DNF	36	TA+2000
45	11	Digby Martland (GB)/Brian Classic (GB)	Chevron-BMW B6	Chevron	118 DNF	26	P
46	58	Fred Andrews, Jr. (USA)/Richard G. Kondracki (USA)	Triumph Spitfire	Richard Cline	106 DNF	63	GT
47	53	Gerhard Mitter (D)/Rolf Stommelen (D)	Porsche 907	Porsche	104 DNF	3	P
48	81	David Piper (GB)/Masten Gregory (USA)	Ferrari 250LM	Luigi Chinetti, Sr.	101 DNF	8	S
49	55	Rico Steinemann (CH)/Dieter Spoerry (CH)	Porsche 907LM	Tartaruga	100 DNF	12	P
50	47	Milo Vega (USA)/John Witt (USA)	Triumph TR4A	John Cameron	96 DNF	56	GT
51	65	George Wintersteen (USA)/Malcolm Starr (USA)	Ford Mustang	Malcolm Starr	90 DNF	28	TA+2000
52	17	Arthur Mollin (USA)/Nick Cone (USA)	TVR Mk IV	Arthur Mollin	86 DNF	65	GT
53	72	Paul Richards (USA)/Tony Adamowicz (USA)/Marvin Davidson (USA)	Porsche 911T	Marvin Davidson	71 DNF	43	TA2000
54	8	Jacky Ickx (B)/Brian Redman (GB)	Ford GT40	John Wyer	58 DNF	1	S
55	46	Steve Payne-Herbert (USA)	Porsche 356B Carrera 2	Grant Miller	46 DNF	52	GT
56	80	Pedro Rodriguez (MEX)	Ferrari Dino 206S	Luigi Chinetti, Sr.	45 DNF	10	P
57	42	Rajah Rodgers (USA)	Jaguar E-type	Richard Robson	43 DNF	53	GT
58	37	William Wonder (USA)/Ray Cuomo (USA)	Ford GT40	William Wonder	42 DNF	25	S
59	76	Ray Heppenstall (USA)/Ed Lowther (USA)	Howmet-Continental TX	Howmet	34 DNF	7	P
60	4	John Moore (USA)	Chevrolet Camaro	HRH	34 DNF	30	+2000
61	5	Bud Sherk (USA)	Dodge Dart	Bud Sherk	20 DNF	46	TA+2000
62	26	Claudio Maglioli (I)	Lancia Fulvia Sport Zagato	Algar Enterprises	6 DNF	50	P
63	14	Bert Everett (USA)	Porsche 911T	Bob Holbert	3 DNF	34	TA2000

24 Hours of Daytona

February 1-2, 1969

24 hour event on the 3.810 mile circuit.

Distance covered: 626 laps for 2385.060 miles.

Winning time: 24 hours, 1 minute, 35.303 seconds for a speed of 99.268 mph.

Margin of victory: 30 laps.

Fastest qualifier: #52 Porsche 908L (Vic Elford), 1:52.2, 122.246 mph.

FIN	CAR NO.	DRIVERS	CAR	ENTRANT	LAPS	START	CLASS
1	**6**	**Mark Donohue (USA)/Chuck Parsons (USA)**	**Lola-Chevrolet T70 Mk3B**	**Roger Penske**	**626**	**2**	**S5000**
2	8	Ed Leslie (USA)/Lothar Motschenbacher (USA)	Lola-Chevrolet T70 Mk3	James Garner	596	11	S5000
3	**26**	**Jerry Titus (USA)/Jon Ward (USA)**	**Pontiac Firebird**	**Jon Ward**	**591**	**16**	**T5000**
4	**20**	**Tony Adamowicz (USA)/Bruce Jennings (USA)/Herb Wetanson (USA)**	**Porsche 911T**	**Herb Wetanson**	**583**	**28**	**GT2000**
5	**14**	**Bert Everett (USA)/Alan Johnson (USA)/E. Linley Coleman (USA)**	**Porsche 911**	**Fine Grinding**	**581**	**29**	**T2000**
6	**39**	**Hugh Kleinpeter (USA)/Bob Beatty (USA)/John Gunn (USA)**	**Chevron-BMW B8**	**Raceco of Miami**	**579**	**22**	**S2000**
7	**9**	**Scooter Patrick (USA)/Dave Jordan (USA)**	**Lola-Chevrolet T70 Mk3**	**James Garner**	**578**	**10**	**S5000**
8	47	Harold Williamson (USA)/George Drolsom (USA)	Porsche 911	Harold Williamson	577	34	T2000
9	68	Jacques Duval (CDN)/George Nicholas (CDN)/* Andre Samson (CDN)	Porsche 911T	Jacques Duval	571	31	GT2000
10	48	Andre Wicky (CH)/Sylvain Garant (F)	Porsche 911T	Andre Wicky	569	36	GT2000
11	**97**	**Claudio Maglioli (I)/Raffaele Pinto (I)**	**Lancia Fulvia HF Zagato**	**Algar Enterprises**	**566**	**45**	**P2000**
12	5	Bob Grossman (USA)/Bob Dini (USA)	Chevrolet Camaro	Randy's Auto Body	549	21	T5000
13	28	Jim Corwin (USA)/Mike Manner (USA)/Carson Baird (USA)	Chevrolet Camaro	Jim Corwin	549	37	T5000
14	86	Pete Harrison (USA)/Jack Ryan (USA)	Porsche 911	Jack Ryan	548	35	T2000
15	61	Masten Gregory (USA)/Richard Brostrom (S)	Porsche 910	Ulf Norinder	544	14	S2000
16	**96**	**Smokey Drolet (USA)/John Tremblay (USA)/Vince Gimondo (USA) John Belperche (USA)**	**Chevrolet Corvette**	**Zorian Productions**	**532**	**48**	**GT+5000**
17	83	Jim Baker (USA)/Clive Baker (GB)/Paul Richards (USA)	Austin-Healey Sprite	Jim Baker	527	63	P2000
18	4	Jim McDaniel (USA)/Steve Pieper (USA)/Bill Scott (USA)	Zink-Volkswagen VSR	HRH	519	52	P2000
19	55	Jim Gammon (USA)/Ray Mummery (USA)/* Reggie Smith, Jr. (USA)	MGB	Chris Waldron	508	53	GT2000
20	62	Rudi Bartling (CDN)/Fritz Hochreuter (CDN)/Rainer Brezinka (CDN)	Porsche 906	Rainer Brezinka	507	24	S2000
21	18	Maurice Carter (CDN)/Nat Adams (CDN)	Chevrolet Camaro	Maurice Carter	501	32	T5000
22	32	Harold Rose (USA)/Mike Richards (USA)/* Steve Hill (USA)	Chevrolet Camaro	Harold Rose	499	40	T5000
23	41	Sam Posey (USA)/Ricardo Rodriguez Cavazos (MEX)	Ferrari 275GTB/4	Luigi Chinetti, Sr.	494	26	GT5000
24	53	Udo Schuetz (D)/Gerhard Mitter (D)/Richard Attwood (GB)	Porsche 908L	Porsche	483 DNF	7	P3000
25	79	Art Riley (USA)/Arthur Mollin (USA)	Volvo 122S	Arthur Mollin	473	58	T2000
26	1	Jacky Ickx (B)/Jackie Oliver (GB)	Ford GT40	John Wyer	470 DNF	8	S5000 NRF
27	81	Bill Pryor (USA)/Jose Marina (USA)	Alfa Romeo Giulia SS	Anatoly Arutunoff	451	55	GT2000
28	15	Larry Bock (USA)/Larry Dent (USA)	Chevrolet Camaro	Larry Drover	449	27	T5000
29	56	Thomas D. Harris (USA)/Chris Waldron (USA)/Ben Scott (USA)	MGB	Chris Waldron	428	54	GT2000
30	50	Jo Siffert (CH)/Hans Herrmann (D)	Porsche 908L	Porsche	415 DNF	3	P3000
31	2	David Hobbs (GB)/Mike Hailwood (GB)	Ford GT40	John Wyer	401 DNF	9	S5000
32	46	John Debo (USA)/E. M. Parkerson (USA)	Triumph TR4	Bud Boles	378 DNF	56	GT5000
33	43	Gary Wright (USA)/Bill Craine (USA)	Porsche 911	Gary Wright	337	33	T2000
34	98	Bruce Hollander (USA)/Robert Clark (USA)/Wayne Marsula (USA)	Lancia Fulvia HF Zagato	Algar Enterprises	331	59	P2000
35	54	Rolf Stommelen (D)/Kurt Ahrens, Jr. (D)	Porsche 908L	Porsche	313 DNF	4	P3000
36	52	Vic Elford (GB)/Brian Redman (GB)	Porsche 908L	Porsche	277 DNF	1	P3000
37	51	Richard Attwood (GB)/Joe Buzzetta (USA)	Porsche 908L	Porsche	273 DNF	6	P3000
38	77	Marty Gifford (USA)/Bill Campbell (USA)	Porsche 911	Lewis Williams, Jr.	272 DNF	46	T2000
39	22	Bob Bailey (USA)/James N. Locke (USA)/Mike Downs (USA)	Porsche 911T	Bob Bailey	249 DNF	47	T2000
40	73	Fred Opert (USA)/Paul Stanford (USA)	Porsche 911	Fred Opert	223 DNF	51	T2000
41	57	David Heinz (USA)/Clarence Moerwald (USA)	MGB	David Heinz	221 DNF	57	GT2000
42	33	John McComb (USA)/Dave Dooley (USA)	Ford Mustang	Harold McComb	219 DNF	23	T5000 DNF
43	91	Norberto Mastandrea (USA)/Doug Silvers (BS)/Robin Ormes (BS)	Chevrolet Camaro	Mar Shipping	210 DNF	41	T5000
44	11	Don Yenko (USA)/Dick Guldstrand (USA)	Chevrolet Camaro	Best Photo	208 DNF	19	T5000
45	67	Jerry Thompson (USA)/Jim Harrell (USA)/Tony DeLorenzo (USA)	Chevrolet Corvette	Tony DeLorenzo	201 DNF	15	GT+5000
46	21	Jim Netterstrom (USA)/John Kelly (USA)	Porsche 911	Porsche America Racing	182 DNF	39	T2000
47	58	Alex Soler-Roig (E)/Rudi Lins (A)	Porsche 907	Alex Soler-Roig	158 DNF	12	P3000
48	40	Charlie Kolb (USA)/Giampiero Biscaldi (I)	Ferrari Dino 206S	Luigi Chinetti, Sr.	152DNF	18	P2000
49	36	Wilbur Pickett (USA)/Mike Downs (USA)/* Bob Tullius (USA)	Porsche 911	Wilbur Pickett	153 DNF	38	T2000
50	17	David H. McClain (USA)/Orlando Costanzo (USA)	Chevrolet Camaro	David H. McClain	145 DNF	43	T5000
51	25	Eduardo Dibos-Chappuis (PE)/Mario Colabattisti (PE)	Alfa Romeo 33/2	Motoritalia	139 DNF	20	P3000
52	59	Peter Gregg (USA)/Sten Axelsson (S)	Porsche 911	Brumos Porsche	137 DNF	30	T2000
53	99	Richard Robson (USA)/Rajah Rodgers (USA)	Jaguar E-type	Richard Robson	116 DNF	49	GT5000

FIN.	CAR NO.	DRIVERS	CAR	ENTRANT	LAPS	START	CLASS
54	69	Ed Lowther (USA)/Robert D. Esseks (USA)/Frank Dominianni (USA)	Chevrolet Corvette	Robert D. Esseks	109 DNF	61	GT+5000
55	93	Richard Cline (USA)/Michael Pickering (USA)	Triumph GT6	Richard Cline	108 DNF	66	GT 2000
56	72	Billy Hagan (USA)/John McVeigh (USA)/Frans Gillebard (USA)	Mercury Cougar	Lafayette Speed Center	88 DNF	42	T5000
57	88	Francis C. Grant (USA)/Dieter Oest (USA)/Barry Batchin (USA)	Lancia Fulvia HF	Francis C. Grant	79 DNF	60	GT2000
58	38	Fausto Merello (EC)/Umberto Maglioli (I)/* Edward Alvarez (USA)	Ferrari 250LM	Raceco of Miami	68 DNF	50	S5000
59	60	Jo Bonnier (S)/Ulf Norinder (S)/* Johnny Servoz-Gavin (F)	Lola-Chevrolet T70 Mk3B	Ulf Norinder	52 DNF	5	S5000
60	16	Wedge Rafferty (USA)/* Jack Gearhart (USA)/* Richard Wisler (USA)	Chevrolet Corvette	Wes Rafferty	48 DNF	44	GT+5000
61	92	Wilton T. Jowett, Jr. (USA)/* Craig Fisher (CDN)	Chevrolet Camaro	Wilton T. Jowett, Sr.	44 DNF	17	T5000
62	66	Tony DeLorenzo (USA)/* Dick Lang (USA)	Chevrolet Corvette	Tony DeLorenzo	23 DNF	13	GT+5000
63	45	George Waltman (USA)/* Wallis Bird (USA)	Osca 1600GT	George Waltman	0 DNF	65	S2000

24 Hours of Daytona

January 31 – February 1, 1970

24 hour event on the 3.810 mile circuit.

Distance covered: 724 laps for 2758.440 miles.

Winning time: 24 hours, 0 minutes, 52.0 seconds for a speed of 114.866 mph.

Margin of victory: 45 laps.

Fastest lap: #1 Porsche 917K (Jo Siffert) 1:48.7, 126.182 mph.

Fastest qualifier: #28 Ferrari 512S (Mario Andretti) 1:51.6, 122.903 mph.

FIN	CAR NO.	DRIVERS	CAR	ENTRANT	LAPS	START	CLASS
1	**2**	**Pedro Rodriguez (MEX)/Leo Kinnunen (SF)/Brian Redman (GB)**	**Porsche 917K**	**John Wyer**	**724**	**3**	**S**
2	1	Jo Siffert (CH)/Brian Redman (GB)	Porsche 917K	John Wyer	679	2	S
3	28	Mario Andretti (USA)/Arturo Merzario (I)/Jacky Ickx (B)	Ferrari 512S	Ferrari	676	1	S
4	**24**	**Sam Posey (USA)/Mike Parkes (GB)**	**Ferrari 312P**	**Luigi Chinetti, Sr.**	**647**	**9**	**P**
5	23	Tony Adamowicz (USA)/David Piper (GB)	Ferrari 312P	Luigi Chinetti, Sr.	632	13	P
6	**7**	**Jerry Thompson (USA)/John Mahler (USA)**	**Chevrolet Corvette**	**Tony DeLorenzo**	**608**	**11**	**GT+2000**
7	21	Gregg Young (USA)/Luigi Chinetti, Jr. (USA)	Ferrari 250LM	Luigi Chinetti, Sr.	603	44	S
8	18	William Wonder (USA)/Ray Cuomo (USA)	Ford GT40	William Wonder	579	41	S
9	40	Greg Loomis (USA)/Bert Everett (USA)/*Pete Harrison (USA)	Porsche 906LE	Greg Loomis	573	43	P
10	33	Francois Cevert (F)/Jack Brabham (AUS)	Matra-Simca MS650	Matra-Simca.	565	7	P
11	89	Cliff Gottlob (USA)/Dave Dooley (USA)	Chevrolet Corvette	Cliff Gottlob	545	34	GT+2000
12	9	Don Yenko (USA)/Bob Grossman (USA)	Chevrolet Camaro	Mamie Reynolds Gregory	542 DNF	24	GT+2000
13	12	Bob Mitchell (USA)/Charlie Kemp (USA)	Chevrolet Camaro	Bob Mitchell	535	29	T+2000
14	**6**	**Tony DeLorenzo (USA)/Dick Lang (USA)**	**Chevrolet Corvette**	**DeLorenzo**	**534**	**20**	**GT+2000**
15	74	Ralph Meaney (USA)/Gary Wright (USA)/Bill Bean (USA)	Porsche 911S	Ralph Meaney	533	39	T2000
16	**90**	**Orlando Costanzo (USA)/David Heinz (USA)**	**Chevrolet Corvette**	**Or Costanzo**	**521**	**27**	**GT+2000**
17	14	Ray Cuomo (USA)/Bernard Gimbel (USA)/George Lissberg (USA)	Ford Mustang	Ray Cuomo	520	46	T+2000
18	95	Michael Brockman (USA)/John Tremblay (USA)	Chevrolet Camaro	Bruce Behrens	511	57	T+2000
19	34	Jean-Pierre Beltoise (F)/Henri Pescarolo (F)	Matra-Simca MS650	Matra-Simca		14	P
20	11	Larry Bock (USA)/Larry Dent (USA)	Chevrolet Camaro	Laurel Racing	507	23	T+2000
21	78	John Belperche (USA)/Tony Lilly (USA)/Don Pickett (USA)	MG B	Chris Waldron	504	55	GT2000
22	79	Chris Waldron (USA)/Lowell Lanier (USA)/Bill Barros (USA)	MG B	Chris Waldron	490	56	GT2000
23	48	Del Russo Taylor (USA)/Hank Sheldon (USA)/* Tom Blank (USA)	Alfa Romeo GTV	Del Russo Taylor	478	64	T2000
24	38	Paul A. Fleming (USA)/Amos Johnson (USA)	Fiat 124	Simone N. Fleming	473	62	T2000
25	25	Dan Gurney (USA)/Chuck Parsons (USA)	Ferrari 512S	Luigi Chinetti, Sr.	464 DNF	6	S
26	76	Scotty Addison (USA)/Erhard Dahm (USA)	Porsche 911S	Scotty Addison	462	49	GT2000
27	8	Robert Johnson (USA)/Robert R. Johnson (USA)/Jim Greendyke (USA)	Chevrolet Corvette	Robert Johnson	457	16	GT+2000
28	47	Jim Bandy (USA)/Fred Stevenson (USA)/Carl Williams (USA)	Lotus Europa	S Motors	442 DNF	36	S
29	30	Corrado Manfredini (I)/Gianpiero Moretti (I)	Ferrari 512S	Corrado Manfredini	412 DNF	33	S
30	98	Norberto Mastandrea (USA)/Smokey Drolet (USA)/Rajah Rodgers (USA)	Chevrolet Camaro	Norberto Mastandrea	409	45	T+2000
31	83	Vincent P. Collins (USA)/Larry E. Wilson (USA)	Ford Mustang	Vincent P. Collins	407	52	T+2000
32	53	Hans Laine (SF)/Gijs van Lennep (NL)	Porsche 908/2	Antti Aarnio-Wihuri	385 DNF	12	P
33	43	William Harris (USA)/Robert E. Lewis (USA)	Austin-Healey Sprite	William Harris	373	51	P

FIN	CAR NO.	DRIVERS	CAR	ENTRANT	LAPS	START	CLASS
34	72	Jacques Duval (CDN)/Bob Bailey (USA)	Porsche 911T	Jacques Duval	365 DNF	40	GT 2000
35	71	Ray Walle (USA)/Bob Speakman (USA)	TVR-Ford Vixen	Ray Walle	364	53	P
36	97	John Elliott (USA)/Don Gwynne, Jr. (USA)	Chevrolet Camaro	Preston Hood	354	50	T+2000
37	3	Kurt Ahrens, Jr. (D)/Vic Elford (GB)	Porsche 917K	Porsche Salzburg	337 DNF	4	S
38	94	Don Cummings (USA)/Warren Stumes (USA)	Shelby GT350	Susan T. Cummings	327	66	GT +2000
39	15	Ed Lowther (USA)/Bob Nagel (USA)/* Robert Fryer (USA)	Chevrolet Camaro	Bob Fryer	320	58	T+2000
40	20	Harley Cluxton (USA)/Gordon Tatum (USA)	Ferrari 275GTB/C	Luigi Chinetti, Sr.	308 DNF	30	S
41	17	Piers Weld Forester (GB)/Andrew Hedges (GB)	Ford GT40	Trevor Graham	299 DNF	17	S
42	77	Bruce Jennings (USA)/Bob Tullius (USA)	Porsche 911T	Jennings/Keyser	279 DNF	35	GT2000
43	88	Barry Batchin (USA)/Dieter Oest (USA)	Lancia Fulvia HF Zagato	Dieter Oest	268 engine	63	T2000
44	84	Walter Brown (USA)/Joe Marcus (USA)/Jim R. Sandman (USA)	BMW 2002	HCAS	257 DNF	54	T2000
45	85	Robert Whitaker (USA)/Richard Krebs (USA)/Harvey Eckoff (USA)	Volvo 122S	Robert Whitaker	243	59	T2000
46	92	Donna Mae Mims (USA)/Jim Corwin (USA)/Fred Pipen (USA)	Chevrolet Camaro	Flem-Cor	220	48	T+2000
47	0	Mark Donohue (USA)/Peter Revson (USA)	American Motors Javelin	Roger Penske	205 DNF	19	T+2000
48	73	Bobby Rinzler (USA)/Charles Reynolds (USA)	Austin-Healey Sprite	Jim Baker	178	47	P
49	22	Ronnie Bucknum (USA)/Wilbur Pickett (USA)	Ferrari 365GTB/4 Daytona	Luigi Chinetti, Sr.	142 DNF	31	S
50	96	Vince Gimondo (USA)/Charles Dietrich (USA)	Chevrolet Camaro	Vince Gimondo	130 DNF	28	T+2000
51	27	Jacky Ickx (B)/Peter Schetty (CH)	Ferrari 512S	Ferrari	115 DNF	5	S
52	16	Jim Baker (USA)/Clive Baker (GB)/* Paul Richards (USA)	Chevron Ford-Cosworth B16	Jim Baker	108 DNF	25	P
53	91	Allan Barker (USA)/John Greenwood (USA)/Richard Hoffman (USA)	Chevrolet Corvette	John Greenwood	101 DNF	18	GT+2000
54	39	Rainer Brezinka (CDN)/Horst Peterman (CDN)/Rudi Bartling (CDN)	Porsche 906	Rainer Brezinka	96 DNF	60	S
55	26	Nino Vaccarella (I)/Ignazio Giunti (I)	Ferrari 512S	Ferrari	89 DNF	8	S
56	93	Jim Harrell (USA)/Len Magner (USA)	Ford Mustang	Jim Harrell	89 DNF	38	T +2000
57	37	Brian Robinson (GB)/Hugh Kleinpeter (USA)/Tony Trimmer (USA)	Chevron Ford-Cosworth B16	Fred Opert	85 DNF	22	P
58	19	Francis C. Grant (USA)/* Ray Heppenstall (USA)/* Joe Marcus (USA)	Ford GT40	Francis C. Grant	82 DNF	21	S
59	66	Ed Matthews (USA)/Don Sesslar (USA)/Al Weaver (USA)	Ford Mustang	Ed Matthews	63 DNF	32	T+2000
60	86	Arthur Mollin (USA)/Art Riley (USA)	Volvo 122S	Arthur Mollin	54 DNF	61	T2000
61	70	James Patterson (USA)/Paul Stanford (USA)	Porsche 911T	Paul Stanford	29 DNF	37	GT2000
62	46	Claibourne Darden (USA)/Warren Matzen (USA)	Shelby GT350	Jack Haywood	26DNF	42	GT+2000
63	55	Don Kearney (USA)/Richard Roberts (USA)/* Wayne Purdy (USA)	Datsun 510	Jack Kearney	24 DNF	65	T2000
64	5	John Cannon (CDN)/* George Eaton (CDN)	Lola-Chevrolet T70 Mk3B	Robin Ormes	0 DNF	10	S
65	54	Carlos A. Pairetti (RA)/* Alain De Cadenet (GB)/* Jorge Omar Del Rio (RA)	Porsche 908/2	Juan Manuel Fangio	0 DNF	26	P

24 Hours of Daytona

January 30-31, 1971

24 hour event on the 3.810 mile circuit.

Distance covered:688 laps for 2621.280 miles.

Winning time: 24 hours, 0 minutes, 58.0 seconds for a speed of 109.147 mph.

Margin of victory: 1 lap.

Fastest lap: #6 Ferrari 512M (Mark Donohue) 1:41.25, 135.467 mph.

Fastest qualifier: #6 Ferrari 512M (Mark Donohue) 1:42.42, 133.919 mph.

FIN	CAR NO.	DRIVERS	CAR	ENTRANT	LAPS	START	CLASS
1	**2**	**Pedro Rodriguez (MEX)/Jackie Oliver (GB)**	**Porsche 917K**	**John Wyer**	**688**	**2**	**S**
2	23	Ronnie Bucknum (USA)/Tony Adamowicz (USA)/* Alain De Cadenet (GB)	Ferrari 512S	Luigi Chinetti, Sr.	687	6	S
3	6	Mark Donohue (USA)/David Hobbs (GB)	Ferrari 512M	Roger Penske	674	1	S
4	**11**	**Tony DeLorenzo (USA)/Don Yenko (USA)/John Mahler (USA)**	**Chevrolet Corvette**	**Tony DeLorenzo**	**613**	**9**	**GT+2500**
5	**21**	**Nestor Garcia-Veiga (RA)/Luigi Chinetti, Jr. (USA)/Alain De Cadenet (GB)**	**Ferrari 312P**	**Luigi Chinetti, Sr.**	**584**	**13**	**P**
6	57	David Heinz (USA)/Orlando Costanzo (USA)	Chevrolet Corvette	David Heinz	581	16	GT+2500
7	**5**	**Jacques Duval (CDN)/George Nicholas (CDN)/Bob Bailey (USA)**	**Porsche 914/6 GT**	**Jacques Duval**	**579**	**28**	**GT2500**
8	19	Stephen Behr (USA)/John Buffum (USA)/Erwin Kremer (D)	Porsche 914/6 GT	Ralph Meaney	571	32	GT2500
9	31	Bert Everett (USA)/James N. Locke (USA)/Jim Netterstrom (USA)	Porsche 911T	James N. Locke	570	27	GT2500
10	50	John Greenwood (USA)/Allan Barker (USA)/Dick Lang (USA)	Chevrolet Corvette	John Greenwood	554	14	GT+2500
11	**17**	**Vince Gimondo (USA)/Charles Dietrich (USA)**	**Chevrolet Camaro**	**Vince Gimondo**	**542**	**17**	**T**

FIN	CAR NO.	DRIVERS	CAR	ENTRANT	LAPS	START	CLASS
12	45	Clive Baker (GB)/Bob Grossman (USA)/Sam Brown (USA) Charles Reynolds (USA)	Chevron Ford-Cosworth B16	Jim Baker	534	18	P
13	42	Javier Garcia (USA)/Luis Sereix (USA)/Richard Small (USA)	Chevrolet Camaro	Garcia Brothers	527	41	T
14	10	Ray Walle (USA)/Michael Sherwin (USA)	Porsche 911S	Ray Walle	498	33	GT2500
15	43	Jean-Pierre Hanrioud (F)/Jean Sage (F)	Chevron Ford-Cosworth B16	Jean-Pierre Hanrioud	488	38	P
16	44	Bob Hindson (USA)/Kendall Noah (USA)/Art Bunker (USA)	Porsche 911T	Art Bunker	488	40	GT2500
17	51	Jim Gammon (USA)/Dean Donley (USA)/Carlos Garza (USA)	MGB GT	Chris Waldron	483	46	GT2500
18	18	Ralph Meaney (USA)/Bill Bean (USA)/Gary Wright (USA)	Porsche 914/6 GT	Ralph Meaney	470 DNF	33	GT2500
19	64	Robert Luebbe (USA)/Robert Baechle (USA)/John Orr (USA)	Chevrolet Corvette	Robert Luebbe	469	20	GT+2500
20	3	Helmut Marko (A)/Rudi Lins (A)	Porsche 917K	Hans-Dieter Dechent	462 DNF	12	S
21	89	Ray Brimble (USA)/Houghton Smith (USA)	Chevrolet Camaro	Houghton Smith	452	37	T
22	72	Bob Mitchell (USA)/Charlie Kemp (USA)	Chevrolet Camaro	Bob Mitchell	408	22	T
23	33	John McComb (USA)/Bob Tullius (USA)	Ford Mustang	John McComb	395 DNF	31	T
24	36	Warren Matzen (USA)/Tom Hayser (USA)/Dick Sears (USA)	Ford Mustang	Dick Sears	369 DNF	25	T
25	16	Michael Keyser (USA)/Bob Beasley (USA)/Bruce Jennings (USA)	Porsche 911S	Michael Keyser	337 DNF	39	GT2500
26	52	Ben Scott (USA)/Lowell Lanier (USA)/Dave Houser (USA)	MGB GT	Chris Waldron	311 DNF	47	GT2500
27	97	Warren Stumes (USA)/Don Cummings (USA)	Shelby GT350	Susan T. Cummings	306 DNF	24	T
28	4	Vic Elford (GB)/Gijs van Lennep (NL)	Porsche 917K	Hans-Dieter Dechent	274 DNF	11	S
29	59	Peter Gregg (USA)/Hurley Haywood (USA)	Porsche 914/6 GT	Brumos Porsche	260 DNF	23	GT2500
30	98	Ed Matthews (USA)/Swede Savage (USA)/Danny Ongais (USA)	Ford Mustang	Ed Matthews	238 DNF	21	T
31	47	John Tremblay (USA)/Bill McDill (USA)/Bob Beatty (USA)	Chevrolet Camaro	Bruce Behrens	230 DNF	15	T
32	88	Norberto Mastandrea (USA)/Tony Lilly (USA)	Chevrolet Camaro	Norberto Mastandrea	215	26	T
33	22	Peter Revson (USA)/Sam Posey (USA)/Chuck Parsons (USA) Luigi Chinetti, Jr. (USA)	Ferrari 512M	Luigi Chinetti, Sr.	202 DNF	3	S
34	15	Peter Kirill (USA)/Ash Tisdelle (USA)	Porsche 911S	Kirill/Tisdelle	163 DNF	30	GT2500
35	28	Arturo Merzario (I)/Jose Juncadella (E)	Ferrari 512S	Jose Juncadella	161 DNF	7	S
36	70	John Belperche (USA)/William A. Davidson (USA)	Triumph GT6	William A. Davidson	157 DNF	48	GT2500
37	14	C. C. Canada (USA)/Joe Hines, Jr. (USA)/Wilbur Pickett (USA)	Chevrolet Camaro	C. C. Canada	137 DNF	29	GT+2500
38	26	Hughes de Fierlant (B)/Gustave Gosselin (B)	Ferrari 512S	Jacques Swaters	124 DNF	8	S
39	92	John Cordts (CDN)/Don Pike (USA)	Pontiac Firebird	B. F. Goodrich	121 DNF	35	T
40	1	Jo Siffert (CH)/Derek Bell (GB)	Porsche 917K	John Wyer	113 DNF	4	S
41	79	Hal Lawrence (USA)/Danny L. Moore (USA)/Gary Bishop (USA)	Shelby GT350	Danny L. Moore	106 DNF	19	T
42	8	Tom Nehl (USA)/Charles Perry (USA)	Porsche 911S	American Racing	88 DNF	39	GT2500
43	12	Jerry Thompson (USA)/John Mahler (USA)	Chevrolet Corvette	Tony DeLorenzo	83 DNF	10	GT+2500
44	40	Fritz Hochreuter (CDN)/Rudi Bartling (CDN)/* Horst Peterman (CDN) * Rainer Brezinka (CDN)	Porsche 911	Fritz Hochreuter	58 DNF	42	GT2500
45	48	Sheldon Dobkin (USA)/* John Maynard (USA)/* John Oliver (USA)	Chevrolet Camaro	John Oliver	37 DNF	45	T
46	74	Al Straub (USA)/* Walter Brown (USA)	Ford Mustang	Al Straub	35 DNF	34	T
47	20	Masten Gregory (USA)/* Gregg Young (USA)/* John Cannon (CDN)	Ferrari 512M	Luigi Chinetti, Sr.	16 DNF	5	S
48	91	Ralph Noseda (USA)/Pepe Nunez (USA)/* Jef Stevens (USA)	Chevrolet Camaro	Ralph Noseda	9 DNF	44	T

24 Hours of Daytona

February 6, 1972

6 hour event on the 3.810 mile circuit. (Weekend races totaled 24 hours.)

Distance covered: 194 laps for 739.140 miles.

Winning time: 6 hours, 1 minute, 40.4 seconds for a speed of 122.620 mph.

Margin of victory: 2 laps.

Fastest lap: #4 Ferrari 312PB (Brian Redman)1:45.0, 130.629 mph.

Fastest qualifier: #2 Ferrari 312PB (Mario Andretti) 1:44.22, 131.606 mph

FINISH	CAR NO.	DRIVERS	CAR	ENTRANT	LAPS	START	CLASS
1	**2**	**Mario Andretti (USA)/Jacky Ickx (B)**	**Ferrari 312PB**	**Ferrari**	**194**	**1**	**S3000**
2	6	Tim Schenken (AUS)/Ronnie Peterson (S)	Ferrari 312PB	Ferrari	192	3	S3000
3	5	Vic Elford (GB)/Helmut Marko (A)	Alfa Romeo 33TT3	Autodelta	190	6	S3000
4	4	Clay Regazzoni (CH)/Brian Redman (GB)	Ferrari 312PB	Ferrari	179	2	S3000
5	9	Giovanni Galli (I)/Andrea de Adamich (I)	Alfa Romeo 33/3	Autodelta	175	8	S3000
DQ	32	Arturo Merzario (I)/Alex Soler-Roig (E)	Abarth 2000SP	Abarth-Osella	166	9	S2000

24 Hours of Daytona

February 1-2, 1975

24 hour event on the 3.810 mile circuit
Distance covered: 684 laps for 2606.040 miles.
Winning time: 24 hours, 0 minutes, 43.0 seconds for a speed of 108.531 mph.
Margin of victory: 15 laps.
Fastest lap: #75 Chevrolet Corvette (John Greenwood) 1:57.3, 116.931 mph.
Fastest qualifier: #75 Chevrolet Corvette (John Greenwood) 1:55.223, 119.039 mph.

FIN	CAR.NO.	DRIVERS	CAR	ENTRANT	LAPS	START	CLASS
1	**59**	**Peter Gregg (USA)/Hurley Haywood (USA)**	**Porsche 911 Carrera RSR**	**Brumos Porsche**	**684**	**7**	**GT**
2	11	Michael Keyser (USA)/Billy Sprowls (MEX)/Andres Contreras (MEX)	Porsche 911 Carrera RSR	Michael Keyser	669	16	GT
3	23	Charlie Kemp (USA)/Carson Baird (USA)	Porsche 911 Carrera RSR	Armor All	668	11	GT
4	30	Jacques Bienvenue (CDN)/George Dyer (USA)	Porsche 911 Carrera RSR	George Dyer	665	12	GT
5	4	Bill Webbe (USA)/George W. Dickinson (USA)/Harry Theodoracopulos (USA)	Porsche 911 Carrera RSR	Bill Webbe	623	20	GT
6	43	John O'Steen (USA)/Dave Helmick (USA)/John Graves (USA)	Porsche 911 Carrera RSR	Dave Helmick	619	10	GT
7	**7**	**Jon Woodner (USA)/Fred Phillips (USA)**	**Ferrari 365GTB/4 Daytona**	**Ted Field**	**613**	**22**	**FIA GT**
8	14	Al Holbert (USA)/Elliott Forbes-Robinson (USA)	Porsche 911 Carrera RSR	Porsche-Audi USA	607 DNF	5	GT
9	5	Guillermo Rojas (MEX)/Hector Rebaque, Jr. (MEX)/Freddie Van Beuren, Jr. (MEX)	Porsche 911 Carrera RSR	Hector Rebaque, Sr.	592	8	GT
10	**60**	**Rusty Bond (USA)/George Rollin (USA)/John Belperche (USA)**	**Porsche 911S**	**Rusty Bond**	**567**	**32**	**GTU**
11	92	Mike Tillson (USA)/Dieter Oest (USA)/Lou Higgins (CDN)	Porsche 911 Carrera RSR	Oest/Tillson	566	34	GT
12	13	Randolph Townsend (USA)/John H. Thomas, Jr. (USA)/Peter Papke (USA)	Porsche 911 Carrera RSR	Randolph Townsend	562	25	GT
13	34	George Drolsom (USA)/Bob Nagel (USA)	Porsche 911S	George Drolsom	558	29	GTU
14	**90**	**Ray Walle (USA)/Tom Reddy (USA)**	**Mazda RX-3**	**Ray Walle**	**557**	**43**	**GTU**
15	67	David H. McClain (USA)/Dave White (USA)/* Frank Harmstad (USA)	Porsche 911 Carrera RSR	David H. McClain	546	23	GT
16	44	John Freyre (USA)/Albert Naon (USA)/Tony Garcia (USA)	Porsche 911 Carrera	Delta Racing	542	50	GT
17	7	Amos Johnson (USA)/Steve Coleman (USA)/Dennis Shaw (USA)	American Motors Gremlin	Amos Johnson	538	46	GT
18	85	John E. Hulen (USA)/Ron Coupland (USA)/Nick Engels (USA)	Porsche 914/6	John E. Hulen	528	37	GTU
19	18	Jerry Thompson (USA)/Andy Bach (USA)/Don Yenko (USA)	Chevrolet Corvette	Jerry Thompson	517 DNF	9	GT
20	22	Dave Mroz (USA)/Richard Mroz (USA)	Ford Mustang	Roaring Moose	497	31	GT
21	73	Bill Arnold (USA)/Bob Bienerth (USA)	Chevrolet Corvette	Bill Arnold	450	36	GT
22	26	Mike Williamson (USA)/Alfred Cosentino (USA)/Charles Gano (USA)	Chevrolet Camaro	Alfred Cosentino	441	44	GT
23	45	Armando Ramirez (USA)/Camilo Mutiz (CO)/Juan Montalvo (C) Mandy Alvarez	Porsche 911S	Delta Racing	435	39	GTU
24	12	Richard C. Hughes (USA)/Robert Whitaker (USA)/Fred Geisel (USA)	Datsun 510	Precision Performance	435	48	GTU
25	41	Herb Jones, Jr. (USA)/Phil Currin (USA)/Steve Faul (USA)	Chevrolet Camaro	Herb Jones, Jr.	427 DNF	17	GT
26	29	Bruce Mabrito (USA)/Jack Steel (USA)	Datsun 240Z	Bruce Mabrito	420	49	GTU
27	95	Ramon de Izaurieta (MEX)/Sergio Tabec (MEX)/Fidel Martinez (MEX)	Porsche 911 Carrera	Hector Rebaque, Sr.	407DNF	28	GT
28	0	Milt Minter (USA)/Claude Ballot-Lena (F)/Giancarlo Gagliardi (I)	Ferrari 365GTB/4 Daytona (NART)	Luigi Chinetti, Sr.	392 DNF	24	GT
29	98	James Alspaugh (USA)/Gene Persinger, Sr. (USA)	Chevrolet Corvette	James W. Persinger	392	41	GT
30	88	Maurice Carter (CDN)/Gene Felton (USA)	Chevrolet Camaro	Maurice Carter	346 DNF	4	GT
31	27	Jon Ward (USA)/Phil Henny (USA)/Dave Barnett (USA)	Chevrolet Camaro	Jon Ward	303 DNF	14	GT
32	46	Spencer Buzbee (USA)/Craig Ross (USA)/William Frates (USA)	Datsun 240Z	Spencer Buzbee	275 DNF	40	GTU
33	24	Sam Posey (USA)/Hans-Joachim Stuck, Jr. (D)	BMW 3.0 CSL	BMW	274 DNF	3	GT
34	64	C. C. Canada (USA)/Russ Boykin (USA)/Guido C. Levetto (USA)	Chevrolet Camaro	Russ Boykin	255 DNF	35	GT
35	56	Harry Jones (USA)/Marcel Mignot (F)/Cyril Grandet (F)	Ferrari 365GTB/4 Daytona	Harry Jones	238 DNF	58	GT
36	51	Leonard Jones (USA)/Robert Kirby (USA)/John Hotchkis, Sr. (USA)	Porsche 914/6	Johnson/Bozzani	229 DNF	30	GTU
37	83	Arthur Mollin (USA)/Michael Gatoff (USA)/Art Riley (USA)	Volvo 142	Arthur Mollin	219 DNF	47	GTU
38	17	Vince Gimondo (USA)/David Heinz (USA)/Bert Everett (USA)	Chevrolet Camaro	Vince Gimondo	201 DNF	26	GT
39	9	Juan Carlos Bolanos (MEX)/Michel Jourdain (MEX)/Hans Heyer (D)	Porsche 911 Carrera RSR	Juan Carlos Bolanos	191 DNF	6	GT
40	89	Don Parish (USA)/Tom Countryman (USA)/Jim Secher (USA)	Porsche 911S	Barrick Motor Racing	158 DNF	33	GTU
41	84	Klaus Selbert (USA)/David Biggs (USA)	Porsche 911S	Klaus Selbert	151 DNF	45	GTU
42	75	John Greenwood (USA)/Vince Muzzin (USA)/Carl Shafer (USA)	Chevrolet Corvette	John Greenwood	148 DNF	1	GT
43	87	Tony DeLorenzo (USA)/Dick Brown (CDN)/Maurice Carter (CDN)	Chevrolet Camaro	Maurice Carter	125 DNF	15	GT
44	28	Anatoly Arutunoff (USA)/Brian Goellnicht (USA)/Alf Gebhardt (USA)	Lotus Europa	Anatoly Arutunoff	114 DNF	42	FIA GT
45	15	Javier Garcia (USA)/George Garcia (USA)	Chevrolet Corvette	Garcia Brothers	110 DNF	13	GT
46	42	John Carusso (USA)/Dick Vreeland (USA)/* Luis Sereix (USA)	Chevrolet Corvette	John Carusso	59 DNF	21	GT
47	110	Tom Nehl (USA)/Milton Moise (USA)	Chevrolet Camaro	Automotive Engineering	41 DNF	27	GT
48	16	Paul Spruell (USA)/Bill Bean (USA)	Porsche 911S	Bill Bean	35 DNF	38	GTU
49	72	Gilberto Jimenez (MEX)/* Patricia Zambrano (MEX)/* Luis Lamberton (MEX)	Mazda RX-2	Cafe Mexicano Racing	34 DNF	51	GTU
50	25	Ronnie Peterson (S)/* Brian Redman (GB)	BMW 3.0 CSL	BMW	29 DNF	2	GT
51	1	Claude Ballot-Lena (F)/* Alain Cudini (F)/* Milt Minter (USA)	Ferrari 365GT4/BB	Luigi Chinetti, Sr.	0 DNF	18	GT

24 Hours of Daytona

January 31-February 1, 1976

24 hour event on the 3.840 mile circuit.

Distance covered: 545 laps for 2092.800 miles

Race was stopped for 3:54:05.784 due to contaminated fuel, then was restarted to positions of 1:10:00 previously; run to 24 hour clock time.

Winning time: 20 hours, 6 minutes, 53.635 seconds for a speed of 104.042 mph.

Margin of victory: 14 laps.

Fastest lap: #76 Chevrolet Corvette (John Greenwood) 1:56.858, 118.297 mph.

Fastest qualifier: # 59 BMW 3.5 CSL (Brian Redman) 1:56.55, 118.610 mph.

FIN.	CAR NO.	DRIVERS	CAR	ENTRANT	LAPS	START	CLASS
1	**59**	**Peter Gregg (USA)/Brian Redman (GB)/John Fitzpatrick (GB)**	**BMW 3.5 CSL**	**BMW**	**545**	**1**	**IMSA GT**
2	14	Al Holbert (USA)/Claude Ballot-Lena (F)	Porsche 911 Carrera RSR	Al Holbert	531	5	IMSA GT
3	61	Jim Busby (USA)/Hurley Haywood (USA)	Porsche 911 Carrera	Brumos Porsche	530	28	IMSA GT
4	56	Bob Hagestad (USA)/Jerry Jolly (USA)	Porsche 911 Carrera RSR	Bob Hagestad	510	15	IMSA GT
5	92	Mike Tillson (USA)/Dieter Oest (USA)/Bruce Jennings (USA)	Porsche 911 Carrera RSR	Oest/Tillson	508	40	IMSA GT
6	71	Chris Cord (USA)/Jim Adams (USA)/Milt Minter (USA)	Ferrari 365GTB/4 Daytona	Ken Starbird	500	34	IMSA GT
7	**42**	**Bob Hindson (USA)/Dick Davenport (USA)/Frank Carney (USA)**	**Porsche 911S**	**Bob Hindson**	**495**	**38**	**IMSA GTU**
8	43	John Graves (USA)/John O'Steen (USA)/Dave Helmick (USA)	Porsche 911 Carrera RSR	Dave Helmick	493	16	IMSA GT
9	99	Phil Currin (USA)/Cliff Gottlob (USA)/Peter Knab (USA)	Chevrolet Corvette	Phil Currin	483	24	IMSA GT
10	24	David Hobbs (GB)/Benny Parsons (USA)	BMW 3.5 CSL	BMW	481	2	IMSA GT
11	29	Charles Mendez (USA)/David Cowart (USA)/Dave Panaccione (USA)	Porsche 911T	Charles Mendez	480	37	IMSA GTU
12	**12**	**Dieter Schmid (D)/Wilhelm Bartels (D)/Heinz Martin (D) Egon Evertz (D)**	**Porsche 911 Carrera**	**Sepp Greger**	**475**	**35**	**Group 5**
13	51	John Hotchkis, Sr. (USA)/Robert Kirby (USA)/Leonard Jones (USA)	Porsche 914/6	Max Dial	467	42	IMSA GTU
14	60	Rusty Bond (USA)/Ren Tilton (USA)/John Belperche (USA)	Porsche 911S	Rusty Bond	465	68	IMSA GTU
15	25	Tom Walkinshaw (GB)/John Fitzpatrick (GB)	BMW 3.5 CSL	BMW	457	3	IMSA GT
16	**21**	**David Pearson (USA)/Larry Pearson (USA)/ Gary Bowsher (USA) Jim Bowsher (USA)**	**Ford Torino (Holman & Moody)**	**Jack Bowsher**	**442**	**17**	**Grand Int.**
17	84	Ara Dube (USA)/Harro Zitza (USA)/Doug Zitza (USA)	Porsche 911	Mike Meldeau	441	59	IMSA GTU
18	90	Ray Walle (USA)/Tom Reddy (USA)/Bill Scott (USA)	Mazda Cosmo	Ray Walle	415	65	IMSA GTU
19	48	James Hylton (USA)/Richard Childress (USA)	Chevrolet Laguna (Banjo's Performance)	James Hylton	414	30	Grand Int.
20	81	Hans Berner (CDN)/Willy Goebbels (CDN)/Fritz Hochreuter (CDN)	Porsche 911S	Motex Auto	412	48	IMSA GTU
21	65	Paul B. May (USA)/Lee Mueller (USA)/David Sauers (USA)	Porsche 911	Stephen Isett	409	55	IMSA GTU
22	15	Javier Garcia (USA)/George Garcia (USA)/Manuel Garcia (C)	Chevrolet Corvette [GM Garcia 76]	Garcia Brothers	399	4	IMSA GT
23	54	Alex Job (USA)/Steve Southard (USA)/Hal Sahlman (USA)	Porsche 914/6	Spirit Racing	392	66	IMSA GTU
24	35	Ted Mathey (USA)/Joe Chamberlain (USA)/Arnstein Loyning (USA)	Chevrolet Corvette	Ted Mathey	380	10	IMSA GT
25	1	Jim Westphal (USA)/Anatoly Arutunoff (USA)/Brian Goellnicht (USA)	BMW 2002	Louis McAlpine	369	64	IMSA GTU
26	89	Don Parish (USA)/Dave Causey (USA)/Wayne Nelson (USA)	Porsche 911S	Barrick Motor Racing	359	53	IMSA GTU
27	52	Bob Bergstrom (USA)/William L. Shaw (USA)/Martin Palmer (USA)	Honda Civic	CACI	352	62	IMSA GTU
28	04	Hershel McGriff (USA)/Doug McGriff (USA)	Chevrolet Nova (McElreath)	Hershel McGriff	336 DNF	26	Grand Int.
29	40	Sam Fillingham (USA)/Bud Sherk (USA)	Chevrolet Corvette	Sam Fillingham	336	33	IMSA GT
30	7	Makoto Kamazuka (J)/Masashi Fukuda (J)/Ron Cortez (USA)	Mazda RX-3	Glen Marckwardt	331 DNF	57	IMSA GTU
31	97	Juan Carlos Bolanos (MEX)/Billy Sprowls (MEX)/Gustavo Bolanos (MEX)	Porsche 911 Carrera	Juan Carlos Bolanos	318 DNF	27	IMSA GT
32	41	Herb Jones, Jr. (USA)/Steve Faul (USA)	Chevrolet Camaro	Herb Jones, Jr.	301 DNF	14	IMSA GT
33	33	Glenn Francis (USA)/Randy Bebout (USA)	Chevrolet Chevelle (Francis)	Glenn Francis	301	29	Grand Int.
34	76	Michael Brockman (USA)/John Greenwood (USA)	Chevrolet Corvette	John Greenwood	298 DNF	8	IMSA GT
35	80	Carmon Solomone (USA)/Ed Maksym (USA)/James Halverson (USA)	Chevrolet Camaro	Carmon Solomone	291	52	IMSA GT
36	36	Rainer Brezinka (CDN)/Gary Hirsch (CDN)/Brian Hardacre (CDN)	Porsche 911S	Rainer Brezinka	286	54	IMSA GTU
37	75	Robert Christiansen (USA)/Billy Hagan (USA)	Chevrolet Camaro	Robert Christiansen	282 DNF	25	IMSA GT
38	0	William Frates (USA)/Craig Ross (USA)/Spencer Buzbee (USA)	Datsun 240Z	William Frates	274	50	IMSA GTU
39	19	Henley Gray (USA)/Bob Burcham (USA)	Chevrolet Laguna (Holman & Moody)	Henley Gray	268 DNF	69	Grand Int.
40	85	John E. Hulen (USA)/Ron Coupland (USA)/Nick Engels (USA)	Porsche 914/6	John E. Hulen	267 DNF	49	IMSA GTU
41	11	Egon Evertz (D)/Sepp Greger (D)/Juergen Laessig (D)	Porsche 934	Sepp Greger	250 DNF	11	Group 5
42	08	Mike Williamson (USA)/Keith Swope (USA)	American Motors Gremlin	Peak Oil	246 DNF	70	IMSA GT
43	22	Dennis Long (USA)/William Jobe (USA)/Tim Startup (USA)	Chevrolet Corvette	Dennis Long	244 DNF	22	IMSA GT
44	55	Joe Ruttman (USA)/Buddy Baker (USA)/Stephen Behr (USA)	Dodge Dart	Car & Driver	240 DNF	21	IMSA GT
45	34	George Drolsom (USA)/Bob Nagel (USA)	Porsche 911S	George Drolsom	200 DNF	45	IMSA GTU
46	74	Ludwig Heimrath (CDN)/Jacques Bienvenue (CDN)/Norm Ridgely (CDN)	Porsche 911 Carrera RSR	Ludwig Heimrath	189 DNF	20	IMSA GT
47	9	Bruce Mabrito (USA)/Jack Steel (USA)	Datsun 240Z	Bruce Mabrito	185 DNF	58	IMSA GTU
48	10	Alf Zellmer (D)/Brian Goellnicht (USA)/Bill Alsup (USA)	BMW 2002	Louis McAlpine	181 DNF	63	IMSA GTU
49	50	Freddie Van Beuren, Jr. (MEX)/Guillermo Rojas (MEX)/Andres Contreras (MEX)	Porsche 911 Carrera	Rebaque, Sr.	172 DNF	19	IMSA GT
50	68	Mike Meldeau (USA)/Bill McDill (USA)/John Tremblay (USA)	Chevrolet Camaro	Mike Meldeau	172 DNF	18	IMSA GT

FIN.	CAR NO.	DRIVERS	CAR	ENTRANT	LAPS	START	CLASS
51	46	Jose Antonio Daher (MEX)/Alfonso Leal (MEX)/Jose Madero (MEX)	Ford Mustang	Jose Antonio Daher	168 DNF	47	IMSA GT
52	67	Dave White (USA)/Frank Harmstad (USA)/* David H. McClain (USA)	Porsche 914/6	David H. McClain	148 DNF	46	IMSA GTU
53	98	Ed Negre (USA)/Bob Mitchell (USA)/Arturo Merzario (I)	Dodge Charger	Ed Negre	144 DNF	44	Grand Int.
54	44	Mauricio de Narvaez (CO)/Albert Naon (USA)/* John Freyre (USA)	Porsche 911 Carrera	Mauricio de Narvaez	141 DNF	23	IMSA GT
55	49	Neil Potter (USA)/Robert M. Gray (USA)/Luis Sereix (USA)	Ford Mustang	Neil Potter	139 DNF	51	IMSA GT
56	2	Bobby Allison (USA)/Donnie Allison (USA)	Chevrolet Nova (Allison)	Bobby Allison	137 DNF	13	Grand Int
57	18	Terry Wolters (USA)/Charles Gano (USA)/Joe Castellano (USA)	Chevrolet Camaro	Terry Wolters	122 DNF	56	IMSA GT
58	53	Arthur Mollin (USA)/Bob Speakman (USA)/* Michael Gatoff (USA)	Volvo 142	Arthur Mollin	121 DNF	61	IMSA GTU
59	20	Richard C. Weiss (USA)/Michael Oleyar (USA)/Jerry Karl (USA)	Porsche 911S	Richard C. Weiss	94 DNF	36	IMSA GT
60	91	Harold Miller (USA)/Johnny Ray (USA)	Chevrolet Chevelle (Holman & Moody)	Debra Lynn Miller	66 DNF	32	Grand Int.
61	72	Bill Arnold (USA)/Al Levenson (USA)/* Tom Brown (USA)	Chevrolet Corvette	Bill Arnold	55 DNF	41	IMSA GT
62	86	Hugh Kleinpeter (USA)/Ron Goldleaf (USA)	De Tomaso Pantera	Hugh Kleinpeter	42 DNF	9	IMSA GT
63	88	Maurice Carter (CDN)/* Gilles Villeneuve (CDN)	Chevrolet Camaro	Maurice Carter	34 DNF	12	IMSA GT
64	4	Stephen E. Bond (USA)/Dale Kreider (USA)	Pontiac Astre	Bill Nelson, Sr.	28 DNF	67	IMSA GT
65	47	Bill Bean (USA)/* Jack Ansley (USA)	Porsche 911S	William Grainger	21 DNF	31	IMSA GTU
66	28	Brian Goellnicht (USA)/Anatoly Arutunoff (USA)/* Jose Marina (USA)	Lotus Europa	Anatoly Arutunoff	20 DNF	71	IMSA GTU
67	64	C. C. Canada (USA)/* Russ Boykin (USA)	Chevrolet Camaro	C. C. Canada	17 DNF	39	IMSA GT
68	93	Larry Flynn (USA)/Bobbie Johnson (USA)	Chevrolet Camaro	Jim Logan	17 DNF	72	IMSA GT
69	73	Clark Howey (USA)/* Tony Kester (USA)/* David Crabtree (USA)	Chevrolet Corvette	Clark Howey	15 DNF	43	IMSA GT
70	23	Charlie Kemp (USA)/* Sam Posey (USA)/* Carson Baird (USA)	Ford Mustang II (Kemp)	Charlie Kemp	6 DNF	73	Le Mans GTX
71	30	George Dyer (USA)/* Michael Keyser (USA)	Porsche 911 Carrera RSR	George Dyer	5 DNF	7	IMSA GT
72	6	Nick Craw (USA)/* Ray Korman (USA)/* Joe Peacock (USA)	BMW 2002	Miller/Norburn	1 DNF	60	IMSA GTU

24 Hours of Daytona

February 5-6, 1977

24 hour event on the 3.840 mile circuit.

Distance covered: 681 laps for 2615.040 miles.

Winning time: 24 hours, 2 minutes, 6.174 seconds for a speed of 108.801 mph.

Margin of victory: 2 laps.

Fastest lap set by #1 Porsche 935 (Jacky Ickx) 1:52.004, 123.424 mph.

Fastest qualifier: #1 Porsche 935 (Jochen Mass), 1:48.289, 127.658 mph.

FIN.	CAR NO.	DRIVERS	CAR	ENTRANT	LAPS	START	CLASS
1	**43**	**Hurley Haywood (USA)/John Graves (USA)/Dave Helmick (USA)**	**Porsche 911 Carrera RSR**	**Dave Helmick**	**681**	**12**	**IMSA GT**
2	**3**	**Carlo Facetti (I)/Martino Finotto (I)/Romeo Camathias (CH)**	**Porsche 935**	**Martino Finotto**	**679**	**5**	**Group 5**
3	8	Reinhold Joest (D)/Bob Wollek (F)/Albrecht Krebs (D)	Porsche 935	Kremer Brothers	670	2	Group 5
4	30	George Dyer (USA)/Brad Frisselle (USA)	Porsche 911 Carrera RSR	George Dyer	663	21	IMSA GT
5	64	Elliott Forbes-Robinson (USA)/Paul Newman (USA)/Milt Minter (USA)	Ferrari 365GTB/4 Daytona	Ramsey Ferrari	631	22	IMSA GT
6	48	John Carusso (USA)/Luis Sereix (USA)/Emory Donaldson (USA)	Chevrolet Corvette	John Carusso	628	34	IMSA GT
7	**42**	**Bob Hindson (USA)/Frank Carney (USA)/Dick Davenport (USA)**	**Porsche 911S**	**Bob Hindson**	**624**	**31**	**IMSA GTU**
8	28	Richard C. Weiss (USA)/Bill Alsup (USA)/Raymond Gage (USA)	Porsche 911S	Richard C. Weiss	596	41	IMSA GTU
9	07	Charles Mendez (USA)/David Cowart (USA)/Dave Panaccione (USA)	Porsche 911T	Charles Mendez	591	37	IMSA GTU
10	61	Peter Gregg (USA)/Jim Busby (USA)	Porsche 934	Brumos Porsche	590	7	IMSA GT
11	60	Rusty Bond (USA)/Ren Tilton (USA)/John H. Thomas, Jr. (USA)	Porsche 911S	Bond/Tilton	586	36	IMSA GTU
12	27	Ray Mummery (USA)/Jack Refenning (USA)/Ralph Noseda (USA)	Porsche 911S	Jack Refenning	581	51	IMSA GTU
13	58	Diego Febles (PR)/Armando Gonzalez (PR)/Hiram Cruz (USA)	Porsche 911 Carrera RSR	Diego Febles	537	18	IMSA GT
14	73	Clark Howey (USA)/David Crabtree (USA)/Dale Koch (USA)	Chevrolet Corvette	Clark Howey	515	49	IMSA GT
15	71	John Higgins (USA)/Chip Mead (USA)/Dave White (USA)	Porsche 911S	Foreign Exchange	508	40	IMSA GTU
16	6	Amos Johnson (USA)/Dennis Shaw (USA)/Steve Anderson (USA)	American Motors Gremlin	Amos Johnson	506	50	IMSA GT
17	18	Jack Swanson (USA)/Terry Wolters (USA)	Chevrolet Camaro	Terry Wolters	484	45	IMSA GT
18	02	Al Levenson (USA)/Dan Rice (USA)/Guido C. Levetto (USA)	Chevrolet Corvette	Al Levenson	475	44	IMSA GT
19	77	Burt Greenwood (USA)/Rick Mancuso (USA)/John Cargill (USA) David Heinz (USA)	Chevrolet Corvette (Protofab)	Rick Mancuso	470	23	IMSA GT
20	10	Marion L. Speer (USA)/Windle Turley (USA)/Hal Sahlman (USA)	Porsche 911S	Race Car	464	33	IMSA GTU
21	1	Jacky Ickx (B)/Jochen Mass (D)/* Juergen Barth (D)	Porsche 935	Porsche	452 DNF	1	Group 5
22	33	Ara Dube (USA)/Harro Zitza (USA)/Joe Castellano (USA)	Porsche 911	Ara Dube	441	46	IMSA GTU

FINISH	CAR NO.	DRIVERS	CAR	ENTRANT	LAPS	START	CLASS
23	50	Tom Waugh (USA)/John Rulon-Miller (USA)/Bob Punch (USA)	American Motors Hornet	Tom Waugh	394	52	IMSA GT
24	72	Bill Arnold (USA)/Carl Thompson (USA)/Billy Hagan (USA)	Chevrolet Corvette	Bill Arnold	378	25	IMSA GT
25	34	George Drolsom (USA)/Bill Scott (USA)/Tom Bagley (USA)	Porsche 911S	George Drolsom	377 DNF	43	IMSA GTU
26	47	John Fitzpatrick (GB)/Kenper Miller (USA)/Paul Miller (USA)	BMW 3.5 CSL	Miller Brothers	368 DNF	9	IMSA GT
27	13	Robert Fryer (USA)/Richard L. Bostyan (USA)/Ed Lowther (USA)	American Motors Javelin	University of Pittsburgh	366	53	IMSA GT
28	9	Klaus Bytzek (CDN)/Harry Bytzek (CDN)/Rudi Bartling (CDN)	Porsche 911 Carrera RSR	Bytzek Brothers	343 DNF	26	IMSA GT
29	20	Jean Rondeau (F)/Jean-Pierre Beltoise (F)/* Al Holbert (USA)	Inaltera Ford-Cosworth	Inaltera	336 DNF	3	FIA Sports
30	05	Jim Trueman (USA)/Jerry Thompson (USA)/Don Yenko (USA)	Chevrolet Monza	Jim Trueman	300 DNF	10	IMSA GT
31	66	Tony Adamowicz (USA)/John Cannon (CDN)/Dick Barbour (USA)	Ferrari 365GTB/4 Daytona	Ramsey Ferrari	286 DNF	29	IMSA GT
32	96	Gene Felton (USA)/Buzz Cason (USA)/James Reeve (USA)	Chevrolet Camaro	Clay Young	251 DNF	14	IMSA GT
33	70	Adrian Gang (USA)/W. K. Gonzalez (USA)/Tim Duke (USA)	Porsche 911 Carrera RSR	Michael Callas	247 DNF	30	IMSA GT
34	14	Al Holbert (USA)/Michael Keyser (USA)/Claude Ballot-Lena (F)	Chevrolet Monza (DeKon)	Al Holbert	246 DNF	8	IMSA GT
35	38	John Paul, Sr. (USA)/John O'Steen (USA)/Bob Hagestad (USA)	Porsche 911 Carrera RSR	John Paul, Sr.	217 DNF	35	IMSA GT
36	46	Mauricio de Narvaez (CO)/Albert Naon (USA)/John Freyre (USA)	Porsche 911 Carrera RSR	Mauricio de Narvaez	199 DNF	32	IMSA GT
37	99	Phil Currin (USA)/Robert H. Hoskins (USA)/Peter Knab (USA)	Chevrolet Corvette	Phil Currin	196 DNF	20	IMSA GT
38	39	Wiley Doran (USA)/Jim Barnett (USA)/Charles Pelz (USA)	Chevrolet Corvette	Wiley Doran	191 DNF	39	IMSA GT
39	40	Andre Sepelon (F)/Bob Lee (USA)/Larry Parker (USA)	Ford Mustang	Robert V. LaMay	180 DNF	59	IMSA GT
40	24	Tom Frank (USA)/Carl Shafer (USA)	Porsche 911 Carrera RSR	Tom Frank	178 DNF	16	IMSA GT
41	2	David Hobbs (GB)/Ronnie Peterson (S)/Sam Posey (USA)	BMW 320i	BMW	177 DNF	19	IMSA GT
42	41	Herb Jones, Jr. (USA)/Steve Faul (USA)	Chevrolet Camaro	Herb Jones, Jr.	154 DNF	13	IMSA GT
43	55	Rick Thompkins (USA)/David Heinz (USA)/Lamar Mann (USA)	Chevrolet Corvette	Rick Thompkins	151 DNF	11	IMSA GT
44	49	Sam Fillingham (USA)/Mike Williamson (USA)/K. P. Jones (USA)	Chevrolet Corvette	Sam Fillingham	117 DNF	48	IMSA GT
45	84	Russ Boykin (USA)/Sam Henderson (USA)/* C. C. Canada (USA)	Chevrolet Camaro	Lenton B. McGill	106 DNF	47	IMSA GT
46	7	Anatoly Arutunoff (USA)/Jose Marina (USA)/Brian Goellnicht (USA)	Lancia Stratos	Anatoly Arutunoff	99 DNF	54	IMSA GTU
47	78	Milton Headley (USA)/Sam Feinstein (USA)/* Skip Panzarella (USA)	Chevrolet Corvette	Milton Headley	85 DNF	15	IMSA GT
48	21	Lella Lombardi (I)/Christine Beckers (B)/* Jean Rondeau (F)	Inaltera Ford-Cosworth	Inaltera	78 DNF	4	FIA Sports
49	63	Ted Field (USA)/Jon Woodner (USA)/* Howdy Holmes (USA) * Danny Ongais (USA)	Porsche 911 Carrera RSR	Ted Field	72 DNF	17	IMSA GT
50	36	Bill Boye (USA)/Jere Gillan (USA)	American Motors Gremlin	Bill Boye	60 DNF	57	IMSA GT
51	98	Ralph Tolman (USA)/* Michael Brockman (USA)/* Sam Sommers (USA)	Lotus Europa	Ralph Tolman	50 DNF	56	IMSA GTU
52	80	Carmon Solomone (USA)/Fred Lang (USA)/* Buzz Fyhrie (USA)	Chevrolet Camaro	Carmon Solomone	48 DNF	28	IMSA GT
53	51	Robert Kirby (USA)/John Hotchkis, Sr. (USA)/* Dennis Aase (USA)	Porsche 914/6	Kirby/Hitchcock	47 DNF	38	IMSA GTU
54	00	Danny Ongais (USA)/* George Follmer (USA)/* Ted Field (USA)	Porsche 911 Carrera RSR	Ted Field	35 DNF	6	FIA Sports
55	01	Bob Bergstrom (USA)/* Jim Cook (USA)	Porsche 911	Bob Bergstrom	29 DNF	42	IMSA GTU
56	17	Vince Gimondo (USA)/* Tim Chitwood (USA)	Chevrolet Nova	Tim Chitwood	20 DNF	58	IMSA GT
57	03	Bruno Beilcke (USA)/* Alf Gebhardt (USA)	BMW 2002	Bavarian Motors Int'l	8 DNF	55	IMSA GTU

24 Hours of Daytona

February 4-5, 1978

24 hour event on the 3.840 mile circuit.

Distance covered: 680 laps for 2611.200 miles.

Winning time: 24 hours, 0 minutes, 45.4 seconds for a speed of 108.743 mph.

Margin of victory: 30 laps.

Fastest lap: #99 Porsche 935-77A (Rolf Stommelen) 1:51.845, 123.600 mph.

Fastest qualifier: #0 Porsche 935 (Danny Ongais) 2:00.152, 115.054 mph.

FINISH	CAR NO.	DRIVERS	CAR	ENTRANT	LAPS	START	CLASS
1	**99**	**Rolf Stommelen (D)/Toine Hezemans (NL)/Peter Gregg (USA)**	**Porsche 935-77A**	**Brumos Porsche**	**680**	**4**	**IMSA GTX**
2	6	Dick Barbour (USA)/Manfred Schurti (FL)/Johnny Rutherford (USA)	Porsche 935-77A	Dick Barbour	650	8	IMSA GTX
3	**58**	**Diego Febles (PR)/Alec Poole (IRL)**	**Porsche 911 Carrera RSR**	**Diego Febles**	**645**	**21**	**IMSA GTO**
4	33	Bonky Fernandez (PR)/John Paul, Sr. (USA)/Phil Currin (USA)	Porsche 911 Carrera RSR	Boricua Racing	637	14	IMSA GTO
5	14	Josef Brambring (D)/John Winter (D)/Dieter Schornstein (D)	Porsche 935-77A	Kremer Brothers	635	10	IMSA GTX
6	09	Doc Bundy (USA)/Gary Belcher (USA)/Al Holbert (USA)	Porsche 935	Gary Belcher	632 DNF	12	IMSA GTX
7	32	Steve Earle (USA)/Bob Akin (USA)/Rick Knoop (USA)	Porsche 911 Carrera RSR	Earle/Akin	632	18	IMSA GTX
8	65	John Morton (USA)/Tony Adamowicz (USA)/Hal Sahlman (USA) Bobby Carradine (USA)	Ferrari 365GTB/4 Daytona	Bobby Carradine	622	16	IMSA GTO
9	59	Peter Gregg (USA)/Claude Ballot-Lena (F)/Brad Frisselle (USA)	Porsche 935	Brumos Porsche	621	6	IMSAGTX
DQ	71	Francisco Romero (YV)/Ernesto Soto (YV)/Hardie Beloff (USA)	Porsche 911S	Bill Scott	617	37	IMSA GTU DQ

FINISH	CAR NO.	DRIVERS	CAR	ENTRANT	LAPS	START	CLASS
10	13	Hal Shaw, Jr. (USA)/Jim Busby (USA)/Howard Meister (USA)	Porsche 935	Hal Shaw, Jr.	608	9	IMSA GTX
11	**01**	**Dave White (USA)/Gary Mesnick (USA)/J. Dana Roehrig (USA)**	**Porsche 911S**	**J. Dana Roehrig**	**604 DNF**	**26**	**IMSA GTU**
12	34	George Drolsom (USA)/Hugh Davenport (USA)/Mark Greb (USA)	Porsche 911S	George Drolsom	592	57	IMSA GTU
13	21	Franz Konrad (A)/Reinhold Joest (D)/Volkert Merl (D)	Porsche 935	Reinhold Joest	590	7	IMSA GTX
14	08	Terry Wolters (USA)/Jack Refenning (USA)/Ray Mummery (USA)	Porsche 911	Terry Wolters	584	55	IMSA GTU
15	24	Tom Frank (USA)/Bob Bergstrom (USA)	Porsche 911 Carrera RSR	Tom Frank	580	19	IMSA GTX
16	84	Chris Doyle (USA)/John Maffucci (USA)/Bob Speakman (USA)	Datsun 260Z	Bob Speakman	577	56	IMSA GTU
17	60	John H. Thomas, Jr. (USA)/Ren Tilton (USA)/Rusty Bond (USA)	Porsche 911	R & R Racing	551	34	IMSA GTU
18	29	Richard C. Weiss (USA)/Bill Alsup (USA)/Bill Follmer (USA)	Porsche 911S	Richard C. Weiss	550	35	IMSA GTU
19	37	Robert Buchler (USA)/Eddie Johnson (USA)/Clay Young (USA)	Chevrolet Camaro	Clay Young	550	45	IMSA GTX
20	46	Mauricio de Narvaez (CO)/Albert Naon (USA)/Tony Garcia (USA)	Porsche 911 Carrera RSR	Mauricio de Narvaez	547 DNF	36	IMSA GTO
21	22	Bill Harriss (USA)/Volker Bruckmann (USA)/Ron Southern (USA)	Porsche 911E	Music City Racing	546	49	IMSA GTU
22	5	Francois Migault (F)/Lucien Guitteny (F)/Gregg Young (USA)	Ferrari 365GT4/BB	Howard O'Flynn	521	17	IMSA GTX
23	68	Luis Mendez (DR)/Armando Gonzalez (PR)/Tato Ferrer (PR)	Porsche 911 Carrera RSR	Luis Mendez	509	66	IMSA GTO
24	91	Bill Cooper (USA)/Steve Cook (USA)/Bob Bondurant (USA) Ron Southern (USA)	Datsun 260Z	Bob Bondurant	508	65	IMSA GTU
25	78	Bobby Hillin (USA)/William Henderson (USA)/Richard Turner (USA)	Ferrari 365GTB/4 Daytona	Western Motor Works	506	52	IMSA GTO
26	9	Brian Goellnicht (USA)/Jose Marina (USA)/Jack May (USA) Anatoly Arutunoff (USA)	Lancia Stratos	Anatoly Arutunoff	505	53	IMSA GTU
27	94	Preston Henn (USA)/Hal Sahlman (USA)/Sandy Satullo (USA)	Ferrari 365GTB/4 Daytona	Preston Henn	502 DNF	31	IMSA GTO
28	**36**	**Ron Case (USA)/Dave Panaccione (USA)**	**Porsche 911**	**Ron Case**	**500**	**46**	**IMSA GTU**
29	53	Jim Downing (USA)/Stu Fisher (USA)/Walt Bohren (USA) Roger Mandeville (USA)	Mazda RX-3	Mazda	498	42	IMSA GTU
30	61	Taku Akaike (J)/Alfred Cosentino (USA)	Mazda RX-3	Alfred Cosentino	498	44	IMSA GTU
31	38	Bill McDill (USA)/Mike Meldeau (USA)	Chevrolet Camaro	Mike Meldeau	497	29	IMSA GTX
32	10	Guy W. Church (USA)/Rick Kump (USA)/Bob Lee (USA)	American Motors AMX	Robert H. Lee	481	62	IMSA GTO
33	50	Charles Kleinschmidt (USA)/Lee Culpepper (USA)	MGB GT	Charles Kleinschmidt	477	68	IMSA GTU
34	77	Amos Johnson (USA)/Dennis Shaw (USA)/Charles J. Woodward (USA)	American Motors Hornet AMX	Amos Johnson	475	41	IMSA GTO
35	7	Ludwig Heimrath (CDN)/Jacques Bienvenue (CDN)/Norm Ridgely (CDN)	Porsche 935	Ludwig Heimrath	466 DNF	11	IMSA GTX
36	07	David Cowart (USA)/Charles Mendez (USA)/Joe Castellano (USA)	Porsche 911 Carrera RSR	Morrison	459 DNF	61	IMSA GTO
37	82	Carmon Solomone (USA)/Fred Lang (USA)/Buzz Fyhrie (USA)	Chevrolet Camaro	Carmon Solomone	456 DNF	24	IMSA GTX
38	15	Bruno Beilcke (USA)/Sepp Grinbold (USA)/Alf Gebhardt (USA)	BMW CSL	Bavarian Motors Int.	427 DNF	48	IMSA GTX
39	55	Emiliano Rodriguez (USA)/Hiram Cruz (USA)	Lotus Europa	Emiliano Rodriguez	402	58	IMSA GTU
40	95	Hurley Haywood (USA)/Bob Hagestad (USA)/Doc Bundy (USA)	Porsche 935	Hagestad	400 DNF	60	IMSA GTX
41	18	Dick Gauthier (USA)/Jack Swanson (USA)/Brad West (USA)	Chevrolet Camaro	Ours & Hours Racing	395	50	IMSA GTX
42	56	Richard J. Valentine (USA)/Craig Carter (USA)/Murray Edwards (CDN)	Chevrolet Camaro	Carter Brothers	361	23	IMSA GTX
43	87	Pedro Vazquez, Jr. (USA)/Ron Oyler (USA)/Joseph Hamilton (USA) Gunter Hamilton (USA)/Gunter Seipolt (USA)	Porsche 911	Pedro Vazquez, Jr.	360	67	IMSA GTU
44	02	Dick Neland (USA)/Al Levenson (USA)/Tom Brown (USA)	Chevrolet Corvette	Al Levenson	353	43	IMSA GTO
45	52	Yoshimi Katayama (J)/Yojiro Terada (J)/Roger Mandeville (USA)	Mazda RX-3	Mazda	271 DNF	28	IMSA GTU
46	19	Chris Cord (USA)/Jim Adams (USA)	Chevrolet Monza (DeKon)	Chris Cord	261 DNF	13	IMSA GTX
47	73	Clark Howey (USA)/Dale Koch (USA)/David Crabtree (USA)	Chevrolet Camaro	Clark Howey	259 DNF	20	IMSA GTX
48	76	Frank Thomas (USA)/Lee Mueller (USA)/Logan Blackburn (USA)	Porsche 911	Frank Thomas	224 DNF	39	IMSA GTU
49	72	Carl Thompson (USA)/Billy Hagan (USA)/Rusty Schmidt (USA)	Chevrolet Corvette	Bill Arnold	169 DNF	22	IMSA GTX
50	20	Richard L. Bostyan (USA)/Jerry Thompson (USA)/Don Yenko (USA)	Chevrolet Corvette	Richard L. Bostyan	152 DNF	15	IMSA GTO
51	25	Kenper Miller (USA)/Paul Miller (USA)/* Oscar Koveleski (USA)	BMW CSL	Kenper Miller	125 DNF	64	IMSA GTO
52	05	Stephen E. Bond (USA)/Dale Kreider (USA)/* Philip Dann (USA)	Chevrolet Monza (Nelson)	Dale Kreider	123 DNF	51	IMSA GTX
53	8	Felice Besenzoni (I)/Luciano Dal Ben (I)/Byron Wever (USA)	Ferrari 308GTB	Jolly Club	117 DNF	33	IMSA GTO
54	48	John Carusso (USA)/Emory Donaldson (USA)/Luis Sereix (USA)	Chevrolet Corvette	John Carusso	90 DNF	27	IMSA GTO
55	80	Herb Adams (USA)/Pat Bedard (USA)/Marv Thomson (USA)	Oldsmobile Cutlass	Herb Adams	89 DNF	30	IMSA GTO
56	0	Danny Ongais (USA)/Ted Field (USA)/Milt Minter (USA)	Porsche 935	Ted Field	88 DNF	1	IMSA GTX
57	12	Bob Wollek (F)/Henri Pescarolo (F)/* Didier Jaunet (F)	Porsche 935-77A	Kremer Brothers	86 DNF	2	IMSA GTX
58	51	John Hotchkis, Sr. (USA)/Robert Kirby (USA)/Dennis Aase (USA)	Porsche 911	Kirby/Hitchcock	85 DNF	63	IMSA GTU
59	4	Dino Mallet (I)/Bob Bondurant (USA)/* Sergio Romolotti (I) * Romeo Camathias (CH)	Ferrari 308GTB	Jolly Club	82 DNF	32	IMSA GTO
60	03	Guido C. Levetto (USA)/Dan Rice (USA)	Chevrolet Camaro	Guido Levetto	79 DNF	69	IMSA GTO
61	54	John Tunstall (USA)/Stephen Behr (USA)/Lou Timolat (USA)	Porsche 911 Carrera	T & C	70 DNF	38	IMSA GTX
62	39	Greg Pickett (USA)/Neil Bonnet (USA)/Bruce Canepa (USA)	Porsche 911 Carrera	Greg Pickett	67 DNF	59	IMSA GTO
63	27	Pierre Honegger (USA)/Bill Scott (USA)/Mark Hutchins (USA) * Robert Dean (USA)	Mazda RX-3	Pierre Honegger	57 DNF	54	IMSA GTU
64	2	David Hobbs (GB)/Ronnie Peterson (S)	BMW 320i	McLaren North America	47 DNF	3	IMSA GTX
65	17	Sam Fillingham (USA)/Tim Chitwood (USA)/* K. P. Jones (USA)	Chevrolet Nova	Tim Chitwood	45 DNF	40	IMSA GTO
66	3	Carlo Facetti (I)/* Martino Finotto (I)	Porsche 935	Martino Finotto	6 DNF	5	IMSA GTX
67	85	John E. Hulen (USA)/* Ron Coupland (USA)/* Nick Engels (USA)	Porsche 914/6	John E. Hulen	0 DNF	47	IMSA GTU
DNS	86	Janet Guthrie (USA)/Hugh Kleinpeter (USA)/Jef Stevens (USA)	De Tomaso Pantera GT4K (Kleinpeter)	Hugh Kleinpeter	DNS	25	IMSA GTX

24 Hour Pepsi Challenge

February 3-4, 1979

24 hour event on the 3.840 mile circuit.
Distance covered: 684 laps for 2626.560 miles/4227.031 kms.
Winning time: 24 hours, 0 minutes, 24.87 seconds for a speed of 109.409 mph.
Margin of victory: 49 laps.
Fastest lap: #1 Porsche 935-77A (Peter Gregg) 1:49.477, 126.273 mph.
Fastest qualifier: #3 Porsche 935 (Carlos Facetti) 1:46.113, 130.276 mph.
1 full-course caution for 8 laps.

FINISH	CAR NO.	DRIVERS	CAR	ENTRANT	LAPS	START	CLASS
1	**0**	**Ted Field (USA)/Danny Ongais (USA)/Hurley Haywood (USA)**	**Porsche 935-79**	**Ted Field**	**684**	**8**	**IMSA GTX**
2	**65**	**John Morton (USA)/Tony Adamowicz (USA)**	**Ferrari 365GTB/4 Daytona**	**Otto Zipper**	**635**	**24**	**IMSA GTO**
3	11	Bruce Canepa (USA)/Rick Mears (USA)/Monte Shelton (USA)	Porsche 935-77A	Bruce Canepa	627	19	IMSA GTX
4	94	Don Whittington (USA)/Bill Whittington (USA)/Juergen Barth (D)	Porsche 935-79	Whittington Brothers	622	6	IMSA GTX
5	**7**	**Yoshimi Katayama (J)/Yojiro Terada (J)/Takashi Yorino (J)**	**Mazda RX-7**	**Mazda**	**617**	**32**	**IMSA GTU**
6	77	Walt Bohren (USA)/Amos Johnson (USA)/Roger Mandeville (USA)	Mazda RX-7	Mazda	615	34	IMSA GTU
7	60	Rusty Bond (USA)/Ren Tilton (USA)	Porsche 911	E. J. Pruitt	612	50	IMSA GTU
8	54	Tony Garcia (USA)/Juan Montalvo (C)/Alberto Vadia, Jr. (USA)	Porsche 911 Carrera RSR	Montura Racing	587	33	IMSA GTO
9	98	Lance Van Every (USA)/Ash Tisdelle (USA)/Robert Overby (USA)	Porsche 911 Carrera RSR	Lance Van Every	579	30	IMSA GTO
10	03	Angelo Pallavicini (CH)/Enzo Calderari (CH)/Marco Vanoli (CH)	Porsche 934	Angelo Pallavicini	577	40	IMSA GTO
11	75	Mike Ramirez (PR)/Manuel Villa Prieto (PR)/Luis Gordillo (PR)	Porsche 911	Mike Ramirez	560	49	IMSA GTU
12	37	Honorato Espinosa (CO)/Francisco Lopez (CO)/Jorge Cortes (CO)	Porsche 911 Carrera	Luis Botero	551	27	IMSA GTO
13	33	Peter Welter (USA)/Richard Aten (USA)/Jack Refenning (USA)	Porsche 911	Peter Welter	550	55	IMSA GTU
14	58	Diego Febles (PR)/Phil Currin (USA)	Porsche 911 Carrera RSR	Diego Febles	543	25	IMSA GTO
15	5	Charles Mendez (USA)/Johnny Rutherford (USA)/Paul Miller (USA)	Porsche 935	Charles Mendez	529 DNF	12	IMSA GTX
16	27	Ray Mummery (USA)/Tom Sheehy (USA)/Luis Sereix (USA)	Porsche 911S	Ray Mummery	522 DNF	44	IMSA GTU
17	62	William Koll (USA)/Jim Cook (USA)	Porsche 914/6	William Koll	511 DNF	39	IMSA GTU
18	95	Stephen E. Bond (USA)/Philip Dann (USA)	Chevrolet Monza (Nelson)	Stephen E. Bond	509	66	IMSA GTO
19	21	John Wood (USA)/Tom Bagley (USA)/Carl Shafer (USA)	Chevrolet Camaro	Gordon Oftedahl	493	14	IMSA GTO
20	42	Tom Ashby (USA)/Bill Bean (USA)/Bob Beasley (USA)	Porsche 911	Bullwinkele Racing	493	45	IMSA GTU
21	08	Terry Wolters (USA)/Nort Northam (USA)/Richard C. Weiss (USA)	Porsche 911	Moran Construction	488	67	IMSA GTU
22	34	George Drolsom (USA)/Mark Greb (USA)/John Maffucci (USA)	Porsche 911	George Drolsom	482	47	IMSA GTU
23	64	C. C. Canada (USA)/Russ Boykin (USA)/Thomas T. Ciccone (USA)	Chevrolet Camaro	Lenton B. McGill	458	54	IMSA GTO
24	61	Alfred Cosentino (USA)/Dick Starita (USA)/Taku Akaike (J)	Mazda RX-3	Alfred Cosentino	444	48	IMSA GTU
25	8	Anatoly Arutunoff (USA)/Jose Marina (USA)/Danny Sullivan (USA)	Lancia Stratos	Anatoly Arutunoff	439 DNF	53	IMSA GTU
26	6	Dick Barbour (USA)/Brian Redman (GB)/Paul Newman (USA)	Porsche 935	Dick Barbour	410 DNF	7	IMSA GTX
27	80	Herb Adams (USA)/Peter Frey (USA)/Louis Spoerl (USA)	Pontiac Firebird	Herb Adams	408 DNF	65	IMSA GTO
28	17	Jim Mederer (USA)/Don Sherman (USA)/Jeff Kline (USA)	Mazda RX-7	Mederer/Oku	393 DNF	43	IMSA GTU
29	93	Dale Whittington (USA)/R. D. Whittington (USA)/Preston Henn (USA)	Porsche 934	Whittington Brothers	389 DNF	35	IMSA GTO
30	71	Bill Scott (USA)/Mark Hutchins (USA)/Pierre Honegger (USA)	Porsche 911S	Bill Scott	388 DNF	41	IMSA GTU
31	40	Steve Southard (USA)/William Koch (USA)/Earl Roe (USA)	Porsche 914/6	Performance Specialists	385 DNF	59	IMSA GTU
32	1	Bob Wollek (F)/Jacky Ickx (B)/Peter Gregg (USA)	Porsche 935-77A	Georg Loos	342 DNF	3	IMSA GTX
33	69	Klaus Bytzek (CDN)/Rudi Bartling (CDN)/Ludwig Heimrath (CDN)	Porsche 911 Carrera RSR	Klaus Bytzek	335 DNF	28	IMSA GTO
34	29	Billy Hagan (USA)/Hoyt Overbagh (USA)/Don Reed (USA)	Chevrolet Monza	Billy Hagan	331 DNF	18	IMSA GTO
35	89	Joseph Hamilton (USA)/Robert H. Hoskins (USA)/Herb Forrest (USA)	Porsche 911	Joseph Hamilton	329 DNF	46	IMSA GTU
36	51	Robert Kirby (USA)/John Hotchkis, Sr. (USA)/Howard Meister (USA)	Porsche 911 Carrera RSR	Kirby/Hitchcock	328 DNF	37	IMSA GTO
37	15	Alf Gebhardt (USA)/Sepp Grinbold (USA)	BMW CSL	Bavarian Motors Int'l	299 DNF	36	IMSA GTO
38	81	Ernesto Soto (YV)/Francisco Romero (YV)/Oscar Notz (YV)	Porsche 911 Carrera	Performance Export	241 DNF	21	IMSA GTO
39	01	Dave White (USA)/J. Kurt Roehrig (USA)/John Hamilton (USA)	Porsche 911	D. R. Racing	223 DNF	38	IMSA GTU
40	13	Hal Shaw, Jr. (USA)/Tom Spalding (USA)/Norm Ridgely (CDN)	Porsche 935	Hal Shaw, Jr.	222 DNF	42	IMSA GTX
41	36	Ron Case (USA)/Dave Panaccione (USA)	Porsche 911	Ron Case	210 DNF	52	IMSA GTU
42	53	Guy Thomas (USA)/Milton Moise (USA)/Tom Nehl (USA)	Chevrolet Camaro	Guy Thomas	201	51	IMSA GTX
43	06	Al Levenson (USA)/Gary Baker (USA)/Lanny Hester (USA)	Chevrolet Corvette	Al Levenson	197 DNF	57	IMSA GTO
44	23	Charlie Kemp (USA)/Carson Baird (USA)/Kees Nierop (CDN)	Ford Cobra II (Kemp)	Charlie Kemp	168 DNF	10	IMSA GTX
45	3	Martino Finotto (I)/Carlo Facetti (I)/Gianpiero Moretti (I)	Porsche 935	Jolly Club	164 DNF	1	IMSA GTX
46	4	Reinhold Joest (D)/Rolf Stommelen (D)/Volkert Merl (D)	Porsche 935J (Joest)	Reinhold Joest	162 DNF	4	IMSA GTX
47	90	Rick Kump (USA)/Bob Lee (USA)/Sam Miller (USA)	American Motors AMX	Bob Lee	156 DNF	56	IMSA GTO
48	12	Gerry Wellik (USA)/Tom Bagley (USA)/Joe Chamberlain (USA) * John Wood (USA)	Chevrolet Camaro	Gordon Oftedahl	147 DNF	26	IMSA GTO
49	56	Craig Carter (USA)/Murray Edwards (CDN)/Richard J. Valentine (USA)	Chevrolet Camaro (Peerless)	Rick Hendrick	144 DNF	17	IMSA GTO
50	2	Manfred Schurti (FL)/John Fitzpatrick (GB)/Bob Wollek (F)	Porsche 935-77A	Georg Loos	135 DNF	2	IMSA GTX
51	57	John Tremblay (USA)/Bob Lapp (USA)	Datsun 240Z	John Tremblay	118 DNF	63	IMSA GTU
52	9	Bob Akin (USA)/Rob McFarlin (USA)/Roy Woods (USA)	Porsche 935-77A	Dick Barbour	117 DNF	9	IMSA GTX

FIN.	CAR NO.	DRIVERS	CAR	ENTRANT	LAPS	START	CLASS
53	66	Jean-Claude Andruet (F)/Spartaco Dini (I)/Claude Ballot-Lena (F)	Ferrari 512BB	Charles Pozzi	103 DNF	15	IMSA GTX
54	67	Claude Ballot-Lena (F)/Michel Leclere (F)/Jean-Claude Andruet (F)	Ferrari 512BB	Charles Pozzi	101 DNF	13	IMSA GTX
55	24	Graham Shaw (USA)/Don Yenko (USA)/Jerry Thompson (USA)	Chevrolet Monza	Graham Shaw	86 DNF	62	IMSA GTX
56	38	Bonky Fernandez (PR)/Chiqui Soldevila (PR)/Tato Ferrer (PR)	Porsche 911 Carrera RSR	Boricua Racing	73 DNF	20	IMSA GTO
57	68	Bob Tullius (USA)/Jean-Pierre Delaunay (F)/Pat Bedard (USA)	Ferrari 512BB	Luigi Chinetti, Sr.	72 DNF	16	IMSA GTX
58	43	Bill McDill (USA)/Stephen Behr (USA)	Chevrolet Camaro	Mike Meldeau	59 DNF	31	IMSA GTX
59	46	Mauricio de Narvaez (CO)/Albert Naon (USA)/Pedro de Narvaez (CO)	Porsche 911 Carrera	Mauricio de Narvaez	46 DNF	23	IMSA GTO
60	07	David Cowart (USA)/David H. McClain (USA)/Kenper Miller (USA)	Porsche 911 Carrera	Morrison	35 DNF	22	IMSA GTO
61	00	Preston Henn (USA)/* Ted Field (USA)/* Danny Ongais (USA)	Porsche 935	Ted Field	29 DNF	11	IMSA GTX
62	14	Stephen Griswold (USA)/* Steve Earle (USA)/* Rick Knoop (USA)	BMW CSL	Bavarian Motors Int.	25 DNF	61	IMSA GTX
63	96	Gary Wonzer (USA)/* Robert Whitaker (USA)/* George Van Arsdale (USA) * Richard C. Hughes (USA)	Triumph GT6	Gary Wonzer	20 DNF	60	IMSA GTU
64	48	Frank Leary (USA)/* Casey Mollett (USA)/* Steve Cook (USA)	Datsun 240Z	Frank Leary	13 DNF	58	IMSA GTU
65	18	John Paul, Sr. (USA)/* Al Holbert (USA)/* Michael Keyser (USA)	Porsche 935JLP-1 (Fabcar)	John Paul, Sr.	12 DNF	5	IMSA GTX
66	79	Bob Bergstrom (USA)/* Brad Frisselle (USA)	Mazda RX-7	Bob Bergstrom	9 DNF	64	IMSA GTU
67	73	Clark Howey (USA)/* Dale Koch (USA)/* Tracy Wolf (USA)	Chevrolet Camaro	Clark Howey	4 DNF	29	IMSA GTX

24 Hour Pepsi Challenge

February 3-4, 1980

24 hour event on the 3.840 mile circuit.

Distance covered: 715 laps for 2745.600 miles

Winning time: 24 hours, 1 minute, 13.33 seconds for a speed of 114.303 mph.

Margin of victory: 33 laps.

Fastest lap: #93 Porsche 935K3 (Bill Whittington) 1:47.964, 128.043 mph.

Fastest qualifier: #93 Porsche 935K3 (Don Whittington) 1:44.411, 132.783 mph.

1 full-course caution for 13 minutes

FIN.	CAR NO.	DRIVERS	CAR	ENTRANT	LAPS	START	CLASS
1	**2**	**Reinhold Joest (D)/Rolf Stommelen (D)/Volkert Merl (D)**	**Porsche 935J (Joest)**	**Reinhold Joest**	**715**	**2**	**IMSA GTX**
2	09	John Paul, Sr. (USA)/Al Holbert (USA)/* Preston Henn (USA)	Porsche 935K3 (Kremer)	Preston Henn	682	13	IMSA GTX
3	0	Ted Field (USA)/Danny Ongais (USA)/Milt Minter (USA)	Porsche 935K3 (Kremer)	Ted Field	664	8	IMSA GTX
4	80	Maurice Carter (CDN)/Craig Carter (USA)/Murray Edwards (CDN)	Chevrolet Camaro (Descon)	Maurice Carter	639	9	IMSA GTX
5	**62**	**William Koll (USA)/Jim Cook (USA)/Greg La Cava (USA)**	**Porsche 914/6**	**William Koll**	**632**	**48**	**IMSA GTU**
6	**54**	**Tony Garcia (USA)/Alberto Vadia, Jr. (USA)/Terry Herman (USA)**	**Porsche 911 Carrera RSR**	**Montura Racing**	**630**	**40**	**IMSA GTO**
7	46	Mauricio de Narvaez (CO)/Albert Naon (USA)/Ricardo Londono (CO)	Porsche 911 Carrera	Mauricio de Narvaez	629	28	IMSA GTO
8	77	Roger Mandeville (USA)/Jim Downing (USA)/Brad Frisselle (USA)	Mazda RX-7	Roger Mandeville	618	38	IMSA GTU
9	9	Skeeter McKitterick (USA)/Bob Garretson (USA)/Anny-Charlotte Verney (F)	Porsche 935	Dick Barbour	599	12	IMSA GTX
10	**4**	**Carlo Facetti (I)/Martino Finotto (I)/* Gianfranco Ricci (I)**	**Lancia Beta Monte Carlo (Dallara)**	**Jolly Club**	**597**	**16**	**IMSA GTX**
11	59	Peter Gregg (USA)/Hurley Haywood (USA)/Bruce Leven (USA)	Porsche 935-80	Brumos Porsche	584	4	IMSA GTX
12	73	Mark Hutchins (USA)/Pierre Honegger (USA)/Fred Apgar (USA)	Mazda RX-7	Pierre Honegger	546	43	IMSA GTU
13	89	Francisco Romero (YV)/Jean-Paul Libert (B)/Ernesto Soto (YV)	Porsche 911 Carrera	Hector Huerta	544	37	IMSA GTO
14	65	John Morton (USA)/Tony Adamowicz (USA)/Bob Bondurant (USA)	Ferrari 365GTB/4 Daytona	Nicholas/McRoberts	539 DNF	29	IMSA GTO
15	78	Robert Giesel (USA)/Bruce Nesbitt (USA)/Alan L. Johnson (USA)	Mazda RX-2	Alan L. Johnson	533	59	IMSA GTU
16	93	Bill Whittington (USA)/Don Whittington (USA)/Dale Whittington (USA)	Porsche 935K3 (Kremer)	Whittington Brothers	509 DQ	1	IMSA GTX
17	81	Lyn St. James (USA)/Mark Welch (USA)/Tom Winters (USA)	Mazda RX-7	Trinity Racing	498	72	IMSA GTU
18	08	Marion L. Speer (USA)/Ray Ratcliff (USA)/Terry Wolters (USA)	Porsche 911	Moran Construction	489	57	IMSA GTU
19	57	Wayne Baker (USA)/Dan Gilliland (USA)/Jeff Scott (USA)	Porsche 914	Wayne Baker	486	67	IMSA GTU
20	82	John Casey (USA)/Steve Dietrich (USA)/Lee Mueller (USA)	Mazda RX-7	Trinity Racing	483	45	IMSA GTU
21	10	David Heinz (USA)/Gerry Wellik (USA)/Bob Young (USA)	Chevrolet Camaro	Gordon Oftedahl	476	25	IMSA GTO
22	22	Volker Bruckmann (USA)/David Goodell (USA)/Rug Cunningham (USA)	Porsche 911 Carrera	Volker Bruckmann	464	55	IMSA GTO
23	37	Honorato Espinosa (CO)/Jorge Cortes (CO)/Francisco Lopez (CO)	Porsche 911 Carrera	Luis Botero	457	35	IMSA GTO
24	39	Allan Moffat (AUS)/Amos Johnson (USA)/Stu Fisher (USA)/* Brad Frisselle (USA)	Mazda RX-7	JLC Racing	440 DNF	42	IMSA GTU
25	28	Tom Nehl (USA)/Peter Kirill (USA)/Kathy Rude (USA)	Chevrolet Camaro	Tom Nehl	435 DNF	64	IMSA GTO
26	68	Luis Mendez (DR)/Tico Almeida (USA)/Rene Rodriguez (USA)	Porsche 911 Carrera RSR	Luis Mendez	423 DNF	41	IMSA GTO
27	15	Alf Gebhardt (USA)/Bruno Beilcke (USA)/* Helmut Trieb (D)	BMW CSL	Bavarian Motors Int'l	420	50	IMSA GTO
28	92	Don Cummings (USA)/Guido C. Levetto (USA)	Shelby GT350	Don Cummings	410	66	IMSA GTO

FIN.	CAR NO.	DRIVERS	CAR	ENTRANT	LAPS	START	CLASS
29	6	John Fitzpatrick (GB)/Manfred Schurti (FL)/Dick Barbour (USA)	Porsche 935K3 (Kremer)	Dick Barbour	405	3	IMSA GTX
30	71	Philip Keirn (USA)/Larry Trotter (USA)/Ed Errington (USA)	Chevrolet Corvette	Philip Keirn	402 DNF	51	IMSA GTO
31	76	Joe Chamberlain (USA)/John Chamberlain (USA)/Richard J. Valentine (USA)	Chevrolet Corvette (Markle)	Richard J. Valentine	393	39	IMSA GTX
32	85	David Deacon (CDN)/Peter Moennick (CDN)/Jacques Bienvenue (CDN)	Porsche 911 Carrera RSR	David Deacon	375 DNF	60	IMSA GTO
33	06	Joe DiBattista (USA)/Thomas T. Ciccone (USA)/Alan Howes (USA)	Porsche 911	Intrepid Design	358	62	IMSA GTU
34	79	Bob Bergstrom (USA)/Pat Bedard (USA)	Mazda RX-7	Bob Bergstrom	355 DNF	47	IMSA GTU
35	56	Rick Borlase (USA)/Don Kravig (USA)/Michael Hammond (USA)	Porsche 911	Rick Borlase	348	52	IMSA GTO
36	69	Preston Henn (USA)/Pierre Dieudonne (B)/* John Paul, Jr. (USA)	Ferrari 512BB	Preston Henn	341 DNF	23	IMSA GTX
37	24	Jack Refenning (USA)/Ray Mummery (USA)/Ren Tilton (USA)	Porsche 934	Glen Kalil	337 DNF	26	IMSA GTO
38	52	Joseph Hamilton (USA)/Tom Cripe (USA)/Fred Snow (USA)	Porsche 911	Fred Snow	301 DNF	63	IMSA GTU
39	5	Charles Mendez (USA)/Brian Redman (GB)/Paul Miller (USA)	Porsche 935K3 (Kremer)	Mendez/Woods/Akin	290 DNF	20	IMSA GTX
40	96	Bob Earl (USA)/William Coykendall (USA)/Fred Stiff (USA)	Datsun 240Z	NTS Racing	281 DNF	65	IMSA GTU
41	42	Dick Neland (USA)/Bill Ferran (USA)/Joe Cotrone (USA)	Chevrolet Camaro	Dick Neland	270 DNF	56	IMSA GTO
42	95	Mike Ramirez (PR)/Manuel Villa Prieto (PR)/Luis Gordillo (PR)	Porsche 911	Mike Ramirez	263 DNF	71	IMSA GTU
43	11	Michael Korten (D)/Patrick Neve (B)/Ian Grob (GB)	BMW M1 (March)	March	260 DNF	17	IMSA GTX
44	70	Chris Doyle (USA)/Charles Guest (USA)/Mike Meyer (USA)	Mazda RX-7	Chris Doyle	250 DNF	58	IMSA GTU
45	13	Elliott Forbes-Robinson (USA)/Randolph Townsend (USA)/Howard Meister (USA)	Porsche 935K3 (Andial-Kremer)	Randolph Townsend	233 DNF	7	IMSA GTX
46	32	Enrique Molins (ES)/Carlos Ernesto Pineda (ES)/Eduardo Barrientos (ES)	Porsche 911 Carrera	Enrique Molins	233 DNF	49	IMSA GTO
47	25	Kenper Miller (USA)/David Cowart (USA)/Christine Beckers (B)	BMW M1	Deren Automotive	222 DNF	21	IMSA GTX
48	55	Ralph Kent Cooke (USA)/Gerard Bleynie (F)/Claude Ballot-Lena (F)	Porsche 935	Charles Mendez	217 DNF	14	IMSA GTX
49	38	Bonky Fernandez (PR)/Tato Ferrer (PR)/Kees Nierop (CDN)	Porsche 911 Carrera RSR	Boricua Racing	211 DNF	36	IMSA GTO
50	19	Chris Cord (USA)/Jim Adams (USA)/* Dick Ferguson (USA)	Chevrolet Monza (DeKon)	Chris Cord	188 DNF	10	IMSA GTX
51	94	Dale Whittington (USA)/Axel Plankenhorn (D)	Porsche 935-79	Whittington Brothers	179 DNF	5	IMSA GTX
52	44	Bob Tullius (USA)/John McComb (USA)/John Kelly (USA)	Triumph TR8	Bob Tullius	171 DNF	27	IMSA GTO
53	75	Dale Kreider (USA)/Billy Hagan (USA)/Stephen E. Bond (USA)	Chevrolet Corvette	Dale Kreider	170 DNF	33	IMSA GTO
54	05	Bob Akin (USA)/Roy Woods (USA)/Bobby Rahal (USA)	Porsche 935K3 (Kremer)	Mendez/Woods/Akin	156 DNF	19	IMSA GTX
55	51	Robert Kirby (USA)/John Hotchkis, Sr. (USA)/John Hotchkis, Jr. (USA)	Porsche 911 Carrera RSR	Kirby/Hitchcock	147 DNF	61	IMSA GTO
56	3	Jim Busby (USA)/Bruce Jenner (USA)/Rick Knoop (USA)	BMW M1 (March)	Jim Busby	139 DNF	18	IMSA GTX
57	23	Don C. Devendorf (USA)/Dick Davenport (USA)/Frank Carney (USA)	Datsun 280ZX	Frank Carney	109 DNF	34	IMSA GTU
58	99	Phil Currin (USA)	Chevrolet Corvette	Kal Showket	89	22	IMSA GTO
59	30	Gianpiero Moretti (I)/* Fernando Cazzaniga (I)/* Bruce Canepa (USA)	Porsche 935J (Joest)	Gianpiero Moretti	72 DNF	11	IMSA GTX
60	58	Diego Febles (PR)/* Chiqui Soldevila (PR)/* Armando Gonzalez (PR)	Porsche 911 Carrera RSR	Coco Lopez	60 DNF	44	IMSA GTO
61	16	Kim Mason (USA)/* Don Yenko (USA)/* Jerry Thompson (USA)	Chevrolet Corvette	Don Yenko	56 DNF	53	IMSA GTO
62	17	Walt Bohren (USA)/* Dennis Aase (USA)/* Jeff Kline (USA)	Mazda RX-7	Mederer/Oku	51 DNF	30	IMSA GTU
63	03	Werner Frank (USA)/* Rudi Bartling (CDN)/* Angelo Pallavicini (CH)	Porsche 934	Werner Frank	51 DNF	31	IMSA GTO
64	83	Harro Zitza (USA)/* John Belperche (USA)/* Doug Zitza (USA)	Porsche 914/6	Harro Zitza	44 DNF	68	IMSA GTU
65	63	Nort Northam (USA)/Hugh Davenport (USA)/* Guy Thomas (USA)	Chevrolet Camaro	Guy Thomas	29 DNF	70	IMSA GTX
66	07	Ludwig Heimrath (CDN)/* Carlos Moran (ES)/* Johnny Rutherford (USA)	Porsche 935	Ludwig Heimrath	24 DNF	6	IMSA GTX
67	18	Anatoly Arutunoff (USA)/* Jose Marina (USA)/* George Drolsom (USA)	Lancia Stratos	Anatoly Arutunoff	20 DNF	69	IMSA GTU
DNS	88	Herb Adams (USA)/Kenny Roberts (USA)/Walker Evans (USA)	Pontiac Fire-Am	Herb Adams	0	54	IMSA GTO
DNS	00	Ted Field (USA)/Danny Ongais (USA)/Milt Minter (USA)	Porsche 935-77A	Ted Field	0	15	IMSA GTX
DNS	14	Pierre Dieudonne (B)/Jorge Koechlin (PE)/Leon Walger (RA)	Porsche 935	Stanton/Barbour	0	24	IMSA GTX
DNS	8	Bob Beasley (USA)/Chuck Grantham (USA)/George Stone (USA)	Porsche 911 Carrera RSR	Bob Beasley	0	32	IMSA GTO
DNS	98	Lance Van Every (USA)/Ash Tisdelle (USA)/Bill Johnson (USA)	Porsche 911 Carrera RSR	Lance Van Every	0	46	IMSA GTO

24 Hour Pepsi Challenge

January 31-February 1, 1981

24 hour event on the 3.840 mile circuit.

Distance covered: 708 laps for 2718.720 miles.

Winning time: 24 hours, 1 minute, 36.871 seconds for a speed of 113.153 mph.

Margin of victory: 13 laps.

Fastest lap: #10 Ferrari 308GTB (Carlos Facetti), 1:48.14, 127.834 mph.

Fastest qualifier: #51 Porsche 935K3 (Rolf Stommelen), 1:43.104, 134.078 mph.

1 full-course caution

FIN	CAR NO.	DRIVERS	CAR	ENTRANT	LAPS	START	CLASS
1	**9**	**Bob Garretson (USA)/Bobby Rahal (USA)/Brian Redman (GB)**	**Porsche 935K3 (Kremer)**	**Bob Garretson**	**708**	**16**	**IMSA GTX**
2	5	Bob Akin (USA)/Craig Siebert (USA)/Derek Bell (GB)	Porsche 935K3 (Kremer)	Bob Akin	695	8	IMSA GTX
3	**62**	**William Koll (USA)/Jeff Kline (USA)/Rob McFarlin (USA)**	**Porsche 911S (Kegel)**	**Kegel Enterprises**	**644**	**31**	**IMSA GTU**
4	23	Dick Davenport (USA)/Frank Carney (USA)/Rameau Johnson (USA)	Datsun 280ZX	Frank Carney	626	42	IMSA GTU
5	**24**	**Martino Finotto (I)/Emanuele Pirro (I)/Carlo Facetti (I)**	**Lancia Beta Monte Carlo (Dallara)**	**Jolly Club**	**609**	**21**	**GTX/G5**
6	**14**	**Hans-Joachim Stuck, Jr. (D)/Alf Gebhardt (USA)/Walter Brun (CH)**	**BMW M1**	**Bavarian Motors Int.**	**608**	**19**	**IMSA GTO**
7	98	Lee Mueller (USA)/Kathy Rude (USA)/Philippe Martin (B)	Mazda RX-7	Dave Kent	606	32	IMSA GTU
8	84	Enrique Molins (ES)/Eduardo Barrientos (ES)/Carlos Gonzalez (ES)	Porsche 935	Enrique Molins	595	24	IMSA GTX
9	55	Roger Mandeville (USA)/Amos Johnson (USA)/Diego Febles (PR)	Mazda RX-7	Roger Mandeville	595	54	IMSA GTU
10	7	Walt Bohren (USA)/Jim Mullen (USA)/J. Kurt Roehrig (USA)	Mazda RX-7	Dave Kent	589	33	IMSA GTU
11	50	Scott Hoerr (USA)/Irv Hoerr (USA)/Jim Downing (USA)	Mazda RX-7	Downing/Maffucci	585	56	IMSA GTU
12	58	Pete Smith (USA)/Chuck Kendall (USA)/Steve Earle (USA)	Porsche 911 Carrera RSR	Chuck Kendall	585	38	IMSA GTO
13	45	Marion L. Speer (USA)/Dwight Mitchell (USA)/Ray Ratcliff (USA)	Porsche 914/6	Autosport Technology	581	58	IMSA GTU
14	07	Ludwig Heimrath (CDN)/Ludwig Heimrath, Jr. (CDN)	Porsche 935	Ludwig Heimrath	575	17	IMSA GTX
15	34	George Drolsom (USA)/Robert H. Hoskins (USA)/Bill Johnson (USA)	Porsche 911 Carrera	George Drolsom	563	62	IMSA GTO
16	**2**	**David Hobbs (GB)/Marc Surer (CH)/Dieter Quester (A)**	**BMW M1 (Sauber)**	**BMW North America**	**555**	**20**	**GTX/G5**
17	27	Steve Southard (USA)/Jay Kjoller (USA)/Jean Kjoller (USA)	Porsche 911 Carrera	Steve Southard	548	61	IMSA GTO
18	3	Riccardo Patrese (I)/Hans Heyer (D)/Henri Pescarolo (F)	Lancia Beta Monte Carlo (Dallara)	Lancia	545	11	IMSA GTX
19	42	Nort Northam (USA)/Ed Kuhel (USA)/Dick Neland (USA)	Chevrolet Camaro	Kend	532	55	IMSA GTO
20	04	Tico Almeida (USA)/Rene Rodriguez (USA)/Miguel Morejon (USA)	Porsche 911 Carrera	Almeida/Rodriguez	526 DNF	35	IMSA GTO
21	02	John Morton (USA)/Tom Klausler (USA)	Ford Mustang (McLaren)	Firestone	517	71	IMSA GTX
22	36	Paul Miller (USA)/Pat Bedard (USA)/Skeeter McKitterick (USA)	Porsche 924 Carrera GTR	Herman/Miller	515	41	IMSA GTO
23	82	Bob Bergstrom (USA)/John Casey (USA)/Jim Cook (USA)	Mazda RX-7	Trinity Racing	513 DNF	30	IMSA GTU
24	51	Rolf Stommelen (D)/Howard Meister (USA)/Harald Grohs (D)	Porsche 935K3 (Andial-Kremer)	Alwin Springer	500 DNF	1	IMSA GTX
25	16	James Burt (USA)/Douglas Grunnet (USA)/Steve Paquette (CDN)	Mazda RX-7	Corp Racing	471	67	IMSA GTU
26	52	Tom Cripe (USA)/Dick Gauthier (USA)/Jack Swanson (USA)	Porsche 911	Beach Ball Racing	450	68	IMSA GTU
27	43	Bob Young (USA)/Leonard Jones (USA)/Bob Gregg (USA)	Porsche 911 Carrera	Bob Gregg	446	44	IMSA GTO
28	81	Tom Winters (USA)/Steve Dietrich (USA)/Carter Alsop (USA)	Mazda RX-7	Trinity Racing	429	63	IMSA GTU
29	70	Chris Doyle (USA)/Hubert Phipps (USA)/Robert Overby (USA)	Mazda RX-7	Chris Doyle	429	49	IMSA GTU
30	46	Honorato Espinosa (CO)/Pedro de Narvaez (CO)/Jorge Cortes (CO)	Porsche 911 Carrera	Pedro de Narvaez	385	36	IMSA GTO
31	65	Tony Adamowicz (USA)/Rick Knoop (USA)	Ferrari 512BB	Ron Spangler	373 DNF	23	IMSA GTX
32	01	Siegfried Brunn (D)/Robert Kirby (USA)/John Hotchkis, Sr. (USA)	Porsche 911 Carrera RSR	Kirby/Hitchcock	361 DNF	57	IMSA GTO
33	25	Kenper Miller (USA)/David Cowart (USA)/Ricardo Londono (CO)	BMW M1	David Cowart	346 DNF	22	IMSA GTO
34	30	Gianpiero Moretti (I)/Mauricio de Narvaez (CO)/Charles Mendez (USA)	Porsche 935-78/81 (Joest)	Gianpiero Moretti	339 DNF	7	IMSA GTX
35	57	Jeff Scott (USA)/David Goodell (USA)/Volker Bruckmann (USA)	Porsche 914/6	Wayne Baker	339 DNF	59	IMSA GTU
36	71	Philip Keirn (USA)/Gail Engle (USA)/Bard Boand (USA)	Chevrolet Corvette	Philip Keirn	328 DNF	50	IMSA GTO
37	67	Dennis Shaw (USA)/Steve Whitman (USA)/Les Blackburn (GB)	American Motors Spirit	Amos Johnson	303 DNF	48	IMSA GTO
38	03	Angelo Pallavicini (CH)/John Sheldon (GB)/Neil Crang (AUS)	Porsche 934	Angelo Pallavicini	290 DNF	40	IMSA GTO
39	0	Ted Field (USA)/Milt Minter (USA)/Danny Ongais (USA)	Porsche 935K3-80 (Kremer)	Ted Field	287 DNF	10	IMSA GTX
40	11	Al Holbert (USA)/Rick Mears (USA)/Doc Bundy (USA)	Porsche 924 Carrera GTR	Al Holbert	263 DNF	26	IMSA GTO
41	4	Michele Alboreto (I)/Piercarlo Ghinzani (I)/Beppe Gabbiani (I)	Lancia Beta Monte Carlo (Dallara)	Lancia	235 DNF	14	IMSA GTX
42	86	Hurley Haywood (USA)/Juergen Barth (D)/Bruce Leven (USA)	Porsche 935-80	Bruce Leven	232 DNF	4	IMSA GTX
43	78	Clark Howey (USA)/Tracy Wolf (USA)/Dale Koch (USA)	Chevrolet Camaro	Tracy Wolf	208 DNF	37	IMSA GTO
44	19	Lance Van Every (USA)/Ash Tisdelle (USA)/Rusty Bond (USA)	Porsche 911 Carrera RSR	Lance Van Every	194 DNF	47	IMSA GTO
45	20	Chris Cord (USA)/Jim Adams (USA)/Bruce Jenner (USA)	Chevrolet Monza (DeKon)	Chris Cord	191 DNF	13	IMSA GTX
46	80	Maurice Carter (CDN)/Eppie Wietzes (CDN)/Richard J. Valentine (USA)	Chevrolet Camaro (Descon)	Maurice Carter	188 DNF	12	IMSA GTX
47	38	Ron Case (USA)/Dave Panaccione (USA)/Ren Tilton (USA)	Porsche 911	Ron Case	169 DNF	65	IMSA GTU
48	1	John Fitzpatrick (GB)/Jim Busby (USA)/Bob Wollek (F)	Porsche 935K3-80 (Kremer)	John Fitzpatrick	167 DNF	2	IMSA GTX
49	22	Wayne Baker (USA)/Dan Gilliland (USA)/Frank Harmstad (USA)	Porsche 914 (Araki)	Wayne Baker	143	53	IMSA GTU
50	33	Harro Zitza (USA)/Doug Zitza (USA)/Ara Dube (USA)	Porsche 914/6	Harro Zitza	128 DNF	64	IMSA GTU
51	17	Bruno Beilcke (USA)/Kurt Koenig (D)/Rudi Walch (D)	BMW 3.5 CSL	Bavarian Motors Int'l	126 DNF	29	IMSA GTO

FIN.	CAR NO.	DRIVERS	CAR	ENTRANT	LAPS	START	CLASS
52	37	Pepe Romero (USA)/Armando Gonzalez (PR)/Luis Mendez (DR)	Porsche 935J (Joest)	Pepe Romero	121 DNF	25	IMSA GTX
53	40	Rudi Bartling (CDN)/Mike Freberg (CDN)/David Deacon (CDN)	BMW M1	David Deacon	118 DNF	27	IMSA GTO
54	54	Tony Garcia (USA)/Albert Naon (USA)/Luis Sereix (USA)	Porsche 911 Carrera RSR	Montura Racing	112 DNF	34	IMSA GTO
55	99	David Heinz (USA)/Chris Gleason (USA)/Joe Cogbill, Jr. (USA) * Michael Gassaway (USA)	Chevrolet Camaro	Gassaway/Oftedahl	108 DNF	28	IMSA GTO
56	60	Vicki Smith (USA)/Sam Miller (USA)/Bob Lee (USA)	American Motors AMX	Bob Lee	87 DNF	60	IMSA GTO
57	94	Don Whittington (USA)/Bill Whittington (USA)/Dale Whittington (USA)	Porsche 935K3 (Kremer)	Whittington Brothers	84 DNF	9	IMSA GTX
58	75	Eddy Joosen (B)/Dirk Vermeersch (B)/Jean-Paul Libert (B)	Mazda RX-7	Pierre Honegger	83 DNF	69	IMSA GTO
59	6	Reinhold Joest (D)/Volkert Merl (D)/* Jochen Mass (D)	Porsche 935J (Joest)	Reinhold Joest	59 DNF	3	IMSA GTX
60	18	John Paul, Sr. (USA)/* John Paul, Jr. (USA)/* Gordon Smiley (USA)	Porsche 935JLP-2 (Kremer)	John Paul, Sr.	53 DNF	5	IMSA GTX
61	44	Terry Labonte (USA)/David Pearson (USA)/* Billy Hagan (USA)	Chevrolet Camaro (Frings)	Billy Hagan	50 DNF	18	IMSA GTX
62	87	George Stone (USA)/* Bob Beasley (USA)/* Werner Frank (USA)	Porsche 911 Carrera RSR	George Beasley	48 DNF	39	IMSA GTO
63	15	Doug Lutz (USA)/Robin Boone (USA)/* Dave White (USA)	Porsche 911 Carrera RSR	Doug Lutz	47 DNF	52	IMSA GTO
64	09	Preston Henn (USA)/Bob Bondurant (USA)/* Dale Whittington (USA)	Porsche 935K3 (Kremer)	Preston Henn	30 DNF	15	IMSA GTX
65	28	Sam Posey (USA)/Fred Stiff (USA)	Datsun 280ZX	NTS Racing	29 DNF	70	IMSA GTO
66	66	Jack Dunham (USA)/John Maffucci (USA)/* Stan Barrett (USA)	Mazda RX-7	Downing/Maffucci	20 DNF	43	IMSA GTU
67	49	Bob Speakman (USA)/* Alfred Cosentino (USA)/Craig Fisher (CDN)	Mazda RX-7	Alfred Cosentino	12 DNF	66	IMSA GTU
68	06	Pete Halsmer (USA)/Jo Crevier (USA)/* Al Unser, Jr. (USA)	Ferrari 365GTB/4 Daytona	Jo Crevier	9 DNF	45	IMSA GTO
69	10	Carlo Facetti (I)/* Martino Finotto (I)	Ferrari 308GTB	Carma FF	4 DNF	6	IMSA GTX
DNS	88	Herb Adams (USA)/Jerry Thompson (USA)/Don Sherman (USA)	Chevrolet Camaro (Riggins)	Herb Adams	0	46	IMSA GTO
DNS	05	Tico Almeida (USA)/Rene Rodriguez (USA)/Fred Flaquer (USA)	Porsche 911 Carrera	Almeida/Rodriguez	0	51	IMSA GTO

24 Hour Pepsi Challenge

January 30-31, 1982

24 hour event on the 3.840 mile circuit.
Distance covered: 719 laps for 2760.960 miles.
Winning time: 24 hours, 3 minutes, 5.301 seconds for a speed of 114.794 mph.
Margin of victory: 9 laps.
Fastest lap: #86 Porsche 935-80 (Hurley Haywood), 1:49.8, 125.902 mph.
Fastest qualifier: #9 March-Chevrolet 82G (Bobby Rahal), 1:43.891, 133.063 mph.

FIN.	CAR NO.	DRIVERS	CAR	ENTRANT	LAPS	START	CLASS
1	**18**	**John Paul, Sr. (USA)/Rolf Stommelen (D)/John Paul, Jr. (USA)**	**Porsche 935JLP-3 (Gaaco)**	**John Paul, Sr.**	**719**	**5**	**GTP**
2	5	Bob Akin (USA)/Craig Siebert (USA)/Derek Bell (GB)	Porsche 935K3-80 (Kremer)	Bob Akin	708	7	GTP
3	46	Mauricio de Narvaez (CO)/Bob Garretson (USA)/Jeff Wood (USA)	Porsche 935K3 (Kremer)	Bob Garretson	683	12	GTP
4	**77**	**Yoshimi Katayama (J)/Takashi Yorino (J)/Yojiro Terada (J)**	**Mazda RX-7**	**Mazda USA**	**644**	**20**	**GTO**
5	05	Ernesto Soto (YV)/Rene Rodriguez (USA)/Tico Almeida (USA)	Porsche 911 Carrera RSR	Almeida/Rodriguez	642	24	GTO
6	**98**	**Kathy Rude (USA)/Lee Mueller (USA)/Allan Moffat (AUS)**	**Mazda RX-7**	**Dave Kent**	**640**	**45**	**GTU**
7	92	Jim Mullen (USA)/Walt Bohren (USA)/Ron Grable (USA)	Mazda RX-7	Dave Kent	632	29	GTU
8	26	Tom Nehl (USA)/Tommy Riggins (USA)/Nelson Silcox (USA)	Chevrolet Camaro (Riggins)	Tom Nehl	626	16	GTP
9	24	Jack Refenning (USA)/Ren Tilton (USA)/Rusty Bond (USA)	Porsche 934	Peter Uria	618	21	GTP
10	38	Roger Mandeville (USA)/Amos Johnson (USA)/Jeff Kline (USA)	Mazda RX-7	Roger Mandeville	615	35	GTU
11	36	Paul Miller (USA)/Pat Bedard (USA)/Juergen Barth (D)	Porsche 924 Carrera	Herman/Miller	608	54	GTO
12	37	Dick Neland (USA)/Ed Kuhel (USA)/Nort Northam (USA)	Chevrolet Camaro	Kendco	602	31	GTO
13	86	Hurley Haywood (USA)/Bruce Leven (USA)/Al Holbert (USA)	Porsche 935-80	Bruce Leven	598	4	GTP
14	63	Tom Waugh (USA)/Jim Downing (USA)/John Maffucci (USA)	Mazda RX-7	Jim Downing	590	36	GTU
15	57	Doug Carmean (USA)/John O'Steen (USA)/Ed Pimm (USA)	Mazda RX-7	Jim Trueman	584	42	GTU
16	35	Marion L. Speer (USA)/Ray Ratcliff (USA)/Terry Wolters (USA)	Porsche 911 Carrera RSR	Marion L. Speer	583	37	GTO
17	01	John Morton (USA)/Tom Klausler (USA)	Ford Mustang	Marketing Corporation	569	23	GTO
18	66	Jack Dunham (USA)/Scott Smith, Jr. (USA)/Scott Smith, Sr. (USA)	Mazda RX-7	Jack Dunham	562 DNF	41	GTU
19	58	Doc Bundy (USA)/Jim Busby (USA)/Manfred Schurti (FL)	Porsche 924 Carrera	Brumos Porsche	558	26	GTO
20	88	Bob Beasley (USA)/George Stone (USA)/Jack Lewis (USA)	Porsche 911 Carrera RSR	Bob Beasley	558	39	GTO
21	44	Bob Tullius (USA)/Bill Adam (CDN)/Gordon Smiley (USA)	Jaguar XJS	Bob Tullius	533	59	GTP
22	72	Jean Kjoller (USA)/Bob Nikel (USA)/Grady Clay (USA)	Porsche 911 Carrera RSR	Carrera Motorsports	529	66	GTO
23	6	Bob Wollek (F)/Edgar Doeren (D)/Randy Lanier (USA)	Ferrari 512BB	Luigi Chinetti, Sr.	523 DNF	15	GTP

FIN.	CAR NO.	DRIVERS	CAR	ENTRANT	LAPS	START	CLASS
24	9	Bobby Rahal (USA)/Bruce Canepa (USA)/Jim Trueman (USA)	March-Chevrolet 82G	Bob Garretson	514 DNF	1	GTP
25	78	Scott Flanders (USA)/Klaus Bitterauf (USA)/Vicki Smith (USA)	Porsche 911	Klaus Bitterauf	511	50	GTU
26	54	Tony Garcia (USA)/Albert Naon (USA)/Rob McFarlin (USA)	BMW M1	Montura Racing	475	18	GTO
27	50	Diego Febles (PR)/Tato Ferrer (PR)/Chiqui Soldevila (PR)	Porsche 911 Carrera RSR	Diego Febles	464	30	GTO
28	80	Leonard Emanuelson (USA)/Roger Mears (USA)/Herb Adams (USA)	Pontiac Firebird	Herb Adams	435	69	GTO
29	84	Francisco Miguel (ES)/Eduardo Barrientos (ES)/Eduardo Galdamez (ES)	Porsche 934	Enrique Molins	420 DNF	71	GTO
30	4	Bob Raub (USA)/Bob Leitzinger (USA)/Art Pasmas (USA)	Pontiac Firebird (Oftedahl)	Gordon Oftedahl	420	19	GTO
31	3	Danny Sullivan (USA)/Gary Belcher (USA)/Hubert Phipps (USA)	Rondeau Ford-Cosworth M382	Gary Belcher	408 DNF	14	GTP
32	65	Rick Knoop (USA)/Carson Baird (USA)/Tom Pumpelly (USA)	Ferrari 512BB	Ron Spangler	377 DNF	51	GTP
33	51	Tom Juckette (USA)/Mike Meldeau (USA)/Bill McDill (USA) * Carl Shafer (USA)	Chevrolet Camaro	Mike Meldeau	351	64	GTP
34	62	William Koll (USA)/Irv Hoerr (USA)/Skeeter McKitterick (USA)	Rondeau Ford-Cosworth M382	William Koll	338 DNF	13	GTP
35	30	Russell Long (USA)/Craig Case (USA)/Ron Case (USA)	Porsche 911	Ron Case	332	47	GTU
36	02	John Bauer (USA)/Gary Pratt (USA)/Milt Minter (USA)	Ford Mustang	Marketing Corporation	321 DNF	72	GTO
37	20	Ron Hunter (USA)/Richard Turner (USA)/Duane Eitel (USA)	Mercury Capri	AutoWest	304	55	GTO
38	44	Billy Hagan (USA)/Terry Labonte (USA)/Gene Felton (USA)	Chevrolet Camaro (Frings)	Billy Hagan	295 DNF	32	GTP
39	29	David Heinz (USA)/Peter Kirill (USA)/Hoyt Overbagh (USA)	Chevrolet Monza (Rickets)	Hoyt Overbagh	276	34	GTO
40	21	Jo Crevier (USA)/Fred Stiff (USA)/Denny Wilson (USA) * Nort Northam (USA)	BMW M1	Jo Crevier	267 DNF	28	GTO
41	42	Gary Wonzer (USA)/Bill Bean (USA)/Chuck Grantham (USA)	Porsche 911	Gary Wonzer	261	46	GTU
42	23	Dick Davenport (USA)/Frank Carney (USA)/John McComb (USA)	Datsun 280ZX	Frank Carney	247 DNF	38	GTU
43	34	George Drolsom (USA)/Bill Johnson (USA)/Werner Frank (USA)	Porsche 924 Carrera	George Drolsom	238	58	GTO
44	10	Carl Shafer (USA)/Joe Mooney (USA)/Tony Brassfield (USA)	Chevrolet Camaro (Oftedahl)	Gordon Oftedahl	231 DNF	52	GTP
45	09	Preston Henn (USA)/Desire Wilson (ZA)/Marty Hinze (USA)	Porsche 935K3 (Kremer)	Preston Henn	229 DNF	6	GTP
46	49	Jerry Jolly (USA)/Bob Copeman (USA)/Tom Alan Marx (USA)	Porsche 911 Carrera RSR	Bob Copeman	220 DNF	63	GTO
47	83	Harro Zitza (USA)/John Belperche (USA)/Doug Zitza (USA)	Porsche 914/6	Harro Zitza	213 DNF	70	GTU
48	13	Anatoly Arutunoff (USA)/Jose Marina (USA)	Lancia Stratos	Anatoly Arutunoff	209 DNF	61	GTU
49	27	Jim Fowells (USA)/Ray Mummery (USA)/John Carusso (USA)	Mazda RX-7	Jim Fowells	168 DNF	49	GTU
50	43	Bob Young (USA)/Bob Gregg (USA)/Ray McIntyre (USA)	Porsche 911 Carrera RSR	Bob Gregg	161 DNF	40	GTO
51	7	Ralph Kent Cooke (USA)/Eppie Wietzes (CDN)/Jim Adams (USA)	Lola-Chevrolet T600	Ralph Kent Cooke	138 DNF	8	GTP
52	67	Les Delano (USA)/Andy Petery (USA)/Jeremy Nightingale (GB)	American Motors Spirit	Amos Johnson	137 DNF	33	GTO
53	70	Larry Chmura (USA)/Jim Schofield (USA)/Brent Regan (USA)	Chevron-Mazda GTP	Genesis Racing	119	56	GTP
54	08	Alan Howes (USA)/Paul Nacthwey (USA)/Oliver Jones (USA)	Porsche 911	Portia Parlor	103 DNF	73	GTU
55	75	Dale Kreider (USA)/Keith Swope (USA)/Peter Knab (USA)	Chevrolet Corvette	Dale Kreider	101 DNF	27	GTO
56	07	Ludwig Heimrath, Jr. (CDN)/Ludwig Heimrath (CDN)	Porsche 924 Carrera	Ludwig Heimrath	91 DNF	25	GTO
57	60	Guy W. Church (USA)/Tom Alan Marx (USA)/* Bob Lee (USA)	American Motors AMX	Bob Lee	91 DNF	57	GTO
58	15	Dave Panaccione (USA)/Chip Mead (USA)/John Graham (CDN)	Porsche 911 Carrera RSR	Doug Lutz	71 DNF	62	GTO
59	73	Clark Howey (USA)/Dale Koch (USA)/Tracy Wolf (USA)	Chevrolet Camaro	Tracy Wolf	70 DNF	67	GTO
60	25	David Cowart (USA)/Kenper Miller (USA)/* Charles Mendez (USA)	March-BMW 82G	David Cowart	68 DNF	11	GTP
61	2	John Fitzpatrick (GB)/* David Hobbs (GB)/* Wayne Baker (USA)	Porsche 935K4 (Kremer)	John Fitzpatrick	59 DNF	2	GTP
62	0	Ted Field (USA)/* Danny Ongais (USA)/* Bill Whittington (USA)	Porsche 935K3-80 (Kremer)	Ted Field	55 DNF	9	GTP
63	89	Gary English (USA)/* Jerry Thompson (USA)/* David Price (USA)	Chevrolet Camaro (Riggins)	Herb Adams	42 DNF	44	GTO
64	87	Armando Ramirez (USA)/Steve Cook (USA)/Bill Cooper (USA)	Mazda RX-7	Ralph Sanchez	26 DNF	48	GTU
65	79	Bob Bergstrom (USA)/* Tom Winters (USA)/* Robert Overby (USA)	Porsche 924 Carrera	Paul Gentilozzi	12 DNF	22	GTO
66	41	Rusty Schmidt (USA)/Scott Schmidt (USA)/Kerry Hitt (USA)	Chevrolet Corvette	Starved Rock Lodge	9 DNF	43	GTO
67	52	Jack Swanson (USA)/* Fred Snow (USA)/* Tom Cripe (USA)	Porsche 911	Ours & Hours Racing	2 DNF	65	GTU
68	11	Dennis Aase (USA)/* Chuck Kendall (USA)/* John Hotchkis, Sr. (USA)	BMW M1	Chuck Kendall	1 DNF	17	GTO
69	47	Bernard de Dryver (B)/* Tom Davis (USA)	Ferrari 512BB	Tom Davis	1 DNF	53	GTP
DNS	00	Bill Whittington (USA)/Ted Field (USA)	Porsche 935K3-80 (Kremer)	Ted Field	0	3	GTP
DNS	8	John Paul, Sr. (USA)	Porsche 935JLP-2 (Kremer)	John Paul, Sr.	0	10	GTP
DNS	53	Francisco Miguel (ES)/Guillermo Valiente (ES)/Wenseslao Kreysa (ES)	BMW CSL	Nemtex	0	60	GTP
DNS	74	Del Russo Taylor (USA)/Bob Arego (USA)/Wayne Dassinger (USA)	Chevron-Buick GTP	Mark Wagoner	0	68	GTP

24 Hour Pepsi Challenge

February 1-2, 1983

24 hour event on the 3.840 mile circuit.
Distance covered: 618 laps for 2373.120 miles.
Winning time: 24 hours, 1 minute, 27.025 seconds for a speed of 98.781 mph.
Margin of victory: 6 laps.
Fastest lap: #6 Porsche 935L (Bob Wollek), 1:49.22, 126.570 mph.
Fastest qualifier: #6 Porsche 935L (Bob Wollek), 1:42.155, 135.324 mph.
Race red flagged for 53 min, 46.6 sec because of rain, time included in total.
8 full-course cautions for 130 minutes.

FIN.	CAR NO.	DRIVERS	CAR	ENTRANT	LAPS	START	CLASS
1	**6**	**Bob Wollek (F)/Claude Ballot-Lena (F)/Preston Henn (USA) A.J. Foyt (USA)**	**Porsche 935L (Andial)**	**Preston Henn**	**618**	**1**	**GTP**
2	88	Terry Wolters (USA)/Randy Lanier (USA)/Marty Hinze (USA)	March-Chevrolet 82G	Marty Hinze	612	15	GTP
3	**7**	**Pete Halsmer (USA)/Bob Reed (USA)/Rick Knoop (USA)**	**Mazda RX-7**	**Mederer/Oku**	**598**	**24**	**GTO**
4	24	Marion L. Speer (USA)/Ken Madren (USA)/Ray Ratcliff (USA)	Porsche 935JLP-2 (Kremer)	Marion L. Speer	578	16	GTP
5	50	Diego Febles (PR)/Kikos Fonseca (CR)/Roy Valverde (CR)	Porsche 911 Carrera RSR	Diego Febles	568	58	GTO
6	10	Ralph Kent Cooke (USA)/Jim Adams (USA)/John Bright (GB)	Lola-Chevrolet T600	Ralph Kent Cooke	563	6	GTP
7	05	Tico Almeida (USA)/Miguel Morejon (USA)/Ernesto Soto (YV)	Porsche 911 Carrera RSR	Almeida/Rodriguez	561	36	GTO
8	77	Walt Bohren (USA)/Pierre Honegger (USA)/David Palmer (GB)	Mazda GTP (Rosemont)	Pierre Honegger	553	32	GTP
9	9	Wayne Baker (USA)/Jim Mullen (USA)/Bob Garretson (USA)	Porsche 934	Wayne Baker	551	52	GTO
10	35	Paul Gilgan (USA)/Al Leon (USA)/Wayne Pickering (USA)	Porsche 911 Carrera RSR	Marion L. Speer	547	56	GTO
11	47	Frank Rubino (USA)/Pepe Romero (USA)/Doc Bundy (USA) Dale Whittington (USA)	Porsche 935	Frank Rubino	546	3	GTP
12	**92**	**Lee Mueller (USA)/Hugh McDonough (USA)/Terry Visger (USA)**	**Mazda RX-7**	**Dave Kent**	**544**	**34**	**GTU**
13	58	Kathy Rude (USA)/Deborah Gregg (USA)/Bonnie Henn (USA)	Porsche 924 Carrera	Brumos Porsche	531	35	GTO
14	90	Mike H. Schaefer (USA)/Jack Refenning (USA)/John Belperche (USA) Doug Zitza (USA)	Porsche 911	Peter Uria	525	70	GTU
15	61	Brent O'Neill (USA)/Don Courtney (USA)/Luis Sereix (USA)	Chevrolet Monza (Baird & Trivette)	Vista Racing	525	31	GTO
16	86	Hurley Haywood (USA)/Bruce Leven (USA)/Al Holbert (USA)	Porsche 935-80	Bruce Leven	515 DNF	5	GTP
17	60	Steve Dietrich (USA)/Chris Ivey (USA)/Jim Cook (USA)	Mazda RX-7	Tommy Morrison	514	67	GTU
18	85	Richard Lloyd (GB)/George Drolsom (USA)/Jonathan Palmer (GB)	Porsche 924 Carrera	Richard Lloyd	500	29	GTO
19	38	Roger Mandeville (USA)/Amos Johnson (USA)/Danny Smith (USA)	Mazda RX-7	Roger Mandeville	476	79	GTU
20	4	Billy Hagan (USA)/Terry Labonte (USA)/Lloyd Frink (USA)	Chevrolet Camaro (Frings)	Billy Hagan	467	10	GTO
21	63	Jim Downing (USA)/John Maffucci (USA)/Steve Potter (USA)	Mazda RX-7	Jim Downing	466	42	GTU
22	29	Robert Overby (USA)/Chris Doyle (USA)/Don Bell (USA)	Chevrolet Camaro	Robert Overby	438	40	GTO
23	37	Tom Burdsall (USA)/Peter Welter (USA)/Al Bacon (USA)	Mazda RX-7	Burdsall/Welter	436	60	GTU
24	26	Tom Nehl (USA)/Nelson Silcox (USA)/Richard J. Valentine (USA)	Chevrolet Camaro (Riggins)	Tom Nehl	426 DNF	20	GTO
25	1	John Paul, Jr. (USA)/Rene Rodriguez (USA)/Joe Castellano (USA)	Porsche 935JLP-4 (Fabcar)	John Paul, Sr.	412 DNF	2	GTP
26	13	Duane Eitel (USA)/Mike Brummer (USA)/Phillip Pate (USA)	Pontiac Firebird (Oftedahl)	Gordon Oftedahl	411 DNF	18	GTO
27	28	Herb Adams (USA)/John Martin (USA)/Joe Ruttman (USA) Leonard Emanuelson (USA)/* Mike Meldeau (USA)	Avanti II (Dillon)	Avanti	410	14	GTO
28	40	Uli Bieri (CDN)/Matt Gysler (CDN)/Duff Hubbard (USA)	BMW M1	Uli Bieri	406	33	GTO
29	97	Wally Dallenbach, Jr. (USA)/Willy T. Ribbs (USA)/Whitney Ganz (USA)	Toyota Celica	Dan Gurney	365	63	GTU
30	75	Bard Boand (USA)/Richard Anderson (USA)/Mike Stephens (USA)	Chevrolet Corvette	Bard Boand	358	38	GTO
31	83	Michael Gassaway (USA)/Scott Smith, Sr. (USA)/Joe Cogbill, Sr. (USA) Joe Cogbill, Jr. (USA)	Chevrolet Camaro	Thomas T. Ciccone	357 DNF	65	GTP
32	52	Tom Cripe (USA)/Dick Gauthier (USA)/David Duncan (USA) Jack Swanson (USA)	Porsche 911	TFC Racing	312	76	GTU
33	71	Charles Morgan (USA)/Bill Johnson (USA)/Jim Miller (USA)	Datsun 280ZX	Charles Morgan	305 DNF	61	GTU
34	27	Jim Fowells (USA)/Ray Mummery (USA)/Tom Sheehy (USA)	Mazda RX-7	Jim Fowells	300 DNF	69	GTU
35	78	Klaus Bitterauf (USA)/Vicki Smith (USA)/Scott Flanders (USA)	Porsche 911	Klaus Bitterauf	299 DNF	75	GTU
36	65	Carson Baird (USA)/Chip Mead (USA)/Tom Pumpelly (USA)	Ferrari 512BB	Ron Spangler	294 DNF	21	GTP
37	23	Raul Garcia (USA)/Vince DiLella (USA)/Armando Fernandez (USA)	Chevrolet Camaro (Superior)	Raul Garcia	285 DNF	81	GTO
38	01	John Morton (USA)/Tom Klausler (USA)/Ronnie Bucknum (USA)	Ford Mustang	Marketing Corporation	284	49	GTO
39	72	Gary Baker (USA)/Sterling Marlin (USA)	Chevrolet Corvette	John Josey	284 DNF	77	GTO
40	41	Rusty Schmidt (USA)/Scott Schmidt (USA)	Chevrolet Corvette	Starved Rock Lodge	263	37	GTO
41	49	Hoyt Overbagh (USA)/Peter Kirill (USA)/David Price (USA)	Chevrolet Monza (Rickets)	Hoyt Overbagh	243	50	GTO
42	66	Jack Dunham (USA)/Jeff Kline (USA)/Jon Compton (USA)	Mazda RX-7	Dunham/Meyer	242 DNF	43	GTU
43	45	Gene Felton (USA)/Tom Williams (USA)/Lloyd Frink (USA)	Chevrolet Camaro (Frings)	Billy Hagan	223 DNF	9	GTO
44	21	Lyn St. James (USA)/John Graham (CDN)/Drake Olson (ZA)	Nimrod-Aston Martin C2	Nimrod	208 DNF	12	GTP
45	79	Tom Winters (USA)/Bob Bergstrom (USA)/Peter Dawe (USA)	Porsche 924 Carrera	Paul Gentilozzi	193 DNF	62	GTO
46	55	Diego Montoya (CO)/Terry Herman (USA)/Tony Garcia (USA)	BMW M1	B de T Racing	172 DNF	25	GTO
47	14	Bob Raub (USA)/Sam Moses (USA)/Carl Shafer (USA)	Pontiac Firebird (Oftedahl	Gordon Oftedahl	165 DNF	17	GTO
48	16	Paul Goral (USA)/Larry Figaro (USA)/Nort Northam (USA)	Porsche 911	Paul Goral	161 DNF	80	GTU
49	74	Del Russo Taylor (USA)/Mike Angus (USA)/Wayne Dassinger (USA)	Chevron-Buick GTP	Mark Wagoner	152 DNF	48	GTP

SunBank 24 At Daytona

FEBRUARY 1-2. 1986

24 hour event on the 3.560 mile circuit.

Distance covered: 712 laps for 2534.720 miles.

Winning time: 24 hours, 1 minute, 45.8 seconds for a speed of 105.484 mph.

Margin of victory: 1:49.150.

Fastest lap: #45 March-Buick 85G Hawk (John Paul Jr.) 1:42.519, 125.011 mph.

Fastest qualifier: #52 Chevrolet T710 Corvette GTP (Sarel van der Merwe) 1:39.318, 129.040 mph.

5 full-course cautions for 24 laps.

FIN.	CAR NO.	DRIVERS	CAR	ENTRANT	LAPS	START	CLASS
1	**14**	**Al Holbert (USA)/Derek Bell (GB)/Al Unser, Jr. (USA)**	**Porsche 962**	**Al Holbert**	**712**	**9**	**GTP**
2	8	A. J. Foyt (USA)/Arie Luyendyk (NL)/Danny Sullivan (USA)/ Preston Henn (USA)	Porsche 962	Preston Henn	712	14	GTP
3	67	Derek Warwick (GB)/Darin Brassfield (USA)/Jim Busby (USA)/ Jochen Mass (D)	Porsche 962	Jim Busby	711	6	GTP
4	**64**	**Lee Mueller (USA)/Maurice Hassey (USA)/Lanny Hester (USA)**	**Ford Mustang (Roush)**	**Raintree Corporation**	**622**	**35**	**GTO**
5	07	Scott Pruett (USA)/Bruce Jenner (USA)/Klaus Ludwig (D)	Ford Mustang (Roush)	Jack Roush	614	17	GTO
6	44	Bob Tullius (USA)/Claude Ballot-Lena (F)/Chip Robinson (USA)	Jaguar XJR-7 (Fabcar)	Bob Tullius	607	10	GTP
7	**13**	**Frank Rubino (USA)/Ray Mummery (USA)/John Schneider (USA)**	**Argo-Mazda JM19**	**Frank Rubino**	**600**	**45**	**GTL**
8	**71**	**Amos Johnson (USA)/Dennis Shaw (USA)/Jack Dunham (USA)**	**Mazda RX-7 (Highball)**	**Amos Johnson**	**597**	**51**	**GTU**
9	35	Armando Gonzalez (PR)/Ernesto Soto (YV)/Basilio Davila (PR)	Royale-Porsche RP40	Diman Racing	579	63	GTL
10	75	Bob Reed (USA)/Tommy Kendall (USA)/John Hogdal (USA)	Mazda RX-7 (Fabcar)	Clayton Cunningham	563 DNF	50	GTU
11	32	Bob Leitzinger (USA)/Mike Carder (USA)/Louis Baldwin/ Steve Alexander (USA) (USA)	Nissan 280ZX	George Alderman	537	59	GTU
12	68	Jan Lammers (NL)/John Morton (USA)/Derek Warwick (GB)	Porsche 962	Jim Busby	512 DNF	7	GTP
13	34	Kikos Fonseca (CR)/Luis Mendez (DR)/Enrique Molins (ES)	Porsche 934	Latino Racing	512	66	GTO
14	27	David Cowart (USA)/Kenper Miller (USA)/Jim Fowells (USA)	Argo-Mazda JM19	Jim Fowells	511	68	GTL
15	76	Nort Northam (USA)/Greg Walker (USA)/Craig A. Rubright (USA)	Chevrolet Corvette (Linderfer)	Greg Walker	506 DNF	43	GTO
16	98	Dennis Aase (USA)/Chris Cord (USA)	Toyota Celica (AAR)	Dan Gurney	489	22	GTO
17	93	Ron Pawley (USA)/Don Marsh (USA)/Kelly Marsh (USA)	Argo-Mazda JM16	Don Marsh	482 DNF	41	GTL
18	17	Al Bacon (USA)/Bill Scott (USA)/Dennis Krueger (USA)	Mazda RX-7 (Chassis Dynamics)	Al Bacon	482	54	GTU
19	66	Jim Rothbarth (USA)/Jeff Kline (USA)/Mike Meyer (USA)	Argo-Mazda JM16	Mike Meyer	477 DNF	33	GTL
20	55	David Heinz (USA)/Steve Zwiren (USA)/Don Yenko (USA)/ Jerry Thompson (USA)	Chevrolet Corvette (Dillon)	David Heinz	472	36	GTO
21	02	Richard Stevens (CDN)/Luis Sereix (USA)/Roy Newsome (USA)/ Dale Kreider (USA)	Mazda RX-7 (MAT)	Roy Newsome	453 DNF	62	GTU
22	47	Steve Millen (NZ)/Elliott Forbes-Robinson (USA)/Tommy Riggins (USA)	Pontiac Firebird (Bemco)	Billy Dingman	438	18	GTO
23	72	Bob Bergstrom (USA)/Gene Felton (USA)/Paul Gentilozzi (USA)	Oldsmobile Toronado (Rocketsports)	Paul Gentilozzi	434 DNF	25	GTO
24	04	Brian Redman (GB)/Vern Schuppan (AUS)/Hurley Haywood (USA)	Jaguar XJR-7 (Fabcar)	Bob Tullius	430 DNF	13	GTP
25	01	Don Bell (USA)/Terry Wolters (USA)/Craig Carter (USA)	Royale-Buick RP40	AT&T	406 DNF	31	GTL
26	00	Jim Adams (USA)/Costas Los (GR)/John Hotchkis, Sr. (USA)	March-Porsche 83G	John Hotchkis, Sr.	402 DNF	20	GTP
27	62	Tim CoConis (USA)/Fernando Robles (DR)/Chris Marte (DR)	Ford Mustang (Roush)	Jack Roush	368 DNF	29	GTO
28	88	Jack Baldwin (USA)/Bob McConnell (USA)/Tommy Morrison (USA)/ Don Knowles (USA)/* Bobby Carradine (USA)	Chevrolet Corvette	Tommy Morrison	365 DNF	48	GTO
29	82	Bill Wessel (USA)/Mark Kennedy (USA)/Dave Fuller (USA)/ Karl Keck (USA)	Chevrolet Corvette (Pratt)	Karl Keck	340	39	GTP
30	87	Ron Grable (USA)/Don Knowles (USA)/John Heinricy (USA)/ Bobby Carradine (USA)	Chevrolet Corvette	Tommy Morrison	331 DNF	46	GTO
31	29	Oma Kimbrough (USA)/Chris Gennone (USA)/ Hoyt Overbagh (USA)/ Peter Baljet (CDN)	Chevrolet Camaro (Stock Car Products)	Hoyt Overbagh	328 DNF	57	GTO
32	16	Drake Olson (ZA)/Price Cobb (USA)/Rob Dyson (USA)	Porsche 962	Rob Dyson	320 DNF	3	GTP
33	45	John Paul, Jr. (USA)/Chip Ganassi (USA)/Ivan Capelli (I)/ Whitney Ganz (USA)	March-Buick 85G Hawk	Phil Conte	310 DNF	11	GTP
34	83	Paul Reisman (USA)/Bob Hebert (USA)/Tom Gaffney (USA)/ Richard Stone (USA)	Pontiac Firebird (Watson)	Charlie Gibson	296 DNF	53	GTO
35	80	Martino Finotto (I)/Ruggero Melgrati (I)/Almo Coppelli (I)	Alba-Ferrari AR6	Carma FF	291 DNF	23	GTL
36	30	Buz McCall (USA)/Pancho Carter (USA)/Jim Mueller (USA)/ Tom Sheehy (USA)	Chevrolet Camaro (Timmons)	Buz McCall	285 DNF	49	GTO
37	6	Charles Morgan (USA)/Logan Blackburn (USA)/David Simpson (USA)	Tiga-Buick GTP286	Charles Morgan	279 DNF	30	GTL
38	33	Bard Boand (USA)/Richard Anderson (USA)/Mike Allen (USA)	Lola-Chevrolet T600	Bard Boand	266 DNF	21	GTP
39	99	David Andrews (GB)/Steve Phillips (USA)/Duncan Bain (GB)	Tiga-Ford GT285	Roy Baker	244 DNF	70	GTP
40	50	Bill Elliott (USA)/Ricky Rudd (USA)/Kyle Petty (USA)/ Ken Schraeder (USA)	Ford Mustang (Roush)	Jack Roush	240 DNF	24	GTO
41	56	Diego Montoya (CO)/Albert Naon, Jr. (USA)/Carlos Migoya (USA)	Pontiac Firebird	Ricardo Londono	238 DNF	61	GTO
42	38	Roger Mandeville (USA)/Danny Smith (USA)/Diego Febles (PR)	Mazda RX-7 (MAT)	Roger Mandeville	229 DNF	47	GTU
43	78	Peter Uria (USA)/Larry Figaro (USA)/Jack Refenning (USA)	Porsche 911 Carrera RSR	Peter Uria	203 DNF	60	GTU
44	26	Ken Bupp (USA)/John Hayes-Harlow (GB)/Del Russo Taylor (USA)	Pontiac Firebird (Python)	Walter Johnston	195 DNF	44	GTO
45	63	Jim Downing (USA)/John O'Steen (USA)/John Maffucci (USA)	Argo-Mazda JM19	Jim Downing	184 DNF	69	GTL
46	3	Thierry Boutsen (B)/Oscar Larrauri (RA)/* Massimo Sigala (I)	Porsche 962	Walter Brun	176 DNF	8	GTP
47	9	Michael Brockman (USA)/Steve Durst (USA)/Deborah Gregg (USA)/ Jim Trueman (USA)	Tiga-Mazda GTP285	Bobby Rinzler	156 DNF	28	GTL
48	77	Leo Franchi (USA)/Steve Gentile (USA)/Rick Knoop (USA)/ * Jack Newsum (USA)	Ford Thunderbird	Brooks Fryberger	150 DNF	42	GTO
49	10	Jim Leeward (USA)/Bill Adam (CDN)/Chip Mead (USA)	March-Chevrolet 82G	Jim Leeward	123 DNF	16	GTP

FINISH	CAR NO.	DRIVERS	CAR	ENTRANT	LAPS	START	CLASS
50	2	Al Leon (USA)/Jim Fitzgerald (USA)/Harald Grohs (D)/ * Art Leon (USA)	March-Porsche 85G	Leon Brothers	117 DNF	15	GTP
51	54	Karl Durkheimer (USA)/Gary Auberlen (USA)/Cary Eisenlohr (USA)/ Peter Jauker (USA)	Porsche 911	Gary Auberlen	117 DNF	67	GTU
52	86	Bob Wollek (F)/Derek Daly (IRL)/Bruce Leven (USA)	Porsche 962 (Holbert)	Bruce Leven	116 DNF	2	GTP
53	4	Lew Price (USA)/Jim Mullen (USA)/Matt Whetstine (USA)	Chevrolet Corvette GTP-T711 (Lola)	Lew Price	104 DNF	19	
54	89	Tom Hunt (USA)/Jim Shelton (USA)/Paul Romano (USA)/ * Russ Boy (USA)	Mazda RX-7	Tom Hunt	85 DNF	64	GTU
55	06	Miguel Morejon (USA)/Joe Varde (USA)/Tico Almeida (USA)	Porsche 935J (Joest)	Bill McDill	83 DNF	38	GTP
56	43	Steve Cohen (USA)/David Christian (USA)/Tom Congleton (USA)	BMW M1	Global Racing	68 DNF	32	GTO
57	90	Les Delano (USA)/Andy Petery (USA)	Pontiac Firebird (Riggins)	Road Circuit Technology	67 DNF	34	GTO
58	37	Peter Welter (USA)/Roy Newsome (USA)/Tom Burdsall (USA)	Tiga-Mazda GT285	Burdsall/Newsome	66 DNF	37	GTL
59	36	Dave Panaccione (USA)/* Ron Case (USA)	Porsche 924	Ron Case	65 DNF	56	GTU
60	11	Paul Lewis (USA)/* Chuck Kendall (USA)/* Tommy Kendall (USA)/ * Max Jones (USA)	Lola-Mazda T616	Chuck Kendall	48 DNF	58	GTL
61	25	Robert Peters (CDN)/* Kent Painter (USA)/* Tom Nehl (USA)/ * Scott Gaylord (USA)	Chevrolet Camaro (Riggins)	Lucas Truck Service	37 DNF	55	GTO
62	5	Hans-Joachim Stuck, Jr. (D)/* Bob Akin (USA)/* Jo Gartner (A)	Porsche 962	Bob Akin	29 DNF	5	GTP
63	46	Whitney Ganz (USA)/Ken Madren (USA)/* Bob Lobenberg (USA)	March-Buick 85G Hawk	Phil Conte	27 DNF	12	GTP
64	0	Paolo Barilla (I)/* Randy Lanier (USA)/* Gianpiero Moretti (I)	Porsche 962	Reinhold Joest	6 DNF	4	GTP
65	92	Ash Tisdelle (USA)/* Lance Van Every (USA)/* Rusty Bond (USA)	Chevrolet Camaro (Riggins)	Lance Van Every	6 DNF	40	GTO
66	28	Terry Labonte (USA)/* Harry Gant (USA)/* Phil Parsons (USA)	Oldsmobile Calais (Powell)	Texas Enterprises	3 DNF	26	GTO
DNS	52	Sarel van der Merwe (ZA)/Doc Bundy (USA)/Wally Dallenbach, Jr. (USA)	Chevrolet Corvette GTP-T710 (Lola)	Rick Hendrick	0	1	GTP
DNS	48	Don Walker (USA)/Brian Goellnicht (USA)/Charles Monk (CDN)	March-Chevrolet 85G	Don Walker	0	27	GTP
DNS	74	Bill McDill (USA)/Richard McDill (USA)/Tom Juckette (USA)	Chevrolet Camaro (Dillon)	Bill McDill	0	52	GTO
DNS	57	Reed Kryder (USA)/Tom Palmer (USA)/Fred Staffilino (USA)/ Rod Whelan (USA)	Nissan 280ZX (Kryderacing)	Reed Kryder	0	65	GTU

SunBank 24 At Daytona

February 1-2, 1987

24 hour event on the 3.560 mile circuit.

Distance covered: 753 laps for 2680.680 miles.

Winning time: 24 hours, 1 minute, 14.67 seconds for a speed of 111.599 mph.

Margin of victory: 8 laps.

Fastest lap: #3 Porsche 962 (Oscar Larrauri), 1:43.07, 124.343 mph.

Fastest qualifier: #86 Porsche 962 (Jochen Mass), 1:41.005, 126.885 mph.

2 full-course cautions for 11 laps.

FINISH	CAR NO.	DRIVERS	CAR	ENTRANT	LAPS	START	CLASS
1	**14**	**Chip Robinson (USA)/Derek Bell (GB)/Al Unser, Jr. (USA)/ Al Holbert (USA)**	**Porsche 962**	**Al Holbert**	**753**	**10**	**GTP**
2	3	Oscar Larrauri (RA)/Gianfranco Brancatelli (I)/Massimo Sigala (I)	Porsche 962	Walter Brun	745	9	GTP
3	16	Price Cobb (USA)/Rob Dyson (USA)/Vern Schuppan (AUS)	Porsche 962	Rob Dyson	742	4	GTP
4	1	A. J. Foyt (USA)/Al Unser, Sr. (USA)/Danny Sullivan (USA)	Porsche 962 (Holbert-Fabcar)	A. J. Foyt	723 DNF	8	GTP
5	10	John Hotchkis, Sr. (USA)/Jim Adams (USA)/John Hotchkis, Jr. (USA)	Porsche 962 (Holbert-Fabcar)	John Hotchkis, Sr.	719	5	GTP
6	5	Hans-Joachim Stuck, Jr. (D)/James Weaver (GB)/Bob Akin (USA)	Porsche 962	Bob Akin	700	12	GTP
7	**11**	**Tom Gloy (USA)/Bill Elliott (USA)/Lyn St. James (USA)/ Scott Pruett (USA)**	**Ford Mustang (Roush)**	**Jack Roush**	**685**	**18**	**GTO**
8	98	Chris Cord (USA)/Steve Millen (NZ)	Toyota Celica (AAR)	Dan Gurney	681	24	GTO
9	22	Deborah Gregg (USA)/Bobby Akin, Jr. (USA)/Scott Pruett (USA)/ Scott Goodyear (CDN)	Ford Mustang (Roush)	Jack Roush	649	66	GTO
10	**71**	**Amos Johnson (USA)/Dennis Shaw (USA)/Bob Lazier (USA)**	**Mazda RX-7 (Highball)**	**Amos Johnson**	**642**	**49**	**GTU**
11	**01**	**Bob Earl (USA)/Don Bell (USA)/Jeff Kline (USA)**	**Spice-Pontiac Fiero GTP**	**Spice Engineering**	**630**	**14**	**GTL**
12	42	Howard Cherry (USA)/John Higgins (USA)/James King (USA)/ Chip Mead (USA)	Fabcar-Porsche	John Higgins	626	42	GTL
13	82	Mike Mees (USA)/Dick Greer (USA)/John Finger (USA)	Mazda RX-7	Dick Greer	622	60	GTU
14	36	John Grooms (USA)/Tom Bagley (USA)/Frank Jellinek, Jr. (USA)/ Augie Pabst (USA)	Lola-Badger Mazda BB	Frank Jellinek, Jr.	621	40	GTL
15	30	Buz McCall (USA)/Walt Bohren (USA)/Paul Dallenbach (USA)	Chevrolet Camaro (Timmons)	Buz McCall	616	29	GTO
16	19	Jim Brown (USA)/Scott Schubot (USA)/Linda Ludemann (USA)	Tiga-Mazda GT285	Schubot/Ludemann	597	39	GTL
17	99	Ricky Rudd (USA)/Jerrill Rice (USA)/Juan Manuel Fangio II (RA)	Toyota Celica (AAR)	Dan Gurney.	591 DNF	25	GTO
18	09	Peter Uria (USA)/Larry Figaro (USA)/John Hayes-Harlow (GB)/ Kyle Rathbun (USA)	Porsche 911 Carrera RSR	Peter Uria	580	51	GTU
19	38	Roger Mandeville (USA)/Kelly Marsh (USA)/Danny Smith (USA)	Mazda RX-7 (Chassis Dynamics)	Roger Mandeville.	572	26	GTO
20	33	Bruce Jenner (USA)/Todd Morici (USA)/Gary Baker (USA)	Ford Mustang (Roush)	Jack Roush	571	26	GTO
21	27	David Cowart (USA)/Kenper Miller (USA)/Jim Fowells (USA)	Argo-Mazda JM19	Jim Fowells	566	67	GTL

FINISH	CAR NO.	DRIVERS	CAR	ENTRANT	LAPS	START	CLASS
22	66	Charles Morgan (USA)/Chris Gennone (USA)/Jim Rothbarth (USA)	Royale-Mazda RP40	RM Racing	554	32	GTL
23	75	Max Jones (USA)/Bart Kendall (USA)/Tommy Kendall (USA)	Mazda RX-7 (Fabcar)	Clayton Cunningham	522 DNF	44	GTU
24	21	Robert Peters (CDN)/Tom Nehl (USA)/Kent Painter (USA)	Chevrolet Camaro (Riggins)	Tom Nehl	520 DNF	53	GTO
25	20	Tom Juckette (USA)/Bill McDill (USA)/Mike Laws (USA)	Chevrolet Camaro (Dillon)	Bill McDill	520	41	GTO
26	26	Ken Bupp (USA)/Guy W. Church (USA)/Del Russo Taylor (USA)/ Mike Hackney (USA)	Pontiac Firebird (Python)	Bob Lee	510	52	GTO
27	68	Steve DePuyster (USA)/Mike Jocelyn (USA)/Jim Kurz (USA)/ Bob Schader (USA)	Mazda RX-7	Bob Schader	503	58	GTU
28	78	Dennis Chambers (USA)/Mike Meyer (USA)/Tom Burdsall (USA)	Mazda RX-7	Dennis Chambers	498	62	GTU
29	29	Gene Felton (USA)/Oma Kimbrough (USA)/Hoyt Overbagh (USA)/ Lee Perkinson (USA)	Chevrolet Camaro (Stock Car Products)	Hoyt Overbagh	470	34	GTO
30	00	Charles Slater (USA)/Ernie Senator (USA)/Davide Duttinger (USA)	Porsche 911 Carrera RSR	S Squared Engineering	414	61	GTU
31	28	Greg Pickett (USA)/Darrell Waltrip (USA)/Terry Labonte (USA)	Chevrolet Camaro (Protofab)	Protofab	410 DNF	15	GTO
32	96	Thomas Hessert (USA)/Keith Rinzler (USA)/Eduardo Dibos, Jr. (PE)	Tiga-Mazda GT287	Thomas Hessert	409 DNF	43	GTL
33	24	Craig A. Rubright (USA)/Garrett Jenkins (USA)/Roy Newsome (USA)	Chevrolet Corvette	Craig A. Rubright	404 DNF	55	GTO
34	6	Wally Dallenbach, Jr. (USA)/John Jones (CDN)/Tommy Riggins (USA)	Chevrolet Camaro (Protofab)	Protofab	402 DNF	19	GTO
35	47	Richard Oakley (USA)/Chaunce Wallace (USA)/Doug Mills (USA)	Mazda RX-7	Chaunce Wallace	386 DNF	68	GTU
36	51	Costas Los (GR)/John Schneider (USA)/David Andrews (GB)	Tiga Ford-Cosworth GC086	Roy Baker	354 DNF	59	GTP
37	63	Jim Downing (USA)/John O'Steen (USA)/John Maffucci (USA)	Argo-Mazda JM19	Jim Downing	352 DNF	30	GTL
38	32	Mark Kennedy (USA)/Karl Keck (USA)/Mark Montgomery (USA)/ Dave Fuller (USA)	Chevrolet Corvette (Pratt)	Karl Keck	346	46	GTO
39	87	Tommy Morrison (USA)/Richard Ceppos (USA)/Don Knowles (USA)/ Stuart Hayner (USA)	Chevrolet Corvette	Tommy Morrison	337 DNF	65	GTO
40	7	Whitney Ganz (USA)/David Hobbs (GB)/Gianpiero Moretti (I)	Ford Probe GTP (Zakspeed)	Zakowski/Moretti	328 DNF	11	GTP
41	83	Tom Gaffney (USA)/Paul Reisman (USA)/Richard Stone (USA)/ Bob Hebert (USA)	Pontiac Firebird (Watson)	Charlie Gibson	316	47	GTO
42	08	Vance Swifts (CDN)/John Drew (USA)/Dean Hall (USA)/ Paul Romano (USA)	Mazda RX-7	Simms/Romano	298	57	GTU
43	8	Brian Redman (GB)/Chris Kneifel (USA)/ Elliott Forbes-Robinson (USA)/ * Kees Nierop (CDN)	Porsche 962 (Holbert-Fabcar)	Primus Motorsports	283 DNF	6	GTP
44	90	Andy Petery (USA)/Les Delano (USA)/Craig Carter (USA)	Buick Somerset (Peerless)	Les Delano	281 DNF	23	GTO
45	17	Al Bacon (USA)/Rod Millen (NZ)/Bob Reed (USA)	Mazda RX-7 (Chassis Dynamics)	Al Bacon	277 DNF	48	GTU
46	89	Steve Durst (USA)/Michael Brockman (USA)/Tony Belcher (USA)/ Mark Abel (USA)	Spice-Pontiac Fiero GTP	Durst/Brockman	273 DNF	17	GTL
47	76	Jack Baldwin (USA)/Eppie Wietzes (CDN)/* John Lloyd (USA)	Chevrolet Camaro (Peerless)	Rick Hendrick	261 DNF	21	GTO
48	52	Sarel van der Merwe (ZA)/Doc Bundy (USA)	Chevrolet Corvette GTP-T710 (Lola)	Rick Hendrick	255 DNF	3	GTP
49	80	Roger Andrey (USA)/Angelo Pallavicini (CH)/Uli Bieri (CDN)	Alba-Ferrari AR2	Gaston Andrey	246 DNF	36	GTL
50	25	Jerry Brassfield (USA)/Michael Roe (IRL)/John Bauer (USA)/ Norton Gaston (USA)	March-Chevrolet 85G	DeAtley Motorsports	245 DNF	16	GTP
51	31	Stanley Dickens (S)/Frank Jelinski (D)/Gary Robinson (USA)/Greg Hobbs (GB)	Gebhardt-BMW JC853	Alf Gebhardt	236 DNF	35	GTL
52	64	Ken Johnson (USA)/Maurice Hassey (USA)/Lanny Hester (USA)	Ford Mustang (Roush)	Raintree Corporation	225 DNF	28	GTO
53	55	Nort Northam (USA)/Scott Lagasse (USA)/Dennis Krueger (USA) * Greg Walker (USA)	Chevrolet Corvette	Jack Wilson	223 DNF	69	GTO
54	44	Bob Tullius (USA)/Hurley Haywood (USA)/John Morton (USA)	Jaguar XJR-7 (Fabcar)	Bob Tullius	216 DNF	7	GTP
55	92	Lance Van Every (USA)/Rusty Bond (USA)/Ash Tisdelle (USA)	Chevrolet Camaro (Riggins)	Lance Van Every	202 DNF	33	GTO
56	86	Klaus Ludwig (D)/Jochen Mass (D)/Bruce Leven (USA)	Porsche 962	Bruce Leven	144 DNF	1	GTP
57	77	Bobby Archer (USA)/Tommy Archer (USA)/ * Robert Lappalainen (SF)/ * Leo Franchi (USA)	Chevrolet Camaro (Protofab)	Brooks Fryberger	121 DNF	22	GTO
58	4	Scott Pruett (USA)/Pete Halsmer (USA)/Tom Gloy (USA)	Ford Mustang Probe II (Roush)	Jack Roush	120 DNF	13	GTP
59	23	George Petrilak (USA)/Graham Duxbury (ZA)/Bill Jacobson (USA)/ * Helmut Silberberger (USA)	Argo-Buick JM16	George Petrilak	119 DNF	38	GTL
60	9	Steve Phillips (USA)/Howard Katz (USA)/Ron Nelson (USA)	Tiga-Mazda GT285	Mike Gue	111 DNF	31	GTL
61	13	Keith Lawhorn (USA)/Vince Gimondo (USA)/Ken Grostic (USA)	Oldsmobile Calais	Vince Gimondo	104 DNF	54	GTO
62	67	Bob Wollek (F)/Jim Busby (USA)/Darin Brassfield (USA)	Porsche 962	Jim Busby	89 DNF	2	GTP
63	50	Paul Canary (USA)/Jerry Winston (USA)/Phil Currin (USA)/ * Richard Bryan (USA)/* Benton Bryan (USA)	Chevrolet Corvette	Paul Canary	88 DNF	56	GTO
64	54	Karl Durkheimer (USA)/Bill Auberlen (USA)/Dieter Oest (USA)/ * Gary Auberlen (USA)	Porsche 911	Gary Auberlen	87 DNF	50	GTU
65	88	John Heinricy (USA)/Bob McConnell (USA)/Bill Adam (CDN)/ * Bobby Carradine (USA)	Chevrolet Corvette	Tommy Morrison	77 DNF	64	GTO
66	74	Paul Gentilozzi (USA)/* Irv Hoerr (USA)/* Ted Boody (USA)	Oldsmobile Toronado (Rocketsports)	Paul Gentilozzi	52 DNF	20	GTO
67	43	Tom Pumpelly (USA)/Robert Overby (USA)/* Tim McAdam (USA)/ * Thomas Schwietz (USA)	Fabcar-Porsche	John Higgins	42 DNF	45	GTL
68	41	Hugo Gralia (USA)/Dennis Dobkin (USA)/* Carlos Padrera (USA)/ * Secondo Tagliero (USA)	Mazda RX-7	Hugo Gralia	30 DNF	63	GTU
69	79	Paul Lewis (USA)/* Skeeter McKitterick (USA)/* Tom Winters (USA)	Alba-Chevrolet AR5	Paul Gentilozzi	28 DNF	37	GTL

SunBank 24 At Daytona

January 30-31, 1988

24 hour event on the 3.560 mile circuit.
Distance covered: 728 laps for 2591.680 miles.
Winning time: 24 hours, 0 minutes, 34.94 seconds for a speed of 107.943 mph.
Margin of victory: 1 lap.
Fastest lap: #16 Porsche 962 (Price Cobb), 1:41.693, 126.026 mph.
Fastest qualifier: #67 Porsche 962 (Mauro Baldi), 1:38.917, 129.563 mph.
10 full-course cautions for 2 hours, 38 minutes.

FINISH	CAR NO.	DRIVERS	CAR	ENTRANT	LAPS	START	CLASS
1	**60**	**Martin Brundle (GB)/Raul Boesel (BR)/John Nielsen (DK)/Jan Lammers (NL)**	**Jaguar XJR-9 (Advanced)**	**Tom Walkinshaw**	**728**	**6**	**GTP**
2	67	Bob Wollek (F)/Mauro Baldi (I)/Brian Redman (GB)	Porsche 962 (Chapman)	Jim Busby	727	1	GTP
3	66	Eddie Cheever (USA)/John Watson (GB)/Johnny Dumfries (GB)	Jaguar XJR-9 (Advanced)	Tom Walkinshaw	713	4	GTP
4	86	Hans-Joachim Stuck, Jr. (D)/Klaus Ludwig (D)/Sarel van der Merwe (ZA)	Porsche 962	Bruce Leven	694	7	GTP
5	15	Jim Rothbarth (USA)/Bernard Jourdain (MEX)/Michel Jourdain (MEX)/ Rob Stevens (USA)	Porsche 962 (Holbert)	John Kalagian	680	12	GTP
6	1	A. J. Foyt (USA)/Al Unser, Jr. (USA)/Elliott Forbes-Robinson (USA)	Porsche 962 (Holbert-Fabcar)	A. J. Foyt	675	9	GTP
7	14	Al Holbert (USA)/Chip Robinson (USA)/Derek Bell (GB)	Porsche 962 (Holbert)	Al Holbert	660 DNF	8	GTP
8	09	Steve Durst (USA)/Michael Brockman (USA)/Bob Earl (USA)/ Gary Belcher (USA)	Spice-Pontiac Firebird GTP	Durst/Brockman	651 DNF	11	GTP
9	16	Price Cobb (USA)/James Weaver (GB)/Rob Dyson (USA)/ Vern Schuppan (AUS)	Porsche 962	Rob Dyson	638	3	GTP
10	**11**	**Scott Pruett (USA)/Paul Miller (USA)/Bobby Akin Jr. (USA)/ Pete Halsmer (USA)**	**Merkur XR4Ti (Roush)**	**Jack Roush**	**634**	**23**	**GTO**
11	03	Buz McCall (USA)/Paul Dallenbach (USA)/Max Jones (USA)/ Mike Meyer (USA)/Jack Baldwin (USA)	Chevrolet Camaro (Riggins)	Buz McCall	634	43	GTO
12	**9**	**David Simpson (USA)/Thomas Hessert (USA)/David Loring (USA)**	**Tiga-Chevrolet GT286**	**Mike Gue**	**617**	**29**	**GTL**
13	63	Howard Katz (USA)/Hiro Matsushita (J)/Jim Downing (USA)	Argo-Mazda JM19	Jim Downing	615	35	GTL
14	55	Terry Visger (USA)/Paul Lewis (USA)/Jon Woodner (USA)	Spice-Pontiac Fiero GTP	Joe Huffaker, Jr.	599	37	GTL
15	**71**	**Amos Johnson (USA)/Dennis Shaw (USA)/Bob Lazier (USA)**	**Mazda RX-7 (Highball)**	**Amos Johnson**	**598**	**52**	**GTU**
16	38	Roger Mandeville (USA)/Kelly Marsh (USA)/Don Marsh (USA)	Mazda RX-7 (Chassis Dynamics)	Roger Mandeville	597	21	GTO
17	04	Gary Auberlen (USA)/Adrian Gang (USA)/Cary Eisenlohr (USA)/ Bill Auberlen (USA)	Porsche 911 Carrera	Gary Auberlen	586	64	GTU
18	89	Peter Uria (USA)/Jack Refenning (USA)/Larry Figaro (USA)/ Rusty Scott (USA)	Porsche 911 Carrera RSR	Peter Uria	577	59	GTU
19	47	Richard Oakley (USA)/Matt Mnich (USA)/Doug Mills (USA)	Mazda RX-7	Chaunce Wallace	573	62	GTU
20	33	Andy Petery (USA)/Les Delano (USA)/Craig Carter (USA)	Lincoln-Mercury Capri (Roush)	Jack Roush	568	36	GTO
21	01	Don Bell (USA)/Charles Morgan (USA)/Costas Los (GR)	Spice-Pontiac Fiero GTP	Spice Engineering USA.	566 DNF	75	GTL
22	19	Ron McKay (USA)/Bill Jacobson (USA)/Jim Brown (USA)	Tiga-Mazda GT286	Mike Gue	557	49	GTL
23	42	Jack Newsum (USA)/Howard Cherry (USA)/Tim McAdam (USA)/ John Higgins (USA)	Fabcar-Porsche	Lorenzo Lamas	554	51	GTL
24	95	Butch Leitzinger (USA)/Chuck Kurtz (USA)/Bob Leitzinger (USA)	Nissan 300ZX (Nash)	Bob Leitzinger	541	63	GTU
25	68	Greg Walker (USA)/King Smith (USA)/Scott Lagasse (USA)	Chevrolet Corvette (Linderfer)	Greg Walker	527	41	GTO
26	61	Davy Jones (USA)/Danny Sullivan (USA)/Jan Lammers (NL)	Jaguar XJR-9 (Advanced)	Tom Walkinshaw	512 DNF	2	GTP
27	80	Martino Finotto (I)/Pietro Silva (I)/Guido Dacco (I)	Alba-Ferrari AR6	Gaston Andrey	506	27	GTL
28	99	Willy T. Ribbs (USA)/Rocky Moran (USA)/Juan Manuel Fangio II (RA)	Toyota Celica (AAR)	Dan Gurney	502 DNF	30	GTO
29	36	John Grooms (USA)/Tom Bagley (USA)/John Fergus (USA)/ Frank Jellinek, Jr. (USA)	Argo-Mazda JM19	Frank Jellinek, Jr.	496 DNF	46	GTL
30	18	Bob Beasley (USA)/Steve Volk (USA)/Jack Lewis (USA)	Porsche 911 Carrera RSR	Jack Lewis	490 DNF	69	GTO
31	84	Bill Wessel (USA)/Craig A. Rubright (USA)/Garrett Jenkins (USA)	Chevrolet Camaro (Dillon)	Craig A. Rubright	479 DNF	53	GTO
32	5	Tommy Archer (USA)/Chip Mead (USA)/Bill Adam (CDN)	Chevrolet Corvette (Protofab)	Protofab	467 DNF	20	GTO
33	56	Karl Durkheimer (USA)/Monte Shelton (USA)/Jim Torres (USA)/ Nort Northam (USA)	Porsche 911 Carrera (Durkheimer)	Karl Durkheimer	455	67	GTU
34	75	Bart Kendall (USA)/Johnny Unser (USA)/Tom Frank (USA)	Mazda RX-7 (Cunningham)	Clayton Cunningham	446 DNF	61	GTU
35	17	Al Bacon (USA)/Bob Reed (USA)/John Hogdal (USA)	Mazda RX-7 (Chassis Dynamics)	Al Bacon	445	56	GTU
36	7	Bruce Jenner (USA)/Scott Goodyear (CDN)/Arie Luyendyk (NL)/ Tom Gloy (USA)/ Calvin Fish (USA)/Thomas Schwietz (USA)	Ford Probe GTP (Zakspeed)	Tom Milner	418 DNF	14	GTP
37	98	Chris Cord (USA)/Dennis Aase (USA)/Steve Millen (NZ)	Toyota Celica (AAR)	Dan Gurney	416 DNF	31	GTO
38	92	Steve Zwiren (USA)/Mark Montgomery (USA)/Anthony Puleo (USA)	Pontiac Firebird (Python)	Anthony Puleo	402 DNF	38	GTO
39	2	Greg Pickett (USA)/John Jones (CDN)/Tommy Riggins (USA)	Chevrolet Corvette (Protofab)	Protofab	398 DNF	19	GTO
40	76	John Morton (USA)/Parnelli Jones (USA)/P. J. Jones (USA)	Mazda RX-7 (Cunningham)	Clayton Cunningham	389 DNF	32	GTO
41	6	Kenper Miller (USA)/Bobby Akin, Jr. (USA)/Paul Gentilozzi (USA)	Merkur XR4Ti (Roush)	Jack Roush	388 DNF	16	GTO
42	23	George Petrilak (USA)/Rex McDaniel (USA)/Bruce MacInnes (USA)	Argo-Buick JM16	George Petrilak	379 DNF	74	GTL
43	4	Jim Miller (USA)/Linda Ludemann (USA)/Scott Schubot (USA)	Spice-Buick SE88P	Schubot/Ludemann	369 DNF	26	GTL
44	22	Mark Martin (USA)/Lyn St. James (USA)/Deborah Gregg (USA)/ Pete Halsmer (USA)	Lincoln-Mercury Capri (Roush)	Ford	349 DNF	25	GTO
45	81	Ken Bupp (USA)/Jack Boxstrom (USA)/Kent Painter (USA)Guy W. Church (USA)	Chevrolet Camaro (Frings)	Ken Bupp	345 DNF	48	GTO
46	72	Michael Allison (USA)/Stephen Hynes (USA)/Chris Ashmore (GB)	Tiga Ford-Cosworth GC286	Roy Baker	329 DNF	39	GTP
47	35	Armando Gonzalez (PR)/Dennis Winfree (USA)/Manuel Villa Prieto (PR)/John Schneider (USA)	Royale-Porsche RP40	Diman Racing	302 DNF	58	GTL
48	79	Skeeter McKitterick (USA)/William Koll (USA)/Tom Winters (USA)/ Claude Ballot-Lena (F)/Mario Hytten (CH)	Spice-Pontiac Fiero GTP	Paul Gentilozzi	297 DNF	24	GTL
49	51	Colin Richard (GB)/Rene Azcona (USA)/Bob Copeman (USA)	Porsche 911 Carrera RSR	Rene Azcona	278	71	GTU
50	3	Oscar Larrauri (RA)/Massimo Sigala (I)/Gianfranco Brancatelli (I)	Porsche 962C	Walter Brun	277 DNF	5	GTP

SunBank 24 At Daytona

February 3-4, 1990

24 hour event on the 3.560 mile circuit.

Distance covered: 761 laps for 2709.160 miles.

Winning time: 24 hours, 0 minutes, 19.049 seconds for a speed of 112.857 mph.

Margin of victory: 4 laps.

Fastest lap: #0 Porsche 962C (Frank Jelinski) 1:41.794, 125.901 mph.

fastest qualifier = # 86 Porsche 962C (Wollek) 1:37.832, 131.000 mph.

4 full-course cautions for 23 laps.

FINISH	CAR NO.	DRIVERS	CAR	ENTRANT	LAPS	START	CLASS
1	**61**	**Davy Jones (USA)/Jan Lammers (NL)/Andy Wallace (GB)**	**Jaguar XJR-12 (Advanced)**	**Tom Walkinshaw**	**761**	**10**	**GTP**
2	60	Price Cobb (USA)/John Nielsen (DK)/Martin Brundle (GB)	Jaguar XJR-12 (Advanced)	Tom Walkinshaw	757	9	GTP
3	86	Bob Wollek (F)/Sarel van der Merwe (ZA)/Dominic Dobson (USA)	Porsche 962	Bruce Leven	755	1	GTP
4	2	Hans-Joachim Stuck, Jr. (D)/Harald Grohs (D)/Hurley Haywood (USA)/Rene Herzog (CH)	Porsche 962 (Chapman)	Rene Herzog.	704	13	GTP
5	**15**	**Robby Gordon (USA)/Calvin Fish (USA)/Lyn St. James (USA)**	**Lincoln-Mercury Cougar XR-7 (Roush)**	**Jack Roush**	**689**	**25**	**GTO**
6	10	Jim Adams (USA)/John Hotchkis, Jr. (USA)/John Hotchkis, Sr. (USA)	Porsche 962 (Fabcar)	John Hotchkis, Sr.	688	15	GTP
7	63	Amos Johnson (USA)/John O'Steen (USA)/Jim Downing (USA)/Pete Halsmer (USA)	Mazda RX-7 (Fabcar)	Jim Downing	671	21	GTO
8	11	Dorsey Schroeder (USA)/Max Jones (USA)/Robert Lappalainen (SF)/Scott Pruett (USA)	Lincoln-Mercury Cougar XR-7 (Roush)	Jack Roush	653 DNF	19	GTO
9	**36**	**John Grooms (USA)/Michael Greenfield (USA)/Frank Jellinek, Jr. (USA)**	**Argo-Mazda JM16**	**Frank Jellinek, Jr.**	**642**	**30**	**GTL**
10	90	Jim Stevens (USA)/Bob Schneider (USA)/James Jaeger (USA)/Robert Lappalainen (SF)	Lincoln-Mercury Capri (Roush)	Jack Roush	634	34	GTO
11	74	Paul Dallenbach (USA)/George Robinson (USA)/Johnny Unser (USA)/Wally Dallenbach, Jr. (USA)	Ford Mustang (Competition Kar)	Harry McMullen	621	22	GTO
12	**71**	**Peter Uria (USA)/Bob Dotson (USA)/Jim Pace (USA)/Rusty Scott (USA)**	**Mazda RX-7 (Highball)**	**Peter Uria**	**620**	**50**	**GTU**
13	55	David Rocha (USA)/Les Delano (USA)/Andy Petery (USA)/Oscar Manautou (MEX)/Craig Carter (USA)	Spice-Pontiac Firebird GTP L	Joe Huffaker, Jr.	609	26	GTL
14	26	Peter Kraft (USA)/Tommy Johnson (USA)/Alex Job (USA)/Buz McCall (USA)	Porsche 911	Alex Job	605	54	GTU
15	82	Dick Greer (USA)/Colin Trueman (USA)/Mike Mees (USA)	Mazda RX-7 (Chassis Dynamics)	Dick Greer	585	51	GTU
16	38	Roger Mandeville (USA)/Kelly Marsh (USA)/John Finger (USA)/Lance Stewart (USA)/John Hogdal (USA)	Mazda MX-6 (MAT)	Roger Mandeville	577	39	GTU
17	4	Scott Schubot (USA)/Tomas Lopez Rocha (MEX)/Linda Ludemann (USA)	Spice-Buick SE88P	Schubot/Ludemann	544 DNF	20	GTL
18	87	Anthony Puleo (USA)/Mark Kennedy (USA)/Jerry Walsh (USA)/Kent Painter (USA)	Chevrolet Camaro (Bemco)	Anthony Puleo	531	60	GTO
19	12	Ron McKay (USA)/Kaming Ko (HK)/Tom Hunter, Jr. (USA)/Marlo Magana (MEX)	Tiga-Chevrolet GT287	Carlos Bobeda	503	35	GTL
20	47	Steven Johnson (USA)/Gary Pierce (USA)	Argo-Buick JM19	Steven Johnson	498	40	GTL
21	43	Donald Wallace (USA)/Bob Young (USA)/Brad Hoyt (USA)/Joe Varde (USA)	Pontiac Fiero (Huffaker)	Joe Varde	469 DNF	47	GTU
22	9	Ferdinand de Lesseps (F)/Jay Cochran (USA)/John Morrison (GB)	Spice-Buick SE89P	Mike Gue	443 DNF	23	GTL
23	8	Charles Morgan (USA)/Hendrick ten Cate (NL)/Thomas Hessert (USA)	Spice-Buick SE89P	Mike Gue	440 DNF	33	GTL
24	97	John Heinricy (USA)/Tim Beverly (USA)/Andy Swett (USA)/Tommy Morrison (USA)	Spice-Pontiac SE87P	Paul Gentilozzi	409	24	GTL
25	67	Kevin Cogan (USA)/John Paul, Jr. (USA)/Mauro Baldi (I)	Nissan GTP-ZXT (Chapman)	Jim Busby	397 DNF	6	GTP
26	04	Henry Brosnaham (USA)/Robert McElheny (USA)/Steve Burgner (USA)	Chevrolet Camaro (Howe)	Henry Brosnaham	369	57	GTO
27	17	Raul Boesel (BR)/Al Unser, Jr. (USA)/Robby Unser (USA)	Porsche 962C	Jochen Dauer	360 DNF	7	GTP
28	84	Derek Daly (IRL)/Bob Earl (USA)/Chip Robinson (USA)/Geoff Brabham (AUS)	Nissan GTP-ZXT (Chapman)	Don C. Devendorf	360 DNF	2	GTP
29	57	Reed Kryder (USA)/Henry Camferdam, Jr. (USA)/Alistair Oag (USA)/Phillip Pate (USA)	Nissan 300ZX (Kryderacing)	Reed Kryder	354 DNF	55	GTU
30	83	Bob Earl (USA)/Chip Robinson (USA)/Geoff Brabham (AUS)/Derek Daly (IRL)	Nissan GTP-ZXT (Chapman)	Don C. Devendorf	327 DNF	3	GTP
31	58	Bill Bean (USA)/Don Abreu (USA)/Bill Wolfe (USA)	Lola-Mazda T616	Gary Wonzer	322 DNF	43	GTL
32	80	Martino Finotto (I)/Paolo Guaitamacchi (I)/Loris Kessel (CH)	Spice-Ferrari SE88P	Bieri/Finotto	306 DNF	29	GTL
33	00	Kal Showket (USA)/Don Knowles (USA)/Neil Hanneman (USA)/Mike Davies (USA)	Dodge Daytona (Showket)	Emory Donaldson	280 DNF	44	GTU
34	01	Michael Allison (USA)/Andrew Hepworth (GB)/Michael Dow (USA)/ George Sutcliffe (USA)/Chris Hodgetts (GB)	Spice-Pontiac SE87P	George Sutcliffe	263 DNF	52	GTL
35	99	Rocky Moran (USA)/Drake Olson (ZA)/Juan Manuel Fangio II (RA)	Eagle-Toyota HF89	Dan Gurney	253 DNF	11	GTP
36	21	Craig A. Rubright (USA)/Kermit Upton (USA)/Daniel Urrutia (USA)	Chevrolet Camaro (Dillon)	Craig A. Rubright	247	49	GTO
37	79	Ken Knott (USA)/Tom Winters (USA)/Claude Ballot-Lena (F)/ Thierry Lecerf (F)	Spice Pontiac-Cosworth SE88P	Roy Roach	243 DNF	27	GTL
38	42	Howard Cherry (USA)/John Higgins (USA)/Charles Monk (CDN)/ Tim McAdam (USA)	Fabcar-Porsche	John Higgins	242 DNF	42	GTL
39	81	Bob Speakman (USA)/David S. Duda (USA)/Mike Speakman (USA)/Jim Novatne (USA)	Datsun 240Z	David S. Duda	231 DNF	56	GTU
40	29	Guy W. Church (USA)/Mark Montgomery (USA)/Del Russo Taylor (USA)/ Don Arpin (USA)/ Hoyt Overbagh (USA)/* Ed De Long (CDN)	Chevrolet Camaro	Hoyt Overbagh	229	38	GTO
41	30	Gianpiero Moretti (I)/Derek Bell (GB)/Stanley Dickens (S)* Costas Los (GR)/* Steve Phillips (USA)	Porsche 962 (Shapiro)	Gianpiero Moretti	186 DNF	14	GTP
42	92	Max Schmidt (USA)/James Briody (USA)/Rusty Schmidt (USA)/Jorge Mendoza (MEX)	Argo-Mazda JM19	Max Schmidt	176 DNF	45	GTL
43	53	Richard McDill (USA)/James Burt (USA)/Bill McDill (USA)	Chevrolet Camaro (Dillon)	Bill McDill	167 DNF	28	GTO
44	95	Bob Leitzinger (USA)/David Loring (USA)/Butch Leitzinger (USA)/ * Chuck Kurtz (USA)	Nissan 240SX (Leitzinger)	Bob Leitzinger	147 DNF	37	GTU
45	0	Frank Jelinski (D)/Henri Pescarolo (F)/Jean-Louis Ricci (F)	Porsche 962C (Joest)	Reinhold Joest	145 DNF	4	GTP
46	07	Stuart Hayner (USA)/Robbie Buhl (USA)/* Mike Davies (USA)	Dodge Daytona (Showket)	Kal Showket	137 DNF	46	GTU
47	33	Bernard Jourdain (MEX)/Jeff Kline (USA)/* Hiro Matsushita (J)/* Scott Atchison (USA)	Spice-Chevrolet SE90P	Spice Engineering USA	90 DNF	8	GTP
48	37	Al Bacon (USA)/John Hogdal (USA)/* John Finger (USA)/* Lance Stewart (USA)	Mazda MX-6 (MAT)	Roger Mandeville	85 DNF	48	GTU
49	70	Bob Hebert (USA)/Paul Reisman (USA)/Richard J. Valentine (USA)	Argo-Mazda JM16	Paul Reisman	84 DNF	31	GTL
50	54	Robert Segall (USA)/Richard Davis (USA)/Gerre Payvis (USA)/Bill Cerveney (USA)/Jeff Davis (USA)	Chevrolet Camaro (Weaver)	Gerre Payvis	74 DNF	36	GTO

FINISH	CAR NO.	DRIVERS	CAR	ENTRANT	LAPS	START	CLASS
51	41	Joe Cogbill, Jr. (USA)/Mark Gibson (USA)/Dale Kreider (USA)/* Clay Young (USA)	Chevrolet Beretta (Baird & Trivette)	Clay Young	67 DNF	41	GTO
52	1	Elliott Forbes-Robinson (USA)/John Morton (USA)/Pete Halsmer (USA)/* Jim Downing (USA)	Mazda RX-7 (Fabcar)	Jim Downing	61 DNF	16	GTO
53	40	Uli Bieri (CDN)/David Tennyson (CDN)/* John Graham (CDN)	Tiga-Ferrari GT286	Uli Bieri	58 DNF	32	GTL
54	23	Bill Adam (CDN)/Richard Laporte (CDN)/* Scott Goodyear (CDN)/* David S. Seabrooke (CDN)	Porsche 962C	David S. Seabrooke	43 DNF	12	GTP
55	16	Rob Dyson (USA)/* James Weaver (GB)/* Scott Pruett (USA)/* Vern Schuppan (AUS)	Porsche 962C	Rob Dyson	6 DNF	5	GTP
DNS	6	Rene Herzog (CH)/Harald Grohs (D)	Ford Probe GTP (Zakspeed)	Tom Milner	0	17	GTP
DNS	31	Costas Los (GR)/Gunther Gebhardt (D)/Hellmut Mundas (D)	Gebhardt-Audi JC853	Moretti/Gebhardt	0	18	GTP
DNS	28	Raul Garcia (USA)/George Garcia (USA)	Pontiac Firebird (Oftedahl)	Raul Garcia	0	53	GTO
DNS	18	Rick Holland (USA)/Mike Green (USA)/Dennis Chambers (USA)	Mazda RX-7	Rick Holland	0	58	GTU
DNS	56	Bill Auberlen (USA)/Nort Northam (USA)/Cary Eisenlohr (USA)/Gary Auberlen (USA)	Porsche 911 Carrera RSR	Gary Auberlen	0	59	GTU
DNS	3	Oscar Larrauri (RA)/Walter Brun (CH)/Massimo Sigala (I)	Porsche 962C (Thompson)	Walter Brun	0		GTP

SunBank 24 At Daytona

February 2-3, 1991

24 hour event on the 3.560 mile circuit.
Distance covered: 719 laps for 2559.640 miles.
Winning time: 24 hours, 0 minutes, 15.399 seconds for a speed of 106.633 mph.
Margin of victory: 8 laps.
Fastest lap: #84 Nissan R90C (Julian Bailey), 1:39.765, 128.462 mph.
Pole winner: #6 Porsche 962C (Bob Wollek), 1:50.87, 115.595 mph.
Fastest qualifier: #1 Nissan R90C (Derek Daly), 1:49.864, 116.653 mph/187.735 kph
3 full-course cautions for 18 laps

FINISH	CAR NO.	DRIVERS	CAR	ENTRANT	LAPS	START	CLASS
1	**7**	**Frank Jelinski (D)/Henri Pescarolo (F)/Hurley Haywood (USA)/Bob Wollek (F)/John Winter (D)**	**Porsche 962C (Joest)**	**Reinhold Joest**	**719**	**7**	**GTP**
2	**83**	**Bob Earl (USA)/Derek Daly (IRL)/Chip Robinson (USA)/Geoff Brabham (AUS)**	**Nissan R90C (Lola)**	**Don C. Devendorf**	**701**	**4**	**LM**
3	10	Chris Cord (USA)/John Hotchkis, Sr. (USA)/Jim Adams (USA)/Rob Dyson (USA)	Porsche 962 (Fabcar)	John Hotchkis, Sr.	692	12	GTP
4	**15**	**Mark Martin (USA)/Wally Dallenbach, Jr. (USA)/Robby Gordon (USA)**	**Ford Mustang (Roush)**	**Jack Roush**	**672**	**22**	**GTO**
5	00	Michael Andretti (USA)/Mario Andretti (USA)/Jeff Andretti (USA)	Porsche 962C (Dauer)	Jochen Dauer	663 DNF	6	GTP
6	12	John Fergus (USA)/Max Jones (USA)/Dorsey Schroeder (USA)	Ford Mustang (Roush)	Jack Roush	658	21	GTO
7	**48**	**Parker Johnstone (USA)/Steve Cameron (NZ)/Doug Peterson (USA)/Bob Lesnett (USA)**	**Spice-Acura SE90P**	**Don Erb**	**654 DNF**	**16**	**GTL**
8	36	John Grooms (USA)/Michael Greenfield (USA)/Frank Jellinek, Jr. (USA)/Peter Greenfield (USA)	Kudzu-Mazda DG-1	Frank Jellinek, Jr.	632	30	GTL
9	54	Michael Dow (USA)/Andrew Hepworth (GB)/Hendrick ten Cate (NL)	Spice-Buick SE89P	Hugh D. Fuller	620 DNF	28	GTL
10	90	Jim Stevens (USA)/Craig Bennett (USA)/Tommy Grunnah (USA)/James Jaeger (USA)	Ford Mustang (Roush)	Jack Roush	619	26	GTO
11	4	Brian Bonner (USA)/Derrick Cope (USA)/Jeff Kline (USA)/Scott Sharp (USA)	Spice-Chevrolet SE88P	Tom Milner	611	14	GTP
12	92	R. K. Smith (USA)/Doc Bundy (USA)/Joe Varde (USA)/Andy Pilgrim (GB)	Chevrolet Corvette	Tommy Morrison	611	24	GTO
13	**82**	**Dick Greer (USA)/Al Bacon (USA)/Mike Mees (USA)/Peter Uria (USA)**	**Mazda RX-7 (Chassis Dynamics)**	**Dick Greer**	**605**	**36**	**GTU**
14	63	Brian Redman (GB)/John O'Steen (USA)/Price Cobb (USA)/Pete Halsmer (USA)	Mazda RX-7 (Fabcar)	Jim Downing	576	17	GTO
15	37	Honorato Espinosa (CO)/Rob Wilson (NZ)/Miguel Morejon (USA)/Felipe Solano (CO)	Mazda MX-6 (MAT)	Luis Botero	576	35	GTU
16	38	Roger Mandeville (USA)/Amos Johnson (USA)/Kelly Marsh (USA)	Mazda RX-7 (MAT)	Roger Mandeville	568	31	GTU
17	42	Geoff Nicol (AUS)/David Tennyson (CDN)/Todd Brayton (USA)	Tiga-Mazda GT286	Geoff Nicol	556	40	GTL
18	09	Stephen Hynes (USA)/Tommy Johnson (USA)/Rob Robertson (USA)/John Sheldon (GB)	Tiga-Buick GT287	Robertson/Johnson	545	23	GTL
19	26	Peter Kraft (USA)/Alex Job (USA)/Joe Pezza (USA)/Jack Refenning (USA)	Porsche 911 (Fabcar)	Alex Job	494	41	GTU
20	84	Julian Bailey (GB)/Steve Millen (NZ)/Arie Luyendyk (NL)/Jeremy Dale (CDN)	Nissan R90C (Lola)	Don C. Devendorf	472 DNF	5	LM
21	91	Stuart Hayner (USA)/Don Knowles (USA)/John Heinricy (USA)/Scott Lagasse (USA)/Tommy Morrison (USA)	Chevrolet Corvette	Tommy Morrison	464	25	GTO
22	16	James Weaver (GB)/John Paul, Jr. (USA)/Tiff Needell (GB)/* Rob Dyson (USA)	Porsche 962C	Dyson	450 DNF	10	GTP
23	72	Steve Volk (USA)/Jay Kjoller (USA)/Patrick Mooney (USA)	Porsche 911	Jay Kjoller	449	44	GTU
24	5	Michael Brockman (USA)/Tim McAdam (USA)/Fred Phillips (USA)/Jeff Davis (USA)	Spice-Chevrolet SE90P	Tom Milner	448 DNF	15	GTP
25	70	Lou Gigliotti (USA)/Boris Said (USA)/Mike Nolan (USA)/Roger Schramm (USA)/Peter Cunningham (USA)	Oldsmobile Cutlass (Frings)	Mike Nolan	445	19	GTO
26	66	Leighton Reese (USA)/Mike Gagliardo (USA)/Brad Hoyt (USA)	Mazda RX-7 (Linderfer)	Brad Hoyt	442 DNF	38	GTU
27	11	Jon Gooding (USA)/John Annis (USA)/Mark Kennedy (USA)/ Nort Northam (USA)/Tom Panaggio (USA)	Chevrolet Camaro (Riggins)	Robert Williams	427	37	GTO
28	98	Mark Dismore (USA)/Rocky Moran (USA)/P. J. Jones (USA)	Eagle-Toyota HF89	Dan Gurney	408 DNF	11	GTP
29	87	Grant Hill (CDN)/Nick Holmes (CDN)/Anthony Puleo (USA)/Daniel Urrutia (USA)	Chevrolet Camaro (Bemco)	Wanda Puleo	399	34	GTO

FIN.	CAR NO.	DRIVERS	CAR	ENTRANT	LAPS	START	CLASS
30	2	Davy Jones (USA)/Scott Pruett (USA)/Raul Boesel (BR)/Derek Warwick (GB)	Jaguar XJR-12 (Advanced)	Tom Walkinshaw	379 DNF	2	GTP
31	6	Bob Wollek (F)/Bernd Schneider (D)/Paolo Barilla (I)/Massimo Sigala (I)	Porsche 962C (Joest)	Reinhold Joest	360 DNF	1	GTP
32	9	Jim Pace (USA)/Thomas Hessert (USA)/Charles Morgan (USA)	Kudzu-Buick DG-1	Mike Gue	359 DNF	20	GTL
33	20	Kaming Ko (HK)/Michael Sheehan (USA)/Ron McKay (USA)/ Charles Monk (CDN)/* Carlos Bobeda (MEX)/* Bill Jacobson (USA)	Tiga-Chevrolet GT287	Carlos Bobeda	328 DNF	32	GTL
34	45	John Forbes (USA)/Ken Fengler (USA)/Bob Hundredmark (USA)/Tom Curren (USA)/* Karl Keck (USA)	Chevrolet Corvette	Bob Hundredmark	315	45	GTO
35	0	Al Unser, Jr. (USA)/Bobby Unser (USA)/Robby Unser (USA)/Al Unser, Sr. (USA)	Porsche 962C	Jochen Dauer	270 DNF	9	GTP
36	28	Don Arpin (USA)/Jon Olch (USA)/Tim Banks (USA)/Scott Watkins (USA)/* Del Russo Taylor (USA)	Chevrolet Camaro (Python)	Del Russo Taylor	234 DNF	46	GTO
37	53	Richard McDill (USA)/Bill McDill (USA)/James Burt (USA)	Chevrolet Camaro (Dillon)	Bill McDill	223 DNF	27	GTO
38	96	Chuck Kurtz (USA)/Bob Leitzinger (USA)/David Loring (USA)/ Don Reynolds (USA)/* Butch Leitzinger (USA)	Nissan 240SX (Leitzinger)	Bob Leitzinger	192 DNF	29	GTU
39	57	Henry Camferdam, Jr. (USA)/Phil Krueger (USA)/Alistair Oag (USA)/Reed Kryder (USA)	Nissan 240SX (Kryderacing)	Reed Kryder	159 DNF	42	GTU
40	60	Jay Cochran (USA)/Derek Bell (GB)/Justin Bell (GB)	Gunnar-Porsche 966 (Chapman)	Kevin Jeannette	83	13	GTP
41	04	Bobby Scolo (USA)/Steve Burgner (USA)/John Macaluso (USA)/* Henry Brosnaham (USA)	Chevrolet Camaro (Howe)	Henry Brosnaham	78	39	GTO
42	99	Juan Manuel Fangio II (RA)/Willy T. Ribbs (USA)/Andy Wallace (GB)	Eagle-Toyota HF89	Dan Gurney	60 DNF	8	GTP
43	62	John Morton (USA)/Calvin Fish (USA)/* Pete Halsmer (USA)	Mazda RX-7 (Fabcar)	Jim Downing	50 DNF	18	GTO
44	1	Arie Luyendyk (NL)/Julian Bailey (GB)/* Derek Daly (IRL)	Nissan R90C (Lola)	Don C. Devendorf	47 DNF	3	LM
45	06	Oma Kimbrough (USA)/Hoyt Overbagh (USA)/* Mark Montgomery (USA)/* Kent Painter (USA)	Chevrolet Camaro (Stock Car Products)	Hoyt Overbagh	37 DNF	43	GTO
46	95	Butch Leitzinger (USA)/* David Loring (USA)/* Chuck Kurtz (USA)/* Bob Leitzinger (USA)	Nissan 240SX (Leitzinger)	Bob Leitzinger	13 DNF	33	GTU
DNS	3	John Nielsen (DK)	Jaguar XJR-12 (Advanced)	Tom Walkinshaw	DNS	0	GTP

Rolex 24 At Daytona

February 1-2, 1992

24 hour event on the 3.560 mile circuit.
Distance covered: 762 laps for 2712.720 miles.
Winning time: 24 hours, 1 minute, 41.598 seconds for a speed of 112.897 mph.
Margin of victory: 9 laps.
Fastest lap: #99 Eagle-Toyota Mk III (Juan Fangio II), 1:40.943, 126.963 mph.
Fastest qualifier: #99 Eagle-Toyota Mk III (Juan Fangio II), 1:35.86, 133.695 mph.
3 full-course cautions for 98 minutes.

FIN.	CAR NO.	DRIVERS	CAR	ENTRANT	LAPS	START	CLASS
1	**23**	**Masahiro Hasemi (J)/Kazuyoshi Hoshino (J)/Toshio Suzuki (J)**	**Nissan R91CP (Lola)**	**Nissan Motorsports**	**762**	**3**	**Gp.C**
2	**2**	**Davy Jones (USA)/Scott Pruett (USA)/David Brabham (AUS)/Scott Goodyear (CDN)**	**Jaguar XJR-12D (Advanced)**	**Tom Walkinshaw**	**753**	**8**	**GTP**
3	52	Hurley Haywood (USA)/Eje Elgh (S)/Roland Ratzenberger (A)/Scott Brayton (USA)	Porsche 962	Vern Schuppan	749	10	GTP
4	98	P. J. Jones (USA)/Rocky Moran (USA)/Mark Dismore (USA)	Eagle-Toyota Mk III	Dan Gurney	739	7	GTP
5	**49**	**Parker Johnstone (USA)/Steve Cameron (NZ)/Jim Vasser (USA)/Dan Marvin (USA)**	**Spice-Acura SE91P**	**Don Erb**	**681**	**15**	**GTL**
6	44	Fermin Velez (E)/Andy Evans (USA)/Lon Bender (USA)/Dominic Dobson (USA)	Kudzu-Buick DG-1	Andy Evans	654	18	GTL
7	**82**	**Al Bacon (USA)/Dick Greer (USA)/Mike Mees (USA)/Peter Uria (USA)**	**Mazda RX-7 (Chassis Dynamics)**	**Dick Greer**	**636**	**38**	**GTU**
8	2	Mauro Martini (I)/Volker Weidler (D)/Jeff Krosnoff (USA)	Nissan R91CP (Lola)	Nova Engineering	635	6	Gp.C
9	**15**	**Dorsey Schroeder (USA)/Wally Dallenbach, Jr. (USA)/Robby Gordon (USA)**	**Ford Mustang (Roush)**	**Jack Roush**	**614 DNF**	**20**	**GTS**
10	51	Jeff Kline (USA)/George Robinson (USA)/Darin Brassfield (USA)/Paul Gentilozzi (USA)	Oldsmobile Cutlass (Rocketsports)	Paul Gentilozzi	590	21	GTS
11	99	Juan Manuel Fangio II (RA)/Andy Wallace (GB)/Kenneth Acheson (GB)	Eagle-Toyota Mk III	Dan Gurney	584	1	GTP
12	24	Eduardo Dibos, Jr. (PE)/Juan Dibos (PE)/Raul Orlandini (PE)/Mario Alberti (PE)	Mazda MX-6 (Bacon)	Mario Alberti	573	36	GTU
13	95	Chuck Kurtz (USA)/Bob Leitzinger (USA)/Butch Leitzinger (USA)/David Loring (USA)	Nissan 240SX (Leitzinger)	Bob Leitzinger	566	32	GTU
14	11	Mark Martin (USA)/Jim Stevens (USA)/Robbie Buhl (USA)/Calvin Fish (USA)	Ford Mustang (Roush)	Jack Roush	539	22	GTS
15	96	Don Knowles (USA)/David Loring (USA)/Chuck Kurtz (USA)/Dan Robson (USA)	Nissan 240SX (Leitzinger)	Bob Leitzinger	538	29	GTU
16	75	John Morton (USA)/Jeremy Dale (CDN)/Johnny O'Connell (USA)	Nissan 300ZX (Cunningham)	Clayton Cunningham	531	16	GTS
17	50	Oma Kimbrough (USA)/Mark Montgomery (USA)/Robert McElheny(USA) Gary Swanander (USA)/Jon Lewis (USA)/Raan Rodriguez (PR)/Hoyt Overbagh (USA)	Chevrolet Camaro (Stock Car Products)	Hoyt Overbagh	529	37	GTS
18	26	Joe Pezza (USA)/Alex Padilla (USA)/John Sheldon (GB)/Jack Refenning (USA)	Porsche 911 (Fabcar)	Alex Job	506	40	GTU
19	30	Hans-Joachim Stuck, Jr. (D)/Frank Jelinski (D)/Gianpiero Moretti (I)/Henri Pescarolo (F)	Porsche 962C	Gianpiero Moretti	503 DNF	4	GTP
20	0	John Fergus (USA)/Bobby Akin, Jr. (USA)/Neil Hanneman (USA)	Dodge Daytona (Showket)	Kal Showket	471	35	GTU
21	37	Rob Wilson (NZ)/Lucio Bernal (CO)/Felipe Solano (CO)/Miguel Morejon (USA)	Mazda MX-6 (MAT)	Luis Botero	465 DNF	33	GTU

FIN.	CAR NO.	DRIVERS	CAR	ENTRANT	LAPS	START	CLASS
22	21	Robert Kahn (USA)/John Annis (USA)/John Macaluso (USA)/Robert Borders (USA)	Chevrolet Camaro (Watson)	Kent Painter	465	45	GTS
23	72	Steve Volk (USA)/Robin Boone (USA)/Jay Kjoller (USA).	Porsche 911	Jay Kjoller	432	48	GTU
24	36	Howard Katz (USA)/John Grooms (USA)/Jim Downing (USA)/Frank Jellinek Jr.(USA)	Kudzu-Mazda DG-1	Jim Downing	426 DNF	25	GTL
25	67	Steve Burgner (USA)/Paul Mazzacane (USA)/Henry Brosnaham (USA)/Bobby Scolo (USA)	Chevrolet Camaro (Howe)	Paul Mazzacane	389	49	GTS
26	13	Pascal Fabre (F)/Lionel Robert (F)/Bob Wollek (F)	Courage-Porsche C28S	Yves Courage	387 DNF	9	Gp.C
27	33	Uli Bieri (CDN)/Heinz Wirth (CH)/Vito Scavone (CDN)/Andrew Hepworth (GB)	Tiga-Ferrari GT287	Uli Bieri	349 DNF	34	GTL
28	57	Frank Del Vecchio (USA)/Joe Danaher (USA)/Mark Kent (USA) Bill Sargis (USA)/Reed Kryder (USA)	Nissan 240SX (Kryderacing)	Reed Kryder	345	46	GTU
29	7	Bernd Schneider (D)/Massimo Sigala (I)/Oscar Larrauri (RA)/John Winter (D)	Porsche 962C (Joest)	Reinhold Joest	327 DNF	5	GTP
30	58	Tim McAdam (USA)/Charles Monk (CDN)/Sam Shalala (USA)/Andre Toennis (USA)/Dan Pastorini (USA)	Porsche 911	Maria Shalala	313	47	GTU
31	41	Jack Baldwin (USA)/Irv Hoerr (USA)/* Paul Gentilozzi (USA)	Oldsmobile Cutlass (Rocketsports)	Paul Gentilozzi	312 DNF	23	GTS
32	25	Bill Adams (USA)/John Duke (USA)/Jon Gooding (USA)/Dale Kreider (USA)	Oldsmobile Cutlass (Kreider)	Dale Kreider	289 DNF	30	GTS
33	6	Ron Zitza (USA)/Rob Robertson (USA)/Mel A. Butt (USA)/Tommy Johnson (USA)	Tiga-Buick GT287	Mel A. Butt	279 DNF	26	GTL
34	83	Geoff Brabham (AUS)/Chip Robinson (USA)/Arie Luyendyk (NL)/Bob Earl (USA)	Nissan R90C (Lola)	Don C. Devendorf	272 DNF	13	GTP
35	12	Francois Migault (F)/David Tennyson (CDN)/Tomas Lopez Rocha (MEX)	Courage-Porsche C28S	Yves Courage	220 DNF	11	GTP
36	05	Henry Camferdam, Jr. (USA)/Phil Krueger (USA)/Gary Drummond (USA)	Mazda MX-6 (Bacon)	Henry Camferdam, Jr.	214 DNF	44	GTU
37	4	Wayne Taylor (ZA)/Jeff Purner (USA)/Hugh D. Fuller (USA)/Hideshi Matsuda (J)	Spice-Chevrolet SE90P	Tom Milner	213 DNF	12	GTP
38	35	Richard McDill (USA)/Chris Schneider (USA)/Bill McDill (USA)/Tom Juckette (USA)	Chevrolet Camaro (Dillon)	Bill McDill	204 DNF	27	GTS
39	69	Brad Hoyt (USA)/Andy Pilgrim (GB)/John Petrick (USA)/* Donald Wallace (USA)	Mazda RX-7 (Linderfer)	Brad Hoyt	195 DNF	43	GTU
40	48	Kazuo Shimizu (J)/Ruggero Melgrati (I)/Bob Lesnett (USA)/Costas Los (GR)/ * Steve Cameron (NZ)/* Doug Peterson (USA)	Spice-Acura SE90P	Don Erb	168 DNF	17	GTL
41	84	Derek Daly (IRL)/Steve Millen (NZ)/Gary Brabham (AUS)	Nissan R90C (Lola)	Don C. Devendorf	150 DNF	14	GTP
42	76	Johnny O'Connell (USA)/John Morton (USA)/* Jeremy Dale (CDN)	Nissan 300ZX (T-Mag)	Clayton Cunningham	144 DNF	19	GTS
43	9	Charles Morgan (USA)/Jim Pace (USA)/Ken Knott (USA)	Kudzu-Buick DG-1	Mike Gue	129 DNF	24	GTL
44	17	Kaming Ko (HK)/Ken Parshauer (USA)/Carlos Bobeda (MEX)/* Paul Debban (USA)/ * Michael Dow (USA)/* Bob Longinetti (USA)/* Bobby Carradine (USA)	Spice-Buick SE90P	Carlos Bobeda	125 DNF	28	GTL
45	73	Jack Lewis (USA)/Bill Ferran (USA)/Taylor Robertson (USA)	Porsche 911 Carrera RSR	Jack Lewis	115 DNF	42	GTU
46	55	Bob Schader (USA)/Phil Mahre (USA)/* Steve Mahre (USA)	Mazda MX-6 (Highball)	Bob Schader	94 DNF	41	GTU
47	71	Amos Johnson (USA)/Scott Hoerr (USA)/* Dennis Shaw (USA)/ * Chuck Hemmingson (USA)/* Paul Hacker (USA)	Oldsmobile Achieva (Highball)	Amos Johnson	89 DNF	39	GTU
48	40	Johnny Unser (USA)/* John Graham (CDN)/* Uli Bieri (CDN)/* Andrew Hepworth (GB)	Alba Ford-Cosworth AR2	Uli Bieri	47 DNF	50	GTL
49	22	Luis Sereix (USA)/* Daniel Urrutia (USA)/* Jorge Polanco (RA)	Chevrolet Camaro (Southern Racing)	John Josey	32 DNF	31	GTS
DNS	3	Davy Jones (USA)/Scott Goodyear (CDN)/David Brabham (AUS)/Scott Pruett (USA)	Jaguar XJR-16 (Advanced)	Tom Walkinshaw	0	2	GTP
DNS	83	Geoff Brabham (AUS)/Chip Robinson (USA)/Arie Luyendyk (NL)	Nissan R90C (Lola)	Don C. Devendorf	0	0	GTP

Rolex 24 At Daytona

January 31, February 1, 1993

24 hour event on the 3.560 mile circuit.

Distance covered: 698 laps for 2484.880 miles.

Winning time: 24 hours, 0 minutes, 27.25 seconds for a speed of 103.504 mph.

Margin of victory: 10 laps.

Fastest lap: #98 Eagle-Toyota Mk III (P.J. Jones), 1:39.363, 128.982 mph.

Fastest qualifier: #98 Eagle-Toyota Mk III (P.J. Jones), 1:33.875, 136.522 mph.

FIN.	CAR NO.	DRIVERS	CAR	ENTRANT	LAPS	START	CLASS
1	**98**	**P. J. Jones (USA)/Rocky Moran (USA)/Mark Dismore (USA)**	**Eagle-Toyota Mk III**	**Dan Gurney**	**698**	**1**	**GTP**
2	**11**	**Wally Dallenbach, Jr. (USA)/Robby Gordon (USA)/Robbie Buhl (USA)/Tommy Kendall (USA)**	**Ford Mustang (Roush)**	**Jack Roush**	**688**	**17**	**GTS**
3	15	John Fergus (USA)/Jim Stevens (USA)/Mark Martin (USA)	Ford Mustang (Roush)	Jack Roush	686	18	GTS
4	1	John Morton (USA)/Johnny O'Connell (USA)/Steve Millen (NZ)	Nissan 300ZX (Cunningham)	Clayton Cunningham	668	16	GTS
5	16	James Weaver (GB)/Rob Dyson (USA)/Price Cobb (USA)/Elliott Forbes-Robinson (USA)	Porsche 962C	Rob Dyson	655	9	GTP
6	30	Gianpiero Moretti (I)/Derek Bell (GB)/Massimo Sigala (I)/John Paul, Jr. (USA)	Nissan NPT-90	Gianpiero Moretti	645 DNF	4	GTP
7	**36**	**John Grooms (USA)/Frank Jellinek, Jr. (USA)/Jim Downing (USA)/Tim McAdam (USA)**	**Kudzu-Mazda DG-1**	**Frank Jellinek, Jr.**	**645**	**22**	**GTL**
8	17	Jon Gooding (USA)/Joe Pezza (USA)/Bill Cooper (USA)	Ford Mustang (Roush)	Jack Roush	638	23	GTS
9	**82**	**Dick Greer (USA)/Al Bacon (USA)/Peter Uria (USA)/Mike Mees (USA)**	**Mazda RX-7 (Chassis Dynamics)**	**Dick Greer**	**623**	**39**	**GTU**
10	**2**	**Scott Goodyear (CDN)/Scott Pruett (USA)/Davy Jones (USA)**	**Jaguar XJR-12D (Advanced)**	**Tom Walkinshaw**	**618 DNF**	**6**	**Gp.C**
11	**28**	**Enzo Calderari (CH)/Luigiano Pagotto (I)/Sandro Angelastri (CH)/Ronny Meixner (D)**	**Porsche 911 Carrera 2**	**Roitmayer Motorsport**	**618**	**41**	**I.GT**

FIN.	CAR NO.	DRIVERS	CAR	ENTRANT	LAPS	START	CLASS
12	71	Peter Harholdt (USA)/Rob Mingay (CDN)/Joseph Hamilton (USA)/Ross Bentley (CDN)/John Mirro (USA)	Tiga-Mazda SC86	Club Zed Motorsports	615	34	GTL
13	27	Edgar Doeren (D)/Oliver Mathai (D)/Wolfgang Mathai (D)	Porsche 911 Carrera 2	Hildesheim Porsche Club	596	48	I.GT
14	41	Stig Amthor (D)/Alfio Marchini (I)/Philippe de Craene (B)/Andreas Fuchs (D)	Porsche 911 Carrera 2	Rudolf Bernt	587	57	I.GT
15	58	Anthony Lazzaro (USA)/Andre Toennis (USA)/Omar Daniel (CH) Alex Tradd (USA)/Frank Beard (USA)/Sam Shalala (USA)	Porsche 911	Frank Beard	577	50	GTU
16	48	Oliver Kuttner (USA)/Danny Marshall (USA)/Weldon Scrogham (USA)/John Biggs (USA)	Porsche 911 Carrera 2	Dave Maraj	572 DNF	56	I.GT
17	5	Peter Cunningham (USA)/Boris Said (USA)/Shawn Hendricks (USA)/Lou Gigliotti (USA)/Jim Minneker (USA)	Chevrolet Corvette	Kim Baker	570 DNF	36	I.GT
18	22	Daniel Urrutia (USA)/Craig A. Rubright (USA)/Gene Whipp (USA)	Chevrolet Camaro (Southern Racing)	John Josey	551 DNF	24	GTS
19	92	Paul Lewis (USA)/Ludwig Heimrath, Jr. (CDN)/Paul Reisman (USA)/Leigh Miller (USA)/John Reisman (USA)	Porsche 944	Scott Clarke	549	56	I.GT
20	45	Fermin Velez (E)/John Marconi (USA)/Thomas Hessert (USA)/Don Bell (USA)	Kudzu-Buick DG-2	Andy Evans	546 DNF	32	GTL
21	21	Bruce Trenery (USA)/Larry Less (USA)/Andrew Osman (AUS)/Kent Painter (USA)	Chevrolet Camaro (Watson)	Bruce Trenery	537	47	GTS
22	87	John Annis (USA)/Bob Kirkland (USA)/Louis Beall (USA)/Dick Downs (USA)/ Bob Deeks (USA)/Eddie Sharp, Jr. (USA)	Chevrolet Camaro (Creative)	John Annis	529	42	GTS
23	95	Butch Leitzinger (USA)/Bob Leitzinger (USA)/Chuck Kurtz (USA)	Nissan 240SX (Leitzinger)	Bob Leitzinger	528	31	GTU
24	42	Buddy Lazier (USA)/Sam Shalala (USA)/Michael Sheehan (USA)/Chris Ivey (USA)/Anthony Lazzaro (USA)	Fabcar-Porsche	Frank Beard	523	58	GTL
25	25	Jorge Oyhanart (RA)/Emilio Satriano (RA)/Fabian Acuna (RA)/ Eduardo Ramos (RA)/Hugo Mazzacane (RA)	Oldsmobile Cutlass (Kreider)	Argentina Racing/Kreider	500	35	GTS
26	08	Henry Taleb (EC)/Alfonso Adarquea (EC)/Marcelo Adarquea (EC)/Ignacio Escobar (EC)	Nissan 300ZX	Henry Taleb	491 DNF	53	GTU
27	99	Juan Manuel Fangio II (RA)/Andy Wallace (GB)/Kenneth Acheson (GB)	Eagle-Toyota Mk III	Dan Gurney	481 DNF	2	GTP
28	44	Andy Evans (USA)/Charles Morgan (USA)/Lon Bender (USA)	Kudzu-Buick DG-2	Andy Evans	461 DNF	20	GTL
29	90	Andy Petery (USA)/Steve Fossett (USA)/Gary Stewart (USA) Les Delano (USA)	Pontiac Firebird (Riggins)	Les Delano	438 DNF	40	GTS
30	26	Mark Sandridge (USA)/Butch Hamlet (USA)/Charles Slater (USA)	Porsche 911 (Fabcar)	Alex Job	435	54	GTU
31	24	Juan Dibos (PE)/Eduardo Dibos, Jr. (PE)/Raul Orlandini (PE) * Roger Mandeville (USA)	Mazda MX-6 (Bacon)	Juan Dibos	435	37	GTU
32	50	Oma Kimbrough (USA)/Robert McElheny (USA)/Bob Hundredmark (USA)/ Mark Montgomery (USA)/David Kicak (USA)/Hoyt Overbagh (USA)	Chevrolet Camaro (Stock Car Products)	Hoyt Overbagh	433 DNF	38	GTS
33	94	John Heinricy (USA)/Stuart Hayner (USA)/Andy Pilgrim (GB) Don Knowles (USA)	Chevrolet Corvette	Tommy Morrison	432	29	I.GT
34	39	Bill Auberlen (USA)/Michael Graham (USA)/David Russell, Jr. (USA)	Mazda RX-7	Charles Wagner	430	51	GTU
35	23	Oscar Aventin (RA)/Juan Landa (RA)/Osvaldo Moressi (RA)/ Osvaldo Lopez (RA)/* Hugo Mazzacane (RA)	Oldsmobile Cutlass (Kreider)	Argentina Racing/Kreider	425	27	GTS
36	12	Henry Camferdam, Jr. (USA)/Dan Robson (USA)/Gary Drummond (USA)	Mazda MX-6 (Bacon)	Henry Camferdam, Jr.	414 DNF	46	GTU
37	76	Geoff Brabham (AUS)/David Loring (USA)/Dominic Dobson (USA)/Tommy Riggins (USA)	Nissan 300ZX (Cunningham)	Clayton Cunningham	332 DNF	19	GTS
38	73	Stephen Hynes (USA)/Jack Lewis (USA)/Joe Cogbill, Jr. (USA)/* Bob Barker (USA)	Porsche 911 Carrera RSR	Jack Lewis	293 DNF	44	GTU
39	10	John Macaluso (USA)/Ed Delong (CDN)/Nick Holmes (CDN)/Bruce MacInnes (USA)	Tiga-Buick SC86	John Macaluso	278	28	GTL
40	66	Dennis Aase (USA)/Carlos Moran (ES)/Chip Hanauer (USA)/ Jay Cochran (USA)/Bobby Carradine (USA)	Gunnar-Porsche 966 (Chapman)	Kevin Jeannette	271 DNF	15	GTP
41	6	Chip Robinson (USA)/Hurley Haywood (USA)/Henri Pescarolo (F)/Danny Sullivan (USA)	Porsche 962C (Joest)	Reinhold Joest	258 DNF	3	GTP
42	57	Frank Del Vecchio (USA)/Joe Danaher (USA)/Guy Kuster (F)/Reed Kryder (USA)	Nissan 240SX (Kryderacing)	Reed Kryder	255	55	GTU
43	93	Del Percilla (USA)/Danny Kellermeyer (USA)/Scott Allman (USA)/ Ron Nelson (USA)/John Heinricy (USA)/Stuart Hayner (USA)/Andy Pilgrim (GB)	Chevrolet Corvette	Tommy Morrison	250 DNF	33	I.GT
44	81	Mark Kennedy (USA)/Jeff Purvis (USA)/Hugh D. Fuller (USA)/Jeff Swindell (USA)/Mike Joy (USA)	Chevrolet Camaro (Dillon)	Mark Kennedy	231 DNF	45	GTS
45	07	Tim Banks (USA)/Paul Reckert, Jr. (USA)/Don Arpin (USA)/ * Guy W. Church (USA)/* David Kicak (USA)	Chevrolet Camaro (Banks)	Don Arpin	213	57	GTS
46	7	Bob Wollek (F)/Manuel Reuter (D)/Frank Jelinski (D)/John Winter (D)	Porsche 962C (Joest)	Reinhold Joest	190 DNF	5	GTP
47	18	Ron Fellows (CDN)/Tomiko Yoshikawa (J)/Peter Baljet (CDN)/ Desire Wilson (ZA)/* Tom Gloy (USA)	Ford Mustang (Riley & Scott)	Tom Gloy	189 DNF	21	GTS
48	67	Paul Mazzacane (USA)/Kenny Wallace (USA)/Chester Edwards (USA)	Chevrolet Camaro (Howe)	Paul Mazzacane	183 DNF	49	GTS
49	40	John Jones (CDN)/Paul Duckworth (USA)/Neil Jamieson (CDN)/ Kenny Wilden (CDN)/Jeffrey Lapcevich (CDN)/* Heinz Wirth (CH)	Alba Ford-Cosworth AR2	Uli Bieri	180 DNF	25	GTL
50	19	Anthony Puleo (USA)/Bill Wessel (USA)/Dave Fuller (USA)/Tim O'Brien (USA)	Chevrolet Camaro (Bemco)	Anthony Puleo	174	30	GTS
51	20	Jim Adams (USA)/Robert Kirby (USA)/Chris Cord (USA)/* John Hotchkis, Sr. (USA)	Porsche 962 (Holbert-Fabcar)	John Hotchkis, Sr.	162 DNF	11	GTP
52	31	Dorsey Schroeder (USA)/Jack Baldwin (USA)/* George Robinson (USA)/ * Calvin Fish (USA)/* Paul Gentilozzi (USA)	Oldsmobile Cutlass (Rocketsports)	Paul Gentilozzi	159 DNF	10	GTS
53	35	Richard McDill (USA)/Tom Juckette (USA)/Bill McDill (USA)	Chevrolet Camaro (Preston)	Bill McDill	156 DNF	26	GTS
54	9	Bob Earl (USA)/Chris Smith (USA)/Bob Schader (USA)	Spice-Acura SE91P	Harry Brix	152 DNF	13	GTL
55	51	Calvin Fish (USA)/George Robinson (USA)/* Darin Brassfield (USA)	Oldsmobile Cutlass (Rocketsports)	Paul Gentilozzi	133 DNF	12	GTS
56	4	Richard J. Valentine (USA)/Max Schmidt (USA)/Jim Minneker (USA)/Ken Payson (USA)/* Kim Baker (USA)	Chevrolet Corvette	Kim Baker	111 DNF	52	I.GT
57	01	John O'Steen (USA)/Larry Schumacher (USA)/Jochen Rohr (USA)/ * Dave White (USA)/* Nick Ham (USA)/* Rich Moskalik (USA)	Porsche 911 Carrera 2 Cup	Jochen Rohr	103 DNF	43	I.GT
58	32	Davy Jones (USA)/David Brabham (AUS)/John Nielsen (DK)/John Andretti (USA)	Jaguar XJR-12D (Advanced)	Tom Walkinshaw	92 DNF	8	Gp.C
59	49	Parker Johnstone (USA)/* Steve Cameron (NZ)/* Dan Marvin (USA)/* Doug Peterson (USA)	Spice-Acura SE91P	Don Erb	DNF	14	GTL
60	3	John Nielsen (DK)/* John Andretti (USA)/* David Brabham (AUS)	Jaguar XJR-12D (Advanced)	Tom Walkinshaw	18 DNF	7	Gp.C

Rolex 24 At Daytona

February 5-6, 1994

24 hour event on the 3.560 mile circuit.
Distance covered: 707 laps for 2516.920 miles.
Winning time: 24 hours, 0 minutes, 54.016 seconds for a speed of 104.806 mph.
Margin of victory: 24 laps.
Fastest lap: #75 Nissan 300ZX (John Morton) 1:51.829, 114.604 mph.
Fastest qualifier: #44 Spice-Chevrolet WSC94 (Fermin Velez) 1:45.934, 120.981 mph.
1 full-course caution for 22 minutes

FIN.	CAR NO.	DRIVERS	CAR	ENTRANT	LAPS	START	CLASS
1	76	Scott Pruett (USA)/Butch Leitzinger (USA)/Paul Gentilozzi (USA)/Steve Millen (NZ)	Nissan 300ZX (Cunningham)	Clayton Cunningham	707	4	GTS
2	86	Bob Wollek (F)/Dominique Dupuy (F)/Jesus Pareja-Mayo (E)/Juergen Barth (D)	Porsche 911S LM	Jack Leconte	683	10	GTS
3	65	Ulrich Richter (D)/Karl-Heinz Wlazik (D)/Dirk-Rainer Ebeling (D)/Gunther Doebler (D)	Porsche 911 Carrera RSR	Dirk-Rainer Ebeling	671	23	GTU
4	02	Harald Grohs (D)/Frank Katthoefer (D)/Bernd Maylaender (D)/Mark Sandridge (USA)	Porsche 911 Carrera RSR	Jochen Rohr	613	13	GTU
5	6	Tommy Riggins (USA)/R. K. Smith (USA)/Price Cobb (USA)/Irv Hoerr (USA)	Oldsmobile Cutlass Supreme (Rocketsports)	Harry Brix	665	63	GTS
6	00	Cor Euser (NL)/Antonio de Azevedo Hermann (BR)/Maurizio Sandro Sala (BR)/Franz Konrad (A)	Porsche 911 Carrera RSR	Franz Konrad	664	16	GTU
7	94	John Heinricy (USA)/Andy Pilgrim (GB)/Stuart Hayner (USA)/Boris Said (USA)	Chevrolet Corvette	Tommy Morrison	658	11	GTS
8	79	Edgar Doeren (D)/Gualtiero Giribaldi (I)/Luigiano Pagotto (I)/Sandro Angelastri (CH)	Porsche 911 Carrera RSR	Manfred Freisinger	656	34	GTU
9	2	Jeremy Dale (CDN)/Ruggero Melgrati (I)/Bob Schader (USA)/Price Cobb (USA)	Spice-Oldsmobile AK93	Harry Brix	651	2	WSC
10	63	Wayne Taylor (ZA)/Hugh D. Fuller (USA)/Charles Morgan (USA)/Jim Downing (USA)	Kudzu-Mazda DG-3	Jim Downing	650	5	WSC
11	5	John Fergus (USA)/Mark Dismore (USA)/Tommy Riggins (USA) Darin Brassfield (USA)	Oldsmobile Cutlass Supreme (Rocketsports)	Harry Brix	634	62	
12	99	Nick Ham (USA)/Mikael Gustavsson (B)/Kalman Bodis (H)/Maurizio Sandro Sala (BR)/ Bernd Netzeband (D)/Franz Konrad (A)	Porsche 911	Franz Konrad	632	24	GTS
13	77	Jay Cochran (USA)/Ferdinand de Lesseps (F)/Michel Aouate (USA)	Porsche 911 Carrera RSR	Kevin Jeannette	630	39	GTU
14	73	Jack Lewis (USA)/John Bourassa (USA)/Bob Beasley (USA)/Joe Cogbill, Jr. (USA)	Porsche 911 Carrera RSR	Jack Lewis	613	29	GTU
15	37	Enzo Calderari (CH)/Lilian Bryner (CH)/Renato Mastroprieto (I)/Ruggero Grassi (I)	Porsche 911 Carrera RSR	Enzo Calderari	612	26	GTU
16	62	Didier Theys (B)/Steve Shelton (USA)/Art Coia (USA)/Tom Shelton (USA)/* Ken Fengler (USA)	Ferrari 348 GTC	Shelton Ferrari	599	42	GTU
17	0	Kat Teasdale (CDN)/John Graham (CDN)/Leigh Miller (USA)	Porsche 968	Leigh Miller	584	55	GTU
18	21	Vic Rice (USA)/Robert Nearn (GB)/David Gooding (GB)/Mauro Borella (I)/* Scott Gaylord (USA)	Chevrolet Camaro (Riggins)	Kent Painter	541	31	GTS
19	51	Andrew Osman (AUS)/Bruce Trenery (USA)/Jeffrey Pattinson (GB)/Thomas Bscher (D)	Oldsmobile Cutlass (Riggins)	Bruce Trenery	538	50	GTS
20	08	Shunji Kasuya (J)/Takamasa Nakagawa (J)/Steven Andskar (S)	Nissan Skyline	Nissan Motorsports	532	43	GTU
21	31	Guy Kuster (F)/Joaquin DeSoto (USA)/John Starkey (GB)/Kent Painter (USA)/* Scott Gaylord (USA)	Chevrolet Camaro (Riggins)	Kent Painter	524	53	GTS
22	71	Jerry Churchill (USA)/Randy Churchill (CDN)/Ken Bupp (USA) Guy W. Church (USA)	Oldsmobile Cutlass (Riggins)	Jerry Churchill	519	41	GTS
23	32	Rob Wilson (NZ)/Felipe Solano (CO)/Luis Rico (CO)/Lucio Bernal (CO)/Luis F. Malkun (CO)	Mazda MX-6 (MAT)	Luis Botero	498	65	GTU
24	13	Anthony Puleo (USA)/Craig Stone (USA)/Ray Irwin (USA)/Daniel Urrutia (USA)	Chevrolet Camaro (Bemco)	Anthony Puleo	490	20	GTS
25	59	Walter Roehrl (D)/Hurley Haywood (USA)/Danny Sullivan (USA)/Hans-Joachim Stuck Jr. (D)	Porsche 911 GT America	Brumos Porsche	467 DNF	8	GTS
26	19	Bill Auberlen (USA)/Les Lindley (USA)/Ron Finger (USA)/Michael Sheehan (USA)	Mazda RX-7 (MAT)	Bill Auberlen.	462	64	GTU
27	87	John Annis (USA)/Louis Beall (USA)/Claude Lawrence (USA)/Chris Funk (USA)/* Duane Neyer (USA)	Chevrolet Camaro (Creative)	John Annis	447	36	GTS
28	25	Scott Watkins (USA)/Brian DeVries (USA)/Dale Kreider (USA)/Nort Northam (USA)/* Don Arpin (USA)	Oldsmobile Cutlass (Kreider)	Dale Kreider	428 DNF	30	GTS
29	57	Reed Kryder (USA)/Tom Miller (USA)/Larry Ray (USA)/ Frank Del Vecchio (USA)/* Joe Danaher (USA)	Nissan 240SX (Kryderacing)	Reed Kryder	413	51	GTU
30	45	Lon Bender (USA)/Steve Fossett (USA)/Andreas Fuchs (D)/Don Bell (USA)	Kudzu-Buick DG-2	Andy Evans	410 DNF	6	WSC
31	69	Gustl Spreng (USA)/Fritz Mueller (D)/Jodexnis Kersten (D)	Porsche 911 Cup	Gustl Spreng	394 DNF	48	GTU
32	68	Art Pilla (USA)/Hugh Johnson (USA)/Joe Danaher (USA)/Charles Coker, Jr. (USA)	Porsche 944	Charles Coker, Jr.	390 DNF	58	GTU
33	93	Jim Minneker (USA)/Jeff Nowicki (USA)/Scott Allman (USA)/Kenny Wilden (CDN)	Chevrolet Corvette	Tommy Morrison	390	22	GTS
34	52	David Murry (USA)/Angelo Cilli (USA)/Tammy Jo Kirk (USA)/Anthony Lazzaro (USA)	Porsche 911	Angelo Cilli	372 DNF	37	GTU
35	96	Don Knowles (USA)/John Mirro (USA)/Rick Sutherland (USA)/ Dirk Layer (USA)/* Bob Leitzinger (USA)	Nissan 240SX (Leitzinger)	John Mirro	359 DNF	18	GTU
36	4	Juan Dibos (PE)/Eduardo Dibos, Jr. (PE)/Raul Orlandini (PE)/Dan Robson (USA)/* Neto Jochamowitz (PE)	Mazda RX-7 (MAT)	Juan Dibos	359 DNF	28	GTU
37	48	Hilton Cowie (ZA)/Stephen Watson (ZA)/George Fouche (ZW)	Lotus Esprit 300	Hugh Chamberlain	354 DNF	21	GTU
38	8	Henry Taleb (EC)/Terry Andrews (EC)/Jean-Pierre Michelet (EC)/Wilson Amador (EC)	Nissan 300ZX	Henry Taleb	352	56	GTU
39	36	Paul Dallenbach (USA)/Oliver Kuttner (USA)	Pegasus-BMW	Oliver Kuttner	343	49	WSC
40	16	James Weaver (GB)/Rob Dyson (USA)/Scott Sharp (USA)/John Paul, Jr. (USA)	Spice-Ferrari DR-3	Rob Dyson	339 DNF	7	WSC
41	75	Steve Millen (NZ)/John Morton (USA)/Johnny O'Connell (USA)	Nissan 300ZX (Cunningham)	Clayton Cunningham	283 DNF	3	GTS
42	82	Dick Greer (USA)/Peter Uria (USA)/Al Bacon (USA)/Mike Mees (USA)/* Terry Lingner (USA)	Mazda RX-7 (Chassis Dynamics)	Dick Greer	258 DNF	25	GTU
43	35	Richard McDill (USA)/Tom Juckette (USA)/Bill McDill (USA)	Chevrolet Camaro (Preston)	Bill McDill	253 DNF	12	GTS
44	26	Jim Pace (USA)/Michael Smith (USA)/Charles Slater (USA)/Butch Hamlet (USA)	Porsche 911 (Fabcar)	Alex Job	238 DNF	33	GTU
45	9	Geoff Brabham (AUS)/Derek Bell (GB)/Andy Wallace (GB)/Morris Shirazi (USA)	Spice-Chevrolet SC89	Morris Shirazi	228 DNF	9	WSC
46	44	Fermin Velez (E)/Ross Bentley (CDN)/Tim McAdam (USA)/Andy Evans (USA)	Spice-Chevrolet WSC94	Andy Evans	223 DNF	1	WSC
47	3	Linda Pobst (USA)/Margy Eatwell (USA)/Tami Rai Busby (USA)/ Kat Teasdale (CDN)/Leigh O'Brien (USA)	Chevrolet Camaro (Dillon)	Leigh O'Brien	219	45	GTS

FIN.	CAR NO.	DRIVERS	CAR	ENTRANT	LAPS	START	CLASS
48	18	Roger Schramm (USA)/Paul Lewis (USA)/Chuck Goldsborough (USA)/ Ludwig Heimrath, Jr. (CDN)/* Leigh Miller (USA)	Porsche 944	Leigh Miller	207 DNF	38	GTU
49	27	Olaf Manthey (D)/Oliver Mathai (D)/Wolfgang Mathai (D)	Porsche 911 Carrera RSR	Porsche Club EV	188 DNF	14	GTU
50	33	Douglas Campbell (USA)/Ralph Thomas (USA)/Frank Jackson (USA)	Mazda RX-7 (Cars)	Ralph Thomas	183	61	GTU
51	72	Bill Adam (CDN)/Juan Manuel Fangio II (RA)/Brian Redman (GB)/Mike Peters, Jr. (USA)	Porsche 911 GT2	Dave Maraj	177 DNF	17	GTS
52	70	Bill Ferran (USA)/Bruce Jones (USA)/Ray Hendricks (USA)/Jay Kjoller (USA)	Porsche 911	Dynamic Air	172 DNF	44	GTU
53	42	Stig Amthor (D)/Rolf Kuhn (CH)/Philippe de Craene (B)/Philippe Olczyk (B)	Porsche 911 Carrera RSR	Rudolf Bernt	171 DNF	27	GTU
54	11	Stan Cleva (USA)/Rob Mingay (CDN)/Joseph Hamilton (USA)/Tony Kester (USA)	Tiga-Mazda Spyder	Tony Kester	160 DNF	47	WSC
55	23	Tom Curren (USA)/Ed Delong (CDN)/Robert Borders (USA)	Oldsmobile Cutlass (Riggins)	Tom Curren	153	59	GTS
56	50	Oma Kimbrough (USA)/David Kicak (USA)/Robert McElheny (USA)/ * Max Schmidt (USA)/*C. J. Johnson (USA)/* Hoyt Overbagh (USA)/* Mark Montgomery (USA)	Chevrolet Camaro (Stock Car Products)	Hoyt Overbagh	61 DNF	35	GTS
57	78	Cameron Worth (USA)/William Weston (USA)/* Sylvain Tremblay (USA)	Mazda RX-7	Cameron Worth	58 DNF	54	GTU
58	24	Alfonso Darquea (EC)/Carlos Paredes (EC)/Marcelo Darquea (EC)/*Andres Izurieta (EC)/* Henry Bradley (USA)	Toyota Corolla	Saeta Racing	51 DNF	60	GTU
59	04	Art Cross (USA)/* Leonard McCue (USA)/* Jim Crist (USA)/* Kerry Hitt (USA)/* Mark Kennedy (USA)	Chevrolet Camaro (Cross)	Art Cross	31 DNF	40	GTS
60	58	Sam Shalala (USA)/Ernie Lader (CDN)/Omar Daniel (CH)/* Alex Tradd (USA)/* Frank Beard (USA)	Porsche 911	Sam Shalala	19 DNF	46	GTU
61	91	C. Lorin Hicks (USA)/* Mel A. Butt (USA)/* Tommy Johnson (USA)/* Ron Zitza (USA)	Porsche 911	Mel A. Butt	12 DNF	32	GTU
62	07	Rick Bye (CDN)/* Harry Hatch (CDN)/* Raymond David (CDN)/* Ludwig Heimrath, Jr. (CDN)	Porsche 968	Rick Bye	8 DNF	52	GTU
DNS	01	Jochen Rohr (USA)/John O'Steen (USA)/Larry Schumacher (USA)/Jeff Zwart (USA)	Porsche 911 Carrera RSR	Jochen Rohr	0	15	GTU
DNS	47	Thorkild Thyrring (DK)/Doc Bundy (USA)/Juergen Laessig (D)/Harry Nuttall (GB)	Lotus Esprit 300	Hugh Chamberlain	0	19	GTU
DNS	61	Danny Marshall (USA)/John Biggs (USA)/Weldon Scrogham (USA)	Porsche 911 Carrera 2	Cole Scrogham	0	57	GTU

Rolex 24 At Daytona

Feburary 4-5, 1995

24 hour event on the 3.560 mile circuit.

Distance covered: 690 laps for 2456.400 miles.

Winning time: 24 hours, 0 minutes, 51.03 seconds for a speed of 102.290 mph.

Margin of victory: 5 laps, weather.

Fastest lap: #3 Ferrari 333SP (Velez) 1:45.464, 121.520 mph/195.567 kph

Fastest qualifier: #33 Ferrari 333SP (Baldi), 1:43.326, 124.035 mph.

6 full-course cautions for 132 minutes.

FIN.	CAR NO.	DRIVERS	CAR	ENTRANT	LAPS	START	CLASS
1	**10**	**Giovanni Lavaggi (I)/Juergen Laessig (D)/Christophe Bouchut (F)/Marco Werner (D)**	**Kremer-Porsche K8 (Thompson)**	**Kremer Brothers**	**690**	**17**	**LM WSC**
2	**2**	**Jeremy Dale (CDN)/Jay Cochran (USA)/Fredrik Ekblom (S)**	**Spice-Oldsmobile BDG-02**	**Harry Brix**	**685**	**4**	**WSC**
3	**70**	**Tommy Kendall (USA)/Paul Newman (USA)/Michael Brockman (USA)/Mark Martin (USA)**	**Ford Mustang (Roush)**	**Jack Roush**	**682**	**15**	**GTS-1**
4	01	Hurley Haywood (USA)/David Murry (USA)/Bernd Maylaender (D)/Jochen Rohr (USA)	Porsche 911 GT2	Jochen Rohr	655	21	GTS-1
5	**54**	**Enzo Calderari (CH)/Lilian Bryner (CH)/Renato Mastroprieto (I)/Ulrich Richter (D)**	**Porsche 911 Carrera RSR**	**Mathias Stadler**	**654**	**36**	**GTS-2**
6	93	Jean-Pierre Michelet (EC)/Henry Taleb (EC)/Rob Wilson (NZ)/John Fergus (USA)	Nissan 240SX (Leitzinger)	Henry Taleb	653	40	GTS-2
7	55	Dennis Aase (USA)/Jorge Trejos (CR)/Javier Quiros (CR)/Martin Snow (USA)	Porsche 911 Carrera RSR	Jorge Trejos	646	46	GTS-2
8	50	Massimo Sigala (I)/Gianfranco Brancatelli (I)/Elton Julian (USA)/Fabrizio Barbazza (I)	Ferrari 333SP (Dallara)	Antonio Ferrari	645	3	WSC
9	40	Karl-Christian Luck (D)/Dieter Lindenbaum (D)/Herrmann Tilke (D)/Edgar Doeren (D)	Porsche 911 Carrera RSR	(no entrant)	645	48	GTS-2
10	96	John Heinricy (USA)/Stuart Hayner (USA)/Don Knowles (USA) Andy Pilgrim (GB)	Chevrolet Corvette	Tommy Morrison	643	29	GTS-1
11	02	Johannes Huber (A)/Lloyd Hawkins (USA)/Andreas Knapp Voith (D)/Nikolaus Siokola (A)	Porsche 911 Carrera RSR	Jochen Rohr	640	41	GTS-2
12	63	Jim Downing (USA)/Butch Hamlet (USA)/Jim Pace (USA)/Tim McAdam (USA)	Kudzu-Mazda DG-3	Jim Downing	637	8	WSC
13	26	Joe Cogbill, Jr. (USA)/Jack Lewis (USA)/Monte Shelton (USA)/Charles Slater (USA)	Porsche 911 (Fabcar)	Alex Job	633	47	GTS-2
14	82	Dick Greer (USA)/Al Bacon (USA)/Peter Uria (USA)/Mike Mees (USA)/Terry Lingner (USA)	Mazda RX-7 (Chassis Dynamics)	Dick Greer	619	57	GTS-2
15	5	Price Cobb (USA)/Mark Dismore (USA)/Darin Brassfield (USA)/Calvin Fish (USA)	Oldsmobile Cutlass Supreme (Rocketsports)	Harry Brix	613	19	GTS-1
16	65	Wally Castro (PR)/Rolando Falgueras (PR)/Magnolo Villa (PR)/Biagio Parisi (YV)/Axel Rivera (PR)	Ford Mustang (Roush)	Jack Roush	607	22	GTS-1
17	53	Bill McDill (USA)/Tom Juckette (USA)/Jim Trotnow (USA)/Richard McDill (USA)	Chevrolet Camaro (Preston)	Bill McDill	602	30	GTS-1
18	85	Wolfgang Land (D)/Arnold Mattschull (D)/Bill Auberlen (USA)/Alexander Mattschull (D)/John Finger (USA)	Porsche 993	Daytona Garage	587 DNF	38	GTS-2
19	91	Bernd Netzeband (D)/Bert Ploeg (NL)/Edgar Althoff (D)/Regis Schuch (BR)/* Franz Konrad (A)	Porsche 911	Franz Konrad	582	45	GTS-1
20	25	Gerry Jackson (USA)/Bruce Barkelew (USA)/Angelo Cilli (USA)/Anthony Lazzaro (USA)	Porsche 911 (Fabcar)	Alex Job	581	44	GTS-2
21	75	Steve Millen (NZ)/Johnny O'Connell (USA)/John Morton (USA)	Nissan 300ZX (Cunningham)	Clayton Cunningham	575	14	GTS-1
22	52	Andy Strasser (USA)/Kevin Wheeler (USA)/Jamie Busby (USA)/	Porsche 911 Carrera RSR	Andy Strasser	566	69	GTS-2

FIN.	CAR NO.	DRIVERS	CAR	ENTRANT	LAPS	START	CLASS
		Dennis DeFranchesci (USA)/Al Ludwig (USA)					
23	08	Weldon Scrogham (USA)/Steve Marshall (USA)/John Biggs (USA)/Danny Marshall (USA)	Porsche 911 Carrera RSR	Marshall/Marshall	564	72	GTS-2
24	09	Craig Conway (GB)/Todd Flis (USA)/Richard Nisbett (USA)/Troy Flis (USA)	Mitsubishi Eclipse	Flis Brothers	562	74	GTS-2
25	69	Fritz Mueller (D)/Ray Mummery (USA)/Gustl Spreng (USA)	Porsche 911 Cup	Gustl Spreng	553	62	GTS-1
26	24	Jarett Freeman (USA)/Simon Gregg (USA)/Max Schmidt (USA)/Nort Northam (USA)	Porsche 993 Supercup	Jarett Freeman	553	73	GTS-2
27	04	Dick Downs (USA)/Larry Schumacher (USA)/Wolfgang Haugg (D)/Richard Raimist (USA)	Porsche 911SC	Jochen Rohr	550	59	GTS-2
28	4	R. K. Smith (USA)/Calvin Fish (USA)/Brian DeVries (USA)/Irv Hoerr (USA)	Oldsmobile Cutlass Supreme (Pratt & Miller)	Harry Brix	547	11	GTS-1
29	99	Karl-Heinz Wlazik (D)/Ira Storfer (CDN)/Helmut Reis (D)	Porsche 911 Carrera RSR	Franz Konrad	524 DNF	51	GTS-2
30	43	Brian Williams (USA)/John Mirro (USA)/Lee Payne (USA)/David Loring (USA)/Don Kitch (USA)	Denali-Oldsmobile	Payne/Williams	512 DNF	10	WSC
31	95	Jim Minneker (USA)/Charles Morgan (USA)/Del Percilla (USA)/Rob Morgan (USA)	Chevrolet Corvette	Tommy Morrison	511	49	GTS-1
32	0	Chuck Cottrell (USA)/Leigh Miller (USA)/Mike Holt (USA)/Chuck Goldsborough (USA)/ Elias Chocron (PAN)/Ted Anderson (USA)/Eric Van Cleef (USA)/Don Kitch (USA)	Kudzu-Buick DG-1	Chuck Cottrell	489	65	WSC
33	64	Mel A. Butt (USA)/Jim Higgs (USA)/Bob Barker (USA)/Ron Zitza (USA)	Chevrolet Camaro (Evans)	Mel A. Butt	480	34	GTS-1
34	61	Enrico Bertaggia (I)/Philippe Olczyk (B)/Josef Wendlinger (D)/Johnny Unser (USA)	Callaway Corvette	Reeves Callaway	473	26	GTS-1
35	30	Gianpiero Moretti (I)/Wayne Taylor (ZA)/Eliseo Salazar (RCH)/Didier Theys (B)	Ferrari 333SP (Dallara)	Gianpiero Moretti	467 DNF	5	WSC
36	31	Robert Nearn (GB)/Nigel Smith (GB)/Juan Gac Soto (RCH)/ Kent Painter (USA)/* Scott Gaylord (USA)	Chevrolet Camaro (Watson)	Kent Painter	450	43	GTS-1
37	7	Dominic Dobson (USA)/Bill Cooper (USA)/Don Bell (USA)/Paul Debban (USA)/* Bobby Brown (USA)/	Spice-Chevrolet HC94	Bobby Brown	447 DNF	9	WSC
38	00	Cor Euser (NL)/Antonio de Azevedo Hermann (BR)/Tiff Needell (GB)/Franz Konrad (A)	Kremer-Porsche K8 (Thompson)	Franz Konrad	436 DNF	23	LMWSC
39	3	Fermin Velez (E)/Andy Evans (USA)/Paul Gentilozzi (USA)/Eric van de Poele (B)	Ferrari 333SP	Andy Evans	417 DNF	2	WSC
40	51	Bruce Trenery (USA)/Vic Rice (USA)/Grahame Bryant (GB)/Buddy Norton (USA)/Jeffrey Pattinson (GB)	Cannibal-Chevrolet	Scott Flatt	407	42	WSC
41	33	Mauro Baldi (I)/Michele Alboreto (I)/Stefan Johansson (S)	Ferrari 333SP (Dallara)	Andy Evans	405 DNF	1	WSC
42	15	Luis Delconte (RA)/Alejandro Spinella (RA)/Fabian Hermoso (RA)/ Facundo Gilbicella (RA)/* Ruben Salerno (RA)	Oldsmobile Cutlass Supreme (Kreider)	Dale Kreider	402	31	GTS-1
43	87	John Annis (USA)/Domenico DeLuca (USA)/David Donavon (USA)/ Tom Paligraf (USA)/* Jim Dunlop (USA)	Chevrolet Camaro (Creative)	John Annis	387	54	GTS-1
44	34	Leonard McCue (USA)/Gary Grubbs (USA)/Greg Cecil (USA)/ Bob Hudgins (USA)/Ray Halin (USA)	Chevrolet Camaro (Creative)	RFF Racing	376	67	GTS-1
45	57	Reed Kryder (USA)/Christian Heinkele (F)/Klaus Roth (D)/Frank Del Vecchio (USA)	Nissan 240SX (Kryderacing)	Reed Kryder	373	61	GTS-2
46	17	Art Pilla (USA)/Kenper Miller (USA)/Charles Mendez (USA)/Dave White (USA)	Porsche 911ME (Fabcar)	Dave White	368 DNF	32	GTS-1
47	88	Ralph Thomas (USA)/John Bourassa (USA)/Douglas Campbell (USA)/Amos Johnson (USA)	Mazda RX-7 (Cars)	Douglas Campbell	335 DNF	68	GTS-2
48	92	Oma Kimbrough (USA)/Mark Montgomery (USA)/Mauro Casadei (I)/ David Kicak (USA)/Steve Golden (USA)/Hoyt Overbagh (USA)/* Robert McElheny (USA)	Chevrolet Camaro (Stock Car Products)	Hoyt Overbagh	317 DNF	50	GTS-1
49	90	Craig Carter (USA)/Andy Petery (USA)/Tommy Riggins (USA)/Les Delano (USA)	Oldsmobile Cutlass Supreme (Riggins)	Tommy Riggins	316	12	GTS-1
50	32	Juan Carlos Carbonell (RCH)/Mike Smellie (USA)/John Finger (USA)/Lambert McLaurin (USA)	Mazda MX-6 (Bacon)	Comprent Motor Sports	294 DNF	60	GTS-2
51	20	Chet Fillip (USA)/Jeff McComb (USA)/Brian Berry (USA)/Mac DeMere (USA)/Don Fuller (USA)	Consulier Intruder	Warren Mosler	291 DNF	27	WSC
52	37	Eric Bachelart (B)/Michael Dow (USA)/Oliver Kuttner (USA)/Rick Ferguson (USA)/* Richard Taylor (USA)	Pegasus-BMW	Oliver Kuttner	290	18	WSC
53	21	Guy Kuster (F)/Sergio Brambilla (I)/Mauro Borella (I)/Kent Painter (USA)/Scott Gaylord (USA)	Chevrolet Camaro (Riggins)	Kent Painter	280	56	GTS-1
54	68	Joe Danaher (USA)/Hugh Johnson (USA)/Charles Coker, Jr. (USA)/Cort Wagner (USA)	Porsche 968 (Frings)	Charles Coker, Jr.	259	71	GTS-2
55	97	Robert Kahn (USA)/Vic Sifton (CDN)/Trevor Seibert (CDN)/Joe Varde (USA)	Chevrolet Lumina (Laughlin)	Vic Sifton	253 DNF	39	GTS-1
56	22	Thomas Hessert (USA)/Steve Durst (USA)/John Higgins (USA)/Mark Abel (USA)	Porsche 911ME (Fabcar)	Fabcar	246 DNF	58	GTS-2
57	77	Don Arpin (USA)/Tim Banks (USA)/Paul Reckert, Jr. (USA)/John Bumb (USA)	Oldsmobile Cutlass Supreme (Laughlin)	Tim Banks	237 DNF	70	GTS-1
58	12	Dieter Quester (A)/John Paul, Jr. (USA)/Pete Halsmer (USA)/David Donohue (USA)	BMW M3	Tom Milner	221 DNF	35	GTS-2
59	86	Mark Mehalic (USA)/John Finger (USA)/Marin Dose (D)/* Bill Auberlen (USA)	Porsche 993	Daytona Garage	207 DNF	52	GTS-2
60	8	Henry Camferdam, Jr. (USA)/Ben Morgenrood (ZA)/Roger Mandeville (USA)/* Dan Robson (USA)	Hawk-Mazda MD3R	Henry Camferdam, Jr.	160 DNF	24	WSC
61	74	Hans-Joachim Stuck, Jr. (D)/Bill Adam (CDN)/Harald Grohs (D)/ Neto Jochamowitz (PE)/Dorsey Schroeder (USA)/* John Fergus (USA)	Porsche 911 GT2	Dave Maraj	159 DNF	20	GTS-1
62	44	Craig T. Nelson (USA)/Ross Bentley (CDN)/Dan Clark (USA)/Margie Smith-Haas (USA)	Spice-Lexus SE90	Craig T. Nelson	156 DNF	28	WSC
63	62	Mark Kennedy (USA)/Billy Bies (USA)/David Rankin (USA)/Tom Curren (USA)	Oldsmobile Cutlass Supreme (Riggins)	Tom Curren	132 DNF	66	GTS-1
64	9	Andy Wallace (GB)/Jan Lammers (NL)/Derek Bell (GB)	Spice-Chevrolet SE90	Morris Shirazi	100 DNF	7	WSC
65	6	Dan Marvin (USA)/Stanley Dickens (S)/Jeff Gray (USA)/* Rick Sutherland (USA)	Spice-Oldsmobile HC93	Rick Sutherland	92 DNF	16	WSC
66	18	Tommy Johnson (USA)/John Sheldon (GB)/Dan Lewis (USA)/Rick Fairbanks (USA)	Mazda MX-6 (Bacon)	Dan Lewis	91 DNF	64	GTS-2
67	23	Bob Hundredmark (USA)/Ken Fengler (USA)/Steve Pfeffer (USA)/Gene Henry (USA)	Oldsmobile Cutlass Supreme (Riggins)	Bob Hundredmark	78 DNF	33	GTS-1
68	58	Michael Smith (USA)/Doug Frazier (USA)/Jim Matthews (USA)/Sam Shalala (USA)/* Frank Beard (USA)	Porsche 911	Sam Shalala	65 DNF	63	GTS-2
69	13	Boris Said (USA)/* Justin Bell (GB)/* Ronny Meixner (D)	BMW M3	Tom Milner	60 DNF	37	GTS-2
70	11	Ken Bupp (USA)/Scott Watkins (USA)/* Luis Sereix (USA)/* Daniel Urrutia (USA)	Ford Mustang (Southern Motorsports)	John Josey	49 DNF	55	GTS-1
71	66	Chapman Root (USA)/* Jonathan Baker (GB)/* Cort Wagner (USA)/* Carlos Moran (ES)	Porsche 911 Carrera RSR	Kevin Jeannette	24 DNF	53	GTS-1
72	38	Tony Ave (USA)/* Ray Irwin (USA)/* Doug Nies (USA)/* Earl Segredahl (USA)	Chevrolet Camaro (Weaver)	Earl Segredahl	17 DNF	13	GTS-1
73	16	James Weaver (GB)/* Rob Dyson (USA)/* Scott Sharp (USA)/ *Butch Leitzinger (USA)/& John Paul, Jr. (USA)	Riley & Scott-Ford Mk III	Rob Dyson	11 DNF	6	WSC
74	72	Neto Jochamowitz (PE)/* Mike Peters, Jr. (USA)/* Jeff Purner (USA)/* Marco Apicella (I)	Porsche 911ME (Fabcar)	Dave Maraj	0 DNF	25	GTS-1

Rolex 24 At Daytona

February 3-4, 1996

24 hour event on the 3.560 mile circuit.
Distance covered: 697 laps for 2481.320 miles.
Winning time: 24 hours, 0 minutes, 53.552 seconds for a speed of 103.324 mph.
Margin of victory: 1:05.518, weather.
Fastest lap set: #30 Ferrari 333SP (Max Papis), 1:41.951, 125.707 mph.
Fastest qualifier: #30 Ferrari 333SP (Didier Theys), 1:41.224, 126.610 mph.
11 full-course cautions for 165 minutes.

FIN.	CAR NO.	DRIVERS	CAR	ENTRANT	LAPS	START	CLASS
1	**4**	**Wayne Taylor (ZA)/Scott Sharp (USA)/Jim Pace (USA)**	**Riley & Scott-Oldsmobile Mk III**	**Dan Doyle**	**697**	**2**	**WSC**
2	30	Gianpiero Moretti (I)/Bob Wollek (F)/Didier Theys (B)/Massimiliano Papis (I)	Ferrari 333SP	Gianpiero Moretti	697	1	WSC
3	63	Tim McAdam (USA)/Barry Waddell (USA)/Butch Hamlet (USA)/Jim Downing (USA)	Kudzu-Mazda DLM	Jim Downing	649	10	WSC
4	**55**	**Enzo Calderari (CH)/Ferdinand de Lesseps (F)/Lilian Bryner (CH)/Ulrich Richter (D)**	**Porsche 911 Carrera RSR**	**Mathias Stadler**	**649**	**40**	**GTS-2**
5	43	Ross Bentley (CDN)/Franck Freon (F)/Lee Payne (USA)/Don Kitch (USA)	Riley & Scott-Oldsmobile Mk III	Lee Payne	645	8	WSC
6	78	Cort Wagner (USA)/Steve Dente (USA)/Mike Doolin (USA)/Richard Raimist (USA)	Porsche 911 Carrera RSR	Richard Raimist	641	45	GTS-2
7	**5**	**Rob Morgan (USA)/Charles Morgan (USA)/Joe Pezza (USA)/Jon Gooding (USA)/ Irv Hoerr (USA)**	**Oldsmobile Aurora (Rocketsports)**	**Harry Brix**	**641**	**15**	**GTS-1**
8	6	Eduardo Dibos, Jr. (PE)/Boris Said (USA)/Johnny O'Connell (USA)/Juan Dibos (PE)/ Raul Orlandini (PE)/Jorge Koechlin (PE)	Ford Mustang (Riley & Scott)	Juan Dibos	639	18	GTS-1
9	06	John Paul, Jr. (USA)/Javier Quiros (CR)/David Donohue (USA)/Pete Halsmer (USA)	BMW M3	Tom Milner	638	32	GTS-2
10	41	Kurt Dujardyn (B)/Franco La Rosa (B)/Michel Neugarten (B)/Kurt Thiers (B)	Porsche 911 Carrera RSR	AD Sport	608	60	GTS-2
11	45	Rick Bye (CDN)/Doug Trott (CDN)/John Ruther (USA)/Phillip Kubik (USA)/ Grady Willingham (USA)	Porsche 993 Carrera RSR	Doug Trott	604	51	GTS-2
12	99	Andy Pilgrim (GB)/Harald Grohs (D)/Larry Schumacher (USA)/Will Pace (USA)	Porsche 911 Carrera RSR	Larry Schumacher	603	36	GTS-2
13	00	Almo Coppelli (I)/Riccardo Agusta (I)/Brian Simo (USA)	Callaway Corvette	Riccardo Agusta	602	22	GTS-1
14	24	Joe Cogbill, Jr. (USA)/Ron Finger (USA)/John Rutherford, Jr. (USA)/Monte Shelton (USA)	Porsche 911 (Fabcar)	Alex Job	599	53	GTS-2
15	86	Steve Marshall (USA)/Martyn Konig (GB)/Peter Chambers (GB)/Danny Marshall (USA)	Porsche 964 Carrera Cup	Marshall/Marshall	598	74	GTS-2
16	73	Jack Lewis (USA)/Edison Lluch (PR)/Kevin Buckler (USA)/Vic Rice (USA)	Porsche 911 Carrera RSR	Jack Lewis	591	49	GTS-2
17	03	Dirk Layer (USA)/Larry Galbo (USA)/Jim McCarthy (USA)/Kelly Collins (USA)	Porsche 911 Carrera RS Cup	Alan Friedman	577 DNF	73	GTS-2
18	35	Richard McDill (USA)/Tom Juckette (USA)/Bill McDill (USA)	Chevrolet Camaro (Preston)	Bill McDill	562	31	GTS-1
19	54	Jean-Francois Hemroulle (B)/Stephane Cohen (B)/Paul Kumpen (B)/Albert Vanierschot (B)	Porsche 993	Peka Racing	560	47	GTS-2
20	20	Butch Leitzinger (USA)/Andy Wallace (GB)/Rob Dyson (USA)/James Weaver (GB)	Riley & Scott-Ford Mk III	Rob Dyson	555	4	WSC
21	75	Cameron Worth (USA)/Roberto Tonetti (I)/Rodger Bogusz (USA)/Hartmut Haussecker (D)	Mazda RX-7	Cameron Worth	554	65	GTS-2
22	42	Jarett Freeman (USA)/Simon Gregg (USA)/Max Schmidt (USA)	Porsche 993 Supercup	Jarett Freeman	546	71	GTS-2
23	26	Charles Slater (USA)/Richard Spenard (CDN)/Thomas Hessert (USA)	Porsche 911ME (Fabcar)	Alex Job	539	48	GTS-2
24	51	Bruce Trenery (USA)/Grahame Bryant (GB)/Nigel Smith (GB)/Jeffrey Pattinson (GB)	Cannibal-Chevrolet	Bruce Trenery	538	59	WSC
25	68	Peter Uria (USA)/Brady Refenning (USA)/John Maffucci (USA)/Jack Refenning (USA)/Tim Vargo (USA)	Porsche 911 Cup	Tim Vargo	526	54	GTS-2
26	47	Juergen Barth (D)/Jesus Pareja-Mayo (E)/Jean-Luc Chereau (F)/Regis Schuch (BR)/Jack Leconte (F)	Porsche 911 GT2 Evo	Jack Leconte	518	27	GTS-1
27	92	Mauro Casadei (I)/Keith Minkhorst (CDN)/Andrea Garbagnati (MC)/ Francesco Ciani (I)/Stefano Bucci (I)	Chevrolet Camaro (Stock Car Products)	Hoyt Overbagh	477	41	GTS-1
28	65	Samuel Brown (USA)/Kurt Thiel (USA)/Vincenzo Polli (I)/Renato Mastroprieto (I)/ * Luigiano Pagotto (I)	Porsche 911 Supercup	Luigino Pagotto	477	68	GTS-2
29	98	Price Cobb (USA)/Tommy Archer (USA)/Shawn Hendricks (USA)/ Mark Dismore (USA)/Vic Sifton (CDN)	Dodge Viper GTS-R	Vic Sifton	472	16	GTS-1
30	8	Henry Camferdam, Jr. (USA)/Roger Mandeville (USA)/Bill Auberlen (USA)/Tony Kester (USA)	Hawk-Chevrolet C8	Henry Camferdam, Jr.	466 DNF	9	WSC
31	21	Mauro Borella (I)/Willie Beck (D)/Alastair Davidson (GB)/Huw Bolle-Jones (GB)/ Kent Painter (USA)	Chevrolet Monte Carlo LM (Watson)	Kent Painter	451	63	GTS-1
32	79	William Robert Farmer (NZ)/Robert Nearn (GB)/Greg Murphy (NZ)/Stephane Ortelli (F)/Alex Tradd (USA)	Porsche 911 GT2	William Robert Farmer	437 DNF	23	GTS-1
33	61	Mark Mehalic (USA)/Chris Cervelli (USA)/Philip Collin (USA)/Gregg Tracy (USA)/ Spencer Sharpe (USA)	Porsche 911 C4S AWD	Mark Alan	428 DNF	64	GTS-2
34	58	Sam Shalala (USA)/Matt Turner (USA)/Robby McGehee (USA)/Mark Hillestad (USA)/ Jim Matthews (USA)	Porsche 911 (Fabcar)	Sam Shalala	420	67	GTS-2
35	10	Anthony Puleo (USA)/Ernst Gschwender (D)/Don Kitch (USA)/Mark Kennedy (USA)/ Craig Conway (GB)	Chevrolet Camaro (Bemco)	Anthony Puleo	391	46	GTS-1
36	15	Facundo Gilbicella (RA)/Luis Delconte (RA)/Edgardo Raul Petrich (RA)/ Eduardo Lavari (RA)/* Rafael Sorrentino (RA)	Oldsmobile Cutlass Supreme (Kreider)	Argentina Racing/Kreider	377 DNF	37	GTS-1
37	25	Anthony Lazzaro (USA)/Gerry Jackson (USA)/Peter Faucetta (USA)/Angelo Cilli (USA)/ * P.J. Jones (USA)	Porsche 911 (Fabcar)	Alex Job	359	55	GTS-2
38	57	Reed Kryder (USA)/Christian Heinkele (F)/Guy Kuster (F)/Manfred Jurasz (A)/ Frank Del Vecchio (USA)	Nissan 240SX (Kryderacing)	Reed Kryder	358	72	GTS-2

FIN.	CAR NO.	DRIVERS	CAR	ENTRANT	LAPS	START	CLASS
39	52	Andy Strasser (USA)/Kevin Wheeler (USA)/David Russell Jr. (USA)/ Rich Peplin (USA)/Al Ludwig (USA)	Porsche 911 Carrera RSR	Andy Strasser	341 DNF	61	GTS-2
40	64	Mel A. Butt (USA)/Jim Higgs (USA)/Dave McTureous (USA)/Ron Zitza (USA)	Chevrolet Camaro (Evans)	Mel A. Butt	321 DNF	28	GTS-1
41	91	Stuart Hayner (USA)/John Heinricy (USA)/Roger Schramm (USA)/Ron Nelson (USA)	Chevrolet Camaro (Auto Concepts)	Roger Schramm	306 DNF	19	GTS-1
42	88	Douglas Campbell (USA)/Carlos Fronti (USA)/Ralph Thomas (USA)/Amos Johnson (USA)	Mazda RX-7 (Cars)	Douglas Campbell	300 DNF	69	GTS-2
43	01	Hurley Haywood (USA)/Scott Goodyear (CDN)/John O'Steen (USA)/David Murry (USA)	Porsche 911 GT2 Evo	Jochen Rohr	284 DNF	20	GTS-1
44	09	Bernd Netzeband (D)/Andre Lara-Resende (BR)/Andre Ahrle (D)/Karel Dolejsi (CZ)/* Franz Konrad (A)	Porsche 911 GT2 Evo	Franz Konrad	281 DNF	50	GTS-1
45	49	Dan Shaver (USA)/Stanton Barrett (USA)/Jack Willes (USA)/* Joe Varde (USA)	Chevrolet Camaro (Rocketsports)	Dan Shaver	272 DNF	34	GTS-1
46	89	Geoff Lees (GB)/Kenneth Acheson (GB)/Tiff Needell (GB)	Lister Storm GTS (G Force)	Brian Lister	254 DNF	17	GTS-1
47	70	Dirk-Rainer Ebeling (D)/Karl-Heinz Wlazik (D)/Markus Oestreich (D)/Ulrich Richter (D)	Porsche 993	Dirk-Rainer Ebeling	231 DNF	44	GTS-2
48	46	James Nelson (USA)/Mark Greenberg (USA)/Nort Northam (USA) John Drew (USA)/ Rob Collings (USA)	Porsche 911 Carrera RS Cup	Rob Collings	231 DNF	76	GTS-2
49	36	Eric van de Poele (B)/Rick Sutherland (USA)/Jean-Paul Libert (B)/Steve Fossett (USA)	Courage-Chevrolet C41	Rick Sutherland	209 DNF	7	WSC
50	1	Irv Hoerr (USA)/Brian Cunningham (USA)/Mike Borkowski (USA)/Darin Brassfield (USA)	Oldsmobile Aurora (Pratt & Miller)	Harry Brix	207 DNF	11	GTS-1
51	90	Andy Petery (USA)/Les Delano (USA)/Tommy Riggins (USA)/Craig Carter (USA)	Oldsmobile Cutlass Supreme (Riggins)	Tommy Riggins	204 DNF	13	GTS-1
52	84	Bertrand Balas (F)/Thierry Lecerf (F)/Marco Spinelli (I)/Jose Close (B)/Bob Hebert (USA)	Dodge Viper	Gilles Gaignault	203 DNF	52	GTS-1
53	07	Dieter Quester (A)/Manfred Wollgarten (D)/Pete Halsmer (USA)/* Kermit Upton (USA)	BMW M3	Tom Milner	198 DNF	33	GTS-2
54	74	Hans-Joachim Stuck, Jr. (D)/Thierry Boutsen (B)/Bill Adam (CDN)	Porsche 911 GT2 Evo	Dave Maraj	181 DNF	14	GTS-1
55	2	Johnny O'Connell (USA)/Craig T. Nelson (USA)/Dan Clark (USA)/Case Montgomery (USA)	Riley & Scott-Ford Mk III	Craig T. Nelson	180 DNF	5	WSC
56	66	Juergen von Gartzen (D)/Bruno Michelotti (CH)/Gualtiero Giribaldi (I)/Luigiano Pagotto (I)	Porsche 993 Carrera RSR	Luigino Pagotto	174 DNF	58	GTS-2
57	7	Elliott Forbes-Robinson (USA)/John Schneider (USA)/Don Bell (USA)/ Lon Bender (USA)/* Bobby Brown (USA)	Spice-Oldsmobile HC94	Bobby Brown	159 DNF	12	WSC
58	97	George Robinson (USA)/Eric Bachelart (B)/Trevor Seibert (CDN)/Vic Sifton (CDN)	Dodge Viper GTS-R	Vic Sifton	157 DNF	29	GTS-1
59	05	Olivier Grouillard (F)/Derek John Hill (USA)/Gildo Pallanca-Pastor (MC)	Bugatti EB110	Gildo Pallanca-Pastor	154 DNF	21	GTS-1
60	67	Jeff Purner (USA)/Dave White (USA)/Karl Singer (USA)/Charles Coker, Jr. (USA)	Porsche 911 Carrera RSR	Charles Coker, Jr.	123 DNF	39	GTS-2
61	33	John Mirro (USA)/Chuck Cottrell (USA)/Mark Neuhaus (USA) Rick Fairbanks (USA)	Kudzu-Buick DG-2	Chuck Cottrell	109 DNF	66	WSC
62	3	Mauro Baldi (I)/Michele Alboreto (I)/Fermin Velez (E)/* Andy Evans (USA)	Ferrari 333SP	Andy Evans	106 DNF	3	WSC
63	02	Jochen Rohr (USA)/Herbert Schuerg (D)/Axel Rohr (D)/Carl Rosenblad (S)	Porsche 911 GT2	Jochen Rohr	105 DNF	35	GTS-1
64	08	Wido Roessler (D)/Antonio de Azevedo Hermann (BR)/Franz Konrad (A)/* Nick Ham (USA)/ * Charles Mendez (USA)	Porsche 911 GT2 Evo	Franz Konrad	105 DNF	26	GTS-1
65	77	Tim Banks (USA)/Mark Montgomery (USA)/Bob Hundredmark (USA)/ Steve Goldin (USA)/Pascal Dro (F)	Oldsmobile Cutlass Supreme (Laughlin)	Tim Banks	96 DNF	75	GTS-1
66	56	Martin Snow (USA)/Dennis Aase (USA)/Jorge Trejos (CR)/P.J. Jones (USA)	Porsche 911 GT2	Martin Snow	91 DNF	24	GTS-1
67	38	Jon Field (USA)/Juan Carlos Carbonell (RCH)/James Briody (USA)	Pegasus-BMW NPTI (Nissan-Chapman)	Oliver Kuttner	86 DNF	42	WSC
68	27	Jack Refenning (USA)/Tim Vargo (USA)/* John Maffucci (USA)/ * Brady Refenning (USA)/* Charles Mendez (USA)	Porsche 993 Carrera RS	Tim Vargo	75 DNF	57	GTS-2
69	72	Derek Bell (GB)/John Fergus (USA)/Dorsey Schroeder (USA)	Porsche 911 GT2 Evo	Dave Maraj	71 DNF	25	GTS-1
70	40	Wolfgang Kaufmann (D)/Yukihiro Hane (J)/* Edgar Doeren (D)/* Klaus Scheer (D)	Porsche 993 Carrera RSR	Manfred Freisinger	48 DNF	38	GTS-1
71	22	Guido Dacco (I)/Alex Caffi (I)/* Fabio Montani (I)/* Gabrio Rosa (I)	Chevron-BMW B73	Fabio Montani	48 DNF	43	WSC
72	16	Andy Wallace (GB)/Rob Dyson (USA)/* James Weaver (GB)/* Butch Leitzinger (USA)	Riley & Scott-Ford Mk III	Rob Dyson	43 DNF	6	WSC
73	62	Billy Bies (USA)/David Perelle (USA)/* Tom Curren (USA)/* James Hildock (USA)	Oldsmobile Cutlass Supreme (Riggins)	Tom Curren	39 DNF	62	GTS-1
74	93	Henry Taleb (EC)/* Jean-Pierre Michelet (EC)/* Wilson Amador (EC)/ * Rob Wilson (NZ)/* Daniel Urrutia (USA)	Nissan 240SX (Leitzinger)	Henry Taleb	28 DNF	56	GTS-2
75	87	John Annis (USA)/* David Donavon (USA)/* Jerry Gillis (USA)/ * David Lacroix (USA)/* Gary Tiller (USA)/* Dana Webster (USA)	Chevrolet Camaro (Creative)	John Annis	8 DNF	78	GTS-1
76	9	Justin Bell (GB)/* Stanley Dickens (S)/* John Shapiro (USA)/* Morris Shirazi (USA)/ * Gustl Spreng (USA)	Spice-Cadillac HC94	Morris Shirazi	7 DNF	70	WSC
DNS	37	Giuseppe Bacigalupe (RCH)/Juan Gac Soto (RCH)/Mauricio Perrot (RCH)/Tim Richardson (USA)	Pegasus-BMW	Oliver Kuttner	0	31	WSC
DNS	44	Michael Jacobs (USA)/Brent Cross (USA)/Michael Duffy (USA)/Pat Sessions (USA)	Pontiac Firebird (Howe)	Michael Jacobs	0	77	GTS-1

Rolex 24 At Daytona

February, 1-2, 1997

24 hour event on the 3.560 mile circuit.
Distance covered: 690 laps for 2456.400 miles.
Winning time: 24 hours, 0 minutes, 48.691 seconds for a speed of 102.292 mph
Margin of victory: 1 lap.
Fastest lap: #3 Ferrari 333SP (Fermin Velez), 1:43.153, 124.243 mph.
Fastest qualifier: #3 Ferrari 333SP (Fermin Velez), 1:40.456, 127.578 mph.
18 full-course cautions.

FIN.	CAR NO.	DRIVERS	CAR	ENTRANT	LAPS	START	CLASS
1	20	Elliott Forbes-Robinson (USA)/John Schneider (USA)/Rob Dyson (USA)/John Paul, Jr. (USA)/ Butch Leitzinger (USA)/Andy Wallace (GB)/James Weaver (GB)	Riley & Scott-Ford Mk III	Rob Dyson	690	5	WSC
2	3	Fermin Velez (E)/Andy Evans (USA)/Charles Morgan (USA) Rob Morgan (USA)	Ferrari 333SP	Andy Evans	689	1	WSC
3	4	Eduardo Dibos, Jr. (PE)/Jim Pace (USA)/Barry Waddell (USA)/*Wayne Taylor (ZA)	Riley & Scott-Oldsmobile Mk III	Eduardo Dibos, Jr.	672	10	WSC
4	99	Ralf Kelleners (D)/Patrice Goueslard (F)/Claudia Huertgen (D)/Andre Ahrle (D)	Porsche 911 GT2	Fabian Roock	665	20	GTS-2
5	01	Jochen Rohr (USA)/Andy Pilgrim (GB)/Harald Grohs (D)/Arnd Meier (D)	Porsche 911 GT2 Evo	Jochen Rohr	663	18	GTS-1
6	74	Hans-Joachim Stuck, Jr. (D)/Bill Adam (CDN)/Thierry Boutsen (B)	Porsche 911 GT2 Evo	Dave Maraj	661	17	GTS-1
7	30	Gianpiero Moretti (I)/Antonio de Azevedo Hermann (BR)/Derek Bell (GB)/Didier Theys (B)	Ferrari 333SP (Dallara)	Gianpiero Moretti	660	2	WSC
8	03	Philippe de Craene (B)/Zak Brown (USA)/Dirk Layer (USA)/Michel Ligonnet (F)	Porsche 911 GT2 Evo	Fabian Roock	651	30	GTS-2
9	10	Javier Quiros (CR)/Derek John Hill (USA)/Boris Said (USA)/Bill Auberlen (USA)/Thomas Hessert (USA)	BMW M3	Tom Milner	640	35	GTS-3
10	39	Jim Matthews (USA)/Hurley Haywood (USA)/David Murry (USA)/Doc Bundy (USA)	Porsche 911	Jim Matthews	638	49	GTS-3
11	76	Kelly Collins (USA)/Mike Doolin (USA)/Scott Peeler (USA)/Cort Wagner (USA)	Porsche 993 Carrera RSR	Richard Raimist	638	42	GTS-3
12	31	Bob Wollek (F)/Yannick Dalmas (F)/Wido Roessler (D)/Franz Konrad (A)	Porsche 911 GT2	Franz Konrad	637	24	GTS-2
13	69	Tim Ralston (USA)/Jeff Gamroth (USA)/Jorge Trejos (CR)/Monte Shelton (USA)	Porsche 911	Jorge Trejos	632	60	GTS-3
14	26	Anthony Lazzaro (USA)/Eric Bretzel (USA)/Michael Conte (USA)/Angelo Cilli (USA)	Porsche 911	Alex Job/Angelo Cilli	631	64	GTS-3
15	94	Olivier Beretta (MC)/Tommy Archer (USA)/Dominique Dupuy (F)	Dodge Viper GTS-R	Hugues de Chaunac	628	12	GTS-1
16	98	Larry Schumacher (USA)/John O'Steen (USA)/Will Pace (USA)/Robert Nearn (GB)	Porsche 911 Carrera RSR	Larry Schumacher	627	66	GTS-2
17	25	Jeff Purner (USA)/Terry Lingner (USA)/Robbie Groff (USA)/Charles Slater (USA)	Porsche 911 Carrera RSR	Alex Job	624	55	GTS-3
18	6	John Fergus (USA)/Ron Finger (USA)/Dan Marvin (USA)/Boris Said (USA)/Derek John Hill (USA)	BMW M3	Tom Milner	622	37	GTS-3
19	46	Geoff Lees (GB)/Tiff Needell (GB)/Anthony Reid (GB)	Lister Storm GTS (G Force)	Brian Lister	615	15	GTS-1
20	53	Axel Rohr (D)/Bruno Michelotti (CH)/Denis Lay (CH)/Uwe Sick (D)	Porsche 911	Jochen Rohr	615	63	GTS-3
21	04	Mike Johnson (USA)/Duke Johnson (USA)/Max Schmidt (USA)/Rusty Schmidt (USA)	Porsche 911	Max Schmidt	609	62	GTS-3
22	55	Enzo Calderari (CH)/Lilian Bryner (CH)/Ellen Lohr (D)/Ulrich Richter (D)	Porsche 911	Mathias Stadler	607	48	GTS-3
23	40	Kurt Thiers (B)/Dirk Schoysman (B)/Jean-Francois Hemroulle (B)/Stephane Cohen (B)	Porsche 911	Paul Kumpen	602	51	GTS-3
24	54	Richard Spenard (CDN)/John Ruther (USA)/Spencer Lane (USA)/Doug Trott (CDN)/ Tom Baldwin (USA)/Grady Willingham (USA)	Porsche 993 Carrera RSR	Doug Trott	600	53	GTS-3
25	56	Martin Snow (USA)/Peter Kitchak (USA)/Ray Lintott (AUS)/Terry Ollila (USA)	Porsche 911 GT2	Martin Snow	591	29	GTS-2
26	63	Tim McAdam (USA)/Yojiro Terada (J)/Joe Castellano (USA)/Jim Downing (USA)	Kudzu-Mazda DLM	Jim Downing	569	13	WSC
27	96	Helmut Reis (D)/Karl Augustin (A)/Manfred Jurasz (A)/Gerold Ried (D)/ Kalman Bodis (H)/* Ernst Gschwender (D)	Porsche 911 GT2	Gerold Ried	565	76	GTS-3
28	97	Edgar Doeren (D)/Leo van Sande (B)/Klaus Scheer (D)/Berndt Neutag (D)	Porsche 911 GT2 Evo	Klaus Scheer	560	43	GTS-1
29	78	Steve Velazquez (USA)/Gary Blackman (USA)/Steve Dente (USA)/Richard Gray (USA)	Porsche 911 Carrera RSR	Richard Raimist	554	44	GTS-3
30	35	Richard McDill (USA)/Tom Juckette (USA)/Giovanni Biava (I)/Bill McDill (USA)	Chevrolet Camaro (Preston)	Richard McDill	540	28	GTS-1
31	09	Ray Kong (USA)/Tom Miller (USA)/Vic Rice (USA)/Chris Neville (USA)	Pontiac Grand Prix (Howe)	Vic Rice	534	39	GTS-1
32	37	Mauro Casadei (I)/Stefano Bucci (I)/Francesco Ciani (I)/Andrea Garbagnati (MC)	Chevrolet Camaro (Stock Car Products)	Hoyt Overbagh	507	52	GTS-1
33	81	Kevin Sherwood (GB)/Michael Millard (GB)/Peter Hardman (GB)/Nigel Greensall (GB)	Pro-Sport Ford 3000 Spyder	Graham Williams	498	31	WSC
34	8	Henry Camferdam, Jr. (USA)/Johnny O'Connell (USA)/Scott Schubot (USA)/Roger Mandeville (USA)	Hawk-Chevrolet C8	Henry Camferdam, Jr.	494 DNF	7	WSC
35	90	Andy Petery (USA)/Les Delano (USA)/Tim J. O'Kennedy (IRL)/Craig Carter (USA)	Oldsmobile Cutlass Supreme (Riggins)	Road Circuit Technology	490	23	GTS-1
36	91	Roger Schramm (USA)/Stuart Hayner (USA)/John Heinricy (USA)/Marty Miller (USA)	Chevrolet Camaro (Auto Concepts)	Roger Schramm	468 DNF	16	GTS-1
37	77	Matthew Cohen (USA)/Pete Halsmer (USA)/John Morton (USA)/Sylvain Tremblay (USA)/* Bobby Brown (USA)	BMW M3	Matthew Cohen	440 DNF	46	GTS-3
38	1	Wayne Taylor (ZA)/Scott Sharp (USA)/Eric van de Poele (B)	Riley & Scott-Oldsmobile Mk III	Dan Doyle	427 DNF	4	WSC
39	42	Jarett Freeman (USA)/Simon Gregg (USA)/Michael Duffy (USA)	Porsche 911	Jarett Freeman	422 DNF	79	GTS-3
40	87	John Annis (USA)/Kelly Toombs (USA)/Neil Tilbor (USA)/Chris Funk (USA)/ Keith Scharf (USA)/David Donovan (USA)	Chevrolet Camaro (Bemco)	John Annis	404	56	GTS-1
41	85	Chris Gleason (USA)/Grant Tromans (GB)/Jack Gratton (GB)Gerard MacQuillan (GBM)	Porsche 911 GT2	Hugh Chamberlain	400 DNF	54	GTS-2
42	24	Don Kitch (USA)/Chris Bingham (USA)/Chip Hanauer (USA)/Chuck Lyford (USA)/Byron Sanborn (USA)	Porsche 911 (Fabcar)	Alex Job/Team Seattle	400	67	GTS-3
43	68	Kevin Buckler (USA)/Charles Nearburg (USA)/Steve Rees (USA)/Fred Seipp (USA)	Porsche 911	Kevin Buckler	393	45	GTS-3
44	29	Alex Caffi (I)/Fabio Montani (I)/Gabrio Rosa (I)	Riley & Scott-Oldsmobile Mk III	Fabio Montani	390 DNF	9	WSC
45	83	Gianfranco Brancatelli (I)/Luca Drudi (I)/Luigiano Pagotto (I)/Renato Mastroprietro (I)/Charles Margueron (F)	Porsche 911	Luigino Pagotto	387 DNF	70	GTS-3
46	47	Nick Longhi (USA)/John Kohler (USA)/Matt Turner (USA)/Joe Safina (USA)/Gary R. Smith (USA)/ Jeffrey Lapcevich (CDN)	Saleen Mustang	T-F Racing	377	80	GTS-2
47	05	Jeff Hays (USA)/Cary Eisenlohr (USA)/Steve Rebeil (USA)/William Stitt (USA)/Kevin Wheeler (USA)	Porsche 911	Auto Sport South	374 DNF	72	GTS-3

FIN.	CAR NO.	DRIVERS	CAR	ENTRANT	LAPS	START	CLASS
48	7	Dieter Quester (A)/Marc Duez (B)/Markus Oestreich (D)/Boris Said (USA)	BMW M3	Tom Milner	373 DNF	40	GTS-3
49	75	George Robinson (USA)/Irv Hoerr (USA)/Jack Baldwin (USA)/Vic Sifton (CDN)	Oldsmobile Aurora (Pratt & Miller)	George Robinson	368 DNF	14	GTS-1
50	27	Marco Polani (I)/Silvino Giarotti (I)/Fabio Rosa (I)/C. J. Johnson (USA)/Marco de Turbe (I)	Chevrolet Camaro (Frings)	Hoyt Overbagh	353	38	GTS-1
51	58	Philip Collin (USA)/Lew Bouchier (USA)/Mauro Borella (I)/Luca Cattaneo (I)/ Sam Shalala (USA)/Alex Tradd (USA)	Porsche 911 (Fabcar)	Sam Shalala	353	75	GTS-3
52	60	Owen Trinkler (USA)/Roberto Quintanilla (MEX)/Jeff Ward (USA)/* David Kopf (USA)	Keiler-Ford KII	David Kopf	348	21	WSC
53	64	Mel A. Butt (USA)/Jim Higgs (USA)/Dave McTureous (USA)/Dennis King (USA)	Chevrolet Camaro (Evans)	Mel A. Butt	339 DNF	26	GTS-1
54	71	Boris Said (USA)/Johnny Unser (USA)/Enrico Bertaggia (I)/Ron Fellows (CDN)	Callaway C7R	Johnny Unser	331 DNF	25	GTS-1
55	44	Lance Stewart (USA)/Brad Creger (VI)/John Bourassa (USA)/John Finger (USA)	Mazda RX-7 (Chassis Dynamics)	Brad Creger	310	71	GTS-3
56	70	Kurt Dujardyn (B)/Koen Wauters (B)/Kris Wauters (B)/Jean-Paul Herreman (B)	Porsche 911 GT2	AD Sport	304 DNF	74	GTS-2
57	19	Mark Montgomery (USA)/Edd Davin (USA)/Butch Brickell (USA)/ *Rael (Claude Vorilhon) (CDN)	Argo-BMW JM17 (Pegasus-Nissan-Chapman)	Edd Davin	279	78	WSC
58	67	Price Cobb (USA)/Phil Andrews (GB)/Rob Rizzo (USA)/David Warnock (GB)/ Robert Schirle (GB)/Tim Allen (USA)	Saleen Mustang	Steve Saleen	274	47	GTS-2
59	92	Raymond Boissoneau (USA)/Peter Goebel (USA)/J. W. Pettigrew (USA)/ David Loring (USA)/Peter Argetsinger (USA)	Mazda RX-7 (Chassis Dynamics)	Raymond Boissoneau	271 DNF	61	GTS-3
60	16	Andy Wallace (GB)/John Paul, Jr. (USA)/Butch Leitzinger (USA)/James Weaver (GB)	Riley & Scott-Ford Mk III	Rob Dyson	227 DNF	3	WSC
61	80	Richard Maugeri (USA)/Sim Penton (USA)/Rob Debartelobeu (USA)/David Perelle (USA)	Oldsmobile Cutlass Supreme (Riggins)	David Perelle	219 DNF	77	GTS-1
62	73	Henry Taleb (EC)/Edison Lluch (PR)/Kurt Mathewson (USA)/Scott Knollenberg (USA)/* Jack Lewis (USA)	Porsche 911 Carrera RSR	Jack Lewis	209 DNF	65	GTS-3
63	28	Jon Field (USA)/A. J. Smith (USA)/Ralph Thomas (USA)/John Mirro (USA)/Rick Ferguson (USA)	Spice-Oldsmobile SC95	Fabian Dressler	182	19	WSC
64	62	Tom Scheuren (USA)/Kerry Hitt (USA)/Bobby Jones (USA)/Gerry Green (USA)	Chevrolet Camaro (Watson)	Tom Scheuren	181	69	GTS-1
65	2	Craig T. Nelson (USA)/Case Montgomery (USA)/Dan Clark (USA)/Darin Brassfield (USA)	Riley & Scott-Ford Mk III	T. Nelson	158 DNF	6	WSC
66	41	Chris Cervelli (USA)/Bruce Busby (USA)/Mark Anderson (USA)/* Ali Basakinci (USA)	Porsche 911 Carrera RSR	Chris Cervelli	138 DNF	58	GTS-3
67	95	Thomas Volk (USA)/Don Bell (USA)/Bill Cooper (USA)/Franck Freon (F)	Kudzu-Chevrolet DL-4	Thomas Volk	121 DNF	22	WSC
68	65	Robert Schirle (GB)/Steve Saleen (USA)/David Warnock (GB)/Tim Allen (USA)	Saleen Mustang	Steve Saleen	109	50	GTS-2
69	51	Bruce Trenery (USA)/Grahame Bryant (GB)/Jeffrey Pattinson (GB)/Patrick van Schoote (B)/ * Buddy Norton (USA)	Chevrolet Monte Carlo (NRP)	Bruce Trenery	101 DNF	68	GTS-1
70	45	Scott Goodyear (CDN)/Ed Davies (USA)/Arie Luyendyk (NL)/* Kerry Hitt (USA)	Porsche 911 GT2 Evo	Ed Davies	95 DNF	32	GTS-1
71	38	Dorsey Schroeder (USA)/Peter Cunningham (USA)/John Green (USA)/ * Mark Hein (USA)/* Greg Loebel (USA)	Acura NSX (Thompson)	Mark Hein	90 DNF	34	GTS-3
72	88	Ross Bentley (CDN)/Danny Sullivan (USA)/Jeff W. Jones (USA)/* Robbie Buhl (USA)	Riley & Scott-Chevrolet Mk III	Peter Kuhn	72 DNF	8	WSC
73	22	Paul Reisman (USA)/John Reisman (USA)/* Shane Lewis (USA)/* Buddy Norton (USA)	Chevrolet Camaro.	Paul Reisman	57 DNF	73	GTS-3
74	15	Ernst Gschwender (D)/Anthony Puleo (USA)/* Mark Kennedy (USA)/* Daniel Urrutia (USA)	Chevrolet Camaro (Bemco)	Anthony Puleo	46 DNF	36	GTS-1
75	50	Alfons Taels (B)/Georges Cremer (B)/* Paul Kumpen (B)/* Albert Vanierschot (B)	Porsche 911	Paul Kumpen	39 DNF	57	GTS-3
76	61	Cor Euser (NL)/* Bernd Netzeband (D)/* Bert Ploeg (NL)/* Wolfgang Kaufmann (D)/* Karel Dolejsi (CZ)	Porsche 911 GT2	Franz Konrad	23 DNF	33	GTS-2
77	00	Almo Coppelli (I)/* Riccardo Agusta (I)/* Carl Rosenblad (S)	Callaway Corvette LM600	Riccardo Agusta	23 DNF	41	GTS-2
78	34	Todd Vallancourt (USA)/Hal Corbin (USA)/* Bill Evans (USA)/ * Toto Lassally (ES)/* Patrick Boidron (F)	Oldsmobile Cutlass Supreme (Riggins)	Todd Vallancourt	22 DNF	59	GTS-1
79	49	Dan Shaver (USA)/* Jack Willes (USA)/* Joe Varde (USA)	Chevrolet Camaro (Rocketsports)	Dan Shaver	16 DNF	27	GTS-1
80	9	Fredrik Ekblom (S)/* Didier Cottaz (F)/* Jerome Policand (F)	Courage-Chevrolet C41	Yves Courage	12 DNF	11	WSC

Rolex 24 At Daytona

January 31-February 1, 1998

24 hour event on the 3.560 mile circuit.
Distance covered: 711 laps for 2531.160 miles.
Winning time: 24 hours, 0 minutes, 52.83 seconds for a speed of 105.401 mph.
Margin of victory: 8 laps.
Fastest lap: #3 Ferrari 333SP (Max Papis) 1:40.545, 127.465 mph.
Fastest qualifier: #3 Ferrari 333SP (Yannick Dalmas) 1:39.195, 129.200 mph.
12 full-course cautions for 172 minutes

FIN.	CAR NO.	DRIVERS	CAR	ENTRANT	LAPS	START	CLASS
1	30	Gianpiero Moretti (I)/Arie Luyendyk (NL)/Mauro Baldi (I)/Didier Theys (B)	Ferrari 333SP (Michelotto)	Gianpiero Moretti	711	2	Can-Am
2	01	Allan McNish (GB)/Danny Sullivan (USA)/Joerg Mueller (D)/Uwe Alzen (D)/Dirk Mueller (D)	Porsche 911 GT1 Evo	Jochen Rohr	703	9	GT1
3	00	Christophe Bouchut (F)/Patrice Goueslard (F)/Carl Rosenblad (S)/Andre Ahrle (D)	Porsche 911 GT1	Jack Leconte	667	16	GT1
4	97	Toni Seiler (CH)/Wido Roessler (D)/Peter Kitchak (USA)/Angelo Zadra (I)/Franz Konrad (A)	Porsche 911 GT2	Franz Konrad	660	30	GT2
5	04	John Morton (USA)/John Graham (CDN)/Patrick Huisman (NL)/Duncan Huisman (NL)	Porsche 911 GT2	John Graham	659	37	GT2
6	10	Bill Auberlen (USA)/Marc Duez (B)/Boris Said (USA)/Peter Cunningham (USA)	BMW M3	Tom Milner	657	33	GT3
7	23	Michael Conte (USA)/Bruno Lambert (B)/Nick Holt (GB)/Darryl Havens (USA)	Porsche 911 Carrera RSR	Alex Job/Team Seattle	639	59	GT3

FIN.	CAR NO.	DRIVERS	CAR	ENTRANT	LAPS	START	CLASS
8	63	Yojiro Terada (J)/Howard Katz (USA)/John O'Steen (USA)/Jim Downing (USA)/Franck Freon (F)	Kudzu-Mazda DLM4	Jim Downing	636	18	Can-Am
9	55	Charles Slater (USA)/Tim Ralston (USA)/Tom Peterson (USA)/Jorge Trejos (CR)	Porsche 911 Carrera RSR	Dennis Aase	629	49	GT3
10	73	Jack Lewis (USA)/Tony Burgess (CDN)/Anthony Lazzaro (USA)/Kurt Matthewson (USA)/ Edison Lluch (PR)	Porsche 911 Carrera RSR	Jack Lewis	626	45	GT3
11	4	Mike Borkowski (USA)/Tony Kanaan (BR)/Robbie Buhl (USA)	Ford Mustang Cobra (Riley & Scott)	Tom Gloy	624 DNF	14	GT1
12	25	Hans-Joerg Hofer (A)/Luca Riccitelli (I)/Raffaele Sangiuolo (I)/Guenther Blieninger (D)	Porsche 993 Supercup	Walch	624	50	GT3
13	77	John Drew (USA)/Dave Friedman (USA)/Beran Peter (USA)/James Nelson (USA)/ Mark Greenberg (USA)	Porsche 911 Carrera RSR	Mark Greenberg	622	63	GT3
14	81	Chris Gleason (USA)/Ray Lintott (AUS)/Matt Turner (USA)/Ashley Ward (GB)	Dodge Viper GTS-R	Hugh Chamberlain	619	38	GT2
15	16	James Weaver (GB)/Rob Dyson (USA)/Dorsey Schroeder (USA)/Elliott Forbes-Robinson (USA)	Riley & Scott-Ford Mk III	Rob Dyson	616 DNF	5	Can-Am
16	7	Ross Bentley (CDN)/Les Delano (USA)/Andy Petery (USA)/Derek John Hill (USA)/Mark Simo (USA)	BMW M3	Tom Milner	616	46	GT3
17	20	Butch Leitzinger (USA)/John Paul, Jr. (USA)/Perry McCarthy (GB)/Rob Dyson (USA)	Riley & Scott-Ford Mk III	Rob Dyson	615 DNF	4	Can-Am
18	07	Price Cobb (USA)/Danny Marshall (USA)/Peter Chambers (GB)/Ulrich Gallade (D)/Martyn Konig (GB)	Porsche 911 GT2 Evo	Cole Scrogham	615	48	GT3
19	38	Thierry Boutsen (B)/Ralf Kelleners (D)/Andy Pilgrim (GB)	Porsche 911 GT1 Evo	Dave Maraj	614 DNF	12	GT1
20	3	Yannick Dalmas (F)/Bob Wollek (F)/Massimiliano Papis (I)/Ron Fellows (CDN)/* Andy Evans (USA)	Ferrari 333SP	Andy Evans	610 DNF	1	Can-Am
21	21	Andre Lara-Resende (BR)/Regis Schuch (BR)/Flavio Trindade (BR)/Maurizio Sandro Sala (BR)	Porsche 911 GT2	Dener Motorsport	604	31	GT2
22	62	John Mirro (USA)/Ralph Thomas (USA)/Douglas Campbell (USA)/Dennis Spencer (USA)/Rich Grupp (USA)	Kudzu-Mazda DLM	Jim Downing	591	17	Can-Am
23	67	Chris Ronson (USA)/Brian Pelke (USA)/Steve Pelke (USA)/Bruce Busby (USA)	Porsche 911 Carrera RSR	Kevin Buckler	567	51	GT3
24	09	Craig Conway (GB)/Eric Van Cleef (USA)/Todd Flis (USA)	Mitsubishi Eclipse	Flis Brothers	563	62	GT3
25	95	Jeret Schroeder (USA)/Thomas Volk (USA)/Lyn St. James (USA)/Pete Halsmer (USA)	Kudzu-Chevrolet DL-4	Thomas Volk	557 DNF	24	Can-Am
26	39	David Murry (USA)/Hurley Haywood (USA)/Derek Bell (GB)/Jim Matthews (USA)	Riley & Scott-Ford Mk III	Colucci/Matthews	550 DNF	11	Can-Am
27	29	Fabio Rosa (I)/Giovanni Vigano (I)/Gabrio Rosa (I)/Pier Angelo Masselli (I)/C. J. Johnson (USA)	Chevrolet Camaro (Frings)	Hoyt Overbagh	547	36	GT1
28	71	Cameron Worth (USA)/Nick Vitucci (USA)/Bill Lester (USA)/Scott Sansone (USA)/Brian Richards (USA)	Mazda RX-7	Cameron Worth	539	61	GT2
29	69	Denis Lay (CH)/Gerd Ruch (D)/William Langhorne (USA)/Gerold Ried (D)	Porsche 911 GT2	Gerold Ried	498	35	GT2
30	8	Johnny O'Connell (USA)/Henry Camferdam, Jr. (USA)/Scott Schubot (USA)	Riley & Scott-Ford Mk III	Henry Camferdam, Jr.	497 DNF	6	Can-Am
31	40	David Rankin (USA)/Hank Scott (USA)/Eric Jensen (USA)/Toto Lassally (ES)/ Nort Northam (USA)	Chevrolet Camaro (Creative)	David Rankin	494	58	GT1
32	99	Eric Bernard (F)/David Brabham (AUS)/Jamie Davies (GB)/*Doc Bundy (USA)	Panoz GTR-1	Don Panoz	472 DNF	8	GT1
33	54	Stuart Hayner (USA)/Henry Taleb (EC)/Scott Neuman (USA)/Terry Borcheller (USA)	BMW M3	James Bell	455 DNF	47	GT3
34	24	Don Kitch (USA)/Byron Sanborn (USA)/Angelo Cilli (USA)/Kim Wolfkill (USA)	Porsche 911 Carrera RSR	Alex Job/Team Seattle	448	55	GT3
35	56	Gaston Aguirre (RA)/Francisco Castillo (RA)/Horacio Paolucci (RA)/ Facundo Gilbicella (RA)	Oldsmobile Cutlass Supreme (Kreider)	Dale Kreider	445	74	GT1
36	87	John Annis (USA)/Lee Hill (USA)/Bill Ladoniczki (USA)/Steve Ladoniczki (USA)/ Randy Pobst (USA)	Chevrolet Camaro (Bemco)	John Annis	438	39	GT1
37	35	Stefano Bucci (I)/Mauro Casadei (I)/Francesco Ciani (I)/Andrea Garbagnati (MC)	Chevrolet Camaro (Preston)	Richard McDill	437	29	GT1
38	0	Scott Maxwell (CDN)/Jason Priestley (USA)/David Empringham (CDN)	Ford Mustang Cobra (Multimatic)	Scott Maxwell	435 DNF	27	GT1
39	5	Andy Wallace (GB)/Scott Pruett (USA)/Raul Boesel (BR)/Doc Bundy (USA)	Panoz GTR-1	Don Panoz	433 DNF	10	GT1
40	28	Jon Field (USA)/Rick Sutherland (USA)/Butch Brickell (USA)/Enrico Bertaggia (I)/ Alex Padilla (USA)	Riley & Scott-Ford Mk III	Jon Field	432 DNF	13	Can-Am
41	51	Bruce Trenery (USA)/Spencer Trenery (USA)/Grahame Bryant (GB)/Steve Pfeifer (USA)/ Kent Painter (USA)	Cannibal-Chevrolet	Bruce Trenery	414	57	Can-Am
42	89	Richard Maugeri (USA)/Anthony Puleo (USA)/Sim Penton (USA)/Daniel Urrutia (USA)	Chevrolet Camaro (Bemco)	Richard Maugeri	385	41	GT1
43	96	Ron Zitza (USA)/Kevin Wheeler (USA)/Mike Davies (USA)	Porsche 964 Carrera Cup	Ron Zitza	381 DNF	64	GT3
44	88	Anthony Lazzaro (USA)/Bill Dollahite (USA)/Paul Dallenbach (USA)	Spice-Chevrolet BDG-02	Bill Dollahite	371 DNF	15	Can-Am
45	59	Simon Gregg (USA)/Oliver Kuttner (USA)/Joaquin DeSoto (USA)/Tim Holt (USA)	Spice-Oldsmobile SC95	Jon Field	344 DNF	28	Can-Am
46	52	David Russell, Jr. (USA)/William Stitt (USA)/Mark Hillestad (USA)/Paul Arnold (USA)/Neil Crilly (D)	Porsche 911	Protosport	342 DNF	67	GT3
47	41	Cort Wagner (USA)/Chris Cervelli (USA)/Marc Basseng (D)/Kelly Collins (USA)	Porsche 911 Carrera RSR	Chris Cervelli	335 DNF	40	GT3
48	36	Eliseo Salazar (RCH)/Jim Pace (USA)/Barry Waddell (USA)/* Jim Matthews (USA)	Riley & Scott-Ford Mk III	Colucci/Matthews	300 DNF	7	Can-Am
49	33	Mike Weinberg (USA)/Jim Michaelian (USA)/Bob Rockwood (USA)/Steve McNeely (USA)	Pontiac Firebird	Joe Aquilante	295	76	GT3
50	19	A.J. Smith (USA)/Mark Montgomery (USA)/Edd Davin (USA)	Kudzu-Buick DG-2/DLM	Edd Davin	287	23	Can-Am
51	27	Steve Goldin (USA)/John G. Thomas (USA)/Todd Vallancourt (USA)/Keith Goldin (USA)	Mazda RX-7 (Linderfer)	Goldin Brothers	277	69	GT3
52	86	Brian Redman (GB)/Steve Marshall (USA)/Arthur Urciuoli (USA)/ Robert Amren (S)/Price Cobb (USA)	Porsche 911 Carrera RSR	Cole Scrogham	272	66	GT3
53	50	J. Robert Johnson (USA)/Tom McGlynn (USA)/James Oppenheimer (USA)/ George Balbach (USA)/Erik Johnson (USA)	Porsche 911	J. Robert Johnson	248 DNF	68	GT2
54	98	Larry Schumacher (USA)/Robert Nearn (GB)/Franz Konrad (A)/Nick Ham (USA)	Porsche 911 GT2	Franz Konrad	245 DNF	26	GT2
55	17	Wayne Taylor (ZA)/Eric van de Poele (B)/Fermin Velez (E)	Ferrari 333SP (Michelotto)	Doyle/Risi	225 DNF	3	Can-Am
56	53	Tom Scheuren (USA)/Gerry Green (USA)/Spencer Pumpelly (USA)/Bobby Jones (USA)	Chevrolet Camaro (Watson)	Tom Scheuren	195 DNF	53	GT1
57	57	Reed Kryder (USA)/Steve Ahlgrim (USA)/Dave Deen (USA)/Frank Del Vecchio (USA)/ Ryan Hampton (USA)	Nissan 240SX (Kryderacing)	Reed Kryder	191 DNF	71	GT3
58	74	George Robinson (USA)/Jack Baldwin (USA)/Irv Hoerr (USA)/Jon Gooding (USA)	Oldsmobile Aurora (Pratt & Miller)	George Robinson	183 DNF	22	GT1
59	45	Stephane Cohen (B)/Paul Kumpen (B)/Marc Schoonbroodt (B)/Michael Funke (D)	Porsche 911	Paul Kumpen	182 DNF	54	GT3
60	90	Koen Wauters (B)/Kris Wauters (B)/Franco La Rosa (B)/Bert Longin (B)/Albert Vanierschot (B)	Porsche 911 GT2	AD Sport	173 DNF	65	GT2

FIN.	CAR NO.	DRIVERS	CAR	ENTRANT	LAPS	START	CLASS
61	2	Shane Lewis (USA)/Vic Rice (USA)/Brian Hornkohl (USA)/Chris Neville (USA)	Mosler Raptor	Mosler	169 DNF	21	GT1
62	37	Dave White (USA)/James Loftis (USA)/Bob Strange (USA)/Richard Howe (USA)	Porsche 968	GTR Motorsports	154 DNF	60	GT3
63	76	Mike Doolin (USA)/Scott Peeler (USA)/John Ruther (USA)/Martin Snow (USA)	Porsche 993 Carrera RSR	Richard Raimist	154 DNF	52	GT3
64	68	Kevin Buckler (USA)/Philip Collin (USA)/Eric Bretzel (USA)/Duncan Dayton (USA)	Porsche 911 Carrera RSR	Kevin Buckler	142 DNF	43	GT3
65	75	Max Schmidt (USA)/Chris Bingham (USA)/Nigel Smith (GB)/Scott Harrington (USA)/ * Karel Dolejsi (CZ)	Porsche 911 Carrera RSR	Bill Radar	115 DNF	56	GT3
66	58	Pascal Dro (F)/Martin Shuster (USA)/Phillipe Lenain (F)	Porsche 944	Al Broadfoot	114 DNF	75	GT2
67	6	Mark Simo (USA)/Dieter Quester (A)/Peter Cunningham (USA)	BMW M3	Milner	87 DNF	42	GT3
68	05	Cor Euser (NL)/Masamitsu Ishihara (J)/Katsunori Iketani (J)/* Harry Bytzek (CDN)	Porsche 911 GT2	Prova Motorsports	79 DNF	32	GT2
69	60	Shane Donley (USA)/Kris Wilson (USA)/* Tim Moser (USA)	Keiler-Ford KII	David Kopf	50 DNF	20	Can-Am
70	46	Julian Bailey (GB)/Tiff Needell (GB)/Craig Baird (NZ)/* Richard Dean (GB)	Lister Storm GTL (G Force)	Brian Lister	45 DNF	19	GT1
71	72	Tim Banks (USA)/Todd Sprinkle (USA)/Kerry Hitt (USA)	Chevrolet Corvette (Banks)	Tim Banks	38 DNF	72	GT1
72	32	John Heinricy (USA)/* Stuart Hayner (USA)/* Scott Harrington (USA)/* Don Knowles (USA)	Pontiac Firebird	Joe Aquilante	9 DNF	70	GT3
73	44	Harald Grohs (D)/* Hans Willems (B)/* Vincent Dupont (B)/* Alfons Taels (B)	Porsche 911	Paul Kumpen	8 DNF	44	GT3
74	11	Rick Fairbanks (USA)/* Mike DeFontes (USA)/* Chuck Goldsborough (USA)/* Dan Lewis (USA)/ * Mark Neuhaus (USA)	Hawk-Mazda MD3R	Rick Fairbanks	5 DNF	25	Can-Am
DNS	65	Steve Saleen (USA)/Ron Anton Johnson (USA)/Will Hoy (GB)	Saleen Mustang	Steve Saleen	0	34	GT2
DNS	15	Jay Cochran (USA)/Michel Aouate (USA)	Porsche 993	Kevin Jeannette	0	73	GT2

Rolex 24 At Daytona

January 30-31, 1999

24 hour event on the 3.560 mile circuit.
Distance covered: 708 laps for 2520.480 miles.
Winning time: 24 hours, 1 minute, 7.146 seconds for a speed of 104.938 mph.
Margin of victory: 2 laps.
Fastest lap: #7 Ferrari 333SP (Allan McNish), 1:42.755, 124.724 mph.
Fastest qualifier: # 16 Riley & Scott-Ford Mk III (James Weaver), 1:40.869, 127.056 mph.
15 full-course cautions for 176 minutes, 56 laps.

FIN.	CAR NO.	DRIVERS	CAR	ENTRANT	LAPS	START	CLASS
1	**20**	**Butch Leitzinger (USA)/Andy Wallace (GB)/Elliott Forbes-Robinson (USA)**	**Riley & Scott-Ford Mk III**	**Rob Dyson**	**708**	**5**	**Can-Am**
2	7	Allan McNish (GB)/Didier de Radigues (B)/Massimiliano Angelelli (I)/Wayne Taylor (ZA)	Ferrari 333SP (Michelotto)	Doyle/Risi	706	3	Can-Am
3	36	Massimiliano Papis (I)/Stefan Johansson (S)/Jim Vasser (USA)/Jim Matthews (USA)	Ferrari 333SP 98 (Michelotto)	Kevin Doran	694	4	Can-Am
4	00	Enzo Calderari (CH)/Angelo Zadra (I)/Lilian Bryner (CH)/Carl Rosenblad (S)	Ferrari 333SP 98 (Michelotto)	Enzo Calderari	679	12	Can-Am
5	8	Eliseo Salazar (RCH)/Duncan Dayton (USA)/Henry Camferdam, Jr. (USA)/Scott Schubot (USA)	Riley & Scott-Ford Mk III	Henry Camferdam, Jr.	643	9	Can-Am
6	**23**	**Kelly Collins (USA)/Cort Wagner (USA)/Anthony Lazzaro (USA)/Darryl Havens (USA)**	**Porsche 911 Carrera RSR**	**Alex Job**	**639**	**36**	**GT3**
7	**83**	**Andre Ahrle (D)/Raffaele Sangiuolo (I)/David Warnock (GB)/Hubert Haupt (D)**	**Porsche 911 GT2**	**Fabian Roock**	**634**	**28**	**GT2**
8	72	Didier Theys (B)/Fredy Lienhard (CH)/Arie Luyendyk (NL)/Mauro Baldi (I)	Ferrari 333SP 98 (Michelotto)	Kevin Doran	632	2	Can-Am
9	02	David Murry (USA)/John Mowlem (GB)/Joel Reiser (USA)/Grady Willingham (USA)	Porsche 911 Carrera RSR	Reiser/Callas	632	42	GT3
10	99	Dirk Mueller (D)/Martin Snow (USA)/John O'Steen (USA)/Larry Schumacher (USA)	Porsche 911 GT2 Evo	Larry Schumacher	626	25	GT2
11	07	Patrick Huisman (NL)/Darren Law (USA)/Steve Marshall (USA)/ Sylvain Tremblay (USA)/Danny Marshall (USA)	Porsche 911 GT2 Evo	Cole Scrogham	625	40	GT3
12	18	Dave Friedman (USA)/Chris Miller (USA)/Vic Rice (USA)/Geoff Auberlen (USA)/ Beran Peter (USA)	Porsche 911 Carrera RSR	David Friedman	623	53	GT3
13	17	Shane Lewis (USA)/Randy Pobst (USA)/Robert Mazzuoccola (USA)/Mark Raccaro (USA)	BMW M3	T. C. Kline	622	44	GT3
14	68	Kevin Buckler (USA)/Michael Conte (USA)/Mike Holt (USA)/Bruno Lambert (B)	Porsche 911 Carrera RSR	Kevin Buckler	617	51	GT3
15	62	Ermanno Ronchi (I)/Ben Treadway (USA)/Fabio Montani (I)/Dennis Spencer (USA)	Kudzu-Mazda DLM	Jim Downing	611	22	Can-Am
16	66	Massimo Morini (I)/Angelo Scarpetta (I)/Luca Cattaneo (I)/Luciano Tamburini (I)/ Antonio Gerolamo de Castro (I)	Porsche 993 Supercup	Carlo Noce	605	71	GT3
17	54	Terry Borcheller (USA)/Tony Kester (USA)/Matt Drendel (USA)/James A. Kenton (USA)/Scott Neuman (USA)	BMW M3	James Bell	602	46	GT3
18	2	Ron Fellows (CDN)/Chris Kneifel (USA)/John Paul, Jr. (USA)	Chevrolet Corvette C5-R	Chevrolet/Pratt & Miller	600	16	GT2
19	77	Andrew Bagnall (NZ)/Renato Mastropietro (I)/Tony Burgess (CDN)/Michel Neugarten (B)	Porsche 911 GT2	Peter Seikel	597	56	GT2
20	49	Michael Irmgartz (D)/Manfred Jurasz (A)/Eric van de Vyver (F)/Klaus Horn (D)	Porsche 911 GT2	Manfred Freisinger	595 DNF	41	GT2
21	95	Jeret Schroeder (USA)/Thomas Volk (USA)/Paul Debban (USA)/Richard J. Valentine (USA)	Riley & Scott-Chevrolet Mk III	Thomas Volk	595	18	Can-Am
22	16	James Weaver (GB)/Rob Dyson (USA)/Dorsey Schroeder (USA)/Stuart Hayner (USA)	Riley & Scott-Ford Mk III	Rob Dyson	593	1	Can-Am
23	3	Hurley Haywood (USA)/Don Whittington (USA)/Dale Whittington (USA)/Danny Sullivan (USA)	Riley & Scott-Ford Mk III	Whittington Brothers	590	11	Can-Am
24	63	Howard Katz (USA)/Yojiro Terada (J)/Chris Ronson (USA)/Jim Downing (USA)	Kudzu-Mazda DLY	Jim Downing	586	17	Can-Am
25	82	Stephane Ortelli (F)/Enrico Bertaggia (I)/Robert Nearn (GB)/Claudia Huertgen (D)	Porsche 911 GT2	Fabian Roock	581	21	GT2
26	44	Jeff Nowicki (USA)/R. K. Smith (USA)/Rick Mancuso (USA)/Tom Murphy (USA)/Mike Farmer (USA)	Chevrolet Corvette	Jack Cauley	578	74	GT3

FIN.	CAR NO.	DRIVERS	CAR	ENTRANT	LAPS	CLASS	
27	39	Spencer Pumpelly (USA)/Chris Mitchum (USA)/David Kicak (USA)/Bill Lester (USA)/ Pascal Dro (F)	Porsche 911 Carrera RSR	Chris Mitchum	575	60	GT3
28	**19**	**Kyle McIntyre (USA)/Gary Stewart (USA)/Andy Petery (USA)/ Craig Carter (USA)/Les Delano (USA)**	**Ford Mustang Cobra (Riley & Scott)**	**GK Group**	**550**	**47**	**GTT**
29	73	Kevin Wheeler (USA)/Jack Lewis (USA)/Ludovico Manfredi (USA)/Kiichi Takahashi (J)/ Ron Henriksen (USA)	Porsche 911 Carrera RSR	Jack Lewis	540	65	GT3
30	75	Cameron Worth (USA)/Scott Sansone (USA)/Steve Pfeifer (USA)/Ryan Hampton (USA)	Mazda RX-7	Cameron Worth	535	68	GT2
31	47	Todd Vallancourt (USA)/Ian James (GB)/John G. Thomas (USA)	Spice-Chevrolet SE90	Jack Beane	528	27	Can-Am
32	42	Pier Angelo Masselli (I)/Marco de Iturbe (MC)/Gian Luca de Lorenzi (MC)/ Giovanni Biava (I)/Franco Scapini (I)	Ferrari F355	Franco Scapini	517	69	GT3
33	60	Kris Wilson (USA)/Tim Moser (USA)/Barry Waddell (USA)	Keiler-Ford KII	David Kopf	510	13	Can-Am
34	55	Toni Seiler (CH)/Gerold Ried (D)/Patrick Vuillaume (F)/Gerd Ruch (D)	Porsche 911 GT2	Gerold Ried	502	31	GT2
35	27	Keith Goldin (USA)/Scott Finlay (USA)/Steve Goldin (USA)/David Russell, Jr. (USA)	Mazda RX-7 (Linderfer)	Goldin Brothers	484	73	GT3
36	45	Peter Baron (USA)/James McCormick (USA)/Barry Graham (AUS)/Leo Hindery (USA)/Brian Till (USA)	BMW M3	James Bell	467	72	GT3
37	89	Neil Crilly (D)/Caroline Wright (USA)/Phillipe Lenain (F)/Mike Borkowski (USA)/Scott Bove (USA)	Porsche 968	Al Broadfoot	465	77	GT3
38	40	Hank Scott (USA)/Toto Lassally (ES)/C. Peter Pope (USA)/David Rankin (USA)/ Richard McDill (USA)	Chevrolet Camaro (Creative)	David Rankin	461	43	GTT
39	09	Craig Conway (GB)/Eric Van Cleef (USA)/Todd Flis (USA)	Mitsubishi Eclipse (Eagle)	Flis Brothers	455	70	GT3
40	33	Altfrid Heger (D)/Peter Kitchak (USA)/Charles Slater (USA)/Battistino Pregliasco (I)/Franz Konrad (A)	Porsche 911 GT2	Franz Konrad	452 DNF	23	GT2
41	79	Richard Maugeri (USA)/Anthony Puleo (USA)/Sim Penton (USA)/Doug Mills (USA)/Ron Zitza (USA)	Chevrolet Camaro (Bemco)	Richard Maugeri	418	48	GTT
42	28	Jon Field (USA)/Ryan Jones (USA)/Sam Hornish (USA)/Mike Shank (USA)	Lola-Ford B98/10	Jon Field	399 DNF	8	Can-Am
43	03	Bret A. Parker (USA)/Kevin Allen (USA)/Neil Hanneman (USA)/Larry Parker (USA)	Dodge Viper GTS-R	Nichols/Parker	390	33	GT2
44	48	Wolfgang Kaufmann (D)/Michel Ligonnet (F)/Lance Stewart (USA)	Porsche 911 GT2	Manfred Freisinger	386 DNF	29	GT2
45	56	Hans Willems (B)/Olaf Manthey (D)/Marc Gindorf (D)/Ulrich Gallade (D)/Ulrich Richter (D)	Porsche 993 Carrera RSR	Olaf Manthey	377 DNF	45	GT3
46	4	Scott Sharp (USA)/Andy Pilgrim (GB)/John Heinricy (USA)	Chevrolet Corvette C5-R	Chevrolet/Riley & Scott	366	20	GT2
47	15	Ross Bentley (CDN)/Chris Bingham (USA)/Didier Andre (F)/Franck Freon (F)	Riley & Scott-Ford Mk III	Rod Everett	349 DNF	19	Can-Am
48	04	Max Schmidt (USA)/Jeff Conkel (USA)/Rusty Schmidt (USA)/* Scott Harrington (USA)	Porsche 993 Carrera RSR	Max Schmidt	343 DNF	59	GT3
49	57	Reed Kryder (USA)/Christian Heinkele (F)/Steve Ahlgrim (USA)	Nissan 240SX (Kryderacing)	Reed Kryder	341	76	GT3
50	53	Tom Scheuren (USA)/Mayo T. Smith (USA)/John McNaughton (USA)/ John Halbing (USA)/Bobby Jones (USA)	Chevrolet Camaro (Watson)	Tom Scheuren	340	66	GTT
51	22	Don Kitch (USA)/Kim Wolfkill (USA)/John Hill (USA)/Wade Gaughran (USA)	Porsche 911 Carrera RSR	Alex Job	327 DNF	52	GT3
52	76	Peter Argetsinger (USA)/Richard Polidori (USA)/Steven Hill (USA)/John McCaig (CDN)	Porsche 993 Carrera RSR	Richard Raimist	326 DNF	50	GT3
53	24	Michael Jacobs (USA)/George Biskup (USA)/John Steinmetz (USA)/Mike DeFontes (USA)/ Frank Del Vecchio (USA)	Ferrari 348	Michael Jacobs	326 DNF	78	GT3
54	67	Steve Pelke (USA)/Brian Pelke (USA)/Ron Herrerias (USA)/Pat DiGiovanni (USA)	Porsche 911 Carrera RSR	Kevin Buckler	312 DNF	62	GT3
55	74	George Robinson (USA)/Jack Baldwin (USA)/Irv Hoerr (USA)/Jon Gooding (USA)	Riley & Scott-Chevrolet Mk III	George Robinson	299 DNF	10	Can-Am
56	81	Chris Gleason (USA)/Christian Glaesel (D)/Brian Hornkohl (USA)/Hans Hugenholtz (NL)	Dodge Viper GTS-R	Hugh Chamberlain	297 DNF	32	GT2
57	96	Gerry Green (USA)/Scott Brunk (USA)/Rich Bell (USA)/Keith Fisher (USA)/Tony Tola (USA)	Chevrolet Camaro (Watson)	Tom Scheuren	273	57	GTT
58	87	John Annis (USA)/John Kohler (USA)/Bill Ladoniczki (USA)/Steve Ladoniczki (USA)/ Mark Kennedy (USA)	Chevrolet Camaro (Bemco)	John Annis	263 DNF	67	GTT
59	52	Paul Arnold (USA)/William Stitt (USA)/Vic Sifton (CDN)/Simon Gregg (USA)	Acura NSX (Thompson)	William Stitt	261 DNF	75	GT2
60	6	Boris Said (USA)/Peter Cunningham (USA)/Mark Simo (USA)/Dieter Quester (A)/* Ernie Irvan (USA)	BMW M3	Tom Milner	247 DNF	38	GT3
61	70	Herman Buurman (NL)/Peter van der Kolk (NL)/Christian Vann (GB)/Cor Euser (NL)	Marcos LM 600 (Euser)	Cor Euser	242 DNF	30	GT2
62	10	Bill Auberlen (USA)/Brian Cunningham (USA)/Johannes van Overbeek (USA) Hans-Joachim Stuck Jr. (D)	BMW M3	Tom Milner	238 DNF	37	GT3
63	29	Samuel Brown (USA)/Butch Brickell (USA)/Jacek Mucha (CDN)/John Mirro (USA)	Riley & Scott-Ford Mk III	Jon Field	225 DNF	15	Can-Am
64	12	Chuck Goldsborough (USA)/Kurt Baumann (USA)/Jeff Altenburg (USA)/Rick Fairbanks (USA)	Hawk-Chevrolet MD3R	Rick Fairbanks	225 DNF	24	Can-Am
65	50	Olivier Beretta (MC)/Tommy Archer (USA)/David Donohue (USA)	Dodge Viper GTS-R	Hugues de Chaunac	188 DNF	14	GT2
66	88	Mike Davies (USA)/Bill Dollahite (USA)/Doc Bundy (USA)/Paul Dallenbach (USA)	Ferrari 333SP	Bill Dollahite	168 DNF	7	Can-Am
67	13	Mark Montgomery (USA)/Martin Shuster (USA)/Spencer Trenery (USA)/Dick Greer (USA)/ Bruce Trenery (USA)	Chevrolet Camaro (Evans)	Davin/Montgomery	167 DNF	58	GTT
68	21	Gabrio Rosa (I)/Roberto Mangifesta (I)/Stefano Zonca (I)/Fabio Rosa (I)	Porsche 911 GT2	Guido Haberthur	128 DNF	63	GT2
69	78	Patrice Roussel (F)/Edouard Sezionale (F)/Sylvain Boulay (F)	Norma-Buick M14	Edouard Sezionale	128 DNF	26	Can-Am
70	08	Rob Wilson (NZ)/Martyn Konig (GB)/Jake Ulrich (USA)/Mike Pickup (GB)	Porsche 911 GT2 Evo	Cole Scrogham	89 DNF	34	GT2
71	32	Jan Lammers (NL)/* Franz Konrad (A)/* Vincenzo Sospiri (I)	Lola-Lotus B98/10	Franz Konrad	43 DNF	6	Can-Am
72	58	Angelo Cilli (USA)/* John Ruther (USA)/* Tom Miller (USA)/* Dale White (USA)/ * Michael Petersen (USA)	Porsche 993 Carrera RSR	Michael Petersen	22 DNF	61	GT3
73	25	Hans-Joerg Hofer (A)/* Luca Riccitelli (I)/* Guenther Blieninger (D)/* Fabio Mancini (I)	Porsche 993 Carrera RSR	Rudi Walch	14 DNF	39	GT3
74	92	John Mowlem (GB)/* Joel Reiser (USA)/* Grady Willingham (USA)/* David Murry (USA)	Porsche 911 Carrera RSR	Reiser/Callas	11 DNF	64	GT3
75	31	Mauro Casadei (I)/* Francesco Ciani (I)/* Stefano Bucci (I)/* Andrea Garbagnati (MC)	Porsche 993 GT2	Guido Haberthur	9 DNF	35	GT2
76	69	Bob Wollek (F)/* Thierry Perrier (F)/* Jean-Louis Ricci (F) * Gerard Larrousse (F)/ * Jean-Paul Richard (F)	Porsche 993 Carrera RSR	Thierry Perrier	7 DNF	49	GT3
77	01	James Nelson (USA)/* John Drew (USA)/* Beran Peter (USA)/* Jim Michaelian (USA)/ * Mark Greenberg (USA)	Porsche 911 Carrera RSR	Mark Greenberg	3 DNF	55	GT3
78	93	Henry Taleb (EC)/* Jean-Pierre Michelet (EC)/* Marcelo Darquea (EC)/* Walter Jimenez (EC)	Nissan 240SX (Leitzinger)	Henry Taleb	0 DNF	54	GT3

Rolex 24 At Daytona

February 5-6, 2000

24 hour event on the 3.560 mile circuit.

Distance covered: 723 laps for 2573.880 miles.

Winning time: 24 hours, 0 minutes, 30.926 seconds for a speed of 107.207 mph.

Margin of victory: 0:30.879.

Fastest lap: # 20 Riley & Scott-Ford Mk III (Weaver), 1:42.541, 124.984 mph.

8 full-course cautions for 32 laps.

FIN.	CAR NO.	DRIVERS	CAR	ENTRANT	LAPS	START	CLASS
1	**91**	**Olivier Beretta (MC)/Karl Wendlinger III (A)/Dominique Dupuy (F)**	**Dodge Viper GTS-R**	**Hugues de Chaunac**	**723**	**21**	**GTO**
2	3	Ron Fellows (CDN)/Justin Bell (GB)/Chris Kneifel (USA)	Chevrolet Corvette C5-R	Chevrolet/Pratt & Miller	723	11	GTO
3	93	David Donohue (USA)/Ni Amorim (P)/Jean-Philippe Belloc (F)/Tommy Archer (USA)	Dodge Viper GTS-R	Hugues de Chaunac	719	18	GTO
4	**20**	**James Weaver (GB)/Rob Dyson (USA)/Massimiliano Papis (I)/Elliott Forbes-Robinson (USA)**	**Riley & Scott-Ford Mk-III**	**Rob Dyson**	**717**	**1**	**SR**
5	92	Tommy Archer (USA)/Marc Duez (B)/Vincent Vosse (B)/ Jean-Philippe Belloc/Olivier Beretta (MC)	Dodge Viper GTS-R	Hugues de Chaunac	691	17	GTO
6	45	Stephen Watson (ZA)/Christian Vann (GB)/Raffaele Sangiuolo (I)/Allison Duncan (USA)	Dodge Viper GTS-R	Hugh Chamberlain	665	41	GTO
7	46	Toni Seiler (CH)/Erik Messley (USA)/Walter Brun (CH	Dodge Viper GTS-R	Hugh Chamberlain	659	28	GTO
8	**56**	**Luca Drudi (I)/Fabio Rosa (I)/Fabio Babini (I) Gabrio Rosa (I)**	**Porsche 996 GT3R**	**Guido Haberthur**	**658**	**43**	**GTU**
9	72	Wolfgang Kaufmann (D)/Ernst Palmberger (D)/Lance Stewart (USA)	Porsche 911 GT2	Manfred Freisinger	657	24	GTO
10	7	Dieter Quester (A)/Philipp Peter (A)/Hans Willems (B)/Hans-Joerg Hofer (A)/Luca Riccitelli (I)	Porsche 996 GT3R	Rudi Walch	657	29	GTU
11	99	Martin Snow (USA)/John O'Steen (USA)/Stuart Hayner (USA)/Larry Schumacher (USA)	Porsche 911 GT2 Evo	Larry Schumacher	654	31	GTO
12	07	Mike Fitzgerald (USA)/Gregory Merril (USA)/Steve Marshall (USA)/Chris MacAllister (USA)/ Danny Marshall (USA)/Darren Law (USA)	Porsche 911 Carrera RSR	Cole Scrogham	651	63	GTU
13	6	Butch Leitzinger (USA)/Andy Wallace (GB)/Franck Lagorce (F)	Cadillac Northstar LMP	Cadillac/Riley & Scott	637 DNF	8	SR
14	5	Massimiliano Angelelli (I)/Wayne Taylor (ZA)/Eric van de Poele (B)	Cadillac Northstar LMP	Cadillac/Riley & Scott	637	5	SR
15	67	Wade Gaughran (USA)/Philip Collin (USA)/Dale White (USA) Kevin Buckler (USA)	Porsche 996 GT3R	Kevin Buckler	623	59	GTU
16	23	Randy Pobst (USA)/Bruno Lambert (B)/Michael Conte (USA)	Porsche 996 GT3R	Alex Job	620 DNF	26	GTU
17	66	Don Kitch (USA)/Steve Miller (USA)/Kiichi Takahashi (J)/Dave Gaylord (USA)	Porsche 996 GT3R	Kevin Buckler		69	GTU
18	41	Peter Hardman (GB)/Philippe Favre (CH)/Stanislas de Sadeleer (B)/Nicolaus Springer (D)	Porsche 996 GT3R	Lecuyer/Recksteiner	606	65	GTU
19	73	Ulrich Gallade (D)/Ray Lintott (AUS)/Manfred Jurasz (A)/Klaus Horn (D)/* Allan Ziegelman (USA)	Porsche 911 GT2	Manfred Freisinger	604	57	GTO
20	90	Christophe Bouchut (F)/Andre Ahrle (D)/Jean-Luc Chereau (F)/Patrice Goueslard (F)	Porsche 996 GT3R	Jack Leconte	597 DNF	34	GTU
21	62	Hugh Plumb (USA)/Mark Hillstadt (USA)/Carlos DeQuesada (USA)/Ross Bluestein (USA)/Joe Safina (USA)	BMW M3	Joseph Safina	597	74	GTU
22	97	Max Schmidt (USA)/Jeff Conkel (USA)/Bob Woodman (USA)/Rusty Schmidt (USA)	Porsche 911 Carrera RSR	Schmidt/Schmidt	594	80	GTU
23	36	Stefan Johansson (S)/Guy Smith (GB)/Jim Matthews (USA)/Memo Gidley (USA)	Reynard-Judd 2KQ	Johansson/Matthews	576	4	SR
24	4	Andy Pilgrim (GB)/Kelly Collins (USA)/Franck Freon (F)	Chevrolet Corvette C5-R	Chevrolet/Pratt & Miller	573 DNF	19	GTO
25	58	Massimo Morini (I)/Antonio Gerolamo de Castro (I)/Luca Cattaneo (I)/Renato Bicciato (I)/ Massimo Frigerio (I)	Porsche 996 GT3R	Carlo Noce	570	73	GTU
26	34	Spencer Pumpelly (USA)/Emil Assentato (USA)/John Steinmetz (USA)/Gregor Fisken (GB)	Porsche 911 Carrera RSR	Spencer Pumpelly	549	72	GTU
27	**84**	**John Finger (USA)/Doug Mills (USA)/Richard Maugeri (USA) Andy McNeil (USA)/Ron Zitza (USA)**	**Chevrolet Camaro**	**James Comer**	**546**	**45**	**AGT**
28	10	Ulrich Richter (D)/Wilhelm Kern (D)/Axel Rohr (D)/Juergen Alzen (D)	Porsche 996 GT3R	Juergen Alzen	542 DNF	54	GTU
29	44	Peter Chambers (GB)/Paul Fuller (GB)/Mike Youles (GB)/Marcus Fothergill (GB)/Adam Simmons (GB)	Porsche 996 GT3R	Mike Pickup	542 DNF	70	GTU
30	2	Shane Lewis (USA)/Robert Mazzuoccola (USA)/Mike Bovaro (USA)/Cort Wagner (USA)	Porsche 996 GT3R	Michael Colucci	540 DNF	42	GTU
31	81	Patrick Huisman (NL)/Uwe Alzen (D)/Duncan Huisman (NL)/Darren Law (USA)	Porsche 996 GT3R	Cole Scrogham	525	30	GTU
32	01	Grady Willingham (USA)/Chris Pennington (USA)/Joel Reiser (USA)/Simon Sobrero (USA)/ Craig Stanton (USA)	Porsche 996 GT3R	Reiser/Callas	523	47	GTU
33	47	Richard McDill (USA)/Todd Vallancourt (USA)/John G. Thomas (USA)/ Les Vallarano (USA)/Ken Stiver (USA)	Spice-Chevrolet SE90	Jack Beane	522	20	SR
34	57	Jean-Luc Maury-Laribiere (F)/Pascal Fabre (F)/Bernard Chauvin (F)/Patrick Cruchet (F)/ Rael (Claude Vorilhon) (CDN)	Porsche 996 GT3R	Guido Haberthur	519	64	GTU
35	74	George Robinson (USA)/Jack Baldwin (USA)/Hurley Haywood (USA)/Irv Hoerr (USA)	Riley & Scott-Chevrolet Mk III	George Robinson	495 DNF	9	SR
36	88	Peter Baron (USA)/Gian Luigi Buitoni (USA)/Tony Kester (USA)/Leo Hindery (USA)/ Mike Borkowski (USA)	Porsche 996 GT3R	Michael Colucci	470 DNF	61	GTU
37	22	Kurt Matthewson (USA)/Tony Burgess (CDN)/Paolo Rapetti (I)/Michel Neugarten (B)	Porsche 996 GT3R	Peter Seikel	443 DNF	48	GTU
38	38	Gerold Ried (D)/Horst Felbermayr, Sr. (A)/Horst Felbermayr, Jr. (A)/Christian Ried (D)	Porsche 911 GT2	Gerold Ried	405	56	GTO
39	70	David Murry (USA)/Lloyd Hawkins (USA)/Rohan Skea (AUS)/John Mowlem (GB)	Porsche 996 GT3R	Rohan Skea	DNF	39	GTU
40	09	Craig Conway (GB)/Troy Flis (USA)/Todd Flis (USA)/Doug Goad (USA)	Chevrolet Camaro (Riggins)	Flis Brothers	397 DNF	32	AGT
41	95	Barry Waddell (USA)/Peter Boss (USA)/Richard J. Valentine (USA)/Thomas Volk (USA)	Riley & Scott-Chevrolet Mk III	Volk	380	16	SR
42	68	Ron Herrerias (USA)/Michael Smith (USA)/Tom McGlynn (USA)/Ludovico Manfredi (USA)	Porsche 911 Carrera RSR	Kevin Buckler	373 DNF	76	GTU
43	17	Chris Bingham (USA)/Boris Said (USA)/Mark Simo (USA)/Rick Sutherland (USA)	Riley & Scott-Ford Mk III	Rod Everett	352 DNF	12	SR
44	33	Marc Schoonbroodt (B)/Luciano Tamburini (I)/Franco Bugane (I) Kurt Thiel (USA)/ Roberto Buonomo (I)/ Italo Ziliani (I)	Porsche 996 GT3R	Carlo Noce	321 DNF	52	GTU
45	59	Roland Berville (F)/Juergen Barth (D)/Michel Ligonnet (F)/Ferdinand de Lesseps (F)	Porsche 996 GT3R	Jack Leconte	314 DNF	49	GTU
46	51	Dirk Mueller (D)/Lucas Luhr (D)/Bob Wollek (F)	Porsche 996 GT3R	Dick Barbour	312 DNF	25	GTU

FIN.	CAR NO.	DRIVERS	CAR	ENTRANT	LAPS	START	CLASS
47	50	Bill Auberlen (USA)/Rick Fairbanks (USA)/Nick Ham (USA)/Chris Gleason (USA)/Chris Miller (USA)	BMW M3	Rick Fairbanks	312 DNF	35	GTU
48	63	Howard Katz (USA)/Chris Ronson (USA)/Steve Pelke (USA/Jim Downing (USA)	Kudzu-Mazda DLY	Jim Downing	303 DNF	15	SR
49	53	Tom Scheuren (USA)/Eric Curran (USA)/Rick DiIorio (USA)/Todd Snyder (USA)/Mayo T. Smith (USA)	Chevrolet Camaro	Ellen Barbara	303 DNF	75	AGT
50	9	Bobby Brown (USA)/Norman Goldrich (USA)/Randy Lenz (USA)/* Brian DeVries (USA)	Spice-Chevrolet HC94	Bobby Brown	292 DNF	53	SR
51	13	Martin Shuster (USA)/Mark Montgomery (USA)/Anthony Puleo (USA)	Chevrolet Camaro	Mark Montgomery	289 DNF	67	AGT
52	48	Mauro Casadei (I)/Stefano Bucci (I)/Andrea Garbagnati (MC)/Renato Mastropietro (I)	Porsche 911 GT2	Guido Haberthur	279 DNF	40	GTO
53	60	Steven Lynn (USA)/Ray Snowdon (USA)/Steve Ahlgrim (USA)/Richard Geck (USA)/ Michael Jacobs (USA)/Frank Del Vecchio (USA)	Kudzu-Chevrolet DLM4	Michael Jacobs	277	66	SR
54	14	R. K. Smith (USA)/Jeff Nowicki (USA)/Bill Lester (USA)/John Heinricy (USA)	Chevrolet Corvette C5	Jack Cauley	261 DNF	46	GTO
55	03	Claudia Huertgen (D)/Hubert Haupt (D)/Hisashi Wada (J)/Robert Nearn (GB)/Nigel Smith (GB)/ Stephen Earle (USA)	Porsche 911 GT2	Fabian Roock	259 DNF	22	GTO
56	32	Juergen von Gartzen (D)/Charles Slater (USA)/Peter Kitchak (USA)Calum Lockie (GB)/Franz Konrad (A)	Porsche 911 GT2	Franz Konrad	248 DNF	27	GTO
57	40	David Rankin (USA)/Dorian Foyil (BS)/Toto Lasally (ES/Hank Scott (USA)/Ian James (GB)	Chevrolet Camaro	David Rankin	240 DNF	33	AGT
58	15	Gaston Aguirre (RA)/Scott Watkins (USA)/Daniel Urrutia (USA)/Rene Villeneuve (USA)	Chevrolet Corvette	Dale Kreider	239 DNF	62	GTO
59	24	Scott Finlay (USA)/Steve Goldin (USA)/Keith Goldin (USA)	Mazda RX-7	Goldin/Goldin	239 DNF	81	GTU
60	35	Pier Angelo Masselli (I)/Franco Scapini (I)/Erich Prinoth (I)/Ivan Capelli (I)	Ferrari F355	Franco Scapini	228 DNF	79	GTU
61	21	John Rutherford Jr. (USA)/Andy Hajducky (USA)/Dave Geremia (USA)/Bob Oneglia (USA)/ Ken Fengler (USA)/Bobby Carradine (USA)	Porsche 911 Carrera RSR	Hajducky/Oneglia	227 DNF	71	GTU
62	75	Michael Brockman (USA)/Paul Newman (USA)/Michael Lauer (D)/Gunnar Jeannette (USA)	Porsche 996 GT3R	Dave Maraj	225 DNF	50	GTU
63	31	Jan Lammers (NL)/Sascha Maassen (D)/Franz Konrad (A)	Lola-Ford B98/10	Franz Konrad	209 DNF	7	SR
64	00	Enzo Calderari (CH)/Angelo Zadra (I)/Marco Zadra (I)/Carl Rosenblad (S)/Lilian Bryner (CH)	Ferrari 333SP	Enzo Calderari	203 DNF	14	SR
65	89	James McCormick (USA)/Kevin Crowder (USA)/Tim Robertson (USA)/Kurt Baumann (USA)	Porsche 996 GT3R	Michael Colucci	192 DNF	55	GTU
66	29	Andy Petery (USA)/Craig Carter (USA)/Gerry Green (USA)/John Mirro (USA)	Riley & Scott-Ford Mk III	Jon Field	175 DNF	36	SR
67	37	Jon Field (USA)/Dale Whittington (USA)/Don Whittington (USA)	Lola-Ford B98/10	Jon Field	164 DNF	10	SR
68	28	Toshio Suzuki (J)/Anders Olofsson (S)/Tsuyoshi Takahashi (J)/Van Peter Hanson (CDN)/ * Tommy Riggins (USA)	Ferrari F355	Masahiro Yamazaki	164 DNF	58	GTU
69	12	Alex Caffi (I)/Allan McNish (GB)/Ralf Kelleners (D)/Mimmo Schiattarella (MC)	Ferrari 333SP	Giuseppe Risi	162 DNF	2	SR
70	55	Felipe Rezk (USA)/Shareef Malnik (USA)/Dennis Crowley (USA)/Chris Miller (USA)/* Rick Fairbanks (USA)	BMW M3	Rick Fairbanks	133 DNF	68	GTU
71	27	Didier Theys (B)/Fredy Lienhard (CH)/Ross Bentley (CDN)/* Mauro Baldi (I)	Ferrari 333SP	Kevin Doran	132 DNF	6	SR
72	04	Zak Brown (USA)/David Warnock (GB)/Spencer Trenery (USA)/* Stephen Earle (USA)/* Vic Rice (USA)	Porsche 911 GT2	Fabian Roock	113 DNF	38	GTO
73	06	Scott Maxwell (CDN)/Harri Toivonen (SF)/John Graham (CDN)	Lola-Ford B98/10	Larry Holt	110 DNF	13	SR
74	69	Derek Bell (GB)/Tim Sugden (GB)/Stephen Day (GB)/* Steve O'Rourke (GB)	Porsche 996 GT3R	O'Rourke/Cane	75 DNF	44	GTU
75	42	Rob Wilson (NZ)/Martin Henderson (GB)/* Martyn Konig (GB)/* Jake Ulrich (USA)	Pilbeam-Nissan MP84	Werner Schroeder	51 DNF	37	SR
76	49	Patrick Vuillaume (F)/Ugo Colombo (USA)/Dieter Faller (CH)/* Anssi Muenz (I)	Porsche 911 GT2	Guido Haberthur	49 DNF	60	GTO
77	8	Scott Schubot (USA)/Henry Camferdam, Jr. (USA)/Duncan Dayton (USA)/*John Burton (GB)	Riley & Scott-Ford Mk III	Philip Creighton	45 DNF	3	SR
78	94	Paul Jenkins (USA)/Steve Lisa (USA)/* Don Arpin (USA)* Bill Beilharz (USA)/* Mark Reed (USA)	Chevrolet Camaro	Don Arpin	40 DNF	78	AGT
79	78	Patrice Roussel (F)/* Edouard Sezionale (F)/* A. J. Smith (USA)	Norma-BMW M14	Edouard Sezionale	13 DNS	23	SR
DNS	79	David Kicak (USA)/Art Pilla (USA)/Skott Burkland (USA)	Porsche 911 GT2	David Kicak	0	77	GTO

Rolex 24 At Daytona

February 3-4, 2001

24 hour event on the 3.560 mile circuit.

Distance covered: 656 laps for 2335.360 miles.

Winning time: 24 hours, 0 minutes, 2.539 seconds for a speed of 97.304 mph.

Margin of victory: 8 laps.

Fastest lap: #12 Ferrari 333SP 98 (Allan McNish), 1:41.875, 125.801 mph.

Pole winner: #16 Riley & Scott-Ford Mk III (James Weaver), 1:47.351, 119.384 mph.

Fastest qualifying lap: #12 Ferrari 333SP 98 (Ralf Kelleners), 1:41.118 ,126.743 mph.

FINISH	CAR NO.	DRIVERS	CAR	ENTRANT	LAPS	START	CLASS
1	**2**	**Johnny O'Connell (USA)/Ron Fellows (CDN)/Chris Kneifel (USA)/Franck Freon (F)**	**Chevrolet Corvette C5-R**	**Chevrolet/Pratt & Miller**	**656**	**14**	**GTS**
2	**31**	**Lucas Luhr (D)/Randy Pobst (USA)/Mike Fitzgerald (USA) Christian Menzel (D)**	**Porsche 996 GT3RS**	**Michael Petersen**	**648**	**39**	**GT**
3	86	Wolfgang Kaufmann (D)/Lance Stewart (USA)/Cyril Chateau (F)	Porsche 996 GT3RS	Manfred Freisinger	644	57	GT
4	3	Andy Pilgrim (GB)/Dale Earnhardt (USA)/Kelly Collins (USA)/Dale Earnhardt, Jr. (USA)	Chevrolet Corvette C5-R	Chevrolet/Pratt & Miller	642	19	GTS
5	56	Gabrio Rosa (I)/Fabio Babini (I)/Alex Caffi (I)/Fabio Rosa (I)	Porsche 996 GT3RS	Peter Seikel	637	40	GT

FINISH	CAR NO.	DRIVERS	CAR	ENTRANT	LAPS	START	CLASS
6	01	Larry Schumacher (USA)/Harry Bytzek (CDN)/John Brenner (CDN)/James Holtom (CDN)	Porsche 911 GT1 Evo	Klaus Bytzek	632	34	GTS
7	43	Peter Baron (USA)/Kyle Petty (USA)/Gian Luigi Buitoni (USA)/Leo Hindery (USA)/Tony Kester (USA)	Porsche 996 GT3RS	Rodger Hawley	630	55	GT
8	81	Darren Law (USA)/Matt Drendel (USA)/David Murry (USA)/Cort Wagner (USA)	Porsche 996 GT3R	Cole Scrogham	629	44	GT
9	10	Bill Auberlen (USA)/Chris Gleason (USA)/Rick Fairbanks (USA)/Chris Miller (USA)	BMW E46 M3	Rick Fairbanks	627	48	GT
10	39	Hugh Plumb (USA)/Kimberly Hiskey (USA)/Michael Culver (CDN)	Porsche 996 GT3R	Michael Petersen	627	53	GT
11	**63**	**Howard Katz (USA)/Chris Ronson (USA)/A. J. Smith (USA)/Jim Downing (USA)**	**Kudzu-Mazda DLY**	**Jim Downing**	**624**	**15**	**SRP**
12	50	Craig Stanton (USA)/Andy Hajducky (USA)/Takaji Suzuki (J)	Porsche 996 GT3R	Dennis Aase	618	41	GT
13	**21**	**Andy Lally (USA)/Paul Macey (CDN)/Martin Henderson (GB)/Peter Seldon (GB)**	**Lola-Nissan B2K/40**	**Michael Johnson**	**600**	**24**	**SRPII**
14	16	James Weaver (GB)/Butch Leitzinger (USA)/Andy Wallace (GB)	Riley & Scott-Ford Mk III	Rob Dyson	598 DNF	1	SRP
15	34	Spencer Pumpelly (USA)/Steve Ivankovich (USA)/Tom Pumpelly (USA)/Rick DiIorio (USA)	Porsche 996 GT3R	Spencer Pumpelly	595	54	GT
16	40	Antonio Gerolamo de Castro (I)/Luca Cattaneo (I)/Renato Bicciato (I)/Franco Bugane (I)	Porsche 996 GT3R	Carlo Noce	593	71	GT
17	57	Stefano Buttiero (I)/Philip Collin (USA)/Andrew Bagnall (NZ)/Tony Burgess (CDN)	Porsche 996 GT3RS	Peter Seikel	590	51	GT
18	71	Yukihiro Hane (J)/Kurt Thiel (USA)/Klaus Horn (D)/Manfred Jurasz (A)	Porsche 996 GT3R	Manfred Freisinger	585	68	GT
19	20	Elliott Forbes-Robinson (USA)/Rob Dyson (USA)/Massimiliano Papis (I)/Niclas Jonsson (S)	Riley & Scott-Ford Mk III	Rob Dyson	584	5	SRP
20	62	Rich Grupp (USA)/Ryan Hampton (USA)/Dennis Spencer (USA)	Kudzu-Mazda DLM	Dennis Spencer	577	20	SRPII
21	37	Jon Field (USA)/Carl Rosenblad (S)/Joel Field (USA)/Clint Field (USA)	Lola-Judd B2K/10	Jon Field	566	4	SRP
22	74	Jack Baldwin (USA)/George Robinson (USA)/Irv Hoerr (USA) Buddy Lazier (USA)	Riley & Scott-Judd Mk III	George Robinson	563 DNF	2	SRP
23	14	Cory Friedman (USA)/Adam Merzon (USA)/Basil Demeroutis (GB)/Lynn Wilson (USA)	Porsche 993 Carrera RSR	Gordon Friedman	563	75	GT
24	24	Cor Euser (NL)/Calum Lockie (GB)/Herman Buurman (NL)	Marcos Mantara LM 600	Cor Euser	562	23	GTS
25	41	Fabio Mancini (I)/Giovanni Luca Collini (I)/Paolo Rapetti (I)/Michel Neugarten (B)	Porsche 996 GT3RS	Carlo Noce	561	56	GT
26	67	Don Kitch (USA)/Dave Parker (USA)/Dave Gaylord (USA)/Mike Oberholtzer (USA)	Porsche 996 GT3R	Kevin Buckler	560	78	GT
27	25	Miguel Angel de Castro (E)/Peter van der Kolk (NL)/Toto Lassally (ES)	Marcos Mantara LM 600	Cor Euser	557	35	GTS
28	**11**	**Ken Bupp (USA)/Dick Greer (USA)/Doug Mills (USA)/Simon Gregg (USA)**	**Chevrolet Camaro**	**Ken Bupp**	**553**	**45**	**AGT**
29	66	Wade Gaughran (USA)/Justin Marks (USA)/Steve Miller (USA)/Kiichi Takahashi (J)	Porsche 996 GT3R	Kevin Buckler	547	72	GT
30	55	Toshio Suzuki (J)/Tsuyoshi Takahashi (J)/Shogo Mitsuyama (J)/Shinichi Yamaji (J)	Ferrari F355	Masahiro Yamazaki	543	73	GT
31	114	Stefano Zonca (I)/Raffaele Sangiuolo (I)/Milka Duno (YV)/David Gooding (GB)	Dodge Viper GTS-R	Hugh Chamberlain	530	49	GTS
32	52	Scooter Gabel (USA)/Joe Safina (USA)/Jonathan Lowman (USA) Carlos DeQuesada (USA)	BMW M3	Joseph Safina	530	69	GT
33	09	Craig Conway (GB)/Erik Messley (USA)/Doug Goad (USA)/Richard Maugeri (USA)	Chevrolet Camaro	Flis Brothers	528	38	AGT
34	9	Marc Bunting (USA)/Emil Assentato (USA)/Philip Shearer (USA)/Steve Ahlgrim (USA)	BMW M3	Rick Fairbanks	510	76	GT
35	05	Francesco Gutierrez (E)/Nigel Smith (GB)/Patrick Vuillaume (F) Jean-Charles Cartier (F)	Porsche 996 GT3R	Guido Haberthur	505 DNF	70	GT
36	30	Fabian Peroni (I)/Tony Ring (S)/Zoblin Sergey (RUS)/Andrea Montermini (MC)	Ferrari F355	Roberto Crugnola	505	79	GT
37	26	Cass Whitehead (USA)/B. J. Zacharias (USA)/Jeff Giangrande (USA)/Chris Hall (USA)	Lola-Nissan B2K/40	Jeff Giangrande	498 DNF	22	SRPII
38	69	Horst Felbermayr, Jr. (A)/Horst Felbermayr, Sr. (A)/Christian Ried (D)/Gerold Ried (D)	Porsche 911 GT2	Gerold Ried	495	42	GTS
39	54	Toney Jennings (USA)/Terry Borcheller (USA)/Boris Said (USA)/Hans-Joachim Stuck Jr. (D)	BMW E46 M3	James Bell	490 DNF	32	GT
40	44	Joe Varde (USA)/David Amick (USA)/Lyndon Amick (USA)/Bill Lester (USA)	Chevrolet Corvette (Hoerr)	David Amick	488 DNF	30	AGT
41	0	Scott Maxwell (CDN)/David Empringham (CDN)/Richard Spenard (CDN)/Klaus Bytzek (CDN)	Porsche 911 GT1 Evo	Klaus Bytzek	479	12	GTS
42	65	Claudia Huertgen (D)/Robert Orcutt (USA)/Juergen Lorenz (D)/Heinrich Langfermann (D)	Porsche 996 GT3R	Robert Schirle	477	61	GT
43	89	Greg Pootmans (CDN)/Bruno St. Jacques (CDN)/Robert Julien (CDN)/Bob Woodman (USA)	Lola-Nissan B2K/40	Andre Gaudet	473 DNF	18	SRPII
44	60	Geoff Lister (GB)/Mike Youles (GB)/Fred Moss (GB)/Matt Turner (USA)	Porsche 996 GT3R	Mike Pickup	471 DNF	74	GT
45	07	Johannes van Overbeek (USA)/Steve Marshall (USA)/Danny Marshall (USA) Tim Holt (USA)	Porsche 911 GT2	Cole Scrogham	470 DNF	47	GTS
46	12	Ralf Kelleners (D)/Allan McNish (GB)/David Brabham (AUS) Eric van de Poele (B)	Ferrari 333SP 98	Giuseppe Risi	462 DNF	3	SRP
47	22	Andrew Davis (USA)/Tony Dudek (USA)/Mike Durand (USA)/Jeff Clinton (USA)	Lola-Nissan B2K/40	Michael Johnson	460 DNF	25	SRPII
48	96	Dave Bacher (USA)/Anthony Puleo (USA)/Hans Hauser (CH)/Robert Dubler (CH)	Oldsmobile Cutlass	Dave Bacher	407	62	AGT
49	68	Kevin Buckler (USA)/Jim Michaelian (USA)/Stephen Earle (USA)/Dilantha Malagamuwa (CL)	Porsche 996 GT3RS	Kevin Buckler	354	46	GT
50	32	Keith Goldin (USA)/Scott Finlay (USA)/David Rankin (USA)/Steve Goldin (USA)	Mazda RX-7	Goldin Brothers	351	77	GT
51	4	Duncan Dayton (USA)/John Burton (GB)/Rick Sutherland (USA)/* Scott Schubot (USA)	Lola-Ford B2K/10	Philip Creighton	347 DNF	8	SRP
52	35	Ulrich Richter (D)/Enzo Calderari (CH)/Lilian Bryner (CH)/Juergen Alzen (D)	Porsche 996 Supercup/GT3R	Juergen Alzen	315 DNF	67	GT
53	17	Luca Riccitelli (I)/Dieter Quester (A)/Marc Duez (B)/Hans-Joerg Hofer (A)	Porsche 996 GT3R	Rudi Walch	310 DNF	37	GT
54	79	Thed Bjork (S)/Niklas Loven (S)/Larry Oberto (USA)/Stanley Dickens (S)	Lola-Nissan B2K/40	Stanley Dickens	241 DNF	13	SRPII
55	18	Jack Willes (USA)/Andy McNeil (USA)/Jon Leavy (USA)/* Les Vallarano (USA)	Chevrolet Corvette	James Comer	238 DNF	43	AGT
56	47	Joe Foster (USA)/Gary Schultheis (USA)/Scott Neuman (USA)/Ross Bluestein (USA)	Porsche 996 GT3RS	Gary Schultheis	233 DNF	52	GT
57	7	Jesus Diez Villarroel (E)/Paco Orti (E)/John Warner (USA)/Ron Zitza (USA)	Porsche 996 GT3R	Al Broadfoot	222 DNF	66	GT
58	48	Shane Lewis (USA)/Bruno Lambert (B)/Toni Seiler (CH)	Pilbeam-Nissan MP84	Alfred Kobacker	216 DNF	29	SRPII
59	38	Dorsey Schroeder (USA)/Bob Wollek (F)/Hurley Haywood (USA)/Sascha Maassen (D)	Lola-Porsche B2K/10	Dave Maraj	209 DNF	6	SRP
60	80	John Morton (USA)/Michael Schrom (USA)/Robert Mazzuoccola (USA)/Stuart Hayner (USA)	Porsche 996 GT3R	Cole Scrogham	185 DNF	60	GT
61	27	Didier Theys (B)/Fredy Lienhard (CH)/Ross Bentley (CDN)/Mauro Baldi (I)	Crawford-Judd SSC2K	Kevin Doran	181 DNF	11	SRP
62	78	Patrice Roussel (F)/John Macaluso (USA)/Edouard Sezionale (F)/Georges Forgeois (F)	Norma-BMW M14	Edouard Sezionale	179 DNF	17	SRP
63	6	Jeff Bucknum (USA)/Brent Sherman (USA)/Travis Duder (USA)/* Gary Tiller (USA)	Lola-Nissan B2K/40	Michael Atkins	138 DNF	21	SRPII
64	53	Eric Curran (USA)/Mayo T. Smith (USA)/Todd Snyder (USA)/Tom Scheuren (USA)	Chevrolet Camaro	Ellen Barbara	125 DNF	65	AGT
65	46	Kerry Hitt (USA)/* Jerry Thompson (USA)/* Joe Nagle (USA)/* Rodger Bogusz (USA)	Chevrolet Corvette	Kerry Hitt	117 DNF	64	AGT
66	06	Todd Snyder (USA)/Peter Argetsinger (USA)/Nick Longhi (USA)/* Michael Jacobs (USA)	Riley & Scott-Ford Mk III	Michael Jacobs	112 DNF	16	SRP
67	92	Hubert Haupt (D)/Anthony Kumpen (B)/Vic Rice (USA)/* John Thomas Young (USA)	Porsche 996 GT3R	Robert Schirle	108 DNF	50	GT
68	36	Angelo Zadra (I)/Pedro Couceiro (P)/Ulrich Gallade (D)/Duncan Huisman (NL)	Porsche 996 GT3RS	Juergen Alzen	106 DNF	63	GT

FIN.	CAR NO.	DRIVERS	CAR	ENTRANT	LAPS	START	CLASS
69	8	Franz Konrad (A)/Alan Heath (AUS)/Charles Slater (USA)/Gualter Salles (BR)	Lola-Ford B2K/10	Franz Konrad	96 DNF	10	SRP
70	83	Norman Simon (D)/Mark Simo (USA)/Brian DeVries (USA)/* Michael Lauer (D)	Riley & Scott-Ford Mk III	Bob Akin	92 DNF	7	SRP
71	23	Mark Montgomery (USA)/Sim Penton (USA)/* Pascal Dro (F) * Patrick Cruchet (F)	Chevrolet Camaro	Gwen Davin	67 DNF	80	AGT
72	28	Spencer Trenery (USA)/Frank Emmett (USA)/Bruce Trenery (USA)/Patrick van Schoote (B)	Riley & Scott-Ford Mk III	Jon Field	62 DNF	28	SRP
73	02	Joao Barbosa (P)/Scott Deware (USA)/John Heinricy (USA)/* Jim Minneker (USA)	Mosler MT900R	Tommy Morrison	61 DNF	31	GT
74	5	Paul Gentilozzi (USA)/Scott Pruett (USA)/* John Miller (USA)/* Anthony Lazzaro (USA)	Saleen S7R	Paul Gentilozzi	50 DNF	26	GTS
75	91	David Warnock (GB)/Ugo Colombo (USA)/* Bernardo Sa Nogueira (P)/* Christian D'Agostin (AUS)	Porsche 911 GT2	Schirle	48 DNF	59	GTS
76	15	Christian Vann (GB)/Chris Bingham (USA)/* Seiji Ara (J)/* Robert Nearn (GB)	Dodge Viper GTS-R	Hugh Chamberlain	45 DNF	33	GTS
77	42	Tommy Byrne (IRL)/* Richard Millman (USA)/* Tony Kester (USA)/* Michael Colucci (USA)	Porsche 996 GT3RS	Rodger Hawley	37 DNF	58	GT
78	76	Gunnar Jeannette (USA)/Wayne Jackson (USA)/* Paul Newman (USA)/* Michael Brockman (USA)	Porsche 911 GT1 Evo	Kevin Jeannette	37 DNF	27	GTS
79	95	Jeret Schroeder (USA)/* Thomas Volk (USA)/* John Mirro (USA)/* Barry Waddell (USA)	Riley & Scott-Chevrolet Mk III	Thomas Volk	3 DNF	9	SRP
DNS	49	Phil Harris (USA)	Pilbeam-Nissan MP84	Alfred Kobacker	0	36	SRPII

Rolex 24 At Daytona

February 2-3, 2002

24 hour event on the 3.560 mile circuit.

Distance covered: 716 laps for 2548.960 miles.

Winning time: 24 hours, 0 minutes, 51.968 seconds for a speed of 106.143 mph.

Margin of victory = 6 laps.

Fastest lap: #2 Crawford-Judd SSC2K (Jan Lammers), 1:42.078, 125.551 mph.

Fastest qualifier: #27 Dallara-Judd LMP (Didier Theys), 1:42.058, 125.576 mph.

11 full course cautions for 32 laps

FIN.	CAR NO.	DRIVERS	CAR	ENTRANT	LAPS	START	CLASS
1	**27**	**Didier Theys (B)/Fredy Lienhard (CH)/Mauro Baldi (I)/Massimiliano Papis (I)**	**Dallara-Judd LMP**	**Doran**	**716**	**1**	**SRP**
2	36	Guy Smith (GB)/Scott Sharp (USA)/Robby Gordon (USA)/Jim Matthews (USA)	Riley & Scott Ford-Elan Mk III-C	Jim Matthews	710	4	SRP
3	**8**	**Anthony Lazzaro (USA)/Terry Borcheller (USA)/Bill Rand (USA)/Ralf Kelleners (D)**	**Lola-Nissan B2K/40**	**Bill Rand/Giuseppe Risi**	**695**	**17**	**SRPII**
4	38	Andy Wallace (GB)/Sascha Maassen (D)/Hurley Haywood (USA)/Lucas Luhr (D)	Lola-Porsche B2K/10	Dave Maraj	681	8	SRP
5	**3**	**Paul Gentilozzi (USA)/Scott Pruett (USA)/Michael Lauer (D)/Brian Simo (USA)**	**Jaguar XKR**	**Paul Gentilozzi**	**675**	**15**	**GTS**
6	22	Chad Block (USA)/Steven Knight (USA)/Brian DeVries (USA)/Mel Hawkins (USA)	Lola-Nissan B2K/40	Michael Johnson	670	25	SRPII
7	**66**	**Kevin Buckler (USA)/Michael Schrom (USA)/Joerg Bergmeister (D)/Timo Bernhard (D)**	**Porsche 996 GT3RS**	**Kevin Buckler**	**669**	**43**	**GT**
8	77	Christophe Bouchut (F)/Patrice Goueslard (F)/Jean-Luc Chereau (F)/Carl Rosenblad (S)	Chrysler Viper GTS-R	Leconte/Chereau	665	24	GTS
9	44	Gary Schultheis (USA)/Tony Kester (USA)/Sylvain Tremblay (CDN)/Selby Wellman (USA)	Porsche 996 GT3RS	Rodger Hawley	664	60	GT
10	86	Ni Amorim (P)/Romain Dumas (F)/Stephane Ortelli (F)/Hans Fertl (D)	Porsche 996 GT3RS	Manfred Freisinger	661	47	GT
11	68	Robert Nearn (GB)/Bob M. Nagel (USA)/B. J. Zacharias (USA)/Larry Schumacher (USA)	Porsche 996 GT3R	Kevin Buckler	657	49	GT
12	63	Charles Nearburg (USA)/Chris Ronson (USA)/John Lloyd (USA)/Jim Downing (USA)	Kudzu-Mazda DLY	Jim Downing	654	14	SRP
13	24	Joao Barbosa (P)/Michel Neugarten (B)/Thierry Perrier (F)	Mosler MT900R	Thierry Perrier	653	30	GT
14	40	Brady Refenning (USA)/Catesby Jones (USA)/Jake Vargo (USA)/Carlos DeQuesada (USA)	BMW E46 M3	Carlos DeQuesada	649	64	GT
15	43	Peter Baron (USA)/Kyle Petty (USA)/Mike Borkowski (USA)/Leo Hindery (USA)	Porsche 996 GT3RS	Rodger Hawley	641	51	GT
16	57	Hugh Plumb (USA)/Tony Burgess (CDN)/Philip Collin (USA)/David Shep (CDN)	Porsche 996 GT3RS	Peter Seikel	641	39	GT
17	31	Charles Slater (USA)/Toni Seiler (CH)/Martin Short (GB)/Gunnar Jeannette (USA)/*Vic Rice (USA)	Saleen S7R (Mallock)	Franz Konrad	634	31	GTS
18	67	Jim Michaelian (USA)/Ludovico Manfredi (USA)/Paul Daniels (GB)/Matthew Talbert (USA)	Porsche 996 GT3RS	Kevin Buckler	618	70	GT
19	35	Gerry Green (USA)/Richard J. Valentine (USA)/Jim Walsh (USA)/Rick DiIorio (USA)	Porsche 996 GT3R	Spencer Pumpelly	608	63	GT
20	04	Stephane de Groodt (NL)/Peter van der Kolk (NL)/Pim van Riet (NL)/Cougar Jacobsen (USA)	Marcos Mantis Plus	Toto Lassally	598	62	GT
21	72	David Murry (USA)/Jack Lewis (USA)/Keith Fisher (USA)/Tom McGlynn (USA)	Porsche 996 GT3 Cup	Jack Lewis	592	45	GT
22	**09**	**Craig Conway (GB)/Doug Goad (USA)/Michael Ciasulli (USA)/Andy Pilgrim (GB)**	**Chevrolet Corvette**	**Flis Brothers**	**591**	**27**	**AGT**
23	37	Jon Field (USA)/Duncan Dayton (USA)/Mike Durand (USA)/Rick Sutherland (USA)	Lola-Judd B2K/10B	Jon Field	590 DNF	10	SRP
24	85	Robert Orcutt (USA)/Ross Bluestein (USA)/Philippe Haezebrouck (F)/Rob Croydon (GB)	Porsche 996 GT3RS	Manfred Freisinger	579	67	GT
25	33	Cort Wagner (USA)/Bill Auberlen (USA)/Costantino Bertuzzi (I)/Derrike Cope (USA)	Ferrari 360 Modena Challenge	Allie Ash Jr.	572	54	GT
26	98	Pierre Bes (B)/Marco Saviozzi (F)/Kurt Thiel (USA)/David Terrien (F)	Porsche 996 GT3R	Carlo Noce	569	48	GT
27	96	Andrea Montermini (MC)/Vincenzo Polli (I)/Franco Bertoli (I)/Sergey Zlobin (RUS)	Ferrari 360 Modena	Erich Prinoth	551 DNF	66	GT
28	10	Todd Snyder (USA)/Rick Fairbanks (USA)/Nick Longhi (USA)/Emil Assentato (USA)	BMW E46 M3	Emil Assentato	547	56	GT
29	62	Dennis Spencer (USA)/Barry Waddell (USA)/Ryan Hampton (USA)/Rich Grupp (USA)	Kudzu-Mazda DLM/FW	Dennis Spencer	533	32	SRPII
30	42	Tommy Byrne (IRL)/Peter Peterson (USA)/Stephen Earle (USA)/Richard Millman (USA)	Porsche 996 GT3RS	Richard Millman	511	65	GTS
31	73	Mike Jordan (GB)/Mark Sumpter (GB)/Graeme Langford (GB)/David Warnock (GB)	Porsche 996 GT3R	Mike Jordan	503	53	GT

FIN.	CAR NO.	DRIVERS	CAR	ENTRANT	LAPS	START	CLASS
32	00	David Empringham (CDN)/Klaus Bytzek (CDN)/Richard Spenard (CDN)/James Holtom (CDN)	Porsche 911 GT1 Evo	Klaus Bytzek	499 DNF	18	GTS
33	46	Charles Morgan (USA)/Andrew Richards (NZ)/Stephen Richards (NZ)/Rob Morgan (USA)	Chevrolet Corvette	Charles Morgan	493 DNF	26	AGT
34	87	Patrice Roussel (F)/Georges Forgeois (F)/Edouard Sezionale (F)/* John Mirro (USA)	Norma-Ford M-2000-02	Edouard Sezionale	492	36	SRP
35	30	Joel Field (USA)/Larry Oberto (USA)/Mark Neuhaus (USA)/Clint Field (USA)	Lola-Judd B2K/10	Jon Field	462 DNF	16	SRP
36	13	Eric van de Poele (B)/David Brabham (AUS)/Stefan Johansson (S)	Ferrari 333SP	Giuseppe Risi	455 DNF	6	SRP
37	4	Grahame Bryant (GB)/Norman Goldrich (USA)/David Gooding (GB)/Kari Maenpaa (SF)	Chrysler Viper GTS-R	Martin Braybrook	434	74	GTS
38	49	Werner Lupberger (ZA)/Timothy J. Bell (USA)/Harri Toivonen (SF)/Klaas Zwart (NL)	Ascari-Judd KZR-1	Klaas Zwart	429 DNF	2	SRP
39	83	Ian McKellar (GB)/Thomas Erdos (BR)/Ron Anton Johnson (USA)/Bobby Verdon-Roe (GB)	Saleen S7R	Graham Nash	428	23	GTS
40	82	Dick Greer (USA)/Jack Willes (USA)/Terry Lingner (USA)/John Finger (USA)	Chevrolet Corvette	Dick Greer	424 DNF	61	AGT
41	56	Luca Drudi (I)/Gabrio Rosa (I)/Fabio Rosa (I)/Alex Caffi (I)	Porsche 996 GT3RS	Peter Seikel	420 DNF	41	GT
42	7	Luca Riccitelli (I)/Dieter Quester (A)/Vincent Vosse (B)/Boris Said (USA)	Porsche 996 GT3R	Rudi Walch	404 DNF	28	GTS
43	51	Chris Bingham (USA)/Peter MacLeod (USA)/Wade Gaughran (USA)/Vic Rice (USA)	Saleen S7R	David Bingham	392	20	GTS
44	20	Elliott Forbes-Robinson (USA)/Rob Dyson (USA)/Chris Dyson (USA)/Dorsey Schroeder (USA)	Riley & Scott-Ford Mk III	Rob Dyson	379 DNF	7	SRP
45	92	Mauro Casadei (I)/Raffaele Sangiuolo (I)/Derek Clark (USA)/Jay Wilton (USA)	Porsche 996 GT3R	Christian Haberthur	352 DNF	68	GT
46	2	Jan Lammers (NL)/John Mowlem (GB)/Tony Stewart (USA)	Crawford-Judd SSC2K	Max Crawford	346 DNF	3	SRP
47	79	Mike Fitzgerald (USA)/Justin Jackson (USA)/Manuel Matos (PR)/Marino Franchitti (GB)	Porsche 996 GT3RS	Justin Jackson	343 DNF	44	GT
48	9	Horst Felbermayr, Jr. (A)/Horst Felbermayr, Sr. (A)/Paul Knapfield (GB)/Andre Ahrle (D)	Porsche 996 GT3R	Rudi Walch	335 DNF	58	GT
49	08	Cor Euser (NL)/Calum Lockie (GB)/Duncan Huisman (NL)	Marcos Mantara LM 600	Cor Euser	330 DNF	22	GTS
50	53	Ross Bentley (CDN)/Bruno Lambert (B)/Don Kitch (USA)/Dave Gaylord (USA)	Saleen S7R	David Bingham	311 DNF	37	GTS
51	39	Tom Papadopoulos (USA)/Dave Friedman (USA)/Matt Plumb (USA)	Porsche 996 GT3R	Tom Papadopoulos	301 DNF	50	GT
52	12	R. K. Smith (USA)/Rodney Mall (USA)/Joey Scarallo (USA)/Douglas Dwyer (USA)	Ultima GTR	Rodney Mall	294 DNF	38	GTS
53	19	Kerry Hitt (USA)/James Briody (USA)/Owen Trinkler (USA)/Shane Lewis (USA)	Chevrolet Corvette	Kerry Hitt	287 DNF	55	AGT
54	21	Jeff Clinton (USA)/Larry Connor (USA)/Jeff Tillman (USA)/Curtis Francois (USA)	Lola-Nissan B2K/40	Michael Johnson	285 DNF	42	SRPII
55	99	Rob Wilson (NZ)/Martyn Konig (GB)/Paul Dawson (GB)/Peter Hannen (GB)	Porsche 996 GT3R	Robert Schirle	284 DNF	59	GT
56	91	Bill Beilharz (USA)/Steve Lisa (USA)/Paul Jenkins (USA)	Oldsmobile Aurora	Bill Beilharz	275 DNF	57	AGT
57	16	James Weaver (GB)/Butch Leitzinger (USA)/Oliver Gavin (GB)	Riley & Scott-Ford Mk III	Rob Dyson	265 DNF	5	SRP
58	54	Brian Cunningham (USA)/Alan van der Merwe (CH)/Andy Petery (USA)/Ron Atapattu (USA)	BMW E46 M3	James Bell	246 DNF	52	GT
59	60	Anthony Puleo (USA)/Robert Dubler (CH)/* Ernst Gschwender (D)/* Hans Hauser (CH)	Chevrolet Corvette	Anthony Puleo	232 DNF	34	AGT
60	18	Dilantha Malagamuwa (CL)/Scott Deware (USA)/* Charles Lamb (GB)/* Martin Short (GB)	Mosler MT900R	Deware	225	72	GT
61	03	Martin Shuster (USA)/Larry Baisden (USA)/John Annis (USA)/Toto Lassally (ES)	Marcos Mantis Plus	Toto Lassally	219 DNF	73	GT
62	95	Jeret Schroeder (USA)/John Macaluso (USA)/John Schneider (USA)/Thomas Volk (USA)	Riley & Scott-Chevrolet Mk III	Thomas Volk	216 DNF	13	SRP
63	2	Irv Hoerr (USA)/Woodson Byron Duncan (USA)/Jack Busch (USA) Darin Brassfield (USA)	Ford Mustang (Hoerr)	Woodson Byron Duncan	196 DNF	19	AGT
64	84	Tom Herridge (GB)/Mike Newton (GB)/Chris Ellis (GB)/Marc Attard (GB)	Porsche 996 GT3R	Graham Nash	184 DNF	69	GT
65	74	Jack Baldwin (USA)/George Robinson (USA)/Wally Dallenbach Jr. (USA)/Mark Simo (USA)	Riley & Scott-Judd Mk III-C	George Robinson	170 DNF	9	SRP
66	89	Robert Julien (CDN)/Lynn Wilson (USA)/Mayo T. Smith (USA)/* Adam Merzon (USA)	Lola-Nissan B2K/40	Andre Gaudet	164 DNF	35	SRPII
67	78	Yannick Roussel (F)/John Mirro (USA)/Jon Krolowitz (USA)/Francois O'Born (F)/* Anthony Kumpen (B)	Norma-BMW M14	Edouard Sezionale	160	71	SRP
68	45	Mike Hezemans (NL)/Simon Gregg (USA)/Stefano Zonca (I)/Marc Bunting (USA)	Dodge Viper GTS-R	Tom Weickardt	132 DNF	29	GTS
69	90	Kevin Harvick (USA)/Rick Carelli (USA)/John Metcalf (USA)/Dave Liniger (USA)	Chevrolet Corvette (Riggins)	Flis Brothers	123 DNF	21	AGT
70	23	Ben Collins (GB)/Klaas Zwart (NL)/Christian Vann (GB)	Ascari-BMW KZR-1	Klaas Zwart	116 DNF	11	SRP
71	07	Darren Law (USA)/Steve Marshall (USA)/Armando Trentini (I)/* Cort Wagner (USA)	Picchio-BMW D-USA	Cole Scrogham	107 DNF	33	SRPII
72	50	Craig Stanton (USA)/* Andy Hajducky (USA)/* Takashi Suzuki (J)/* Javier Quiros (CR)	BMW E46 M3	Dennis Aase	54 DNF	40	GT
73	34	Spencer Pumpelly (USA)/* Steve Ivankovich (USA)/* Randy Pobst (USA) * Kimberly Hiskey (USA)	Porsche 996 GT3RS	Spencer Pumpelly	15 DNF	46	GT

Rolex 24 At Daytona

February 1-2, 2003

24 hour event on the 3.560 mile circuit.

Distance covered: 695 laps for 2474.200 miles.

Winning time: 24 hours, 1 minute, 7.001 seconds for a speed of 103.012 mph.

Margin of victory: 9 laps.

Fastest lap set by # 59 Fabcar-Porsche FDSC/03 (Sharp) 1:50.618, 115.858 mph/186.455 kph

Fastest qualifier = # 88 Multimatic-Ford Focus (Maxwell) 1:50.512, 115.969 mph/186.634 kph

10 full-course cautions for 29 laps.

FIN.	CAR NO.	DRIVERS	CAR	ENTRANT	LAPS	START	CLASS
1	66	Kevin Buckler (USA)/Michael Schrom (USA)/Timo Bernhard (D)/Joerg Bergmeister (D)	Porsche 996 GT3RS	The Racer's Group	695	16	GT
2	35	Ralf Kelleners (D)/Anthony Lazzaro (USA)/John Mowlem (GB)	Ferrari 360 Modena	Risi Competizione	686	17	GT
3	83	Johannes van Overbeek (USA)/David Murry (USA)/Dave Standridge (USA)/Richard Steranka (USA)	Porsche 996 GT3R	Rennwerks Motorsports	684	37	GT
4	88	Scott Maxwell (CDN)/David Empringham (CDN)/David Brabham (AUS)	Multimatic-Ford Focus	Multimatic	679	1	DP
5	59	Hurley Haywood (USA)/Jamie C. France (USA)/Scott Goodyear (CDN)/Scott Sharp (USA)	Fabcar-Porsche FDSC/03	Brumos Racing	661	3	DP
6	43	Peter Baron (USA)/Leo Hindery (USA)/Marc Lieb (D)/Kyle Petty (USA)	Porsche 996 GT3RS	Hawley (Orbit Racing)	656	13	GT
7	5	Ross Bentley (CDN)/Don Kitch (USA)/Joseph Pruskowski (USA)/Justin Pruskowski (USA)	Lola-Nissan B2K/40	Essex Racing/Team Seattle	652	26	SRPII
8	15	Wade Gaughran (USA)/Steve Gorriaran (USA)/Peter MacLeod (USA)/Dave Gaylord (USA)	Lola-Nissan B2K/40	Essex Racing/Team Seattle	648	33	SRPII
9	24	Jerome Policand (F)/Joao Barbosa (P)/Michel Neugarten (B)/Andy Wallace (GB)	Mosler MT900R	Perspective Racing	641	10	GTS
10	46	Charles Morgan (USA)/Lance Norick (USA)/Jim Pace (USA)/Rob Morgan (USA)	Chevrolet Corvette	Morgan Dollar Motorsports	639	11	GTS
11	34	Mauro Baldi (I)/Justin Keen (GB)/Eric van de Poele (B)/Ryan Hampton (USA)	Ferrari 360 Modena	Risi Competizione/ Ferri Competizione	638	23	GT
12	31	Rob Barff (GB)/Richard Stanton (GB)/Andrew Britnell (GB)/Rick Sutherland (USA)	Mosler MT900R	Rollcentre Racing	635	20	GTS
13	69	Brian Cunningham (USA)/Hugh Plumb (USA)/Cory Friedman (USA)/Chris Mitchum (USA)	BMW M3	Marcus Motorsports	633	32	GT
14	20	Augusto Farfus (BR)/Emmanuel Collard (F)/Massimiliano Papis (I)/Andrea Garbagnati (MC)	Ferrari 360 Modena Challenge	JMB Racing USA	621	31	GT
15	30	Martin Short (GB)/Tom Herridge (GB)/John Burton (GB)/David Shep (CDN)	Mosler MT900R	Rollcentre Racing	601	21	GTS
16	7	Franz Konrad (A)/Toni Seiler (CH)/Airton Dare (BR)/Jean-Francois Yvon (F)	Saleen S7R (Mallock)	Konrad Motorsport	600	12	GTS
17	49	Roberto Orlandi (I)/Michele Merendino (I)/Derek Clark (USA)/Ron Atapattu (USA)	Porsche 996 GT3RS	Mac Racing	595	42	GT
18	21	Larry Oberto (USA)/Chris Bingham (USA)/Derrike Cope (USA)/Brian DeVries	(USA)Lola-Nissan B2K/40	Archangel Motorsport Services	589 DNF	29	SRPII
19	44	Mike Fitzgerald (USA)/Manuel Matos (PR)/Joseph Policastro, Sr. (USA)/Joseph Policastro, Jr. (USA)	Porsche 996 GT3RS	Orbit Racing	566 DNF	24	GT
20	97	Mirko Savoldi (I)/Piergiuseppe Peroni (I)/Filippo Francioni (I)	Lucchini-Nissan SR2002	Lucchini Engineering	548 DNF	44	SRPII
21	09	Doug Goad (USA)/Paul Menard (USA)/Paul Mears, Jr. (USA)/James Briody (USA)	Chevrolet Corvette	Flis Motorsports	542 DNF	38	GTS
22	68	Jim Michaelian (USA)/Richard J. Valentine (USA)/Thomas Hessert III (USA)/Thomas Hessert (USA)	Porsche 996 GT3RS	The Racer's Group	501 DNF	41	GT
23	03	Cor Euser (NL)/Rob Knook (NL)/Donny Crevels (NL)/Peter van der Kolk (NL)	Marcos Mantis Plus	Marcos Racing USA	465 DNF	40	GT
24	8	Boris Said (USA)/Darren Law (USA)/Dieter Quester (A)/Luca Riccitelli (I)	Picchio-BMW DP2	G & W Motorsports	451 DNF	5	DP
25	3	Darius Grala (PL)/Oswaldo Negri (USA)/Josh Rehm (USA)/Guy Cosmo (USA)	Fabcar-Toyota FDSC/03	Cegwa Sport	403 DNF	4	DP
26	19	Anthony Puleo (USA)/Kerry Hitt (USA)/Robert Dubler (CH)/Mark Kennedy (USA)	Chevrolet Corvette	ACP Motorsports	391 DNF	14	GTS
27	05	Craig Conway (GB)/John Metcalf (USA)/Rick Carelli (USA)/Dave Liniger (USA)	Chevrolet Corvette	Team Re/Max Racing	378 DNF	9	GTS
28	77	Alex Vassiliev (RUS)/Tetsuya Tanaka (J)/Walter Lechner, Jr. (A)/Nikolai Fomenko (RUS)	Porsche 996 GT3R	RWS Motorsport/ Yukos Motorsport	361 DNF	34	GTS
29	99	Jim Hamblin (USA)/Barry Brensinger (USA)/James Nelson (USA)/Mark Greenberg (USA)	Porsche 996 GT3RS	NETTS Racing	316 DNF	27	GT
30	40	Justin Bell (GB)/Kenny Wilden (CDN)/Derek Bell (GB)/Simon Gregg (USA)	Chevrolet Corvette	Derhaag Motorsports	260 DNF	7	GTS
31	33	Cort Wagner (USA)/Brent Martini (USA)/Sylvain Tremblay (CDN)/Selby Wellman (USA)	Ferrari 360 Modena	Ferrari of Washington	214 DNF	18	GT
32	73	Rob Wilson (NZ)/Mike Newton (GB)/David Gooding (GB)/Martyn Konig (GB)	Porsche 996 GT3R	Graham Nash Motorsport	211 DNF	36	GT
33	10	David Terrien (F)/Gian Luca de Lorenzi (I)/Didier Delalande (F)/Marco Saviozzi (F)	Porsche 996 GT3R	Mac Racing	206 DNF	19	GT
34	58	David Donohue (USA)/Mike Borkowski (USA)/Randy Pobst (USA)/Chris Bye (CDN)	Fabcar-Porsche FDSC/03	Brumos Racing	160 DNF	2	DP
35	67	Andrew Davis (USA)/Robert Julien (CDN)/Tom Nastasi (USA)/David Lacey (CDN)	Porsche 996 GT3RS	The Racer's Group	151 DNF	39	GT
36	98	Sascha Maassen (D)/Lucas Luhr (D)/Martin Snow (USA)/Larry Schumacher (USA)	Porsche 996 GT3RS	Schumacher Racing	135 DNF	15	GT
37	80	Shawn Bayliff (USA)/Steve Marshall (USA)/Robert Prilika (USA)/Andy Lally (USA)	Picchio-BMW D-USA	G & W Motorsports	121 DNF	45	SRPII
38	57	Alex Caffi (I)/Gabrio Rosa (I)/Andrea Chiesa (CH)/Fabio Rosa (I)	Porsche 996 GT3RS	Seikel Motorsport	101 DNF	25	GT
39	54	Didier Theys (B)/Forest Barber (USA)/Terry Borcheller (USA)/Christian Fittipaldi (BR)	Doran-Chevrolet JE4	Bell Motorsports	67 DNF	6	DP
40	22	Stephen Earle (USA)/* Philip Shearer (USA)/* Stephane Gregoire (F)/ * Ludovico Manfredi (USA)	Ferrari 360 Modena Challenge	JMB Racing USA	54 DNF	35	GT
41	48	Tommy Riggins (USA)/Dave Machavern (USA)/* Kevin Lepage (USA)/* Scott Lagasse (USA)	Ford Mustang	Heritage Motorsports	49 DNF	8	GTS
42	18	Ken Stiver (USA)/* Scott Deware (USA)/* Don Bell (USA) * Jeff Kline (USA)	Mosler MT900R	Boston Motorsports Group	14 DNF	43	GTS
43	6	Gunnar Jeannette (USA)/* Duncan Dayton (USA)/* Peter Kitchak (USA)/* Ron Zitza (USA)	Porsche 911 GT1	Gunnar Racing	9 DNF	28	GTS
44	51	Mauro Casadei (I)/* Gerold Ried (D)/* Christian Ried (D)/* Manfred Jurasz (A)	Porsche 911 GT2	Proton Competition	2 DNF	22	GTS
DNS	61	Peter van Merksteijn (NL)/Charles Brugman (NL)/Frans Munsterhuis, Jr. (NL)/Cougar Jacobsen (USA)	Porsche 996 GT3RS	Peter van Merksteijn (System Force Motorsport)	0	30	GT

Index of Winning Drivers

Complete Index of Daytona Drivers

Bachelart, Eric 95-96
Bacher, Dave 01
Bacon, Al 83-95
Baechle, Robert 71, 73
Baghetti, Giancarlo 68
Bagley, Tom 77, 79, 87-88
Bagnall, Andrew 99, 01
Bagration, Jorge de 72
Bailey, Bob 69-73
Bailey, Julian 91, 98
Bain, Duncan 86
Baird, Carson 69, 75, 79, 82-85
Baird, Craig 98
Baisden, Larry 02
Baker, Buck 65, 72
Baker, Buddy 76
Baker, Clive 69-72
Baker, Freddy 85, 89
Baker, Gary 79, 83-85, 87
Baker, Jim 69-70
Baker, Larry 72
Baker, Wayne 80-81, 83-85
Balas, Bertrand 96
Balbach, George 98
Baldi, Mauro 88-90, 95-96, 98-03
Baldwin, Jack 84-89, 92-93, 97-02
Baldwin, Louis 86
Baldwin, Tom 97
Baljet, Peter 86
Baljet, Pieter 89, 93
Ballot-Lena, Claude 73-80, 83-86, 88-90
Bandini, Lorenzo 67
Bandy, Jim 70
Banks, Tim 91, 93, 95-96, 98
Barbazza, Fabrizio 95
Barber, Bill 72-73
Barber, Forest 03
Barber, Jr., George 65
Barbosa, Joao 01-03
Barbour, Dick 77-80
Barff, Rob 03
Barilla, Paolo 86, 91
Barkelew, Bruce 95
Barker, Allan 70, 71
Barker, Bob 95
Barnard, George 64
Barnett, Bob 84
Barnett, Dave 75, 85
Barnett, Jim 77
Baron, Peter 99-03
Barrett, Stanton 96
Barrientos, Eduardo 80-83
Barros, Bill 70
Bartels, Wilhelm 76
Barth, Edgar 64
Barth, Jürgen 79, 81-82, 94, 96, 00
Bartlett, Kevin 85
Bartling, Rudi 69 –71, 73, 77, 79, 81
Barton, Buzz 68
Basseng, Marc 98
Batchin, Barry 69-70
Bauer, Andre 85
Bauer, John 82, 85, 87
Baumann, Kurt 99-00
Bayliff, Shawn 03
Beall, Louis 93-94
Bean, Bill 66, 68, 70-71, 73-76, 79, 82-83, 88-90
Beard, Frank 93
Beasley, Bob 71-73, 79, 82-85, 88, 94
Beatty, Bob 69, 71
Bebout, Randy 76
Beck, Willie 96
Beckers, Christine 77, 80
Bedard, Pat 78-84
Beddow, Brian 67
Behr, Stephen 71-73, 76, 78, 79
Beilcke, Bruno 77, 78, 80-81
Beilharz, Bill 02
Belcher, Gary 78, 82, 88
Belcher, Tony 87, 89
Bell, Derek 71, 73, 81-82, 84-91, 93-98, 00, 03
Bell, Don 83-84, 86-88, 93-
Bell, Justin 91, 96, 00, 03
Bell, Rich 99
Bell, Timothy J. 02
Belloc, Jean-Philippe 00
Beloff, Hardie 78
Belperche, John 69-72, 75-76, 82-83
Beltoise, Jean-Pierre 70, 73, 77
Bencker, Bill 62-68
Bender, Lon 92-94, 96
Bender, Mitch 84
Bennett, Craig 91
Bentley, John 66-67
Bentley, Ross 93-03
Beretta, Olivier 97, 99-00
Berg, Allen 89
Bergmeister, Jörg 02-03
Bergstrom, Bob 73, 76-84, 86
Bernal, Lucio 92, 94
Bernard, Eric 98
Berner, Hans 76
Bernhard, Timo 02, 03
Berry, Brian 95
Bertaggia, Enrico 95, 97-99
Bertoli, Franco 02
Bertuzzi, Costantino 02
Berville, Roland 00
Bes, Pierre 02
Besenzoni, Felice 78
"Beurlys" (see Jean Blaton)
Beverly, Tim 90
Bianchi, Lucien 64, 66-68
Bianchi, Mauro 63
Biava, Giovanni 97, 99
Bicciato, Renato 00-01
Bienerth, Bob 75
Bienvenue, Jacques 73-76, 78, 80
Bieri, Uli 83-84, 87-90, 92
Bies, Billy 95-96
Biggs, David 75
Biggs, John 93, 95
Bighouse, Roger 84
Bingham, Chris 97-03
Biscaldi, Giampiero 68-69
Bishop, Gary 71
Biskup, George 99
Bitterauf, Klaus 82-83
Bjork, Thed 01
Black, Newt 64
Blackaller, Tom 84
Blackburn, Les 81
Blackburn, Logan 78, 85-86
Blackman, Gary 97
Blancpain, Paul 73
Blaton, Jean 66-67
Bleynie, Gerard 80
Blieninger, Günther 98
Block, Chad 02
Bluestein, Ross 00-02
Boand, Bard 81, 83-86
Bobeda, Carlos 92
Bock, Larry 69, 70, 72, 73
Bodis, Kalman 94, 97
Boesel, Raul 88-91, 98
Boggs, David 72
Bogusz, Rodger 96
Bohren, Walt 78-85, 87
Boissoneau, Raymond 97
Bolander, John 66
Bolanos, Gustavo 76
Bolanos, Juan Carlos 75-76
Bolle-Jones, Huw 96
Bolton, Don 64-65
Bond, Rusty 75-79, 81-82, 84, 87-89
Bond, Stephen E. 76, 78-80
Bondurant, Bob 65-66, 78, 78, 81
Bonner, Brian 91
Bonnet, Neil 78, 85
Bonnier, Jo 62-64, 66, 69, 72
Boo, Dick 66
Boone, Robin 81, 92
Borcheller, Terry 98-99, 01-03
Borders, Robert 92, 94
Borella, Mauro 94-97
Borkowski, Mike 96, 98-00, 02-03
Borlase, Rick 80
Boss, Peter 00
Bostyan, Richard L. 77-78
Bouchard, Ron 85
Bouchier, Lew 97
Bouchut, Christophe 95, 98, 00, 02
Bouharde, Robert 65
Boulay, Sylvain 99
Bourassa, John 94-95, 97
Boutsen, Thierry 85-86, 96-98
Bouverat, Alan 64
Bovaro, Mike 00
Bove, Scott 99
Bowsher, Gary 76
Bowsher, Jim 76
Boxstrom, Jack 88-89
Boye, Bill 68, 77
Boykin, Russ 75, 77, 79
Brabham, David 92, 93, 98, 01-03
Brabham, Gary 92
Brabham, Geoff 89-94
Brabham, Jack 70
Brainard, Mark 84
Brambilla, Sergio 95
Brambring, Josef 78
Brancatelli, Gianfranco 87-88, 95, 97
Brassfield, Darin 85-87, 92, 94-97, 02
Brassfield, Jerry 87
Brassfield, Tony 82
Brayton, Scott 89, 92
Brayton, Todd 89, 91
Bremmer, Ross L. 67
Bren, Steve 89
Brenner, John 01
Brensinger, Barry 03
Bretzel, Eric 97-98
Brezinka, Rainer 69-70, 76
Brickell, Butch 97-99
Bright, John 83
Brimble, Ray 71
Briody, James 88, 90, 96, 02-03
Britnell, Andrew 03
Brockman, Michael 70, 76, 86-89, 91, 95, 00
Brooker, Brad 68
Broomall, Jack 88
Brosnaham, Henry 89-90, 92
Brostrom, Richard 69
Brown, Bob 67, 72
Brown, Bobby 88, 00
Brown, Dick 75
Brown, Jim 87-88
Brown, Robert Ryan 63, 66-67
Brown, Sam 71
Brown, Samuel 96, 99
Brown, Tom 78
Brown, Walter 70
Brown, Zak 97, 00
Bruckmann, Volker 78, 80-81
Brummer, Mike 83-85
Brun, Walter 81, 89, 00
Brundle, Martin 88, 90
Brunk, Scott 99
Brunn, Siegfried 81
Bryant, Grahame 95-98, 02
Bryner, Lilian 94-97, 99-01
Bscher, Thomas 94
Bucci, Stefano 96-98, 00
Buchler, Robert 78
Buchman, Bill 64, 67
Buckler, Kevin 96-03
Bucknum, Jeff 01
Bucknum, Ronnie 66-68, 70-72, 83
Buffum, John 71-72

C

D

Flux, Ian 88
Flynn, Larry 76
Follmer, Bill 78
Follmer, George 66, 73
Fomenko, Nikolai 03
"Fomfor" (see Francisco Miguel)
Fonseca, Kikos 83-84, 86
Forbes, John 91
Forbes-Robinson, Elliott 75, 77, 80, 83-90, 93, 96-02
Fordyce, Robert 72
Forester, Piers Weld 70
Forgeois, Georges 01-02
Forlong, Duncan 66
Forrest, Herb 79
Forte, John W. 66
Fossett, Steve 93-94, 96
Foster, Joe 01
Fothergill, Marcus 00
Fouche, George 94
Fowells, Jim 82-84, 86-89
Foyil, Dorian 00
Foyt, A. J. 62, 67, 83-88
Fraim, John 66
France, Jamie C. 03
Franchi, Leo 86
Franchitti, Marino 02
Francioni, Filippo 03
Francis, Glenn 76
Francois, Curtis 02
Frank, Tom 77-78, 88
Frank, Werner 80, 82-83
Fraser, Tom 72
Frates, William 75-76
Frazier, Doug 95
Freberg, Mike 81
Freed, Alan 89
Freeman, Chet 66-67
Freeman, Jarett 95-97
Freon, Franck 96-01
Frey, George 65
Frey, Jean-Pierre 89
Frey, Peter 79
Freyre, John 75, 77
Friedman, Cory 01, 03
Friedman, Dave 98-99, 02
Frigerio, Massimo 00
Frink, Lloyd 83
Frisselle, Brad 77-78, 80
Fronti, Carlos 96
Fry, Harry 66
Fryer, Robert 77
Fuchs, Andreas 93-94
Fukuda, Masashi 76
Fuller, Dave 86-87, 93
Fuller, Don 95
Fuller, Hugh D. 92-94
Fuller, Lewis 85
Fuller, Paul 00
Fulp, John 62, 66-67
Funk, Chris 94, 97
Funke, Michael 98
Fyhrie, Buzz 78

G

Gabbiani, Beppe 81
Gabel, Scooter 01
Gac Soto, Juan 95-96
Gaffney, Tom 86-87
Gafford, Bert 72
Gage, Raymond 73, 77
Gagliardi, Giancarlo 75
Gagliardo, Mike 91
Galbo, Larry 96
Galdamez, Eduardo 82-83, 85
Gallade, Ulrich 98-01
Galli, Giovanni 72
Gammon, Jim 69, 71, 73
Gamroth, Jeff 97
Ganassi, Chip 86
Gang, Adrian 77, 88
Ganger, Dick 67
Ganley, Howden 73
Gano, Charles 75-76
Ganz, Whitney 83-88
Garant, Sylvain 68-69
Garbagnati, Andrea 96-00, 03
Garcia, Fernando 84-85
Garcia, George 75-76
Garcia, Javier 71-72, 75-76
Garcia, Manuel 72, 76
Garcia, Raul 83, 85
Garcia, Tony 75, 78-84
Garcia-Veiga, Nestor 71
Gardner, Bill 84
Gardner, Frank 67
Garretson, Bob 80-83
von Gartzen, Jürgen 96, 00
Garza, Carlos 71
Gassaway, Michael 83
Gaston, Norton 87
Gatoff, Michael 75
Gaughran, Wade 99-03
Gauthier, Dick 78, 81, 83
Gavin, Oliver 02
Gaylord, Dave 00-03
Gaylord, Scott 95
Gebhardt, Alf 75, 78-81
Geck, Richard 00
Geisel, Fred 75
Gelles, William 84-85
Gendebien, Olivier 62
Generotti, E. J. 88
Gennone, Chris 85-88
Gentile, Steve 86
Gentilozzi, Paul 85-88, 92, 94-95, 01-02
Gerber, Dan 66
Geremia, Dave 00
Gethin, Peter 67
Ghinzani, Piercarlo 81
Giangrande, Jeff 01
Giarotti, Silvino 97
Gibson, Mark 90
Gidley, Memo 00
Giesel, Robert 80
Gifford, Marty 68-69
Gigliotti, Lou 91, 93
Gilbicella, Facundo 95-96, 98
Gilgan, Paul 83-84
Gillan, Jere 77
Gillebard, Frans 68-69
Gilliland, Dan 80-81
Gimbel, Bernard 70
Gimondo, Vince 69-75, 77, 87
Gindorf, Marc 99
Ginther, Richie 65-67
Giribaldi, Gualtiero 94, 96
Giunti, Ignazio 70
Gläsel, Christian 99
Gleason, Chris 81, 97-01
Glenn, Pete 67
Glenn, Walter 66
Glick, Allen 85
Gloy, Tom 73, 87-88
Goad, Doug 00-03
Goebbels, Willy 76
Goebel, Peter 97
Goellnicht, Brian 72, 75-78, 84
Golden, Steve 95
Goldin, Keith 98-01
Goldin, Steve 96, 98-01
Goldleaf, Ron 76
Goldrich, Norman 00, 02
Goldsborough, Chuck 94-95, 99
Goldsmith, Paul 62-63
Gonzalez, Armando 77-78, 81, 86, 88-89
Gonzalez, Carlos 81
Gonzalez, Victor 84
Gonzalez, W. K. 77
Goodell, David 80-81
Gooding, David 94, 01-03
Gooding, Jon 91-93, 96, 98-99
Goodman, Ken 67
Goodwin, Brian 89
Goodyear, Scott 87-88, 92-93, 96-97, 03
Goral, Paul 83, 85
Gordillo, Luis 79-80
Gordon, Robby 90-93, 02
Gorriaran, Steve 03
Gosselin, Gustave 71
Gottlob, Cliff 70, 76
Goueslard, Patrice 97-98, 00, 02
Grable, Ron 82-84, 86
Graham, Barry 99
Graham, John 82-83, 94, 98, 00
Graham, Michael 93
Grala, Darius 03
Gralia, Hugo 84-85, 87
Grandet, Cyril 75
Grant, Allen 65
Grant, Francis C. 69-70
Grant, Jerry 63-66, 68
Grantham, Chuck 82, 85
Grassi, Ruggero 94
Gratton, Jack 97
Graves, John 75-77
Gray, Henley 76
Gray, Jeff 95
Gray, Richard 97
Gray, Robert M. 76
Greb, Mark 78-79
Green, Gerry 97-00, 02
Green, Jeff 88
Green, John 97
Green, Jonathan 88
Greenberg, Mark 96, 98, 03
Greendyke, Jim 70
Greenfield, Michael 90-91
Greenfield, Peter 91
Greensall, Nigel 97
Greenwood, Burt 77
Greenwood, John 70-76
Greer, Dick 87-95, 99, 01-02
Greger, Sepp 73, 76
Gregg, Bob 81-82, 84
Gregg, Deborah 83-84, 86-88
Gregg, Peter 64-69, 71-80
Gregg, Simon 95-99, 01-03
Gregory, Masten 66-69, 71
Griffin, Jack 84-85
Grimaldi, Joe 68
Grinbold, Sepp 78-79
Griswold, Stephen 79
Grob, Ian 80
Groff, Robbie 97
Grohs, Harald 81, 85-86, 90, 94-98
de Groodt, Stephane 02
Grooms, John 87 88 89 90 91 92 93
Grossman, Bob 64-71, 73
Grostic, Ken 87
Grouillard, Olivier 96
Grubbs, Gary 95
Grunnah, Tommy 85, 91
Grunnet, Douglas 81
Grupp, Rich 98, 01-02
Gschwender, Ernst 96-97
Guaitamacchi, Paolo 88-90
Guest, Charles 80, 84-85
Guichet, Jean 64, 67
Guitteny, Lucien 78
Guldstrand, Dick 66, 68-69
Gunn, John 68-69
Gurney, Dan 62-67, 70
Gustavsson, Mikael 94
Guthrie, Janet 66-67
Gutierrez, Francesco 01
Gwynne, Jr., Don 70, 72
Gysler, Matt 83-84

H

Habegger, Walter 67
Hackman, Gene 83
Haezebrouck, Philippe 02
Hagan, Billy 68-69, 76-80, 82-85, 88
Hagestad, Bob 76-78, 84
Hailwood, Mike 68-69, 73
Hajducky, Andy 00-01
Halbing, John 99
Halin, Ray 95
Hall, Chris 01

Johnson, Rameau 81
Johnson, Robert 62-68, 70
Johnson, Robert R. 70, 72-73
Johnson, Ron Anton 02
Johnson, Steven 88-90
Johnson, Tommy 88-92, 95
Johnstone, Parker 89, 91-93
Jolly, Jerry 76, 82, 84
Jones, Bobby 97-99
Jones, Bruce 94
Jones, Catesby 02
Jones, Davy 88-93
Jones, Gene 66
Jones, Harry 75
Jones, Jeff W. 97
Jones, John 85, 87-88, 93
Jones, K. P. 77
Jones, Leonard 75-76, 81
Jones, Max 87-91
Jones, Oliver 82
Jones, P. J. 88, 91-93, 96
Jones, Parnelli 88
Jones, Ryan 99
Jones, Jr., Herb 75-77
Jonsson, Niclas 01
Joosen, Eddy 81
Jordan, Dave 68-69
Jordan, Mike 02
Jourdain, Bernard 88-90
Jourdain, Michel 75, 88
Jowett, Jr., Wilton T. 69
Joy, Mike 93
Juckette, Tom 82, 87-88, 92-97
Julian, Elton 95
Julien, Robert 01-03
Juncadella, Jose 71
Junco, Rodolfo 72
Jurasz, Manfred 96-97, 99-01

K

Kahn, Robert 89, 92, 95
Kalagian, John 84-85
Kamazuka, Makoto 76
Kanaan, Tony 98
Karl, Jerry 76
Kasuya, Shunji 94
Katayama, Ukyo 98
Katayama, Yoshimi 78-79, 82, 85, 89
Katthoefer, Frank 94
Katz, Howard 87-89, 92, 98-01
Kauffman, Jim 68
Kaufmann, Wolfgang 96, 99-01
Kearney, Don 66-67, 70
Keck, Harold 65-66
Keck, Karl 83-87
Keen, Justin 03
Keirn, Philip 80-81
Kelder, Dana 63-68
Kelleners, Ralf 97-98, 00-03
Keller, Paul 73
Kellermeyer, Danny 93
Kelly, John 68-69, 80
Kelly, T. J. 67
Kemp, Charlie 69-76, 79
Kendall, Bart 87-89
Kendall, Chuck 81, 85
Kendall, Jerry 84
Kendall, Tommy 86, 87, 89, 93, 95
Kennedy, Jerry 84
Kennedy, Mark 85-88, 90-91, 93-96, 99, 03
Kent, Mark 92
Kenton, James A. 99
Kern, Wilhelm 00
Kerrison, Chris 64
Kersten, Jodexnis 94
Kessel, Loris 90
Kessler, Ray 73
Kester, Tony 94, 96, 99-02
Keyes, Robert 62
Keyser, Michael 71-75, 77
Kicak, David 88, 93-95, 99
Kimbrough, Oma 86-89, 91-95
King, Dennis 97
King, James 87
King, Perry 88
Kinnunen, Leo 70
Kirby, Robert 75-81, 93
Kirill, Peter 71-73, 80, 82-83
Kirk, Tammy Jo 94
Kirkland, Bob 93
Kitch, Don 95-00, 02-03
Kitchak, Peter 97-00
Kjoller, Jay 81, 89, 91-92, 94
Kjoller, Jean 81-82
Klass, Günther 66
Klausler, Tom 81-82
Kleinpeter, Hugh 66, 68-70, 72-73, 76
Kleinschmidt, Charles 78
Klempel, Robert 73
Kline, Jeff 79, 81-87, 89-92
Knab, Jack 62
Knab, Peter 76-77, 82
Knapfield, Paul 02
Kneebone, Tom 63
Kneifel, Chris 87, 99-01
Knight, Steven 02
Knollenberg, Scott 97
Knook, Rob 03
Knoop, Rick 78-86
Knott, Ken 85, 90, 92
Knowles, Don 86 -87, 90-95
Knupp, Ike 73
Ko, Kaming 90-92
Koch, Dale 77-78, 81-82, 85
Koch, William 79
Koechlin, Jorge 96
König, Kurt 81
Kohler, John 97, 99
Kolb, Charlie 62-65, 67
van der Kolk, Peter 99, 01-03
Koll, William 79-82, 88
Kondracki, Richard G. 68
Kong, Ray 97
Konig, Mark 66, 68
Konig, Martyn 96, 98-99, 02-03
Konrad, Franz 78, 94-01, 03
Korten, Michael 80
Koveleski, Oscar 66
Kraft, Chris 89-91
Krages, Louis 78, 91-93
Krause, Billy 63
Krause, Conrad M. 64
Kravig, Don 80, 85
Krebs, Albrecht 77
Krebs, Richard 70
Kreider, Dale 76, 78, 80, 82-84, 86, 89-90, 92, 94
Kremer, Erwin 71, 73
Krolowitz, Jon 02
Krosnoff, Jeff 92
Krueger, Charles 67
Krueger, Dennis 84, 86-87
Krueger, Phil 91-92
Kryder, Reed 89-96, 98-99
Kubik, Phillip 96
Kuehne, Bert 73
Kuhel, Ed 81-82
Kuhn, Rolf 94
Kump, Rick 78-79
Kumpen, Anthony 01
Kumpen, Paul 96, 98
Kurkjian, Mike 63, 64
Kurtz, Chuck 88-89, 91-93
Kurz, Jim 87
Kuster, Guy 93-96
Kuttner, Oliver 93-95, 98
Kwech, Horst 68

L

La Cava, Greg 80
La Rosa, Franco 96 98
Labonte, Terry 81-87
Lacey, David 03
Lacroix, David 89
Lader, Ernie 94
Ladoniczki, Bill 98-99
Ladoniczki, Steve 98-99
Lässig, Jürgen 76, 95
Lafosse, Jean-Louis 73
Lagasse, Scott 87-88, 91
Lagorce, Franck 00
Laine, Hans 70
Lally, Andy 01, 03
Lamas, Lorenzo 88-89
Lambert, Bruno 98-02
Lammers, Jan 86, 88-90, 95, 99-00, 02
Land, Wolfgang 95
Landa, Juan 93
Lane, David 62, 65-66
Lane, Spencer 97
Lanfranchi, Tony 68
Lang, Dick 70-71
Lang, Eric 85
Lang, Fred 77-78
Langfermann, Heinrich 01
Langford, Graeme 02
Langhorne, William 98
Langlois von Ophem, Gerard 66
Lanier, Lowell 70-71
Lanier, Randy 82-85
Lapcevich, Jeffrey 93, 97
Laporte, Richard 90
Lapp, Bob 79
Lappalainen, Robert 90
Lara-Resende, Andre 96, 98
Larrauri, Oscar 86-89, 92
Larrousse, Gerard 72
Lassally, Toto 98-02
Latta, Arthur M. 65
Lauer, Michael 00, 02
Lavaggi, Giovanni 95
Lavari, Eduardo 96
Law, Darren 99-03
Lawhorn, Keith 87
Lawrence, Claude 94
Lawrence, Hal 71
Laws, Mike 84, 87
Lay, Denis 97-98
Layer, Dirk 94, 96-97
Lazier, Bob 87 -89
Lazier, Buddy 89, 93, 01
Lazzaro, Anthony 93-99, 02-03
Leal, Alfonso 76
Learch, Peter 66
Leary, Frank 79
Leavy, Jon 01
Lecerf, Thierry 90, 96
Lechner, Jr., Walter 03
Leclere, Michel 79
Leconte, Jack 96
Lee, Bob 77-79, 81, 85
Lees, Geoff 96-97
Leeward, Jim 86
Leibler, Scott 89
Leitzinger, Bob 82, 86, 88-93
Leitzinger, Butch 88-94, 96-02
Lenain, Phillipe 98-99
van Lennep, Gijs 67, 70-71
Lenz, Randy 00
Leon, Al 83-86
Leon, Art 84-85
Leris, Pierre 77
Leslie, Ed 65, 68-69
Lesnett, Bob 89, 91-92
Less, Larry 93
de Lesseps, Ferdinand 90, 94, 96, 00
Lester, Bill 98-01
Leven, Bruce 80-86, 89
Levenson, Al 76-79
Levetto, Guido C. 65, 67, 73, 75, 77-78, 80
Levetto, Mario 73
Lewis, Dan 95
Lewis, Jack 82, 84-85, 88, 92-96, 98-99, 02
Lewis, John D. 65
Lewis, Jon 92
Lewis, Paul 84-88, 93-94
Lewis, Robert E. 70
Lewis, Shane 98-02

Libert, Jean-Paul 80-81, 83, 89, 96
Lieb, Marc 03
Lienhard, Fredy 99-02
Ligonnet, Michel 97, 99-00
Lilly, Tony 70-71
Lindenbaum, Dieter 95
Lindley, Les 85, 89, 94
Linge, Herbert 64, 66
Lingner, Terry 95, 97, 02
Liniger, Dave 02-03
Lins, Rudi 69, 71
Lintott, Ray 97-98, 00
Lisa, Steve 00, 02
Lisberg, George 70
Lister, Geoff 01
Lloyd, John 85, 02
Lloyd, Richard 83
Lluch, Edison 96-98
Lobenberg, Bob 84
Locke, James N. 69, 71-73
Lockie, Calum 00-02
Loftis, James 98
Lohr, Ellen 97
Lollobrigida, Guido 62
Lombardi, Lella 77
Londono, Ricardo 80-81
Long, Dennis 76
Long, H. J. 84
Long, Russell 82
Longhi, Nick 97, 01-02
Longin, Bert 98
Loomis, Greg 70
Lopez, Aurelio 89
Lopez, Francisco 79-80
Lopez, Osvaldo 93
Lopez Rocha, Tomas 89-90, 92
Lorenz, Jürgen 01
de Lorenzi, Gian Luca 99, 03
Loring, David 84, 88, 90-93, 95, 97
Los, Costas 86-89, 92-93
Lott, Pat 84
Loven, Niklas 01
Lowman, Jonathan 01
Lowther, Ed 66, 68-70, 77
Loyning, Arnstein 76
Luck, Karl-Christian 95
Ludemann, Linda 87-90
Ludwig, Al 95-96
Ludwig, Klaus 86-89
Luebbe, Robert 71-72
Luhr, Lucas 00-03
Lund, Tiny 73
Lupberger, Werner 02
Lutz, Doug 81, 83
Luyendyk, Arie 86, 88-89, 91-92 97-99
Lyford, Chuck 97
Lynn, Steven 00
Lyon, Charles 67

M

Maassen, Sascha 00-03
Mabrito, Bruce 75-76
MacAllister, Chris 00
MacDonald, Randy 89
MacGrotty, Ross 66
MacInnes, Bruce 88, 93
MacLeod, Peter 02-03
MacQuillan, Gerard 97
Macaluso, John 91-93, 01-02
Macey, Paul 01
Machavern, Dave 03
Macon, Richard 66
Madero, Jose 76
Madren, Ken 83-86
Maenpaa, Kari 02
Maffucci, John 78-79, 81-89, 96
Magana, Marlo 90
Maglioli, Claudio 68-69
Maglioli, Umberto 67, 69
Magner, Len 70
Maher, Rich 85
Mahler, John 70-71
Mahre, Phil 88, 92
Mairesse, Willy 67
Maksym, Ed 76
Malagamuwa, Dilantha 01-02
Maldonado, Guillermo 83
Malkun, Luis F. 94
Mall, Rodney 02
Mallet, Dino 78
Mallock, Ray 84
Malnik, Shareef 00
Manautou, Oscar 89-90
Mancini, Fabio 01
Mancuso, Rick 77, 85, 99
Mandeville, Roger 78-91, 95-97
Manfredi, Ludovico 99, 00, 02
Manfredini, Corrado 70
Mangifesta, Roberto 99
Mann, Lamar 77
Manner, Mike 69
Mannino, Tony 63
Manthey, Olaf 94, 99
Marchini, Alfio 93
Marconi, John 93
Marcus, Joe 70
Margueron, Charles 97
Marina, Jose 69, 77 -79, 82
Marinelli, J. Peter 67
Marko, Helmut 71-72
Marks, Justin 01
Marlin, Sterling 83-84
Marsh, Don 84-86, 88
Marsh, Kelly 84-91
Marshall, Danny 93, 95-96, 98-01
Marshall, Steve 95-96, 98-03
Marsula, Wayne 69
Marte, Chris 86
Martin, Heinz 76
Martin, John 83
Martin, Mark 88-89, 91-93, 95
Martin, Philippe 81
Martin, Tony 84-85
Martin, William J. 65-68
Martinez, Fidel 75
Martini, Brent 03
Martini, Mauro 92
Martland, Digby 68
Marvin, Dan 89, 92, 95, 97
Marx, Tom Alan 82, 82
Mason, Kim 80, 84
Mass, Jochen 77, 81, 85-87
Masselli, Pier Angelo 98-00
Mastandrea, Norberto 69-71
Mastropietro, Renato 94-97, 99-00
Mathai, Oliver 93-94
Mathai, Wolfgang 93-94
Mathewson, Kurt 97
Mathey, Ted 76
Mathis, Charles 63-65
Matienzo, Eugenio 85
Matos, Manuel 02-03
Matsuda, Hideshi 92
Matsushita, Hiro 88
Matthews, Ed 70-71
Matthews, Jim 95-00, 02
Matthewson, Kurt 98, 00
Mattschull, Alexander 95
Mattschull, Arnold 95
Matzen, Warren 70-71
Maugeri, Richard 97-01
Maury-Laribiere, Jean-Luc 00
Maxwell, Scott 98, 00-01, 03
Maxwell, Jr., Ike A. 64-68
May, Jack 78
May, Paul B. 76
May, Spurgeon 66
Maylaender, Bernd 94-95
Mazzacane, Hugo 93
Mazzacane, Paul 92-93
Mazzuoccola, Robert 99-01
McAdam, Tim 88-97
McCaig, John 99
McCaig, Maurice 72
McCaig, Roger 72
McCall, Buz 84, 86-90
McCall, Robin 85
McCarthy, Jim 96
McCarthy, Perry 98
McClain, David H. 65, 69, 75, 79
McCloud, Peter 85
McClure, Bob 73
McClure, Jack 67
McCluskey, Roger 65
McComb, Jeff 95
McComb, John 67, 69, 71, 73, 80, 82, 85, 88
McConnell, Bob 86-87
McCormick, James 99-00
McCue, Leonard 95
McDaniel, Jim 68-69
McDaniel, Rex 88
McDill, Bill 71, 73, 76, 78-79, 82-83 87-97
McDill, Richard 88-97, 99-00
McDonald, Dave 63-64
McDonald, Lee 72
McDonough, Hugh 83
McElheny, Robert 90, 92-94
McFarlin, Rob 79, 81-82, 84
McGehee, Robby 96
McGlynn, Tom 98, 00, 02
McGriff, Doug 76
McGriff, Hershel 76
McIntyre, Kyle 99
McIntyre, Ray 82, 85
McKay, Ron 88-91
McKellar, Ian 02
McKemie, William 66
McKitterick, Skeeter 80-82, 85, 88
McLaren, Bruce 66-67
McLaurin, Lambert 95
McNaughton, John 99
McNeely, Steve 98
McNeil, Andy 00-01
McNish, Allan 98-01
McTureous, Dave 96-97
McVeigh, John 68-69
Mead, Chip 77, 82-83, 85-89
Meaney, Ralph 70-71
Mears, Rick 79, 81
Mears, Roger 82
Mears, Jr., Paul 03
Mederer, Jim 79
Mees, Mike 87-95
Mehalic, Mark 95-96
Meier, Arnd 97
Meister, Howard 78-81, 84
Meixner, Ronny 93
Meldeau, Mike 76, 78, 82
Melgrati, Ruggero 86, 89, 92, 94
Mena, Alfredo 84
Menard, Paul 03
Mendez, Charles 76-81, 95
Mendez, Luis 78, 80-81, 86
Mendoza, Jorge 90
Menzel, Christian 01
Merello, Fausto 68-69
Merendino, Michele 03
Merino, Victor 64
Merl, Volkert 78-81
Merril, Gregory 00
van der Merwe, Alan 02
van der Merwe, Sarel 84-85, 87-90
Merzario, Arturo 70-73, 76
Merzon, Adam 01
Mesnick, Gary 78
Messley, Erik 00-01
Metcalf, John 02-03
Meyer, Mike 80, 86-89
Michaelian, Jim 98, 01-03
Michelet, Jean-Pierre 94-95
Michelotti, Bruno 96-97
Migault, Francois 73, 78, 92
Mignot, Marcel 75
Migoya, Carlos 86
Miguel, Francisco 84
Miles, Ken 65-66
Millard, Michael 97
Millen, Rod 87, 89

Millen, Steve 85-88, 91-95
Miller, Chris 99-01
Miller, Harold 76
Miller, Jack 84
Miller, Jim 83, 85, 88
Miller, Kenper 77-88, 95
Miller, Leigh 93-95
Miller, Marty 97
Miller, Paul 77-83, 85, 88
Miller, Sam 79, 81
Miller, Steve 00- 01
Miller, Tom 94, 97
Millman, Richard 02
Mills, Doug 87-88, 99-01
Mims, Donna Mae 66-67, 70
Mingay, Rob 93-94
Minkhorst, Keith 96
Minneker, Jim 93-95
Minter, Milt 73-78, 80-83
Mirro, John 93-00, 02
Mitchell, Bob 70-73, 76
Mitchell, Dwight 81
Mitchum, Chris 99
Mitsuyama, Shogo 01
Mitter, Gerhard 66-69
Mnich, Matt 88
Moennick, Peter 80
Moerwald, Clarence 69
Moffat, Allan 68, 80, 82, 85
Moise, Milton 75, 79
Molins, Enrique 80-86
Mollin, Arthur 67-70, 72, 75-76
Molnar, Jerry 84
Monk, Charles 88, 90-92
Monneret, Pierre 65
Montalvo, Juan 75, 79
Montani, Fabio 97, 99
Montermini, Andrea 01-02
Montgomery, Case 96-97
Montgomery, Mark 87-88, 90, 92, 93, 95-01
Montoya, Diego 83-84, 86
Mooney, Joe 82
Mooney, Patrick 91
Moore, Ben 66
Moore, Danny L. 71
Moore, Jack 64
Moore, John 68
Moore, Rick 89
Moran, Carlos 93
Moran, Rocky 88, 90-93
Morehead, Bruce 68
Morejon, Miguel 81, 83-84, 86, 91-92
Moressi, Osvaldo 93
Moretti, Gianpiero 70, 79-81, 85, 87-90, 92-93, 95-98
Morgan, Charles 83, 85-97, 02-03
Morgan, Dave 62, 68
Morgan, Jerry H. 64
Morgan, Rob 95-97, 02-03
Morgenrood, Ben 95
Morici, Todd 87
Morini, Massimo 99-00
Morrison, John 89-90
Morrison, Tommy 84, 86-87, 90-91
Morton, John 78-88, .90-95, 97-98, 01
Moser, Tim 99
Moses, Sam 83
Mosiman, Jere 63
Moss, Fred 01
Moss, Stirling 62
Motschenbacher, Lothar 69
Mowlem, John 99-00, 02-03
Mroz, Dave 75
Mroz, Richard 75
Mucha, Jacek 99
Müller, Dirk 98-00
Müller, Fritz 94-95
Mueller, Jim 86
Müller, Jörg 98
Mueller, Lee 76, 78, 80-84, 86
Mullen, Jim 81-86
Mummery, Ray 68-69, 73, 77-80, 82-84, 86, 88, 95
Mundas, Hellmut 88
Muniz, Daniel 72-73
Murphy, Greg 96
Murphy, Tom 99
Murray, Ken 83-84
Murry, David 94-03
Muther, Rick 65
Mutiz, Camilo 75
Muzzin, Vince 75
Myers, Bruce 68

N

Nacthwey, Paul 82
Nagel, Bob 70, 75-76, 88
Nagel, Bob M. 02
Nakagawa, Takamasa 94
Naon, Albert 75-82, 84
Naon, Jr., Albert 85-86, 89
de Narvaez, Mauricio 76-82, 84-85
de Narvaez, Pedro 79, 81
Nastasi, Tom 03
Nearburg, Charles 97, 02
Nearn, Robert 94-00, 02
Needell, Tiff 91, 95-98
Neerpasch, Jochen 68
Negre, Ed 76
Negri, Oswaldo 03
Nehl, Tom 71-75, 79-80, 82-85, 87
Neland, Dick 78, 80-83
Nelson, Craig T. 95-97
Nelson, Edward 67-68
Nelson, James 96, 98-99, 03
Nelson, Ron 87-89, 93, 96
Nelson, Wayne 76
Nesbitt, Bruce 80
Netterstrom, Jim 68-69, 71
Netzeband, Bernd 94-96
Neugarten, Michel 96, 99-03
Neuhaus, Mark 96, 02
Neuman, Scott 98-99, 01
Neutag, Berndt 97
Neve, Patrick 80
Neville, Chris 97-98
Newman, Paul 77, 79, 95, 00
Newsome, Roy 83-84, 86-87
Newsum, Jack 84-85, 88
Newton, Mike 02-03
Nicholas, George 69, 71
Nicholson, Nick 84-85
Nicol, Geoff 88, 91
Nielsen, John 88-90, 93
Nierop, Kees 79-80, 85
Nightingale, Jeremy 82
Nikel, Bob 82
Nisbett, Richard 95
Noah, Kendall 71
Nolan, Mike 91
Norburn, Russ 72-73
Norick, Lance 03
Norinder, Ulf 64, 69
Northam, Nort 79-84, 86-89, 91, 94-96, 98
Norton, Buddy 95
Norwood, John 65, 67
Noseda, Ralph 64, 66, 71-73, 77, 85
Notz, Oscar 79
Novatne, Jim 90
Novoa, Ruben 72
Nowicki, Jeff 94, 99-00
Nunez, Pepe 71

O

O'Born, Francois 02
O'Brien, Leigh 94
O'Brien, Tim 93
O'Connell, Johnny 92-98, 01
O'Kennedy, Tim J. 97
O'Neill, Brent 83-85, 88
O'Steen, John 73-77, 82-84, 86-87, 89, 91, 93, 96-00
Oag, Alistair 90-91
Oakley, Richard 87-88
Oberholtzer, Mike 01
Oberto, Larry 01-03
Oest, Dieter 69-70, 73-76, 87
Oestreich, Markus 96-97
Olch, Jon 91
Olczyk, Philippe 94-95
Oleyar, Michael 72, 76
Oliver, Jackie 69, 71
Ollila, Terry 97
Olofsson, Anders 00
Olson, Drake 83-86, 88-90
Olson, John 66
Oneglia, Bob 00
Ongais, Danny 71, 77-82
Opert, Fred 66-69
Oppenheimer, James 98
Orcutt, Robert 01-02
Orlandi, Roberto 03
Orlandini, Raul 92-94, 96
Ormes, Robin 69
Orr, John 71
Ortega, Guillermo 68
Ortelli, Stephane 96, 99, 02
Orti, Paco 01
Osman, Andrew 93-94
Overbagh, Hoyt 79, 82, 83, 85-93, 95
van Overbeek, Johannes 99, 01, 03
Overby, Robert 79, 81, 83-84, 87
Owen, Buell 67
Oyhanart, Jorge 93
Oyler, Ron 78

P

Pabst, Augie 63-64, 87
Pace, Jim 90-92, 94-98, 03
Pace, Will 96-97
Padilla, Alex 92, 98
Pagotto, Luigiano 93-94, 96-97
Painter, Kent 85, 87-90, 93-96, 98
Pairetti, Carlos A. 70
Paligraf, Tom 95
Pallanca-Pastor, Gildo 96
Pallavicini, Angelo 79, 81, 83-84, 87-88
Palmberger, Ernst 00
Palmer, David 83
Palmer, Jonathan 83
Palmer, Martin 76
Panaccione, Dave 76-79, 81-83, 86
Panaggio, Tom 91
Panch, Marvin 62
Panch, Ritchie 73
Paolucci, Horacio 98
Papadopoulos, Tom 02
Papis, Massimiliano 96, 98-03
Papke, Peter 75
Paquette, Steve 81
Paredes, Carlos 94
Pareja-Mayo, Jesus 94, 96
Parish, Don 75-76
Parisi, Biagio 95
Parker, Bret A. 99
Parker, Dave 01
Parker, Larry 77, 99
Parkerson, E. M. 69
Parkes, Mike 67, 70
Parshauer, Ken 92
Parsons, Benny 76
Parsons, Chuck 69-71
Parsons, Gene 65
Parsons, George 64, 66
Pasmas, Art 82
Pastorini, Dan 92
Pate, Phillip 83, 90
Patrese, Riccardo 81
Patrick, Scooter 68-69
Patterson, James 70
Pattinson, Jeffrey 94-97
Paul, Jr., John 81-83, 85-86, 90-91, 93-99

Q

R

Spencer, Dennis 98-02
Spencer, G. C. 64
Spinella, Alejandro 95
Spinelli, Marco 96
Spirgel, Robert 72
Spoerl, Louis 79
Spoerry, Dieter 67-68
Spreng, Gustl 94-95
Springer, Nicolaus 00
Sprinkle, Todd 98
Sprowls, Billy 75-76
Spruell, Paul 75
St. Jacques, Bruno 01
St. James, Lyn 80, 83, 85, 87-88, 90, 98
St. John, Harold 64
Stafford, R. Sheldon 72
Stalder, Fred 77
Standridge, Dave 03
Stanford, Paul 69-70
Stanton, Craig 00-03
Stanton, Richard 03
Starita, Dick 79
Starkey, John 94
Starr, Malcolm 68
Startup, Tim 76
Steel, Jack 75-76
Steinemann, Rico 67-68
Steinmetz, John 99-00
Stephens, Mike 83
Steranka, Richard 03
Stevens, Jef 62-64
Stevens, Jim 90-93
Stevens, Richard 84, 86
Stevens, Rob 88
Stevenson, Fred 70
Stevenson, Kenneth 64
Stewart, Gary 93, 99
Stewart, Lance 89-90, 97, 99-01
Stewart, Paul 89
Stewart, Tony 02
Stiff, Fred 80-82
Stitt, William 97-99
Stiver, Ken 00, 03
Stoddard, Robert 65, 68
Stommelen, Rolf 67-69, 72, 78-82
Stone, Craig 94
Stone, George 72-73, 81-82
Stone, Richard 86-87
Storey, William 62-63
Storfer, Ira 95
Stott, Phil 68
Stoutenburg, Raymond 66-67
Strait, Bob 88
Strange, Bob 98
Strasser, Andy 88, 95-96
Straub, Al 71-72
Streeter, Don 64
Stuck, Jr., Hans-Joachim 75, 81, 85-90, 92, 94-97, 99, 01
Stumes, Warren 70-71
Sugden, Tim 00
Sullivan, Danny 79, 82, 86-88, 93-94, 97-99
Sullivan, Glen 68
Sumpter, Mark 02
Surer, Marc 81
Surtees, John 65
Sutcliffe, George 90
Sutcliffe, Peter 66
Sutherland, Rick 94, 96, 98, 00-03
Suzuki, Takaji 01
Suzuki, Toshio 92, 00-01
Swan, Herb 62
Swan, Tony 83-85
Swanander, Gary 92
Swanson, Arthur W. 66
Swanson, Jack 77, 78, 81-83, 89
Swett, Andy 90
Swifts, Vance 87
Swindell, Jeff 93
Swope, Keith 76, 82

T

Tabec, Jaeid 75
Taels, Alfons 97
Takahashi, Kiichi 99-01
Takahashi, Tsuyoshi 00-01
Talbert, Matthew 02
Taleb, Henry 93-99
Tamburini, Luciano 99-00
Tanaka, Tetsuya 03
Tapy, Yvon 87
Tatum, Gordon 70
Taylor, Del Russo 67-68, 70, 83-88, 90
Taylor, Wayne 88, 92, 94-00
Taylor-Matthews, Anita 67
Tchkotoua, Zourab 64
Teasdale, Kat 94
Tennyson, David 90-92
Terada, Yojiro 78-79, 82, 85, 97-99
Terrien, David 02-03
Theodoracopulos, Harry 66-67, 75
Thetford, Dick 67
Theys, Didier 94-03
Thiel, Kurt 96, 00-02
Thiem, Doug 62
Thiers, Kurt 96-97
Thomas, Frank 78
Thomas, Guy 79
Thomas, John G. 98-00
Thomas, Ralph 94-98
Thomas, Jr., John H. 75, 77-78
Thompkins, Rick 77
Thompson, Carl 77-78
Thompson, Jerry 68-75, 77-79, 82, 84-86
Thompson, Richard 62-63, 65-67
Thomson, Marv 78
Thorpe, Bob 66
Tidwell, Ted 65
Tilbor, Neil 97
Tilke, Herrmann 95
Till, Brian 99
Tillman, Jeff 02
Tillson, Mike 73-76
Tilton, Ren 76-82, 84-85
Timanus, John 65
Timolat, Lou 78
Tisdelle, Ash 71, 79, 81, 84-87
Titus, Jerry 68-69
Toennis, Andre 92-93
Toivonen, Harri 00, 02
Tola, Tony 99
Tolman, Ralph 77
Tonetti, Roberto 96
Toombs, Kelly 97
Torgersen, Anthony 72
Torres, Jim 85, 88
Townsend, Randolph 75, 80
Tracy, Gregg 96
Tradd, Alex 93, 96-97
Treadway, Ben 99
Trejos, Jorge 95-98
Tremblay, John 67, 69-72, 76, 79
Tremblay, Sylvain 97, 99, 02, 03
Trenery, Bruce 93-99, 01
Trenery, Spencer 98-01
Trentini, Armando 02
Trimmer, Tony 70
Trindade, Flavio 98
Trinkler, Owen 97, 02
Tromans, Grant 97
Trotnow, Jim 95
Trott, Doug 96-97
Trotter, Larry 80
Trueman, Colin 90
Trueman, Jim 77, 82, 84-86
Tullius, Bob 65, 70-71, 79-80, 82-88
Tunstall, John 78
de Turbe, Marco 97
Turley, Windle 77
Turner, Billy 67
Turner, Matt 96-98, 01
Turner, Richard 78, 82

U

Ullom, Garth 88
Ulrich, Jake 99
Unser, Bobby 91
Unser, Johnny 88-90, 92, 95, 97
Unser, Robby 90-91
Unser, Jr., Al 83, 85-88, 90-91
Unser, Sr., Al 85, 87, 91
Upton, Kermit 89-90
Urciuoli, Arthur 98
Uria, Peter 85-96
Urrutia, Daniel 88-91, 93-94, 98, 00
Utt, Brian 84

V

Vaccarella, Nino 68, 70
Vadia, Jr., Alberto 79-80
Valentine, Richard J. 78-81, 83-84, 90, 93, 99-00, 02-03
Vallancourt, Todd 97-00
Vallarano, Les 00
Valverde, Roy 83
Van Beuren, Jr., Freddie 67, 73-76
Van Cleef, Eric 95, 98-99
Van Every, Lance 79, 81, 83-85, 87
Vanierschot, Albert 96, 98
Vann, Christian 99-02
Vanoli, Marco 79
Varde, Joe 83-86, 89-91, 95, 01
Vargo, Jake 02
Vargo, Tim 96
Vasser, Jim 92, 99
Vassiliev, Alex 03
Vazquez, Jr., Pedro 78
Vega, Milo 62, 64, 66, 68
Velazquez, Steve 97
Velez, Fermin 92-98
Verdon-Roe, Bobby 02
Vermeersch, Dirk 81
Verney, Anny-Charlotte 80
Vestey, Paul 68
Vigano, Giovanni 98
Villa, Magnolo 95
Villa Prieto, Manuel 79-80, 88-89
Villarroel, Jesus Diez 01
Villeneuve, Rene 00
Visger, Terry 83-84, 88
Vitolo, Dennis 84-85, 88
Vitucci, Nick 98
Vögele, Charles 67
Voith, Andreas Knapp 95
Volk, Steve 88, 91-92
Volk, Thomas 97-00, 02
Vorilhon, Claude 00
Vose, Hamilton 65
Vosse, Vincent 00, 02
Vreeland, Dick 75
Vuillaume, Patrick 99-01
van de Vyver, Eric 99

W

Wada, Hisashi 00
Waddell, Barry 96-00, 02
Wagner, Cort 95-03
Wagoner, Dennis 85
Walch, Rudi 81
Waldron, Chris 68-70
Walker, Don 85
Walker, Greg 86, 88
Walkinshaw, Tom 76
Wallace, Andy 89-03
Wallace, Chaunce 87, 89
Wallace, Donald 85, 90
Wallace, Kenny 93
Walle, Ray 70-71, 75-76
Walsh, Jerry 90
Walsh, Jim 02
Waltman, George 66, 68-69
Waltrip, Darrell 83 87
Ward, Ashley 98
Ward, Jeff 97

Y

Z

Following page: The No. 59 Triumph TR-3 of George Cornelius is passed by the No. 5 Corvette of NASCAR driver Johnny Allen during 1963 race action. Allen went on to finish sixth overall and second in the big-engine class, while Cornelius placed twentieth overall and third in his class.

5
Shell